An impressive collection of research papers and sound analysis covering the trajectory of the elaboration of the International Covenant on the Right to Development, the impediments for its realization, the prospects for its actualisation and implications for the global balance of power and justice. A major scholarly contribution to making the right to development a reality for all and raising the right to development to the same level as and on a par with all other human rights and fundamental freedoms.

– Ayuush Bat-Erdene, Chief of the Right to Development Section at the United Nations Human Rights Office, Geneva, Switzerland

This powerful edited volume on the International Covenant on the Right to Development offers insightful perspectives on questions of global power, sustainable development, international cooperation and assistance, and (new) human rights (right to development) duty-bearers and right holders.

– Wouter Vandenhole, Law and Development Research Group, University of Antwerp, Belgium

International Covenant on the Right to Development

Studies in Critical Social Sciences

VOLUME 326

The titles published in this series are listed at *brill.com/scss*

International Covenant on the Right to Development

Implications for Developing Countries and the Global Balance of Power

Edited by

Carol Chi Ngang

BRILL

LEIDEN | BOSTON

Cover illustration: “Scales of Justice” generated by AI and available in the public domain at: https://stockcake.com/i/scales-of-justice_205615_37293.

Library of Congress Cataloging-in-Publication Data

Names: Ngang, Carol Chi editor
Title: International covenant on the right to development : implications for developing countries and the global balance of power / edited by Carol Chi Ngang.
Description: Leiden ; Boston : Brill, 2025. | Series: Studies in critical social sciences, 1573-4234 ; volume 326 | Includes index.
Identifiers: LCCN 2025020037 (print) | LCCN 2025020038 (ebook) | ISBN 9789004734340 hardback | ISBN 9789004734357 ebook
Subjects: LCSH: Right to development | Right to development--Developing countries | Law and economic development | Law and economic development--Developing countries | International economic relations | International law and human rights
Classification: LCC K3821 .I58 2025 (print) | LCC K3821 (ebook) | DDC 343.07--dc23/eng/20250424
LC record available at https://lccn.loc.gov/2025020037
LC ebook record available at https://lccn.loc.gov/2025020038

Typeface for the Latin, Greek, and Cyrillic scripts: “Brill”. See and download: brill.com/brill-typeface.

ISSN 1573-4234
ISBN 978-90-04-73434-0 (hardback)
ISBN 978-90-04-73435-7 (e-book)
DOI 10.1163/9789004734357

This book is printed on acid-free paper and produced in a sustainable manner.

Contents

Foreword

This timely book explores the implications for developing countries and for the global balance of power of the imminent adoption of an International Covenant on the Right to Development by the United Nations General Assembly. This Covenant would undoubtedly mark an epochal moment in the evolution of international human rights law. I had the distinct honour to serve as the Chair-Rapporteur of the five-members Expert Drafting Group appointed by the United Nations to elaborate its text. Having been intricately involved in the process since the outset, I am convinced that the Covenant will have immense positive implications for the human rights project in general by establishing a normative framework that is built on the acknowledgement that development is not charity or a privilege but a human right of all individuals and peoples. It challenges the existing global order that was largely constructed after the second World War (WWII) by its victors when most of today's developing countries did not even exist as independent countries. Its fundamental premise is that for development to be realised as a human right, it is important to eliminate obstacles that emanate from both the national and the international levels. It fleshes out the obligation of international cooperation for development, which States have undertaken under Articles 55 and 56 of the Charter of the United Nations.

To understand the magnitude of the International Covenant on the Right to Development, it is useful to recall that the right to development was first articulated by the Senegalese diplomat Doudou Thiam, who in a landmark speech delivered at the 21st Session of the United Nations General Assembly on 23 September 1966, made a fervent appeal to lay the foundations of a revolutionary new world society where all the practices, institutions and rules on which international economic relations were constructed pursuant to WWII, and which perpetuated economic subjugation of the previously colonised countries, to be dismantled. He demanded that not only must we affirm our *right to development*, but we must also take the steps that will enable this right to become a reality. It is unsurprising that the African continent took the lead in incorporating development as a guaranteed right of all peoples and a binding obligation on States under Article 22 of the African Charter on Human and Peoples Rights adopted in 1981.

It took five more years for the United Nations General Assembly to adopt the 1986 Declaration on the Right to Development. This Declaration was adopted by an overwhelming 146 countries voting in its favour. Eight countries—Denmark, Finland, Germany, Iceland, Israel, Japan, Sweden and the United Kingdom—abstained, and only the United States of America voted against. Since then, the right to development has unanimously been reaffirmed by all countries in over 22 instruments, including the 1992 Rio Declaration on Environment and Development, 1993 Vienna Declaration and Programme of Action, 2030 Agenda for Sustainable Development, and Paris Agreement on Climate Change. However, there continue to be deep divisions between the Global North and the Global South on the normative scope and content of this right and the appropriate means for its operationalisation.

The principal forum for discussing these aspects since the mid-1990s has been the Intergovernmental Working Group on the Right to Development which meets annually in Geneva. The Working Group is a subsidiary body of the Human Rights Council, but participation in it is open to all States and is not limited only to the 47 members of the Council. Until 2015, the Working Group proved to be a theatre where disagreements on fundamental aspects of the right and the corresponding duties were on full display, thereby impeding any meaningful progress. It was the adoption of the 2030 Agenda in 2015 by the General Assembly that ultimately catapulted the right to development agenda to the centre stage. Developing countries, represented mostly through groupings such as the Non-Aligned Movement (NAM) and the G77, were frustrated that despite their efforts since 1986, developed countries had continued to stall operationalisation of the right. Thus, four things occurred at the behest of the NAM in a very short time that broke the stalemate viz. the appointment for the first time of a Special Rapporteur on the Right to Development by the Human Rights Council in 2016, the adoption of a Resolution in 2018 mandating the Working Group to commence the discussion to elaborate a draft legally binding instrument, and the adoption of a Resolution in 2019, establishing first, an Expert Mechanism on the Right to Development as another subsidiary body of the Council, and second, a high-level biennial panel at the Council to discuss the right. Interestingly, developed countries voted against all these resolutions.

The Chair-Rapporteur of the Working Group, Ambassador Zamir Akram from Pakistan, was requested by the Human Rights Council to submit a draft instrument to the Working Group for negotiations by member States, and in turn, he requested the High Commission for Human Rights to appoint an Expert Drafting Group of international lawyers to assist him with this process. In addition to myself as its Chair and Rapporteur, the Drafting Group also comprised of the late Koen de Feyter (Belgium), Diane Desierto (Philippines); Margarette May Macaulay (Jamaica); and Makane Moïse Mbengue (Senegal). My task was not only to prepare the zero draft but also to develop elaborate legal commentaries on each provision to be considered first by the other four members and then by the member States. Four rounds of transparent and intense negotiations took place at the Working Group on every revised version that was accompanied by updated commentaries, before the final draft "International Covenant on the Right to Development" was ultimately submitted to the Human Rights Council for its consideration. In October 2023, the Council forwarded the draft Covenant to the General Assembly for its "consideration, negotiation and subsequent adoption". The Resolution was adopted at the Human Rights Council with 29 countries voting in favour (member States of the NAM and G77), 13 against (developed countries), and 5 abstaining (all South American countries).

While the lightning speed at which the process moved between 2018 and 2023 is remarkable, it also masks the intense divisions still persisting between developed and developing countries. Although the NAM was convinced that the only way to move away from the business-as-usual approach towards development as charity or development cooperation being donor-driven was to adopt a legally binding instrument, developed countries contended that the 1986 Declaration accompanied by non-binding frameworks such as the 2030 Agenda for sustainable development were the appropriate path. In normative terms as well, there were clear differences. Developed countries, mostly represented during the inter-governmental negotiations through the European Union, adopted some positions that were not only unflinching but also plainly contrary to international human rights law. For instance, the European colleagues adopted a rigid position that the right to development was acceptable to them only if it was articulated as an individual right but not also as a collective right of peoples. This infuriated several African diplomats who saw traces of a colonial attitude in the European position because it implied to them that only the latter's ideas of human rights can be considered valid and that the African understanding of collective rights as incorporated in the African Charter was unworthy of being accepted as international law.

Even purely on aspects of law, on numerous occasions, I pointed out during the negotiations that the European Union's contention was contradictory to the very first article of the International Covenant on Civil and Political Rights, which is identical to Article 1 of the International Covenant on Economic, Social and Cultural Rights viz. "*All peoples* have the right of self-determination. By virtue of that right they freely determine their political status and *freely pursue their economic, social and cultural development*" (emphasis added). There was an evident sense among delegates from NAM member states and from civil society organisations during the negotiations that the opposition to the right of peoples to self-determined development was not an ideological or a legal one; it was a political position of obstinacy. There were other instances where negotiating positions greatly differed. Developed countries opposed extraterritorial obligations as well as the duty of States to cooperate as incorporated in the zero draft and insisted that States only had obligations to individuals within their jurisdictions. The NAM member States strongly rejected these arguments and contended that realisation of the right to development as a "common concern of humankind" implies discharge of duties by States across three levels viz. internal, extraterritorial, as well as collective. Developed countries equally rejected the recognition in the zero draft of an obligation on legal persons, including business corporations and international organisations to respect the right to development of individuals and peoples (that is, do no harm). For concrete reasons provided in the commentaries, the Expert Drafting Group did not agree with the European positions on these aspects.

Following numerous resolutions of the Human Rights Council and the General Assembly calling for the right to development to be brought at the same level as and on a par with civil, political, economic, social and cultural rights, the Drafting Group with support from Ambassador Akram and the NAM, named the instrument as a "Covenant" rather than as a "Convention" (as the core human rights treaties other than the two Covenants currently existing are called). The concrete objective is to ensure that the future International Covenant on the Right to Development is added to what is considered as the "International Bill of Human Rights", currently comprising cumulatively of the Universal Declaration on Human Rights, the International Covenant on Civil and Political Rights, and the International Covenant on Economic, Social and Cultural Rights.

There is power in numbers. The NAM and the G77 had the majority in voting for the draft Covenant on the Right to Development at the Human Rights Council and has an even larger majority at the General Assembly where the Covenant is being considered for adoption. Having engaged with member States also at the United Nations Headquarters in New York in 2024, it will profoundly surprise me if the draft Covenant does not get adopted, at the latest by 2026, which will mark the 40th anniversary of the 1986 Declaration on the Right to Development. The threshold for the Covenant to enter into force is low since it requires only 20 ratifications.

Undoubtedly, the Covenant, once in force, will have great implications for how the international order is structured. Under its framework, individuals and peoples are the principal rights holders of the right to development, which entitles them to define what development means to them and what their priorities ought to be. Governments are obliged to adopt appropriate national development policies as well as development plans and programmes based on these priorities. International organisations such as the International Monetary Fund or the World Bank are also prohibited from violating these rights, for instance, by imposing counterproductive conditionalities on loans. With its focus on the three levels of obligations on States, the duty to cooperate, and the obligation of businesses and international organisations to respect human rights, the draft Covenant is inherently disruptive of the existing *status quo* and thus, evokes discomfort among those who may rather prefer to maintain it.

There is no doubt that merely adopting a normative framework is generally not sufficient for addressing gaping holes in the global architecture. It is however, equally true that without an enabling normative framework, any reform in how development is conceived of and operationalised, including through the financial and trade institutions of global governance, will only be based on moral demands. As history has unequivocally demonstrated since the decolonisation process began in the 1950s, moral grounds have consistently failed in reforming a lopsided global order that is dominated by developed countries, which at every instance, want to dictate the pace for development that developing countries must pursue.

During the negotiations in Geneva, I was often asked about the value-added of a Covenant on the Right to Development, to which, I would invite States to consider the counter-factual, "What would happen in the absence of a Covenant?". The answer is simple and evident, "business-as-usual". It is in this context that I believe this book is both timely and useful. It is timely because it comes at an important stage in the process of elaboration and adoption of the Covenant. It is useful because its chapters explore various themes addressed by the Draft Covenant. This book is undoubtedly a valuable contribution to enhancing our collective understanding of the significant implications an International Covenant on the Right to Development will have, especially for eliminating obstacles to development at both the national and international levels.

Dr. Mihir Kanade
Chair-Rapporteur of the Expert Drafting Group, and Member of the Expert Mechanism on the Right to Development

In Memoriam

While this book project was underway, the cold hands of death snatched Professor Koen de Feyter in a sudden and unexpected manner. He was the first to submit his chapter contribution to the book, having taken research leave (retreat) in May/June 2024 at the University of Palermo in Italy purposely to write the chapter. He had encouraged some of the authors in this collection to equally contribute a chapter. His dedication and contribution in advancing the right to development is immense and immeasurable. He passed on, on 20 September 2024. He was an exceptional personality and will be greatly missed.

"I am Not Ready"

I am not ready. That is the first thought that entered my mind as I was rushing to the train station to get to Antwerp's Law Faculty on Friday, 20 September. I am not ready for a faculty without Koen, for a research group without Koen, not ready to continue our projects without Koen. When we were on a study trip together, he told me about his daughter. The conversation was about independence and approval. Koen could give both simultaneously. He could differ respectfully. He could explain his views without judging others for theirs.

He could act as if I were ready, and by acting make it so.

When he asked me to take over the coordination of the Master of Laws programme (LLM), I said I was not ready. Several of us tried tirelessly to convince him to continue, but he thought we were ready. When he planned a study trip to Palestine, I was not ready. I was not ready to reform the LLM programme he masterminded. Yet, when he asked about it (as incoming Dean), it was only out of curiosity and not out of a sense of controlling.

So was Koen ready? I don't know.

He was in the middle of planning: projects with Birzeit University on the Palestinian West Bank, with partners in Bolivia, and with the Law and Development Research Network. His world will never shrink. He was in the middle of running staff matters and solving challenges related to increased student numbers. He was going to open the academic year in three days' time. He will never close his academic tasks.

Koen listened and learned.

He will never tire of listening, he will never be too old to learn. He was interested in people. He will never lose his fascination. Koen took time for tasks and people, but he will never become bored for having too much time. He looked and analysed. He will never lose his vision. He was patient, but will never become a patient. Koen was serious and rigorous, but he will never become cynical. He was generous. He will never have to stop giving and sharing. He was socially engaged. He will never become worn out. Koen was a loyal colleague and a wise and empowering mentor. He will never become powerless.

Are we ready? No, I am not.

But something deep inside me hears Koen saying that we are ready and that we will be able to carry on our common work.

Professor Dr. Thalia Kruger
Faculty of Law, University of Antwerp

Acknowledgements

The idea for this book was conceived at the Advanced Human Rights Course on the Right to Development in Africa, which took place from 2 to 7 October 2023. Offered by the Centre for Human Rights, Faculty of Law, University of Pretoria in collaboration with the Law and Development Research Group, Faculty of Law, University of Antwerp, the Advanced Human Rights Course on the Right to Development in Africa has held annually since 2012. The annual courses bring together academics, field experts and participants from different walks of life into an intensive full week session of robust engagements on various aspects of the right to development. During the 2023 course, the draft International Covenant on the Right to Development was extensively discussed, which inspired the writing of this collection. We are extremely grateful to the Centre for Human Rights for the devotedness in providing the academic space for advancing the right to development.

Enormous thankfulness is extended to all the chapter contributors, including for the sacrifices and demonstration of academic citizenship in internally peer-reviewing the manuscripts and providing insightful comments that enabled the fine-tuning of the revised versions and thus, certifying the quality of this final output. The enthusiasm to set aside other important commitments and prioritise contribution to this project especially, within the tight timeframes, is sincerely appreciated. The elaborate Foreword to the book, written by Dr Mihir Kanade (Chair-Rapporteur, Expert Drafting Group, member of the UN Expert Mechanisms on the Right to Development and Academic Director of the University for Peace), is acknowledged with profound gratitude.

As the project intensified at the final stages of peer review and editing, it required two weeks of retreat from 8 to 20 December 2024 to complete compilation of the chapter contributions into the full manuscript. The full cost for the retreat was covered by the Free State Centre for Human Rights, University of the Free State without which, the project might have delayed. The support is acknowledged with immense gratitude.

Deep appreciations also go to the editorial and production team at De Gruyter Brill for the heavy lifting in transforming the manuscript into a book. Particularly instrumental in this regard was David Fasenfest, editor of the *Studies in Critical Social Sciences* series under which this volume is published and Katie Short who played an enormously supportive role. Every other person whose support contributed in one way or another, to the realisation of this book project, is also greatly appreciated.

Tables and Figures

Tables

Figures

Abbreviations and Acronyms

4IR	Fourth industrial revolution
ACHPR	African Charter on Human and Peoples' Rights
ACTCJ	African Centre for Transnational Criminal Justice
AfCFTA	African Continental Free Trade Area
AHRLR	African Human Rights Law Review
AoA	Agreement on Agriculture
ASEAN	Association of South East Asian Nations
ATAF	African Tax Administration Forum
AU	African Union
AUABC	African Union Advisory Board on Corruption
AUC	African Union Commission
AUCPCC	African Union Convention on Preventing and Combating Corruption
AUDA	African Union Development Agency
AYC	African Youth Charter
BBBEE	Broad-Based Black Economic Empowerment
BoP	Balance of payment
BYAP	Braga Youth Action Plan
CAP	Common Agricultural Policy
CESCR	Committee on Economic, Social and Cultural Rights
COP	Conference of the Parties
CPI	Corruption Perception Index
CRC	Convention on the Rights of the Child
DRC	Democratic Republic of Congo
ECHR	European Convention of Human Rights
ECJ	European Court of Justice
ESS	Environmental and Social Standards
EU	European Union
FAO	Food and Agricultural Organisation
FDI	Foreign direct investment
FRACCK	Framework for the Return of Assets from Corruption and Crime in Kenya
G20	Group of 20 of the world's major economies
G77	Group of 77 (now 134) developing countries
GATS	General Agreement on Trade in Services
GATT	General Agreement on Tariffs and Trade
GDP	Gross domestic product
GDPR	General Data Protection Regulation

GFI	Global Financial Integrity
GSP	Generalised System of Preferences
HDI	Human development index
HLP	High Level Panel
IACYR	Ibero-American Convention on Young People's Rights
IADB	Inter-American Development Bank
IBRD	International Bank for Reconstruction and Development
ICC	International Criminal Court
ICCPR	International Covenant on the Right to Development
ICESCR	International Covenant on Economic, Social and Cultural Rights
ICJ	International Court of Justice
ICT	Information and communication technology
IDA	International Development Association
IDPS	Internally displaced persons
IFF	Illicit financial flows
IFI	International financial institutions
ILA	International Law Association
IMF	International Monetary Fund
IsDB	Islamic Development Bank
LSC	London School of Economics
MDGS	Millennium Development Goals
MTS	Multilateral trading system
NAM	Non-Aligned Movement
NATO	North Atlantic Treaty Organisation
NEPAD	New Partnership for Africa's Development
NIEO	New international economic order
NSC	North-South Cooperation
OAU	Organisation of African Unity
OECD	Organisation for Economic Cooperation and Development
PAPSS	Pan-African Payment and Settlement System
PRSPS	Poverty Reduction Strategy Programmes
PSC(AU)	Peace and Security Council (African Union)
RECS	Regional economic communities
RIS	Information System for Developing Countries
RTD	Right to development
SADC	Southern Africa Development Community
SAMIM	Southern African Development Commission Mission in Mozambique
SAPS	Structural Adjustment Programmes
SCM	Agreement on Subsidies and Countervailing Measures
SDGS	Sustainable Development Goals

SDT (S&DT)	Special and Differential Treatment
SERAC	Social and Economic Rights Action Centre
SPS	Agreement on the Application of Sanitary and Phytosanitary Measures
SSA	sub-Saharan Africa
SSC	South–South Cooperation
TBT	Technical barriers to trade
TFA	Trade Facilitation Agreement
TRACECA	Transport Corridor Europe-Caucasus-Asia
TRALAC	Trade Law Centre
TRIMS	Agreement on Trade-Related Investment Measures
TRIPS	Agreement on Trade-Related Aspects of Intellectual Property Rights
UDHR	Universal Declaration on the Right to Development
UK	United Kingdom
UN	United Nations
UNCHR	United Nations Commission on Human Rights
UNCITRAL	United Nations Commission on International Trade Law
UNCTAD(CTAD)	United Nations Conference on Trade and Development
UNDP	United Nations Development Programme
UNDRIP	United Nations Declaration on the Rights of Indigenous Peoples
UNDRTD(DRTD)	United Nations Declaration on the Right to Development
UNECA(ECA)	United Nations Economic Commission for Africa
UNESCO	United Nations Educational, Scientific and Cultural Organisation
UNFCCC(FCCC)	United Nations Framework Convention on Climate Change
UNGA (Gen Ass)	United Nations General Assembly
UNHRC	United Nations Human Rights Council
UNICEF	United Nations Children's Fund
UNIDO	United Nations Industrial Development Organisation
UNOCHA(OCHA)	United Nations Office for the Coordination of Humanitarian Affairs
UNOHCHR(OHCHR)	United Nations Office of the High Commissioner for Human Rights
USA (US)	United States of America
USD	United States Dollar
WFP	World Food Programme
WHO	World Health Organisation
WPAY	Word Programme of Action for the Youth
WTO	World Trade Organisation

Notes on Contributors

Elisabeth Achancho Etagha

is a postdoctoral fellow at the Free State Centre for Human Rights, Faculty of Law, University of the Free State. She was research assistant at the School of Law, University of KwaZulu-Natal, South Africa where she obtained her PhD. She has previously served as Director of Academic Affairs and Dean at the Catholic University Institute of Buea, Cameroon. She has received many awards, including: The UKZN Research Grant Award, 2022; National Institute for the Humanities and Social Sciences—CODESRIA Doctoral Scholarship Award, 2017; Successful Leadership Award, 2016; Outreach Award, 2015; Best Dean Award, 2015 and Administrative Excellence Award, 2014 from the Catholic University Institute of Buea. She has been an entrepreneurial coach and mentor in Business and Legal Studies and guest lecturer at Vives University College, Kortrijk, Belgium.

Clement Agyemang

is a doctoral researcher at the Centre for Human Rights, Faculty of Law, University of Pretoria where he delves into the human rights mandate of national parliaments. His research explores the impact of parliamentary functions on domestic implementation of human rights. He holds a Master of Philosophy in Human Rights and Democratisation in Africa from the University of Pretoria and a Bachelor of Arts in Political Studies from Kwame Nkrumah University of Science and Technology, Ghana. His expertise spans key areas, including international human rights law, African human rights system, right to development, constitutionalism, parliament, and democratisation.

Munyai Anzanilufuno

is a Senior Lecturer at the African Centre for Transnational Criminal Justice (ACTCJ) at the University of the Western Cape, South Africa. She holds an LLD (2017) on corruption in Africa and LLM in International Criminal Law (2015) both obtained at the North-West University, Mafikeng Campus and an LLB (2014) from the University of Venda. Her research focuses on Afrocentric approaches to the right to development, anti-corruption, and decolonisation.

Dorcas Basimanyane

(LLD) is a development lawyer of about 10 years' experience. She is currently serving as academic project coordinator of International Trade and

Investments Law (TILA) programme and a post-doctoral researcher in the International Development Law Unit (IDLU) of the Centre for Human Rights, University of Pretoria in South Africa. Her specialises in technology law, development and human rights.

Carol Chi Ngang
(LLD, LLM, LLB, PGD-HE, IDHA, SUSTLAW) is Associate Professor of Laws in the Department of Public Law, National University of Lesotho, Research Fellow at Free State Centre for Human Rights, University of the Free State and Guest Lecturer at the Centre for Human Rights, University of Pretoria. He is UNDP Human Rights Chair for Lesotho and National Research Foundation of South Africa Category C2-rated Researcher. He has been a visiting researcher at the Van Vollenhoven Institute, Leiden University in 2022; Law and Development Research Group, University of Antwerp in 2025 and 2016 and Cegla Centre for Interdisciplinary Research in Law, University of Tel-Aviv in 2015. His research interests combine human rights and development with a niche on the right to development. He has published extensively including books, book chapters, journal articles and policy briefs. He is a member of the Law and Society Association, Law and Development Research Network, Associate Editor of the *Lesotho Law Journal* and *Turf Law Journal*, Editorial Board member of the *Journal of the Institute of African Studies* and Advisory Board member of the *International Journal of Ethiopia Legal Studies*. He has also previously worked within the NGO sector in Cameroon and South Africa.

Serges Djoyou Kamga
is full Professor of Human Rights Law and Dean of the Faculty of Law at the University of the Free State, South Africa. He is currently the Vice President of the African Network of Constitutional Lawyers (ANCL) (Central Africa Region) and member of the Executive Committee of the International Association of Constitutional Lawyers. Prof Kamga previously worked at the Thabo Mbeki African School of Public and International Affairs (University of South Africa) (UNISA), the Centre for Human Rights (University of Pretoria) and at the South African Institute for Advanced Constitutional Law (SAIFAC), University of Johannesburg. His research is multi and transdisciplinary. Over the years he has demonstrated a profound and sustained commitment to advancing knowledge about Africa's development, African renaissance, human rights particularly, the right to development in the African human rights system, human rights from a cross-cultural perspective and disability rights. His research also includes illicit financial flows and their impact on human rights in Africa.

Koen de Feyter
(of blessed memory) was Professor of public international law, Director of the Law and Development Research Group and Chair of the LLM Programme, Faculty of Law, University of Antwerp. He had also headed the Pieter Gills Centre on Active Pluralism and Interdisciplinarity at the same university. He was a member of the United Nations Expert Mechanism on the Right to Development and of the Expert Drafting Group of the International Covenant on the Right to Development. He assumed the office of Dean of the Faculty of Law, University of Antwerp on 1 September 2024 just before his sudden demise. As a law and development scholar, Prof Koen taught a range of courses on public international law, sustainable development, human rights, development cooperation, the rights of indigenous peoples, business and human rights, the right to development and global legal systems at universities in Europe, Africa, Asia and Latin American and published widely in those disciplines. He initiated many long-term collaborations with academic partners across the Global South. He is co-founder of the Law and Development Research Network.

Bonny Ibhawoh
is Professor and the Senator William McMaster Chair in Global Human Rights at McMaster University, Canada. He serves as an Independent Expert of the United Nations Expert Mechanism on the Right to Development. He is the founding Director of the McMaster University Centre for Human Rights and Restorative Justice. With over 30 years of experience as a human rights educator, policymaker, and practitioner, he has taught in Universities in Africa, Europe, the United States and Canada. He coordinates the Confronting Atrocity Project, a transnational study of truth and reconciliation processes. He is also the Project Director of Participedia, a global research network on public participation and democratic innovations. He has authored several books and journal articles on human rights, international development studies, and transitional justice.

Amal Jawad
holds three master degrees, including an MA in Globalisation from McMaster University. With over five years of experience in the public and private sectors, he has developed expertise in management consulting, team building, and strategic implementation. He is pursuing a PhD in Global Health at McMaster University, focusing on addressing healthcare disparities in rural Canadian communities. His research explores how these disparities impact the right to development, intending to propose strategies for equitable healthcare access.

He is also involved in global projects, including a UN initiative on the right to development and climate justice. Additionally, he serves as a Teaching Assistant, supporting various courses and mentoring students.

Linda Mushoriwa
is researcher at the African Centre for Transnational Criminal Justice (ACTCJ), in the Faculty of Law, University of the Western Cape, South Africa where she teaches the LLM module on International Criminal Law. She is Associate Editor for the African Student Law Journal published by the University of the Western Cape. She is a member of the South African Coalition for Transitional Justice. Linda obtained her PhD in international criminal law from the University of KwaZulu Natal, South Africa; LLM (International Economic Law) from the University of South Africa and LLB from the University of Zimbabwe. Her research focuses on law and development; conflict management, peace and security from an African perspective; the "Agenda 2063: The Africa We Want" Framework; women and children's rights and international criminal justice.

Bamisaye Olutola
is a Senior Lecturer at the Department of Public Law, College of Law, Caleb University, Lagos State, Nigeria. He obtained his LLD (2019) and LLM (2014) degrees from the Centre for Human Rights, University of Pretoria, South Africa and LLB degree from the University of Lagos, Nigeria. He is a member of the Nigerian Bar as a Barrister and Solicitor of the Supreme Court of Nigeria. He has published widely in both local and international journals and presented papers at several international conferences. In 2019, he presented a paper at the Global Youth International Programme for Young Constitutional Law Scholars and recently, at the First International Conference on Children's Rights organised by the University of Stellenbosch, South Africa, 10–11 August 2024. His research areas include international human rights law, public international law, comparative constitutional law, and comparative criminal law.

Denis Nfor Yuni
holds a PhD in Economics from Nnamdi Azikiwe University in Awka, Nigeria. He has a rich blend of research and teaching experience; having worked in 3 research centres for about 5 years and has served as a university lecturer for the last 9 years. He is currently a senior lecturer in the Department of Economics, National University of Lesotho (2021–date). His research interests are in Development Finance, International Economics and Environmental Economics. He has published over forty journal articles and over ten working papers

and technical reports. He has consulted for local and international organisations like TetFund, Civil Resource Development and Documentation Centre, Nigerian Communications Commission, Centre for Environmental Economics and Policy in Africa, African Economic Research Consortium; Climate analytics GMBH Berlin Germany, UN University Institute for Natural Resources in Africa, World Bank Sub National Doing Business, United Nations Development Programme, European Union and the United Nations Industrial Development Organisation. He was the Deputy Director, Centre for Internationalisation and Advancement, AEFUNA and is now the research pillar coordinator of the National University of Lesotho—World Trade Organisation Research Chair.

Rita Nkiruka Ozoemena
is a Research Fellow at the Free State Centre for Human Rights, University of the Free State, South Africa. She was an Associate Professor at the University of South Africa (UNISA) where she taught fundamental rights and fundamental rights litigation. She previously practised as a legal practitioner at the Johannesburg Bar and was the legal division coordinator for the Free State Centre for Human Rights where the offfice dealt with public interest litigation. Prof Ozoemena has research interests in gender justice, the right to development and African law. She has published several articles in these areas in peer-reviewed international journals.

Pratyush Sharma
is a Consultant at the Global South Centre of Excellence incubated at Research and Information System for Developing Countries (RIS), New Delhi in India. He has a background in International Relations and has completed his PhD from the United Nations mandated University for Peace, Costa Rica. He has also been a Queen Elizabeth Scholar for International Development at the University of Calgary, Canada, and a Global Governance Fellow at the Institute of Development and Sustainability, Bonn in Germany. Assistant Editor for Development Cooperation Review.

Mofihli Teleki
is a PhD candidate at the School of Public Leadership, Stellenbosch University, South Africa. He holds an MPA (cum laude) in Public Policy Analysis (Stellenbosch) and BA (UNISA), BPA (Hons) (Stellenbosch). Teleki is a former member of UNESCO's Communication and Information Sub-Committee in South Africa. He was a Fellow of the Mellon Foundation's Ubuntu Fellowship in 2018 offered by the Michigan State University (United States) and Stellenbosch

University (South Africa). He works at the Department of Trade, Industry and Competition as Director for Stakeholder Relations and Communication at the Black Economic Empowerment Commission, South Africa. He has authored/co-authored several books, book chapters and journal articles and presented academic papers at conferences in South Africa, Cameroon, China, Scotland and Canada. His research interests include the right to development, public policy, governance, human rights and gender equality.

Daniel M. Walyemera
is an Advocate of the High Court of Uganda. He has taught, published, and practiced law for over 20 years. He is admitted on the Lists of Counsel of the African Court on Human and Peoples' Rights and the International Criminal Court, where he occasionally practices law. Walyemera holds a Doctor of Laws (LLD) from the University of the Western Cape, South Africa. He is currently a Postdoctoral Researcher at the College of Law, University of South Africa.

CHAPTER 1

Introduction: Trajectory to the International Covenant on the Right to Development

Carol Chi Ngang

1 Background Overview

The concept of the right to development has, from as far back as can possibly be traced, evolved through a checkered and controversial history that has comprehensively been articulate in an extensive range of academic literature and other commentaries on the subject.[1] After over five decades of heavily polarised disagreements over the origins, conceptual clarity, legal nature, the normative and substantive contents, and the question of rights holders and duty bearers among others, many of the contentions have in effect, died down and are ultimately being put to rest. Notwithstanding the angle from which the right to development has been conceived by various stakeholders, and despite the divergences in perceptions; the debates eventually converged into both a tacit and explicit acceptance that there is indeed, a legitimate claimable human right to development, which is not unlike any other universally recognised human right.[2] The idea of the right to development derives from a human rights reading of the amorphous concept of development embodied in the undertakings under international law as enshrined in the UN Charter, "to promote social progress and better standards of life in larger freedom" and to promote respect for the full realisation of all human rights, including entitlement to the highest attainable standards of living as a fundamental prerequisite in the processes for development.[3]

1 See for example, Ngang, Carol Chi (2021) *The Right to Development in Africa*. Leiden/Boston: Brill Publishers, 18–53; Subedi, Surya (2021) Declaration on the Right to Development. *United Nations Audiovisual Library of International Law* 1.

2 UN Commission on Human Rights, Resolution 4 (XXXIII), Adopted Without a Vote on 21 February 1977.

3 Report of the Secretary General (2013) Emergence of the Right to Development. In: UN Human Rights (ed) *Realizing the Right to Development: Essays in Commemoration of 25 Years of the United Nations Declaration on the Right to Development*. Geneva/New York: UN Publication, 7–8.

 | DOI:10.1163/9789004734357_002

The right to development is conceptualised from this viewpoint as guaranteeing entitlement to better quality of life and improved standards of living for everyone and for all peoples, necessitating at the national level, the primary obligation of state governments to ensure its realisation and in its international dimension, the collective action of states through international cooperation. Being a human right means that the right to development deserves legal recognition and protection as an integral component of international human rights law. As envisaged in the Millennium Development Goal Declaration in 2000, to make the right to development a reality for everyone,[4] attention has increasingly focused on ensuring its legal recognition and protection at the international level. The key milestone on this front, included the Declaration on the Right to Development adopted in 1986,[5] which however, imposed no binding obligations on states for its implementation and enforcement. It therefore, necessitated the drafting of the International Covenant on the Right to Development (Covenant), which is currently in process for intergovernmental negotiations at the United Nations General Assembly.[6]

Majorly significant about the Covenant is its value addition to international law as a legally binding instrument with a unique inclination of not only imposing obligations on state parties but also on a broader range of actors and stakeholders, including non-state entities and as it is argued in chapter 9, third states by virtue of its external and extraterritorial dimensions with respect to the pursuit of development objectives at the national and global levels.[7] Also crucial about the Covenant is that, by reaffirming the legal nature of right to development as a human right pertaining to, and claimable by individuals

4 UN Millennium Declaration Resolution A/55/L.2 adopted by the General Assembly on 18 September 2000 Para III(11).

5 Declaration on the Right to Development, Resolution A/RES/41/128, Adopted by the UN General Assembly on 4 December 1986.

6 Human Rights Council Adopts Five Resolutions, Submits to General Assembly Draft International Covenant on the Right to Development for its Negotiation and Adoption, and Extends Mandate on Burundi. *The United Nations Office at Geneva*, 12 October 2023. Available at: https://www.ungeneva.org/en/news-media/meeting-summary/2023/10/le-conseil-adopte-cinq-resolutions-dont-celle-transmettant (consulted 7 March 2024); United Nations (2023) Third Committee Underscores Need for Legally Binding Tool to Enforce Right to Development, Unrealized by Millions Worldwide, Directed Also at Businesses' Meetings, Coverage and Press Releases Seventy-eighth Session, 20th and 21st Meeting (AM and PM) GA/SHC/4383, 13 October 2023. *United Nations*. Available at: https://press.un.org/en/2023/gashc4383.doc.htm (consulted 7 March 2024).

7 Draft International Covenant on the Right to Development—Report by the Chair-Rapporteur of the Working Group on the Right to Development, Zamir Akram (Pakistan) Human Rights Council A/HRC/54/50 54th Session, 6 October 2023.

and collectively by peoples and importantly also, by states on behalf of their peoples, the Covenant marks another breakthrough in the evolution of international human rights law, which has hitherto, predominantly uphold and promoted the individualistic nature of human rights. Unambiguously referred to as "Covenant"—a change from "Convention" by which it was initially named, upon adoption, it is intended to have the same status in law as the International Covenant on Economic, Social and Cultural Rights (ICESCR) and the International Covenant on Civil and Political Rights (ICCPR) and hence, an integral part of the corpus of legally binding instruments that make up the International Bill of Human Rights and international human rights law more broadly.[8]

The absence of a binding instrument to protect the development aspirations of all peoples especially, those of the developing world has regrettably given way to scenarios where some of the peoples particularly, those of the developed world, have enjoyed the liberty (with impunity) to subjugate other peoples through slavery, colonialism, apartheid, neocolonialism, economic globalisation, unfettered expansion of the global market economy and other contemporary forms of imperial domination. This has meant unjust deprivations, impoverishments and development imbalances for the seething billions of peoples who are disproportionately disadvantaged and denied opportunities for advancement. If the norms of international law were to apply rigorously in upholding the reaffirmation of faith in fundamental human rights, the solemn commitment to establishing conditions for global justice and the obligation to promote social progress and better standards of living in larger freedoms, and in accordance, to employ the international machinery to promote the economic and social advancement of all peoples,[9] development among nations would probably, have been much more balanced. Asserting the sovereign equality and self-determination right to development has aimed to fix the age-old dilemma of lopsided rules and suppressive operational models that have bedevilled the international legal system over the decades.

History cautions against losing sight of the deeply entrenched operational modalities of the global system that have constituted a setback to the right to development. The contributions in this book proceed from the starting point that without a robust safeguard mechanism in the form of a binding treaty

8 By Resolution 52/136 of 12 of December 1997, the UN General Assembly affirmed that the inclusion of the Declaration on the Right to Development in the International Bill of Human Rights would be an appropriate means of celebrating the fiftieth anniversary of the Universal Declaration of Human Rights.

9 See the Preamble and Art 1 of the Charter of the United Nations, 1945.

on the right to development, aspirations for advancement for many of the peoples around the world will remain elusive. The discussions centre on, and broadly explore questions around the International Covenant on the Right to Development: What the Covenant represents especially, for developing countries? How and to what extent the Covenant will, as an instrument of international law, shape the global balance of power? Whether the adoption and coming into force of the Covenant will enable sufficient rupturing of the lopsidedness and power imbalances that have enabled a compartmentalisation of nations into a hierarchical ordering of first, second and third worlds, which are further pigeon-holed into levels-of-development categories as developed (high income), emerging (middle-income), and least-developed or developing (low-income) countries? Of interest is whether developing countries will be able to leverage on the Covenant in exerting sovereignty and self-determination under the imminent new right to development dispensation? The book responds broadly to the central concern whether, how, and to what extent the Covenant on the Right Development (when it becomes enforceable), would facilitate the processes of redressing longstanding development injustices and/or contribute to equalising opportunities for development to the benefit of the peoples in the developing parts of the world.

2 Made for Purpose

Bonny Ibhawoh has correctly illustrated that the rhetoric on the right to development has mainly centred on the politics and polemics of power and resistance that puts proponents from the global south against opponents from the global north at variance.[10] In characterising the right to development as a language of power, Ibhawoh points out how developing countries of the Global South assert entitlement thereto as a demonstration of sovereignty, which conflicts with the resistant position of developed countries of the Global North that contest and object to the existence of such a right.[11] The power dynamics equally goes the other way round in terms of developing countries of the Global South insistently asserting the right to development as a form of resistance to the hegemonic global system that is dominated and exclusively managed by developed countries of the Global North.

---

10 Ibhawoh, Bonny (2011) The Right to Development: The Politics and Polemics of Power and Resistance. *Human Rights Quarterly* 33(1): 86–102.

11 Ibid at 97–102.

The International Covenant on the Right to Development is admittedly made for such purpose—to create a new international economic order (NIEO), entailing global balance in the exercise of power between developed and developing countries, which ought to be regulated by the norms of international law that espouse the principles of self-determination, sovereign equality, non-interference, permanent sovereignty over natural resources and international cooperation in the pursuit of development objectives. The right to development evolved from the abortive campaign for a NIEO, championed in the 1970s by the community of developing countries that make up the Non-Aligned Movement (NAM) and the G77 (now consisting of 134 member states) that aimed to upset the *status quo* of dominance and patronage, advance the cause for global equity and redistributive justice and establish an impartial global dispensation that reflects the development aspirations of the disadvantaged and impoverished peoples around the world.[12]

The right to development, it must be re-emphasised, is conceptually formulated as an assertion of self-determination and the quest for self-actualisation in the pursuit of economic, social and cultural development and in enhancing political sovereignty with respect to the interwoven international law principles of sovereign equality and non-interference. Besides being a stand-alone human right, the right to development also serves as a mechanism for the full realisation of the three composite categories of human rights: civil and political, socio-economic and cultural and other collective rights like the right to permanent sovereignty over natural resources, the to a clean and health environment and the right to peace and stability. In commemorating the 25th Anniversary of the Declaration on the Right to Development over a decade ago, the Office of the High Commission for Human Rights, already noted that the right to development is "a development paradigm for a globalized future" that has been overshadowed by dominant economic development models, which despite engineering considerable progress, tend to overlook crucial social concerns, including human rights.[13] Acknowledging the right to development as a paradigm for development makes much sense at this stage with the global development landscape envisaged to be governed and regulated by the Covenant on the Right to Development, which promises equitable opportunities and aspirations for better standards of living and a threshold

12 Ngang 2021, supra note 1, 41–43; Declaration on the Right to Development, supra note 5, Art 3(3).

13 UN Human Rights (ed) (2013) *Realizing the Right to Development: Essays in Commemoration of 25 Years of the United Nations Declaration on the Right to Development*. Geneva/New York: UN Publication, 495.

quality of life which no human person anywhere around the world should fall below.

Like for all other human rights, states parties will have the primary duty to ensure realisation of the Covenant on the Right to Development. However, bearing in mind the disagreements and divergence of stance between developed and developing countries regarding the Covenant, the question of its adoption and ratification is crucial but does not provide any room to despair. Haven championed the cause for its legally binding status, it is predictable that adoption of the Covenant will largely be endorsed by the NAM and G77 member states that form the bulk of member states of the UN General Assembly and equally accelerate its ratification and coming into force in the shortest time possible and hence, also activate the framework for implementation.[14] It is stated that

> The object and purpose of the present Covenant is to promote and ensure the full, equal and meaningful enjoyment of the right to development by every individual and all peoples everywhere, and to guarantee its effective operationalization and full implementation at the national and international levels.[15]

Aside the progress in pushing for legal recognition of the right to development at the international level, the past couple of years have witnessed structural transformation in global geopolitics and a progressive decoupling from, and dismantling of the unipolar world that has hitherto, exclusively been defined by power configurations that defy established rules, norms and principles of international law. The distorted ordering on how the world has been constrained to operate under conditions of power asymmetries has not only created imbalances of enormous proportions, but also alienated relatively weaker countries from a place "at the table in the international system" and accordingly, dispossessed of sovereignty and reduced to a "menu" to be devoured by the most powerful states.[16] The right to development has from inception, characteristically aimed to redress the disproportionate power dynamics that has stood in the way of the developing regions of the world and their prospects

14 Millennium Development Goals Declaration, supra note 4.

15 Draft Covenant on the Right to Development, supra note 7, Art 1.

16 At the Munich Security Conference in February 2024, U.S. Secretary of State, Anthony Blinken gave a culinary view of how world politics world by stating frankly that "if you're not at the table in the international system, you're going to be on the menu".

for advancement. Strikingly significant about the Covenant on the Right to development when it becomes enforceable is that, besides imposing binding obligations on state parties for its realisation, it is envisaged to have important implications for developing countries in terms of imposing new rules that will regulate global governance and hence also, in terms of birthing new geostrategic power configurations with the potential to accelerate realisation of the right to development.

3 Honour to the Vanguards

The book is conceived and written in honour of the following members of the Expert Drafting Group: Dr Mihir Kanade (India), who acted as Chair-Rapporteur; Prof Koen de Feyter (Belgium), Prof Diane Desierto (Philippines); Mrs Margarette May Macaulay (Jamaica); and Prof Makane Moïse Mbengue (Senegal), commissioned by the UN Human Rights Council. Over the last couple of years, these imminent personalities consecrate time and their expertise in drafting the Covenant ensuring that the right to development acquires international legal status on a par with other universally recognised human rights that make up the international bill of human rights. Besides their involvement in the drafting of the Covenant on the Right to Development, each of the members of the Expert Drafting Group have also contributed enormously in several other ways, including through scholarship, consultancy and thematic expertise in advancing the conceptual formulation of the right to development globally and advising on best practices and modalities for its implementation. In addition to serving in the Expert Drafting Group, Prof Mihir Kanade and Prof Koen de Feyter also doubled as members of the Expert Mechanism on the Right to Development.[17] Their contributions will remain indelible in the history of the right to development.

Regarding the convoluted processes leading up to the drafting of the International Covenant on the Right to Development, credit is indeed, owed to early proponents like Kéba M'baye who published the pioneer seminal thesis

17 At the time of writing this book, the members of the Expert Mechanism on the Right to Development were Prof Mihir Kanade—current Chair (India), Prof Bonny Ibhawoh (Nigeria), Ms Klentiana Mahmutaj (Albania), Ms Liliana Valiña (Argentina) and Ms Isabelle Durant (Belgium); see UN Human Rights (1996–2024) Independent Experts: Expert Mechanism on the Right to Development. Available at: https://www.ohchr.org/en/hrc-subsidiaries/expert-mechanism-on-right-to-development/independent-experts (consulted 30 October 2024).

on the right to development in 1972.[18] The expertise of Independent Expert on the Right to Development—Arjun Sengupta (1999–2004) and UN Special Rapporteurs on the Right to Development—Saad Alfarargi (2017–2023) and Surya Deva (2023 to present)—has been instrumental in respectively, broadening understanding of the right and developing guidelines and practical modalities for its implementation. The Centre for Human Rights at the University of Pretoria in collaboration with the Law and Research Group at the University of Antwerp have played a major educational role in promoting the right to development through the annual Advanced Human Rights Course on the Right to Development.[19]

The steadfastness of the NAM and the G77 member states in championing the cause for legal recognition and protection of the right to development has not only materialised but also marked an indelible milestone in the advancement of international law. It is also worth recognising that by enshrining the right to development in the African Charter on Human and Peoples' Rights adopted in 1981, and ancillary treaty instruments,[20] the African human rights system, has through an evolving jurisprudence, laid the foundation for its justiciability as a legitimate entitlement enforceable through judicial processes.[21] Numerous scholars and commentators have equally made valuable theoretical contributions in advancing the right to development in significant ways. While they cannot all be mentioned here, their impactful inputs cannot be ignored.

Despite the numerous efforts highlighted above in codifying the right to development into an internationally binding treaty instrument, resistance and

---

18 M'baye, Kéba (1972) Le Droit au Développement Comme un Droit de l'Homme: Leçon Inaugural de la Troisième Session d'Enseignement de l'Institut International des Droits de l'Homme. *Revue des Droits de l'Homme* 5: 505–534.

19 Centre for Human Rights (2024) Advanced Human Rights Course: The Right to Development in Africa. Available at: https://www.chr.up.ac.za/courses-presented/right-to-development-in-africa (consulted 26 December 2024).

20 African Charter on Human and Peoples' Rights adopted in Nairobi, Kenya on 27 June 1981 OAU Doc CAB/LEG/67/3 Rev.5 (1981); Art 22; African Youth Charter adopted in Banjul, the Gambia on 2 July 2006, Art 10; Protocol to the African Charter on Human and Peoples' Rights on the Rights of Women in Africa adopted by the Assembly of Heads State and Government in Maputo, Mozambique on 11 July 2003, Art 19.

21 *African Commission on Human and Peoples' Rights v Republic of Kenya* (2017) Appl No 006/2017 Paras 207–211; *Centre for Minority Rights Development (Kenya) and Minority Rights Group International on Behalf of Endorois Welfare Council v Kenya* Comm 276/2003 (2009) AHRLR 75 (ACHPR 2009), Para 298; *Democratic Republic of Congo v Burundi, Rwanda and Uganda* (2009) AHRLR 9 (ACHPR 2009) Para 95; *Sudan Human Rights Organisation and Another v Sudan* (2009) AHRLR 153 (ACHPR 2009), Para 224.

roadblocks have continued to be mounted by the key gatekeepers of international law, which has repeatedly been marked by their reluctance in agreeing to a binding treaty on the right to development. It is anticipated that when the Covenant is eventually adopted and comes into force, it will provide a legal framework by which both developed and developing countries can be held to the same standard of compliance, responsiveness and accountability. The relevance of the Covenant on the Right to Development cannot be overemphasised especially because since inception several decades back, implementation of the right to development remains elusive in many of developing countries particularly, those in Africa that have championed the cause for its recognition and protection.

With the shifting dynamics in global geopolitics, and the effects thereof on international law, the book delves to a great length in looking at the modalities for implementing the right to development at the domestic, regional and international levels. In synchronising the diverse narratives, which involves looking back in retrospect on crucial highlights and milestones, and projecting into the possible future of a new global dispensation governed by the right to development paradigm, the chapter contributions provide a comprehensive coverage of the intricacies and the dialectics in the understanding of the crucial role that the Covenant on the Right to Development is envisaged to play in redefining the global balance of power, and the implications of that in the lives of the billions of adversely affected peoples in the developing regions of the world who are disproportionately denied and deprived of opportunities for development, which are guaranteed in abundance to the peoples in the developed parts of the world.

4 Structure of the Book and Synopsis of the Chapters

The book is an inspiring collection of chapter contributions by a diverse range of authors comprising of leading experts, distinguished scholars and emerging researchers on the right to development and related disciplines. While the discussions converge on the central theme on the right to development, the deeply explored perspectives articulated in each of the chapters zoom in from varying academic viewpoints, including law, development economics, environmental justice, and gender studies among others. The discussions are thus, essentially interdisciplinary in scope, with sufficient depth of research, analysis and argumentation on the various interconnected aspects relating to the subject matter. The chapter contributions are mostly constructed using qualitative methods in analysing legal texts and existing literature. As to the structural layout, in addition to the introductory and concluding chapters, the substantive chapters are grouped into four major thematic parts. Part 1 focuses on the nature of the right to development. Part 2 explores the global cooperation framework for development and the matrix of power between developed and developing countries. In Part 3, the discussions revolve around perspectives on right to development justice. Part 4 looks at systemic impediments to realising the right to development. The chapters in each part, are arranged in as seamless a manner as possible, which allows for a comprehensible flow of the discussions.

4.1 *Introduction*

The introductory chapter provides a broad background overview of the trajectory to the International Covenant on the Right to Development. It highlights what the Covenant is envisaged to accomplish, pays tribute and honour to the drafters of the Covenant and the several other vanguards whose distinguished contributions to the advancement of the right to development laid the solid foundation on which the Covenant has been erected. It also provides a summary of the various chapter contributions, arranged in a manner that allows for coherent flow of the analysis.

4.2 *Part 1—Nature of the Right to Development*

In chapter 2, Amal Jawad and Bonny Ibhawoh draw attention to the fact that the right to development is intrinsically linked to self-determination and the collective rights of peoples whose control over their economic, social, and cultural development is a prerequisite for realising all fundamental human rights. While the Declaration on the Right to Development laid the foundation for a rights-based approach to development founded on self-determination, equity, equality, and justice as primary determinants of development, the draft Convention on the Right to Development goes a step further by introducing concrete, detailed, and implementable norms. Centring on self-determination and the collective rights of people, the authors show how the right to development agenda bridges the gap between human rights and sustainable development. Locating the discussion in struggles for self-determination and demands for a NIEO by states of the Global South, they argue that the normative content of the right to development as outlined in the draft Convention, holds promise for a more just and equitable international human rights agenda.

In chapter 3, Koen de Feyter provides a comprehensive account of the holders of the right to development, which are recognised in the UN Declaration on the Right to Development and the draft Covenant on the Right to Development, as both individuals and peoples. Attributing the same right to individuals and to peoples alike as he argues, offers opportunities to strengthen the existing international human rights regime, which however, has not been explored given the political impasse between the global North and the global South that has persisted since 1979 the UN General Assembly first proclaimed the right. The chapter illustrates that the concurrent application of the individual and the peoples' right to development renders the best possible way out in terms of the protection of human dignity. The chapter also discusses the vexed issue of whether States should be considered holders of the right to development, next to being a duty bearer. He argues that this issue can best be addressed through a proper interpretation of the duty to cooperate, itself a cornerstone of the right to development.

Clement Agyemang expands the conversation in chapter 4 by looking at attainment of the sustainable development through a binding right to development. He illustrates that outside of the African human rights system, where the right to development enjoys legally binding status, its application has been the subject of debates among human rights scholars and development practitioners. He argues in this regard that the proposal to have the International Covenant on the Right to Development is imperative considering the gains it offers in not only redressing development problems especially, in developing countries but also ensuring that development is sustainable as envisaged in the Covenant. Noting that the right to development cannot be achieved if development is unsustainable, the chapter explores the practicality and the extent to which the RTD as a binding law can ensure development that meets the needs of the present, without compromising the ability of future generations to meet their own needs.

Pratyush Sharma examines the power asymmetries in the politics of international development and the quest for global balance in the cooperation framework for development in chapter 5. He points out that the current international development architecture and the incumbent development cooperation ecosystem is lopsided in favour of developed countries with respect to the quantum of foreign aid, its conceptualisation and framework of delivery, leashed operationalisations (conditionalities), and the temporality of cooperation (delay in delivery). He illustrates that South–South model of cooperation is more practicable in realising sustainable development as it is devoid of the North-South model conceptual and operational handicaps. He argues that the normative framework of the right to development has the potential to revolutionise the global development architecture in ensuring that development is genuinely sustainable and inclusive. He concludes with some actionable points as to how to make the right to development more relevant within the policy circles of the Global South and the Global North.

4.3 *Part 2—Global Cooperation Framework for Development and the Matrix of Power*

In the exploratory analysis in chapter 6, Carol Chi Ngang advances a theoretical argument with the purpose of extrapolating answers to some intricate questions regarding the extraterritorial obligations of third states on the right to development. He points out that as far as prescriptive obligations of outcome are concerned, the Covenant on the Right to Development, when it is eventually adopted and comes into force, will in terms of the insulative provisions of the Vienna Convention on the Law of Treaties, not apply to third states. However, basing on an expansive reading of international law, he illustrates that third states have a presumptive obligation to refrain from conduct that may impair realisation of the right to development and therefore, are susceptible to accountability when, in their extraterritorial operations, they contravene that obligation.

Elizabeth Etagha's reflection on the right to development obligations of international organisations is articulately captured in chapter 7. She notes that international organisations play a crucial role in realising the right to development by fostering cooperation, providing development financing and technical assistance, and supporting member states in ensuring that development policies are inclusive and sustainable. Noting that international organisations traditionally, do not have human rights obligations under international law like states do, she observes that operating based on their objectives and mandate, international organisations are under no compulsion to comply with the right to development in their operations. She draws attention to the fact that the Covenant on the Right to Development however, recognises that international organisations do have obligations arising from their international legal personality and constituent agreements, to not operate in a manner that inhibits the right to development.

Noting that resource mobilisation is crucial for implementing the right to development, which is hampered by economic inequalities between the Global North and the Global South, Daniel Walyemera provides in chapter 8, an analysis on development financing in the Global South. He draws attention to the fact that development, which is recognised in various international law instruments as a human right, cannot occur without financing. He alludes to several soft law instruments that outline the possibilities of finding resources to finance development that benefits humanity regardless of geographical location. Hence, in addition to the need for democratising governance of the International Monetary Fund (IMF) and the World Bank to enable effective financing for development in the global south, he argues that philanthropic causes could be an alternative source of financing for development in the Global South if harnessed effectively.

4.4 *Part 3—Perspectives on Right to Development Justice*

Rita Ozoemena's contribution in chapter 9, highlights some gender considerations in operationalising the right to development in African continental free trade. The chapter examines the critical issues that must be put in place to foster the participation of women and ultimately reduce gender inequalities through harnessing socio-economic development for the effective integration of the continent. Ozoemena argues that proficient monitoring of the impact of free trade on all workers, especially women in all sectors is imperative in ensuring the successful implementation of the free trade agreement. She posits that the fight for women's rights to equality constitutes the bedrock for equity, fairness, choice and accountability and the right to development guaranteed to them in the African Charter and the Protocol on the Rights of Women in Africa. She notes that the African Continental Free Trade Area offers incredible opportunities, including for women entrepreneurs and aspirants. Cognisance of the fact that a one-size-fits-all policy may not suffice, she suggests that equity-driven considerations are vital in addressing existing inequalities.

Discussing the necessity to bridge the divide in chapter 10, Dorcas Basimanyane examines the potential impact of technology advancement on the right to development in Africa. She notes that in the mobile internet era, the right to development assumes new relevance, prompting a re-evaluation of its principles in the context of increasingly rapid digital transformation. The chapter explores how mobile internet technology influences and reshapes understanding of the right to development by enhancing the creation of inclusive and accessible virtual development environments. It investigates what the principles of the right to development mean and entail in a world that is increasingly driven by digital connectivity and more so, how advancements in technology impact on the associated rights to self-determination, sovereignty over natural resources, and international cooperation in fostering human-centred development in Africa.

In chapter 11, Mofihli Teleki looks at constitutional remedies in the practice of the right to development in South Africa. He affirms South Africa's commitment to the right to development by virtue of it being a state party to the African Charter, its adherence to the UN Declaration to the Right to Development and obligations under the national Constitution, which embodies aspirations for the right to development in an indirect manner and by implication. Teleki however, notes that the implied framing of the right to development in the South

African constitutional order as some scholars have argued, is problematic and poses a challenge with respect to accountability and remedial action, which are crucial in advancing the right to development. Within the backdrop of the adoption of the International Covenant on the Right to Development, regarding domestic enforcement, Teleki argues that the South African Constitution needs to be explored at length for the numerous provisions therein that can strengthen accountability and remedial actions.

Chapter 12 delves into investigating the and challenges related to litigating youth right to development wherein, Bamisaye Olutola shows that the prospects youth are among the most disadvantaged segment of the populations whose rights have not been given proper attention as far as the human rights agenda is concerned. He draws attention to some UN instruments, including Resolution 2037 adopted in 1965, the World Programme of Action for Youth adopted in 1995, and the Lisbon Declaration of 1998, which all aim at advancing youth rights globally. He contends that implementation of these instruments has not been effective in protecting youth rights apparently, because they are not legally binding. He notes that the African Youth Charter has legally binding status, but is only applicable in Africa, which limits litigating youths' right to development within the UN and other regional human rights systems. Litigation, as he observes, is crucial in promoting youths' right to development, which may only become possible for the youth population around the world with the adoption of the Covenant on the Right to Development.

4.5 *Part 4—Systemic Impediments to Realising the Right to Development*

Writing on illicit financial flows, development assistance and the realisation of the right to development in Africa in chapter 13, Serges Djoyou Kamga points out that while the right to development remains controversial at the global level, it is recognised as a human right within the African human rights system. He notes that to enhance prospects for its realisation, the African Charter equally guarantees the right to ownership over natural resources, which can be tapped into in advancing development on the continent. Unfortunately, Africa is being robbed of the proceeds of the natural resources through illicit financial flows (IFFs). The chapter examines the measures undertaken by the African institutions in safeguarding the continent against IFF practice.

Denis Nfor Yuni's discussion in chapter 14 dwells on the international trade restrictions for developing countries wherein, from a right to development point of view, he provides a critique of the trade policies. He illustrates that trade restrictions stem back to the mercantilist era of the 16th to 18th centuries, characterised by national laws that simply promoted exports and prevented imports, driven by the zero-sum game principle. He notes that trade restrictions have from inception, evolved in form, scope and type. He contends that trade restrictions minimise global trade and erodes benefits, necessitating a regulatory multilateral trade system with the mandate to determine trade rules and to facilitate trade negotiations, which under the World Trade Organisation (WTO), tends to favour countries with higher bargaining powers. He interrogates existing global trade rules, in determining the implications for developing countries with relatively low industrial capacity to compete with developed countries.

In chapter 15, Anzanilufuno Munyai assesses the impact of corruption on the social, and redistributive justice aspects of the right to development in Africa. She explains that in addition to the historical legacies of colonialism, corruption has become an arduous impediment to development, which is aggravated by compromises in efforts at redistributive justice resulting from diversion of public resources for private gains instead of for societal advancement. She notes that the prospective Covenant on the Right to Development, which is crafted to achieve redistributive justice, faces significant obstacles due to corruption. Through a meticulous analysis of data obtained from Transparency International and Afrobarometer, she sheds light on the extend of corruption on the realisation of the right to development in Africa.

In chapter 16, Linda Mushoriwa explores the threats to peace and security that persist in Africa. Focusing on the conflict in the Cabo Delgado region in Mozambique, she illustrates how armed conflicts and insurgencies, which she notes, are triggered by the obsession for natural resource extraction including by external actors, pose a hindrance to the right to development on the continent. Perceived in light of the evolving dynamics of the conflict and the aspiration for a "prosperous Africa" and a "peaceful and secure Africa" as stated in the Agenda 2063 framework for development, Mushoriwa avers that adoption of the Covenant on the Right to Development is likely to shift the goalposts in geopolitical relations between politically powerful states and their former colonies in Africa, necessitating effective strategies in confronting the problem of armed conflicts and insurgencies that hinder development on the continent.

4.6 *Conclusion*

The last chapter provides some concluding reflexions and a forward-looking projection on what actualisation of the International Covenant on the Right to Development would entail when it eventually becomes law but also in terms of global power balancing between developed and developing countries. It looks at overarching issues relating to how international law and global dynamics are likely to be reshaped significantly. It illustrates the value-add of the Covenant on the Right to Development expectantly becoming an integral part of the International Bill of Rights, giving credibility to the argument in favour of rights-based development and the pursuit of it as a development paradigm for the new global dispensation that will be stablished.

References

African Charter on Human and Peoples' Rights adopted in Nairobi, Kenya on 27 June 1981 OAU Doc CAB/LEG/67/3 Rev.5 (1981).

African Commission on Human and Peoples' Rights v Republic of Kenya (2017) Appl No 006/2017.

African Youth Charter adopted in Banjul, the Gambia on 2 July 2006.

Centre for Human Rights (2024) Advanced Human Rights Course: The Right to Development in Africa. Available at: https://www.chr.up.ac.za/courses-presented/right-to-development-in-africa (consulted 26 December 2024).

Centre for Minority Rights Development (Kenya) and Minority Rights Group International on Behalf of Endorois Welfare Council v Kenya Comm 276/2003 (2009) AHRLR 75 (ACHPR 2009).

Declaration on the Right to Development, Resolution A/RES/41/128, Adopted by the UN General Assembly on 4 December 1986.

Democratic Republic of Congo v Burundi, Rwanda and Uganda (2009) AHRLR 9 (ACHPR 2009).

Draft International Covenant on the Right to Development—Report by the Chair-Rapporteur of the Working Group on the Right to Development, Zamir Akram (Pakistan) Human Rights Council A/HRC/54/50 54th Session, 6 October 2023.

Human Rights Council Adopts Five Resolutions, Submits to General Assembly Draft International Covenant on the Right to Development for its Negotiation and Adoption, and Extends Mandate on Burundi. *The United Nations Office at Geneva*, 12 October 2023. Available at: https://www.ungeneva.org/en/news-media/meeting-summary/2023/10/le-conseil-adopte-cinq-resolutions-dont-celle-transmettant (consulted 7 March 2024).

Ibhawoh, Bonny (2011) The Right to Development: The Politics and Polemics of Power and Resistance. *Human Rights Quarterly* 33(1): 76–104.

M'baye, Kéba (1972) Le Droit au Développement Comme un Droit de l'Homme: Leçon Inaugural de la Troisième Session d'Enseignement de l'Institut International des Droits de l'Homme. *Revue des Droits de l'Homme* 5: 505–534.

Ngang, Carol Chi (2021) *The Right to Development in Africa*. Leiden/Boston: Brill Publishers.

Protocol to the African Charter on Human and Peoples' Rights on the Rights of Women in Africa adopted by the Assembly of Heads State and Government in Maputo, Mozambique 11 July 2003.

Report of the Secretary General (2013) Emergence of the Right to Development. In: UN Human Rights (ed) *Realizing the Right to Development: Essays in Commemoration of 25 Years of the United Nations Declaration on the Right to Development*. Geneva/New York: UN Publication.

Subedi, Surya (2021) Declaration on the Right to Development. *United Nations Audiovisual Library of International Law*, 1–9.

Sudan Human Rights Organisation and another v Sudan (2009) AHRLR 153 (ACHPR 2009).

UN Human Rights (1996–2024) Independent Experts: Expert Mechanism on the Right to Development. Available at: https://www.ohchr.org/en/hrc-subsidiaries/expert-mechanism-on-right-to-development/independent-experts (consulted 30 October 2024).

United Nations (2023) Third Committee Underscores Need for Legally Binding Tool to Enforce Right to Development, Unrealized by Millions Worldwide, Directed also at Businesses' Meetings, Coverage and Press Releases Seventy-eighth Session, 20th and 21st Meeting (AM and PM) GA/SHC/4383, 13 October 2023. *United Nations*. Available at: https://press.un.org/en/2023/gashc4383.doc.htm (consulted 7 March 2024).

United Nations Commission on Human Rights, Resolution 4 (XXXIII), Adopted Without a Vote on 21 February 1977.

United Nations Human Rights (ed) (2013) *Realizing the Right to Development: Essays in Commemoration of 25 Years of the United Nations Declaration on the Right to Development*. Geneva/New York: UN Publication.

United Nations Millennium Declaration Resolution A/55/L.2 adopted by the General Assembly on 18 September 2000.

PART 1

Nature of the Right to Development

CHAPTER 2

Self-Determination and the Collective Rights of Peoples in the Right to Development Agenda

Amal Jawad and Bonny Ibhawoh

1 Introduction

The right to development (RTD) represents a transformative paradigm in international human rights and development discourse, intricately linking self-determination with peoples' collective rights.[1] Central to this framework is the assertion that actual development cannot be achieved solely through individual liberties but must also encompass the collective aspirations and self-governance of communities and nations.[2] This integrative approach acknowledges that individual freedoms are deeply intertwined with the collective capacity of peoples to determine their own economic, social, and cultural destinies.[3] By emphasising individual and collective dimensions, the RTD broadens the scope of human rights, fostering a more holistic and inclusive understanding of development.

This chapter employs a normative legal analysis combined with a comparative approach to dissect the foundational principles of the RTD and their practical implications. The analysis situates the RTD within the broader human rights and sustainable development context by systematically reviewing international instruments, legal precedents, and scholarly literature. It includes case studies and theoretical perspectives, which provide a nuanced understanding of how self-determination and collective rights operate within different socio-political landscapes. The research contributes to existing literature by bridging gaps between normative theories and

1 Declaration on the Right to Development Resolution A/RES/41/128 adopted by UN General Assembly on 4 December 1986.

2 Ibid.

3 United Nations General Assembly (2024) Individual and Collective Dimensions of the Right to Development. Available at: https://documents.un.org/doc/undoc/gen/g24/107/20/pdf/g2410720.pdf (consulted 6 June 2024).

 | DOI:10.1163/9789004734357_003

practical implementations of the RTD. It offers a comprehensive examination of the dual dimensions of the RTD, highlighting the interplay between individual and collective rights in fostering inclusive development. Furthermore, the chapter advances the discourse by proposing actionable recommendations for enhancing international cooperation and state obligations, promoting a more just and equitable global development framework. Integrating historical contexts with contemporary challenges underscores the enduring relevance of self-determination and collective rights in shaping the future of international development and human rights. It provides a critical lens through which policymakers, scholars, and practitioners can evaluate and advance the RTD agenda, ensuring that development processes are people-centred and sustainable.

The chapter delves into the intricate relationship between self-determination and peoples' collective rights within the RTD agenda. It begins by establishing the normative foundations of the RTD, exploring how it encompasses both individual and collective rights and situating it within the historical context of post-colonial struggles and the advocacy for a new economic order by states of the Global South. Building on this foundation, the discussion transitions to examining the collective RTD, highlighting the integration of individual and collective rights and analysing key case studies that illustrate the operationalisation of these rights. Subsequently, the chapter thoroughly explores the concept of self-determination, emphasising its legal affirmations and role in facilitating collective development. This is followed by an analysis of peoples' RTD, where the chapter examines the legal and theoretical definitions of "peoples" as collective rights holders and discusses the challenges and opportunities arising from the ambiguity in defining the concept in international law. Further, it addresses state obligations and the duty to cooperate, outlining the multi-layered responsibilities of states at global, regional, and national levels in fostering inclusive development. It underscores the necessity of international cooperation and the reform of the international economic order to support the realisation of the RTD. Finally, the chapter discusses participatory and sustainable development themes, emphasising the importance of inclusive and equitable growth aligned with human rights principles. By integrating these elements, the chapter analyses how self-determination and collective rights underpin the RTD agenda, offering insights into the global challenges and opportunities for advancing equitable and sustainable development.

2 Normative Foundations of the Right to Development

2.1 *Definition and Dimensions of the Right to Development*

The Declaration on the Right to Development (DRTD) defines the RTD as encompassing individual and collective aspects.[4] It emphasises that every person has the right to engage in and reap the benefits of development while recognising this right as shared among all communities and nations.[5] The United Nations General Assembly formally endorsed the DRTD in 1986 as "an inalienable human right under which every human person and all peoples are entitled to participate in, contribute to, and enjoy economic, social, cultural and political development, in which all human rights and fundamental freedoms can be fully realised".[6] The intersection of human rights and development began to take shape after the decolonisation movement in the 1950s and 1960s, as formerly colonised nations gained independence and voiced the RTD as an essential element accompanying their new political freedom.[7]

Initial interpretations of the RTD framed the right as primarily or even exclusively a collective right of peoples, reflecting a principle applicable to all.[8] The perspective presented departs from the conventional emphasis on individual rights within the discourse on human rights.[9] Nevertheless, the RTD is concurrently acknowledged as a personal right.[10] This dual recognition underscores a nuanced understanding of human rights that integrates collective and individual dimensions, broadening the traditional scope of human rights discourse.[11] Such a broadened interpretation of rights includes comprehensive developmental considerations that identify "every individual" and "all peoples" as entitled to the RTD.[12]

---

4 Declaration on the Right to Development, supra note 1.

5 Arts, Karin and Tamo, Atabongawung (2016) The Right to Development in International Law: New Momentum Thirty Years Down the Line? *Netherlands International Law Review* 63: 221–249; Declaration on the Right to Development, supra note 1.

6 Declaration on the Right to Development, supra note 1.

7 Arts and Tamo, supra note 5, 221–249.

8 Declaration on the Right to Development, supra note 1.

9 UNGA, Individual and Collective Dimensions of the Right to Development, supra note 3.

10 Arts and Tamo, supra note 5, 221–249.

11 UNGA, Individual and Collective Dimensions of the Right to Development, supra note 3.

12 Ibid.

Although all United Nations (UN) member states have endorsed the RTD either in the DRTD or related instruments affirming it,[13] the specifics of their obligations and enforcement strategies remain widely debated. Despite this, the declaration is recognised as a non-legally binding resolution.[14] Over the past three decades, political disputes and considerations have significantly impeded the realisation and enactment of the RTD. Developed countries have generally dismissed any reading of the RTD that would require them to allocate assistance for development to less developed countries; developed countries usually have rejected interpretations of the RTD that require assistance to less developed nations due to economic, political, and strategic concerns.[15]

Economically, they argue that mandatory financial commitments would strain their budgets and divert resources from domestic priorities.[16] Politically, there is a disinclination to relinquish control over international development agendas to multilateral institutions, fearing it could undermine their sovereignty and national interests. Additionally, concerns about the effectiveness and accountability of aid distribution led developed nations to worry that funds might be mismanaged or fail to produce desired outcomes.[17] Strategically, developed countries often oppose the RTD provisions that mandate aid to nations with complex geopolitical ties, such as those involving security or trade dependencies. They also tend to favour market-driven development initiatives over rights-based frameworks, advocating for private sector-led solutions rather than state-directed aid. The resistance has resulted in a consistent reluctance to support legally binding RTD obligations. Instead, developed countries prefer voluntary or non-binding commitments, allowing them to contribute to global development without stringent enforcement.[18]

A shift is occurring toward conditional aid, linking assistance to specific policy reforms or governance improvements rather than recognising the RTD

13 Arts and Tamo, supra note 5, 221–249.

14 Declaration on the Right to Development, supra note 1.

15 Sengupta, A. (2017) On the Theory and Practice of the Right to Development. In: Kamminga, M.T. (ed) *Challenges in International Human Rights Law*. New York: Routledge, 667–720.

16 Oduwole, Olajumoke (2014) International Law and the Right to Development: A Pragmatic Approach for Africa. *International Institute of Social Studies*.

17 Ozoemena, Rita (2021) Misappropriated Development: Exploring Accountability as the Rate-determining Step to the Realisation of the Right to Development in Select African Countries. *Comparative and International Law Journal of Southern Africa* 54(3): 21–43.

18 Lorenzo, Johanna Aleria (2021) A Path Toward Sustainable Development Along the Belt and Road. *Journal of International Economic Law* 24(3): 591–608.

as an unconditional human right. These trends reflect a broader hesitancy to fully integrate the RTD into international law, challenging the traditional donor-recipient dynamic and necessitating a more equitable redistribution of resources. Consequently, opposition from developed nations has hindered the implementation of the RTD, perpetuating global inequalities and limiting the establishment of a just and equitable development framework.[19] Conversely, developing countries have persistently called for enhanced global cooperation, seeking development assistance, equitable trade conditions, access to technology, and relief from debt burdens from developed nations.[20] This divergence has impeded the actualisation of the RTD agenda. This divergence has impeded the actualisation of the RTD agenda by creating significant barriers to consensus and coordinated action.

The reluctance of developed countries to commit to binding financial and policy obligations has constrained the availability of essential resources and support that developing nations need to achieve their development goals.[21] Additionally, disagreements over trade policies and technology transfer have hindered the establishment of fair and inclusive economic systems.[22] The persistent debt burdens imposed on developing countries further restrict their ability to invest in critical areas such as education, healthcare, and infrastructure. These conflicting priorities and lack of mutual commitment have resulted in fragmented efforts and insufficient progress towards realising the comprehensive and equitable development envisioned by the RTD framework.[23]

The discussion on the RTD after the 1960s centred on several critical issues, including the absence of democracy at the international level, unfair international systems disadvantaging developing nations, compromised self-determination and sovereignty over resources in these countries due to interference by powerful states, and structural impediments that weaken the role of states in the Global South in crafting and executing economic policies.[24] Advocacy for the RTD as a principle has focused on rectifying these systemic

---

19 Mamah, Wilfred (2013) Traps and Tools: A Contextual Critique of the Right to Development in International Law. PhD Dissertation, University of Westminster.

20 Muchhala, Bhumika (2022) The Structural Power of the State-Finance Nexus: Systemic Delinking for the Right to Development. *Society for International Development* 65(2–4): 124.

21 Mamah, supra note 19.

22 Sam, Emmanuel and Fredah, Luareen (2024) Legal and Economic Implications of China's Utilization of the Right to Development (RTD) in Africa to Further its Debt-Trap Diplomacy. *Science and Economics Research Journal* 3(3): 1–10.

23 Mamah, supra note 19.

24 Arts and Tamo, supra note 5, 221–249.

imbalances and remedying the disparities in the global economic framework, particularly those stemming from the uneven dynamics between developed and developing nations. The new international economic order (NIEO), an agenda by developing countries in the 1970s to restructure global economic relations, exemplifies such advocacy. The NIEO agenda focused on promoting fair trade practices, increasing development aid, granting greater control over natural resources, and ensuring equitable economic growth.[25] It sought to redress imbalances between developed and developing countries, fostering an environment where all nations could participate equitably in the global economy.[26] The NIEO laid the groundwork for the 1967 Charter of Algiers, in which the Group of 77 (now comprising of 134) developing nations recognised the RTD and the adoption of the DRTD by the UN General Assembly in 1986.[27] This DRTD marked a significant milestone in international efforts to integrate human rights and economic development objectives.

Since the adoption of the DRTD, it has been affirmed in several UN instruments, including the Rio Declaration on Environment and Development of 1992, the Vienna Declaration and Programme of Action of 1993, the United Nations Millennium Declaration of 2000, the United Nations Declaration on the Rights of Indigenous Peoples (UNDRIP) of 2007, the 2030 Agenda for the Sustainable Development Goals (SDGs) and the Paris Agreement on Climate Change of 2015.[28] Additionally, the SDGs highlight key aspects of the RTD, and it has been noted that achieving the SDGs could significantly advance realisation of the RTD.[29] For example, Goals 16 and 17 of the SDGs, which focus on fostering inclusive societies, justice access, building strong institutions, and enhancing global partnerships and resources for sustainable development, are particularly aligned with the RTD principles.

---

25 Gordon, Ruth (2009) The Dawn of a New, New International Economic Order? *Law and Contemporary Problems* 72(4): 131–162.

26 Kamga, Serges Djoyou (2015) The G77 and the Right to Development. *Latin American Report* 31(1): 58–76.

27 United Nations Commission on Human Rights, Res. 4 (XXXIII), 21 February 1977.

28 Kanade, Mihir and Puvimanasinghe, Shyami (2023) The Right to Development and the 2030 Agenda for Sustainable Development. In: *Operationalizing the Right to Development in Implementing the Sustainable Development Goals*, E-Learning Module, Right to Development Section of the Office of the United Nations High Commissioner for Human Rights (OHCHR).

29 Arts and Tamo, supra note 5, 221–249.

The RTD had gained significant recognition within regional legal frameworks, notably through the 1981 African Charter on Human and Peoples' Rights.[30] Article 22 of the Charter stands out as the only legally binding provision acknowledging the RTD as an individual and collective right, complete with enforceable state obligations. It underscores the significance of the RTD in its Preamble and elaborates on the right of peoples to pursue economic, social, and cultural development while maintaining their freedom, identity, and equal access to the shared legacy of humanity.[31] The African Charter's provisions have been used in legal proceedings to enforce peoples' collective rights.

2.2 *Collective Right to Development*

By providing for a broad range of individual and collective rights, the RTD brings a holistic view to human rights. It affirms that each person and every community is entitled to play an active role in and derive advantages from development across various dimensions—economic, social, cultural, and political.[32] This principle underscores the imperative for inclusive progress that incorporates contributions from all sectors of society and addresses their diverse needs, fostering a comprehensive approach to development where no individual or group is neglected.[33] This comprehensive approach ensures that marginalised and vulnerable groups receive the necessary attention and resources, thereby reducing disparities and promoting social equity.[34] The RTD framework prevents excluding individuals or groups by actively involving diverse communities in decision-making processes and tailoring development initiatives to meet their needs.[35]

The inclusive strategy enhances the effectiveness of development programmes and fosters social cohesion and stability, ensuring that the benefits of progress are shared broadly across society. Based on the understanding that individual rights form the foundation of human dignity, the RTD also acknowledges that sovereignty over natural resources should be exercised

30 Ibid.

31 UNGA, Individual and Collective Dimensions of the Right to Development, supra note 3.

32 Arts and Tamo, supra note 5, 221–249.

33 Chen, Weiqi and Wang, Linbin (2024) A Holistic View of Human Rights and its Application in the Context of Infectious Disease Pandemics. *Heliyon* 10(9): 1–11.

34 Arts and Tamo, supra note 5, 221–249.

35 Giralt, Laura (2024) A Comprehensive Analysis of the European Union's Integration of the Right to Development and the Sustainable Development Goals: EU Development: From Policy to Practice. *Journal of International Development* 12(1): 45–60.

for the collective benefit of the entire community.[36] Within the RTD framework, individual rights enable each person to benefit from their enforcement directly, fostering personal empowerment and autonomy.[37] Simultaneously, collective rights under the RTD ensure communal welfare and the sustainable management of shared resources, promoting equitable development and social cohesion.[38] This dual recognition underscores the necessity of balancing personal freedoms with collective responsibilities, thus facilitating a holistic development approach that benefits individuals and communities alike. Based on the understanding that individual rights form the foundation, this principle also acknowledges that sovereignty over natural resources should be exercised for the collective benefit of the entire community.[39] Individual rights benefit the right holders directly, whereas collective rights ensure communal welfare and sustainable management of shared resources. In the case of collective rights like self-determination, even though the right may belong to a group or nation, its application ultimately promotes the well-being of its members.[40]

Development aims to enhance individuals' capabilities to improve overall societal well-being.[41] However, balancing individual and collective rights can lead to conflicts, especially in resource-limited settings.[42] The RTD can be contrasted with rights traditionally seen through an individual lens, such as the right to liberty of speech or the exact right to a fair trial.[43] These rights protect individual freedoms and ensure that the state or other actors do not infringe on personal liberties.[44] Individual rights are usually upheld individually, and breaches of these rights frequently lead to personal and direct experiences.[45]

36 UNGA, Individual and Collective Dimensions of the Right to Development, supra note 3.

37 Ibid.

38 Ibid.

39 Schmidt, Hendrik (2023) The Legal Meaning of State Custodianship in the Context of the Mineral and Petroleum Resources Development Act 28 of 2002. PhD Thesis, University of Cape Town.

40 O'Sullivan, D. (2023) Self-Determination, Participation and Leadership. In: O'Sullivan, D. (ed) *Indigeneity, Culture and the UN Sustainable Development Goals*. Singapore: Springer Nature Singapore, 159–188.

41 Plagerson, Sophie (2021) Human Well-being and Capabilities. *United Nations Research Institute for Social Development*, 1–25.

42 Ibid.

43 Chaturvedi, Ipshita (2014) A Critical Study of Free, Prior and Informed Consent in the Context of the Right to Development—Can Consent Be Withheld. *Journal of Indian Law and Society* 5(winter): 37.

44 Oestreich, Joel (2017) *Development and Human Rights: Rhetoric and Reality in India*. Oxford: Oxford University Press, 9.

45 UNGA, Individual and Collective Dimensions of the Right to Development, supra note 3.

Though collective rights pertain to groups, their violation can have significant implications for individuals within those groups. For instance, when collective rights are undermined—such as Indigenous peoples' rights to maintain their cultural heritage or workers' rights to form unions—the affected individuals may experience a loss of identity, reduced economic opportunities, and diminished access to essential services.[46] These collective infringements can lead to personal hardships, including psychological distress, financial instability, and limited personal development.

Additionally, the erosion of collective rights can weaken community structures, making it more difficult for individuals to advocate for their rights effectively.[47] Therefore, violations of collective rights impact the group as a whole and have prefund individual consequences, underscoring the interconnectedness of individual and collective rights within the RTD framework. Violation is often a direct, personal experience. The collective rights pertaining to groups can have implications for individual rights. Development projects like building infrastructure or improving public health systems illustrate how collective action can lead to the individual enjoying a higher quality of life. Furthermore, collective rights like those of Indigenous peoples to maintain their social legacy or of workers to form unions illustrate the RTD's necessity for collective rights.[48] These rights often require group recognition and action to realise them, highlighting how a community's development can enhance its capabilities and rights.

The essence of the RTD lies in its integrative approach, which seeks to amalgamate development with human rights, positioning the individual at the core of developmental processes.[49] This is distinct from other human rights frameworks, which may not explicitly connect development with enhancing human freedoms.[50] For instance, the Universal Declaration of Human Rights and the International Covenant on Civil and Political Rights (ICCPR), primarily focus on protecting individual liberties without explicitly linking development to enhancing human freedoms. Unlike these frameworks, the RTD emphasises the interconnectedness of economic, social, cultural, and political development

46 Ibid.

47 Ibid.

48 Bunn, Isabella (2000) The Right to Development: Implications for International Economic Law. *American University International Law Review* 15(6): 1425–1467.

49 Sengupta, supra note 15, 667–720.

50 UNGA, Individual and Collective Dimensions of the Right to Development, supra note 3.

by realising human rights, thereby fostering a more holistic and inclusive approach to human dignity and societal progress.

Echoing the views of the former UN Independent Expert on the RTD and economist, Amartya Sen, it is worth stressing that development is characterised as a progression of enlarging people's actual liberties described as "substantial freedoms," and the expansion of "capabilities of persons to lead the kind of lives they value or have reasons to value".[51] Sen also posits that effective public policies should foster the construction of social, economic, and political institutions that boost individuals' capabilities, ensuring that rights across different domains are realised concurrently for the complete enjoyment of all rights.[52] Compared to individual rights, which can be claimed and enforced by single individuals, the RTD insists on an integrated individual and collective approach where states and international bodies must collaborate to create conditions that allow for the comprehensive development of societies.[53] The collective approach is especially, relevant in addressing systemic issues such as poverty and inequality, which affect large groups and require coordinated resolution efforts.

The RTD debate persists despite established frameworks, reflecting differing views on development's meaning, assessment, and implementation responsibilities.[54] Discussions extend to balancing personal rights with collective advancement and the role of global influences.[55] The complexities of balancing individual and collective rights ensure that the RTD is not just a legal concept but also a dynamic and evolving conversation reflecting the changing landscape of global politics, economics, and social justice. The persistent debates surrounding the RTD, which reflect differing views on its definition, assessment, and implementation responsibilities, underscore the importance of clearly conceptualising and effectively operationalising individual and collective rights within this framework.

51 Sengupta, supra note 15, 667–720.

52 Ibhawoh, Bonny (2011) The Right to Development: The Politics and Polemics of Power and Resistance. *Human Rights Quarterly* 33(1): 76.

53 United Nations (2024) Individual and collective dimensions of the right to development, Thematic study by the Expert Mechanism on the Right to Development A/HRC/57/40, Geneva.

54 Ibhawoh, supra note 53, 76.

55 Sengupta, supra note 15, 667–720.

3 Self-Determination and the Right to Development

3.1 *Embodiment of Individual Rights into Collective Rights*

Collective human rights, epitomised by the right to self-determination, are essential for protecting and realising individual rights. This is grounded in the understanding that no individual is isolated from their community; individual autonomy and freedom are intrinsically linked to the collective.[56] The suppression of collective rights, particularly the right to self-determination, thus, inevitably infringes on individual liberties. Indigenous peoples, whose identities and livelihoods are inextricably tied to their collectives, experience this infringement most acutely.[57] Self-determination, as recognised in international legal instruments, is a fundamentally collective right with profound implications for individual rights.[58] Collective rights, recognised in international legal frameworks, are essential for Indigenous peoples, whose identities and livelihoods are deeply tied to their groups and for other communities globally. These rights, such as self-determination, hold profound implications for the individual rights of all members within such collectives, including ethnic minorities and communal societies.[59] This broader application demonstrates the universal importance of collective rights in safeguarding diverse groups' cultural, social, and economic foundations worldwide.[60]

The right to self-determination is foundational to international human rights law architecture, prominently enshrined in Article 1 of the ICCPR and the International Covenant on Economic, Social, and Cultural Rights (ICESCR).[61] This articulation underscores the primacy of the RTD in the hierarchy of rights, establishing a legal precedent that enables all peoples to freely determine their political, economic, social, and cultural development. Beyond the ICCPR and ICESCR, the universality of this right is further supported by its inclusion in other key instruments such as the Declaration on the Granting

56 Norton, Anthony Dean (2024) Beyond Right and Recognition: Toward a History of Collective Self-Determination as the Authorship of Political Personhood. PhD Dissertation, University of California.

57 Williams, Lewis (2021) *Indigenous Intergenerational Resilience: Confronting Cultural and Ecological Crisis*. New York: Routledge.

58 Ibhawoh, supra note 53, 76.

59 UNGA, Individual and Collective Dimensions of the Right to Development, supra note 3.

60 De Matos, M.M. (2018) Cultural Identity and Self-Determination as Key Concepts in Concurring Legal Frameworks for the International Protection of the Rights of Indigenous Peoples. In: Lagrange, E., Oeter, S. and Uerpmann-Wittzack, R. (eds) *Cultural Heritage and International Law: Objects, Means and Ends of International Protection*. Cham: Springer Nature, 273–292.

61 Ibhawoh, supra note 53, 76.

of Independence to Colonial Countries and Peoples (General Assembly Resolution 1514) and the Vienna Declaration and Programme of Action.[62] These documents collectively affirm that the realisation of the RTD is an essential condition for protecting and enhancing individual human rights and crucial for fostering international peace and security. By anchoring the discussion in these broader legal contexts, the interconnectedness of the RTD with the global human rights framework becomes apparent, emphasising its role as the bedrock upon which all other rights are realised.

The DRTD further reinforces the centrality of self-determination to collective human rights. The DRTD underscores the fundamental role of self-determination within the context of collective human rights, highlighting it as central to the framework of international legal standards.[63] The DRTD further elaborates on this theme by proposing more defined mechanisms and obligations for states to ensure the practical application of the principles of self-determination. The DRTD and the draft Covenant on the Right to Development emphasise the growing recognition of self-determination as a theoretical right and a practical imperative, which states are expected to support and implement actively.[64] Such instruments are pivotal in framing self-determination as a dynamic element of international law that supports the broader agenda of human rights and sustainable development.[65] It emphasises that the RTD is inseparable from peoples' right to self-determination, including their inalienable right to full sovereignty over their natural wealth and resources.[66] This principle is rooted in the historical context of decolonisation, where newly independent states sought to reclaim control over their political, economic, and social destinies free from external domination. The DRTD reflects the demand for a NIEO to empower nations, particularly those emerging from colonial rule, to manage their resources to achieve development legitimately. The exercise of self-determination in this context enables

62 Cerqueira, D. (2023) Cultural Rights. In Cantú Rivera, H. (ed) *The Universal Declaration of Human Rights*. Leiden/Boston: Brill Nijhoff, 710–732.

63 Human Rights Committee, General Comment No 12: The Right to Self-Determination of Peoples (Art 1), 1984.

64 Nakagiri, Masashi (2021) The Zero Draft Convention on the Right to Development as a Non-consensual Lawmaking: International and Domestic Dimension. *Faculté de Droit et de Science Politique—Aix Marseille Université*.

65 Human Rights Committee, General Comment No 12, supra note 64, (Art 1).

66 Bedjaoui, M. (1992) The Right to Development. In: Mayor F. and Bedjaoui, M. *International Law: Achievements and Prospects*. Paris: UNESCO and Dordrecht: Martinus Nijhoff, 1177–1203.

collectives, particularly states and their citizens, to pursue development pathways aligned with their values and priorities.

The dual focus of self-determination—on individual autonomy and collective welfare—lies at the heart of the RTD.[67] It is a right that encompasses the freedom to pursue individual aspirations and the collective capacity to shape communal futures. This collective dimension is notably highlighted in the UNDRIP,[68] which acknowledges the historical injustices suffered by indigenous peoples as a result of colonisation and the dispossession of their lands, territories, and resources.[69] Such dispossession has directly impacted their ability to exercise the RTD according to their needs and interests.[70] Articles 3 and 4 of the UNDRIP explicitly reaffirm the right of indigenous peoples to self-determination and autonomy in managing their internal affairs, underscoring their authority to pursue economic, social, and cultural development according to their values and priorities. In the context of the DRTD, these provisions are crucial.[71] The draft Covenant on the Right to Development advocates for a supportive international environment that enhances national capacities for self-determination.[72] By examining the provisions of the UNDRIP alongside the draft Covenant, it becomes evident that both instruments emphasise the fundamental role of self-determination in enabling Indigenous communities to achieve their developmental aspirations. The alignment suggests that the draft Covenant supports and reinforces the principles outlined in the UNDRIP, thereby providing a broader framework for interpreting indigenous rights to self-determination under international law. This underscores the importance of self-determination as a political right and a key development driver for marginalised and historically oppressed communities.

In a more recent reaffirmation of the right to self-determination, the UN's Summit of the Future highlighted the global community's renewed

---

67 Evans, Joane et al (2015) Self-determination and Archival Autonomy: Advocating Activism. *Archival Science* 15(4): 337–368.

68 United Nations Declaration on the Rights of Indigenous Peoples, Resolution 61/295 adopted on 13 September 2007.

69 Ibid.

70 Ibid at Arts 3–4.

71 Zadorin, Maxim Yu and Gladun, Elena (2022) Primary Elements of the Indigenous Peoples' Right to Self-Determination and Their Reflection in International Cases. *Law Enforcement Review* 6(4): 121–138; see also Barelli, Mauro (2011) Shaping Indigenous Self-Determination: Promising or Unsatisfactory Solutions? *International Community Law Review* 13(4): 413–436.

72 Draft International Covenant on the Right to Development—Report by the Chair-Rapporteur of the Working Group on the Right to Development, Zamir Akram (Pakistan) Human Rights Council A/HRC/54/50 54th Session, 6 October 2023.

commitment to this principle.[73] The Pact for the Future, adopted at the Summit, reinforced member states' obligation to respect the sovereign equality of all nations and to uphold the principles of equal rights and self-determination of peoples, as enshrined in the UN Charter.[74] The Summit highlighted the essential role of multilateral cooperation in tackling our era's critical challenges. These challenges are fundamentally linked to the broader goal of pursuing development through self-determination.[75] This renewed commitment recognises that self-determination remains as relevant today as it was during the decolonisation era, especially in light of contemporary global inequities in wealth, power, and access to resources.

The principle of self-determination is thus, essential for the fulfilment of individual human rights and for the realisation of comprehensive sustainable development.[76] As the DRTD asserts, the RTD must be understood as the full realisation of the right to self-determination, which enables peoples and communities to determine their political, economic, and cultural futures.[77] This is especially significant in the contexts where basic human rights—such as access to water, healthcare, and education—remain unfulfilled. The RTD, grounded in self-determination, provides a framework for communities to assert control over their destinies, ensuring that development processes are responsive to their unique needs and aspirations. Self-determination embodies the right of peoples to determine their political, economic, social, and cultural status without external interference. This principle, central to international law, advocates for the autonomy and agency of groups to navigate their developmental pathways following their unique values and priorities.

Although primarily associated with national and ethnic sovereignty, self-determination also underpins various international human rights doctrines, asserting that sustainable development can only occur when people have the power to influence the laws and policies that govern them. The connection between self-determination and broader human rights frameworks is thus

73 United Nations (2024, 22 September) A Pact for the Future, Global Digital Compact and a Declaration on Future Generations. Available at: https://www.un.org/sites/un2.un.org/files/sotf-pact_for_the_future_adopted.pdf (consulted 30 September 2024).

74 Ibid.

75 Ibid.

76 Ryan, R.M. and Deci, E.L. (2022) Self-Determination Theory. In: Maggino, F. (ed) *Encyclopedia of Quality of Life and Well-Being Research*. Cham: Springer International Publishing, 6229–6235.

77 Schrijver, N. (2013) Self-determination of Peoples and Sovereignty over Natural Wealth and Resources. In: UN Human Rights (ed) *Realizing the Right to Development*. Geneva/New York: UN Publication, 95–102.

integral, providing a foundation upon which equitable development can be built. Building upon the principle of self-determination, the RTD is recognised as an inalienable human right that extends individuals' and communities' ability to improve their well-being without discrimination. The DRTD asserts that this right must be fulfilled through the practical application of self-determination, enabling communities to direct their development agendas. This is especially crucial in regions where access to essential services like water, healthcare, and education is compromised.[78] By embedding self-determination in the framework for development, the RTD ensures that progress is sustainable and equitable, reflecting each community's specific needs and aspirations. Therefore, realising the right to self-determination is about autonomy and empowering communities to forge sustainable development paths that respect and fulfil their fundamental human rights.

At its core, the RTD seeks freedom, which is both the foremost goal and the principal means of development. Freedom, in this sense, is not merely individual autonomy but encompasses the collective capacity of communities to shape their futures. While individual freedom is vital for asserting personal autonomy, the full potential of individuals can only be realised in the context of collective social freedoms.[79] In this context, freedom transcends mere individual autonomy to encompass the collective capacity of communities to shape their futures.[80] This broader understanding of freedom is fundamental to sustainable development, which asserts that people must have the authority to determine their political, economic, and cultural destinies. This collective dimension of freedom is integral to sustainable development, as it empowers communities, not just individuals, to participate actively in making decisions that impact their lives. Moreover, this expansive view of freedom directly informs the RTD, which advocates for the conditions necessary for all people to develop their full potential.[81]

The RTD emphasises that development needs to be comprehensive and human-centred, enabling every community member to contribute to and benefit from economic and social progress. The interdependence of sustainable development and the RTD illustrates that actual development requires harmony between individual liberties and collective aspirations. It highlights

78 Declaration on the Right to Development, supra note 1.

79 Hummels, C.C.M. and Frens, J.W. (2011) Designing Disruptive Innovative Systems, Products and Services: RTD Process. In: Coelho, D. (ed) *Industrial Design—New Frontiers*. InTech, 147–172.

80 Ibid.

81 Mannelli, Caludio (2021) *The Ethics of Rapid Tissue Donation* (RTD). Cham: Springer International Publishing.

that development should be measured by economic growth and by enhancing people's ability to lead a life they value, which is the essence of freedom.[82] Therefore, the realisation of self-determination and the RTD hinges on fostering an environment where individual and collective freedoms are respected and nurtured.[83] Thus, the RTD, anchored in the principle of self-determination, calls for a holistic approach to human rights that recognises the interdependence of individual and collective rights in pursuing meaningful, inclusive, and sustainable development. In this context, collective rights are framed in terms of peoples' RTD.

Thus, the RTD, anchored in the principle of self-determination, necessitates a holistic approach to human rights that acknowledges the interdependence of individual and collective rights. This integrated perspective is essential for achieving meaningful and inclusive sustainable development. Within this framework, collective rights are conceptualised as the right of communities to pursue development that aligns with their values and needs. Such an approach ensures that development initiatives strengthen communal capacities, thereby fostering a comprehensive realisation of human potential across development's social, economic, and cultural dimensions.

3.2 *People's Rights to Development*

The concept of "peoples" as rights holders has emerged as a fundamental principle in international law, most notably within the framework of the RTD.[84] This notion is rooted in the post-World War II geopolitical context, and it is intricately linked with the broader understanding of "nations" in international law, as distinguished from the political and juridical concept of "states".[85] The UN Charter begins with the words "we the peoples of the United Nations"[86] and thus, situates "peoples" as international law and development subjects. The RTD has evolved within this context as embodying not only the rights of individuals but also the collective rights of "peoples".[87]

82 Sengupta, supra note 15, 667–720.

83 Rauna, Koukkanen (2019) *Restructuring Relations: Indigenous Self-Determination, Governance, and Gender*. Oxford: Oxford University Press.

84 Ibid.

85 Ibid.

86 Charter of the United Nations and Status of the International Court of Justice, adopted in San Francisco, United States of America on 26 June 1945, Preamble.

87 UNGA, Individual and Collective Dimensions of the Right to Development, supra note 3.

The UN Charter explicitly identifies the promotion of the "economic and social advancement of all peoples"[88] as a central goal. Article 1(2) articulates the UN's mission "to develop friendly relations among nations based on respect for the principle of equal rights and self-determination of peoples".[89] This fundamental purpose is reiterated in Article 55, which emphasises that the UN shall promote higher living standards, economic progress, and universal respect for human rights to create conditions of stability conducive to peaceful international relations.[90] Significantly, under Article 56, all member states must collaborate, individually and collectively, to achieve these aims. Thus, the UN Charter lays the groundwork for understanding peoples as collective entities with rights, particularly within the self-determination and development framework.

Beyond the UN Charter, several key international instruments further reinforce the recognition of peoples as collective rights holders. The ICCPR and the ICESCR affirm the right of all peoples to self-determination. The concept of "peoples" as collective rights holders is central to the RTD framework in international law. Rooted in post-World War II principles and explicitly emphasised within the UN Charter, this notion underpins the collective dimension of the RTD, which extends beyond individual rights to encompass the rights of communities and groups to self-determined development. The UN Charter's commitment to "the economic and social advancement of all peoples"[91] reflects a foundational goal of promoting development that respects collective rights. Article 1 highlights the UN's mission to enable conditions conducive to stable, peaceful international relations through inclusive development.

Furthermore, both the ICCPR and the ICESCR affirm the right of all peoples to self-determination, reinforcing the RTD's emphasis on collective agency in the development process.[92] By recognising "peoples" as the central beneficiaries of development rights, the RTD framework underscores that sustainable development must be community-centred and inclusive. This perspective aligns with the obligation of states, as outlined in Article 56 of the UN Charter, to work collaboratively to achieve equitable development outcomes that serve the interests of all peoples collectively, thus fostering global solidarity and respect

---

88 United Nations Executive Committee of Economic and Social Affairs (2024) Objective. Available at: https://www.un.org/esa/ecesa/objective.html (consulted 10 June 2024).

89 United Nations Charter, supra note 87, Chapter I: Purposes and Principles.

90 Ibid at Chapter IX: International Economic and Social Cooperation.

91 United Nations, Executive Committee of Economic and Social Affairs, supra note 89.

92 Munene, Andrew William (2019) *Realising the Right to Development in Kenya under the 2010 Constitution through Poverty Alleviation, Anti-Corruption and Public Participation Interventions*. Doctoral Dissertation, University of the Witwatersrand, South Africa.

for collective rights.[93] Similarly, the DRTD affirms peoples' collective rights to development. However, a significant lacuna exists across these instruments: none offer a definitive legal definition of "peoples". This absence has generated considerable ambiguity in interpreting who qualifies as a "peoples" under international law, especially concerning the RTD's operationalisation.[94]

Scholars like Alfredsson argue that this ambiguity is not necessarily detrimental but instead reflects the evolving and fluid nature of the term, particularly in response to global transformations in politics, culture, and society.[95] As conceived in international law, peoples have adapted to changes driven by globalisation, migration, and technological advancements. The absence of a rigid definition allows for flexibility, accommodating the diverse and complex realities in which claims to peoples' rights are made.[96] The notion of peoples is particularly crucial in interpreting collective rights within the context of the RTD. In this context, development is not solely an individual entitlement; it also represents a collective process through which peoples pursue social, economic, and cultural advancement. As noted in the DRTD, peoples have the right to participate in and contribute to development and the right to enjoy the benefits of development. The DRTD affirms that all peoples have an inherent right to participate actively in the development process, contribute meaningfully, and enjoy its benefits. This principle emphasises that development must be inclusive and equitable, ensuring that the fruits of progress are shared among all members of society and that every group has a voice in shaping development initiatives that impact their lives.[97]

Yet, whether a particular group qualifies as "peoples" to claim RTD is complex and requires careful examination. This qualification is critical, as it directly impacts the group's legal standing to claim collective development rights under international law. Such recognition involves assessing shared characteristics like cultural identity, historical continuity, and collective self-identification, affirming the group's claim to exercise collective rights within the development framework. In some cases, entire populations, such as

93 United Nations Charter, supra note 87, Art 56.

94 UNGA, Individual and Collective Dimensions of the Right to Development, supra note 3.

95 Summers, James (2014) *Peoples and International Law*. Leiden/Boston: Brill Nijhoff, 7; Alfredsson, Gudmundur (2022) Indigenous Peoples, Treaties With. *Max Planck Encyclopedias of International Law*.

96 Opeskin, Brian (2009) The Influence of International Law on the International Movement of Persons. *Munich Personal RePEc Archive Aper No 19200*.

97 Charter of the United Nations, Arts 73, 76, and 80 (regarding the Trusteeship System).

those of colonised territories, have asserted their RTD under the umbrella of self-determination.

In some cases, more minor, distinct groups within a state—such as Indigenous peoples—have claimed their RTD in response to marginalisation or exclusion from national development processes. For instance, in Brazil, Indigenous communities have consistently advocated for the protection of the Amazon rainforest, which is central to their livelihoods and cultural identity, against deforestation and industrial projects that primarily benefit non-Indigenous populations.[98] Similarly, in Canada, First Nations groups have demanded the right to control development on their traditional lands to ensure that resource extraction activities do not harm their environment or infringe on their cultural heritage.[99] These examples underscore how the RTD is crucial for marginalised communities to preserve their resources, uphold their way of life, and achieve equitable participation in the broader national economy.[100]

In other cases, smaller, distinct groups within a state—such as Indigenous peoples—have claimed their RTD in response to marginalisation or exclusion from national development processes. For instance, in Bolivia, indigenous groups have advocated for greater control over the development of their ancestral lands, especially in the context of large-scale infrastructure projects that threaten their territories.[101] These cases highlight how the RTD is invoked by marginalised communities to protect their cultural and environmental interests and to ensure that development initiatives benefit them equitably. The African Commission on Human and Peoples' Rights, in the landmark *Endorois* case, underscored this distinction by recognising the *Endorois* community as a distinct people with the RTD despite the Kenyan government's contestation.[102]

Further guidance on the definition of peoples in the context of the RTD is offered in a UNESCO study, which states that peoples are generally characterised by common historical traditions, racial or ethnic identities, linguistic unity,

98 Carstens, Martin (2021) Indigenous Rights and COVID-19: Indigenous Land and Health Under Serious Threat in Brazil. *International Journal on Minority and Group Rights* 29(3): 528–576.

99 Flanagan, Thomas (2019) *First Nations? Second Thoughts*. Montreal/Kingston: McGill-Queen's University Press.

100 Massad, Joseph (2018) Against Self-Determination. *Humanity* 9(2): 161–191.

101 Fabricant, Nicole (2012) *Mobilizing Bolivia's Displaced: Indigenous Politics and the Struggle Over Land*. Chapel Hill: University of North Carolina Press.

102 *Centre for Minority Rights Development (Kenya) and Minority Rights Group International on behalf of Endorois Welfare Council v Kenya* Comm 276/2003 (2009) AHRLR 75 (ACHPR 2009), Para 151.

cultural homogeneity, religious or ideological affinity, territorial connection, and shared economic life.[103] An additional critical element in determining peoples' rights is the group's collective consciousness and its will to be identified as a people. The African Commission on Human and Peoples' Rights has relied on these criteria in several cases, including *Gumne v Cameroon*, where the people of the Southern Cameroons were recognised as a distinct people based on shared history, language, and identity.[104] However, these defining characteristics applied in case law are not intended to be applied rigidly or cumulatively. Certain characteristics may carry more weight in specific contexts, such as territorial connection for indigenous peoples whose survival often depends on their relationship to their ancestral lands and natural resources.[105]

The ambiguity surrounding the definition of peoples presents challenges and opportunities for advancing the RTD. On one hand, the lack of a universal definition complicates the task of enforcing peoples' rights under international law. States may resist recognising distinct groups within their borders as peoples, fearing that doing so could undermine national sovereignty or territorial integrity. This tension is particularly evident in situations of secessionist movements or indigenous claims to autonomy.[106] On the other hand, the fluidity of the concept allows for a more inclusive and adaptable approach to development, ensuring that diverse groups—whether entire populations or smaller communities—can exercise the RTD in ways that reflect their needs and aspirations.

The recognition of peoples as rights holders within the RTD framework is well-established and continually evolving. Although no universally accepted definition of "peoples" exists, international law has articulated criteria to facilitate the identification of peoples on a case-by-case basis.[107] The collective nature of the RTD emphasises the significance of acknowledging collective identities and ensuring that all peoples—irrespective of their size or political status—are able to pursue their development without coercion,

---

103 UNESCO (1990) Final Report and Recommendation of Experts on Further Study of the Concept of the Rights of Peoples. UNESCO, Paris 27–30 November 1989.

104 *Kevin Mgwanga Gumne and Others v Cameroon* Comm 266/2003 (2009) AHRLR 9 (ACHPR 2009); see also, Ngang, Carol Chi (2021) Self-determination and the Southern Cameroons Quest for Sovereign Statehood. *African Journal of International and Comparative Law* 29(2): 304–307.

105 *Endorois* case, supra note 103, Para 151.

106 Gat, Azar (2012) *Nations: The Long History and Deep Roots of Political Ethnicity and Nationalism*. Cambridge: Cambridge University Press.

107 Sengupta, supra note 15, 667–720.

marginalisation, or exclusion. International courts and regional bodies have successfully operationalised this approach. However, ongoing vigilance and adaptation are essential to ensure that the RTD remains inclusive, equitable, and responsive to the needs of all peoples.[108] In addition to the role of judicial bodies and other enforcement mechanisms, the practical implementation of the RTD largely depends on the policies and actions of states, which are the primary duty-bearers.

3.3 *States' Obligations and the Duty to Cooperate*

The realisation of the RTD, encompassing both individual and collective dimensions, is fundamentally anchored in the obligations of states.[109] As one of the most comprehensive and interdisciplinary human rights, the RTD underscores the interconnectedness of all human rights, making state obligations central to its fulfilment.[110] States are bound by their duty to respect, protect, and fulfil the RTD through three interrelated levels of obligation: (1) their participation in global and regional partnerships aimed at fostering development; (2) policies that affect individuals and communities beyond their territorial jurisdiction; and (3) national policies and programmes designed to uplift individuals and communities within their borders.[111] These multi-layered obligations highlight development's complex and interdependent nature and the need for a holistic approach to state responsibility.

Crucially, realising the RTD requires robust international cooperation, which is not merely aspirational but a legal duty. Realising the RTD depends on strong international cooperation, which is a hopeful goal and a legally binding obligation recognised by various international agreements. In our interconnected world, challenges like poverty, climate change, and health crises cannot effectively be addressed by any nation alone. International legal instruments, such as the DRTD and the UN Charter, mandate countries to collaborate, share resources, and support each other's development efforts. This legal duty ensures that nations are accountable for contributing to global progress, fostering a cooperative environment where sustainable and equitable development can thrive for all, as enshrined in various international instruments. The DRTD stipulates that:

---

108 Shany, Yair (2012) Assessing the Effectiveness of International Courts: A Goal-Based Approach. *American Journal of International Law* 106(2): 225–270.

109 Declaration on the Right to Development, supra note 1.

110 Kanade, and Puvimanasinghe, supra note 29.

111 Ibid.

> States have the duty to cooperate with each other in ensuring development and eliminating obstacles to development. States should realise their rights and fulfil their duties in such a manner as to promote a new international economic order based on sovereign equality, interdependence, mutual interest, and cooperation among all States, as well as to encourage the observance and realisation of human rights.[112]

This provision is fundamental in articulating the need for collective action, recognising that development is a global concern that transcends national borders. Furthermore, Article 4 of the DRTD emphasises that states must take both individual and collective action to formulate international development policies to facilitate the full realisation of the RTD.[113] Practical international cooperation: effective international cooperation with developing countries involves financial support, technology sharing, and capacity building to drive comprehensive and sustainable development. It means providing essential funds and investments to build infrastructure, create jobs, and improve education and healthcare systems. Sharing advanced technologies and innovative practices helps boost productivity and sustainability while training and strengthening local institutions ensure that development initiatives are managed effectively.

Additionally, aligning policies and promoting fair trade practices enable developing nations to access global markets and compete on an equal footing. Collaborative efforts to address environmental challenges and promote inclusive social development ensure equitable and environmentally responsible growth. By integrating these elements, international cooperation creates the necessary resources and frameworks for sustainable progress, benefiting all nations involved, particularly developing countries, which is essential to providing the necessary means and facilities to foster comprehensive sustainable development.[114] The duty to cooperate necessitates a paradigm shift from an individualistic, state-centric development model to one that embraces collective responsibility.[115] This shift is grounded in recognising the world as a unified global community rather than a collection of isolated sovereign entities. In this

---

112 Declaration on the Right to Development, supra note 1, Art 3(3).

113 Ibid at Art 4(1); see also, Art 10. "Steps should be taken to ensure the full exercise and progressive enhancement of the right to development, including the formulation, adoption and implementation of policy, legislative and other measures at the national and international levels".

114 Declaration on the Right to Development, supra note 1, Art 4.

115 Owuor, Mayiwa Maxwel (2020) Towards Development Justice: Re-visiting the Accountability of the World Bank and the IMF from a Right to Development Perspective. PhD Dissertation, York University.

context, the RTD challenges the traditional Westphalian model of sovereignty, which prioritises state autonomy and non-interference in domestic affairs.[116] As articulated in the DRTD, the RTD calls for states to engage in cooperative and collective action, both within multilateral institutions and through bilateral arrangements, to address global development challenges such as poverty, inequality, climate change, and global health crises.[117]

The DRTD places significant emphasis on reforming the international economic order to ensure equitable development for all.[118] It envisions a new international economic order based on principles of sovereign equality, mutual benefit, and interdependence. This vision is aligned with the aspirations of the Global South, particularly, in the aftermath of decolonisation when decolonised territories sought to assert their sovereignty and reclaim control over their natural resources.

According to Amin, the RTD emerged as a response to the global inequalities perpetuated by the existing international economic system, which privileged the Global North at the expense of the Global South.[119] Amin argues that the RTD, if fully realised, has the potential to redress these historical injustices by empowering states and communities in the Global South to chart their development paths.[120] In line with this vision, the duty to cooperate under the RTD is not limited to economic assistance but extends to creating an enabling environment for sustainable development. This involves addressing structural inequalities in the global economic system, such as unfair trade practices, debt burdens, and unequal access to technology and markets. The DRTD recognises that the RTD cannot be fully realised without addressing these systemic issues. The duty to cooperate also encompasses states' responsibilities to individuals and groups beyond their borders. This extraterritorial dimension of the RTD has gained increasing attention in recent years, particularly in the context of globalisation and the rise of transnational challenges such as climate change,

116 Weber, Martin (2007) On the Critique of the Subject of Development: Beyond Proprietary and Methodological Individualism. *Globalizations* 4(4): 460–474.

117 Salomon, Margot (2007) *Global Responsibility for Human Rights: World Poverty and the Development of International Law*. Oxford: Oxford University Press, 89–91.

118 Carabias-Hütter, Vicente et al (2007) Enhancing Regional RTD and Innovation Development through Foresight and Mentoring: Scenario Development and Action Plan for RTD and Innovation Promotion up to 2020 in Zurich, Switzerland. *Zurich University of Applied Sciences*.

119 Amin, Samir (1997) *Capitalism in the Age of Globalization: The Management of Contemporary Society*. London: Zed Books, 53–54.

120 Ibid.

pandemics, and migration.[121] Margot Salomon argues that the duty to cooperate in the context of the RTD requires states to "move beyond their traditional conception of obligations as territorially limited" and to recognise their responsibility for the global impacts of their actions.[122] This requires shifting from a narrow focus on national interests to a broader recognition of global interdependence and shared responsibility for addressing common challenges.

At the national level, the RTD imposes specific obligations on states to ensure that their domestic policies and programs are designed to promote inclusive and sustainable development.[123] This includes adopting policies prioritising poverty eradication, social inclusion, environmental sustainability, and realising economic, social, and cultural rights. States are also required to ensure that marginalised and vulnerable groups, such as women, indigenous peoples, and persons with disabilities, are actively involved in decision-making processes related to development.[124] This participatory dimension of the RTD is critical, as it empowers individuals and communities to take ownership of their development and to hold states accountable for their obligations.[125]

The duty to cooperate provisions of the DTRD represent a transformative vision of global governance that prioritises collective responsibility and mutual accountability. It challenges traditional notions of state sovereignty and calls for a reimagining of international law to reflect the interdependence of states and the need for global solidarity in addressing development challenges. The realisation of the RTD requires a fundamental shift from a state-centric, individualistic governance model to one that embraces collective action within and beyond national borders. The DTRD introduces a duty to cooperate with provisions that fundamentally reshape how nations interact on the global stage. These provisions move beyond traditional notions of sovereignty and unilateral action, advocating for a transformative vision of global governance centred on collective responsibility and mutual accountability. Traditionally, global governance has been characterised by individual nations pursuing their interests, often leading to fragmented and inconsistent approaches to international challenges. The DTRD's duty to cooperate provisions propose a shift

121 Ibid.

122 Salomon, M. (2011) Globalization, Human Rights, and Development. In: Evans, T. (ed) *Human Rights, Development and Globalization: Law and Policy Issues*. London: Routledge, 104–106.

123 Damman, Siri (2007) Indigenous Vulnerability and the Process Towards the Millennium Development Goals—Will a Human Rights-Based Approach Help? *International Journal on Minority and Group Rights* 14(4): 489–539.

124 Ibid.

125 Declaration on the Right to Development, supra note 1, Art 8(1).

towards a more integrated and collaborative framework, where countries work together towards common development goals. This vision recognises that many of today's most pressing issues—such as poverty, climate change, and public health crises—are inherently transnational and cannot effectively be addressed in isolation. As the global community grapples with pressing issues such as climate change, inequality, and pandemics, the duty to cooperate will be more crucial than ever in ensuring that the RTD is realised for all.

4 Participatory and Sustainable Development

Participation and sustainability have emerged as central themes in both academic and policy debates concerning the operationalisation of the RTD, highlighting the dual focus on the individual and collective dimensions.[126] Participation has long been a cornerstone of development, rooted in the foundational DRTD. Participation and sustainable development are deeply interconnected concepts essential for realising the RTD. Participatory development emphasises the active involvement of all stakeholders, including marginalised communities, in the decision-making processes that shape their lives.[127] This ensures that development initiatives are inclusive, equitable, and tailored to the specific needs of diverse populations.[128] Fundamental characteristics of meaningful participation include inclusivity, empowerment, transparency, and accountability, ensuring that every voice is heard and respected. Key participants typically include local communities, government agencies, civil society organisations, the private sector, and international partners collaborating to create comprehensive and effective development strategies. On the other hand, the concept of sustainable development focuses on meeting present needs without compromising the ability of future generations to meet their own, encompassing economic growth, social inclusion, and environmental protection.[129] When combined with participatory approaches, sustainable development becomes more robust and resilient, incorporating diverse perspectives and fostering a sense of ownership among stakeholders. Approaches to participatory development can be either top-down, where initiatives are driven by government or large organisations, or bottom-up, originating from

126 Ibid.

127 Ibid.

128 Ibid.

129 Mensah, Justice (2019) Sustainable Development: Meaning, History, Principles, Pillars, and Implications for Human Action: Literature Review. *Cogent Social Sciences* 5(1): 1–21.

local communities. An integrative approach that blends both methods often proves most effective, balancing strategic direction with local relevance and ownership.

This synergy supports state obligations and the duty to cooperate by promoting collective responsibility and mutual accountability. Governments are encouraged to facilitate and engage in collaborative efforts, ensuring that development projects align with national and global sustainability goals. Additionally, participatory and sustainable development intersect by enhancing resource management, policy development, and community resilience, reinforcing RTD principles. By embracing these intertwined frameworks, nations can address global challenges more effectively, fostering a just and sustainable global community where development benefits all.[130]

Meanwhile, the focus on sustainability, anchored in the SDGs, has more recently gained prominence in discussions on development.[131] Both themes converge in debates around state obligations to respect, protect, and fulfil the RTD, underscoring the necessity of a holistic approach to human rights and development that integrates people-centred participation and sustainable practices.[132] This highlights the need for a comprehensive strategy that simultaneously addresses human rights and development. A holistic approach ensures that development initiatives are not only environmentally sustainable but also inclusive and responsive to the needs of all individuals. By integrating people-centred participation, communities actively participate in decision-making, leading to more equitable and effective outcomes. Sustainable practices ensure that development meets present needs without compromising the needs of future generations, thus fostering long-term stability and resilience. These elements create a balanced framework where social justice and environmental stewardship go hand in hand, promoting well-being and equitable growth for all.

The DRTD affirms that development must be a participatory and people-driven process.[133] It emphasises that development cannot be imposed from above but must be grounded in human rights principles that respect individual and collective rights. The DRTD affirms that "the human person is the central subject

---

130 Declaration on the Right to Development, supra note 1.
Sen, Amartya (1999) *Development as Freedom*. Oxford: Oxford University Press, 36.

131 Mahajan, Ritika et al (2024) The Role of Business and Management in Driving the Sustainable Development Goals (SDGs): Current Insights and Future Directions from a Systematic Review. *Business Strategy and the Environment* 33(5): 4493–4529.

132 Ngang, Carol Chi (2015) Indigenous Peoples' Right to Sustainable Development and the Green Economy Agenda. *Africa Insight* 44(4): 31–46.

133 Declaration on the Right to Development, supra note 1; Sen, supra note 131, 36.

of development and should be the active participant and beneficiary of the right to development".[134] This understanding of development as a human right entails not only the fulfilment of basic needs but also the empowerment of people to shape their development trajectory through participation in decision-making processes at both local and global levels. This participatory approach is integral to creating development frameworks that are equitable and just, as it ensures that marginalised groups have a voice in shaping policies that impact their lives.[135]

However, economic growth, traditionally measured by increases in gross domestic product, industrial output, or export expansion, does not automatically translate into sustainable development. From a human rights perspective, development must be inclusive, equitable, and sustainable, addressing economic growth and development's broader social, political, and environmental dimensions.[136] Sustainable development requires policies that promote equality of opportunity and equitable distribution of resources, ensuring that all segments of society share the benefits of growth, particularly the most vulnerable.[137] The SDGs emphasise this need for inclusive growth, highlighting goals such as poverty reduction, gender equality, quality education, and climate action as essential components of sustainable development.[138] In this context, sustainable development seeks to improve living standards and aims to protect civil and political rights, ensuring that economic progress does not exacerbate inequalities or undermine human dignity.

The RTD framework, which emerged in response to the limitations of traditional economic development models, takes a fundamentally different approach. Unlike conventional development strategies prioritising economic growth over social justice and human rights, the RTD framework places human rights at the centre of development. It emphasises that development should be a means to realise all human rights—civil, political, economic, social, and cultural. The RTD calls for development strategies that are participatory, people-centred, and sustainable, recognising that development is not just

134 Declaration on the Right to Development, supra note 1; Sen, supra note 131, 36.

135 Declaration on the Right to Development, supra note 1.

136 Hamm, Bonnie (2001) A Human Rights Approach to Development. *Human Rights Quarterly* 23(4): 1005–1031.

137 Sen, supra note 131, 36.

138 United Nations, Transforming Our World: The 2030 Agenda for Sustainable Development, A/RES/70/1 (2015), Goals 1–17.

about increasing national income but also about improving the quality of life for all peoples.[139]

Historically, the development strategies promoted by industrialised nations often prioritised economic growth at the expense of equity and justice. For instance, during the colonial era, European powers implemented extractive economic policies in their colonies, focusing primarily on extracting natural resources and establishing cash-crop economies. This approach led to significant economic gains for the colonial powers but resulted in the exploitation and marginalisation of local populations. Indigenous communities were frequently displaced from their lands, and labour was coerced under harsh conditions, undermining social equity and justice. Additionally, structural adjustment programmes imposed by international financial institutions like the International Monetary Fund (IMF) and the World Bank in the late 20th century emphasised rapid economic liberalisation and privatisation in developing countries.[140] While these policies aimed to stimulate economic growth, they often led to increased income inequality, reduced access to essential services, and weakened labour rights, disproportionately affecting the most vulnerable segments of society. These examples illustrate how industrialised nations' emphasis on economic expansion frequently neglected the principles of equity and justice, resulting in long-term social and economic disparities.[141] These strategies, which focused on capital accumulation, industrialisation, and the expansion of trade, were frequently pursued without regard for the broader social and environmental impacts.[142] Developing countries were encouraged to follow the same path to economic growth, often with the support of international financial institutions such as the IMF and the World Bank, which provided loans and development assistance to increase the gross national product.[143] However, these development models failed to address the

139 Ngang, Carol Chi (2019) Systems Problem and a Pragmatic Insight into the Right to Development Governance for Africa. *African Human Rights Law Journal* 19(1): 390–393.

140 Konadu-Agyemang, Kwaku (ed) (2018) *IMF and World Bank Sponsored Structural Adjustment Programs in Africa: Ghana's Experience, 1983–1999*. New York: Routledge.

141 Ferguson, James (1981) *The Anti-Politics Machine: Development, Depoliticization, and Bureaucratic Power in Lesotho*. Cambridge: Cambridge University Press.

142 Ibid.

143 Obstfeld, M. (2013) The International Monetary System: Living with Asymmetry. In: Feenstra, R.C. and Taylor, A.M. (ed) *Globalization in an Age of Crisis: Multilateral Economic Cooperation in the Twenty-First Century*. Chicago/London: University of Chicago Press, 301–336.

deep-seated inequalities and injustices faced by marginalised groups in these countries.[144]

Historically, development models promoted by industrialised nations have often emphasised economic growth and modernisation without adequately addressing social equity and justice. For example, during the colonial era, European powers focused on extracting natural resources from their colonies, which led to the exploitation and marginalisation of indigenous populations.[145] These strategies prioritised the economic interests of the colonisers over the well-being of local communities, resulting in significant social disparities. Relatively recently, the structural adjustment programmes imposed by the IMF and the World Bank have aimed to stimulate economic growth in developing countries through policies such as privatisation and deregulation. These measures rather led to reduced funding for essential public services like healthcare and education, disproportionately impacting vulnerable and marginalised groups. As a result, income inequalities widened, and access to necessities became more limited for those already disadvantaged.

Additionally, top-down development approaches often ignore communities' unique cultural and social contexts, failing to engage marginalised groups in the decision-making process. This lack of participation meant that development initiatives were not tailored to the specific needs of these populations, perpetuating cycles of poverty and exclusion. Consequently, while overall economic indicators might have improved, the benefits were unevenly distributed, leaving marginalised communities further entrenched in inequality and injustice.[146] The RTD framework, by contrast, insists that development must be about more than just economic growth; it must also promote justice, equity, and participation, ensuring that all people have access to the benefits of development.[147] The participatory approach to development emphasises the need for an inclusive and equitable development process.[148] It stresses that the poor and marginalised must be empowered to take an active role

144 Malavisi, Anna (2022) *Global Development, Ethics, and Epistemic Injustice: Rethinking Theory and Practice*. New York: Rowman and Littlefield.

145 Ojala, Carl-Gösta and Nordin, Jonas (2015) Mining Sápmi: Colonial Histories, Sámi Archaeology, and the Exploitation of Natural Resources in Northern Sweden. *Arctic Anthropology* 52(2): 6–21.

146 Gunder, Andre Frank (1967) *Capitalism and Underdevelopment in Latin America*. New York: Monthly Review Press, 12.

147 Sen, A. (2000) What is Development About? In: Meier, G.M. and Stiglitz, J.E. (eds) *Frontiers of Development Economics: The future in Perspective*. New York: World Bank and Oxford University Press, 506–513.

148 Ibid.

in shaping their futures rather than being passive recipients of development aid. This approach is based on recognising that development is a complex, multi-dimensional process involving economic growth and social, cultural, and political changes. Participatory development is, therefore, essential to ensuring that development policies are responsive to the needs and aspirations of the people they are intended to benefit.[149]

The RTD framework and the SDGs both recognise the critical role of international cooperation in achieving sustainable development.[150] The DRTD asserts that development is a global responsibility and that states have an obligation to work together to create an international environment conducive to development.[151] The SDGs similarly call for revitalising global partnerships for sustainable development, emphasising the need for collective action to address global challenges such as poverty, inequality, and climate change.[152] Therefore, the RTD framework is not just about achieving specific development targets; it is about transforming the way we think about development. Hence, the RTD framework transcends merely achieving specific development targets; it fundamentally transforms our understanding and approach to development. Instead of focusing solely on economic indicators like gross domestic product (GDP) growth, the RTD emphasises the holistic well-being of individuals and communities, integrating social, political, and environmental dimensions. This shift encourages inclusive participation, ensuring all stakeholders, especially marginalised groups, have a voice in shaping development policies.

The RTD promotes sustainable practices that balance present needs with preserving resources for future generations. By prioritising human rights, equity, and collective responsibility, the RTD framework fosters a more just and equitable global society, redefining development as a comprehensive and transformative process rather than a set of isolated goals. It calls for a shift from focusing on economic growth to human well-being, emphasising the importance of participation, equity, and justice in the development process. As such, the RTD framework provides a powerful tool for promoting a more just and equitable world where all peoples can fulfil their potential and live in dignity. This approach aims to enhance material well-being through economic growth

149 Gready, Paul and Ensor, Jonathan (2005) *Reinvisioning Development: Good Governance, Human Rights and Social Justice*. London: Zed Books, 123–127.

150 De Feyter, Koen (2013) Towards a Framework Convention on the Right to Development. *International Policy Analysis/Dialogue on Globalization*, 1.

151 Ibid.

152 United Nations. Sustainable Development Goals: 17 Goals to Transform Our World. Available at: https://www.un.org/en/exhibits/page/sdgs-17-goals-transform-world (consulted 30 September 2024).

and ensures that such development is sustainable, respects all human rights, and prioritises the most vulnerable and marginalised groups. It emphasises the need for participatory processes, where development policies are crafted with the direct involvement of those who impact the most, thereby promoting ownership and accountability. Ultimately, the RTD framework underscores the interconnectedness of human rights and development, advocating for policy coherence at the national and international levels to create synergies that benefit all everywhere.

5 Conclusion

The RTD is a complex blend of individual and collective rights, emphasising that genuine development must go beyond state sovereignty and governance to reflect the valid will and interests of the population. It underscores the necessity of integrating both dimensions of self-determination—internal and external—to ensure that development policies are made at the state level and genuinely incorporate the diverse voices and aspirations of the people they affect. This approach stresses that actual development is achieved through participatory, equitable, and universally beneficial strategies that respect and promote human rights.

The RTD integrates individual and collective dimensions, emphasising the necessity of a collaborative approach involving states and global bodies to generate conducive situations for comprehensive societal development. This collective approach is pivotal for addressing systemic issues like poverty and inequality, which are widespread and require coordinated actions for resolution. The RTD's essence lies in its holistic framework, which fosters individual freedoms and enhances collective capabilities, guaranteeing that development is equitable and inclusive for all global community members. The holistic and integrative nature of the RTD aligns individual and collective human rights with participatory sustainable development. It highlights the necessity for worldwide cooperation and adherence to human rights standards to effectively implement development strategies that are just, inclusive, and equitable. This approach ensures that development processes focus on economic growth and foster social, cultural, and political advancements that benefit all members of society, particularly in developing nations.

Ultimately, the RTD framework offers a transformative vision for the future of human rights and development. It calls for a paradigm shift from a narrow focus on economic growth to a broader emphasis on human well-being, freedom, and justice. The RTD provides a powerful tool for addressing systemic inequalities and fostering a more just and equitable international order by centring on self-determination and peoples' collective rights. This framework challenges traditional notions of development, urging the global community to embrace a more holistic and inclusive approach and recognising the interdependence of human rights, development, and sustainability. By advancing self-determination and collective autonomy, the RTD has the potential to shape a more equitable world in which all peoples can fully participate in and benefit from development.

References

Alfredsson, Gudmundur (2022) Indigenous Peoples, Treaties With. *Max Planck Encyclopedias of International Law.*

Amin, Samir (1997) *Capitalism in the Age of Globalization: The Management of Contemporary Society*. London: Zed Books.

Arts, Karin and Tamo, Atabongawung (2016) The Right to Development in International Law: New Momentum Thirty Years Down the Line? *Netherlands International Law Review* 63: 221–249.

Barelli, Mauro (2011) Shaping Indigenous Self-Determination: Promising or Unsatisfactory Solutions? *International Community Law Review* 13(4): 413–436.

Bedjaoui, M. (1992) The Right to Development. In: Mayor F. and Bedjaoui, M. *International Law: Achievements and Prospects*. Paris: UNESCO and Dordrecht: Martinus Nijhoff, 1177–1203.

Bunn, Isabella D. (2000) The Right to Development: Implications for International Economic Law. *American University International Law Review* 15(6): 1425–1467.

Carabias-Hütter, Vicente et al (2007) Enhancing Regional RTD and Innovation Development through Foresight and Mentoring: Scenario Development and Action Plan for RTD and Innovation Promotion up to 2020 in Zurich, Switzerland. *Zurich University of Applied Sciences.*

Charter of the United Nations and Status of the International Court of Justice, adopted in San Francisco, United States of America on 26 June 1945.

Carstens, Martin (2021) Indigenous Rights and COVID-19: Indigenous Land and Health Under Serious Threat in Brazil. *International Journal on Minority and Group Rights* 29(3): 528–576.

Centre for Minority Rights Development (Kenya) and Minority Rights Group International on behalf of Endorois Welfare Council v Kenya Comm 276/2003 (2009) AHRLR 75 (ACHPR 2009).

Cerqueira, D. (2023) Cultural Rights. In: Cantú Rivera, H. (ed) *The Universal Declaration of Human Rights*. Leiden/Boston: Brill Nijhoff, 710–732.

Chaturvedi, Ipshita (2014) A Critical Study of Free, Prior and Informed Consent in the Context of the Right to Development—Can Consent be Withheld. *Journal of Indian Law and Society* 5(winter): 37–60.

Chen, Weiqi and Wang, Linbin (2024) A Holistic View of Human Rights and its Application in the Context of Infectious Disease Pandemics. *Heliyon* 10(9): 1–11.

Damman, Siri (2007) Indigenous Vulnerability and the Process Towards the Millennium Development Goals—Will a Human Rights-Based Approach Help? *International Journal on Minority and Group Rights* 14(4): 489–539.

De Feyter, Koen (2013) Towards a Framework Convention on the Right to Development. *International Policy Analysis/Dialogue on Globalization.*

De Matos, M.M. (2018) Cultural Identity and Self-Determination as Key Concepts in Concurring Legal Frameworks for the International Protection of the Rights of Indigenous Peoples. In: Lagrange, E., Oeter, S. and Uerpmann-Wittzack, R. (eds) *Cultural Heritage and International Law: Objects, Means and Ends of International Protection.* Cham: Springer Nature, 273–292.

Declaration on the Right to Development Resolution A/RES/41/128 adopted by UN General Assembly on 4 December 1986.

Draft International Covenant on the Right to Development—Report by the Chair-Rapporteur of the Working Group on the Right to Development, Zamir Akram (Pakistan) Human Rights Council A/HRC/54/50 54th Session, 6 October 2023.

Evans, Joane et al (2015) Self-determination and Archival Autonomy: Advocating Activism. *Archival Science* 15(4): 337–368.

Fabricant, Nicole (2012) *Mobilizing Bolivia's Displaced: Indigenous Politics and the Struggle Over Land.* Chapel Hill: University of North Carolina Press.

Ferguson, James (1981) *The Anti-Politics Machine: Development, Depoliticization, and Bureaucratic Power in Lesotho.* Cambridge: Cambridge University Press.

Flanagan, Thomas (2019) *First Nations? Second Thoughts.* Montreal/Kingston: McGill-Queen's University Press.

Gat, Azar (2012) *Nations: The Long History and Deep Roots of Political Ethnicity and Nationalism.* Cambridge: Cambridge University Press.

Giralt, Laura (2024) A Comprehensive Analysis of the European Union's Integration of the Right to Development and the Sustainable Development Goals: EU Development: From Policy to Practice. *Journal of International Development* 12(1): 45–60.

Gordon, Ruth (2009) The Dawn of a New, New International Economic Order? *Law and Contemporary Problems* 72(4): 131–162.

Gready, Paul and Ensor, Jonathan (2005) *Reinvisioning Development: Good Governance, Human Rights and Social Justice.* London: Zed Books, 123–127.

Gunder, Andre Frank (1967) *Capitalism and Underdevelopment in Latin America.* New York: Monthly Review Press.

Hamm, Bonnie (2001) A Human Rights Approach to Development. *Human Rights Quarterly* 23(4): 1005–1031.

Human Rights Committee, General Comment No 12: The Right to Self-Determination of Peoples, 1984.

Hummels, C.C.M. and Frens, J.W. (2011) Designing Disruptive Innovative Systems, Products and Services: RTD Process. In: Coelho, D. (ed) *Industrial Design—New Frontiers*. InTech, 147–172.

Ibhawoh, Bonny (2011) The Right to Development: The Politics and Polemics of Power and Resistance. *Human Rights Quarterly* 33(1): 76–104.

Kamga, Serges Djoyou (2015) The G77 and the Right to Development. *Latin American Report* 31(1): 58–76.

Kanade, Mihir and Puvimanasinghe, Shyami (2023) The Right to Development and the 2030 Agenda for Sustainable Development. In: *Operationalizing the Right to Development in Implementing the Sustainable Development Goals*. E-Learning Module, Right to Development Section of the Office of the United Nations High Commissioner for Human Rights (OHCHR).

Kevin Mgwanga Gumne and Others v Cameroon Comm 266/2003 (2009) AHRLR 9 (ACHPR 2009).

Konadu-Agyemang, Kwaku (ed) (2018) *IMF and World Bank Sponsored Structural Adjustment Programs in Africa: Ghana's Experience, 1983–1999*. New York: Routledge.

Lorenzo, Johanna Aleria (2021) A Path Toward Sustainable Development Along the Belt and Road. *Journal of International Economic Law* 24(3): 591–608.

Mahajan, Ritika et al (2024) The Role of Business and Management in Driving the Sustainable Development Goals (SDGs): Current Insights and Future Directions from a Systematic Review. *Business Strategy and the Environment* 33(5): 4493–4529.

Malavisi, Anna (2022) *Global Development, Ethics, and Epistemic Injustice: Rethinking Theory and Practice*. New York: Rowman and Littlefield.

Mamah, Wilfred (2013) Traps and Tools: A Contextual Critique of the Right to Development in International Law. PhD Thesis, University of Westminster School of Law.

Mannelli, Caludio (2021) *The Ethics of Rapid Tissue Donation (RTD)*. Cham: Springer International Publishing.

Massad, Joseph (2018) Against Self-Determination. *Humanity* 9(2): 161–191.

Mensah, Justice (2019) Sustainable Development: Meaning, History, Principles, Pillars, and Implications for Human Action: Literature Review. *Cogent Social Sciences* 5(1): 1–21.

Muchhala, Bhumika (2022) The Structural Power of the State-Finance Nexus: Systemic Delinking for the Right to Development. *Society for International Development* 65(2–4): 124–135.

Munene, Andrew William (2019) *Realising the Right to Development in Kenya under the 2010 Constitution through Poverty Alleviation, Anti-Corruption and Public*

Participation Interventions. Doctoral Dissertation, University of the Witwatersrand, South Africa.

Nakagiri, Masashi (2021) The Zero Draft Convention on the Right to Development as a Non-consensual Lawmaking: International and Domestic Dimension. *Faculté de Droit et de Science Politique—Aix Marseille Université.*

Ngang, Carol Chi (2015) Indigenous Peoples' Right to Sustainable Development and the Green Economy Agenda. *Africa Insight* 44(4): 31–46.

Ngang, Carol Chi (2019) Systems Problem and a Pragmatic Insight into the Right to Development Governance for Africa. *African Human Rights Law Journal* 19(1): 365–394.

Ngang, Carol Chi (2021) Self-determination and the Southern Cameroons Quest for Sovereign Statehood. *African Journal of International and Comparative Law* 29(2): 288–308.

Norton, Anthony Dean (2024) Beyond Right and Recognition: Toward a History of Collective Self-Determination as the Authorship of Political Personhood. PhD Dissertation, University of California.

O'Sullivan, D. (2023) Self-Determination, Participation and Leadership. In: O'Sullivan, D. (ed) *Indigeneity, Culture and the UN Sustainable Development Goals*. Singapore: Springer Nature Singapore, 159–188.

Obstfeld, M. (2013) The International Monetary System: Living with Asymmetry. In: Feenstra, R.C. and Taylor, A.M. (ed) *Globalization in an Age of Crisis: Multilateral Economic Cooperation in the Twenty-First Century*. Chicago/London: University of Chicago Press, 301–336.

Oduwole, Olajumoke (2014) International Law and the Right to Development: A Pragmatic Approach for Africa. *International Institute of Social Studies.*

Oestreich, Joel (2017) *Development and Human Rights: Rhetoric and Reality in India*. Oxford: Oxford University Press.

Ojala, Carl-Gösta and Nordin, Jonas (2015) Mining Sápmi: Colonial Histories, Sámi Archaeology, and the Exploitation of Natural Resources in Northern Sweden. *Arctic Anthropology* 52(2): 6–21.

Opeskin, Brian (2009) The Influence of International Law on the International Movement of Persons. *Munich Personal RePEc Archive Aper No 19200.*

Owuor, Mayiwa Maxwel (2020) Towards Development Justice: Re-visiting the Accountability of the World Bank and the IMF from a Right to Development Perspective. Doctoral Dissertation, York University.

Ozoemena, Rita (2021) Misappropriated Development: Exploring Accountability as the Rate-determining Step to the Realisation of the Right to Development in Select African Countries. *Comparative and International Law Journal of Southern Africa* 54(3): 21–43.

Plagerson, Sophie (2021) Human Well-being and Capabilities. *United Nations Research Institute for Social Development*, 1–25.

Rauna, Koukkanen (2019) *Restructuring Relations: Indigenous Self-Determination, Governance, and Gender*. Oxford: Oxford University Press.

Ryan, R.M. and Deci, E.L. (2022) Self-Determination Theory. In: Maggino, F. (ed) *Encyclopedia of Quality of Life and Well-Being Research*. Cham: Springer International Publishing, 6229–6235.

Salomon, M. (2011) Globalization, Human Rights, and Development. In: Evans, T. (ed) *Human Rights, Development and Globalization: Law and Policy Issues*. London: Routledge.

Salomon, Margot (2007) *Global Responsibility for Human Rights: World Poverty and the Development of International* Law. Oxford: Oxford University Press.

Sam, Emmanuel and Fredah, Luareen (2024) Legal and Economic Implications of China's Utilization of the Right to Development (RTD) in Africa to Further its Debt-Trap Diplomacy. *Science and Economics Research Journal* 3(3): 1–10.

Schmidt, Hendrik (2023) The Legal Meaning of State Custodianship in the Context of the Mineral and Petroleum Resources Development Act 28 of 2002. Doctoral Thesis, University of Cape Town.

Schrijver, N. (2013) Self-determination of Peoples and Sovereignty over Natural Wealth and Resources. In: UN Human Rights (ed) *Realizing the Right to Development*. Geneva/New York: UN Publishers, 95–102.

Sen, A. (2000) What is Development About? In: Meier, G.M. and Stiglitz, J.E. (eds) *Frontiers of Development Economics: The future in Perspective*. New York: World Bank and Oxford University Press, 506–513.

Sen, Amartya (1999) *Development as Freedom*. Oxford: Oxford University Press.

Sengupta, Arjun (2017) On the Theory and Practice of the Right to Development. In: Kamminga, M.T. (ed) *Challenges in International Human Rights Law*. New York: Routledge, 667–720.

Shany, Yair (2012) Assessing the Effectiveness of International Courts: A Goal-Based Approach. *American Journal of International Law* 106(2): 225–270.

Summers, James (2014) *Peoples and International Law*. Leiden: Brill Nijhoff.

Transforming Our World: The 2030 Agenda for Sustainable Development, UN General Assembly Resolution A/RES/70/1 (2015) (Sustainable Development Goals Framework).

UNESCO (1990) Final Report and Recommendation of Experts on Further Study of the Concept of the Rights of Peoples. UNESCO, Paris 27–30 November 1989.

United Nations (2024) Individual and collective dimensions of the right to development, Thematic study by the Expert Mechanism on the Right to Development A/HRC/57/40, Geneva.

United Nations (2024, 22 September) A Pact for the Future, Global Digital Compact and a Declaration on Future Generations. Available at: https://www.un.org/sites/un2.un.org/files/sotf-pact_for_the_future_adopted.pdf (consulted 30 September 2024).

United Nations Commission on Human Rights, Res. 4 (XXXIII), 21 February 1977.

United Nations Declaration on the Rights of Indigenous Peoples, Resolution 61/295 adopted on 13 September 2007.

United Nations General Assembly (2024) Individual and Collective Dimensions of the Right to Development. Available at: https://documents.un.org/doc/undoc/gen/g24/107/20/pdf/g2410720.pdf (consulted 6 June 2024).

United Nations, Executive Committee of Economic and Social Affairs (2024) Objective. Available at: https://www.un.org/esa/ecesa/objective.html (consulted 10 June 2024).

United Nations. Sustainable Development Goals: 17 Goals to Transform Our World. Available at: https://www.un.org/en/exhibits/page/sdgs-17-goals-transform-world (consulted 30 September 2024).

Weber, Martin (2007) On the Critique of the Subject of Development: Beyond Proprietary and Methodological Individualism. *Globalizations* 4(4): 460–474.

Williams, Lewis (2021) *Indigenous Intergenerational Resilience: Confronting Cultural and Ecological Crisis*. New York: Routledge.

Zadorin, Maxim Yu and Gladun, Elena (2022) Primary Elements of the Indigenous Peoples' Right to Self-Determination and Their Reflection in International Cases. *Law Enforcement Review* 6(4): 121–138.

CHAPTER 3

The Holders of the Right to Development

Koen de Feyter

1 Introduction

This chapter perceives of the right to development as an instrument to protect the human dignity of the rights holders. It puts forward an interpretation of the right to development that adds value to the protection already offered by current international human rights treaties. The emphasis is thus, not on the politics of the right to development. States take conflicting positions on who the right to development belongs to. These positions are acknowledged, but not elaborated upon.[1] The chapter relies mainly on primary sources. The UN Declaration on the Right to Development[2] remains the foundational document on the right to development at the global level. At the time of writing, an International Covenant on the Right to Development[3] is *in statu nascendi*. Drafting at the level of the United Nations Human Rights Council was completed. The further process is now in the hands of the United Nations General Assembly. On the topic of the rights holders of the right to development, the current draft Covenant does not diverge significantly from the Declaration.

Article 1(1) of the UN Declaration on the Right to Development designates "every human person and all peoples" as the holders of the right to development. The chapter provides an interpretation of the individual and collective dimensions of the right in the light of normative developments that have occurred since the adoption of the Declaration. The Declaration is a living instrument that should contribute to effective protection today—within the limits of what soft law can provide and pending the adoption of a legally binding instrument. The individual human right to development builds on existing human rights

1 On the politics on right to development, see at more length: Marks, Stephen (2011) *The Politics of the Possible: The Way Ahead for the Right to Development*. Berlin: Friedrich-Ebert-Stiftung; De Feyter, Koen (2003) The Convention on the Right to Development: Drafting a New Global Human Rights Treaty. *La Comunità Internazionale* 77(3): 413–440.

2 Declaration on the Right to Development Resolution A/RES/41/128 adopted by UN General Assembly on 4 December 1986, adopted by a 146-1-8 vote.

3 A/HRC/54/50/Add.1: Draft International Covenant on the Right to Development, with Commentaries—Report by the Chair-Rapporteur of the Working Group on the Right to Development, Zamir Akram (Pakistan), 4 September 2023.

 | DOI:10.1163/9789004734357_004

treaty law. It offers protection against development interventions[4] that entail human rights violations. It enables making use of human rights mechanisms that are available for the protection of individual human rights.

Depending on the circumstances, the peoples' right to development may refer to the entire population of a state, or to peoples within a state, including indigenous peoples and to local communities not accommodated by dominant development paradigms. As the right to development is both an individual and a collective right, groups that are connected socially rather than territorially may opt to rely on the right to development either as individuals or as a collective. Future generations are not considered in the Declaration on the Right to Development but have emerged in the literature as potential rights holders.

States are not holders of the human right to development—but have the duty to cooperate with each other to ensure the right to development to the rights holders. The duty of states to cooperate consists of reciprocal obligations: states are thus, not only obligated, but also entitled to cooperation by other states. This is of particular importance given the persistent factual inequality between states. The duty to cooperate extends beyond states. In line with Article 3(3) of the Declaration, the elimination of obstacles to development requires an enabling international environment. The "international environment" today includes intergovernmental organisations, businesses, and other non-state actors that impact on the realisation of the right to development.

2 The Individual Right to Development

The individual right to development can be understood as the right of a person to self-develop, much as the right to self-determination could be understood as a right of a person to determine one's own life. Article 2(2) of the UN Declaration acknowledges self-development by referring to the free and complete fulfilment of the human being as the goal that development seeks to achieve.

The right to development nevertheless, emerged in the specific historical context of postcolonialism. Governments of newly independent states claimed that after colonisation, they lacked the means to implement development

4 Building on Belcher, Brian and Palenberg, Marcus (2018) Outcomes and Impacts of Development Interventions: Toward Conceptual Clarity. *American Journal of Evaluation* 39(4): 479. Development interventions are understood here as deliberate involvement in a process or system impacting on sustainable development. The term may refer to a single activity, or a set of activities organised within a project, program, or instrument, and may be undertaken by a domestic or an external actor that may be public or private in nature.

policies that would result in the realisation of human rights for their people without global solidarity and changes to the international economic system. The right to development permitted seeing (the lack of) global development efforts as a human rights issue. If the right to self-determination was about peoples under colonial domination achieving independence or self-government, then the right to development was about enabling a people to make its own development choices. In this historical context, individual self-development did not stand high on the agenda, and this has to a large extent, remained so.

The individual right to development takes on significance in the face of interventions made in the name of development that result in human rights violations. Article 6(3) of the UN Declaration on the Right to Development thus, admonishes states to "take steps to eliminate obstacles to development resulting from failure to observe civil and political rights, as well as economic, social and cultural rights". Development interventions generating human violations can originate from a variety of actors. In principle, the scope of the individual right to development extends to any actor engaging in a development intervention.

It could be argued that when the domestic state engages in a development intervention resulting in human rights violations, an individual right to development is largely redundant because existing international human rights treaty law suffices. Human rights treaty law applies to any area of government policy, including development policy. Martin Scheinin thus, argues that the individual right to development could be realised under existing human rights treaties and their monitoring mechanisms provided that an interdependence-based and development-informed reading can be given to the treaties in question.[5]

The individual right to development makes very clear that individual human rights are an integral part of development. This is not a luxury. Civil society organisations defending marginalised peoples within their own society regularly associate "development" with development aggression and hence, not with something that one would wish to have a right to. Elite capture results in a discreditation of the concept of development. Development carries a negative connotation as well in a strand of the international literature on law and development. Adelman and Paliwala write:

> Development theory has failed to overturn the dominance of neoliberal, extractive, growth-driven development that drives the climate and

5 Scheinin, M. (2010) Advocating the Right to Development through Complaint Procedures under Human Rights Treaties. In: Andreassen, B. and Marks, S. (eds) *Development as a Human Right: Legal, Political and Economic Dimensions*. Antwerp: Intersentia, 339–352.

> environmental crises. The postwar rhetoric of development as modernity and progress camouflaged the entrenchment of underdevelopment and injustice in much of the global South, which intensified with neoliberalism. It failed to eliminate injustices because it was rooted in injustice.[6]

In the authors' view, the addition of modifiers such as "human", "alternative" or "sustainable" still does not address the structural causes of under-development, inequality, and injustice. They suggest replacing the phrase law and development by law and global justice.[7] It may be unwise however, to abandon the use of the term development to those favouring neo-liberal approaches to growth that disregard human rights. Surely, the risk that the concept substituting for development will equally fall prey to hegemonic capture is real. If anything, the disillusionment with the practice of development points to the need to reaffirm that there cannot be development without human rights, as the right to development emphasises.

Development interventions should not discriminate against human persons based on their individual characteristics. The exclusion of categories of persons based on their individual characteristics when policies are designed, and benefits are shared is not uncommon. The duty to ensure equal access to participation and benefit-sharing remains a basic tenet of the individual dimension of the right to development. In the Arab Charter on Human Rights, the right to development is an individual right that is limited to citizens, (several other rights in the treaty are as well) thus, rendering other persons within the state's jurisdiction invisible.[8]

It is true that development interventions tend to affect groups of people rather than a single person. The agency of individuals to claim the right to development is of particular importance in legal contexts where only individual rights are held to be justiciable in court and/or where access to legal procedures for collectivities is limited. Successful individual claims with a communitarian dimension may well result in an outcome that benefits the community. The European Court of Human Rights has for instance, acknowledged that in interpreting individual human rights, "the principle of proportionality requires that [...] situations, where a whole community and a long

---

6 Adelman, S. and Abdul, P. (2021) Beyond Law and Development. In: Adelman, S. and Abdul, P. (eds) *The Limits of Law and Development*. Abingdon: Routledge, 16.

7 Ibid at 36.

8 Arab Charter on Human Rights adopted in Cairo, Egypt on 15 September 1994, Art 37; note Art 43 which safeguards higher levels of protection of rights when provided for in applicable domestic and international law, but these may not always be available for the right to development.

period are concerned, be treated as being entirely different from routine cases of removal of an individual from unlawfully occupied property".[9] Such an approach is aligned with the individual dimension of the right to development. The individual human right to development is of added value in holding actors beyond the domestic state accountable for having failed to cooperate for the realisation of the right to development. As explained *infra*, the duty to cooperate is an integral part of the right to development and extends to third states, intergovernmental organisations, and non-state actors. Current international human rights treaty law remains limited in this respect.

Finally, the inclusion of both the individual and the collective dimensions of the right to development ensures that neither dimension overrides the other. Both dimensions stand next to each other without hierarchy. If the right to development is to be realised, the agency of both individuals and peoples as rights holders needs to be guaranteed. In a development context, individuals benefit from being members of a community, and thus, of the collective dimension of the right. By preserving their own rights, they have initiative to contribute to the welfare of the community. The individual right to development is important too for persons marginalised within their own community. As a measure of last resort, this includes the individual right to leave. Ultimately however, the understanding of the right to development as both an individual and a collective right is based on a vision of the human as a person associated with a community in seeking self-fulfilment.

3 The Collective Right to Development

At the time of adoption, the Declaration on the Right to Development received strong support because the right development was conceived both as an individual and a peoples' right. While the European Union (EU) no longer subscribes to this historical near consensus in the on-going negotiations on a treaty on the right to development and insists that the right to development is an individual right only, corresponding closely to the EU's own human rights approach to development, the collective dimension of the right adds

9 *European Court of Human Rights, Yordanova and others v Bulgaria* (Appl No 25446/06), 5 June 2012, Para 121. Analogously, the UN Human Rights Committee has under its Optional Protocol (which provides jurisdiction for individual claims only) interpreted the right to use one's culture and the right to privacy to provide protection to an indigenous people against the impact of climate change (UN Human Rights Committee, Communication No 3624/2019 *Daniel Billy et al v Australia*, CCPR/C/135/D/3624/2019, 22 September 2022).

significant value to the protection current international human rights treaty law offers.

The Declaration on the Right to Development contains no definition of peoples. No international legal instrument does. The term "peoples" is therefore, open to interpretation. Over time international instruments and judgements have recognised an increasing number of groups sharing common characteristics as peoples.[10] The term "peoples" in the Declaration on the Right to Development should be interpreted accordingly, in an evolutive manner. The various meanings of "peoples" discussed below coexist. The most pertinent meaning of the term depends on the situation. Different meanings may apply simultaneously. In the context of foreign investment for instance, the state is called upon to protect the rights of the entire population (in relation to the home state of the investor) as well as the rights of the communities that may directly be affected by the investor's activities.

3.1 *The Entire Population*

As a condition of statehood, the people equal the population. During decolonisation, the right to self-determination was the right of the population of a colonial territory to achieve self-government through independence or another freely determined political status. Upon independence, the population of the colonial territory became the peoples of the newly independent state. The people retained the right to self-determination in the post-colonial context as a safeguard against foreign interference and as an accountability mechanism vis-à-vis the government. The common characteristic of peoples was the shared colonial history. In other regards, the population could be diverse as the borders of the newly independent states had often been determined in agreements between the colonial powers. The challenge for the new governments was to create a sense of unity. This nation-building[11] exercise, a

10 A UNESCO Expert study described a people as a group of individual human beings who enjoyed all or some common features: a common historical tradition; racial or ethnic identity; cultural homogeneity; linguistic unity; religious or ideological affinity; territorial connection, common economic life. The will to be identified as a people or the consciousness of being a people was also deemed an important characteristic (UNESCO International Meeting of Experts on further study on the concept of the rights of peoples. Final report and Recommendations, SHS-89/CONF.602/7, 22 February 1990, 7–8).

11 The former UN Special Rapporteur on the Right to Development Mr. Saad Alfarargi took the view that nations were included among the collectivities holding the right to development (e.g., see Saad, Alfarargi (2017) United Nations Special Rapporteur on the Right to Development: An Introduction to the Mandate. New York: United Nations, 4). The final preambular paragraph of the UN Declaration on the Right to Development provides that "equality of opportunity for development is a prerogative both of nations and of

process of inculcating a shared sense of belonging, proved hazardous, including in terms of its human rights implications.

The understanding of peoples as the population of a state permeated the Declaration on the Right to Development. In Article 2(3), the duty of a state to aim at the improvement of the well-being of the "entire population"[12] appears. The Declaration emphasises that the right to development implies the full realisation of the right of peoples to self-determination, including the right of full sovereignty over the natural wealth and resources (in Article 1(2)). Full sovereignty over natural resources was attributed to the whole population, represented by the government in international relations. Strikingly (at least with hindsight), there are no references in the Declaration to indigenous peoples, minorities, or local communities within a state. This approach coincided with the view of the post-colonial governments. Their primary interest was in the creation of human rights obligations for developed countries to facilitate the right to development for the populations in developing countries.

The right to development as a right of the population of a state remains relevant today. In line with the post-colonial version of the right to self-determination, the right to development of the population of a state has an internal and an external dimension. The internal dimension requires that the state demonstrates that the national development policy is the result of a participatory process that involves the population in decision-making and fair benefit-sharing. The external dimension requires that the state shields the population from interferences by external actors that result in obstacles to the realisation of the right to development. The state's duty to protect[13] its population thus, applies to how the state conducts its relations with other actors impacting on the right to development such as other states, intergovernmental organisations, foreign investors, state and non-state development agencies.

---

individuals who make up nations" but does not designate nations as holders of the right to development and steers clear of the term in the operative part of the text. The term "nation" remains an elusive concept in public international law. It may coincide with the entire population of an existing state, but also with a community seeking statehood, or as a description of a historical community sharing a sense of belonging and endowed with certain institutions and connected with a territory.

12 The term "entire population" is also used in the second preambular paragraph of the Declaration. For a confirmation that the collective dimension of the right to development originally targeted the improvement of the well-bring of the entire population, see Sengupta, Arjun (2002) On the Theory and Practice of the Right to Development. *Human Rights Quarterly* 24(4): 837–889.

13 Draft International Covenant on the Right to Development, with Commentaries, supra note 3, compare Art 11.

Ensuring compliance with the state's duty to protect may well necessitate domestic or international legal action to safeguard the right to development of the population.[14]

3.2 *Peoples as Collectivities*

The terms used in the Declaration on the Right to Development should be interpreted in the light of the evolution of international and regional law after the adoption of the Declaration almost four decades ago. The international recognition of indigenous rights; environmental treaties as well as intergovernmental organisations acknowledging participatory rights of local communities; the case-law of the African Commission and African Court on Human and Peoples' Rights on the concept of "peoples", and the caselaw of the Inter-American Court of Human Rights on Afro-descendants in Latin America all inform the meaning of the term "peoples" in the Declaration.[15] International law does not provide a definition of indigenous peoples. The African Court on Human and Peoples Rights, in its judgment on the merits in the *Ogiek Community* case listed several factors for the identification of indigenous peoples based on pertinent international documents:

> the relevant factors to consider are the presence of priority in time with respect to the occupation and use of a specific territory; a voluntary perpetuation of cultural distinctiveness, which may include aspects of language, social organisation, religion and spiritual values, modes of production, laws and institutions; self-identification as well as recognition by other groups, or by State authorities that they are a distinct collectivity; and an experience of subjugation, marginalisation, dispossession, exclusion or discrimination, whether or not these conditions persist.[16]

---

14 The external dimension of the right to development as the right of the entire population of a State remains largely unexplored in the jurisprudence under the African Charter on Human and Peoples Rights. See African Charter on Human and Peoples' Rights adopted in Nairobi, Kenya on 27 June 1981 OAU Doc CAB/LEG/67/3 Rev.5 (1981), Art 22.

15 The same approach is taken in the draft Covenant on the Right to Development, supra note 3, as the Commentary explains; see A/HRC/54/50/Add.1 (4 September 2023), 28. See also Expert Mechanism on the Right to Development, Commentary on Art 1(1) of the Declaration on the Right to Development, A/HRC/EMRTD/7/CRP.1 (1 March 2023), Para 5; 15–16.

16 *African Commission on Human and Peoples' Rights v Republic of Kenya*, Application No 006/2012, ACtHPR Judgment of 26 May 2017, Para 107.

Article 23 of the United Nations Declaration on the Rights of Indigenous Peoples attributes the right to development to indigenous peoples.[17] This is uncontroversial. As per the Declaration on the Right to Development, indigenous peoples are entitled to active, free, and meaningful participation in development and in the fair distribution of the benefits resulting therefrom (Article 2(3)).[18] In international legal practice[19] however, the higher standard of free, prior, and informed consent applies to development interventions affecting indigenous peoples. The UN Declaration on the Rights of Indigenous Peoples stipulates that no relocation shall take place without the free, prior and informed consent of the indigenous peoples concerned (Article 10) and that states shall consult and cooperate in good faith with the indigenous peoples concerned through their own representative institutions in order to obtain their free and informed consent prior to the approval of any project affecting their lands or territories and other resources, particularly in connection with the development, utilisation or exploitation of mineral, water or other resources (Article 32(2)).[20]

In international law, the higher standard applicable to indigenous peoples is grounded in their right to self-determination, a right not attributed to other groups that qualify as holders of the right to development. In exercising the right to self-determination, indigenous peoples are entitled to autonomy or self-government.[21] This entitlement goes beyond the participatory rights envisaged in the Declaration on the Right to Development. The UN Expert

17 The provision reads: "Indigenous peoples have the right to determine and develop priorities and strategies for exercising their right to development. Indigenous peoples have the right to be actively involved in developing and determining health, housing and other economic and social programmes affecting them and, as far as possible, to administer such programmes through their own institutions". See United Nations Declaration on the Rights of Indigenous Peoples, General Assembly Resolution 61/295 (13 September 2007), adopted by a 144-4-11 vote, Art 23.

18 Note that Draft International Covenant on the Right to Development, supra note 3, Art 4(3) provides more explicitly than the Declaration that "very individual and all peoples *have the right to* active, free and meaningful participation in development and in the fair distribution of benefits resulting therefrom" (emphasis added).

19 For examples on case-law acknowledging free, prior and informed consent under the regional human rights treaties, see the *Saramaka People v Suriname*, Inter-Am Ct Hum Rts Judgment of 28 November 2007 (Preliminary Objections, Merits, Reparations, and Costs), Para 194(d); *Centre for Minority Rights Development (Kenya) and Minority Rights Group International on behalf of Endorois Welfare Council v Kenya* Comm 276/2003 (2009) AHRLR 75 (ACHPR 2009), Para 291. For a recent overview of international practice, see Barrie, G. (2024) The 'Right' to Free, Prior and Informed Consent: Evolving Customary International Law. In: De Villiers, B.; Isra, S. and Faiz, P.M. (eds) *Courts and Diversity*. Leiden: Brill, 195–227.

20 See in addition, United Nations Declaration on the Rights of Indigenous Peoples, supra note 17, Art 12, 27 and 30.

21 Ibid at Art 4.

Mechanism on Indigenous Rights thus, perceives of instances of indigenous peoples dissenting or refusing to consent to development projects on their land as an expression of their right to self-determination.[22]

In litigation, a claim is often brought by a single or several indigenous communities rather than by an indigenous people as a whole. In the Inter-American system, this does not create a problem: under the American Convention on Human Rights any group of persons is entitled to lodge a petition regarding a violation of the Convention.[23] A community therefore, does not need to show that it represents the whole indigenous people. This is relevant both from a conceptual point of view—communities are included as rights holders—but also from a practical point of view as states and corporate actors regularly employ divide and rule strategies when dealing with indigenous peoples. By offering benefits to some communities, they seek to demonstrate consent by the people as a whole.

Regional human rights mechanisms and development practice gradually extended rights originally granted to indigenous peoples only to other groups that were similarly situated. The Inter-American Court of Human Rights developed case law on Afro-descendants in Latin America. In these judgements, previous interpretations on the right to property in cases involving indigenous peoples were applied to a non-indigenous group. The Maroons are descendants of West Africans taken to Surinam to work as slaves on Dutch plantations in the 17th century. Escapees formed their own communities that exist until today.[24] The Inter-American Court acknowledges that these communities are not indigenous to the region they inhabit, but designates them as "tribal' given that their "social, cultural and economic characteristics are different from other sections of the national community, particularly because of their special relationship with their ancestral territories, and because they regulate themselves, at least partially, by their own norms, customs, and/or traditions".[25]

22 Expert Mechanism on the Rights of Indigenous Peoples, Efforts to implement the United Nations Declaration on the Rights of Indigenous Peoples: Indigenous Peoples and the Right to Self-determination, A/HRC/48/75 (4 August 2021), Para 29; Draft International Covenant on the Right to Development, with Commentaries, supra note 3, Art 17(1) spells out "the right of indigenous peoples in exercise of the right to self-determination, to freely pursue their development".

23 American Convention on Human Rights adopted in San José, Costa Rica on 22 November 1969, Art 40.

24 *Moiwana Community v Suriname*, Inter-Am Ct Hum Rts Judgment of 15 June 2005 (Preliminary Objections, Merits, Reparations and Costs), Para 86.

25 *Saramaka People v Suriname*, supra note 19, Para 84; International Labour Organisation Convention No 169—Convention Concerning Indigenous and Tribal Peoples in Independent Countries adopted on 7 June 1989 deals with indigenous and tribal people

The Court then finds that due to their special relationship to land, the tribal communities are entitled to the same special measures as indigenous peoples:

> Hence, this Tribunal declares that the members of the Saramaka people are to be considered a tribal community, and that the Court's jurisprudence regarding indigenous peoples' right to property is also applicable to tribal peoples because both share distinct social, cultural, and economic characteristics, including a special relationship with their ancestral territories, that require special measures under international human rights law in order to guarantee their physical and cultural survival.[26]

The African Charter on Human and Peoples' Rights attributes the right to development to "peoples". The African Commission and the African Court have given a broad meaning to the concept. While drawing inspiration from international law on indigenous rights when an application is filed by a people that qualifies as indigenous under international instruments,[27] the concept of peoples under the African Charter is broader, and there is some sensitivity in distinguishing indigenous peoples from other peoples, as the term "indigenous people" is absent from the treaty.

According to the African Commission on Human and Peoples' Rights, a collective of individuals should manifest certain features to be considered a people: a common historical tradition, racial or ethnic identity, cultural homogeneity, linguistic unity, religious and ideological affinities, territorial connection, and a common economic life or other bonds, identities and affinities they collectively enjoy; suffer from the deprivation of collective rights; and express a desire to be identified as a people or have the consciousness that they are a people.[28] Importantly, the African Commission noted in the *Endorois* case that:

> some marginalised and vulnerable groups in Africa are suffering from particular problems. It is aware that many of these groups have not been accommodated by dominating development paradigms and in many

---

without distinction. There is a tendency to avoid the term "tribal" in contemporary international standards, as it perceived of as upholding stereotypes.

26 *Saramaka People v Suriname*, supra note 19, Para 86.

27 *African Commission on Human and Peoples' Rights v Republic of Kenya*, supra note 16, Para 108.

28 *Centre for Minority Rights Development (Kenya) and Another v The Republic of Kenya*, supra note 19, Para 154.

> cases, they are being victimised by mainstream development policies and thinking and their basic human rights violated.[29]

Groups not accommodated by dominant development paradigms are entitled to protection as a people under the African Charter, and thus qualify as holders of the right to development. The *Southern Cameroons* case is an example of a dispute involving a non-indigenous group that was found to be a people under the African Charter. The Government of Cameroon argued that the Southern Cameroonians were not a people and alleged that nothing set them apart from other Cameroonians except their language (English), which was introduced during the colonial period. The African Commission disagreed and identified several other factors that qualified the South Cameroonians as a dominated people. The Commission admitted that the group was not ethnically different from the rest of the population. This, however, did not deprive the group of the collective rights in the African Charter:

The African Commission agreed with the respondent state that a "people" may manifest ethno-anthropological attributes. Ethno-anthropological attributes may be added to the characteristics of a "people". Such attributes are necessary only when determining indigeneity of a "people" but cannot be used as the only determinant factor to accord or deny the enjoyment or protection of peoples' rights. Was it the intention of the state parties to rely on ethno-anthropological roots only to determine "peoples' rights," they would have said so in the African Charter. As it is, the African Charter guarantees equal protection to peoples on the continent, including other racial groups whose ethnoanthropological roots are not African.[30] Indigeneity is a relevant, but not a decisive factor in the determination of whether a group constitutes a people under the African Charter.

The protection of groups not accommodated by dominant development paradigms by means of the right to development makes eminent sense, not only at the regional, but also at the global level. Peoples' rights as rights of marginalised groups respond to the failure of states to create conditions favourable to the realisation of the right to development. Individuals turn to their community for support when development is not forthcoming from the state. In such circumstances, communities deliver to the extent possible the protection that the state is duty-bound under international human rights law to provide

29 Ibid at Para 148.

30 *Kevin Mgwanga Gumne and Others v Cameroon* Comm 266/2003 (2009) AHRLR 9 (ACHPR 2009), Para 178.

and therefore, the communities themselves require protection to safeguard the right to development.

In a right to development context, groups not accommodated by dominant development paradigms are deserving of protection regardless of the nature of the dominant actor. The dominant actor will often be the domestic state (either directly or because it fails in its duty to protect), but it may also be an external actor, such as a third state, an intergovernmental organisation, a governmental or non-governmental agency providing official development assistance, or a private investor dealing directly with the group.

The World Bank Environmental and Social Standard (ESS) No 7 on "Indigenous Peoples and Sub-Saharan African Historically Underserved Traditional Local Communities"[31] equally takes a broad approach in defining the groups that fall within the scope of the instrument. The World Bank's ESS set out the requirements for borrowers to identify and assess the environmental and social risks and impacts associated with projects financed by the Bank. The ESS7 specifically, deals with indigenous peoples and sub-Saharan African historically underserved traditional local communities (or similar groups that "may be referred to in the national context using an alternative terminology"). The requirements set by the Bank vis-à-vis borrowing states are the same for all groups covered by the ESS. What matters is that the group possesses certain characteristics "in varying degrees".[32] All these groups are said to be disadvantaged by traditional models of development, and this explains why they are dealt with jointly:

> Their economic, social, and legal status frequently limits their capacity to defend their rights to, and interests in, land, territories, and natural and cultural resources, and may restrict their ability to participate in and benefit from development projects. In many cases, they do not receive equitable access to project benefits, or benefits are not devised or delivered in a form that is culturally appropriate, and they may not always

31 The World Bank Environmental and Social Standard (ESS) No 7 on Indigenous Peoples/ Sub-Saharan African Historically Underserved Traditional Local Communities in: The World Bank Environmental and Social Framework, 2017, World Bank, 75–83.

32 Ibid at Para 8; The characteristics are self-identification as members of a distinct indigenous social and cultural group and recognition of this identity by others; collective attachment to geographically distinct habitats, ancestral territories, or areas of seasonal use or occupation, as well as to the natural resources in these areas: customary cultural, economic, social, or political institutions that are distinct or separate from those of the mainstream society or culture; and a distinct language or dialect, often different from the official language or languages of the country or region in which they reside.

> be adequately consulted about the design or implementation of projects that would profoundly affect their lives or communities.[33]

In several or all, be it strictly defined circumstances, the ESS7 requires that the borrower obtains their free, prior, and informed consent.[34] Participatory rights of local communities are increasingly recognised in international environmental law.[35] These instruments too tend not to differentiate between indigenous and local communities. They perceive of their participatory rights as a safeguard against environmental harm.

Article 8(j) of The Convention on Biological Diversity (5 June 1992) recognises the relevance of knowledge, innovations and practices of indigenous and local communities embodying traditional lifestyles for the conservation and sustainable use of biological diversity. The Convention promotes the wider application of their expertise with their approval and involvement and encourages the equitable sharing of the benefits arising from the utilisation of their knowledge, innovations, and practices.[36] The Paris Agreement (12 December 2015) in its Preamble, recognises that states when taking action to address climate change should take into account their obligations to (among others) local communities.[37] The Conference of the Parties subsequently, established a Local Communities and Indigenous Peoples Platform to *inter alia*, facilitate the integration of diverse knowledge systems, practices and innovations in designing and implementing international and national actions, programmes and policies "in a manner that respects and promotes the rights and interests of local communities and indigenous peoples".[38] Article 3(a) of the United Nations Convention to Combat Desertification in those Countries Experiencing Serious Drought and/or Desertification, Particularly in Africa (14 October 1994) provides that state parties should ensure that decisions on the design and implementation of programmes to combat desertification

---

33 Ibid at Para 3.

34 Ibid at Para 24.

35 Compare Urbinati, S. (2017) The Community Participation in International Law. In: Adell, N. et al (eds) *Between Imagined Communities and Communities of Practice: Participation, Territory, and the Making of Heritage*. Göttingen: Göttingen University Press, 123–140.

36 See further, Nagoya Protocol on Access to Genetic Resources and the Fair and Equitable Sharing of Benefits arising from their Utilization adopted at the 10th Meeting of the Conference of the Parties in Nagoya, Japan on 29 October 2010, Art 6.

37 See, Paris Agreement adopted at the UN Climate Change Conference (COP21) in Paris, France, on 12 December 2015, Preamble Para 12.

38 See Art 6(c), Decision 2/CP.23 (17 November 2017), FCCC/CP/2017/11/Add.1, 12.

and/or mitigate the effects of drought are taken with the participation of "populations and local communities".

At the regional level, the revised[39] African Convention on the Conservation of Nature and Natural Resources (11 July 2003), adopted by the African Union Assembly, includes participatory rights for local communities as well. The objectives of the Convention include the enhancement of environmental protection and sustainable use of natural resources "with a view to achieving ecologically rational, economically sound, and socially acceptable development policies and programmes" (Article II). Article III reprises elements from the African Charter on Human and Peoples' Rights' provisions on the right to a satisfactory environment and on the right to development. Article XVII is somewhat unusually entitled: "Traditional Rights of Local Communities and Indigenous Knowledge". The second paragraph of the Article equates indigenous knowledge with knowledge of local communities. Article XVII(3) states:

> The Parties shall take the measures necessary to enable active participation by the local communities in the process of planning and management of natural resources upon which such communities depend, with a view to creating local incentives for the conservation and sustainable use of such resources. There is no doubt that the global concept of development includes an environmental dimension. Inferences can be drawn from environmental instruments for the interpretation of the right to development, regarding both the concept of people and the scope of participatory rights in decision-making and benefit-sharing.

3.3 *Social Groups*

The groups discussed so far all have a shared connection with territory and with the exploitation of natural resources. They manage the resources, develop knowledge, and share a way of life and identity that is strongly connected to land. Other social groups self-identify based on other characteristics and may also suffer exclusion from dominant development paradigms. These characteristics include sex and gender, age or disability, ethnicity or race; the group's position in the economy (such as the poor, peasants, fisherfolk, and more generally, people practising a subsistence economy); the exercise of a profession that is deemed unworthy in a specific societal context (scavengers, butchers);

39 For background on the revision process, see Erinosho, Bolanle (2013) The Revised African Convention on the Conservation of Nature and Natural Resources: Prospects for a Comprehensive Treaty for the Management of Africa's Natural Resources. *African Journal of International and Comparative Law* 21(3): 378–397.

lack of citizenship or of a residence permit (e.g. migrants) or even a shared experience, such as proximity to a waste facility. In addition, different aspects of identity may expose the same persons to intersecting disadvantages.

Social groups may wish to invoke either the individual or collective dimension of the right to development. They are entitled to formulate a claim based on the individual right to development, either alone or in association with others, arguing that their exclusion is of a discriminatory nature. Alternatively, they may argue that all groups disregarded by dominant development paradigms should be recognised as collective holders of the right to development. An interesting, but atypical example is the recognition of peasants "and other people working in rural areas" as a social group that holds the right to development. The United Nations Declaration on the Rights of Peasants and Other People Working in Rural Areas[40] includes the right to development.[41] It is an atypical example, because the Declaration defines a peasant in part as a person who has a special dependency on and attachment to land, so the territorial connection is still present.

Other characteristics included in the definition are connected to the position of peasants in the economy: engagement in small-scale agriculture, significant reliance on household or family labour and other non-monetised ways of organising labour.[42] Article 3(2) of the Declaration lays down that peasants and other people working in rural areas have the right to determine and develop priorities and strategies to exercise their right to development, leaving open the options to claim the right to development individually or as a group. The impact of development interventions on peasants is addressed in a number of provisions: international cooperation, including international development programmes should be inclusive, accessible and pertinent to peasants and other people working in rural areas;[43] the right of active and free participation in the preparation and implementation of policies, programmes and projects that may affect their lives, land and livelihoods is recognised;[44] and intergovernmental organisations are called upon to contribute to the realisation of the Declaration "including through the mobilisation of, inter alia, development assistance and cooperation".[45]

40 UN Declaration of Rights of Peasants and other People Working in Rural Areas, adopted by General Assembly Resolution 73/165 on 17 December 2018, adopted by a 121-8-54 vote.

41 The right to development of peasants and other people working in rural areas is also included in the draft Covenant on the Right to Development, supra note 3, Art 18.

42 Ibid at Art 1(1).

43 Ibid at Art 2(6a).

44 Ibid at Art 10(1).

45 Ibid at Art 27(1); also note Art 26 on the right to freely pursue cultural development.

Article 1(3) of the Declaration stipulates that the text also applies to indigenous peoples and local communities working on the land. Specific legislation on indigenous peoples should not be disregarded.[46] In practice tensions between indigenous peoples and rural populations over the use of land may well arise.[47] Other groups are included too: transhuman, nomadic, and semi-nomadic communities, and the landless engaged in the rural work covered by the Declaration. Members of these groups are thus holders of the right to development as spelled out in Article 3(2).

One final remark on groups as rights holders. Group bonds may extend beyond a single country. Cross border solidarity may come about based on a shared condition. Transboundary groups can support members that face marginalisation in development.[48] It is not self-evident to locate such cross-border organising groups in a single place in the current right to development framework because this framework still builds on the distinction between domestic and external actors. Transboundary groups are both within and outside. They may be considered as collectivities of rights holders but may also act as external actors carrying out development interventions.

3.4 *Future Generations*

Principle 3 of the 1992 Rio Declaration on Environment and Development (12 August 1992)[49] prescribes that the right to development must be fulfilled to equitably meet developmental and environmental needs of present and future generations. Identical language is included in Paragraph 35 of the Association of South East Asian Nations (ASEAN) Human Rights Declaration (19 November 2012). Article 24(c) of the Draft International Covenant on the Right to Development explicitly attributes the right to development to future generations. The draft provision requires States to ensure that "their decisions

46 Ibid at Art 2(3).

47 For a recent example and strategies to deal with these tensions, see Vallejo, Juan (2022) Indigenous Peoples versus Peasants: Land disputes in Colombia and the Search for an Alternative Approach. *Drake Journal of Agricultural Law* 27(3): 386–430.

48 For example, *La Via Campesina* describes itself as "an international movement bringing together millions of peasants, landless workers, indigenous people, pastoralists, fishers, migrant farmworkers, small and medium-size farmers, rural women, and peasant youth from around the world. Built on a solid sense of unity and solidarity, it defends peasant agriculture for food sovereignty"; see, About La Via Campesina. Available at: https://viacampesina.org/en/international-peasants-voice/ (consulted 15 June 2024).

49 Rio Declaration on Environment and Development, Resolution A/CONF.151/26 (Vol. I) adopted at the United Nations Conference on Environment and Development at Rio de Janeiro, Brazil, on 12 August 1992.

and actions do not compromise the ability of present and future generations to realise their right to development".[50]

The Maastricht Principles on the Human Rights of Future Generations (July 2023), a recommendatory text adopted by an international group of experts suggest that states must necessarily impose reasonable restrictions on activities that undermine the rights of future generations, including the unsustainable use of natural resources and the destruction of nature. According to the experts, these restrictions must not undermine the human rights of present generations, but they must rectify the vastly disproportionate levels of control over and use of resources by some members of the present generation, neither must they impose disproportionate burdens on disadvantaged groups.[51]

4 The Role of the State

Should the state (and the government acting on its behalf) be considered a holder of the right to development? One could argue that the state as a social institution does not markedly differ from an indigenous people or a community. The state too is a value-based institution, organises social life and provides structure and order. Since the start of the global debate on the right to development in the seventies of the previous century, part of the literature and some governments have argued that the state, and more specifically, developing countries hold the right to development. Former President of the International Court of Justice, Mohammed Bedjaoui wrote:

50 At the time of writing, a Declaration on Future Generations was under preparation as part of the UN Summit of the Future (planned for September 2024). For the currently available draft, see "REV 1 Declaration on Future Generations". Available at: https://www.un.org/sites/un2.un.org/files/sotf-declaration-on-future-generations-rev1.pdf (consulted 15 June 2024). This draft does not include a right to development of future generations. It acknowledges the need to guarantee the ability of future generations to thrive in prosperity and achieve sustainable development, including by addressing intergenerational transmission of poverty and hunger, inequality, and injustice (Para 13). Future generations are described as all those generations that do not yet exist, and who will inherit this planet (Para 3).

51 See Maastricht Principles on the Human Rights of Future Generations (July 2023), Art 7(c). Available at: https://www.rightsoffuturegenerations.org/the-principles (consulted 15 June 2024). According to the Maastricht Principles, future generations include persons, groups, and peoples (Principle 1). They are entitled to human rights (Principle 2), including the right to development (see Principle 5(b)).

> the present writer in 1969 affirmed a right to development in its international dimensions, placing in particular on the advanced countries a real "obligation" for the development of the less economically advanced State, but in the framework of a "new international law"; […] Thus were identified, first the State which owes the legal "obligation", the developed State, next the State that is the possessor of the right, the "proletarian nation" and lastly the new legal framework of this relationship, which was "a new international law" of solidarity and co-operation.[52]

Decades later, in 2017, in the run up to the drafting process on a legally binding instrument on the right to development at the United Nations Human Rights Council, the Non-Aligned Movement proposed a Set of Standards on the implementation and realisation of the right to development that adheres to Bedjaoui's approach. The proposed standards focus entirely on the provision by developed countries and the international community of appropriate means and facilities to developing countries to foster their comprehensive development[53] and ignore the right to development of individuals and peoples.[54] Bonny Ibhawoh criticises the exclusively statist interpretation of the right to development, but still subscribes to the notion that states, "can also claim development as a human rights entitlement against other states or the international community".[55]

The proposition that the human right to development is held by states cannot be supported. As a subject of international law, a state cannot be equated either with an individual or a people. Both peoples and individuals have a legal personality that is entirely distinct from the state. In public international law, states hold state rights, not human rights. As the International Court of Justice points out, differently from any other subjects of international law, a state possesses the totality of international rights and duties recognised by international law.[56] It is precisely because of the uniquely privileged position of the state in the international legal system that international human rights law provides state obligations to safeguard individuals and peoples against

52 See Bedjaoui, M. (1992) The Right to Development. In: Mayor, F. and Bedjaoui, M. (eds) *International Law: Achievements and Prospects*. Leiden: Brill, 1178.

53 In line with the Declaration on the Right to Development, supra note 2, Art 4(2).

54 See NAM Proposal on Set of Standards Regarding the Implementation and Realization of the Right to Development A/HRC/WG.2/18/G/1 of 5 April 2017.

55 Ibhawoh, Bonny (2011) The Right to Development: The Politics and Polemics of Power and Resistance. *Human Rights Quarterly* 33(1): 86.

56 International Court of Justice, Advisory Opinion on Reparation for Injuries suffered in the Service of the United Nations (11 April 1949), ICJ Reports 1949.

injurious state actions and omissions. Also, as a social institution, the state (and the government acting on its behalf) has an overarching meta role in organising and exercising control over other social institutions, including through the monopoly of violence.

A so-called state held human right to development would diminish states' responsibility as a duty bearer. It would put the state on an equal footing with the individuals and peoples as holders of the right to development and thus, shatter the protection that the right to development is meant to provide them with. It would also cast doubt upon the obligations states hold under current international human rights treaty law. It would resurrect the argument that the effective compliance by a state (and particularly by a developing country) with its existing human rights treaty law obligations depends on compliance (particularly by developed countries) with the so-called state human right to development (of developing countries).

Article 1(1) of the Declaration on the Right to Development does not recognise states as holders of the right to development. Draft Article 4(1) of the current draft International Covenant also does not include states as holders of the right to development, nor does the Commentary on the draft Covenant suggest otherwise.[57] States are duty bearers of the human right to development and as Carol Ngang puts it, are "directly attributed the central role to ensure the realisation of the right to development".[58] In this respect, the right to development does not differ from other human rights. Some confusion may arise from the duty to cooperate, a crucial state duty corresponding to the right to development. Article 3(3) of the Declaration on the Right to Development reads (in part) as follows: States have the duty to cooperate with each other in ensuring development and eliminating obstacles to development.[59]

In line with the Declaration, the Committee on Economic, Social and Cultural Rights confirmed that international cooperation for development and thus, for the realisation of economic, social, and cultural rights is an obligation of all states. The Committee commented that the duty to cooperate was "particularly incumbent upon those States which are in a position to assist others in this regard".[60] The duty to cooperate is a duty that applies between states.

57 See Draft International Covenant on the Right to Development, with Commentaries, supra note 3, Arts 28, 37–40.

58 Ngang, Carol Chi (2021) *The Right to Development in Africa*. Leiden: Brill, 73.

59 Note that the obstacles referred to in the provision include the failure to observe human rights; see Declaration on the Right to Development, supra note 2, Art 6(3).

60 UN Committee on Economic, Social and Cultural Rights, General Comment No 3: The Nature of States Parties' Obligations (Art 2(1) of the Covenant), E/1991/23 of 14 December 1990, Para 14.

It belongs to the realm of classic public international law. States owe this duty to each other. The duty to cooperate expresses a mutual commitment to achieve a shared goal. Arguably it establishes for each state a (state) right to receive cooperation from any other state bound by the duty. Under the duty to cooperate, the "other" state is required to engage in best efforts to achieve the goal and to refrain from unilateral action that obstructs its achievement. Ideally, the duty to cooperate entails a negotiation process on equal terms resulting in a legally binding agreement with legal commitments on action that needs to be undertaken to achieve the shared objective.

From the perspective of the holders of the right to development, the purpose of the inter-state duty to cooperate is to contribute to the realisation of their rights.[61] The duty of the state exercising jurisdiction over the rights holders is thus, complemented by an additional duty of states to cooperate for the achievement of the same goal. The inter-state duty to cooperate stemming from the realm of classic public international law connects to the duty of states vis-à-vis the rights holders. Requirements at the level of the horizontal relationship between states contribute to the fulfilment of the states' vertical obligations to the rights holders. In this way, the right to development facilitates complementarity between the legal regimes of development and of human rights. The vertical obligations of states to the rights holders are however, not altered by the failure of states to cooperate with each other.

In a world marred by global inequality, cooperation between states is essential to ensure equal human rights protection to all. Human rights protection is resource intensive, and resources are distributed unevenly among states. Yet, current human rights treaty law remains largely dependent on each state acting unilaterally to realise the human rights of the rights holders for which it is responsible. Given the pivotal role of state sovereignty, the need arises for an inter-state duty to cooperate—each state according to its ability—to achieve the universal realisation of human rights. As the Committee on Economic, Social and Cultural Rights has pointed out, the principle of common but differentiated responsibility applies to the inter-state duty to cooperate. All states bear the duty to cooperate, but what is required in terms of implementation differs depending on a state's ability to assist.

As argued above, the language of a state held right to development is best avoided in international treaty law, as it may create the erroneous impression that the state is the holder of the human right to development. Article 3(4) of

61 Note that according to Arts 3(3) and 4(2) of the Declaration, states are required to cooperate internationally on all aspects of development, including in situations where there is no or little impact on the holders of the right to development.

the United Nations Framework Convention on Climate Change (9 May 1992) provides that the "parties have a right to, and should, promote sustainable development".[62] The paragraph appears to provide for an uncontroversial state right to promote sustainable development, at least if my interpretation of the placing of the commas in the text is correct. Article 3 deals with the principles that the Framework Convention is based on; first and foremost, the principle of common but differentiated responsibility of states, including the need for developed countries to take the lead in efforts combating climate change. The inter-state duty to cooperate in efforts combating climate change mirrors the duty to cooperate for the realisation of the right to development.

5 The Role of the International Community

Article 3(3) of the Declaration on the Right to Development on the duty to cooperate continues as follows: "States should realise their rights and fulfil their duties in such a manner as to promote a new international economic order based on sovereign equality, interdependence, mutual interest and co-operation among all States, as well as to encourage the observance and realization of human rights". In the 2030 Agenda, the parties commit in contemporary language to pursue "an enabling environment for sustainable development at all levels and by all actors, and to reinvigorating the Global Partnership for Sustainable Development".[63]

Already in 1948, the Universal Declaration of Human Rights was intended as a common standard of achievement for every organ of society. The Global Partnership envisaged in the 2030 Agenda seeks to attain the sustainable development goals by bringing together "governments, the private sector, civil society, the United Nations system, and other actors".[64] The Declaration on the Right to Development, states that all human beings have a responsibility for

62 The United Nations Framework Convention on Climate Change was one of three treaties adopted at the Rio Conference on Environment and Development (next to the treaties on biodiversity and desertification) that focused on the normative consequences of the concept of sustainable development.

63 See Transforming Our World: The 2030 Agenda for Sustainable Development, Annex to General Assembly Resolution 70/1 (20 September 2015), no vote, Para 63. The 2030 Agenda is "grounded" in the Universal Declaration of Human Rights and international human rights treaties and "informed" by other instruments such as the Declaration on the Right to Development. The sixth but last paragraph of the preamble of the Draft International Covenant on the Right to Development suggests the language of an "international environment conducive to just, equitable and participatory development".

64 Ibid at Para 39.

development, individually and collectively.[65] The right to development and the corresponding duty to cooperate speak to any actor engaging in development interventions.

The lived experience of the holders of the right to development certainly confirms the need for non-state actors to cooperate for the realisation of the right to development. The activities of non-state actors such as foreign investors, international organisations, and both public and private donor agencies frequently affect the human dignity of rights holders. This is particularly the case in peripheral lands or poor urban neighbourhoods where state institutions are largely absent. In such circumstances the duty to cooperate of non-state actors, resulting in legal commitments that provide accountability to the rights holders, is of crucial importance for the realisation of the right to development. The Expert Mechanism on the Right to Development has suggested that the duty to cooperate of non-state actors[66] can be broken down into several practical components: the duty to give notice; the duty to consult and agree; the duty to assist; and the duty to repair harm.

The current draft Covenant on the Right to Development includes a provision obliging intergovernmental organisations (as institutionalised forms of inter-state cooperation) to refrain from conduct that would result in a state or another organisation breaching its obligations pertaining to the right to development. The draft treaty is open to accession by intergovernmental organisations.[67] Businesses are included as duty bearers among the legal persons addressed in both draft Articles 3k and 7. Accordingly, businesses have a duty to respect human rights and to refrain from violating the right to development. States have the obligation to ensure that businesses do not impair the exercise or enjoyment of the right to development (draft Article 11).[68]

---

65 Declaration on the Right to Development, supra note 2, Art 2(2).

66 Expert Mechanism on the Right to Development, The Duty to Cooperate and Non-State Actors, A/HRC/54/84, 5 July 2023.

67 Draft International Covenant on the Right to Development, with Commentaries, supra note 3, Arts 9 and 31 respectively.

68 A concurrent drafting process is taking place at the UN Human Rights Council on a treaty on business and human rights (in full: the Draft Legally Binding Instrument to Regulate, in International Human Rights Law, the Activities of Transnational Corporations and other Business Enterprises) that will offer much more detail on corporate human rights responsibility. The latest draft (July 2023) was published as https://www.ohchr.org/sites/default/files/documents/hrbodies/hrcouncil/igwg-transcorp/session9/igwg-9th-updated-draft-lbi-clean.pdf (consulted 15 June 2024).

6 Conclusion

Individuals and peoples are the holders of the right to development. The realisation of the right to development depends on the agency of both individuals and peoples. The individual right to development offers protection against interventions made in the name of development that result in human rights violations. This is particularly important when development interventions discriminate against persons based on their individual characteristics. The agency of individuals to claim the individual right to development is essential in the legal contexts where, only individual rights are held to be justiciable and/or access to legal procedures for collectivities is limited.

Peoples' rights are of substantial value in the context of development. In current international human rights treaty law, only the right to self-determination speaks to (aspects of) development from a collective rights perspective. Over time several international and regional instruments and judgements have recognised an increasing number of groups sharing common characteristics as peoples. The term "peoples" in the Declaration on the Right to Development should be interpreted accordingly, in an evolutive manner. Populations of states, indigenous peoples and similarly situated groups as well as local communities and social groups not accommodated by dominant development paradigms are recognised holders of the right to development. Various meanings and perceptions of the concept of "peoples" coexist.

States have the duty to realise the right to development of individuals and peoples within their jurisdiction. They also have the duty to cooperate with each other for the realisation of the right to development. The duty to cooperate establishes for each state a right to receive cooperation from any other state bound by the duty, and particularly from a state that can assist. The objective of both the obligations of the state exercising jurisdiction and of the inter-state duty to cooperate is to ensure the enjoyment of right to development to the rights holders.

The duty to cooperate also requires the creation of an enabling international environment for the realisation of the right to development. The international environment consists not only of states, but also of non-state actors carrying out development interventions such as intergovernmental organisations, foreign investors, and public and private development agencies. The right to development offers protection against development interventions by all these actors: both in terms of requiring that their interventions do not adversely affect the rights of individuals and peoples, as well as regarding their duty to cooperate for the realisation of the right to development.

Two final reflections conclude this chapter. Peoples confronted with development interventions that threaten their human dignity represent the beating heart of the right to development. When development is understood as a human right, it is ultimately for the rights holders to define development and for the intervening actor to respect their understanding of development. This is not unusual in international human rights law. Concepts such as family, privacy or property have been interpreted in a context-specific manner to protect human dignity as effectively as possible. When considering development as a plural concept, the only limitations that apply flow from the current global consensus that development is a multidimensional concept (economic, ecological, social) and that it includes human rights.

The right to development deals with a complex web of relationships in comparison with human rights codified earlier that strongly focus on the relationship between the state and the individuals within its jurisdiction. This complex web of relationships certainly reflects the reality of the situations in which development interventions take place. The actions of the duty bearers are interconnected, and it is precisely to this interconnectedness that the right to development seeks to respond to. There is a risk though, that the right to development collapses under its own weight. One may question whether one right can really deal with the varying (non-)cooperative interactions between so many different actors that may act in diverse constellations. For sure, in litigation forums and to some extent in international organisations as well, compartmentalisation will occur. Situations will be approached from the perspective of a specific branch of international law. The responsibility of actors will be dealt with in separation. The added value of the right to development then is to bring back the whole and to stress the centrality of the rights holders. Seen from this perspective, the right to development strengthens the ability of public international law (including human rights law)—as a legal regime grounded in the sovereign state as the supreme legal person—to deal with the multi-actor reality of global development.

References

A/HRC/54/50/Add.1: Draft International Covenant on the Right to Development, with Commentaries—Report by the Chair-Rapporteur of the Working Group on the Right to Development, Zamir Akram (Pakistan), 4 September 2023.

About La Via Campesina. Available at: https://viacampesina.org/en/international-peasants-voice/ (consulted 15 June 2024).

Adelman, S. and Abdul, P. (2021) Beyond Law and Development. In: Adelman, S. and Abdul, P. (eds) *The Limits of Law and Development*. Abingdon: Routledge.

African Charter on Human and Peoples' Rights adopted in Nairobi, Kenya on 27 June 1981 OAU Doc CAB/LEG/67/3 Rev.5 (1981).

African Commission on Human and Peoples' Rights v Republic of Kenya, Application No 006/2012, ACtHPR Judgment of 26 May 2017.

American Convention on Human Rights adopted in San José, Costa Rica on 22 November 1969.

Arab Charter on Human Rights adopted in Cairo, Egypt on 15 September 1994.

Barrie, G. (2024) The 'Right' to Free, Prior and Informed Consent: Evolving Customary International Law. In: De Villiers, B.; Isra, S. and Faiz, P.M. (eds) *Courts and Diversity*. Leiden: Brill, 195–227.

Bedjaoui, M. (1992) The Right to Development. In: Mayor, F. and Bedjaoui, M. (eds) *International Law: Achievements and Prospects*. Leiden: Brill.

Belcher, Brian and Palenberg, Marcus (2018) Outcomes and Impacts of Development Interventions: Toward Conceptual Clarity. *American Journal of Evaluation* 39(4): 479.

Centre for Minority Rights Development (Kenya) and Minority Rights Group International on behalf of Endorois Welfare Council v Kenya Comm 276/2003 (2009) AHRLR 75 (ACHPR 2009).

Compare Urbinati, S. (2017) The Community Participation in International Law. In: Adell, N. et al (eds) *Between Imagined Communities and Communities of Practice: Participation, Territory, and the Making of Heritage*. Göttingen: Göttingen University Press, 123–140.

De Feyter, Koen (2003) The Convention on the Right to Development: Drafting a New Global Human Rights Treaty. *La Comunità Internazionale* 77(3): 413–440.

Declaration on the Right to Development Resolution A/RES/41/128 adopted by UN General Assembly on 4 December 1986, adopted by a 146-1-8 vote.

Draft Legally Binding Instrument to Regulate, in International Human Rights Law, the Activities of Transnational Corporations and other Business Enterprises (latest draft, July 2023). Available at: https://www.ohchr.org/sites/default/files/documents/hrbodies/hrcouncil/igwg-transcorp/session9/igwg-9th-updated-draft-lbi-clean.pdf (consulted 15 June 2024).

Erinosho, Bolanle (2013) The Revised African Convention on the Conservation of Nature and Natural Resources: Prospects for a Comprehensive Treaty for the Management of Africa's Natural Resources. *African Journal of International and Comparative Law* 21(3): 378–397.

European Court of Human Rights, Yordanova and others v Bulgaria Appl No 25446/06, 5 June 2012.

Expert Mechanism on the Right to Development, Commentary on Art 1(1) of the Declaration on the Right to Development, A/HRC/EMRTD/7/CRP.1, 1 March 2023.

Expert Mechanism on the Right to Development, The Duty to Cooperate and Non-State Actors, A/HRC/54/84, 5 July 2023.

Expert Mechanism on the Rights of Indigenous Peoples, Efforts to implement the United Nations Declaration on the Rights of Indigenous Peoples: Indigenous Peoples and the Right to Self-determination, Resolution A/HRC/48/75, 4 August 2021.

Ibhawoh, Bonny (2011) The Right to Development: The Politics and Polemics of Power and Resistance. *Human Rights Quarterly* 33(1): 76–104.

International Court of Justice, Advisory Opinion on Reparation for Injuries suffered in the Service of the United Nations (11 April 1949), ICJ Reports 1949.

International Labour Organisation Convention No 169—Convention Concerning Indigenous and Tribal Peoples in Independent Countries adopted on 7 June 1989.

Kevin Mgwanga Gumne and Others v Cameroon Comm 266/2003 (2009) AHRLR 9 (ACHPR 2009).

Maastricht Principles on the Human Rights of Future Generations (July 2023). Available at: https://www.rightsoffuturegenerations.org/the-principles (consulted 15 June 2024).

Marks, Stephen (2011) *The Politics of the Possible: The Way Ahead for the Right to Development*. Berlin: Friedrich-Ebert-Stiftung.

Moiwana Community v Suriname, Inter-Am Ct Hum Rts Judgment of 15 June 2005 (Preliminary Objections, Merits, Reparations and Costs).

Nagoya Protocol on Access to Genetic Resources and the Fair and Equitable Sharing of Benefits arising from their Utilization adopted at the 10th Meeting of the Conference of the Parties in Nagoya, Japan on 29 October 2010.

NAM Proposal on Set of Standards Regarding the Implementation and Realization of the Right to Development A/HRC/WG.2/18/G/1 of 5 April 2017.

Ngang, Carol Chi (2021) *The Right to Development in Africa*. Leiden: Brill.

Paris Agreement adopted at the UN Climate Change Conference (COP21) in Paris, France, on 12 December 2015.

Rio Declaration on Environment and Development, Resolution A/CONF.151/26 (Vol. I) adopted at the United Nations Conference on Environment and Development at Rio de Janeiro, Brazil, on 12 August 1992.

Saad, Alfarargi (2017) United Nations Special Rapporteur on the Right to Development: An Introduction to the Mandate. New York: United Nations.

Saramaka People v Suriname, Inter-Am Ct Hum Rts Judgment of 28 November 2007 (Preliminary Objections, Merits, Reparations, and Costs).

Scheinin, M. (2010) Advocating the Right to Development through Complaint Procedures under Human Rights Treaties. In: Andreassen, B. and Marks, S. (eds) *Development as a Human Right: Legal, Political and Economic Dimensions*. Antwerp: Intersentia, 339–352.

Sengupta, Arjun (2002) On the Theory and Practice of the Right to Development. *Human Rights Quarterly* 24(4): 837–889.

The World Bank Environmental and Social Standard (ESS) No 7 on Indigenous Peoples/Sub-Saharan African Historically Underserved Traditional Local Communities in: The World Bank Environmental and Social Framework, 2017, World Bank, 75–83.

Transforming Our World: The 2030 Agenda for Sustainable Development, Annex to General Assembly Resolution 70/1 adopted on 20 September 2015.

United Nations Declaration of Rights of Peasants and other People Working in Rural Areas, adopted by General Assembly Resolution 73/165 on 17 December 2018, adopted by a 121-8-54 vote.

United Nations Human Rights Committee, Communication No 3624/2019 *Daniel Billy et al v Australia*, CCPR/C/135/D/3624/2019, 22 September 2022.

UNESCO International Meeting of Experts on further Study on the Concept of the Rights of Peoples. Final Report and Recommendations, SHS-89/CONF.602/7, 22 February 1990.

United Nations Committee on Economic, Social and Cultural Rights, General Comment No 3: The Nature of States Parties' Obligations (Art 2(1) of the Covenant), E/1991/23 of 14 December 1990.

United Nations Declaration on the Rights of Indigenous Peoples, General Assembly Resolution 61/295 (13 September 2007), adopted by a 144-4-11 vote.

Vallejo, Juan (2022) Indigenous Peoples versus Peasants: Land disputes in Colombia and the Search for an Alternative Approach. *Drake Journal of Agricultural Law* 27(3): 386–430.

CHAPTER 4

Realising Sustainable Development through a Binding Right to Development

Clement Agyemang

1 Introduction

Development that is sustainable is one that may be desired by all as it ensures continuous provision of what one needs. Sustainable development is development that meets the needs of society. According to the World Commission on Environment and Development, sustainable development is development that "meets the needs of the present without compromising the ability of future generations to meet their own needs".[1] States must, therefore, achieve sustainable development through strategic development plans and policies that can provide for every apparent need of society at all times. Efforts by states in realising this kind of development has led to the adoption of development goals such as the Millennium Development Goals (MDGs) and the ongoing Sustainable Development Goals (SDGs), which are envisaged to be achieved by 2030. Although the MDGs among others significantly lifted more than one billion people out of extreme poverty, made inroads against hunger, and enabled more girls to attend school than ever before and to protect our planet, inequalities persist and progress has been uneven.[2] While the ongoing SDGs is known to be the clearest blueprint of humanity's highest aspirations, its comprehensive assessment of global progress towards it paints a sobering picture due to factors including the Covid-19 pandemic, wars and dysfunctional and unfair international financial architecture.[3] Achieving the SDGs in the remaining years would therefore, need extra efforts from the actors involved. Considering factors including unexpected ones that sometimes stunt development, always

1 Brundtland Commission (1987) Report of the World Commission on Environment and Development: Our Common Future. Available at: https://sustainabledevelopment.un.org/content/documents/5987our-common-future.pdf (consulted 4 September 2024), Para 27.

2 United Nations Millennium Declaration Resolution A/55/L.2 adopted by the United Nations General Assembly on 8 September 2000, 3.

3 Ibid.

 | DOI:10.1163/9789004734357_005

having ongoing developing policies even in time of crises can ensure development continuity and sustainability which may be possible through a binding RTD. It can thus, be deduced that sustainable development is a process of continuously ensuring development through policies and goals. While this may entail short, medium, and long-term plans, there is need to establish the importance of development, how to realise it and make it sustainable.

Related to the concept of sustainable development is the right to development (RTD), conceived as a fundamental human right that offers a framework within which development should take place in a sustainable manner if the RTD is respected, protected, and fulfilled. The Declaration on the Right to Development (DRTD)[4] is however, only recognised internationally in its soft law form, making provisions on the RTD enshrined therein, unenforceable. Achieving sustainable development through the RTD therefore, requires a change of the status of the right from soft to hard law, making it an international legally binding instrument. The draft Covenant on the Right to Development when adopted, will give the RTD its needed strength in enhancing sustainable development. The possibility of achieving sustainable development through a binding RTD is what this chapter seeks to demonstrate in six parts. Part one introduces the topic and explores its background. Part two examines the interplay and interdependence of the RTD with sustainable development and the potential contribution of the RTD to sustainable development. Part three explores the status and the impact of the RTD. Part four looks at the importance of realising sustainable development through the RTD. Part five evaluates the proposed Covenant on the RTD, and how its binding status could simultaneously facilitate realisation of the RTD and sustainable development. It also explores some potential challenges in implementing the RTD and offers recommendations. Part six sums up the chapter.

2 Interdependence between the RTD and Sustainable Development

The global development framework is currently characterised by two interdependent and complementary framings comprising of the RTD framing on the one hand and of the sustainable development framing on the other hand. While these development framings have evolved separately as illustrated

4 Declaration on the Right to Development Resolution A/RES/41/128 adopted by UN General Assembly on 4 December 1986.

in the subsections below, they are by every conceivable measure, mutually reinforcing.

2.1 *Mutuality of the RTD and Sustainable Development*

2.1.1 The Right to Development

The RTD is defined in the DRTD as

> an inalienable human right by virtue of which every human person and all peoples are entitled to participate in, contribute to, and enjoy economic, social, cultural, and political development, in which all human rights and fundamental freedoms can be fully realised.[5]

From this definition flows three principles; first, that the RTD is an inalienable human right like any other right; second, that it is a process of economic, social, cultural, and political development, in which all human rights and fundamental freedoms can be fully realised; and third, that it is a human right through which every individual and all peoples are entitled to participate in, contribute to and enjoy the development process.[6] According to Sengupta, the first principle affirms the RTD as an inalienable right which cannot be taken or bargained away; the second defines a process of development through which all international and regional human rights can be realised; and the third conceives of the RTD as that process of development in terms of claims or entitlements of rights holders, which duty bearers must protect and promote.[7]

In the same vein, the High-Level Task Force came up with a core norm to the RTD as the right of peoples and individuals to the constant improvement of their well-being and to a national and global environment conducive to just, equitable, participatory, and human-centred development respectful of all human rights. Three attributes are identified from this core norm namely, a comprehensive and human-centred development policy, participatory

5 Declaration on the Right to Development, supra note 4, Art 1.

6 Sengupta, Arjun (2000) Realizing the Right to Development. *Development and Change* 31(3): 663; Dąbrowska, Anna Olga (2010) Legal Status of the Right to Development. *Haskoli Island University*. Available at: https://scholar.google.com/scholar?hl=en&as_sdt=0%2C5&q=Legal+Status+of+the+Right+to+Development+by+Anna+Olga+D%C4%85browska&btnG= (consulted 5 September 2024); Sengupta, A. (2013) Conceptualizing the Right to Development for the Twenty-First Century. In: United Nations Human Rights (ed) *Realizing the right to development: Essays in Commemoration of 25 Years of the United Nations Declaration on the Right to Development*. Geneva/New York: UN Publishing, 68.

7 Sengupta 2000, supra note 6, 68.

human rights processes, and social justice in development.[8] A principle that runs through the definition of the RTD is participation, which according to Kamga, is the cornerstone of the RTD in that it "ensures that no one is left out on any ground, whatsoever".[9] To him, the right to participation promotes non-discrimination and stresses the need for transparency and accountability in the development process.[10] While participation is emphasised in international and regional human rights instruments, its place in the RTD seems to be that without which the right cannot stand. In other words, the RTD seems to lose its substance without the idea of participation. This is corroborated by Manouchehr Ganji, the former Special Rapporteur of the Commission on Human Rights that

> the basic principle governing the question of human rights in development should be the participation of the people in deciding their own style of individual and corporate life in general, and particularly their participation in decision-making in connection with development programmes, in the implementation of those programmes and in the benefits derived from them.[11]

Although the RTD is said to be implied in the 1944 Philadelphia Declaration[12] and many international human rights instruments,[13] it was first coined by leaders of developing countries following the period of decolonisation in the

8 De Feyter, Koen (2013) Towards a Framework Convention on the Right to Development. *Friedrich-Ebert-Stiftung—International Policy Analysis*. Available at: http://library.fes.de/pdf-files/bueros/genf/09892.pdf (consulted 5 September 2024), 2; Report of the High-Level Task Force on the Implementation of the Right to Development on its Sixth Session. Available at: https://documents.un.org/doc/undoc/gen/g10/118/37/pdf/g1011837.pdf (consulted 5 September 2024).

9 Kamga, Serges Djoyou (2011) Human Rights in Africa: Prospects for the Realisation of the Right to Development under the New Partnership for Africa's Development. PhD thesis, University of Pretoria, 188–190.

10 Ibid at 122.

11 United Nations Human Rights (2013) *Realizing the right to development: Essays in Commemoration of 25 Years of the United Nations Declaration on the Right to Development*. Geneva/New York: UN Publishing, 14.

12 Hallgren, Ragnar (1990/1991) The UN and the Right to Development. *Peace Research* 22(4)/23(1): 32; Sengupta 2000, supra note 6, 554–555.

13 Li, Yuefen; Uribe, Daniel and Danish (2022, 8 March) The International Discourse on the Right to Development and the Need to Reinvigorate its Implementation. *South Centre Research Paper No 149*.

1960s.[14] While addressing a conference in Algiers in 1967, Doudou Thiam, former Senegalese Minister for Foreign Affairs, stated that "the old colonial past, of which the present is merely an extension, should be denounced" and states should "proclaim, loud and clear, the right to development for the nations of the Third World".[15] This highlights the unfair colonial treatments that were meted out to Africa and from which the continent must be freed. Similarly, in 1969 in Algiers, Cardinal Leon-Etienne Duval made a public statement to the effect that "the right to development should be proclaimed for the Third World".[16] In concrete terms, it is:

> the codification of international law, which recognizes the right to self-determination, legitimized the cause for decolonization. The adoption of international human rights instruments further guaranteed that justice could be achieved through the assertion of rights, which in turn informed the emerging argument that development in Africa could be claimed as a matter of right.[17]

The official proclamation of the RTD is however, credited to Kéba M'baye in 1972.[18] Despite these glaring shreds of evidence that the RTD emerged from developing countries,[19] others consider it to be a western idea. To them, the RTD was implicitly expressed by Eleanor Roosevelt, who while leading the US delegation, described the drafting of the UDHR in the following terms: "we will have to bear in mind that we are writing a bill of rights for the world and that one of the most important rights is the opportunity for development".[20]

14 Suzanne van der Have, Nieke (2013) The Right to Development and State Responsibility Can States be Held to Account? *University of Amsterdam—Amsterdam Law School Research Paper No 2013–23*, 2; Kirchmeier, Felix (2006) The Right to Development—Where Do We Stand?: State of the Debate on the Right to Development. *Dialogue on Globalization Occasional Papers No 23*: 8.

15 Ouguergouz, Fatsah (2003) *The African Charter on Human and Peoples' Rights: A Comprehensive Agenda for Human Dignity and Sustainable Democracy in Africa*. Dordrecht: Martinus Nijhoff Publishers, 298.

16 Ibid.

17 Ngang, Carol Chi (2018) Towards a Right-to-Development Governance in Africa. *Journal of Human Rights* 17(1): 109.

18 M'baye, Kéba (1972) Le Droit au Développement Comme un Droit de l'Homme: Leçon inaugural de la troisième session d'enseignement de l'Institut International des Droits de l'Homme. *Revue des Droits l'Homme* 5: 505–534.

19 Ibhawoh, Bonny (2011) The Right to Development: The Politics and Polemics of Power and Resistance. *Human Rights Quarterly* 33(1): 101.

20 Sengupta 2000, supra note 6, 554–555.

While the RTD may be implied in Mrs Roosevelt's statement, it was not framed and recognised as such. Nonetheless, it appears indisputable that it is Kéba M'baye's proclamation that gave the RTD its enormous reputation in the field of academia as well as the politics of development by providing a framework that clarifies the concept of development as a human right.[21] It is this framework that informed the DRTD as well as the proposed Covenant on the Right to Development.

2.1.2 Sustainable Development

Despite, the debate among development scholars and practitioners over its meaning,[22] sustainable development remains a global agenda driven by the UN General Assembly as a solution to global development problems. Although, sustainable development is implied in the development literature[23] prior to the 1987 Report of the World Commission on Environment and Development titled "Our Common Future", it owes its definition and popularity to this report.[24] It became a global agenda following the report by the World Commission on Environment and Development. It is recorded that the UN General Assembly, in its Resolution 38/161 of 19 December 1983, welcomed among others, the idea to set up a special commission, which later became the World Commission on Environment and Development, to produce a report on the environment and the global problematic to the year 2000 and beyond,

---

21 Ngang, supra note 17, 112.

22 McNeill, D. (2004) The Concept of Sustainable Development. In: Schmidt, J D. (ed) *Development Studies and Political Ecology in a North South Perspective*. Aalborg, Denmark: Aalborg University Research Center on Development and International Relations Development Research Series, Occasional Papers No 5; Ozili, Peterson (2022) Sustainability and Sustainable Development Research Around the World. *Munich Personal RePEc Archive aper No 115767*. Available at: https://mpra.ub.uni-muenchen.de/115767/1/MPRA_paper_115767.pdf (consulted 4 September 2024), 4; Ruggerio, Carlos Alberto (2021) Sustainability and Sustainable Development: A Review of Principles and Definitions. *Science of the Total Environment* 786(147481): 2–3; Tufaner, Mustafa Batuhan and Türker, Taner (2016) The Importance of the Sustainable Development in Terms of Quality of Life of the Future Generations. *Journal of Social and Administrative Sciences* 3(4): 301–302.

23 Hulme, David (2009) The Millennium Development Goals (MDGs): A Short History of the World's Biggest Promise. *Brooks World Poverty Institute Working Paper 100*. Available at: https://papers.ssrn.com/sol3/papers.cfm?abstract_id=1544271 (consulted 4 September 2024); Mensah, Justice (2019) Sustainable Development: Meaning, History, Principles, Pillars, and Implications for Human Action: Literature Review. *Cogent Social Sciences* 5(1): 6–7; Pezzey, John (1992) *Sustainable Development Concepts: An Economic Analysis*. Washington DC: The World Bank, 1.

24 Emas, Rachel (2015) The Concept of Sustainable Development: Definition and Defining Principles. *Brief for GSDR 2015*; McNeill, supra note 22, 26; Ozili, supra note 22.

including proposed strategies for sustainable development.[25] In accordance with the resolution, and pursuant to the mandate and purview of the United Nations Environment Programme, the report was considered by the Governing Council of the Programme, and transmitted to the Assembly together with its comments, before being adopted as environmental perspective to the year 2000 and beyond.[26] At its fourteenth session from 8 to 19 June 1987 in Nairobi, Kenya, the Governing Council of the UN Environment Programme adopted Decision 14/14 of 16 June 1987 titled "Report of the World Commission on Environment and Development" and transmitted it to the General Assembly together with a draft resolution annexed to the decision for consideration and adoption.[27] The Report was adopted during the forty-second session of the UN General Assembly on 4 August 1987.[28]

The Commission was mandated among others to formulate "A global agenda for change" by proposing long-term environmental strategies towards achieving sustainable development by the year 2000 and beyond.[29] The definition of sustainable development embodies two concepts namely, needs reflecting the basic exigencies of the world's poor, which should be urgently prioritised and the idea of constraints stemming from the state of technology and social organisation regarding the environment's capacity to meet present and future needs.[30] It can be deduced therefrom, the idea to meet the basic needs of the world's poor by ensuring a decent standard of living and human dignity with due regard to technological capacity and social organisation to ensure efficient use, distribution and management of resources. The report suggests that socio-economic goals must be defined in terms of sustainability in developed and developing countries, market-oriented or centrally planned. Although, interpretations may vary, they do share similar characteristics and should be based on a common understanding of sustainable development and a broad strategic framework for achieving it.[31]

Indeed, development involves a gradual transformation of the economy and society, ensuring physical sustainability. However, policies must consider resource access, cost-benefit distribution, and social equity between generations, extending to equity within each generation.[32] Since development which

25 Brundtland Commission Report, supra note 1, Para 1.
26 Ibid.
27 Ibid at 1.
28 Ibid.
29 Ibid at 11.
30 Ibid.
31 Ibid.
32 Ibid.

is about meeting human needs and aspirations seems difficult to achieve in developing countries, sustainable development appears a viable strategy by which to tackle development problems as it entails providing for the basic needs of everyone and extending the opportunity to meet their aspirations for a better life.[33] It is about sustainable living standards in line with long-term sustainability in consumption, where perceived needs are socially and culturally determined as well as promoting values that encourage ecologically acceptable consumption standards.[34] It also requires economic growth in areas where essential needs are not being met, while maintaining sustainability and non-exploitation principles. However, high productive activity and widespread poverty often coexist, endangering the environment and requiring equitable opportunities for all.[35]

While sustainable development deals with every foreseeable sector that impacts the environment and human conditions, with different requirements, objectives and goals, achieving it involves a harmonious process of resource exploitation, investment direction, technological development, and institutional change, aiming to enhance current and future potential to meet human needs.[36] Among the various ways to achieve sustainable development, the MDGs and the SDGs have been promoted globally. Although, the MDGs ended in 2015 without achieving all the objectives set, the lessons learnt paved the way for the SDGs, which are more promising and will end in 2030 despite global challenges such as the COVID-19 pandemic and wars hindering their effective implementation. Unlike the goals that are set towards achieving it, sustainable development is generally not bound by time. It is something that must always happen and hence, support realisation of the RTD.

2.2 *Interplay between the RTD and Sustainable Development*

Based on the definitions and characteristics of the RTD and of sustainable development, both concepts are inherently, interconnected and reinforce each other. Development, which remains the main objective of both concepts is with respect to the RTD, a comprehensive economic, social, cultural and political process that seeks to ensure the constant improvement of the well-being of everyone based on their active, free and meaningful participation in development and a fair sharing of its benefits. Sustainable development seeks to ensure development for everyone now and in the future through judicious

33 Ibid at 54.
34 Ibid at 54–55.
35 Ibid at 55.
36 Ibid at 57.

management of available resources. While the development process within the RTD framework is expressed and implied in that of sustainable development, it is argued that the former ensures the realisation of the latter. Indeed, the pursuit of constant improvement in the well-being of the beneficiaries of the RTD as stipulated in Article 2(3) of the DRTD is inherently aligned with the principles of sustainable development since both aim at the continuous enjoyment of better quality of life for present and future generations. This indicates that what is constant goes beyond the present and inevitably provides for the future. In a nutshell, sustainable development is nothing but the constant enjoyment of the RTD.

Moreover, sustainable development creates a conducive environment for the enjoyment of the RTD. It must be noted that the RTD cannot be fully enjoyed within an unsafe and resource deficit environment which sustainable development seeks to prevent. This makes the RTD and sustainable development, two sides of the same coin. While the RTD can contribute to realising sustainable development, the latter can also facilitate the realisation of the former. While the RTD ensures participation of all citizens in their individual capacities and groups of peoples in their collective capacity in the development process, there cannot be fair distribution of the benefits therefrom, without constant availability of sufficient resources, which is what sustainable development aims to achieve. In fact, it is the participation of every individual and all peoples with the aim to constantly improving the wellbeing of everyone that makes development sustainable. In other words, development cannot be sustainable without constant improvement in human well-being.

Further, the economic, social, cultural and political aspects of the development embodied in the RTD fall among the key elements of sustainable development. Economically and socially, the framework of sustainable development strongly suggests that socio-economic development be defined in terms of sustainability irrespective of a country's political and economic system.[37] That is because "development involves a progressive transformation of economy and society".[38] Culturally, the sustainable development framework indicates that the perceived needs of individuals and of peoples are socially and culturally determined and that sustainable development entails promoting the values that support sustainable consumption within the ecological limits, attainable by all.[39]

Equity in the distribution of resources in the context of sustainable development, is conceived to be achievable through "political systems that secure

37 Ibid at 54.
38 Ibid.
39 Ibid at 55.

effective citizen participation in decision making and by greater democracy in international decision making".[40] In much the same way, realising sustainable development requires among others, "a political system that secures effective citizen participation in decision making; an economic system that is able to generate surpluses and technical knowledge on a self-reliant and sustained basis; and a social system that provides for solutions for the tensions arising from disharmonious development".[41]

As can be observed, participation which is key to realising the RTD, is not less an important factor in efforts to achieve sustainable development. In the same way as participation is an entitlement and a critical element in the development process under the RTD,[42] it remains inevitable in the context of sustainable development.[43] Human-centredness, which cuts across the RTD and sustainable development have greater impact and are more felt through the principle of participation. While the RTD makes the human person the central subject of development, entailing their active participation in, contribution to and benefit from the development process, sustainable development ensures a political system where citizens can effectively participate in decision making. Based on this relationship between the RTD and sustainable development, it is important to discuss how the former contributes to achieving the latter.

2.3 *How the RTD Contributes to Sustainable Development*

Because the relationship between the RTD and sustainable development indicates how they reinforce each other, the RTD is thus, crucial and instrumental in achieving sustainable development. Simply put, the RTD is the means to an end and sustainable development is the end goal. By its nature and status as a universal human right, the RTD does not only ensure participation in the development process, but also aims at the constant improvement in well-being, which by inference, means sustainable development. In other words, sustainable development entails the constant improvement in well-being economically, socially, and environmentally and in an inclusive, balanced, and integrated manner and in harmony with nature. It guarantees in sum, a minimum threshold for collective well-being.[44] To achieve sustainable development therefore, boils down to recognising the RTD. This means that to achieve sustainable development, states must respect, protect, fulfil and

40 Ibid at 25.

41 Ibid at 74.

42 Declaration on the Right to Development, supra note 4, Art 1.

43 Brundtland Commission Report, supra note 1, Para 113.

44 Ngang, Carol Chi (2019) Systems Problem and a Pragmatic Insight into the Right to Development Governance for Africa. *African Human Rights Law Journal* 19(2): 390–391.

promote the RTD for their peoples. The challenge however, is that the RTD is currently only recognised under international law as soft law and therefore, needs to be elevated to the status of a legally binding instrument, which the draft Covenant aims to achieve.

3 Status and Impact of the RTD

Although the Universal Declaration of Human Rights makes provisions for socio-economic and cultural rights, they are not written in the context of development.[45] Development in the era of decolonisation and the spring-up of newly established nations in the Global South, focused primarily on economic growth rather than human rights.[46] The concept of development then excluded the human rights aspect and its bearing on development.[47] The distinction between human rights and development only became evident in the 1970s, following the emergence of the concept of the RTD.[48] Located under the taxonomy of the third generation of human rights or solidarity rights,[49] the RTD is comprehensively articulated in the DRTD adopted by the UN General Assembly Resolution 41/128 on 4 December 1986. The Declaration was adopted by 146 votes in favour, 1 vote against (USA), 8 abstentions (Denmark, Finland, Iceland, Sweden, Israel, Japan, Great Britain and the Federal Republic of Germany) with Norway being the only Nordic country that voted in favour of the Declaration.

Furthermore, the 1993 Vienna Declaration and Programme of Action (Vienna Declaration) confirmed the "RTD as a universal and inalienable right and an integral part of fundamental human rights".[50] The RTD is also recognised in regional human rights systems, including in particular, the African human rights system.[51] Subsequently, the RTD received the blessing of all UN member states, including the USA during the second World Conference on

45 Ibhawoh, supra note 19.

46 Ibid.

47 Uvin, Peter (2007) From the Right to Development to the Rights-Based Approach: How "Human Rights" Entered Development. *Development in Practice* 17(4/5): 597.

48 Ibhawoh, supra note 19.

49 Vasak, Karel (1997) A Thirty-Year Struggle: The Sustained Efforts to Give Force of Law to the Universal Declaration on Human Rights. *UNESCO Courier* 32: 28–29.

50 Vienna Declaration and Programme of Action, adopted by the World Conference on Human Rights in Vienna on 25 June 1993, Para 10.

51 African Charter on Human and Peoples' Rights adopted in Nairobi, Kenya on 27 June 1981 OAU Doc CAB/LEG/67/3 Rev.5 (1981), Art 22.

Human Rights in 1993, which culminated in the adoption by consensus of the Vienna Declaration and Programme of Action.[52] It must be emphasised that the RTD has given the world a new approach to development thinking by integrating human rights into the domestic and global development frameworks.[53] It has equally inspired many states to include the RTD in their national constitutions and enforcement mechanisms[54] and thus, provided "a reference point for demands for a more equitable distribution of wealth and resources within and between states".[55]

The controversy on whether the RTD is a human right can be considered settled following the adoption of the Vienna Declaration and Programme of Action among other major developments, including the drafting of the Covenant on the Rights to Development, which is currently undergoing intergovernmental negotiations at the level of the UN General Assembly. This is further, corroborated by the submission of Navi Pillay, former UN High Commissioner for Human Rights, who observed that the RTD is neither superior nor inferior but is of the same standard as all other human rights.[56] Regrettably, the RTD has for long, remained non-binding at the international level.[57] The DRTD has since its adoption in 1986, remained a soft law instrument and therefore, by nature unenforceable.[58] Despite the tireless efforts of the Commission on Human Rights (now the Human Rights Council), through the open-ended Intergovernmental Working Group and the Independent Expert on the RTD[59]

52 Sengupta, Arjun (2004) The Human Right to Development. *Oxford Development Studies* 32(2): 179.

53 Declaration on the Right to Development, supra note 4.

54 Constitution of the Republic of Cameroon 1972, Preamble read with Art 65; Constitution of the Republic of Uganda 1995, Objective IX; Constitution of the Democratic Republic of Congo 2005, Preamble and Art 58; Constitution of the Republic of Malawi 1994, Art 30; Constitution of the Federal Democratic Republic of Ethiopia 1994, Art 43; Constitution of the Democratic Republic of Benin 1990, Art 9; Constitution of the Federal Republic of Nigeria (Promulgation) Act 24 of 1999 Cap C23 Vol 3 (LFN 2004 Revised); Constitution of Zimbabwe Amendment Act No 20 of 2013, Sect 13(3).

55 Ibhawoh, supra note 19, 103.

56 United Nations Human Rights 2013, supra note 11, iii–iv.

57 Piron, Laure-Helene (2002) The Right to Development: A Review of the Current State of the Debate for the Department for International Development. *Overseas Development Institute Global.* Available at: https://media.odi.org/documents/2317.pdf (consulted 20 October 2024).

58 Ngang, Carol Chi; Kamga, Serge Djoyou and Gumede, Vusi (2018) *Perspectives on Right to Development.* Pretoria: Pretoria University Law Press, 2.

59 Office of the High Commission for Human Rights—The Right to Development Commission for Human Rights Resolution 1998/72, adopted without a vote on 22 April 1998.

as well as the work of the Special Rapporteur on the RTD,[60] implementation of the RTD remains a problem.[61] Although the RTD is implicitly enshrined in binding human rights instruments such as the International Covenant on Civil and Political Rights and the International Covenant on Economic, Social and Cultural Rights, it still remains a soft law.[62] Considering its guarantees, making the RTD a universally binding treaty, as suggested by Teshome, would be a remarkable achievement.[63] It is in this direction that the proposed Covenant on the Right to Development comes in handy in not only ensuring concrete realisation of the RTD but also envisaging realisation of sustainable development.[64]

4 Envisaging Sustainable Development through the RTD

The DRTD defines development as "a comprehensive economic, social, cultural, and political process, which aims at the constant improvement of the well-being of the entire population and of all individuals on the basis of their active, free and meaningful participation in development and in the fair distribution of benefits resulting therefrom".[65] It is expected that the full realisation of the RTD will culminate in the achievement of sustainable development. It is therefore, incumbent on the United Nations (UN) to concretely ensure the exercise of such an important right, which could bring about sustainable development particularly, in Africa where "poverty, hunger, malnutrition, inequality, suppression, decrepit infrastructure, debilitating educational services, and socio-economic cum political turmoil"[66] are the order of the day. In other words, it is universally known that many developing countries are in

60 United Nations Human Rights Council Resolution 33/14, adopted on 29 September 2016, on the Appointment of a Special Rapporteur.

61 Udombana, Nsungurua (2000) The Third World and the Right to Development: Agenda for the Next Millennium. *Human Rights Quarterly* 22(3): 753.

62 Kirchmeier, supra note 14, 8.

63 Teshome, Roman Girma (2022) The Draft Convention on the Right to Development: A New Dawn to the Recognition of the Right to Development as a Human Right? *Human Rights Law Review* 22(2): 6.

64 Draft International Covenant on the Right to Development—Report by the Chair-Rapporteur of the Working Group on the Right to Development, Zamir Akram (Pakistan) Human Rights Council A/HRC/54/50 54th Session, 6 October 2023, Art 24.

65 Declaration on the Right to Development, supra note 4, Preamble.

66 Bedjaoui, M. (1991) The Right to Development. In: Bedjaoaui, M. (ed) *International Law: Achievements and Prospects*. Dordrecht/Paris: Martinus Nijhoff and UNESCO 1177–1204; Ejembi, Paul Adole (2017) Decrypting the Approaches of Eastern and Western

a deplorable state as they wrestle with poverty, disease, and many other problems that our generation is confronted with.[67]

There may be many ways to achieve sustainable development, which entails providing for current and future needs, an objective which every state seeks to achieve. Adoption of the MDGs and currently the SDGs saddled by the above-mentioned challenges indicate the failure of these global policies to achieve sustainable development. Although achieving sustainable development appears herculean, the RTD seems to have what it takes to ensure its attainment, hence its importance in the process as explained in this subsection. First, the RTD, makes development an inalienable human right[68] like any other human right which must be respected, protected, and fulfilled. Despite its current soft law status, its connectedness and interdependence with other fundamental human rights constitutes an obligation for its realisation by duty bearers. Second, it entitles every person and groups of persons to participate in, contribute to and enjoy economic, social, cultural, and political development, a process through which all human rights and fundamental freedoms are envisaged to be fully realised.[69] By ensuring participation in, contribution to, and enjoyment of the development process, the entitlements of the RTD can be expected. In terms of the DRTD, "The human person is the central subject of development and should be the active participant and beneficiary of the right to development".[70] It further emphasises the individual and collective responsibility of all persons for development, the respect for their human rights and fundamental freedoms, and their duties to the community they live in.[71] Hence, individuals and communities are required to promote and protect an appropriate political, social, and economic order for development.[72]

In much the same way, states are mandated to design national development policies to ensure the constant improvement of the wellbeing of individuals and communities by guaranteeing "their active, free and meaningful participation in development and in the fair distribution of the benefits resulting therefrom".[73] To the extent that national development polices ensure the foregoing, sustainable development can be expected through the RTD.

Geo-Political Blocs in Africa's Quest for Development under International Law. *Nnamdi Azikiwe University Journal of International Law and Jurisprudence* 8(1): 56.

67 Udombana, supra note 61.

68 Declaration on the Right to Development, supra note 4, Art 1.

69 Ibid.

70 Ibid at Art 2(1).

71 Ibid at Art 2(2).

72 Ibid.

73 Ibid at Art 2(3).

The obligation of states to formulate, adopt and implement policies, including legislative and other measures nationally and internationally to ensure the full exercise and progressive enhancement of the RTD,[74] can significantly contribute to sustainable development.

While development facilitates the enjoyment of all human rights including the RTD, the lack of it may not be used to limit internationally recognised human rights.[75] As an internationally recognised human right, the RTD which aims at ensuring economic, social, cultural, and political development can simultaneously give effect to sustainable development. In other words, if the lack of development cannot justify limiting the RTD, respecting the RTD therefore, envisages that development and human rights are achieved. This cyclical process between the RTD and development can contribute to sustainable development. Achieving sustainable development would, therefore, entail constant respect for, protection and fulfilment of the RTD. Since the RTD remains soft law at the international level, it is strongly argued that the proposed Convention on the RTD when it is eventually adopted by the UN General Assembly as binding law, can significantly facilitate sustainable development.

5 Draft International Covenant on the RTD and Sustainable Development

5.1 *Provisions on Sustainable Development in the Covenant*

The draft International Covenant on the RTD is contained in the report by the Chair-Rapporteur of the Working Group on the Right to Development, Zamir Akram from Pakistan which forms part of efforts to have a binding treaty on the RTD that will apply internationally.[76] Unlike the DRTD and the Vienna Convention and Programme of Action which only recognise the RTD as an inalienable human right and an integral component of international human rights law, the draft Covenant on the RTD goes a mile further in enshrining express provisions on sustainable development.[77] In a nutshell, it makes sustainable development a human right.

---

74 Ibid at Art 10.

75 Vienna Declaration and Programme of Action, supra note 50, Para 10.

76 A/HRC/54/50: Draft International Covenant on the Right to Development—Report by the Chair-Rapporteur of the Working Group on the Right to Development, Zamir Akram (Pakistan), 11 July 2023.

77 Draft International Covenant on the Right to Development, supra note 64, Art 24.

First, the draft Covenant mandates states parties to individually and collaboratively ensure that laws, policies and practices relating to development nationally and internationally, contribute to the realisation of sustainable development in ways that align with their obligations under international law.[78] Considering that the RTD is a human right; in realising sustainable development, particular attention should be given to states' human rights obligations. In this regard, state laws, policies and practices on development must be human rights oriented. They must be designed and implemented with a human rights-based approach with the understanding that the implementation of the RTD leads to the realisation all human rights and fundamental freedoms.[79]

Second, the draft Covenant enjoins state parties to take decisions and actions that do not compromise the ability of present and future generations to realise their RTD.[80] This provision embodies the idea of intergenerational equity in the conceptualisation of the RTD[81] and thus, affirms the inextricable link between the RTD and sustainable development to the effect that state decisions and actions relating to sustainable development have a bearing on the RTD.

Third, the draft Covenant provides that in formulating, adopting and implementing laws, policies and practices to realise development, states parties must fully comply with provisions of the Covenant and other obligations under international law for realising sustainable development.[82] It is worthy to note that, compliance with the Covenant and other instruments of international law, can significantly contribute to realising sustainable development. The RTD is therefore, crucial in achieving sustainable development, necessitating looking at how the draft Covenant makes provision for the specific aspects of sustainable development namely, economic, social, and environmental.

5.2 *Economic, Social, and Environmental Dimensions of Sustainable Development*

The draft Covenant on the RTD guarantees that

> every individual and all peoples have the inalienable right to development, by virtue of which they are entitled to participate in, contribute to

78 Ibid at Art 24(a).

79 Declaration on the Right to Development, supra note 4, Art 1.

80 Draft International Covenant on the RTD, note 64, Art 24(b).

81 Ngang, C.C. (2021) Urban Landownership and the Right to Sustainable Development for Women in Africa. In: Home, R. (ed) *Land Issues for Urban Governance in Sub-Saharan Africa*. Geneva: Springer International Publishing, 97–99.

82 Draft International Covenant on the RTD, note 64, Art 24(c).

> and enjoy civil, cultural, economic, environmental, political and social development that is indivisible from and interdependent and interrelated with all other human rights and fundamental freedoms.[83]

It further recognises that to achieve sustainable development, "development must be achieved in its three dimensions namely, economic, social and environmental, in an inclusive, balanced and integrated manner and in harmony with nature".[84] As noted in the Preamble to the DRTD and reaffirmed in the draft Covenant, development is conceived as a comprehensive economic process[85] among others to constantly improve the wellbeing of everyone, which can be achieved in many ways.

On the economic dimensions, every individual and all peoples are entitled to *inter alia*, participate in, contribute to, and enjoy economic development that fully realises all human rights and fundamental freedoms.[86] Not only does it urge states to take appropriate economic and social reforms to eradicate all social injustices nationally,[87] but it also calls for a new international economic order[88] that guarantees equitability and global balance between developed and developing countries. In this way, the RTD is envisaged to contribute to sustainable development by ensuring inclusive economic growth that benefit both individuals and group of peoples through strategies that aim at eradicating poverty and inequality. Realising the RTD has the potential to increase economic opportunities by creating jobs, stimulating entrepreneurship and expanding access to the equitable distribution of resources.

On the social dimension, the draft Covenant on the RTD enjoins state parties to put in place social reforms aimed at eradicating social injustices.[89] States parties are also mandated to cooperate to create a domestic social and international order conducive to the realisation of the RTD[90] whose impact on sustainable development cannot be underestimated. Equally critical is the definition of development in the framework of the RTD as a comprehensive social process among others, to constantly improve the well-being of everyone and all peoples.[91] By this, the draft Covenant on the RTD promises social

83 Ibid at Art 4(1).
84 Ibid at Art 3(g).
85 Declaration on the Right to Development, supra note 4, Preamble.
86 Ibid at Art 1.
87 Ibid at Art 8.
88 Ibid at Art 3(3).
89 Draft International Covenant on the RTD, note 64, Art 12(2).
90 Ibid at Art 13(4).
91 Declaration on the Right to Development, supra note 4, Preamble.

inclusion, which guarantees participation and inclusion of marginalised groups and thus, curb social exclusion. This not only protects human dignity and the worth of everyone, but it also enables every individual and all peoples to take ownership and control of the development process and reap the benefit from its outcomes.

On the environmental dimension, the draft Covenant entitles everyone to participate in, contribute to and enjoy among others, environmental development that is indivisible from and interdependent and interrelated with all other human rights and fundamental freedoms.[92] It recognises among others, a comprehensive environmental process to development, to constantly improve the well-being of everyone based on their active, free and meaningful participation in development and in the fair distribution of the benefits resulting therefrom.[93] In this register, the RTD can significantly impact sustainable development by ensuring environmental protection through sustainable natural resource management. This can equally ensure climate change mitigation, and investments in renewable energy to reduce carbon emissions. The RTD can in this instance, promote environmentally sustainable development, reduce poverty, and ensure a healthy environment for present and future generations.

5.3 *Potential of a Binding Treaty on the RTD in Achieving Sustainable Development*

The potential benefits of a binding treaty on the RTD are enormous. This subsection examines how the binding nature of the Covenant on the RTD can contribute to the achievement of sustainable development.

5.3.1 Legal Benefits

A binding treaty on the RTD will obligate states parties to formulate appropriate national development policies,[94] and more so, to respect,[95] protect[96] and fulfil[97] the RTD of every individual and all peoples, including the socially marginalised, the economically disadvantaged and the environmentally vulnerable and consequently, guarantee that development is achieved in a sustainable manner. The need for accountability will arise and states will have to put in place mechanisms for monitoring, reporting and remedial action for the

92 Draft International Covenant on the RTD, note 64, Art 4(1).
93 Ibid at Preamble.
94 Declaration on the Right to Development, supra note 4, Art 2(3).
95 Draft International Covenant on the RTD, note 64, Art 10.
96 Ibid at Art 11.
97 Ibid at Art 12.

implementation of the RTD. As an instrument of international human right law, depending on each country's legal system, and approach to international law, the extent of its justiciability, when adopted, the Covenant on the RTD will equip and empower judicial and quasi-judicial bodies to address violations of the RTD and provide appropriate remedies to individuals and communities that may be affected.[98] Indeed, every individual and all peoples will be able to seek justice for the violation of their RTD through domestic, regional and international human rights judicial or quasi-judicial bodies.[99] It will set a standard for development policies and practices within the framework of the RTD and thus, enhance sustainability in the development process.

5.3.2 Development Benefits

The benefits of development, which is the end goal of the RTD and sustainable development are worth mentioning. A binding treaty on the RTD will ensure economic development benefits across all segments of society and thereby, curb inequalities, social exclusion and development injustices. As a rights-based human-centred law, the envisaged treaty on the RTD will prioritise the well-being, dignity and quality of life of everyone and all peoples.[100] The draft Covenant envisages poverty eradication by enshrining provisions that seek to address the roots causes of poverty and inequality and promote sustainable livelihoods for all particularly, those living and working in rural areas, including indigenous peoples.[101] The expected binding treaty on the RTD will ensure social justice by promoting equity, non-discrimination, and participatory governance, which is estimated to empower the marginalised, the disadvantaged and the vulnerable[102] and enhance the capacities of every individual and all peoples and communities for sustainable development.

5.3.3 Sustainable Development Benefits

A binding RTD as it is anticipated with the coming into force of the International Covenant, which is pending adoption by the UN General Assembly will equip and obligate states parties to adopt an integrated approach to sustainable development by enabling them to balance the economic, social and environmental dimensions in ensuring holistic development.[103] This will encourage

---

98 Ibid at Art 15.

99 Ibid.

100 Declaration on the Right to Development, supra note 4, Preamble; Draft International Covenant on the RTD, note 64, Preamble.

101 Draft International Covenant on the RTD, note 64, Art 18.

102 Ibid at Art 3(b).

103 Ibid at Art 3(g).

sustainable development planning and decision making that considers not only present but future generations. Not only does the Covenant on the RTD seek to address the impacts of climate change on vulnerable populations and promote climate resilience,[104] it also aims to protect the environment by ensuring sustainable natural resource management and the conservation of biodiversity.[105]

The binding Covenant on the RTD is envisioned to create an economically conducive and enabling environment for responsible investments,[106] promote sustainable development, ensure economic growth through inclusive growth strategies, stimulate economic development and consequently, eradicate poverty.[107] This can equally address economic disparities, promote social equity and foster decent job opportunities. Socially, the Covenant on the RTD, when it is adopted, will equip and empower every individual, all peoples and communities, including in particular women and girls to legitimately claim their rights.[108] It will offer expanded opportunities for participation in decision making processes and community engagement;[109] social cohesion by promoting unity, solidarity and shared responsibility; strengthening social fabrics; and ensuring the preservation of cultural values through respect and promotion of cultural diversity.[110] The anticipated binding Covenant on the RTD will guarantee environmental and climate justice for vulnerable communities and guarantee access to appropriate remedies for victims.[111] When the Covenant on the RTD is adopted and comes into force, it is envisaged, based on the related provisions therein, to enjoin states parties to adopt appropriate national environmental laws and policies, which in combination, will facilitate the attainment of sustainable development objectives.

5.4 *Challenges in Realising Sustainable Development through the RTD*

While a binding treaty on the RTD may obligate states parties to respect, protect and fulfil the right, and promote sustainable development, certain challenges may be expected in the process. These challenges include power imbalances among state governments; resource constraints where states have positive obligations; management of the tensions between the economic, social and

104 Ibid at Art 15(2).
105 Ibid at Art 5(3).
106 Ibid at Art 8(5).
107 Ibid at Art 13(1)(b).
108 Ibid at Art 16(1).
109 Ibid at Art 4(2).
110 Ibid at Preamble.
111 Ibid at Arts 13(4)(h) and 15(2).

environmental dimensions of sustainable development and ensuring effective implementation of the RTD during conflicts and crisis situations. The challenges are however, not insurmountable.

To deal with the issue of power imbalances, states parties must strengthen local governance by empowering local authorities through capacity-building and adequate resource allocation. They should also decentralise development policies to ensure that decision-making power and resource distribution are equitable. In dealing with intergovernmental agreements towards implementing the RTD, states must establish clear roles, responsibilities, and coordination mechanisms.

In addressing the problem of resource constraints, states parties must in addition to generating development financing internally, also consider international cooperation in mobilising supplementary resources through global partnerships and development assistance. It is worth emphasising that states have the obligation to first endeavour to mobilise the requisite resources for development at the domestic level by implementing progressive taxation, reducing corruption, and increasing transparency before proceeding to explore the opportunities available through international cooperation. To effectively coordinate the economic, social, and environmental dimensions of sustainable development, states may adopt integrated policy frameworks to balance the related legislative and policy considerations and ensure that global development objectives that are embodied in the SDGs align with domestic development plans and policies. Moreover, stakeholder engagement should be prioritised by involving civil society organisations, the private sector, and local communities in decision-making on matters of development that affect their lives.

To ensure effective implementation of the RTD during conflicts and crisis situations, states may and indeed, as expected to bridge humanitarian responses with long-term development strategies; and accordingly, design programmes that respond adequately to the conflict dynamics as well as to the human rights and development exigencies. The protection of marginalised, disadvantaged and vulnerable groups must be prioritised under such circumstances by prioritising their human rights and freedoms and most importantly, their livelihood sustainability needs.

6 Conclusion

The lack of development and its importance for a meaningful and qualitative living in many parts of the world particularly, in developing countries has led to the understanding that development is a fundamental human right which has been conceptualised as the RTD. For development to be achieved in a sustainable matter requires that the RTD be guaranteed legal recognition and protection. The African human rights system has successfully done so by enshrining the RTD in the African Charter and ancillary human rights instruments and affirmed its enforceability through a robust evolving jurisprudence.

However, at the international level, the RTD has remained unenforceable due to its status as soft law, which dilutes its potential to contribute to the realisation of sustainable development. Because the RTD and sustainable development are mutually reinforcing, making the RTD legally binding at the international level through adoption of the International Covenant on the RTD, is envisaged to facilitate the processes for sustainable development as envisaged under the SDG framework. Giving the RTD legally binding status, will not only keep development on states' agenda as a matter of obligation but also ensure that national development policies are designed, implemented and monitored through a human rights approach.

References

A/HRC/54/50: Draft International Covenant on the Right to Development—Report by the Chair-Rapporteur of the Working Group on the Right to Development, Zamir Akram (Pakistan), 11 July 2023.

African Charter on Human and Peoples' Rights adopted in Nairobi, Kenya on 27 June 1981 OAU Doc CAB/LEG/67/3 Rev.5 (1981).

Bedjaoui, M. (1991) The Right to Development. In: Bedjaoaui, M. (ed) *International Law: Achievements and Prospects*. Dordrecht/Paris: Martinus Nijhoff and UNESCO, 1177–1204.

Brundtland Commission (1987) Report of the World Commission on Environment and Development: Our Common Future. Available at: https://sustainabledevelopment.un.org/content/documents/5987our-common-future.pdf (consulted 4 September 2024).

Constitution of the Democratic Republic of Benin 1990.

Constitution of the Democratic Republic of Congo 2005.

Constitution of the Federal Democratic Republic of Ethiopia 1994.

Constitution of the Federal Republic of Nigeria (Promulgation) Act 24 of 1999 Cap C23 Vol 3 (LFN 2004 Revised).

Constitution of the Republic of Cameroon 1972.

Constitution of the Republic of Malawi 1994.

Constitution of the Republic of Uganda 1995.

Constitution of Zimbabwe Amendment Act No 20 of 2013.

Dąbrowska, Anna Olga (2010) Legal Status of the Right to Development. *Haskoli Island University*. Available at: https://scholar.google.com/scholar?hl=en&as_sdt=0%2C5&q=Legal+Status+of+the+Right+to+Development+by+Anna+Olga+D%C4%85browska&btnG= (consulted 5 September 2024).

De Feyter, Koen (2013) Towards a Framework Convention on the Right to Development. *Friedrich-Ebert-Stiftung—International Policy Analysis*. Available at: http://library.fes.de/pdf-files/bueros/genf/09892.pdf (consulted 5 September 2024).

Declaration on the Right to Development Resolution A/RES/41/128 adopted by UN General Assembly on 4 December 1986.

Draft International Covenant on the Right to Development—Report by the Chair-Rapporteur of the Working Group on the Right to Development, Zamir Akram (Pakistan) Human Rights Council A/HRC/54/50 54th Session, 6 October 2023.

Ejembi, Paul Adole (2017) Decrypting the Approaches of Eastern and Western Geo-Political Blocs in Africa's Quest for Development under International Law. *Nnamdi Azikiwe University Journal of International Law and Jurisprudence* 8(1): 56–63.

Emas, Rachel (2015) The Concept of Sustainable Development: Definition and Defining Principles. *Brief for GSDR 2015*.

Hallgren, Ragnar (1990/1991) The UN and the Right to Development. *Peace Research* 22(4)/23(1): 32.

Hulme, David (2009) The Millennium Development Goals (MDGs): A Short History of the World's Biggest Promise. *Brooks World Poverty Institute Working Paper 100*. Available at: https://papers.ssrn.com/sol3/papers.cfm?abstract_id=1544271 (consulted 4 September 2024).

Ibhawoh, Bonny (2011) The Right to Development: The Politics and Polemics of Power and Resistance. *Human Rights Quarterly* 33(1): 76–104.

Kamga, Serges Djoyou (2011) Human Rights in Africa: Prospects for the Realisation of the Right to Development under the New Partnership for Africa's Development. PhD thesis, University of Pretoria, 188–190.

Kirchmeier, Felix (2006, July) The Right to Development—Where Do We Stand?: State of the Debate on the Right to Development. *Dialogue on Globalization Occasional Papers No* 23: 1–28.

Li, Yuefen; Uribe, Daniel and Danish (2022, 8 March) The International Discourse on the Right to Development and the Need to Reinvigorate its Implementation. *South Centre Research Paper No 149*.

M'baye, Kéba (1972) Le Droit au Développement Comme un Droit de l'Homme: Leçon Inaugural de la Troisième Session d'Enseignement de l'Institut International des Droits de l'Homme. *Revue des Droits l'Homme* 5: 505–534.

McNeill, D. (2004) The Concept of Sustainable Development. In: Schmidt, J.D. (ed) *Development Studies and Political Ecology in a North South Perspective*. Aalborg,

Denmark: Aalborg University Research Center on Development and International Relations Development Research Series, Occasional Papers No 5.

Mensah, Justice (2019) Sustainable Development: Meaning, History, Principles, Pillars, and Implications for Human Action: Literature Review. *Cogent Social Sciences* 5(1): 1–21.

Ngang, C.C. (2021) Urban Landownership and the Right to Sustainable Development for Women in Africa. In: Home, R. (ed) *Land Issues for Urban Governance in Sub-Saharan Africa*. Geneva: Springer International Publishing, 89–102.

Ngang, Carol Chi (2018) Towards a Right-to-Development Governance in Africa. *Journal of Human Rights* 17(1): 107–122.

Ngang, Carol Chi (2019) Systems Problem and a Pragmatic Insight into the Right to Development Governance for Africa. *African Human Rights Law Journal* 19(2): 365–394.

Ngang, Carol Chi; Kamga, Serge Djoyou and Gumede, Vusi (2018) *Perspectives on Right to Development*. Pretoria: Pretoria University Law Press.

Office of the High Commission for Human Rights—The Right to Development Commission for Human Rights Resolution 1998/72, adopted Without a Vote on 22 April 1998.

Ouguergouz, Fatsah (2003) *The African Charter on Human and Peoples' Rights: A Comprehensive Agenda for Human Dignity and Sustainable Democracy in Africa*. Dordrecht: Martinus Nijhoff Publishers.

Ozili, Peterson (2022) Sustainability and Sustainable Development Research Around the World. *Munich Personal RePEc Archive Paper No 115767*. Available at: https://mpra.ub.uni-muenchen.de/115767/1/MPRA_paper_115767.pdf (consulted 4 September 2024).

Pezzey, John (1992) *Sustainable Development Concepts: An Economic Analysis*. Washington DC: The World Bank.

Piron, Laure-Helene (2002) The Right to Development: A Review of the Current State of the Debate for the Department for International Development. *Overseas Development Institute Global*. Available at: https://media.odi.org/documents/2317.pdf (consulted 20 October 2024).

Report of the High-Level Task Force on the Implementation of the Right to Development on its Sixth Session. Available at: https://documents.un.org/doc/undoc/gen/g10/118/37/pdf/g1011837.pdf (consulted 5 September 2024).

Ruggerio, Carlos Alberto (2021) Sustainability and Sustainable Development: A Review of Principles and Definitions. *Science of the Total Environment* 786(147481): 1–11.

Sengupta, A. (2013) Conceptualizing the Right to Development for the Twenty-First Century. In: United Nations Human Rights (ed) *Realizing the right to development: Essays in Commemoration of 25 Years of the United Nations Declaration on the Right to Development*. Geneva/New York: UN Publishing, 67–87.

Sengupta, Arjun (2000) Realizing the Right to Development. *Development and Change* 31(3): 553–578.

Sengupta, Arjun (2004) The Human Right to Development. *Oxford Development Studies* 32(2): 179–203.

Suzanne van der Have, Nieke (2013) The Right to Development and State Responsibility Can States be Held to Account? *University of Amsterdam—Amsterdam Law School Research Paper No 2013–23*, 1–18.

Teshome, Roman Girma (2022) The Draft Convention on the Right to Development: A New Dawn to the Recognition of the Right to Development as a Human Right? *Human Rights Law Review* 22(2): 1–24.

Tufaner, Mustafa Batuhan and Türker, Taner (2016) The Importance of the Sustainable Development in Terms of Quality of Life of the Future Generations. *Journal of Social and Administrative Sciences* 3(4): 300–310.

Udombana, Nsungurua (2000) The Third World and the Right to Development: Agenda for the Next Millennium. *Human Rights Quarterly* 22(3): 753–787.

United Nations Human Rights (2013) *Realizing the right to development: Essays in Commemoration of 25 Years of the United Nations Declaration on the Right to Development.* Geneva/New York: UN Publishing.

United Nations Human Rights Council Resolution 33/14, adopted on 29 September 2016, on the Appointment of a Special Rapporteur.

United Nations Millennium Declaration Resolution A/55/L.2 adopted by the United Nations General Assembly on 8 September 2000.

Uvin, Peter (2007) From the Right to Development to the Rights-Based Approach: How "Human Rights" Entered Development. *Development in Practice* 17(4/5): 597–606.

Vasak, Karel (1997) A 30-Year Struggle: The Sustained Efforts to Give Force of Law to the Universal Declaration on Human Rights. *UNESCO Courier* 32: 28–29.

Vienna Declaration and Programme of Action, adopted by the World Conference on Human Rights in Vienna on 25 June 1993.

PART 2

Global Framework for Development and the Matrix of Power

CHAPTER 5

Power Asymmetries in the Politics of International Development Cooperation and the Quest for Global Balance

Pratyush Sharma

1 Introduction

The current international development architecture and the development cooperation ecosystem is lopsided in favour of developed countries with respect to the quantum of foreign aid (Official Development Assistance), conceptualisation and the Washington Consensus framework for delivery, leashed operationalisations (conditionalities), and the temporality of cooperation (delays in delivery). Meanwhile, development cooperation between developing countries, which is generally referred to as South–South cooperation (SSC) is one of the most successful models of partnership for realising sustainable development as it is devoid of North-South cooperation's (NSC) conceptual and operational handicaps. With the economic and political rise of the Global South and the rise in the voice of the Global South, the development cooperation landscape has also been evolving where a convergence has emerged in NSC and SSC. Conceptually, the right to development (RTD) has the potential to revolutionise the global development architecture through fostering SSC, NSC, and triangular cooperation as envisaged in the draft International Covenant on the Right to Development.[1]

This chapter delves into the historical origins of the power asymmetries in the field of international development followed by the emergence of SSC, and the RTD which emanated through the challenges faced by countries of the Global South in their quest for development justice and an international economic order that guarantees global balance. The following sections, showcase through case study analyses, how the normative framework of the RTD provides the answer for better operationalisation of the SSC framework than what currently exists. The chapter also discusses the current debates in the

1 Draft International Covenant on the Right to Development—Report by the Chair-Rapporteur of the Working Group on the Right to Development, Zamir Akram (Pakistan) Human Rights Council A/HRC/54/50 54th Session, 6 October 2023, Art 13(4)(g).

 | DOI:10.1163/9789004734357_006

development cooperation ecosystem and how the RTD could respond to some of the burning contemporary issues within the global political economy where the RTD is increasingly being conceived as a solution driven approach to development thinking. The chapter ends with actionable points as to how to make the RTD more relevant in the policy circles of the Global South and the Global North and more so, in enhancing SSC.

2 South–South Cooperation

The SSC framework of international cooperation for carrying out projects in the developing world originated as soon as countries in Asia and Africa got independence from colonial rule from the 1940s. Lived experiences and the shared history of colonialism brought together, countries that were experiencing similar challenges with respect to development and lack of skilled human resources.[2] Solidarity driven assistance started between these countries, which in various occasions were deprived of financial transfer as the assistance were operationalised in the form of barter driven exchanges.[3] Just as with trade, in SSC, comparative advantage of the countries involved play a significant role. For example, in the initial phases of SSC, India, owing to better human resources in the field of education and engineering, assisted different nations in the South in developing their education systems through capacity building programmes.[4] Similarly, Cuba has been instrumental in strengthening the health sector in different African countries by sending teams of medical practitioners to the beneficiary countries.[5] Brazil has assisted other countries through their policy transfers[6] and China in the recent decades has built infrastructure in various countries in the South.[7] The SSC framework has continued to grow with the economic rise of the Global South. Complementary to

2 Chaturvedi, Sachin (2016) *The Logic of Sharing: Indian Approach to South–South Cooperation.* Cambridge: Cambridge University Press, 16.

3 Romero, C. (2010) South–South Cooperation between Venezuela and Cuba. In: The Reality of Aid (ed) *South–South Development Cooperation: A Challenge to the Aid System.* Philippines: IBON Books 108.

4 Ibid.

5 Brouwer, Steve (2011) *Revolutionary Doctors: How Venezuela and Cuba Are Changing the World's Conception of Health Care.* New York: New York University Press, 2.

6 De Morais, Michelle Graciela (2005) South–South Cooperation, Policy Transfer and Best-Practice Reasoning: The Transfer of the Solidarity in Literacy Program from Brazil to Mozambique. *International Institute of Social Studies Working Paper Series No 406*, 2.

7 Abdenur, Adiana Erthal and Da Fonseca, João Moura (2013) The North's Growing Role in South–South Cooperation: Keeping the Foothold. *Third World Quarterly* 34(8): 1475–1491.

bilateral SSC, the emergence of SSC at a multinational level took place in 1955 at the Bandung Conference where 24 newly independent nations from Asia and Africa laid the foundation of the Non-Aligned Movement (NAM).[8]

It is important to discuss the other form of development cooperation which is different from SSC. North-South Cooperation (NSC) is a development concept in which there is a linear transfer of resources from a developed country to developing countries. It has its origins from the reconstruction activities led by the United States of America (USA) and its economic recovery plans for Europe which had been ravaged by the Second World War. Under the Marshall Plan initiated in 1948, the USA granted USD 15 billion (nearly USD 140 billion in 2024) to Europe for a period of four years for rebuilding the war-torn regions, removing trade barriers, modernising industries, improving European prosperity, and preventing the spread of communism.[9] The reasons behind the Marshall Plan were, both altruistic and strategic. While the USA aspired on the one hand, for the development of Europe, on the other hand, its fear of the spread of communism from the Soviet Union was palpable.[10] After the development activities in Europe, the attention of the USA shifted to the developing world with the intention of replicating the successes of the Marshall Plan in Asia, Africa, and Latin America. The foundation of NSC was laid with the establishment of the Organisation of Economic Cooperation and Development (OECD) in 1961.[11] Its members are high income developed countries in the Global North with high human development indices.

In contrast with NSC, SSC is a non-western construct for inter-state and inter-social relations. Its pillars of shared identity, involving countries with similar levels of economic development, common goals and aspirations of equitable exchange situates SSC at a different level. Global International Relations[12]

---

8 Yu, Vincente Paolo (2019) Key Issues for BAPA+40: South–South Cooperation and the BAPA+40 Subthemes. *South Centre Research Paper No 91*, 3.

9 Rosseel, Peter et al (2009) Approaches to North-South, South–South and North-South-South Collaboration: A policy Document. Available at: file:///C:/Users/ngang/Downloads/POLICY_PAPER_VLIR_UWC__NSS.pdf (consulted 30 November 2024), 11.

10 Hogan, Morgan (1987) *The Marshall Plan: America, Britain and the Reconstruction of Western Europe, 1947–1952*. Cambridge University Press, 34.

11 Abdenur and Da Fonseca, supra note 7, 1478.

12 It is pertinent to point out that the discipline of International Relations emerged after the ravages of the Great War (1914–1918) with the intention of spreading peace, attaining peaceful settlement of disputes between countries and stopping a repeat of such devastating wars. The developmental (trade, finance, peace and human rights) angle in IR was realised only when previous set of beliefs could not stop the Second World War (1939–1945). The victors of Second World War set the stage for IR in post 1945 era with establishment of various international and inter-governmental organisations. Emergence

as a framework of cooperation, encourages interactions that deviate from the mainstream northern idea of international relations and seeks to uncover indigenously driven patterns of interactions around the world, paying attention to local, regional and interregional interactions. True universalism, according to global international relations, recognises the diversity of human interactions, rather than the one that legitimises imposition of the Anglo-Saxon world.[13]

Most of the major countries involved in SSC were once the recipients of foreign aid from OECD member countries. The guiding principles of SSC that emerged over the years were a response against the hardships and challenges faced by countries of the Global South recipients of aid from the Global North.[14] It came to mean that countries in the Global South would not subject fellow developing countries to the same treatment they suffered at the hands of developed nations. It meant the absence of any political and macro-economic conditionalities attached to development cooperation within the SSC framework. However, on many occasions the guiding principles have either come under stress or a controversy has erupted where observers claimed SSC to be neo-colonial in nature.[15] Conditionalities attached to foreign aid in NSC have mainly been in the form of structural adjustment programmes (SAPs), which are in essence, policy interventions in the domestic affairs of recipient countries.[16] Research conducted in the period from 1980s to 1990s, reveal that the SAPs and conditionalities were counterproductive and the fiscal conservativeness were harming essential sectors like education, healthcare and agriculture in Africa and Asia.[17]

---

of the Global South ushered in a different set of value systems in existing IR. The IR now appears to be global in nature with infusion of ideas and principles from countries that were still under colonial rule right after 1945. This can be viewed as transition of the discipline from IR to Global IR.

13 Acharya, Amitav (2016) Studying the Bandung Conference from a Global IR Perspective. *Australian Journal of International Affairs* 70(4): 342–357.

14 Mawdsley, Emma (2012) *From Recipients to Donors: Emerging Powers and the Changing Development Landscape*. London: Zed Books Ltd, 18.

15 Chahoud, Tatjana (2007) South–south cooperation-opportunities and challenges for international cooperation. German Institute of Development and Sustainability—Briefing Paper No 7/2007, 1–7.

16 International Policy Centre for Inclusive Growth (2010) Poverty in Focus. Available at: https://ipcig.org/pub/IPCPovertyInFocus20.pdf (consulted 29 November 2024), 3.

17 Cornia, Giovanni Andrea; Jolly, Richard and Stewart, Frances (1987) *Adjustment with a Human Face*. Oxford: Clarendon Press; Riddell, Barry (1992) Things Fall Apart Again: Structural Adjustment Programmes in sub-Saharan Africa. *The Journal of Modern African Studies* 30(1): 53–68; Mathur, Ajeet (1993) The Experience of Consultation During Structural Adjustment in India (1990–92). *International Labour Review* 132: 331;

In contrast, in line with the principle of respect for national sovereignty, SSC was developed based on the idea that the partner or the recipient countries initiate, organise and manage their cooperation activities, which hinge on interdependences, not new dependencies. The basic tenet that supports SSC that international cooperation never ought to interfere with the internal dynamics of the partner countries, such as providing policy recommendations that challenge the national sovereignty of the partners. It also does not seek to withhold and/or rescind partnerships due to changes in the policy and legislative frameworks within the partner country. However, these basic tenets of SSC have been questioned in the recent past, mainly with respect to China with its ambitious Belt and Road Initiative (BRI) for infrastructure and connectivity projects in developing countries. Interestingly, the criticisms have come both from countries in the Global North[18] and those from the Global South[19] alike that perceive the BRI to be debt-trap diplomacy.[20]

It has been observed that on many occasions, development project activities within the NSC framework take place unilaterally without consulting the recipient countries or without taking their demands and aspirations

Upendranadh, C. (1993) Structural Adjustment and Education: Issues Related to Equity. *Economic and Political Weekly* 28(44): 2415–2419; Mosley, Paul; Harrigan, Jane and Toye, John (1995). *Aid and Power: The World Bank and Policy-Based Lending*. 2nd Edn London: Routledge; Prabhu, K.S. (1996) The Impact of Structural Adjustment on Social Sector Expenditure: Evidence from Indian States. In: Rao, C.H.H. and Linnemann H. (eds) *Economic Reforms and Poverty Alleviation in India*. New Delhi: Sage Publication.

18 US Department of Defense (2019) Indo-Pacific Strategy Report: Preparedness, Partnerships, and Promoting a Networked Region. Available at: https://media.defense.gov/2019/Jul/01/2002152311/-1/-1/1/DEPARTMENT-OF-DEFENSE-INDO-PACIFIC-STRATEGY-REPORT-2019.PDF (consulted 20 November 2024), 1.

19 Ministry of External Affairs, India (2020) Media Centre. Available at: https://www.mea.gov.in/lok-sabha.htm?dtl/32353/QUESTION+NO606+BRI+AND+CPEC (consulted 20 November 2024).

20 Chellaney, Brahma (2017, 23 January) China's Debt-Trap Diplomacy. *Project Syndicate*. Available at: https://www.project-syndicate.org/commentary/china-one-belt-one-road-loans-debt-by-brahma-chellaney-2017-01 (consulted 20 November 2024); Ferchen, Matt (2018, 16 August) China, Venezuela, and the Illusion of Debt-Trap Diplomacy. *Asia Global Online*. Available at: https://carnegieendowment.org/posts/2018/10/china-venezuela-and-the-illusion-of-debt-trap-diplomacy?lang=en (consulted 20 November 2024); Lindberg, Kari and Lahiri, Tripti (2018, 28 December) From Asia to Africa, China's "Debt-Trap Diplomacy" was Under Siege in 2018. *Quartz Daily Brief*. Available at: https://www.google.com/amp/s/qz.com/1497584/how-chinas-debt-trap-diplomacy-came-under-siege-in-2018/amp (consulted 20 November 2024).

TABLE 5.1 Major differences between NSC and SSC

Parameters	North–South Cooperation	South–South Cooperation
Aim/purpose	Historically altruistic endeavour	Solidarity-driven mutual benefit endeavour
Geopolitical origin	Emerged under Cold War rhetoric	Emerged during Non-Aligned Movement
Political aspiration	Maintenance of North led international order	Democratisation of international order
Primary drivers	OECD-DAC members	Global South (Tri-continentalism: Asia, Africa and Latin America)
Nature of partners	Donors from an industrialised state with high per-capita income	Partnership between states with similar levels of development
Theoretical basis	Theory of change	Lacks theorisation
Philosophical basis	Framework approach	Ingredient approach
Conditionalities	Extensive political and macro-economic conditionalities	Presence of soft procedural conditionalities
Operational sovereignty	Multilayered time-consuming bureaucratic structures, hence added transaction cost	Highly decentralised and relatively fast with few implications for transaction cost
Institutional oversight	No global body. OECD acts as a Secretariat	No global body. Tri-continental multi-stakeholder partnership on the rise
Public perception	Negative, with inward-looking tendencies in donor countries	Positive, with belief in globalisation in partner countries

SOURCE: ADAPTED FROM CHATURVEDI (2014) AND LENGYEL AND MALACALZA (2011)

into account.[21] To get rid of this paternalistic and patronising treatment, the demand-driven approach took shape as one of the operational principles within the SSC framework. Within the SSC, it is the partner or the recipient, rather than the provider or the source of funds that determines the priorities in the project. The selection of projects and the methods for implementation are decided in consultation with the partner and is never imposed on the recipient country. Furthermore, it is important to note that all the SSC partners carrying out projects in the developing world were/are themselves developing and

21 Moyo, Dambisa (2009) *Dead Aid: Why Aid is not Working and How There is a Better Way for Africa*. Macmillan Publishers, 44.

had/have development challenges. Assisting other countries within the SSC framework is thus, not a charity-based model but driven by altruism and solidarity.[22] It means that SSC is based on genuine partnership devoid of hierarchy in development cooperation. The spirit of sharing through capacity building and technology transfer has been a principal driver of SSC. It is for these reasons that SSC was conceived and developed, adhering to the principle of "mutual benefit" wherein some benefit is expected for the provider country as well thereby, rejecting an unequal dependent relationship. The aim of cooperation is to create a higher level of capability and economic opportunity for both the partners, aimed at mutually beneficial interdependency.

The SSC framework evolved and expanded during the decades when NSC was the primary development channel for the Global South. Not only is the quantum of development assistance through NSC much higher than with SSC, it is also spread out across different countries and sectors. All the international and inter-governmental organisations like the United Nations, the World Bank, the International Monetary Fund, and the World Trade Organisation are still under the control of the USA and other countries of the North.[23] As a result, the development cooperation landscape has for a long time, been under the hegemonic control of the Global North. Despite this, as mentioned previously, countries of the Global South were, in their own way contributing towards the development of other developing countries. It was during the first decade of the 21st Century when the emerging economies of the Global South experienced a sustained spurt in economic growth, while countries in the Global North faced economic downturn in 2008 and beyond that there was a sincere interest by the Global North to seek to understand development interventions of the South by the South and for the South.[24] The surge in economic growth of countries in the Global South enabled them increase their developmental activities in other countries of the Global South.

The SSC framework, however, lacks an institutionalised approach to development cooperation, unlike the NSC framework which has the organisational backing of the OECD. Plurality within the SSC framework is celebrated and encouraged to come up with local solutions to the problems and diversity in

---

22 Chaturvedi, Sachin and Mulakala, Anthea (eds) (2016) *India's Approach to Development Cooperation*. London/New York: Routledge.

23 Foot, Rosemary; Macfarlane, Neil and Mastanduno, Michael (2000) US Hegemony and International Organisations. New York: Oxford University Press.

24 Gosovic, Branislav (2016) The Resurgence of South–South Cooperation. *Third World Quarterly* 37(4): 739.

terms of modalities when it comes to the operationalisation of development projects.[25] For example, India carries its development cooperation projects under the rubric and principles of SSC within the modality of "development compact" which includes capacity building for sustainable growth, trade for development, project specific concessional finance, grants, and technology sharing. These modalities are then manifested across various sectors. Traditionally, the sectors where India carries out projects in other countries of the Global South include health, education, agriculture, and digital solutions.[26]

Other Southern countries follow a different modality set-up and concentrate on different sectors. For example, Brazil, Indonesia, and Turkey engage in areas of SSC to which they bring expertise and capacity such as entrepreneurial education, tropical agriculture, or disaster prevention and response,[27] while Cuba[28] and Nigeria[29] put great emphasis on technical cooperation initiatives. Through these specialisations, these countries can draw on their unique experiences, which add greater value to development initiatives. This diversity and plurality within the SSC framework are both, a boon and a bane. Such diversity and plurality bring flexibility to development interventions and has a better chance of course correction, not only at the end of the project cycle but, also during the project cycle. On the flip side, different countries that are engaged in SSC have imagined SSC differently. Such a diversity has impeded a theoretical or normative framework for SSC from emerging. A detailed discussion on this is provided in the section on theoretical framework below.

Apart from economic growth in the emerging countries of the Global South, increase in geographical expanse and in quantum of SSC, the economic downturn faced by major economies of the Global North, and the success stories of South–South projects grabbing headlines, another major reason for the prominent positioning of SSC in recent decades has been adoption of the SDGs by

25 Milani, Carlos (2014) Brazil's South–South Co-operation Strategies: From Foreign Policy to Public Policy. *South African Institute of International Affairs: African Perspectives, Global Insights—Occasional Paper No 179*.

26 Chaturvedi, Sachin (2011) *South–South Cooperation in Health and Pharmaceuticals: Emerging Trends in India-Brazil Collaborations*. New Delhi: Research and Information System for Developing Countries.

27 De Renzio, Paolo and Seifert, Jurek (2014) South–South Cooperation and the Future of Development Assistance: Mapping Actors and Options. *Third World Quarterly* 35(10): 1864.

28 Gómez, A.F.R. (2016) Cuba and South–South Cooperation. In: Verzola Jr, P. (ed) *Country Case Studies on South–South Cooperation*. Philippines: Reality of Aid, 90.

29 Lechini, Gladys (2007) Middle Powers: IBSA and the New South–South Cooperation. *NACLA Report on the Americas*, 40(5), 28–32.

the world community in 2015.[30] The SSC framework has explicitly been mentioned as one of the means of implementation for realising the SDGs, meaning that apart from other modes available for realising the goals, SSC is one of the operational tools at the disposal of the global community in seeking to achieve the SDGs by 2030. Through several years of on-the-ground operationalisation of SSC, countries of the South have amassed knowledge about development, cooperation and ideas that can be shared with the global community in realising the SDGs.

The year 2015 was quite significant not only because of adoption of the 2030 Agenda but also for another important agenda-setting conference where relevant stakeholders met in Addis Ababa in July 2015 to agree on and adopt the Addis Ababa Action Agenda of the Third International Conference on Financing for Development. It laid out the steps for the global community to take towards funding the 2030 Agenda which were adopted in September of the same year.[31] The focus of the Addis Ababa Action Agenda has been in the areas of taxation; the system of development banks; trade, investment and technology; and international monetary and financial architecture.[32] As far as the operationalisation tool required for the realisation of the Addis Ababa Action Agenda (which would equally contribute to the SDGs) is concerned, the outcome document mentions SSC as its complementary mechanism.[33] For a proper understanding of the operational framework, it is important to examine the concept of the right to development (RTD) in relation to SSC.

3 The Right to Development as a Normative Framework for SSC

As discussed previously, in the absence of a normative framework for SSC, countries of the Global South have carried out cooperation according to their

30 Transforming Our World: The 2030 Agenda for Sustainable Development, UN General Assembly Resolution A/RES/70/1 (2015) (Sustainable Development Goals Framework).

31 Hurley, Gail (2015) The Addis Ababa Action Agenda: A Step Forward on Financing for Development? Available at: https://www.undp.org/content/undp/en/home/blog/2015/7/21/The-Addis-Ababa-Action-Agenda-A-step-forward-on-financing-for-development-.html (consulted 24 November 2024).

32 Ocampo, Gaviria (2016) The Contribution of the Addis Ababa Action Agenda to Agenda 2030, 1.

33 Addis Ababa Action Agenda of the Third International Conference on Financing for Development adopted at the Third International Conference on Financing for Development (Addis Ababa, Ethiopia, 13–16 July 2015) and endorsed by the General Assembly Resolution 69/313 of 27 July 2015, Paras 28, 56, 57 and 120.

own understanding of it. These countries have varying operational frameworks, different modalities, and sector specificities under which the projects are operationalised, and as earlier noted, this diversity and plurality is both a boon and a bane for SSC. Both the development process, and its outcomes are vital aspects of realising development. Thus, development is described as a process, indicating that it must not be measured based only on *what* is achieved (the outcomes) but also on *how* it is achieved (the process).[34] Before embarking on the journey to establish the relationship between the RTD, SSC, sustainability, and the SDGs, it is important to look at the historical evolution of the RTD from being merely an idea to its eventual incorporation in the global discourse on development.

3.1 *Normative Framework on the Right to Development*

Senegalese diplomat, Doudou Thiam, first articulated the idea of the RTD in a speech delivered at the opening session of the 21st UN General Assembly in 1966.[35] The urge of delivering such a speech emanated from the frustration of the failure of the international community to meet the goals of the UN's First Development Decade which was launched in December 1961 by the UNGA. In his speech, Doudou Thiam alluded to the fact that political sovereignty has not translated into economic sovereignty and the imbalance between developed and developing countries have continued to persist. Thus, the RTD was framed in the post-colonial critique of the established modernisation theory of development.[36] The modernisation theory explains that sovereign countries traverse similar stages of development on their way to a mature and industrial society.[37] Rostow enumerated the stages of development as: traditional economies, involving (a) the transition to take-off (adoption of scientific methods of technology), (b) the take-off (rapid capital accumulation and early industrialisation), (c) the drive to maturity (high industrialisation in which standard of

34 UN General Assembly (1999) Study on the Current State of Implementation of the Right to Development Submitted by Mr. Arjun Sengupta, Independent Expert, E/CN.4/1999/WG.18/2, Para 36.

35 UN General Assembly (1966) United Nations General Assembly, Official Records, Twenty-first Session, 1414th Plenary Meeting, 23 September 1966.

36 Whelan, Daniel; Kanade, Mihir; Puvimanasinghe, Shyami (2018) Operationalizing the Right to Development in Implementing the Sustainable Development Goals. E-Learning Module, 2.

37 Rostow, W.W. (1990) *The Five Stages of Growth: A Summary*. In: Rostow, W.W. (ed) *The Five Stages of Growth: A Non-Communist Manifesto*. 3rd Edn, Cambridge: Cambridge University Press, 4–16.

living of the masses remains low), and (d) the stage of high consumption. Many social scientists are predicting a sixth stage (e), "post-industrial" society.[38]

The modernisation theory posits that present day developed countries were once backward; hence underdeveloped societies in the 1950s and 1960s would follow similar paths of development as was followed by developed countries of today and their transition would be hastened through close contact with already developed societies.

The modernisation theory has however, being challenged by Raúl Prebisch who propounded the dependency theory in describing the contemporary framework for development.[39] Prebisch is considered the father of dependency theory, which articulates the idea that resources flow from a "periphery" of poor and exploited states to a "core" of wealthy states, enriching the latter at the expense of the former.[40] He was an Argentinian economist who headed the United Nations Economic Commission for Latin America in the

TABLE 5.2 Societies I–V, seen at times 1–6, in developmental stages A–E

Societies	Timelines					
	1	2	3	4	5	6
I	Traditional	A2	B3	C4	D5	E6
II	Traditional		A3	B4	C5	D6
III	Traditional			A4	B5	C6
IV	Traditional				A5	B6
V	Traditional					A6

A = Take-off from the traditional society (the adoption of scientific methods of technology)
B = Take-off (rapid capital accumulation and early industrialisation)
C = Maturity (high industrialisation in which the standard of living of the masses remains low)
D = Age of high consumption
E = Post-Industrial Society
SOURCE: CHIROT AND HALL (1982)

38 Bell, Daniel (1973) The Coming of Post-Industrial Society: A Venture in Social Forecasting. New York: Basic Books, 507.

39 Prebisch, Raúl (1962) The Economic Development of Latin America and its Principal Problems. *Economic Commission for Latin America and the Caribbeans*. Available at: https://repositorio.cepal.org/entities/publication/9a00fa5b-ad04-4520-ae4c-e3adbe791790 (consulted 26 December 2024).

40 Chaturvedi, Sachin and Chakrabarti, Milindo (eds) (2019) *Raúl Prebisch and Development Strategy*. New Delhi: Research and Information Systems for Developing Countries.

late 1940s and early 1950s and became the Secretary-General of the United Nations Conference on Trade and Development (UNCTAD) from 1964 to 1969. He showed in his studies that the terms of trade had run against agricultural exporting countries from the late 19th century until the late 1930s.[41] He further suggested that there was a tendency for terms of trade to decline as against those of manufactured goods and argued that this was because of intense competition that existed between many primary goods producers (agriculture produce, minerals and natural resources), as opposed to the relatively few manufactured goods producers.[42] This was also accentuated by a low-income elasticity of demand for primary goods, so that as average incomes increased, people spent a proportionately lower amount of their income on primary goods.[43]

The scope of trade export for developing countries are primary products like agriculture produce, minerals and natural resources. Thus, one of the earliest articulations of the RTD and its fundamental root was incidentally linked to the right of self-determination. The discussion continued as to how this right could be realised and/or enforced, especially in its economic instantiation: the right to permanent sovereignty over natural resources.[44] Emergence of a unified Third World approach to development policy further solidified the positioning of the RTD. Though, the journey through different conferences and declarations (see Table 5.3 for timelines), the idea of the RTD was shaped, re-shaped and even sometimes derailed and distorted.[45] The journey of iteration and re-iteration of the RTD led to its incorporation in the global discourse on development where the moral imperative on Third World demands for global economic justice as a right have continuously been emphasised.[46] Ultimately, the RTD was adopted as General Assembly Resolution 41/128 titled "Declaration on the Right to Development" (DRTD) on a vote of 146-1-8, with the US casting the sole dissenting vote.[47]

41 Love, Joseph (1980) Raúl Prebisch and the Origins of the Doctrine of Unequal Exchange. *Latin American Research Review* 15(3): 46.

42 Sharma, Pratyush (2019) Dependency Theories in the Era of BAPA+40. *Special Issue: Development Cooperation Review* 4(2): 37.

43 Ibid.

44 Whelan, Kanade and Puvimanasinghe, supra note 38, 3.

45 Ngang, Carol Chi (2021) *The Right to Development in Africa*. Leiden/Boston: Brill Koninklijke, 47–48.

46 Whelan, Kanade and Puvimanasinghe, supra note 38, 8.

47 Ibid at 12.

3.2 *Timelines on the RTD Linked to Third World Stance on Development Policy*

As the RTD was adopted by member states at the United Nations General Assembly (UNGA) in 1986, the discussions around development experienced significant change. The first of those changes were emergence of the concept of sustainable development a year later in 1987, as a global objective to be achieved. Also, any apprehensions regarding the status of the RTD as a human right were quashed by the unanimous adoption of the Vienna Declaration and Programme of Action in 1993, which made explicit reference to the DRTD and reaffirmed the RTD as a universal and inalienable right and an integral part of fundamental human rights, thereby settling the status of the RTD as a recognised human right.[48] During the same period, the UN Commission on Human Rights (UNCHR) instituted an open-ended Working Group of Government Experts on the RTD and in 1996, it established an Inter-governmental Working

TABLE 5.3 Timelines on the RTD from 1962 to 1986

No.	Name	Major outcome	Remark
1.	Conference on the Problems of Economic Development, Cairo (1962)	~ Cairo Declaration of Developing Countries focussed on the international structural obstacles to development in developing countries. ~ The Conference resulted in the UN establishing the UNCTAD	The Cairo Declaration focused on setting guidelines for the First UNCTAD Conference held in Geneva in 1964.
2.	UNGA 21, 1966	~ First articulation of the RTD by Senegalese diplomat, Doudou Thiam.	Out of frustration due to unfulfilled goals of the UN Development Decade.
3.	1st Ministerial Meeting of the G77, Algiers (1967)	~ The Charter of Algiers focussed on the worsening conditions of trade for developing countries. ~ It also underlined the obligations of the international community to rectify the unfavourable trends.	Development and aid were given the status of juridical obligation, which until then were viewed as charity.

48 Whelan, Kanade and Puvimanasinghe, supra note 38, 14.

TABLE 5.3 Timelines on the RTD from 1962 to 1986 (*cont.*)

No.	Name	Major outcome	Remark
4.	UNCTAD II Summit, New Delhi (1968)	~ The language of the RTD was conspicuously absent in the official declaration. ~ The official document hinged on a narrowly defined economic growth model of development.	The excitement from the G77 meeting in Algiers regarding juridical obligation towards development was lost.
5.	2nd Ministerial Meeting of the G77, Lima (1971)	~ Special Committee on Latin America (Consensus of Lima) embraced the idea of the RTD and concretised it through articulation of the rights of developing countries and the obligations of developed countries and the international community.	Despite progress on the RTD in the Consensus of Lima, it failed to be mentioned in the outcome document of the 2nd Ministerial Meeting.
6.	UNCTAD III Summit, Santiago (1972)	~ Lobbying by Latin American States and Mexico resulted in adoption of elements of the RTD in the form of the Charter on Economic Rights and Duties.	This was the last instance of focus on human-centred development and economic justice. The NIEO had no mention of such terms.
7.	Commission on Human Rights (UNCHR) led seminars on human rights in developing countries	~ Between 1964–1970 seminars in Kabul and Dakar led to discussions on the enjoyment of economic and social rights in developing countries. ~ Led to appointment of Iranian diplomat, Manouchehr Ganji as a Special Rapporteur	Ganji had the task of preparing a report on the realisation of all the economic, social, and cultural rights set forth in the UDHR and the ICESCR.
8.	30th Session of the Commission on Human Rights, 1974	~ Ganji's revised report majorly emphasis the international dimensions of underdevelopment. ~ The report emphasised poverty reduction and hunger.	The Ganji Report led to the conclusion that the UNCHR should accord greater importance to economic and social rights.

TABLE 5.3 Timelines on the RTD from 1962 to 1986 (*cont.*)

No.	Name	Major outcome	Remark
9.	31st Session of the Commission on Human Rights, 1975	~ The general feeling of the Commission echoed Senegalese jurist, Kéba M'Baye's assertion of "right to development". This got further credence as the NIEO and CERD got adopted in 1974.	Developed countries led the discussion in a different way. This led to the emergence of "rights-based development" or "human rights-based approach" to development.
10.	UNGA Resolution 32/130, 1977	~ Directed the UNCHR to study alternate ways and means to respect human rights with emphasis on economic, social and cultural rights. ~ Led to preparation of the report "The International Dimensions of the Right to Development."	The report by Theo van Boven advocated a synthesis of political and economic, and individual and collective rights as the ideal approach to development.
11.	Working Group on the RTD, 1981	The UNCHR created a 15 member WG to study the scope and content of the RTD to ensure realisation of economic, social and cultural rights.	The idea was to work towards a draft international instrument on the RTD.
12.	African Charter on Human and Peoples' Rights adopted in 1981	Enumerated the collective right (of "peoples") to "their economic, social and cultural development.	African bloc created a *fait accompli* which the rest of the world could not ignore.
13.	UNGA, 1981	The UNGA Resolution 36/133 declared the RTD to be an "inalienable human right."	Despite differences between the WG, members were convinced that holders of the right are peoples and states.
14.	UNGA, 1986	The UNCHR presented to the UNGA and through Resolution 41/128, the "Declaration on the Right to Development" was adopted.	The WG issued a 17-page report in 1983, which was not accepted in whole by the WG.

SOURCE: AUTHOR'S COMPILATION BASED ON WHELAN, KANADE, PUVIMANASINGHE (2018)

Group on the RTD. In 1997, the UNGA passed a resolution wherein a call was made to include the DRTD as part of the International Bill of Human Rights.[49] Thereafter, the UNCHR recommended to the Economic and Social Council to establish an open-ended Working Group on the RTD which led to the appointment of Arjun Sengupta as first Independent Expert on the RTD.[50]

Alongside the institutional evolution of the RTD at the level of the UN including, there was also simultaneous policy shifts and academic progress in terms of reconceptualising development with a focus on the human dimension. In 1990, the UNDP published the first Human Development Report in which it introduced the human development index (HDI). The HDI embodied Amartya Sen's capabilities approach to understanding human well-being[51] thereby, emphasising the importance of ends (decent standard of living) over the means (GDP growth and per capita income).[52] Another landmark transformative shift happened through the seminal work of Amartya Sen in his book *Development as Freedom*.[53] The book has been instrumental in altering the understanding of development in economics, which shifted from the narrowly focussed economic perspective to a more holistic perspective of development conceived as a process of enhancing human well-being and the freedoms they enjoy, rather than just the maximisation of income or wealth.[54] The book emphasises that if income or wealth does not lead to enhancing lives and freedoms, then it is pretty much useless. In Sen's view, any adequate conception of development must not ignore economic growth but must look beyond it.[55] As such, he argued that enhancement of human freedoms is both the primary end and the principal means of development.[56] This is in sync with the DRTD which provides that "every human person and all peoples are entitled to participate in, contribute to, and enjoy economic, social, cultural and political development, in which all human rights and fundamental freedoms can be fully realised".[57] The DRTD is the first international instrument to bridge the ideological schism that saw the Universal Declaration of Human Rights split

---

49 Ibid at 15.

50 Ibid.

51 Sen, Amartya (1985) *Commodities and Capabilities*. Amsterdam: North Holland.

52 Stanton, Elizabeth (2007, February) The Human Development Index: A History. *University of Massachusetts Working Papers Series No 127*, 85: 3.

53 Sen, Amartya (1990) *Development as Freedom*. Oxford: Oxford University Press.

54 Whelan, Kanade and Puvimanasinghe, supra note 38, 27.

55 Sen 1990, supra note 56.

56 Whelan, Kanade and Puvimanasinghe, supra note 38, 15; Sen, supra note 56.

57 Declaration on the Right to Development Resolution A/RES/41/128 adopted by UN General Assembly on 4 December 1986, Art 1(1).

into two separate international covenants on Economic, Social and Cultural Rights on the one hand and Civil and Political Rights on the other. Thus, the elements within the RTD and Sen's work coincided.

The book converged the economic and the human rights perspectives of development into the contemporary formulation and understanding of the RTD. Also, the works of Arturo Escobar,[58] Martha Nussbaum,[59] and the concepts of human development and human security[60] led to the understanding that the human dimension must become the central element for development debates. Around the same period, 189 world leaders adopted the UN Millennium Declaration in 2000, which led to adoption of the MDGs, which highlighted as a principal objective, to make the RTD a reality for everyone.[61] This meant that achievement of development goals would have been realised by keeping the RTD in sharp focus. However, it remains highly debatable whether the actual implementation of the MDGs on the ground by states over the 15-year timeframe was undertaken within the overarching framework of the RTD.[62]

In his capacity as the UN Independent Expert on the RTD, Arjun Sengupta authored five reports which clarified the meaning and scope of the RTD and dealt with the vital questions regarding implementation thereof. Drawing on his reports and other important contributions from scholars on the RTD, the following points best summarise the normative framework of the RTD:[63]

a. The RTD is an inalienable self-standing human right. Development, and as will be pointed out below, sustainable development, are thus not mere privileges enjoyed by human beings, nor are they just subjects of charity or generosity.
b. The RTD denotes the entitlement of the rights holders to three things viz. to participate in, contribute to, and enjoy economic, social, cultural, and political development.
c. The RTD also implies the full realization of the right of peoples to self-determination.

58 Escobar, Arturo (1995) *Encountering Development: The Making and Unmaking of the Third World*. Princeton University Press.

59 Nussbaum, Martha (2000) *Women and Human Development: The Capabilities Approach*. Cambridge University Press.

60 UNDP (1990) *Human Development Report 1990*. Oxford: Oxford University Press.

61 United Nations Millennium Declaration Resolution A/55/L.2 adopted by the United Nations General Assembly on 8 September 2000, Para 11.

62 Whelan, Kanade and Puvimanasinghe, supra note 38, 18.

63 Ibid at 5–6.

d. Operationalising the RTD involves respecting, protecting, and fulfilling all other human rights—civil, political, economic, social, and cultural—along with generating the resources of growth such as GDP, technology etc. This means that given the very nature of development as a human right, it cannot be realised when there are violations of other human rights.
e. The RTD requires focusing not only on outcomes which are sought to be achieved as a result of a development plan (the "what" question), but also on the process by which those outcomes are achieved (the "how" question). Both the processes and outcomes of development must be consistent with and based on all other human rights.
f. Human beings are individually (all human persons) and collectively (all peoples) the rights holders of the RTD against their States as well as other States. Every State is entitled, as an agent of all persons and peoples subject to its jurisdiction, to demand respect for their RTD by other States and international organizations.
g. The DRTD entails duties on all States to respect, protect and fulfil the RTD across the following three levels:
   i. States acting individually as they formulate national development policies and programmes affecting persons within their jurisdiction,
   ii. States acting individually as they adopt and implement policies that affect persons not strictly within their jurisdiction, and
   iii. States acting collectively in global and regional partnerships.
h. The RTD imposes an obligation on States, individually and collectively, to eliminate existing obstacles to its realisation, refrain from making policies which are adverse to its realisation, and to positively create conditions favourable to its realisation.
i. Most importantly, the RTD imposes a duty on States with respect to international cooperation to realise the RTD.

It is clear from the above that in the context of SSC, the RTD provides an important normative framework wherein development is viewed not as charity but as a duty within the context of international cooperation. Before ending this section with the institutional changes within the UN system related to the RTD, it is important to discuss the normative core of the RTD which represents the integration of human rights principles into economic planning as Felice[64] among other scholars have drawn attention to as illustrate in this analysis.

---

64 Felice, William (2018, January) Operationalizing the Right to Development in Implementing the Sustainable Development Goals. E-Learning Module, Chapter 2, 4.

The right to equal opportunity: The onset of the post-World War II era with its economic, financial and trade related organisations like the World Bank, the IMF and the GATT resulted in continuation of the lopsided word order, including economic disparity between the developed and the developing countries. This world order did not do away with the social injustices of colonialism and neo-colonialism.[65] In the backdrop of such imbalances, the DRTD included the provision that development must be for all, and all peoples must enjoy the fair-distribution of the benefits of development. The RTD further claimed that it is a call for equal opportunity and a call to give an equal chance to participate fully in an economic system that can be exploitative and unjust if protective measures are not adhered to.[66] This resulted in the incorporation of state's duties and obligations to create a mechanism for equal opportunities for all.

Development as a process to realise all human rights: Development has been described as the core human right from which all other human rights stem.[67] In other words, realisation of the RTD would ultimately result in realisation of all human rights pertaining to economic, social, cultural, civil and political rights. These debates and discussions around the RTD have led to the articulation of human development.[68] Sen's capabilities approach further added to the understanding that development must be seen beyond the economic sense, which led to the conceptualisation of the rights-based approach to development.[69]

Legal accountability: The idea of the RTD is to view development cooperation and assistance from a legal perspective of rights and duties and away from its understanding based on charity and guilt. This is captured as:

> Before giving me charity or offering me your aid, give me my due. Perhaps I shall then have no need of your aid. Perhaps charity is no more than the screen behind which you expropriate what is due to me. Such charity does not deserve to be so called; it is my own property you are handing back to me in this way and, what is more, not all of it.[70]

---

65 Felice, William (2010) *The Global New Deal: Economic and Social Rights in World Politics*. 2nd Edn, Lanham, Maryland: Rowman and Littlefield Publishers, 51–52.

66 Felice 2018, supra note 67, 5.

67 Bedjaoui, M. (1991) The Right to Development. In: Bedjaoui, M. (ed) *International Law: Achievements and Prospects*. Paris: UNESCO.

68 Felice 2018, supra note 67, 6.

69 Sen 1990, supra note 56.

70 Bedjaoui, supra note 70, 1191–1192.

With such background, the DRTD ascribes duties and obligations on states (elaborated in the following sections). From the perspective of legal accountability, some scholars argue that the RTD has achieved the status of international customary law and is thus, binding on all states.[71] Others claim that the RTD can be seen as an emerging norm of international law with corresponding legal duties and obligations. Affirmation of the RTD in the 2030 Agenda for Sustainable Development makes a case for the RTD to be understood as soft law.[72] In any case, one cannot dispute the fact that irrespective of its status as soft law or customary international law, the RTD is a human right of all persons and peoples and thus, provides a strong normative foundation for development policy and practice.

Link between human development and civil and political rights: The Cold War era resulted in global conflict over the state of human rights. Western countries felt more comfortable with the idea of civil and political rights, whereas the socialistic states paid emphasis on economic, social and cultural rights. The RTD attempts to bridge this gap between human development and civil and political rights. Article 6(3) of the RTD provides that states must "take steps to eliminate obstacles to development resulting from the failure to observe civil and political rights, as well as economic, social and cultural rights".[73] Moreover, democratic participation is seen as critical to human development. As development is a subjective concept, a singular universal model of development is difficult to fathom and thus, development strategies must be determined by the peoples involved and adapted to their local conditions and needs.[74] Indeed, the DRTD establishes the framework for development to be conceived from the perspective of the rights holders. They are the authors of what development means to them.

The UN human rights system underwent institutional changes in the initial years of the new millennium. The Independent Expert, which used to support the inter-governmental Working Group on RTD was replaced by the High-Level Task Force on the Implementation of the RTD. This task force was composed of five experts from five geographical regions.[75] The mandated work of the Task Force was to assess and observe the realisation of MDG 8 on global partnership in compliance with the DRTD. In 2006, the Task Force was replaced

71 Chimni, B. (2003) Development and Migration. In: Aleinikoff, A. and Chetail, V. (eds) *Migration and International Legal Norms*. The Hague: T.M.C. Asser Press, 260.

72 Felice 2018, supra note 67, 8.

73 Declaration on the Right to Development, supra note 60, Art 6(3).

74 Felice 2018, supra note 67, 10.

75 UN Commission on Human Rights (2004) Resolution 2004/7 and ECOSOC Decision 2004/249.

by the UN Human Rights Council (UNHRC), which further established the Special Rapporteur on the RTD in 2016.[76]

The mandate of the Special Rapporteur is to contribute to the promotion, protection and fulfilment of the RTD in the context of the 2030 Sustainable Development Goals, the Addis Ababa Action Agenda, the Paris Agreement on Climate Change and the Sendai Framework for Disaster Risk Reduction 2015–2030; engaging and supporting efforts to mainstream the RTD among various stakeholders aimed at strengthening the revitalised global partnership for sustainable development; contributing to the work of the Working Group on the RTD; submitting studies requested by the UNHRC and an annual reports to the UNHRC and the UNGA.[77]

It is important to remember that these institutional changes did not alter the regional understanding of the RTD. Elements of the RTD are present in the 1948 Charter of the Organisation of American States.[78] Moreover, the African Charter on Human and People's Rights adopted in 1981, the Arab Charter on Human Rights of 2004, ASEAN Human Rights Declaration of 2012, and the 2016 the Abu Dhabi Declaration adopted by the Organisation of Islamic Cooperation Independent Permanent Human Rights Commission all affirm that the RTD is an indivisible, interdependent, interrelated and mutually inclusive individual and collective right.[79]

Moreover, the COVID-19 pandemic threatened to derail progress in the realisation of the SDGs as it posed immense negative socio-economic impact on societies globally, making the issue of rights and responsibilities for peoples and states more evident than ever before. Adoption of the 2030 Agenda gave the much-needed push to and reinvigoration of the RTD, which has been recognised by relevant stakeholders as a normative framework necessary for the realisation of the SDGs. It has led to a flurry of activities at the UNHRC and the Office of the High Commissioner for Human Rights (OHCHR).[80] It is a situation where the dual causality is at play. On the one hand, the 2030 Agenda could be seen as an implementation of states' duty as mentioned in the DRTD and on the other hand, operationalisation of the RTD can in turn, significantly bolster realisation of the SDGs by providing it with a normative framework.[81]

76 Whelan, Kanade and Puvimanasinghe, supra note 38, 18.

77 Ibid at 19.

78 Ibid at 22.

79 Ibid at 23.

80 Kanade, Mihir (2020, July) Towards a Legally Binding Instrument on the Right to Development. *University of Peace—Ideas of Peace Series No 15.*

81 Ibid at 2.

In the past couple of years, the UNHRC has undertaken three concrete steps in advancing the RTD.[82] In 2016, the UNHRC appointed a Special Rapporteur on the RTD (after a gap of ten years) with the mandate of contributing to the promotion, protection and fulfilment of the RTD within the context of implementation of the SDGs. In 2018, the UNHRC's commissioned the Working Group on the RTD in its 20th Session, to explore prospects of formulating a legally binding instrument on the RTD and thus, requested its advisory committee to prepare a research-based report on the importance of such a binding instrument on the RTD. In 2019, the UNHRC established a subsidiary expert mechanism to provide thematic expertise on the right to development; in searching for, identifying and sharing best practices with member states and promote implementation of the right to development worldwide.[83] The recently appointed Expert Mechanism has five independent experts elected for a term of three years with the possibility of extension by one term.[84]

The historical evolution of the RTD from its conceptualisation to its declaration along with the associated institutional changes related with the RTD clearly shows its embeddedness in the global policy framework. The adoption of the SDGs in 2015 has advanced the MDGs with quantitative and qualitative improvements. As mentioned previously, the RTD was supposed to play a central role in realisation of the MDGs, but its implementation left much to be desired. In the context of the SDGs, it is crucial that involvement of the RTD in the operationalisation of the goals is carried out in an efficient manner. At this stage, it is important to clearly layout the symbiotic relationship between the RTD and SSC.

3.3 *Relation between the Right to Development and South–South Cooperation*

As explained in the previous sections, traditional forms of development cooperation, notably the NSC framework has not lived up to the expectations of countries of the Global South. They have proven to be ill-equipped and insufficient in addressing development challenges in the Global South and thus also caught off guard in terms of the realisation of the MDGs, and SDGs. The SSC framework has meanwhile, not only expanded in quantum but also in geographical spread and is now considered to be an important means of implementation and complementary mechanism for achieving the SDGs. However, the plurality and diversity within the SSC framework has meant that

---

82 Ibid at 3.

83 UN Human Rights Council Resolution on the Right to Development A/HRC/RES/42/23 adopted on 27 September 2019, Paras 29–34.

84 Ibid at Para 4.

a universal definition of SSC cannot be achieved. An operational definition was nonetheless, agreed on in the 2012 UN operational guidelines on supporting South–South and triangular cooperation. The operational definition of SSC reads as:

> A process whereby two or more developing countries pursue their individual and/or shared national capacity development objectives through exchanges of knowledge, skills, resources and technical know-how, and through regional and interregional collective actions, including partnerships involving Governments, regional organizations, civil society, academia and the private sector, for their individual and/or mutual benefit within and across regions.[85]

The definition was derived from Paragraphs 18 and 19 of the 2009 Nairobi outcome document of the High-level United Nations Conference on South–South Cooperation[86] which stipulates as follows:

> We reaffirm that South–South cooperation is a common endeavour of peoples and countries of the South, born out of shared experiences and sympathies, based on their common objectives and solidarity, and guided by, inter alia, the principles of respect for national sovereignty and ownership, free from any conditionalities. South–South cooperation should not be seen as official development assistance. It is a partnership among equals based on solidarity. In that regard, we acknowledge the need to enhance the development effectiveness of South–South cooperation by continuing to increase its mutual accountability and transparency, as well as coordinating its initiatives with other development projects and programmes on the ground, in accordance with national development plans and priorities. We also recognize that the impact of South–South cooperation should be assessed with a view to improving, as appropriate, its quality in a results-oriented manner.
>
> South–South cooperation embraces a multi-stakeholder approach, including non-governmental organizations, the private sector, civil society, academia and other actors that contribute to meeting development challenges and objectives in line with national development strategies and plans.

85 UN (2012) Framework of Operational Guidelines on United Nations Support to South-South and triangular Cooperation. Para 9.

86 UN (2009) Nairobi Outcome Document of the High-Level United Nations Conference on South–South Cooperation. Paras 18 and 19.

International cooperation as a means of implementation has always been mentioned in various international instruments and development frameworks. The obligation on international cooperation in the context of development and human rights is derived from Article 1(3) of the UN Charter, which states as a foundational principle, "To achieve international cooperation in solving international problems of an economic, social, cultural, or humanitarian character, and in promoting and encouraging respect for human rights and for fundamental freedoms for all without distinction as to race, sex, language, or religion".[87] Article 55 of the UN Charter further states:

> With a view to the creation of conditions of stability and well-being which are necessary for peaceful and friendly relations among nations based on respect for the principle of equal rights and self-determination of peoples, the United Nations shall promote:
> a. higher standards of living, full employment, and conditions of economic and social progress and development,
> b. solutions of international economic, social, health, and related problems; and international cultural and educational cooperation, and
> c. universal respect for, and observance of, human rights and fundamental freedoms for all without distinction as to race, sex, language, or religion.

Article 56 of the UN Charter also stipulates that "All Members pledge themselves to take joint and separate action in co-operation with the Organization for the achievement of the purposes set forth in Article 55". It is provided in Article 22 of the Universal Declaration of Human Rights that "Everyone, as a member of society, has the right to social security and is entitled to realization, through national effort and international co-operation and in accordance with the organization and resources of each State, of the economic, social and cultural rights indispensable for his dignity and the free development of his personality".[88] Article 2(1) of the International Covenant on Economic, Social and Cultural Rights provides that

> Each State Party to the present Covenant undertakes to take steps, individually and through international assistance and co-operation, especially

87 Charter of the United Nations and Statute of the International Court of Justice, adopted in San Francisco, United States of America on 26 June 1945, Art 1(3).

88 Universal Declaration of Human Rights, UN General Assembly Resolution A/RES/217(III), adopted in Paris, France on 10 December 1948, Art 22.

> economic and technical, to the maximum of its available resources, with a view to achieving progressively the full realization of the rights recognized in the present Covenant by all appropriate means, including particularly the adoption of legislative measures.[89]

These, along with other international human rights treaties; and commitments undertaken by states in resolutions and international policy instruments place international cooperation at the centre of achieving various development goals. International cooperation has thus, been understood to be a cornerstone for development.

Although SSC is often not explicitly mentioned with respect to international cooperation, currently and for the future, all international cooperation is understood to include SSC as an acceptable form of international cooperation.[90] Under contemporary international law, other major declarations incorporating international cooperation are the 1992 Rio Declaration on Environment and Development. Principle 5 of the Rio Declaration asserts that

> all States and all people shall cooperate in the essential task of eradicating poverty as an indispensable requirement for sustainable development, in order to decrease the disparities in standards of living and better meet the needs of the majority of the people of the world.[91]

The 1993 Vienna Declaration and Programme of Action

> calls upon the international community, States, international organizations and non-governmental organizations to cooperate effectively, including with regard to the enjoyment of human rights, the realization of the right to development and the elimination of obstacles to development.[92]

---

89 International Covenant on Economic, Social and Cultural Rights adopted by the UN General Assembly, Resolution 2200A (XXI) of 16 December 1966, 999 UNTS 171 UN Doc A/6316 (1966), Art 2(1).

90 Report of the Special Rapporteur on the Right to Development on the Promotion and Protection of all Human Rights, Civil, Political, Economic, Social and Cultural Rights, including the Right to Development. Human Rights Council, 39th Session A/HRC/39/51, 10–28 September 2018, Para 12.

91 Rio Declaration on Environment and Development, Report of the United Nations Conference on Environment and Development A/CONF.151/26 (Vol. I) adopted in Rio de Janeiro, Brazil on 14 June 1992, Principle 5.

92 Report of the Special Rapporteur on the Right to Development, supra note 93, Para 22.

The Addis Ababa Action Agenda of the Third International Conference on Financing for Development specifically mentions SSC. It "explicitly reiterates the importance of South–South cooperation as a complement to North-South cooperation and as a vital element of international cooperation for development".[93] The Sendai Framework for Disaster Risk Reduction "highlights that a combination of various forms of cooperation has proven to be key in supporting States, communities and businesses in reducing disaster risk".[94] The Paris Agreement on Climate Change "recognizes the importance of international cooperation on adaption efforts, paying special attention to the needs of developing countries".[95] Ultimately, the 2030 Agenda for Sustainable Development "recognizes that sustainable development can only be realized with a strong commitment to global partnerships and cooperation".[96] To grasp the relationship between the RTD and SSC, it is important to reiterate and map out the rights holders and the duty bearers of the RTD as illustrated in Table 5.4.

TABLE 5.4 Rights holders and duty bearers on the RTD

RIGHTS HOLDERS
Who is the rights holder? Human beings are the rights holders of RTD. RTD is both an individual right and collective right.
Individual right Human person is the central subject of development. Human person should be the active participant and beneficiary of RTD. Human person should have access to free, active and meaningful participation in development decisions. There should be fair distribution of benefits of development with ultimate objective of fulfilling all human rights for all.

93 Ibid at Para 24.
94 Ibid at Para 25.
95 Ibid at Para 26.
96 Ibid at Para 27.

TABLE 5.4 Rights holders and duty bearers on the RTD (*cont.*)

Collective right
RTD is linked to the fundamental right of peoples to self-determination.
This includes peoples' right to full sovereignty over all their natural wealth and resources.

Women, children and other groups
RTD specifically states that women and children should have an active role in the development process.
RTD calls for elimination of sex-based discrimination in access to all human rights and fundamental freedoms

DUTY BEARERS

Who is the duty bearer?
RTD imposes duty on states and the international community.
And on all those whose actions and/or omissions have an impact on human rights and on the environment in which these rights are to be fulfilled.

States as primary duty bearer
States have the primary responsibility for respecting, protecting and fulfilling human rights.
They also have the primary responsibility for creating national and international conditions favourable for the realisation of the RTD.
It means that states have obligations at 3 levels:
Domestic: through the formulation of national development policies and programmes affecting persons within their jurisdictions.
International: through the adoption and implementation of policies extending beyond their jurisdictions.
Collective: through global and regional partnerships.

Human beings
All human beings, apart from being active participants in development, have a duty to promote and protect their human rights and fundamental freedoms.

SOURCE: AUTHOR'S COMPILATION BASED ON OHCHR (2016)

TABLE 5.5 Principles of the RTD in relation to the guiding principles of SSC

Principles of the RTD	Guiding principles of SSC
People-centred development: The human person is the central subject, participant, and beneficiary of development.	Solidarity and Ownership: SSC is solidarity and demand-driven approach to cooperation based on mutual-benefit among equal partners who share common experiences and objectives. SSC does not adhere to political and macro-economic conditionalities.
Participation: Active, free and meaningful participation of all individuals and peoples irrespective of race, sex, language or religion with fair distribution of the benefits of development along with adherence to accountability and transparency.	Multi-stakeholder Approach: SSC involves cooperation among peoples and countries, including partnerships involving governments, regional organisations, civil society actors, academia and the private sector.
State as primary duty-bearer: States have a duty to formulate an enabling local and global environment for development and to eliminate obstacles to development.	Modalities: SSC is not limited to financial aid but comprises of trade, investment, financial and humanitarian support, technical cooperation and capacity-building, technology transfer and knowledge exchange among others.
Good governance and global partnership: through the duty of international cooperation both, national and international dimensions of development.	Development impact and effectiveness: SSC should be evidence-based, result-oriented, based on mutual accountability and transparency and coordinated with other development programmes and projects on the ground.

SOURCE: OHCHR

The issue of international cooperation and global partnerships are central to the ideas SDG 17 whereas, the duties and responsibilities are central to the idea of the RTD. In this regard, it becomes imperative to view SSC from the perspective of the "duty of international cooperation".[97] Also, as mentioned previously the guiding/operational principles of SSC overlap with the principles

97 Kanade, M. (2021) From the Means of Implementation to Implementation of the Means: Realizing the Sustainable Development Goals as if they Matter In: Kakar, N.; Popovski,

of the RTD such as equality, inclusiveness, participation, national ownership, and self-determination. It is worth emphasising that SSC does not adhere to political and macro-economic conditionalities.[98] Table 5.5 puts the principles in perspective and elaborates on what it entails to promote the RTD as the normative framework for SSC.

3.4 *Draft International Covenant on the RTD and SSC*

The draft International Covenant on the RTD was released on 18 July 2023, during the 54th Session of the Human Rights Council. It is conceived to become a legally binding instrument to address issues relating to development as a human right under the United Nations framework. It builds on the 1986 Declaration on the Right to Development, which recognises that development is a universal and inalienable right. The Covenant provides the opportunity for ensuring the collective commitment of states in promoting equitable development while addressing structural inequalities at the national and global levels. It emphasises the inalienable nature of individual and peoples' right to equitable development and highlights the instrumental role of SSC in achieving this goal. SSC aligns with the principles of solidarity, mutual benefit, and non-conditionality, and accordingly, offers an alternative to the dominant North-South paradigms in global development. The draft Covenant provides the normative framework for operationalising the right to development, including through leveraging SSC in addressing shared challenges among developing countries. In envisaging realisation of the right to development, South–South and triangular cooperation are not intended to become substitutes for, but rather a complement to, North-South cooperation.[99] A further mention of SSC appears in Article 13 on the duty to cooperate, which incorporates

> Enhancing North-South, South–South, triangular and other forms of regional and international cooperation in all spheres, particularly on access to science, technology and innovation, and also enhancing knowledge-sharing on mutually agreed terms, including through improved coordination among existing mechanisms, in particular at

---

V. and Robinson N.A. (eds) *Fulfilling the Sustainable Development Goals: On a Quest for a Sustainable World.* London: Routledge, 3.

98 Research and Information System for Developing Countries (2013) Report of Conference of Southern Providers South–South Cooperation: Issues and Emerging Challenges. Research and Information System for Developing Countries, New Delhi. Available at: http //ris .org.in/pdf/SSC_report_web.pdf (consulted on 28 November 2024).

99 Draft Covenant on the Right to Development, supra note 1, Art 3(j).

the United Nations level and through existing and new mechanisms for global technology facilitation.[100]

4 Conclusion: Integrating the RTD into SSC

For the RTD to act as the normative framework for SSC, it is important that the guiding/operational principles adhere to the principles of the RTD. In this context, SSC operations must seek to achieve the SDGs on the ground, bearing in mind the following:

- The sections on the historical evolution of the RTD and SSC are clear on the fact that development must not be seen through the perspective of guilt/charity given to developing countries or development being enjoyed by a few as a matter of privilege. Development is a human right. Table 5.4 is illustrative of who the rights holders and duty bearers of the RTD are.
- From the perspective of SSC, it means that partner (recipient) countries must act as agents/representatives of the rights holders (citizens of the recipient countries) when it receives development assistance.
- It entails that in responding to the development priorities of partner countries, SSC operations must not in any way, undermine or violate the rights of the rights holders. Thus, SSC must ensure that its primary concern is enhancement of the well-being of the rights holders and not the interest of the partner countries.

The RTD framework means that SSC must not be viewed only from the political or economic point of view of self-interest but from the perspective that states are duty-bearers, entailing obligations at three-levels:

- To ensure that SSC initiatives in the partner (recipient) countries do not impair or nullify the partner country's obligations on the RTD. It means that the provider country must not impose SSC initiatives and projects on partner countries but must be directed by their development priorities. Policy conditionalities must not be imposed on a partner country, which will impede their realisation of the RTD. The RTD framework requires respecting the policy space of recipient countries, not as a matter of good behaviour but as a duty under international law, to respect state sovereignty.
- To ensure that unilateral domestic policies do not have adverse extra-territorial impact on the RTD of peoples elsewhere.

---

100 Ibid at 11.

– To ensure that on the global and collective front, SSC is operationalised at the regional and global levels for the realisation of the RTD and that obstacles to development are eliminated.

The above three points are underpinned by the duty to cooperate, which in essence forms the basis of the RTD. Not only does the duty to cooperate necessitate advancing the RTD of every individual and all peoples everywhere around the world, it also imposes the duty to eliminate existing obstacles to development. The framework of the RTD for SSC implies that development cooperation initiatives must be compatible with human rights standards and does not allow for the violation of any human rights in the process of cooperation and/or as a development outcome. Any trade-off between the successful completion of a SSC project and human rights violation goes against the principles of the RTD.

Tools for impact assessment and for monitoring and evaluation must accordingly, be employed to assess whether SSC initiatives do promote or undermine the RTD. This will not only assist states in ensuring better and sustainable project delivery but also help in making necessary adjustments, if the development cooperation processes are found to be detrimental to the RTD.

References

Abdenur, Adiana Erthal and Da Fonseca, João Moura (2013) The North's Growing Role in South–South Cooperation: Keeping the Foothold. *Third World Quarterly* 34(8): 1475–1491.

Acharya, Amitav (2016) Studying the Bandung Conference from a Global IR Perspective. *Australian Journal of International Affairs* 70(4): 342–357.

Addis Ababa Action Agenda of the Third International Conference on Financing for Development adopted at the Third International Conference on Financing for Development (Addis Ababa, Ethiopia, 13–16 July 2015), endorsed by the General Assembly Resolution 69/313 of 27 July 2015.

Bedjaoui, M. (1991) The Right to Development. In: Bedjaoui, M. (ed) *International Law: Achievements and Prospects*. Paris: UNESCO.

Bell, Daniel (1973) The Coming of Post-Industrial Society: A Venture in Social Forecasting. New York: Basic Books.

Brouwer, Steve (2011) *Revolutionary Doctors: How Venezuela and Cuba Are Changing the World's Conception of Health Care*. New York: New York University Press.

Chahoud, Tatjana (2007) South–South Cooperation-Opportunities and Challenges for International Cooperation. German Institute of Development and Sustainability—Briefing Paper No 7/2007, 1–7.

Charter of the United Nations and Statute of the International Court of Justice, adopted in San Francisco, United States of America on 26 June 1945.

Chaturvedi, Sachin (2011) *South–South Cooperation in Health and Pharmaceuticals: Emerging Trends in India-Brazil Collaborations*. New Delhi: Research and Information System for Developing Countries.

Chaturvedi, Sachin (2014, 1 January) Features of South–South Cooperation and Global Dynamics. *Forum for Indian Development Cooperation Policy Brief No 1*. Available at: http://ris.org.in/images/RIS_images/pdf/FIDC%20policy%20brief_1.pdf (consulted 24 November 2024).

Chaturvedi, Sachin (2016) *The Logic of Sharing: Indian Approach to South–South Cooperation*. Cambridge: Cambridge University Press.

Chaturvedi, Sachin and Chakrabarti, Milindo (eds) (2019) *Raúl Prebisch and Development Strategy*. New Delhi: Research and Information Systems for Developing Countries.

Chaturvedi, Sachin and Mulakala, Anthea (eds) (2016) *India's Approach to Development Cooperation*. London/New York: Routledge.

Chellaney, Brahma (2017, 23 January) China's Debt-Trap Diplomacy. *Project Syndicate*. Available at: https://www.project-syndicate.org/commentary/china-one-belt-one-road-loans-debt-by-brahma-chellaney-2017-01 (consulted 20 November 2024).

Chimni, B. (2003) Development and Migration. In: Aleinikoff, A. and Chetail, V. (eds) *Migration and International Legal Norms*. The Hague: T.M.C. Asser Press, 255–270.

Chirot, Daniel and Hall, Thomas (1982) World-System Theory. *Annual Review of Sociology* 8(1): 81–106.

Cornia, Giovanni Andrea; Jolly, Richard and Stewart, Frances (1987) *Adjustment with a Human Face*. Oxford: Clarendon Press.

De Morais, Michelle Graciela (2005) South–South Cooperation, Policy Transfer and Best-Practice Reasoning: The Transfer of the Solidarity in Literacy Program from Brazil to Mozambique. *International Institute of Social Studies Working Paper Series No 406*.

De Renzio, Paolo and Seifert, Jurek (2014) South–South Cooperation and the Future of Development Assistance: Mapping Actors and Options. *Third World Quarterly* 35(10): 1860–1875.

Declaration on the Right to Development Resolution A/RES/41/128 adopted by UN General Assembly on 4 December 1986.

Draft International Covenant on the Right to Development—Report by the Chair-Rapporteur of the Working Group on the Right to Development, Zamir Akram (Pakistan) Human Rights Council A/HRC/54/50 54th Session, 6 October 2023.

Escobar, Arturo (1995) *Encountering Development: The Making and Unmaking of the Third World*. Princeton University Press.

Felice, William (2010) *The Global New Deal: Economic and Social Rights in World Politics*. 2nd Edn, Lanham, Maryland: Rowman and Littlefield Publishers, 51–52.

Felice, William (2018, January) Operationalizing the Right to Development in Implementing the Sustainable Development Goals. E-Learning Module Chapter 2.

Ferchen, Matt (2018, 16 August) China, Venezuela, and the Illusion of Debt-Trap Diplomacy. *Asia Global Online*. Available at: https://carnegieendowment.org/posts/2018/10/china-venezuela-and-the-illusion-of-debt-trap-diplomacy?lang=en (consulted 20 November 2024).

Foot, Rosemary; Macfarlane, Neil and Mastanduno, Michael (2000) US Hegemony and International Organisations. New York: Oxford University Press.

Gómez, A.F.R. (2016) Cuba and South–South Cooperation. In: Verzola Jr, P. (ed) *Country Case Studies on South–South Cooperation*. Philippines: Reality of Aid, 88–112.

Gosovic, Branislav (2016) The Resurgence of South–South Cooperation. *Third World Quarterly* 37(4): 733–743.

Hogan, Morgan (1987) *The Marshall Plan: America, Britain and the Reconstruction of Western Europe, 1947–1952*. Cambridge: Cambridge University Press.

Hurley, Gail (2015) The Addis Ababa Action Agenda: A Step Forward on Financing for Development? Available at: https://www.undp.org/content/undp/en/home/blog/2015/7/21/The-Addis-Ababa-Action-Agenda-A-step-forward-on-financing-for-development-.html (consulted 24 November 2024).

International Covenant on Economic, Social and Cultural Rights adopted by the UN General Assembly, Resolution 2200A (XXI) of 16 December 1966, 999 UNTS 171 UN Doc A/6316 (1966).

International Policy Centre for Inclusive Growth (2010) Poverty in Focus. Available at: https://ipcig.org/pub/IPCPovertyInFocus20.pdf (consulted 29 November 2024).

Kanade, M. (2021) From the Means of Implementation to Implementation of the Means: Realizing the Sustainable Development Goals as if they Matter In: Kakar, N.; Popovski, V. and Robinson N.A. (eds) *Fulfilling the Sustainable Development Goals: On a Quest for a Sustainable World*. London: Routledge.

Kanade, Mihir (2020, July) Towards a Legally Binding Instrument on the Right to Development. *University of Peace—Ideas of Peace Series No 15*.

Lechini, Gladys (2007) Middle Powers: IBSA and the New South–South Cooperation. *NACLA Report on the Americas*, 40(5): 28–32.

Lengyel, Miguel and Malacalza, Bernabé (2011) What do we Talk when we Talk about South–South Cooperation?: The Construction of a Concept from Empirical Basis. Available at: https://www.researchgate.net/publication/265152002_What_do_we_talk_when_we_talk_about_South-South_Cooperation_The_construction_of_a_concept_from_empirical_basis (consulted 24 November 2024).

Lindberg, Kari and Lahiri, Tripti (2018, 28 December) From Asia to Africa, China's "Debt-Trap Diplomacy" was Under Siege in 2018. *Quartz Daily Brief*. Available at: https://www.google.com/amp/s/qz.com/1497584/how-chinas-debt-trap-diplomacy-came under-siege-in-2018/amp (consulted 20 November 2024).

Love, Joseph (1980) Raúl Prebisch and the Origins of the Doctrine of Unequal Exchange. *Latin American Research Review* 15(3): 45–72.

Mathur, Ajeet (1993) The Experience of Consultation During Structural Adjustment in India (1990–92). *International Labour Review* 132: 331–345.

Mawdsley, Emma (2012) *From Recipients to Donors: Emerging Powers and the Changing Development Landscape*. London: Zed Books Ltd.

Milani, Carlos (2014) Brazil's South–South Co-operation Strategies: From Foreign Policy to Public Policy. *South African Institute of International Affairs: African Perspectives, Global Insights—Occasional Paper No 179*.

Ministry of External Affairs, India (2020) Media Centre. Available at: https://www.mea.gov.in/lok-sabha.htm?dtl/32353/QUESTION+NO606+BRI+AND+CPEC (consulted 20 November 2024).

Mosley, Paul; Harrigan, Jane and Toye, John (1995) *Aid and Power: The World Bank and Policy-Based Lending*. 2nd Edn London: Routledge.

Moyo, Dambisa (2009) *Dead Aid: Why Aid is not Working and How There is a Better Way for Africa*. Macmillan Publishers.

Ngang, Carol Chi (2021) *The Right to Development in Africa*. Leiden/Boston: Brill Koninklijke.

Nussbaum, Martha (2000) *Women and Human Development: The Capabilities Approach*. Cambridge: Cambridge University Press.

Ocampo, Gaviria (2016) The Contribution of the Addis Ababa Action Agenda to Agenda 2030.

Office of the High Commissioner for Human Rights (2016) Frequently Asked Questions on the Right to Development. Available at: https://www.ohchr.org/Documents/Publications/FSheet37_RtD_EN.pdf (consulted 28 November 2024).

OHCHR (d.n.a) The Right to Development and The Sustainable Development Goals: Mutual Reinforcement and Synergy in Action.

Prabhu, K.S. (1996) The Impact of Structural Adjustment on Social Sector Expenditure: Evidence from Indian States. In: Rao, C.H.H. and Linnemann H. (eds) *Economic Reforms and Poverty Alleviation in India*. New Delhi: Sage Publication.

Prebisch, Raúl (1962) The Economic Development of Latin America and its Principal Problems. *Economic Commission for Latin America and the Caribbeans*. Available at: https://repositorio.cepal.org/entities/publication/9a00fa5b-ad04-4520-ae4c-e3adba791790 (consulted 26 December 2024).

Report of the Special Rapporteur on the Right to Development on the Promotion and Protection of all Human Rights, Civil, Political, Economic, Social and Cultural Rights, including the Right to Development. Human Rights Council, 39th Session A/HRC/39/51, 10–28 September 2018.

Research and Information System for Developing Countries (2013) Report of Conference of Southern Providers South–South Cooperation: Issues and Emerging Challenges.

Research and Information System for Developing Countries, New Delhi. Available at: http://ris.org.in/pdf/SSC_report_web.pdf (consulted on 28 November 2024).

Riddell, Barry (1992) Things Fall Apart Again: Structural Adjustment Programmes in sub-Saharan Africa. *The Journal of Modern African Studies* 30(1): 53–68.

Rio Declaration on Environment and Development, Report of the United Nations Conference on Environment and Development A/CONF.151/26 (Vol. I) adopted in Rio de Janeiro, Brazil on 14 June 1992.

Romero, C. (2010) South–South Cooperation between Venezuela and Cuba. In: The Reality of Aid (ed) *South–South Development Cooperation: A Challenge to the Aid System*. Philippines: IBON Books.

Rosseel, Peter et al (2009) Approaches to North-South, South–South and North-South-South Collaboration: A policy Document. Available at: file:///C:/Users/ngang/Downloads/POLICY_PAPER_VLIR_UWC__NSS.pdf (consulted 30 November 2024).

Rostow, W.W. (1990) *The Five Stages of Growth: A Summary*. In: Rostow, W.W. (ed) *The Five Stages of Growth: A Non-Communist Manifesto*. 3rd Edn, Cambridge: Cambridge University Press, 4–16.

Sen, Amartya (1985) *Commodities and Capabilities*. Amsterdam: North Holland.

Sen, Amartya (1990) *Development as Freedom*. Oxford: Oxford University Press.

Sharma, Pratyush (2019) Dependency Theories in the Era of BAPA+40. *Special Issue: Development Cooperation Review* 4(2): 32–43.

Stanton, Elizabeth (2007, February) The Human Development Index: A History. *University of Massachusetts Working Papers Series No 127*, 1–36.

Transforming Our World: The 2030 Agenda for Sustainable Development, UN General Assembly Resolution A/RES/70/1 (2015) (Sustainable Development Goals Framework).

United Nations (2009) Nairobi Outcome Document of the High-Level United Nations Conference on South–South Cooperation.

United Nations (2012) Framework of Operational Guidelines on United Nations Support to South–South and triangular Cooperation.

United Nations Commission on Human Rights (2004) Resolution 2004/7 and ECOSOC Decision 2004/249.

United Nations Development Programme (1990) *Human Development Report 1990*. Oxford: Oxford University Press.

United Nations General Assembly (1966) United Nations General Assembly, Official Records, Twenty-first Session, 1414th Plenary Meeting, 23 September 1966.

United Nations General Assembly (1999) Study on the Current State of Implementation of the Right to Development Submitted by Mr. Arjun Sengupta, Independent Expert, E/CN.4/1999/WG.18/2.

United Nations Millennium Declaration Resolution A/55/L.2 adopted by the United Nations General Assembly on 8 September 2000.

United Nations Human Rights Council Resolution on the Right to Development A/HRC/RES/42/23 adopted on 27 September 2019.

United States Department of Defense (2019) Indo-Pacific Strategy Report: Preparedness, Partnerships, and Promoting a Networked Region. Available at: https://media.defense.gov/2019/Jul/01/2002152311/-1/-1/1/DEPARTMENT-OF-DEFENSE-INDO-PACIFIC-STRATEGY-REPORT-2019.PDF (consulted 20 November 2024).

Universal Declaration of Human Rights, UN General Assembly Resolution A/RES/217(III), adopted in Paris, France on 10 December 1948.

Upendranadh, C. (1993) Structural Adjustment and Education: Issues Related to Equity. *Economic and Political Weekly* 28(44): 2415–2419.

Whelan, Daniel; Kanade, Mihir; Puvimanasinghe, Shyami (2018) Operationalizing the Right to Development in Implementing the Sustainable Development Goals. E-Learning Module.

Yu, Vincente Paolo (2019) Key Issues for BAPA+40: South–South Cooperation and the BAPA+40 Subthemes. *South Centre Research Paper No 91.*

CHAPTER 6

Third States' Extraterritorial Obligations on the Right to Development

Carol Chi Ngang

1 Introduction

In the exploratory analysis in this chapter, I advance a theoretical argument with the purpose of extrapolating answers to some intricate questions regarding the extraterritorial obligations of third states with respect to the International Covenant on the Right to Development (draft), which is envisaged to become an additional instrument to the international bill of human rights. Anthony Aust defines a third state as one that is not eligible to become a party to a treaty and/or one that has ratified a treaty but for which the treaty is, for legitimate reasons not yet in force and therefore, not legally binding.[1] By this definition, the conception of a third state as used in this chapter, does not include other subjects of international law such as international organisations, corporate multinationals and individuals. The third states referred to in this analysis are states that will not have ratified the Covenant of the Right to Development or consent to be bound by it, but as it is argued, would with respect to their extraterritorial operations, have a prohibitive obligation to refrain from actions or conduct that may impair the right to development protected by the Covenant and ancillary legally binding instruments.

Conceptually, the right to development has, besides other orthodox interpretations, evolved as an assertion of self-determination and a quest for development justice by peoples who have over the decades, systematically been deprived of, and/or denied opportunities for development. Notwithstanding the provisions of Articles 34 to 37 of the Vienna Convention on the Law of Treaties that insulate third states from obligations under international treaties, it is argued in this chapter that the Covenant on the Right to Development

1 Vienna Convention on the Law of Treaties, adopted by the United Nations at Vienna on 22 May 1969, United Nations, Treaty Series, Vol. 1155, p. 331, Art 2(1)(h); Aust, Anthony (2007) *Modern Treaty Law and Practice*. Cambridge: Cambridge University Press, 256.

 | DOI:10.1163/9789004734357_007

envisages extraterritorial obligations for third states.[2] Article 7 of the Covenant on the Right to Development, which outlines the responsibility of everyone to respect human right under international law, provides that:

> Nothing in the present Covenant may be interpreted as implying for any natural or legal person, people, group or State any right to engage in any activity or perform any act aimed at the destruction, nullification or impairment of any of the rights and freedoms set forth herein or at their limitation to a greater extent than is provided for in the Covenant. To that end, States Parties agree that all natural and legal persons, peoples, groups and States have the general duty under international law to refrain from participating in the violation of the right to development.

Admittedly, it is the primary duty of every state to create development and hence, guarantee the right to development for its peoples. As stated in the citation above, the right to development may not in any way be hindered, including by third states. It is crucial to be reminded that the claim to the right to development was born out of resentment against the domineering conduct of developed countries, which over the centuries has disrupted, obstructed and stripped developing countries of their prospects to create development.[3] Basing on the international law principles of self-determination, sovereign equality of states and of non-interference in the internal affairs of sovereign states, in addition to the general principles outlined in Article 3 of the draft Covenant on the Right to Development, I contend that there is no basis under international law why a third state, would in pursuit of its development objectives, asphyxiate the development aspirations of other sovereign states as has been the practice over the decades.

With anticipated disruptions to the lopsided global power dynamics, which the coming into force of the Covenant on the Right to Development is likely to engender, it is apparent, though not conclusively certain that the developed countries that perpetuate global development injustices and have consistently demonstrated reluctance to the idea of a treaty on the right to development, are likely to shun ratification of the Covenant, with the hope to enjoy third state protection under Articles 34–37 of the Vienna Convention. It is admitted that the Covenant will not apply to third states as far as prescriptive positive

2 Draft International Covenant on the Right to Development—Report by the Chair-Rapporteur of the Working Group on the Right to Development, Zamir Akram (Pakistan) Human Rights Council A/HRC/54/50 54th Session, 6 October 2023, Art 7.

3 Ngang, Carol Chi (2021) *The Right to Development in Africa* Leiden/Boston: Brill Publishers, 20–38.

obligations of outcome are concerned. However, basing on a critical reading of international law, I illustrate with reference to applicable instruments that in relation to their extraterritorial operations, third states have a presumptive obligation of conduct to refrain from actions that may impair realisation of the right to development. The analysis responds to the question whether it is rational for third states to enjoy the liberty to contravene the right to development with impunity?

On how the discussion unfolds, I commence by looking at the general rules of international law regarding treaty obligations. The Vienna Convention on the Law of Treaties and the generic obligations deriving from international human rights law are examined, entailing states parties to human rights treaties to shoulder the primary duties to ensure full realisation of the provisions contained therein. In juxtaposition, I explore exceptions to the conventional rule to illustrate that third states indeed, have a presumptive obligation under international law. In justification of this argument, I undertake an expansive reading of Article 2(6) of the UN Charter, the rules of customary international law and the general principles of law as they apply to third states. I then proceed to examine the prohibitive obligations on third states, which incorporates an account of the development injustices that hinder realisation of the right to development and a *lex feranda* argument against impunity. In conclusion, I reiterate the point that third states are susceptible to accountability when, in their extraterritorial operations, they contravene the prohibitive obligation to refrain from conduct that may impair the right to development.

2 General Rule of International Law on Treaty Obligations

2.1 *Prescriptive State Party Obligations*

International human rights treaties lay down rules that oblige states parties to adhere to and comply with the human rights standards they commit to. The triad obligations that obtain from human rights law have generally been described as the obligations to respect, to protect and to fulfil. The UN Office of the High Commissioner for Human Rights explains the obligation to respect to mean that states must refrain from interfering with or curtailing the enjoyment of human rights, the obligation to protect as requiring states to protect individuals and groups against abuse and the obligation to fulfil to mean that states are enjoined to take positive action to facilitate the enjoyment of basic human rights.[4]

4 International Human Rights Law. *UNOHCHR*. Available at: https://www.ohchr.org/en/instruments-and-mechanisms/international-human-rights-law (consulted 18 June 2024).

Human rights obligations are essentially prescriptive in nature in terms of what concrete actions or inactions are envisaged of states with respect to their human rights commitments. Unlike other human rights instruments, which do not specifically define the obligation imposed on state parties (the obligations are only inferred), the International Covenant on the Right to Development explicitly outlines a contextual formulation of the obligations to respect, protect and fulfil, and also adds the duty to cooperate and what their realisation entails for states parties.

2.1.1 Obligation to Respect

On the obligation to respect, the Covenant on the Right to Development provides that state parties shall refrain from any form of conduct, including through law, policy or practice that may nullify or impair the exercise and enjoyment of the right to development; conduct that may not impair the ability of another state or international organisation from accomplishing their obligations on the right to development; conduct that may not in any way through persuasion or coercion, with full knowledge of the circumstance and consequences of the act, cause another state or international organisation to breach their obligations on the right to development, as well as conduct that may cause an international organisation of which it is a member to commit an act that, if committed by the state party, would constitute a breach of its obligation under the present Covenant.[5]

The obligation to respect has conceptually been formulated as amounting to a negative duty not to act or better still, the prohibitive obligation to do no harm.[6] It is essentially, an obligation of conduct much more than an obligation of outcome/result.[7] While the obligation to respect, which translates to a negative, prohibitive obligation of conduct would apply directly to state parties to the Covenant on the Right to Development, it ought to be understood as imposing a presumptive obligation of indirect applicability to third states. Otherwise, the right to development entitlements and aspirations contained in the Covenant will simply be laid bare and susceptible of violation with impunity by third states. The obligation to respect forbids harmful

5 Draft Covenant on the Right to Development, supra note 2, Art 10.

6 Shelton, D. (2022) Negative and Positive Obligations. In: Binder, C. et al (eds) *Elgar Encyclopedia of Human Rights*. London: Edward Elgar Publishing, 545–550; Wibye, Johand (2022) Reviving the Distinction between Positive and Negative Human Rights. *Ratio Juris* 35(4): 363–382; Karp, David (2020) What is the Responsibility to Respect Human Rights? Reconsidering the "Respect, Protect, and Fulfil" Framework. *International Theory* 12(1): 83.

7 Skogly, Sigrun and Gibney, Mark (2002) Transnational Human Rights Obligations. *Human Rights Quarterly* 24(3): 795–798.

conduct and consequently, serves as a crucial safeguard in limiting the extent to which a third state may exert extraterritorial leverage and dominance that may encroach on the right to development in a home state. The international law principle of non-interference bars third states from conduct that may interfere with the right to development within the jurisdiction of other states.

2.1.2 Obligation to Protect

Regarding the obligation to protect, the Covenant prescribes that states parties shall adopt and enforce all necessary, appropriate and reasonable measures, including administrative, legislative, investigative, judicial, diplomatic among others, to ensure that natural or juristic persons, peoples, groups or any other state or non-state entities that the state is in a position to regulate, do not impair the exercise and enjoyment of the right to development, either within or outside their territories.[8] The Covenant further elucidates on the circumstances or instances where states parties ought to perform the obligation to protect, including but not limited to when the conduct in questions occurs, partially or fully, on the territory of the state party; when the natural or juristic person/persons involved have the nationality of the state party; or when the state party has the requisite legal duty under either domestic or international law to supervise, regulate or otherwise exercise oversight, through among others things, requiring human rights due diligence of the conduct of the juristic person engaging in business operations, including those of a transnational character.[9] The obligation to protect thus, clearly prescribes requisite actions that must be taken to ensure that the right to development is not contravened.

Assuming that states parties have the legal duty under domestic law (based on legislation in place) and under international law (based on the principles of self-determination, sovereign equality, non-interference and territorial integrity) to ensure adherence to and compliance with the provisions of the Covenant, the obligation to protect equips and empowers the home state to regulate not only persons and non-state entities but also third states when their extraterritorial operations pose a threat to the right to development. This will apply more concretely in the instance where states parties have domesticated and incorporated the Covenant into domestic law. The obligation to protect entails putting in place mechanisms, which though may not produce any direct substantive outcomes, will ensure that existing entitlements are not taken away. It entails that the right to development is not lowered below the threshold standards set out in the Covenant.

8 Draft Covenant on the Right to Development, supra note 2, Art 11.
9 Ibid.

2.1.3 Obligation to Fulfil

The obligation to fulfil enjoins each states parties to take legislative and other policy measures individually at the national level, and collectively through international cooperation and assistance, with a view to progressively enhancing the right to development, without prejudice to the associated obligations, which states parties are required to give immediate effect to.[10] As duty bearers with the primary obligation to ensure the constant improvement in living standards for their populations, states parties are obligated to take necessary measures and adequate national development policies to ensure equality of opportunity for development to everyone without discrimination or distinction, including through digital inclusion.[11] The obligation additionally, requires appropriate reforms with a view to eradicating the social injustices that may limit realisation of the right to development.

The obligation to fulfil is a prescriptive requirement to take positive action and thus, creates expectation of specific right to development outcomes, including increased popular participation in, and contribution to the processes for development; equitable (re)distribution of natural resources; fair sharing of the benefits of development; guaranteed equality of opportunities for development; reduced poverty and inequalities; improved well-being; and better standards of living. Noting that development is a composite process envisaging long term realisation of the full range of human rights and freedoms and hence, constant improvement in well-being for every individual and all peoples; the obligation to fulfil envisages that the right to development is only achievable over time. While instant realisation is obviously not practicable, the obligation necessitates that relevant legislative and policy reforms and programmatic measures are taken and operational systems established to enable progressive realisation.

2.1.4 Duty to Cooperate

The international dimension of the right to development creates the duty to cooperate as stated in the Covenant on the Right to Development, which outlines the rationale, commonality of purpose, and the operational modalities for solidarity and cooperation with a view to creating the requisite enabling international environment and conditions favourable for realising the right to development.[12] The duty to cooperate binds states parties to a commitment to undertake joint and separate actions, including through collaboration with

---

10 Ibid at Art 12.

11 Ibid.

12 Ibid at Art 13 *et seq.*

international organisations and engagement with civil society and the corporate sector. The duty to cooperate is aimed at resolving global development challenges of a socio-economic and cultural, political, environmental, public health, educational, technological or humanitarian character; eradicating poverty in all its forms; promoting the highest attainable standards of living; and upholding respect for universally recognised human rights and fundamental freedoms.[13]

The commitment implies a prescriptive obligation of outcomes, necessitating concrete, targeted and calculated steps and measures to prevent impairments that may diminish realisation of the right to development, eliminate obstacles to the full realisation of the right to development, ensure development practice and policy compliance with right to development standards, formulate appropriate international operational systems and mobilise the requisite natural, financial, material and human resources to enable realisation of the right to development particularly, in developing and least developed countries.[14]

Arjun Sengupta highlights the point that the duty to cooperate should be read in conjunction with Paragraph 1(10) of the Vienna Declaration of 1993 that established universal consensus on the right to development, and reaffirms with respect to the UN Charter that obligates member states to cooperate in ensuring development and in eliminating obstacles to development, that the international community ought to promote effective international cooperation for the realisation of the right to development.[15] He notes that progress towards implementation of the right to development requires effective development policies at the national level, and in essence also, a conducive environment at the international level, requiring the international community to make efforts in alleviating specific problems such as the debt burden on developing countries and to support the development efforts of these countries.[16]

The international community refers to the ensemble of sovereign states and international organisations that are subjects of international law. The international community's obligation to cooperate for the realisation of the right to development extends beyond the Covenant on the Right to Development and is conceptualised within the broader framework of international law to the

13 Ibid at Art 13(1)(2).

14 Ibid at Art 13(2).

15 Sengupta, Arjun (2001) Right to Development as a Human Right. *Economic and Political Weekly* 36(27): 2529.

16 Ibid at 2529.

effect that while a third state may not be subject to the prescriptive obligations of action and of outcome, they are at minimum, obligated to cooperate with respect to the commitment to abide by the prohibitive obligation to refrain from conduct that may compromise the right to development. This argument notwithstanding, the international law rules on treaty obligations rather seem to set insulating standards for third states.

2.2 *Conventional Rules Regarding Third States*

The Vienna Convention is explicit in stating that "A treaty does not create either obligations or rights for a third State without its consent",[17] which translates unambiguously to the fact that third states are not legally bound by treaties which they are not parties to. To be bound requires that a state would have signed and/or ratified the treaty in question or give formal consent to be bound by it absent which, the state enjoys the insulative protection guaranteed to third states as enshrine in Article 34 of the Vienna Convention. In terms of Articles 35 and 36 of the Vienna Convention, an obligation or right would arise for a third state in the instance where a provision of the treaty is intended by the states parties as establishing the obligation and/or the right, and the third state is required to expressly accept in writing to be bound by the obligation and/or right. Article 37 makes provision to the effect that any obligation and/or right that accrues to a third state may at any time, be revoked or modified with consent of the state parties and the third state involved.

Dörr and Schmalenbach explain that the whole notion of treaty obligations for third states, is based on the principle of consent[18] against which the principle of persistent objection has evolved to ensure that consent is not assumed based on indeterminate factors.[19] The draft Covenant on the Right to Development does not have any such provisions requiring third states to consent to be bound by it and therefore, creates no rights for third states. However, to overlook obligations that ought to be inputted to third states is an

17 Vienna Convention, supra note 1, Art 34.

18 Dörr, O. and Schmalenbach, K. (2012) Article 35: Treaties Providing for Obligations for Third States. In: Dörr, O. and Schmalenbach, K. (eds) *Vienna Convention on the Law of Treaties: A Commentary*. Cham, Switzerland: Springer, 645.

19 On the principle of persistent objection, see generally Yeini, Shelly (2021) The Persistent Objector Doctrine: Identifying Contradictions. *Chicago Journal of International Law* 22(2): 581–620; Lepard, B. (2010) The Persistent Objector Exception. In: Lepard, B. (ed) *Customary International Law: A New Theory and Practical Applications*. Cambridge: Cambridge University Press, 229–242; Lau, Holning (2005) Rethinking the Persistent Objector Doctrine in International Human Rights Law. *Chicago Journal of International Law* 6(1): 495–510.

inopportune oversight, considering that their extraterritorial operations often impact on the right to development in other states.

2.3 *Extraterritoriality and Lapses in the Orthodoxy on Treaty Obligations*

It is trite law that treaties (written international agreements between states, which are governed by international law) exclusively bind state parties that have consented to be bound and for which the treaty is in force and accordingly, allocate rights and impose obligations, which the state parties must comply with. This precept draws from the Vienna Convention, which as earlier noted, conveys the rule that a treaty only binds the state parties thereto and by virtue of the *pacta sunt servanda* principle, are enjoined to perform the treaty obligations in good faith (sincerity of intention in entering into the treaty).[20] In formulating treaty obligations in this manner, assumes that the issues intended for regulation and/or protection only implicate states parties, which sometimes, is not necessarily the case. For instance, the Covenant on the Right to Development seeks to regulate global development injustices and the ensuing imbalances, impoverishment and underdevelopment and in so doing, protect the right to development. When adopted, the Covenant will subject state parties to responsiveness and accountability regarding performance of the obligations they have committed to.

It is crucial to point out that the development injustices in question—comprising of the iniquities of slavery, colonialism, contempt for the rights to sovereignty, violation of the right to self-determination and disruptions in natural resource ownership as well as the ills of neocolonialism, paternalism, and economic globalisation—that affect large numbers of peoples and roll back development gains in many parts of the world, are usually not directly imputable to the home state. In their extraterritorial operations, third states often encroach on human rights and the development landscape in the home state, either positively or adversely and in the latter instance, the actions may cause major disruptions to standards of living or substantial regression in the enjoyment of existing human rights and freedoms. Because the formulation of treaty obligations overlook realities of this nature, I contend that to cause a home state to shoulder the burden of a development injustice created by a third state is not only prejudicial but also undermines justice and the international rule of law.

Insulating third states from treaty obligations, obtains from the assumption that states' operations are confined to their territorial jurisdictions and

---

20 Vienna Convention, supra note 1, Art 26.

in accordance, state parties to treaties are enjoined to undertake requisite actions in demonstration of the obligation of performance.[21] This is certainly not exhaustive of how treaty obligations ought to be conceived, which I argue, should take into account the fact that states often have extraterritorial reach and therefore, their international law obligations with respect to human rights, including the right to development naturally extends into the extraterritorial jurisdiction. Extraterritorial obligation is defined as "the situation when a state extends its legal power beyond its territorial boundaries".[22] It is referred to more precisely as "obligations of a global character that are set out in the Charter of the United Nations and human rights instruments to take action, separately, and jointly through international cooperation, to realize human rights universally".[23] When a third state extends its operations into the jurisdiction of a state party to the Covenant on the Right to Development, the third state will definitely, not have any prescriptive obligation of performance under the Covenant. There is however, a presumptive obligation that prohibits third states from conduct that may impair the right to development in the home state.

In analysing the right to development as a composite of all human rights achievable in an integrated manner and also as the right to both the process and the outcome of development, Arjun Sengupta illustrates that its realisation would be attained if, at least one of the component rights is fulfilled and none are violated.[24] In a similar reading, the African Commission on Human and People's Rights observed in the *Endorois* case that realisation of the right to development is subject to a two-pronged test, implying that it is on the one hand, procedural and thus, instrumental in ensuring that the processes for development fulfil legitimate expectations and on the other hand, substantive and hence, constitutive of anticipated concrete outcomes, which must be met

21 See generally Türkelli, G.E. (2021) Extraterritorial Human Rights Obligations and Responsibility under International Law. In: Gibney, M. et al (eds) *The Routledge Handbook on Extraterritorial Human Rights Obligations*. London: Routledge, 40–52; Langford, M.; Coomans, F. and Gómez, I.F. (2013) Extraterritorial Duties in International Law. In: Langford, M. et al (eds) *Global Justice and State Duties: The Extraterritorial Scope of Economic, Social and Cultural Rights in International Law*. Cambridge: Cambridge University Press, 51.

22 Extraterritorial Obligation. *National Action Plans on Business and Human Rights*. Available at: https://globalnaps.org/issue/extraterritorial-jurisdiction/ (consulted 20 June 2024).

23 Maastricht Principles on Extraterritorial Obligations of States in the Area of Economic, Social and Cultural Rights 2013, Para 8(b).

24 Sengupta, Arjun (2004) The Human Right to Development. *Oxford Development Studies* 36(2): 183.

simultaneously.[25] If only the substantive component is met and the procedural component is violated, the right to development would have been violated.

By inference, if all state parties to the Covenant on the Right to Development demonstrate good faith in their commitments to development, and none of the obligations discussed above is violated, the right to development would in principle, be achieved. If however, an impediment to development occurs (not caused by states parties to the Covenant), but resulting from the extra-territorial operations of a third state, such an operation will disrupt the full realisation of the right to development and thus, constitute a violation of the same nature as a violated committed by state parties. For state parties, legal accountability in view of redressing a violation is discernibly indisputable. Of concern is, what should happen in the instance where the violation is committed by a third state? It would be contrary to international law, to hold a third state to account under the Covenant on the Right to Development, on account of the insulation they enjoy in terms of Article 26 of the Vienna Convention. While this is the *lex lata* (the law as it is) position under international law, I contend that such a position compounds the legal problem by perpetuating the same development injustices that motivated claims for a right to development and recourse to a legally binding instrument for its protection.

Sellers and Chibundu make a compelling argument to the effect that the purpose, nature and value of international law is to advance justice and that international law would have no legitimacy unless it accomplishes the goal of advancing justice.[26] The UN Charter affirms the commitment, "to establish conditions under which *justice* and respect for the obligations arising from treaties and other sources of international law can be maintained" (emphasis added).[27] It suggests as Rilmayer and Tesfalidet indicate, a commitment to "general lawfulness of the international community", entailing the "Responsibility to Protect" under Chapter VII of the UN Charter and hence, a normative role for the international community in enforcing the rule of law against massive human rights atrocities.[28] The object of international law thus, incorporates

---

25 *Centre for Minority Rights Development (Kenya) and Minority Rights Group International on behalf of Endorois Welfare Council v Kenya* Comm 276/2003 (2009) AHRLR 75 (ACHPR 2009), Para 277.

26 Seller, Mortimer and Chibundu, Maxwell (2017) The Purpose of International Law is to Advance Justice—And International Law Has no Value Unless it Does So. *Proceedings of the Annual Meeting—American Society of International Law* 111: 301–303.

27 Charter of the United Nations and Statute of the International Court of Justice adopted in San Francisco, United States of America on 26 June 1945, Preamble Para 3.

28 Rilmayer, Lea and Tesfalidet, Isaias (2011) Third State Obligations and the Enforcement of International Law. *International Law and Politics* 44(1): 11 and 27.

advancing global development justice in accordance with the fundamental objectives set out in the UN Charter, "to promote social progress and better standards of life in larger freedom", achievable through the "promotion of economic and social advancement of all peoples".[29] To this end, third states' obligations ought to be perceived through a broader prism by looking at exceptions to the conventional rule.

3 Exceptions to the Conventional Rule

3.1 *Expansive Reading of the* erga omnes *Nature of Article 2(6) of the UN Charter*

The UN Charter, as the foundational instrument of contemporary international law codifies the major principles that regulate relations between states and binds all member states, which are accordingly obligated to comply with all the provisions of the Charter.[30] Besides applying lawfully to all member states in terms of Article 26 of the Vienna Convention, the UN Charter also applies to non-member states (third states). The Charter provides in Article 2(6) that: "The organization shall ensure that *states which are not Member States of the United Nations* act in accordance with these principles [of international law] so far as may be necessary for the maintenance of international peace and security" (emphasis added).

By this, the UN sets the norm that despite not being a state party to the UN Charter, a non-member state (third state) is compelled to respect the principles of international law laid down in the Charter. It does not compel non-member states to take positive actions but rather only imposes a prohibitive obligation, enjoining non-state parties to refrain from acting in a manner that may contravene or impair the international law principles enshrined in the UN Charter. In as much as it may be crucial for states—recognised as such under international law—to safeguard their sovereignty and accordingly, exercise the right to be selective regarding the treaties they commit to, opting for third state status does not grant such states the leeway to contravene treaties they are not parties to.

This is more comprehensible within the context of international humanitarian law and international criminal justice where, the Rome Statute of the International Criminal Court (ICC) has exceptionally, been applied in holding

29 UN Charter, supra note 28, Preamble.

30 United Nations Charter. *United Nations*. Available at: https://www.un.org/en/about-us/un-charter (consulted 18 April 2024).

perpetrators from states that are not parties to the Rome statute criminally responsible for committing genocide, war crimes, crimes against humanity, and crimes of aggression. Typical examples include, the *Rohingya Genocide* case wherein, in 2019, the ICC pronounced on its jurisdictional competence to hold Myanmar (alongside Bangladesh) accountable for gross human rights violations committed against the Rohingyas in Myanmar even though Myanmar is not a state party to the Rome Statute.[31] In 2020, the ICC equally adjudged on its jurisdictional competence to investigate war crimes committed by the United States (US) military in Afghanistan notwithstanding that the US is not a state party to the Rome Statute.[32] There is also the ICC prosecution instituted in 2023 against Russia for war crimes, crimes against humanity, crimes of aggression in the war in Ukraine even though, neither Russia nor Ukraine are states parties to the Rome Statute.[33] The Office of the ICC Prosecutor has since 2014, exercised jurisdiction over Israel, and is undertaking investigations for war crimes, crimes against humanity, and crimes of aggression committed in Gaza/Palestine despite Israel not being a state party to the Rome Status.[34]

---

31 Decision Pursuant to Art 15 of the Rome Statute on the Authorisation of an Investigation into the Situation in the People's Republic of Bangladesh/Republic of the Union of Myanmar. Pre-Trial Chamber III Decision ICC-01/19-27 of 14 November 2019; Takemura, Hitomi (2023) *The Rohingya Crisis and the International Criminal Court.* Singapore: Springer, 27–61.

32 Beavers, Elizabeth (2021) Where Do They Go for Justice? The United States-International Criminal Court and Crimes Against Humanity in Afghanistan. *California Western International Law Journal* 52(1): 85–114; Hashimy, Sayed (2021) Analysis of the United States' Liability for War Crime in Afghanistan. *Indian Journal of Law and Legal Research* III(I): 1–17; Ochs, Sara (2019) The United States, the International Criminal Court, and the Situation in Afghanistan. *Notre Dame Law Review Reflection* 95(2): 89–100; International Criminal Court Prosecutor Recommends Investigation of Potential War Crimes in Afghanistan, Including Actions by U.S. Military and Central Intelligence Agency. *American Journal of International Law* (2017) 111(2): 517–523.

33 Rynkun-Werner, Robert; Kozicki, Bartosz; Zelkowski, Jarosław and Krzewniak, Daria (2023) Jurisdiction of the International Criminal Court in The Hague and War Crimes in Ukraine in the Face of Security. *Journal of Security and Sustainability Issues* 13(1): 325–336; Sarkins, Jeremy (2023) Will the International Criminal Court (ICC) be Able to Secure the Arrest of Vladimir Putin When He Travels? *International Human Rights Law Review*, 12(1): 26–68; Bogush, Gleb (2023) Taking Russia to Court: Prosecution of International Crimes. *Russian Analytical Digest*, 307: 2–8; Frulli, Micaela (2023) International Criminal Justice at the Russia-Ukraine Crossroads. *The Italian Yearbook of International Law Online* 32(1): 231–247; Marchuk, Iryna and Wanigasuriya, Aloka (2022) The ICC and Russia-Ukraine War. *American Society of International Law Insights* 26(4): 1–6.

34 Statement of ICC Prosecutor Karim A.A. Khan KC: Applications for Arrest Warrants in the Situation in the State of Palestine, Statement, 20 May 2024. Available at: https://www.icc-cpi.int/news/statement-icc-prosecutor-karim-aa-khan-kc-applications-arrest

With the illustrations highlighted above, the question is whether, the law contemplates a lesser threshold or a contrary standard for other aspects of international law, notably the right to development which is the subject of discussion in this chapter? In responding to this question, it is crucial to allude to the International Covenant on Economic, Social and Cultural Rights (ICESCR) regarding international obligations for realising the rights enshrined therein. The Committee on Economic, Social and Cultural Rights (CESCR) has in its General Comments No 3, pointed out with respect to international cooperation for development that the realisation of socio-economic and cultural rights, is an unavoidable obligation of state parties.[35] However, because of globalisation, the role of the classical Westphalian state in assuming obligations under international law has increasingly been overshadowed by powerful global actors. As far as respect for human rights within the development context is concerned, the CESCR has in its General Comment No 2, identified two general principles that ought to apply to third party international organisations;[36] entailing on the one hand, a negative obligation on third parties to refrain from, and to "scrupulously avoid" actions that may impair or compromise realisation of the socio-economic rights enshrined in the ICESCR and on the other hand, prohibit ill-conceived and counter-productive development cooperation operations undertaken in the name of "development", which do not in anyway, contribute to the realisation of socio-economic, and cultural rights.[37]

These obligations are certainly not otherwise for the right to development for which, the CESCR further notes in General Comment 3, the need to take full account of the principles recognised in the 1986 Declaration on the Right to Development.[38] Not being a legally binding instrument, the Declaration on the Right to Development however, imposes a compelling moral obligation on all states and also on the international community, including actors whose

-warrants-situation-state (consulted 25 June 2024); Soraya, Ninda; Muhammad, Ali and Ladiqi, Suyatno (2024) ICC Jurisdiction: Against Israeli War and Humanitarian Crimes Targeting Palestinian Civilians 2023. *Jurnal Media Hukum* 31(1): 59–77.

35 CESCR General Comment No 3, The Nature of States Parties Obligations (Art 2, Para 1 of the Covenant) (5th Session, 1990), Compilation of General Comments and General Recommendations Adopted by Human Rights Treaty Bodies, UN Doc. HRI/GEN/1/Rev.1 (1994), Para 14.

36 Third party international organisations, includes third states, which engage in international cooperation for development through their development agencies or otherwise.

37 CESCR, General Comment 2, International Technical Assistance Measures (Art 22 of the Covenant) (4th Session, 1990), Compilation of General Comments and General Recommendations Adopted by Human Rights Treaty Bodies, UN Doc. HRI/GEN/Rev.1 (1994), Para 6.

38 CESCR General Comment No 3, supra note 35, Para 14.

actions and/or omissions have an impact on the right to development.[39] The international dimension on the right to development is read in function of Article 2(6) of the UN Charter to imply an *erga omnes* obligation that extends to third states in terms of prohibition from conduct that may transgress the right to development, which is further explained by the rules of customary international law.

3.2 *Customary Rules of International Law*

In furtherance of the argument articulated above, Article 38 of the Vienna Convention states that "Nothing in articles 34 to 37 precludes a rule set forth in a treaty from becoming binding upon a third State as a customary rule of international law, recognized as such".[40] Customary international law consists of binding rules that emanate from a general and consistent practice by states, which is accepted as law, and applies indiscriminately to all states irrespective of treaty law. While the right to development is envisaged to become legally binding under international law with the eventual coming into force of the International Covenant on the Right to Development, it has existed as soft law. The UNOHCHR has noted that in as much as the Declaration on the Right to Development is not legally binding, many of its provisions are enshrined in legally binding instruments and more so, anchored on principles that form an integral part of customary international law, which is binding on all states.[41] By this, the UNOHCHR hints that the right to development can be read into customary international law, which in terms of Article 38 of the Statute of the International Court of Justice (ICJ), is a binding source of international law. Being embodied in customary international law equally implies that the right to development imposes a binding obligation on all states, including third states that would not have ratified the Covenant on the Right to Development or any other legal instruments that protect the right to development.

In the UN Secretary General's report on the emergence of the right to development, it is noted that the right to self-determination, which is enshrined in common Article 1 of both International Covenants on Human Rights, imposes on states the obligation to respect the rights of peoples under their jurisdiction to freely choose their political status and to pursue their economic, social and

39 UNOHCHR (d.n.a) Frequently Asked Questions on the Right to Development: Fact Sheet No 37. *UNOHCHR*. Available at: https://www.ohchr.org/sites/default/files/Documents/Publications/FSheet37_RtD_EN.pdf (consulted 27 April 2024), 3.

40 Vienna Convention, supra note 1, Art 38. Arts 34 to 37 provide the terms by which a treaty may allocate rights and obligations to state states.

41 UNOHCHR, supra note 39, 5.

cultural development without any form of discrimination.[42] It must be emphasised that self-determination, which denotes the right of peoples to govern themselves politically and to decide their own socio-economic and cultural development destiny, is not only a core principle of international law but also, a rule of customary international law.[43] More so, the right to self-determination is of the same *sui generis* nature as the right to development[44] and therefore, as a component of customary international law, obligates all states—third states inclusive—to respect the provisions enshrined in the Covenant on the Right to Development, albeit that they might not become parties to the Covenant when it is adopted.

As an extension of the international law principle of sovereign equality, the right to self-determination incorporates the right to development, which guarantees to all states, the sovereignty to freely make their own development choices. The Declaration on the Right to Development stipulates that the human right to development implies the full realisation of "the right of peoples to self-determination", which includes "the exercise of their inalienable right to full sovereignty over all their natural wealth and resources" and accordingly, equips states with "the right and the duty to formulate appropriate national development policies that aim at the constant improvement of the well-being of the entire population and of all individuals [...]".[45] The contravention of a negative obligation has the same implication as the contravention of a positive obligation. With respect to the self-determination rule of customary international law, if a third state conducts itself in a manner that impairs the right to development, such conduct contravenes customary international law and

42 Report of the Secretary General (2013) Emergence of the Right to Development. In: UN Human Rights (ed) *Realizing the Right to Development: Essays in Commemoration of 25 Years of the United Nations Declaration on the Right to Development*. New York/Geneva: UN Publication, 13.

43 Jones, Natalie (2021) Self-Determination and the Right of People to Participate in International Law-Making. *The British Yearbook of International Law* 00(0): 4; *Legal Consequences for States of the Continued Presence of South Africa in Namibia (South West Africa) notwithstanding Security Council Resolution 276 (1970)* (Advisory Opinion) [1971] ICJ Rep 16, 31; *Western Sahara* (Advisory Opinion) [1975] ICJ Rep 12, 31–33; *Case Concerning East Timor (Portugal v Australia)* (Merits) [1995] ICJ Rep 90, 102; *Legal Consequences of the Construction of a Wall in the Occupied Palestinian Territory* (Advisory Opinion) [2004] ICJ Rep 136, 182–83.

44 Udombana, Nsongurua (2000) The Third World and the Right to Development: Agenda for the Next Millennium. *Human Rights Quarterly* 22(3): 769–770.

45 Declaration on the Right to Development Resolution A/RES/41/128 adopted by the UN General Assembly on 4 December 1986, Art 1(2) and Art 2(3).

accordingly, implicates the third state in the same manner as it would implicate a state party to the Covenant on the Right to Development.

Anthony Aust notes that the law of treaties does not preclude the continuous application of the rules of customary international law in governing questions not regulated by the Vienna Convention.[46] He explains that

> if a norm which is created by a treaty is followed in the practice of non-parties, it can, provided there is *opinion juris*, lead to the evolution of a customary rule which will be applicable between states which are not parties to the treaty and between parties and non-parties.[47]

Aust further remarks that an accumulation of bilateral treaties on the same subject may be considered as evidence of a customary rule.[48] The proliferation of bilateral treaties through international development agencies like the Japan International Cooperation Agency, German Agency for International Cooperation, US Agency for International Development, the United Kingdom Department for International Development, Swiss Agency for Development and Cooperation, African Union Development Agency; Swedish International Development Cooperation Agency, Brazilian Cooperation Agency; China International Development Cooperation, Russian Cooperation Agency; Canadian International Development Agency and Australian Agency for International Development among many others, provides evidence of a customary rule on development practice among nations.

Acknowledging that development is in terms of Paragraph 1(10) of the Vienna Declaration, universally recognised as a human right, the argument can be made that prevailing state practices in promoting development through bilateral cooperation treaties has become a rule of customary international law to uphold the right to development, which obviously, is a prerogative of every nation. To go against development standards established through state practice, amounts to a violation of the right to development and hence, would mean a contravention of customary international law, which binds and is applicable to all states, including third states irrespective of the insulative protection they enjoy under Articles 34–37 of the Vienna Convention.

46 Aust, supra note 1, 9–10.

47 Ibid at 1 and 10.

48 Thirlway, Hugh (1990) The Law and Procedure of the International Court of Justice. *British Yearbook of International Law* 61(1): 86.

3.3 *General Principles of Law*

One of the principal sources of international law as set out in the Statute of the ICJ is "the general principles of law" recognised by the community of nations.[49] While it is not apparently clear as to what general principles of law are or refer to in concrete terms, which leaves it to legal interpretation, Eirik Bjorge points out that general principles of law include acceptable rules of legal conduct that are formed within the international legal system and those that derive from national legal systems.[50] On the positive side general principles of law oblige compliance with the law and on the negative side, prohibit contraventions to the law. It translates into a conception of legality and the rule of law and most importantly, into the global pursuit of justice, which Mortimer Sellers affirms, forms the foundational purpose of international law and equally constitutes "[...] the foundational claim of every other legal system".[51]

As a source of public international law recognised in Article 38 of the ICJ Statute, general principles of law are conceived and understood as an embodiment of the standards set out in instruments of international law and precedent laid down in international law jurisprudence, which are upheld as such by the community of nations regarding what is legitimately acceptable as applicable law. The instruments of international law referred to, include on the one hand, hard law instruments like treaties, conventions and agreements that impose legally binding obligations and on the other hand, soft law instruments like declarations, resolutions and guiding principles that provide compelling moral guidelines for implementation. Noting that international law aims to regulate relations between states, entailing respect for states' equal rights to sovereignty, the right to self-determination and the duty to cooperate for the realisation of the right to development;[52] general principles of law would in this instance, incorporate standards that uphold these expectations and of course, forbid conduct that go against the set expectations.

General principles of law necessitate recourse to equity and justice and jurisprudence in developing the common law to the extent that existing instruments of law do not provide explicit provisions on a legal issue such as third states' extraterritorial obligations on the right to development. With respect to established and universally acknowledged principles of international law,

---

49 UN Charter, supra note 28, Art 38(1)(c); Chapter VIII—General Principles of Law. UN General Assembly Report of the International Law Commission A/76/10 Seventy-Second Session of 6 August 2021, 162–163.

50 Bjorge, Eirik (2023) General Principles of Law Formed Within the International Legal System. *International and Comparative Law Quarterly* 72(4): 846.

51 Seller and Chibundu, supra note 27, 301–302.

52 Declaration on the Right to Development, supra note 45, Art 3(3).

it would be contrary to the general principles of law to entrench a rule or condone state conduct that may interfere with, threaten realisation of, or constitute an obstacle to development anywhere around the world. The African Commission noted in the *Social and Economic Rights Action Centre and Another* (SERAC) *v Nigeria* case that "Governments have a duty to protect their citizens, not only through appropriate legislation and effective enforcement, but also by protecting them from damaging acts that may be perpetrated by private parties".[53] Logically, the state's role as a duty bearer is not limited to protecting citizens against private actors but also against third states. It is stated in Article 13(2)(a) of the Covenant on the Right to Development that states parties have a primary responsibility "To ensure that natural and legal persons, groups and States do not impair the enjoyment of the right to development".

By the standard of justice embodied in general principles of law, it will constitute development injustice to condone a contravention of the right to development by a third state on the grounds of the insulation under Articles 34 to 37 of the Vienna Convention. Motimer Seller notes that:

> Justice is the attribute that makes legal systems legitimate. Legitimacy in this context is the status of being justified, according to the standard of legitimacy that applies to the practice in question. Legal systems are legitimate when they establish or at least advance justice, but otherwise are not. If they fail to establish or at least advance justice, then legal systems are not legitimate according to the standards of legitimacy that justify laws and legal systems. [...] The claim of justice is not only what makes international law legitimate in theory, it is also what makes the law effective in fact.[54]

By this reading, international law will lose legitimacy if it fails to advance justice in ensuring that while third states are under no prescriptive obligation of outcome to take action in actualising the right to development, they should at minimum, as a matter of development justice, be obliged to honour the prohibitive obligation to respect, and therefore, refrain from conduct that may impair the right to development in any other state where the right is protected by law.

---

53 *Social and Economic Rights Action Centre* (SERAC) *and Another v Nigeria* Comm 155/96 (2001) AHRLR 60 (ACHPR 2001), Paras 57–58.

54 Seller and Chibundu, supra note 27, 302.

4 Prohibitive Obligations on Third States

4.1 *Persisting Development Injustices*

Despite introduction of the right to self-determination into international law in the late 1950s and early 1960s, which occasioned sovereign statehood for decolonised territories and hence, recognising the equal right of all states to "freely determine their political status and freely pursue their economic, social and cultural development",[55] the global political economy has continued to generate injustices that hinder development in most countries around the world. These injustices manifest in many forms, including through capitalist market expansion and the extraction of natural resources from other sovereign states, unfair international trade rules, irrational currency devaluations, debt enslavement, lopsided representation in the global structures of policy making. The right to development envisages confronting these injustices and the economic imbalances that have, in opposition to the rules and principles of international law, become the barometer for gauging statehood.

Even as the right to development is generally guaranteed to every individual and to all peoples in developed and developing countries alike, several substantive provisions of the Covenant on the Right to Development as well as the Preamble to the Covenant portray the right to development as a right that is most relevant for developing countries.[56] To achieve the right to development entails redressing the development injustices that hold back developing countries. As noted above, the processes necessitate emphasis on the international dimension where relations between all actors in addition to other relevant actors ought to be regulated. For instance, in drawing attention to the two levels of state obligations on the right to development, Ramola Adeola points out that Article 22(2) of the African Charter has an extraterritorial dimension, which enjoins state parties, to collectively take action in view of actualising the right to development.[57] This would apply directly to the 54 African Union (AU) member states that have ratified the African Charter and are in terms of the obligation provision in Article 1, bound to give effect to the right to development enshrined therein. The intricacy arises in case of Morocco, which although an AU member state, is not a state party to the African Charter but

55 Declaration on the Granting Independence to Colonial Countries and Peoples, adopted by the UN General Assembly Resolution 1514 (XV) of 14 December 1960.

56 See for example, Arts 13(2)(e); 13(4)(b, d–h); 15(2) and 18 of the Draft Covenant on the Right to Development.

57 Adeola, R. (2018) The Right to Development under the African Charter: Is There an Extraterritorial Reach? In: Ngang, C.C.; Kamga, S.D. and Gumede, V. (eds) *Perspectives on the Right to Development*. Pretoria: Pretoria University Press, 46.

has extraterritorial operations with implications on the right to development in the Sahrawi Arab Democratic Republic (Western Sahara), which is a state party to the African Charter. Of interest is whether the extraterritorial dimension of the right to development extends to Morocco, which has been in illegal occupation of the Sahrawi Republic since 1975 but has not given any documented consent to be bound by the African Charter.[58]

Quite clearly, Article 22(2) of the African Charter does not impose any prescriptive obligation of performance of the right to development on Morocco. However, enjoying third state status and thus, in terms of Article 26 of the Vienna Convention, insulated from obligations under the Africa Charter does not allow Morocco the liberty to transgress the right to development in the Saharawi Republic. The Charter provides in Article 22(1), entitlement to the equal enjoyment of the common heritage, which allows state parties to utilise their natural resource endowments for realising the right to development. Morocco has in its extraterritorial operations, engaged in illicit exploitation of natural resources in the Sahrawi Republic in contravention of Article 22 of the African Charter.[59] Therefore, because Morocco is in occupation and exercises effective control in the Sahrawi Republic, it bears responsibility for securing the entire range of substantive rights in the territory in question as was decided by the European Court of Human Rights in the *Cyprus v Turkey* case.[60]

Rilmayer and Tesfalidet explain that third states' obligations are limited to situations where the third state perpetrated or contributed to the violation and does not apply in the instance where the third state is a stranger to the dispute.[61] To count as a violation, the third state's involvement should have a causal effect and the legal basis for making such a determination is that the third state's violation is related to the same substantive law under which the primary violator (state party) would be held accountable.[62] The argument suggests that Morocco's violation would be determined by its extraterritorial operations (direct involvement) in the illicit extraction of natural resources from the Sahrawi Republic and therefore, can be held accountable under the African Charter, which is the substantive law that protects the right to development and the instrument by which Sahrawi Republic would equally be held accountable for a violation of the right. Rilmayer and Tesfalidet however,

58 International Court of Justice, Reports of Judgments, Advisory Opinions and Orders—Western Sahara Advisory Opinion ICJ Reports of 16 October 1975, 12.

59 Allan, Joanna and Ojeda-García, Raquel (2022) Natural Resource Exploitation in Western Sahara: New Research Directions. *The Journal of North African Studies* 27(6): 1107–1136.

60 *Cyprus v Turkey*, 35 Eur. Ct. H.R. 967 (2001), Para 77.

61 Rilmayer and Tesfalidet, supra note 29, 38.

62 Ibid at 43.

contend that third states' obligation prohibit one state from contributing to a violation in another state.[63]

4.2 Lex feranda *Argument against Impunity*

Haven looked at the *lex lata* angle in the reading of third states' obligations, the question of extraterritoriality and the lapses in the orthodoxy of treaty obligations and also pointed out the exceptions to the general rule under international law, it is of essence to construct a *lex ferenda* argument against impunity by third states regarding the right to development. It is argued to this end that third states have an implied prohibitive obligation to refrain from conduct that may infringe on the right to development in any home state where the third state has an extraterritorial reach. For a comprehensible understanding of the core argument, it is necessary to look at the African human man rights system where the right to development is enshrined as a legally binding entitlement in the African Charter and ancillary treaty instruments,[64] which has often been violated with impunity by third states.

Taking the US involvement in violating international human rights and humanitarian law for example, which has resulted in hundreds of thousands of civilian deaths and suffering for millions around the world in addition to silencing the voices of victims, Trevor Rice makes a cogent argument that when impunity is ignored, history tends to repeat itself.[65] The US is known for evading most international human rights treaties and for shunning the rules of international law in their intractable *ultra vires* extraterritorial operations in many countries around the world,[66] including in Africa. As an illustration to Rice's

---

63 Ibid at 1–54.

64 African Charter on Human and Peoples' Rights adopted in Nairobi, Kenya on 27 June 1981 OAU Doc CAB/LEG/67/3 Rev.5 (1981); Art 22; African Youth Charter adopted by the 7th Ordinary Session of the AU Assembly of Heads of State and Government in Banjul, the Gambia on 2 July 2006, Art 10; Protocol to the African Charter on Human and Peoples' Rights on the Rights of Women in Africa adopted by the Assembly of Heads State and Government in Maputo, Mozambique on 11 July 2003, Art 19.

65 Rice, Trevor (2023) Ending Impunity for All: Why the ICC's Office of the Prosecutor Should use their Prosecutorial Discretion to Prioritize the Crimes of the Powerful. *Columbia Human Rights Law Review* 54(2): 939–941; Western Sahara Resource Watch (2021) P for Plunder: Morocco's Export of Phosphate from Occupied Western Sahara. *WSRW Report*, April 2021, 1–25.

66 Schaack, Beth Van (2014) The United States' Position on the Extraterritorial Application of Human Rights Obligations: Now is the Time for Change. *International Law Studies* 90(20): 53–65. Vilken, Marie (2017) U.S. Aversion to International Human Rights Treaties. *Global Justice Centre*. Available at: https://www.globaljusticecenter.net/u-s-aversion-to-international-human-rights-treaties/ (consulted 2 July 2024).

point, without being subject to any form of accountability under international law for the atrocities committed in other countries like the invasion of Iraq in 2003, purportedly to disarm Saddam Hussein of weapons of mass destruction, the United States found justification to carry out a similar invasion of Libya in 2011, where in alliance with Britain and France, caused significant regression on the right to development in the country.

Libya is a state party to the African Charter, which protects the right to development as stated in Article 22. By virtue of that right, Libya prioritised the well-being of its peoples and consequently, was able to accomplish significant socio-economic development gains. Prior to the North Atlantic Treaty Organisation (NATO) invasion in 2011 on the pretext of protecting human rights, the peoples of Libya enjoyed the highest standards of living on the African continent with per capital income ranking among the highest globally.[67] By 2010, Libya's gross national income stood at USD 76.75 billion, which fell drastically to USD 29.32 in 2011 and by 2020, has only slightly recovered to USD 34.1 billion.[68] From a debt-free country prior to the US-led NATO invasion, Libya's debt stock has risen exponentially to an all-time high of government debt to GDP of 155% in 2020.[69] Of concern is the fact that Libya is not a NATO member state and therefore, not subject to accountability under the NATO treaty, raising a critical question about the third state principle that seems to apply selectively.

If the African Charter were to be invoked against NATO and its member states, objection on jurisdiction is likely to be raise based on the third state argument, which logically does not hold water. Reiterating Rilmayer and Tesfalidet's reasoning that third states' obligations prohibit one state from contributing to a violation in another state,[70] by extending their operations into Libya, the NATO member states involved assumed a presumptive obligation to not violate the human and peoples' rights protected by the African Charter. Article 22 will obviously not apply in obligating NATO member states to take

67 Cramer, Mary (2011) Before US-NATO Invasion, Libya Had the Highest Human Development Index, the Lowest Infant Mortality, the Highest Life Expectancy in all of Africa. *Counter Currents.Org*. Available at: https://www.countercurrents.org/cramer040511.htm (consulted 19 April 2024); Ngang 2021, supra note 3, 238.

68 Ngang, Carol Chi (2014) Right to Development and the Role of DAC OECD Foreign Aid to Development in Africa. *Journal of the Institute of African Studies* 67(2): 44; Gross National Income (GNI) in Libya from 2010 to 2020 (in Billion U.S. Dollars). *Statista* 2014. Available at: https://www.statista.com/statistics/1292068/gross-national-income-in-libya/ (consulted 3 July 2014).

69 Libya Government Debt to GDP. *Trading Economics* 2024. Available at: https://tradingeconomics.com/libya/government-debt-to-gdp (consulted 31 July 2024).

70 Rilmayer and Tesfalidet, supra note 29, 1–54.

positive action in ensuring realisation of the right to development in Libya. It is the primary duty of the Libyan government to do so. However, the negative obligation to respect, obliged the NATO member states that carried out the operations in Libya, to have refrained from the lethal invasion, which not only decimated the country's leader among many others but also reversed socio-economic development in the country by several decades.

As noted earlier, Article 2(6) of the UN Charter compels non-member states to adhere to and comply with the international law principles enshrined in Article 2 of the Charter. The principle of non-interference contained in Article 2(4) guarantees that "All Member shall refrain in their international relations from the threat or use of force against the territorial integrity or political independence of any state, or in other manner inconsistent with the Purposes of the United Nations". The rules of customary international law equally impose an *erga omnes* obligation on all states to respect human rights, the right to development inclusive. If a case against a third state should come before the Africa Court alleging violation of the right to development enshrined in Article 22 of the African Charter, the conclusive argument is that the Court would have both subject matter and jurisdictional competence to entertain such a case and should in terms of Article 3(2) of the Protocol on the Establishment of the African Court and Rule 29(3) of the Rules of the Court, be able to rule on its competence to do so.[71]

5 Conclusion

It is vital to conclude by reiterating that realisation of the right to development does not depend exclusively on the extent to which states parties adhere to their treaty commitments but in essence also, on the extent to which third states refrain from extraterritorial operations that may compromise the right to development aspirations of the large number of states around the world that have remained trapped in the development conundrum. Jurisprudence on the right to development from the African human rights system has demonstrated that states have the primary obligation to ensure attainment of the right to development, which entails constant improvement in living standards.[72] In addition to this, attention must insistently be drawn to the development

71 Protocol to the African Charter on Human and Peoples' Rights on the Establishment of an African Court on Human and Peoples' Rights adopted by the Assembly of Heads of States and Government in Addis Ababa, Ethiopia on 10 June 1998.

72 Declaration on the Right to Development, supra note 45, Art 2(3).

injustices inflicted on developing countries by developed countries that operate beyond the peripheries of international law.

The fact cannot be overlooked that when the early proponents advocated for recognition of the right to development for developing countries of the "third world", the idea was not necessarily to pit the peoples against their own state governments. Rather, it was an assertion against continued foreign domination, external influences and contempt for the principles of sovereign equality, self-determination and permanent ownership of natural resources, which have continually been violated with impunity to this day. To the extent that third states enjoy the liberty to generate obstacles to development, states parties' obligations under the Covenant on the Right to Development will not be achieved. The argument thus, centres on the submission that third states do have extraterritorial obligations and therefore, are susceptible to accountability when, in their extraterritorial operations, they contravene the prohibitive obligation to refrain from conduct that may undermine the right to development. Protecting the right to development is crucial as a redress mechanism in securing a balanced world free from the perpetuation of development injustices.

References

Adeola, R. (2018) The Right to Development under the African Charter: Is there an Extraterritorial Reach? In: Ngang, C.C.; Kamga, S.D. and Gumede, V. (eds) *Perspectives on the Right to Development*. Pretoria: Pretoria University Press 34–46.

African Charter on Human and Peoples' Rights adopted in Nairobi, Kenya on 27 June 1981 OAU Doc CAB/LEG/67/3 Rev.5 (1981).

African Youth Charter adopted by the 7th Ordinary Session of the AU Assembly of Heads of State and Government in Banjul, the Gambia on 2 July 2006.

Allan, Joanna and Ojeda-García, Raquel (2022) Natural Resource Exploitation in Western Sahara: New Research Directions. *The Journal of North African Studies* 27(6): 1107–1136.

Aust, Anthony (2007) *Modern Treaty Law and Practice*. Cambridge: Cambridge University Press.

Beavers, Elizabeth (2021) Where do They Go for Justice? The United States-International Criminal Court and Crimes Against Humanity in Afghanistan. *California Western International Law Journal* 52(1): 85–114.

Bjorge, Eirik (2023) General Principles of Law Formed Within the International Legal System. *International and Comparative Law Quarterly* 72(4): 845–867.

Bogush, Gleb (2023) Taking Russia to Court: Prosecution of International Crimes. *Russian Analytical Digest* 307: 2–8.

Case Concerning East Timor (*Portugal v Australia*) (Merits) [1995] ICJ Rep 90.

Centre for Minority Rights Development (*Kenya*) *and Minority Rights Group International on behalf of Endorois Welfare Council v Kenya* Comm 276/2003 (2009) AHRLR 75 (ACHPR 2009).

CESCR General Comment No 3, The Nature of States Parties Obligations (Art 2, para. 1 of the Covenant) (5th session, 1990), Compilation of General Comments and General Recommendations Adopted by Human Rights Treaty Bodies, UN Doc. HRI/GEN/1/Rev.1 (1994).

CESCR, General Comment 2, International Technical Assistance Measures (Art 22 of the Covenant) (4th session, 1990), Compilation of General Comments and General Recommendations Adopted by Human Rights Treaty Bodies, UN Doc. HRI/GEN/Rev.1 (1994).

Chapter VIII—General Principles of Law. UN General Assembly Report of the International Law Commission A/76/10 Seventy-second Session of 6 August 2021, 162–163.

Charter of the United Nations and Statute of the International Court of Justice, adopted in San Francisco, United States of America on 26 June 1945.

Cramer, Mary (2011) Before US-NATO Invasion, Libya had the Highest Human Development Index, the Lowest Infant Mortality, the Highest Life Expectancy in all of Africa. *Counter Currents.Org*. Available at: https://www.countercurrents.org/cramer040511.htm (consulted 19 April 2024).

Cyprus v Turkey, 35 Eur. Ct. H.R. 967 (2001).

Decision Pursuant to Article 15 of the Rome Statute on the Authorisation of an Investigation into the Situation in the People's Republic of Bangladesh/Republic of the Union of Myanmar. Pre-Trial Chamber III Decision ICC-01/19-27 of 14 November 2019.

Declaration on the Granting Independence to Colonial Countries and Peoples, adopted by the UN General Assembly Resolution 1514 (XV) of 14 December 1960.

Declaration on the Right to Development Resolution A/RES/41/128 adopted by UN General Assembly on 4 December 1986.

Dinah, S. (2022) Negative and Positive Obligations. In: Binder, C. et al (eds) *Elgar Encyclopedia of Human Rights*. London: Edward Elgar Publishing, 545–550.

Dörr, Oliver and Schmalenbach, Kirsten (2012) Article 35: Treaties Providing for Obligations for Third States. In: Dörr, O. and Schmalenbach, K. (eds) *Vienna Convention on the Law of Treaties: A Commentary*. Cham, Switzerland: Springer, 645–654.

Draft International Covenant on the Right to Development—Report by the Chair-Rapporteur of the Working Group on the Right to Development, Zamir Akram (Pakistan) Human Rights Council A/HRC/54/50 54th Session, 6 October 2023.

Extraterritorial Obligation. *National Action Plans on Business and Human Rights*. Available at: https://globalnaps.org/issue/extraterritorial-jurisdiction/ (consulted 20 June 2024).

Frequently Asked Questions on the Right to Development: Fact Sheet No 37. *United Nations Office of the High Commissioner for Human Rights* 2016. Available at: https://www.ohchr.org/sites/default/files/Documents/Publications/FSheet37_RtD_EN.pdf (consulted 27 April 2024).

Frulli, Micaela (2023) International Criminal Justice at the Russia-Ukraine Crossroads. *The Italian Yearbook of International Law Online* 32(1): 231–247.

Gross National Income (GNI) in Libya from 2010 to 2020 (in Billion US Dollars). *Statista* 2014. Available at: https://www.statista.com/statistics/1292068/gross-national-income-in-libya/ (consulted 3 July 2024).

Hashimy, Sayed (2021) Analysis of the United States' Liability for War Crime in Afghanistan. *Indian Journal of Law and Legal Research* III(I): 1–17.

International Court of Justice, Reports of Judgments, Advisory Opinions and Orders—Western Sahara Advisory Opinion ICJ Reports of 16 October 1975.

International Criminal Court Prosecutor Recommends Investigation of Potential War Crimes in Afghanistan, Including Actions by U.S. Military and Central Intelligence Agency. *American Journal of International Law* (2017) 111(2): 517–523.

International Human Rights Law. UNOHCHR, 2024. Available at: https://www.ohchr.org/en/instruments-and-mechanisms/international-human-rights-law (consulted 18 June 2024).

Karp, David Jasop (2020) What is the Responsibility to Respect Human Rights? Reconsidering the "Respect, Protect, and Fulfil" Framework. *International Theory* 12(1): 83–108.

Langford, M.; Coomans, F. and Gómez, I.F. (2013) Extraterritorial Duties in International Law. In: Langford, M. et al (eds) *Global Justice and State Duties: The Extraterritorial Scope of Economic, Social and Cultural Rights in International Law*. Cambridge: Cambridge University Press, 51–113.

Lau, Holning (2005) Rethinking the Persistent Objector Doctrine in International Human Rights Law. *Chicago Journal of International Law* 6(1): 495–510.

Legal Consequences for States of the Continued Presence of South Africa in Namibia (South West Africa) Notwithstanding Security Council Resolution 276 (1970) (Advisory Opinion) [1971] ICJ Rep 16.

Legal Consequences of the Construction of a Wall in the Occupied Palestinian Territory (Advisory Opinion) [2004] ICJ Rep 136.

Lepard, B. (2010) The Persistent Objector Exception. In: Lepard, B. (ed) *Customary International Law: A New Theory and Practical Applications*. Cambridge: Cambridge University Press, 229–242.

Libya Government Debt to GDP. *Trading Economics* 2014. Available at: https://tradingeconomics.com/libya/government-debt-to-gdp (consulted 31 July 2024).

Maastricht Principles on Extraterritorial Obligations of States in the Area of Economic, Social and Cultural Rights 2013.

Marchuk, Iryna and Wanigasuriya, Aloka (2022) The ICC and Russia-Ukraine War. *American Society of International Law Insights* 26(4): 1–6.

Natalie, Jones (2021) Self-Determination and the Right of People to Participate in International Law-Making. *The British Yearbook of International Law* 00(0): 1–33.

Ngang, Carol Chi (2014) Right to Development and the Role of DAC OECD Foreign Aid to Development in Africa. *Journal of the Institute of African Studies* 67(2): 40–59.

Ngang, Carol Chi (2021) *The Right to Development in Africa.* Leiden/Boston: Brill Publishers.

Ochs, Sara (2019) The United States, the International Criminal Court, and the Situation in Afghanistan. *Notre Dame Law Review Reflection* 95(2): 89–100.

Protocol to the African Charter on Human and Peoples' Rights on the Rights of Women in Africa adopted by the Assembly of Heads of States and Government in Maputo, Mozambique on 11 July 2003.

Protocol to the African Charter on Human and Peoples' Rights on the Establishment of an African Court on Human and Peoples' Rights adopted by the Assembly of Heads of States and Government in Addis Ababa, Ethiopia on 10 June 1998.

Report of the Secretary General (2013) Emergence of the Right to Development. In: UN Human Rights (ed) *Realizing the Right to Development: Essays in Commemoration of 25 Years of the United Nations Declaration on the Right to* Development. New York/Geneva: UN Publication.

Rilmayer, Lea and Tesfalidet, Isaias (2011) Third State Obligations and the Enforcement of International Law. *International Law and Politics* 44(1): 1–54.

Rynkun-Werner, et al (2023) Jurisdiction of the International Criminal Court in the Hague and War Crimes in Ukraine in the Face of Security. *Journal of Security and Sustainability Issues* 13(1): 325–336.

Sarkins, Jeremy (2023) Will the International Criminal Court (ICC) be able to Secure the Arrest of Vladimir Putin when he Travels? *International Human Rights Law Review* 12(1): 26–68.

Schaack, Beth Van (2014) The United States' Position on the Extraterritorial Application of Human Rights Obligations: Now is the Time for Change. *International Law Studies* 90(20): 50–65.

Seller, Mortimer and Chibundu, Maxwell (2017) The Purpose of International Law is to Advance Justice—And International Law has no Value Unless it Does So. *Proceedings of the Annual Meeting—American Society of International Law* 111: 301–308.

Sengupta, Arjun (2001) Right to Development as a Human Right. *Economic and Political Weekly* 36(27): 2527–2536.

Sengupta, Arjun (2004) The Human Right to Development. *Oxford Development Studies* 36(2): 179–203.

Skogly, Sigrun and Gibney, Mark (2002) Transnational Human Rights Obligations. *Human Rights Quarterly* 24(3): 781–798.

Social and Economic Rights Action Centre (SERAC) *and Another v Nigeria* Comm 155/96 (2001) AHRLR 60 (ACHPR 2001).

Soraya, Ninda; Muhammad, Ali and Ladiqi, Suyatno (2024) ICC Jurisdiction: Against Israeli War and Humanitarian Crimes Targeting Palestinian Civilians 2023. *Jurnal Media Hukum* 31(1): 59–77.

Statement of ICC Prosecutor Karim A.A. Khan KC: Applications for Arrest Warrants in the Situation in the State of Palestine, Statement, 20 May 2024. Available at: https://www.icc-cpi.int/news/statement-icc-prosecutor-karim-aa-khan-kc-applications-arrest-warrants-situation-state (consulted 25 June 2024).

Takemura, Hitomi (2023) *The Rohingya Crisis and the International Criminal Court*. Singapore: Springer, 27–61.

Thirlway, Hugh (1990) The Law and Procedure of the International Court of Justice. *British Yearbook of International Law* 61(1): 1–133.

Trevor, Rice (2023) Ending Impunity for All: Why the ICC's Office of the Prosecutor Should use their Prosecutorial Discretion to Prioritize the Crimes of the Powerful. *Columbia Human Rights Law Review* 54(2): 905–951.

Türkelli, G.E. (2021) Extraterritorial Human Rights Obligations and Responsibility under International Law. In Gibney, M. et al (eds) *The Routledge Handbook on Extraterritorial Human Rights Obligations*. London: Routledge, 40–52.

Udombana, Nsongurua (2000) The Third World and the Right to Development: Agenda for the Next Millennium. *Human Rights Quarterly* 22(3): 753–787.

United Nations Charter. *United Nations*. Available at: https://www.un.org/en/about-us/un-charter (consulted 18 April 2024).

Vienna Convention on the Law of Treaties, adopted by the United Nations at Vienna on 22 May 1969, United Nations, Treaty Series, Vol. 1155.

Vilken, Marie (2017) U.S. Aversion to International Human Rights Treaties. *Global Justice Centre*. Available at: https://www.globaljusticecenter.net/u-s-aversion-to-international-human-rights-treaties/ (consulted 2 July 2024).

Western Sahara (Advisory Opinion) [1975] ICJ Rep 12.

Western Sahara Resource Watch (2021) P for Plunder: Morocco's Export of Phosphate from Occupied Western Sahara. *WSRW Report*, April 2021, 1–25.

Wibye, Johand Vorland (2022) Reviving the Distinction between Positive and Negative Human Rights. *Ratio Juris* 35(4): 363–382.

Yeini, Shelly (2021) The Persistent Objector Doctrine: Identifying Contradictions. *Chicago Journal of International Law* 22(2): 581–620.

CHAPTER 7

Right to Development Obligations for International Organisations

Elisabeth Achancho Etagha

1 Introduction

The right to development (RTD) is a multifaceted human right that integrates economic, social, cultural, and political dimensions. It emphasises as stipulated in the United Nations Declaration on the Right to Development 1986 (UNDRTD) the creation of an enabling environment where all human rights and fundamental freedoms can be fully realised.[1] It asserts in Article 1(2) of the UNDRTD that every human being and all peoples are entitled to participate in, contribute to, and enjoy economic, social, cultural, and political development. In addition to being the preserve of states, international organisations are, in terms of the draft International Covenant on the Right to Development, required to assume obligations, including in fostering the RTD, given the pivotal role they play within the global development framework.[2] International organisations are conceived to be instrumental in achieving the RTD, requiring them to adopt and implement policies and programmes that promote equitable sustainable development that is respectful of human rights.

The term international organisation is defined in the Draft Covenant as "an organisation established by a treaty or other instrument governed by international law and possessing its own international legal personality; international organisations may include, in addition to States, other entities as members".[3]

1 United Nations Declaration on the Right to Development adopted by General Assembly Resolution A/RES/41/128 on 4 December 1986, Art 1(1).

2 Draft International Covenant on the Right to Development—Report by the Chair-Rapporteur of the Working Group on the Right to Development, Zamir Akram (Pakistan) Human Rights Council A/HRC/54/50 54th Session, 6 October 2023, Art 25(2); UN Sustainable Development Group (2003) The Human Rights Based Approach to Development Cooperation Towards a Common Understanding Among UN Agencies. Available at: https://unsdg.un.org/sites/default/files/6959The_Human_Rights_Based_Approach_to_Development_Cooperation_Towards_a_Common_Understanding_among_UN.pdf. (consulted 25 April 2025).

3 Draft Covenant on the Right to Development, supra note 2, Art 2(b).

 | DOI:10.1163/9789004734357_008

In accordance with this definition, the United Nations (UN) and its specialised agencies, the World Trade Organisation (WTO), Organisation for Economic Cooperation and Development (OECD), the World Bank, International Monetary Fund (IMF), European Union (EU) and African Union (AU) among many others, could be listed as prominent examples of international organisations. The definition of international organisation in the draft Covenant is similar to the definition adopted by the UN International Law Commission in 2011.[4] It indicates that the obligations of international organisations arise from their international legal personality status and constituent agreement. The intriguing question is, if international organisations are not parties to the Covenant on the RTD, how do they become bound by it? States do have clearly stipulated primary obligations to respect, protect and fulfil the RTD.[5] This is however, not the case with international organisations, which are not under a positive obligation to achieve the RTD. The UNDRTD, apart from referring to all human beings as having a responsibility for development, only recognise states as duty bearers. It does not include international organisations as having obligations for development.

An examination of the RTD obligations in international law demonstrates that international organisations operate based on the objectives and mandate set out in their constituent treaties and therefore, do not have direct development responsibilities under international law like states do. However, with the shifting global dynamics, international organisations admittedly do engage in development operations, which sometimes impact adversely on individuals and communities and therefore, should be allocated development obligations under international law. The IMF and World Bank for example, are influential in shaping and directing the trajectory for development around the world and the global financial order.[6] They remain the most authoritative norm-setters, and influencers of the international development landscape.[7]

It is the aim of this chapter to determine whether and to what extent RTD obligations apply to international organisations as envisioned in the draft

4 Draft Articles on the Responsibility of International Organisations 2011, adopted by the UN International Law Commission (ILC) Art 2; Faix, Martin (2014) Are International Organisations Bound by International Human Rights Obligations. *Czech Yearbook of Public and Private International Law* 5: 267–290.

5 UN Declaration on the Right to Development Resolution A/RES/41/128 adopted by UN General Assembly on 4 December 1986, Art 2(3) and 3–8.

6 Bretton Woods Project (2019) What are the Main Criticisms of the World Bank and IMF? Available at: https://www.brettonwoodsproject.org/wp-content/uploads/2019/06/Common-Criticisms-FINAL.pdf (consulted 17 September 2024).

7 Ibid.

Covenant on the RTD. The chapter explores the legal obligations of international organisations on the RTD and advances the argument that in addition to the negative obligations envisaged by the draft Covenant on the RTD for international organisations to refrain from actions that may impair the RTD, they also have an obligation for development cooperation, which entails prioritising the RTD in their policies and programmes in a way that is respectful of human rights. The issues are articulated as follows: Section 2 that follows, provides a conceptual underpinning of the RTD in international law. Sections 3 discusses the legal framework on the RTD, while Section 4 examines the RTD obligations of international organisations under the draft Covenant and Section 5 concludes the discussion.

2 The Right to Development in International Law

The RTD represents a significant evolution in international human rights law, reflecting the interconnectedness of economic, social, and cultural rights, civil and political rights, the right to self-determination, the right to peace and security and the right to a clean and healthy environment among others. It underscores the importance of a holistic approach to development that prioritises human well-being and equitable growth. The UNDRTD defines the RTD as an inalienable human right by which every person and all peoples are entitled to participate in, contribute to, and enjoy economic, social, cultural, and political development.[8] The RTD accordingly, aims to ensure the full realisation of all human rights and fundamental freedoms within the development process and it is primarily, the obligation of states to do so. It emphasises the need for an enabling environment at both the national and international levels, where development policies and programmes are envisaged to improve the well-being of every individual and all peoples. However, the UNDRTD does not explicitly mandate international organisations to ensure the realisation of the RTD. It should be underscored that international organisations are significantly involved in and they majorly influence all sectors of human development and therefore, form an integral part of the development process and consequently, ought to be attributed equivalent obligations under international law.

The RTD emerged in the context of decolonisation and the global struggle for development justice.[9] Post-World War II, newly independent states

8 UNDRTD, supra note 5, Art 1(1).

9 Ngang, Carol Chi (2021) *The Right to Development in Africa*. Leiden/Boston: Brill Publishers, 22–52.

in Africa, Asia, and Latin America began advocating for a new international economic order to address the inequalities between developed and developing countries. Algeria was one of the first countries where the idea of the RTD emerged in the 1960s as a collective right that should benefit all peoples, which however, was suppressed by the international system of unfair and inequitable economic relations.[10] It has been argued that economic growth in Algeria was largely influenced by its detachment from inequitable multilateral constraints and promoting the RTD of all peoples in its economic measures and activities on the international stage.[11] The RTD gained favour among the G77 (currently consisting of 134 developing countries) member states that advocated for, defended and upheld the idea, which has progressively shaped a new normative foundation for international law. The RTD was accordingly, perceived to place a development obligation on advanced countries towards the less advanced and economically disadvantaged countries. The concept of the RTD was therefore, not welcomed without resistance by advanced nations who argued that the RTD rests exclusively on each state towards its citizens and not on developed nations toward developing ones.

While the discourse on the RTD culminated in the adoption of the UNDRTD in 1986, it also ignited heated debates and controversies. While developing countries argued for recognition and protection of the RTD, developed nations rejected the existence of such a right.[12] The United States for example, outrightly voted against the UNDRTD in 1986. Initially, the RTD was seen as a new right different from other human rights enshrined in the international human rights covenants.[13] It was later described as a "third-generation, solidarity or collective rights" different from the first (civil and political rights) and second (economic, social and cultural rights) generations of rights.[14] Third generation rights belong to individuals and peoples and focuses on development, humanitarian assistance, common heritage, communication, peace and environment.[15] The principal obligations relating to these rights rest exclusively on states. International organisations are not mentioned in the UNDRTD

10 Bedjaoui, M. (1991) The Right to Development. In: Mayor, F. and Bedjaoui, M. (eds) *International Law: Achievements and Prospects*. Leiden: Brill/Nijhoff, 1177–1203.

11 Ibid at 1178.

12 Ngang, supra note 9; Reza, Ghaebi (2015) Realization of the Right to Development: Prospects for Drafting a Convention on the Right to Development. *Journal of Human Rights* 14(6): 548–558; Mark, Stephen (2004) The Human Right to Development: Between Rhetoric and Reality. *Harvard Human Rights Journal* 17: 137–168.

13 Reza, supra note 12, 549.

14 Ibid at 549.

15 Marks, supra note 12, 138.

as duty bearers of the RTD, which has evolved as a milestone achievement after a long struggle for balance and equitability in the global economic order.

Affirmation of the RTD in the 1993 Vienna Declaration and Programme of Action and other international instruments, transformed the idea of a human right to development from rhetoric to universal recognition.[16] The UNDRTD and the Vienna Declaration among other relevant instruments laid the groundwork for the draft Covenant on the RTD, which emphasises the inalienable right of every human person and all peoples to development. Besides being a stand-alone right, the RTD embodies all the generations of rights, including emphasis both on individuals, and on peoples as rights holders. It is of essence to reiterate that the debate on the RTD is now focus on implementation, which necessitates looking at relevant legal instruments to determine the obligation of international organisations in ensuring its full realisation.

3 International Legal Framework on the RTD

3.1 *Omission in Allocating Obligations to International Organisations*

This section explores the omission in allocating obligations to international organisations by the existing international legal frameworks on the RTD, which currently consist of just few instruments, including the UNDRTD, which articulates the concept of the RTD in the most comprehensive manner. It asserts that development is a comprehensive process aimed at the constant improvement of the well-being of the entire population and of every individual. The UNDRTD places the primary obligation for creating conditions favourable for development on states. While the UNDRTD attributes no obligations on international organisations, it places an emphasis on international cooperation, which is read in the broadest sense to include international organisations as key actors in actualising the international dimension of the RTD.

Before the adoption of the UNDRTD, the African Charter on Human and Peoples' Rights already enshrined the RTD in 1981,[17] and it remains the only regional human rights instrument besides the Arab Charter that gives the RTD

16 Nwauche, E.S. and Nwobike, J.C. (2004) Implementing the Right to Development. *Sur—International Journal on Human Rights* 2(2): 93–112.

17 African Charter on Human and Peoples' Rights adopted in Nairobi, Kenya on 27 June 1981 OAU Doc CAB/LEG/67/3 Rev.5 (1981), Art 22 states: 1. All peoples shall have the right to their economic, social and cultural development with due regard to their freedom and identity and in the equal enjoyment of the common heritage of mankind. 2. States shall have the duty, individually or collectively, to ensure the exercise of the right to development.

a legally binding status. The obligation to ensure realisation of the RTD contained in the African Charter rests exclusively on states parties as stated in Article 22(2) of the Charter, which provides that "States shall have the duty, individually or collectively, to ensure the exercise of the right to development". The RTD obligation of international organisations is not addressed in the African Charter albeit that many of such organisations operate in Africa and their actions often contravene the RTD across the continent. The RTD is also enshrined in the African Youth Charter and the Protocol on the Rights of Women in Africa.[18]

Several other international and regional instruments recognise and/or reaffirm commitment to the RTD. They include: the Additional Protocol to the American Convention on Human Rights in the Area of Economic, Social and Cultural Rights,[19] Rio Declaration on the Environment and Development,[20] Vienna Declaration and Programme of Action,[21] Millennium Declaration,[22] Inter-American Democratic Charter,[23] Monterrey Consensus,[24] Arab Charter on Human Rights,[25] Human Rights Declaration of the Association of Southeast Asian Nations,[26] American Declaration on the Rights of Indigenous Peoples[27]

18 African Youth Charter adopted by the 7th Ordinary Session of the AU Assembly of Heads of State and Government in Banjul, the Gambia on 2 July 2006, Art 10; Protocol to the African Charter on Human and Peoples' Rights on the Rights of Women in Africa adopted by the Assembly of Heads of States and Government in Maputo, Mozambique on 11 July 2003, Art 19.

19 Additional protocol to the American Convention on Human Rights in the area of Economic, Social and Cultural Rights (Protocol of San Salvador), adopted the General Assembly of the Organisation of American States in San Salvador, El Salvador on 16 November 1999, Preamble.

20 Rio Declaration on Environment and Development adopted at the United Nations Conference on Environment and Development at Rio de Janeiro, Brazil, 3 to 14 June 1992, Principle 3.

21 Vienna Declaration and Programme of Action adopted by the United Nations World Conference on Human Rights UN Doc. A/CONF.157/24, 25 June 1993, Para I(10 and 11) and II (72 and 73).

22 Ibid at III(11), V(24).4.

23 Inter-American Democratic Charter adopted by Special Session of the General Assembly of the Organisation of American States in Lima, Peru on 1 September 2001, Art 6.

24 Monterrey Consensus of the International Conference on Financing for Development, adopted by the United Nations in Monterrey, Mexico, 18–22 March 2002, Sect II(A)(11).

25 Arab Charter on Human Rights adopted in Cairo, Egypt on 15 September 1994, Art 37.

26 Association of South East Asian Nations (ASEAN) Human Rights Declaration adopted in Phnom Penh, Cambodia on 9 November 2012, Art 35–37.

27 United Nations Declaration on the Rights of Indigenous Peoples, Resolution 61/295 adopted by the UN General Assembly on 13 September 2007, Preamble and Art XXIX.

World Summit Outcome Document,[28] and the UN Declaration on the Rights of Indigenous Peoples.[29]

There is currently no legally binding instrument and/or enforcement mechanism on the RTD at the international level, which means no legal claim can be made at that level, when the RTD is violated. Apart from states parties to the African Charter which are subject to legal accountability on the RTD, all other states around the world as well as international organisations cannot be held legally accountable for any contraventions of the RTD. Thus, despite universal recognition, the RTD has remained a moral or political obligation within the international community. The advent of the International Covenant on the Right to Development, though still in draft form, gives prospects of a binding instrument that will impose legally binding obligations at the international level. There is no doubt that the Covenant will eventually be adopted and thus, form an integral part of international human rights law.

Given the controversy and reticence that has characterised the discourse on the RTD at the international level, implementation and enforcement of the Covenant on the RTD when it is adopted and comes into force remains uncertain. To increase prospects of ensuring full realisation of the RTD at the international level, drafters of the Covenant on the RTD envisage obligations for international organisations which is discussed in the next section.

3.2 *Obligations of International Organisations on the RTD*

As international organisations continue to exercise greater authority and power over national and international affairs, there has been reflections on the obligations they ought to assume under international law. As a background to this debate, in the 1980s, the International Court of Justice (ICJ) in the *World Health Organisation (WHO) and Egypt Advisory Opinion* case, stated that "international organisations are subjects of international law and, as such, are bound by any obligations incumbent upon them under general rules of international law, under their constitutions or under international agreements to which they are parties".[30] This decision has been used to justify allocating obligations to international organisations under customary international law and general principles of law. The most authoritative source of obligations under international law comes from Article 38 of the ICJ Statute, which provides that the Court shall decide international disputes based on international

28 Vienna Declaration and Programme of Action, supra note 21, Para II(24)(b), IV (123).

29 UN Declaration on the Rights of Indigenous Peoples, supra note 27, Preamble and Art 23.

30 *Interpretation of the Agreement of 25 March 1951 Between the WHO and Egypt, Advisory Opinion*, 1980 I.C.J. Rep. 73, pp. 89–90 (Dec 20) (emphasis added).

treaties (conventions), international custom and general principles of law. International organisations, being subjects of international law, are bound by these obligations, though not absolutely because to a greater extent, the human rights obligations of international organisations are different from the obligations attributed to states.

Over the years, scholars have debated on the sources of the legal obligations of international organisations relating to the realisation of international human rights, including the RTD. These debates centres on three principles: first that their legal obligations emanate from the provisions of international treaties; second, from customary international law, (*jus cogens* norms) and lastly, from general principles of international law.[31]

In the first place, the obligations of international organisations arising from international treaties and their constituent agreements are easy to decipher and this corresponds to the definition of international organisations as contained in the draft Covenant on the RTD. Here, the scope of application and the mechanisms of implementation and enforcement can easily be established. However, there are two distinctive elements that can be identified with regards to obligations arising from international treaty engagements. One is the constituent treaty of the organisation and the second is accession to an international treaty. With respect to the constituent treaty, it is easier to hold international organisations accountable for the human rights violations they commit as reference will be made directly to their mandate and purpose. In this instance, the organisations are obligated to carry out their functions as stipulated in the founding treaties and ensure compliance with the obligations arising from the constitutive agreement they have concluded. As such, the organisations are subject to accountability when they fail to respect the treaty obligations.

The problem arises when it comes to accession or ratification of an international treaty, which normally fall under the jurisdictional competence of states. Generally, international organisations do not have the capacity or competence to accede to an international treaty based on international rules applicable to the law of treaties. The rule has however, changed as some international instruments currently, give international and regional organisations the right of signatory and accession to international treaties. For example, the EU is signatory to the UN Convention on the Rights of Persons with Disabilities adopted in 2006. Such a right is however, contested by some courts on grounds of the capacity and competence of organisations to become parties to international

31 Faix, supra note 4, 267–290.

treaties. For instance, Protocol No 14 of June 2010 to the European Convention on Human Rights amended the Convention to permit the EU to accede to it.[32] In opposition, the European Court of Justice in its Opinion 2/94 rejected the idea that the EU could accede to the European Convention on Human Rights based on competence.[33] According to the principle of *lex specialis*, the capacity of international organisations depends on the nature of their material competences in international cooperation, which are not the same as states. It is essential for international organisations to be party to the international treaties that fall within the scope of their material competence based on the principle of *lex specialis*. International organisations specialised in human rights and development have the capacity to become signatories to the Covenant on the RTD, which indeed, makes provision for the right of signatory and accession of international organisations in Articles 30 and 31 based on their competence.

Secondly, it is generally accepted that international organisations have obligations under customary international law and there are of a *jus cogens* nature.[34] This is because international organisations are subjects of international law, and international customary norms are part of general international law. This position was affirmed in the *WHO and Egypt ICJ Opinion* cited earlier. The same approach was adopted by the International Law Association Committee on the Accountability of International Organisations.[35] It recognised the fact that the primary rules and peremptory norms of international law are applicable both to international organisations and to member states. The principle of *lex specialis* and customary international norms may, however, not apply *mutatis mutandis*. As Martin Faix argues, the application of international customary rules differ regarding the possession of certain legal capacities and material competences of the specific organisation.[36] Where the principle of *lex specialis* is implemented, it takes precedence over customary rules, which raises the question to what extent a particular customary rule should apply.

32 Ibid at 281.

33 Ibid at 282.

34 Ibid at 284; Neuman, Gerald (2019) International Organizations and Human Rights: The Need for Substance. *Research Working Paper Series Vol. 9, HRP 19-001—Harvard Law School* 5; Freedman, Rosa (2014) UN Immunity or Impunity? A Human Rights Based Challenge. *European Journal of International Law* 25(1): 239–254; Schmitt, Pierre (2017) *Access to Justice and International Organizations: The Case of Individual Victims of Human Rights Violations*. London: Edward Elgar Publishing.

35 International Law Association (2004) Committee on Accountability of International Organisations, Berlin Conference Final Report. Available at: https://www.ila-hq.org/en_GB/documents/final-conference-report-berlin-2004-1 (consulted 26 August 2024).

36 Faix, supra note 4, 286.

Thirdly, principles of general international law apply to international organisations. As noted earlier, the origin or source of the obligation of international organisations comes from Article 38 of the ICJ Statute. However, international organisations cannot be bound by all human rights obligations as they apply to states. For instance, international human rights covenants require of states to protect and fulfil the rights contained therein, which obligations cannot be imposed on international organisations in the sense that they only play a secondary role to what states are obligated to do.[37] This is justified with respect to the mandate and objectives of each organisation.

It becomes more complicated when states transfer authority to international organisations. The issue of transfer of authority or power conferral from states to international organisations without a corresponding transfer of obligations has meant that many human rights violations committed by these international organisations go unaccounted for. Mateja Platise notes that there is a lack of international authority in establishing responsibility for human rights violations committed by international organisations because of the transfer of powers from states to international organisations.[38]

Transfer of authority or power conferral here means a situation where states cannot exercise direct authority over the organisation and the states consent are bound by the decisions of the organisations.[39] There are different approaches through which states transfer their treaty obligations to international organisations, including through an act of establishment whereby, the organisation is bound by the law of treaties to comply with the treaty obligations or as a duty of international cooperation, to observe the human rights treaty obligations of its member states.[40] It is not the object of this chapter to examine the different ways through which states transfer their authority to international organisation as there is extensive literature on it.[41] Nonetheless, it is important to say that states have used these approaches to circumvent their human rights obligations. There has been lack of corresponding transfer of

37 Neuman, supra note 34, 5.

38 Platise, Mateja (d.n.a) Responsibility of International Organizations for Human Rights Violations. Available at: https://www.mpil.de/en/pub/research/areas/public-international-law/ipa/responsibility-organizations.cfm#publications (consulted 27 August 2024).

39 Sarooshi, D. (2007) Transfers of Powers to International Organizations. In: Sarooshi, D. (ed) *International Organizations and their Exercise of Sovereign Powers*. London: Oxford University Press.

40 Zagel, Gudrun Monika (2018) International Organisations and Human Rights: The Role of the UN Covenants in Overcoming the Accountability Gap. *Nordic Journal of Human Rights* 36(1): 74–90.

41 Schmitt, P. (2017) Setting the Scene: The Case of Individual Victims of Human Rights Violations. In: Schmitt, P. (ed) *Access to Justice and International Organizations*. London: Edward Elgar Publishing, 1–52.

responsibility to international organisations. This is the issue that Article 10(d) of the draft Covenant on the RTD is concerned about. However, the extend of international organisations' accountability for human rights violations is limited, necessitating the Covenant on the RTD to emphasise on imposing corresponding obligations on organisations with a RTD mandate.

4 Right to Development Obligations for International Organisations

4.1 *Obligations under the International Covenant on the RTD*

The Covenant on the RTD is envisaged to make the RTD justiciable and legally enforceable at the international level. This sub-section examines the RTD obligations of international organisations as established in the Covenant and responds to the question whether the prescribed obligations are legally binding on international organisations and if so, to what extend? When adopted, the Covenant on the RTD will formally end the debates and controversies surrounding the RTD at the international level and ensure effective operationalisation and its full implementation as indicated in Article 1 thereof. The definition of an international organisation is provided in Article 2 as earlier illustrated. With respect to the general principles of the Covenant, international organisations are required to cooperate with other stakeholders in the protection and promotion of a social and international order that will facilitate realisation of the RTD.[42] The obligations of international organisations are enumerated in Article 7.[43] These obligations though not specific to international organisations, emanate from general principles of international human rights law as they apply to natural and legal persons. Article 9 provides for the general obligations of international organisations as follows:

> Without prejudice to the general duty contained in article 7, States Parties agree that international organisations also have the obligation to refrain from conduct that aids, assists, directs, controls or coerces, with

42 Draft Covenant on the Right to Development, supra note 2, Art 3(l).

43 Ibid at Art 7 states that "Nothing in the present Covenant may be interpreted as implying for any natural or legal person, people, group or State any right to engage in any activity or perform any act aimed at the destruction, nullification or impairment of any of the rights and freedoms set forth herein or at their limitation to a greater extent than is provided for in the Covenant. To that end, States Parties agree that all natural and legal persons, peoples, groups and States have the general duty under international law to refrain from participating in the violation of the right to development".

> knowledge of the circumstances of the act, a State or another international organisation to breach any obligation that the State or the latter organisation may have with regard to the right to development.

Here, international organisations are designated as having the duty to abstain from any activity that will make a state or another international organisation to hinder or impede the RTD. While international organisations are not responsible for fulfilling the RTD, they must not hinder its realisation. The obligation is nevertheless, too general and therefore, raises concerns that need to be examined. In the first place, the Covenant does not oblige international organisations, including those with a RTD mandate to promote, protect and fulfil the RTD. It seems a bit insulating on the basis that international organisations are supposed to have corresponding obligations especially, where there is transfer of rights and authority by states, the states' obligations ought to equally pass over to the international organisations. This is because it is usually difficult, if not impossible to bind international organisations to human rights treaties which they are not parties to.

The idea of general obligations applicable to all international organisations irrespective of their mandate and purpose is problematic. It is understandable that the Covenant cannot oblige every organisation to fulfil the RTD, but it is the responsibility of every organisation with a RTD mandate to do so. The general obligations can reasonably be directed to organisations performing different functions with different mandates other than human rights and development. The tone of Article 31(2) indicates that any international organisation that becomes signatory or accedes to the Covenant shall have the duty to fulfil the RTD and consequently, have the same responsibilities as states parties within the limits of their competence. Emphasis on the words "within the limits of their competence" is necessary to signify the unequal nature of the obligations between states and international organisations. International organisations like the UN, WHO, WTO, the World Bank, IMF and EU are supranational organisations with more executive authority than many sovereign states. They are extensively involved in the field of human rights, and they make decisions that are binding on states and other international organisations.

The question then is whether these organisations can really be perceived to have a limit competence? To what extent can their obligations be limited? The answer to these questions lie in the extensive authority, influence and the power of control wielded by international organisations over individuals, states and other organisations. It is worth noting that Article 31(1) of the draft Covenant requires international organisations to declare the extent of their competence in relation to the RTD.[44] In my opinion, such a declaration does not sufficiently bind and render international organisations legally accountable for breaches of individual or collective human rights within the development context.

The draft Covenant when it is adopted, will be open for signature or accession by international organisations.[45] International organisations currently exert greater power and influence over states especially, in the formulation of international policies and therefore, those with a RTD mandate should assume corresponding obligations. Article 10(b) and (c) of the draft Covenant obligates states to abstain from any activity that will make another state or international organisation hinder the realisation of the RTD. The Covenant is quite specific as far as obligations of a member state of an international organisation and the said international organisation is concern. It provides in Article 10(d) that a member state shall refrain from legal, policy or practical conduct that may:

> cause an international organisation of which it is a member to commit an act that, if committed by the State Party, would constitute a breach of its obligation under the present Covenant, and does so to circumvent that obligation by taking advantage of the fact that the international organisation has competence in relation to its subject matter.

The obligation offers a partial solution to the problem of accountability and justice where the legal basis of international organisations responsibility for the violation of human rights remains unsettled. There have been accountability gaps where victims of human rights violations have been left without a remedy because of failure to attribute responsibility to international organisations and/or their member states that commit the violations. For instance, the UN Security Council resolution listing individuals for sanctions without the

44 Art 31(1) states that "International organizations shall declare, in their instruments of formal confirmation or accession, the extent of their competence with respect to matters governed by the present Covenant. Subsequently, they shall inform the depositary of any substantial modification in the extent of their competence".

45 Draft Covenant on the Right to Development, supra note 2, Arts 29 and 30(2) and (3). Art 29 states that "The present Covenant shall be open for signature by all States and international organizations at United Nations Headquarters in New York as of [....]" and Art 30(2) and (3) states: 2. Notwithstanding the obligations of international organizations existing under international law and the present Covenant, the consent of signatory international organizations to be bound by the present Covenant shall be expressed through an act of formal confirmation. 3. The present Covenant shall be open for accession by any State or international organization that has not signed the Covenant.

possibility of judicial review goes against the International Covenant for Civil and Political rights (ICCPR).[46] However, the UN could not be held accountable in this instance because, it is neither a state party to the ICCPR nor could its member states be held responsible as they are not the UN.[47] Furthermore, the WTO has been criticised for constraining its members' policy freedoms in implementing their human rights obligations.[48] Here, the WTO rules strictly hinder America (Clove Cigarettes) and Australia (Tobacco Products) from adopting anti-smoking rules required by the right to health guaranteed in the International Covenant on Economic, Social and Cultural Rights.[49] Holding international organisations responsible for human rights violations has proved difficult especially because, establishing responsibility for international organisations that are not parties to international treaties is problematic, and this has left victims of human rights violations to suffer without the opportunity for redress. This concern invokes the question about the feasibility of implementation of the International Covenant on the RTD when it comes into force especially, if these organisations decline to become parties to it.

If international organisations with a RTD mandate are not properly regulated, individuals and peoples will continue to suffer human rights violations, including the RTD resulting from the actions of these extensively powerful entities, which because of their influence, cannot be held to account. It becomes even more complex when the victims of human rights violations are individuals or peoples and not a state or another international organisation, which obviously do not have human rights entitlements. Individuals and peoples often do not have the avenue of holding international organisations accountable for breach of their human rights. States on the most part, are reluctant to hold international organisations accountable on account of national interests, which they are keen on protecting.

The cholera outbreak in Haiti in 2010 can be exemplified.[50] Management of the epidemic, which involved instances of human rights violations illustrate

46 Zagel, supra note 40, 74; International Covenant on Civil and Political Rights adopted by the UN General Assembly, Resolution 2200A (XXI) of 16 December 1966, 993 UNTS 3 UN Doc A/6316 (1966) on judicial review, Art 14.

47 Ibid at 75.

48 Ibid at 74.

49 Ibid at 75; International Covenant on Economic, Social and Cultural Rights adopted by the UN General Assembly, Resolution 2200A (XXI) of 16 December 1966, 999 UNTS 171 UN Doc A/6316 (1966), Art 12.

50 As a background to this legal problem, in October 2010, the UN peacekeeping mission brought cholera to Haiti. This was seen as the world's worst modern cholera epidemics. The epidemic resulted in more than 2,500 deaths within the first three months;

how the policies of international organisations have not been carried out in a way that is respectful of human rights. It is reported that the UN Peacekeeping Mission to Haiti infected the population with cholera that killed thousands of Haitians.[51] The UN denied any legal obligation to compensate the victims and invoked its immunity.[52] Although the Secretary-General, Ban Ki-Moon acknowledged in 2016 that the UN had a moral obligation to eliminate the cholera epidemic in Haiti and provide material assistance and support to the affected individuals and communities, no significant actions were taken.[53] The Secretary-General announced a new approach to reduce the incidence of the cholera outbreak and proposed a USD 400 million assistance but as noted, not up to 10% of the assistance was ever supplied. The UN only assumed a moral obligation with no legal commitment to make the new approach enforceable. The UN rejected having any legal obligation to compensate victims irrespective of its obligation under Section 29 of the Convention on the Privileges and Immunities of the UN, 1946.[54] The Haitian government equally did little or nothing to fight for the rights of its citizens who were affected by the cholera epidemic.[55] The introduction of cholera in Haiti by the UN Peacekeeping Mission violated the fundamental human rights of Haitians, including but not limited to the rights to life, sanitation, health, water, good living standards and freedom from degrading treatment.[56] These right form part of the RTD,

---

Ceccarelli, Daniela et al (2011) Origin of Vibrio Cholerae in Haiti. *The Lancet Infectious Diseases* 11(4): 262. The epidemic killed more than 9,700 people and infected over 819,000; Institute for Justice and Democracy in Haiti's Report (2020) Years on: A "New Approach"? The Ongoing Violation of Victims' Rights in the UN's Response to Cholera in Haiti. It provides a comprehensive report of the decade-long efforts to hold the UN accountable for human rights violations; Luquero, Francisco et al (2016) Mortality Rates During Cholera Epidemic, Haiti, 2010–2011. *Emerging Infectious Diseases* 22(3): 410; Gladstone, Rick (2016) Cholera Deaths in Haiti Could Far Exceed Official Count. *New York Times*.

51 Daugirdas, K. (2021) States' Due Diligence Obligations to Supervise International Organizations. In: Krieger, H.; Peters, A. and Kreuzer, L. (eds) *Due Diligence in the International Legal Order*. Oxford: Oxford University Press.

52 Ibid at 62.

53 Ibid at 73.

54 Sect 29 states that "The United Nations shall make provisions for appropriate modes of settlement of: (a) disputes arising out of contracts or other disputes of a private law character to which the United Nations is a party; (b) disputes involving any official of the United Nations who by reason of his official position enjoys immunity, if immunity has not been waived by the Secretary-General".

55 Daugirdas, Kristina (2019) Reputation and Accountability: Another Look at the United Nations' Response to the Cholera Epidemic in Haiti. *International Organizations Law Review* 16(1): 11–41.

56 Harvard Law School International Human Rights Clinic, Institute for Justice and Democracy in Haiti, Bureau des Avocats Internationaux (2020) Violations of the Right

implying that the RTD was equally violated and there has been no effective compensation to victims. As Barbanel Dove puts it, despite mobilisation by human rights advocates, more than one million victims have not seen justice.[57]

Article 25 of the draft Covenant provides that without impairing the obligations of the UN and its specialised agencies as provided for in the UN Charter and the constitutions of its specialised agencies, the UN and its specialised agencies are under the obligation to promote the right to development.[58] This is a reaffirmation of the UN's obligations as stipulated in the UN Charter and the constitutions of its specialised agencies. The provision, however, only provides a partial and incomplete solution to the question regarding the RTD obligations of other international organisations. The obligations of the UN in the UN Charter and the constitutions of its specialised agencies have not prevented them from violating human rights as shown above. The UN has always found a way to circumvent justice when accused of human rights violations. Other instances where such has happened are reflected in the *Bosnia and Herzegovina v Serbia and Montenegro*[59] and the *Askir v Boutros-Ghali and Others* cases.[60]

---

to Effective Remedy: The UN's Responsibility for Cholera in Haiti. Available at: https://humanrightsclinic.law.harvard.edu/wp-content/uploads/2022/10/HLS-IHRC-IJDH-BAI-Submission-to-Special-Procedures_Cholera.pdf (consulted 25 April 2025).

57 Barbanel, Dove (2021) No Remedy to Cholera in Haiti: How the UN Undermines Human Rights. *Journal of Human Rights Practice* 13(2): 386–406.

58 Draft Covenant on the Right to Development, supra note 2, Art 25(2).

59 *Application of the Convention on the Prevention and Punishment of the Crime of Genocide (Bosnia and Herzegovina v Serbia and Montenegro)*, Judgment, 26 February 2007, ICJ Rep. (2007) Para 297. In June 1995, some 7,600 male Muslim civilian inhabitants of Srebrenica in Bosnia were killed by Bosnian Serb forces. A small and lightly armed Dutch peacekeeping force—part of the United Nations Protection Force (UNPROFOR)—had been deployed to guard Srebrenica as a "safe area". However, it did to prevent the massacre. The question was raised whether the UN had failed in its mission by allowing the Dutch to send a small military contingent and refusing airstrikes against the Bosnian Serb forces. In 2007, the "Mothers of Srebrenica" Foundation (*Stichting*)—representing some 6,000 relatives of the victims of the massacre—started judicial proceedings before Dutch jurisdictions to condemn both the UN and the Dutch State for their failure to prevent the massacre and to claim financial compensation. In addition, individual Srebrenica survivors and victims' families filed claims for compensation against the Dutch Government. The domestic jurisdictions rejected the claims as far as the UN's responsibility was concerned because of the latter's absolute immunity before national jurisdictions; see Schmitt, supra note 41, 2.

60 *Abdi Hosh Askir v Boutros Boutros-Ghali*, 933 F Supp 368 (SDNY, 1996). A Somali citizen brought a claim against the UN, seeking damages for unlawful possession of property during UN operations in Somalia in April 1992. The complaint was dismissed based on UN absolute immunity.

These cases and other situations in which individuals have been deprived of their right of access to justice have led to the question whether the immunity and lack of accountability of international organisations should not be equated with impunity.[61] By enjoining these organisations to become parties to the Covenant on the RTD when it is adopted particularly because of the development impact they exert is imperative.

4.2 *Duty to Cooperate and the Developmental Impacts of International Organisations*

The analysis on the RTD obligations of international organisations cannot be complete without looking at the developmental impacts of these organisations in relation to the duty to cooperate with states as envisaged in Article 13(2) of the draft Covenant.[62] Several international organisations have made significant contributions to realising the right to development as this was considered merely as a moral and/or political commitment to provide developmental assistance. This section examines the impact of current developmental programmes undertaken by international organisations like the United Nations Development Programme (UNDP), the United Nations Children's Fund (UNICEF), IMF, the World Bank and the AU. Although most of the initiatives by these organisations are considered developmental programmes, the extent of their impacts with respect to human rights and meeting the provisions of Article 13(2) leaves much to be desired. Most of the assistance provided by international organisations especially, in the name of financial aid, comes in the form of loans with exorbitant interest rates and conditionalities which the impoverished recipient countries often struggle with and in most instances,

61 Freedman, supra note 34.

62 Draft Covenant on the Right to Development, supra note 2, Art 13(2) provides that 2. To this end, States Parties have primary responsibility, in accordance with the general principle of international solidarity described in the present Covenant, for the creation of international conditions favourable for the realization of the right to development for all, and shall take deliberate, concrete and targeted steps, individually and jointly, including through cooperation within international organizations and engagement with civil society: (a) To ensure that natural and legal persons, groups and States do not impair the enjoyment of the right to development; (b) To eliminate obstacles to the full realization of the right to development, including by reviewing international legal instruments, policies and practices; (c) To ensure that the formulation, adoption and implementation of States Parties' international legal instruments, policies and practices are consistent with the objective of fully realizing the right to development for all; (d) To formulate, adopt and implement appropriate international legal instruments, policies and practices aimed at the progressive enhancement and full realization of the right to development for all; (e) To mobilize appropriate technical, technological, financial, infrastructural and other necessary resources to enable States Parties, particularly in developing and least developed countries, to fulfil their obligations under the present Covenant.

are not able to comply with the conditionalities and terms of repayment. This raises the issue of development justice to recipient countries and communities. Donor conditionalities and the development programmes they fund and support, have often seriously violated human rights in local communities but the organisations continue to argue that they do not have a legal obligation towards human rights.[63] It is suggested that when the Covenant on the RTD eventually comes into force, there should be a robust streamlining of the conditionalities on development assistance coming from international organisations to safeguard the rights and dignity of those receiving such assistance. At the end of this sub-section, specific reference will be made to the AU to show the justiciability of the RTD in the promotion and protection of human rights in Africa.

Meanwhile, it is important to first look at how other international organisations undertake the duty to cooperate for development. The UNDP has been instrumental in promoting sustainable development and reducing poverty in developing countries through various initiatives. In line with what is envisaged in Article 13(2) of the Covenant on the RTD on the duty to cooperate, some of UNDP initiatives fall within a tripartite agreement between the UNDP, the beneficiary country and international and/or regional banks to provide technical assistance to developing countries. For example, UNDP is providing technical assistance for sustainable landscaping and ecotourism in Cambodia,[64] tackling disasters and climate change in Papua New Guinea,[65] strengthening the healthcare sector in Cameroon and Turkmenistan during COVID-19,[66]

63 The World Bank and IMF for example, argue that they have no legal obligations under international human rights law; see Bretton Woods Project 2019, supra note 6, 7.

64 In May 2021, UNDP entered a tripartite partnership with the government of Cambodia and the World Bank to provide technical assistance to the Sustainable Landscape and Ecotourism Project in Cambodia, supported by a $1.1M loan from the World Bank to the Cambodian government. The project duration is from May 2021 to December 2025; see UNDP (2022) Strong Partnerships, Stronger Impact: Governments, International Financial Institutions and UNDP Working Together for Development Results. Available at: https://www.undp.org/sites/g/files/zskgke326/files/2022-03/Web-Tripartite%20Brochure.pdf (consulted 6 September 2024).

65 In March 2020, the government of Papua New Guinea requested UNDP's support to implement a $3M Asian Development Bank loan for the project Building Resilience to Climate Change. UNDP came in at a point when the project had been underway for several years with limited progress and results; see UNDP (2022) Strong Partnerships, Stronger Impact: Governments, International Financial Institutions and UNDP Working Together for Development Results. Available at: https://www.undp.org/sites/g/files/zskgke326/files/2022-03/Web-Tripartite%20Brochure.pdf (consulted 6 September 2024).

66 In July 2020, a tripartite collaboration between the Islamic Development Bank, Cameroon, and 3 UN agencies (UNDP, UNOPS, UNICEF) made available $27.4M to help improve Cameroon's testing capacity, and early detection and support of COVID-19 to promote a

innovating to save lives in Yemen,[67] striving for quality education in Panama,[68] and integrating border management in Amenia.[69]

UNICEF has been instrumental in promoting the rights of children, education and healthcare in many countries. Just like the UNDP, UNICEF's current strategic plan envisages cooperating with International Financial Institutions (IFIs) in protecting children's rights.[70] For UNICEF to meet its

---

strengthened health system. From the total funds available, UNDP signed the larger agreement for $13.8M with Cameroon to strengthen the health system and the logistics chain of the Ministry of Health. In the same period, the World Bank approved a $20M loan from the International Bank for Reconstruction and Development (IBRD) for the Turkmenistan COVID-19 Response Project. The government of Turkmenistan partnered with UNDP to serve as a project implementing entity, with a focus on providing technical advice and strengthening the capacity of Turkmenistan Ministry of Health to respond to the pandemic; see UNDP (2022) Strong Partnerships, Stronger Impact: Governments, International Financial Institutions and UNDP Working Together for Development Results. Available at: https://www.undp.org/sites/g/files/zskgke326/files/2022-03/Web-Tripartite%20Brochure.pdf (consulted 06 September 2024.)

67 Yemen is facing one of the largest crises in the world with immense development and humanitarian challenges. Since 2016, UNDP has mobilized nearly $500M in grant financing from the World Bank's International Development Association to Yemen (as of the end of 2021). See UNDP (2022) Strong Partnerships, Stronger Impact: Governments, International Financial Institutions and UNDP Working Together for Development Results. Available at: https://www.undp.org/sites/g/files/zskgke326/files/2022-03/Web-Tripartite%20Brochure.pdf (consulted 6 September 2024.)

68 In May 2019, the Inter-American Development Bank (IADB) loaned $100M to Panama to improve the quality of education. On behalf its ministry of education, UNDP has been implementing $47M of the total loan to strengthen technical and operational capacity; improve agility and transparency in process and procedures; and develop a platform for the ministry to work with counterparts and development actors; see UNDP (2022) Strong Partnerships, Stronger Impact: Governments, International Financial Institutions and UNDP Working Together for Development Results. Available at: https://www.undp.org/sites/g/files/zskgke326/files/2022-03/Web-Tripartite%20Brochure.pdf (consulted 6 September 2024.)

69 In 2012, UNDP was tasked with improving three Border Crossing Points in Armenia, which together account for 80% of the country's trade. These borders play a big role not just in the country but also the continent: the EU identified them as a section of the proposed intercontinental trade and transport network TRACECA (Transport Corridor Europe-Caucasus-Asia). The project, called "The Modernization of Bagratashen, Bavra and Gogavan Border Crossing Points," received $53.7M from EIB, comprised of a $37.4M loan to the government of Armenia and $14.5M grant to UNDP from the EU's Neighbourhood Investment Facility. In addition, UNDP provided $1.8M to the project; UNDP (2022) Strong Partnerships, Stronger Impact: Governments, International Financial Institutions and UNDP Working Together for Development Results. Available at: https://www.undp.org/sites/g/files/zskgke326/files/2022-03/Web-Tripartite%20Brochure.pdf (consulted 6 September 2024).

70 UNICEF (2023) Update on UNICEF Engagement with International Financial Institutions. Available at: https://www.unicef.org/executiveboard/media/14836/file/2023-EB7

core commitments to children and its twin development and humanitarian mandate, it is working with IFIs in humanitarian crises and fragile situations. In 2017, UNICEF partnered with the World Bank to provide life-saving assistance to 1.5 million vulnerable families in Yemen. It worked with partners like the WHO to provide vital healthcare and nutrition facilities to about 17 million recipients in the Yemen Emergency Human Capital Project. More so, under the Restoring Education and Learning Project, UNICEF collaborated with the World Food Programme (WFP) and Save the Children to maintain access to basic education and improve conditions of learning for 360,000 children in 1,200 schools in Yemen. Again in 2018, UNICEF worked with the World Bank, the WHO and the International Committee of the Red Cross to deliver life-saving vital health amenities in South Sudan. UNICEF is equally supporting the government of Haiti in responding to the humanitarian crisis following the earthquake in August 2021 and cholera outbreak in October 2022.

It is common knowledge that the policy conditions promoted by these international organisations in the form of loans (especially by IFIs like the World Bank and the IMF), development projects, technical and humanitarian assistance or financial surveillance comes with huge costs and most of the times, do not align with the states' national development priorities. These conditionalities undermine the sovereignty of recipient nations, restraining their authority to make policy decisions, and subsequently, stripping them of ownership of national development strategies.[71] It also undermines the RTD, the right to self-determination and the right to permanent sovereignty over victim states' natural resources. These are the ills that Article 13(2) envisage to regulate. Cooperation projects that violate the RTD are not encouraged.

The IMF and the World Bank share the goal of economic development and in raising living standards in their member states.[72] They have provided significant development financing for infrastructure projects and providing policy advice to developing countries but not without a cost, owing to their conditionalities and lack of transparency. They were established to promote international economic cooperation. Their interests have however, been seen as serving Western political and economic power than the developing countries they purport to assist.[73] Most of the initiatives in Africa have not had any positive impact on development, rather they have continued to widen the poverty

-Update_on_UNICEF_engagement_with_IFI-EN-2023.01.09.pdf (consulted 6 September 2024).

71 Bretton Woods Project, supra note 8, 4.

72 International Monetary Fund (2022) The IMF and the World Bank. Available at: https://www.imf.org/en/About/Factsheets/Sheets/2022/IMF-World-Bank-New (Consulted on 17 September 2024).

73 Bretton Woods Project, supra note 6, 2.

gap. I describe these initiatives as "poverty development programmes" in the sense that they sustain poverty and not reduce it. According to the London School of Economies, the World Bank structural adjustment initiative had a dismal record on development, which basically destroyed the poor countries that implemented the initiative instead of helping them develop.[74] It further notes that "countries that have come under the sway of the World Bank—and its sister institution, the IMF—have experienced declining development outcomes over the past 30 years or so". The healthcare system and healthcare infrastructure in Africa have deteriorated as a result of the failed development programmes of these international organisations. The IMF and the World Bank introduced the Structural Adjustment Programmes (SAPs) and the Poverty Reduction Strategy Programmes in Africa with policies and conditionalities that required recipient countries to restructure their economies, which undermined investment in the health sector.[75] Not even the Millenium Development Goals, the Sustainable Development Goals or any other such framework mechanisms for development have had any significant impact

74 London School of Economics (2012) The World Bank and the Development Delusion. Available at: https://blogs.lse.ac.uk/africaatlse/2012/11/16/the-world-bank-and-the-development-delusion-2/ (consulted 18 September 2024).

75 London School of Economics (2015) The Ebola Crisis in West Africa and the Enduring Legacy of the Structural Adjustment Policies. Available at: https://eprints.lse.ac.uk/75575/1/Africa%20at%20LSE%20%E2%80%93%20The%20Ebola%20crisis%20in%20West%20Africa%20and%20the%20enduring%20legacy%20of%20the%20Structural%20Adjustment%20Policies.pdf (consulted 25 April 2025). The origin of these failed development programmes started with the World Bank publishing the Berg report in 1981, in response to the global debt crisis of the late 1970s and the economic distress it had exerted on poor countries. The study anchored the crisis on excessive government spending on social programmes, including healthcare. Accordingly, despite acknowledging that in many African countries, hospitals, clinics, and equipment had "fallen into disrepair" with facilities often "staffed at levels far below what is needed," the Bank proceeded to advocate deep cuts in public spending on healthcare services, including health infrastructure. As a result, following the introduction of SAPs, government expenditure as a percentage of GDP on health plunged. According to the Berg Report, in 1979, government expenditure on health as percentage of GDP in Africa averaged between 5 to 7 percent (see London School of Economics 2015). A WHO study shows the rate at between 5.6% to 6.2%; London School of Economics (2015) Today, the physician-to-patient ratio in Africa hovers at 2 per 10,000 of the population, and nurses and midwives-to-patient at 12 per 10,000, with minor variations among countries, according to the World Bank and WHO; see, LSE (2015). That ratio is less than 1 physician per 10,000 people in Liberia, less than 2 in Uganda, and about 4 in Nigeria—the second highest in the region after South Africa, with seven physicians per 10,000 population. It is worth noting that at the height of the Ebola crisis in West Africa some World Bank and IMF officials seemed to acknowledge their past mistakes, albeit only implicitly; see London School of Economics 2015.

on development in any community in Africa or other developing regions of the world.

The AU is currently the only international organisation that has made the RTD justiciable and therefore, lived up to its legal obligation in ensuring that the RTD is achieved across the continent. The landmark *Endorois Welfare Council v the Republic of Kenya* case[76] consolidated and concretised the African Commission on Human and Peoples Rights' position on the RTD.[77] It laid an important precedent in the recognition and protection of the RTD of indigenous peoples and ordered for compensation to be paid to the affected community for the violations they suffered. This makes the AU the first international organisation to take its legal obligation to promote, protect and fulfil the RTD as established in the African Charter seriously. The AU example is an important lesson to other international organisations to be proactive in complying with their RTD obligations. Suffice to say that unlike many other international organisations, the AU has largely been successful in protecting the RTD. Violations have no doubt been committed by AU member states like Kenya acting in their individual capacity and not as the AU.

5 Conclusion

I conclude the discussion in this chapter by highlighting the fact that international organisations do have human rights obligations under international law. Nonetheless, it is the extent to which they are bound by these obligations

---

76 *Centre for Minority Rights Development (Kenya) and Minority Rights Group International on behalf of the Endorois Welfare Council v The Republic of Kenya* 276/2003 ACHPR (2009). Regarding the facts of the case, the Kenyan government in 1973 gazetted the Endorois land as a game reserve and the Endorois community were later forcibly and illegally strip-off of their ancestral land without proper compensation. The Endorois people exhausted all national avenues without a legal solution. Under the African Charter, the allegations against the Kenya government included violations of the Endorois right to practise religion (Art 8), right to culture (Arts 7(2) and (3)), right to property (Art 14), right to dispose freely of their natural resources (Art 21) and right to development (Art 22). The Kenyan government failed respond on time and later denied responsibility. The ACHPR in 2010 decided in favour of the Endorois people and requested the Kenyan government to return the land to the Endorois community and compensate them for losses suffered: Ashamu, Elizabeth (2011) Centre for Minority Rights Development (Kenya) and Minority Rights Group International on Behalf of Endorois Welfare Council v Kenya: A Landmark Decision from the African Commission. *Journal of African Law* 55(2): 300–313.

77 The African Commission establish a violation on the RTD of the Endorois indigenous people in Kenya.

that is the subject of contestation especially, if the organisation is not a party to the relevant human rights treaty. It is not inappropriate that the Covenant on the RTD envisages obligations for international organisations, which are mostly only formulated as negative obligation not to hinder or impair realisation of the RTD. International organisations also have a duty to cooperate for the realisation of the RTD, implying that they must prioritise the RTD in their policies and programmes to ensure that development is equitable, sustainable and respectful of human rights. The obligations arise from the fact that international organisations often do not respect human rights in their development endeavours. The obligations entail that in carrying out their mandate, international organisations refrain from activities that inhibit the fundamental human right to development. As primary duty bearers, states are enjoined to take proactive measures in dismantling barriers to development that arise from human rights violations, including those committed by international organisations. Of concern is the fact that states are generally reluctant to hold international organisations accountable. The Haiti cholera case is instructive.

The RTD is a critical human right that requires concerted efforts from all stakeholders, including international organisations. In addition to the duty to cooperate, by fulfilling their negative obligation, which entails refraining from actions that may impair the RTD, international organisations have the potential to contribute significantly in creating the enabling environment where all human rights and fundamental freedoms can be fully realised. Thus, adopting policies that clearly indicate their commitment not to violate the RTD during their operations, international organisations can play a pivotal role in promoting sustainable and inclusive development.

References

Additional protocol to the American Convention on Human Rights in the area of Economic, Social and Cultural Rights (Protocol of San Salvador), adopted the General Assembly of the Organisation of American States in San Salvador, El Salvador on 16 November 1999.

African Charter on Human and Peoples' Rights adopted in Nairobi, Kenya on 27 June 1981 OAU Doc CAB/LEG/67/3 Rev.5 (1981).

African Youth Charter adopted by the 7th Ordinary Session of the AU Assembly of Heads of State and Government in Banjul, the Gambia on 2 July 2006.

Arab Charter on Human Rights adopted in Cairo, Egypt on 15 September 1994.

Ashamu, Elizabeth (2011) Centre for Minority Rights Development (Kenya) and Minority Rights Group International on Behalf of Endorois Welfare Council v Kenya:

A Landmark Decision from the African Commission. *Journal of African Law* 55(2): 300–313.

Association of South East Asian Nations (ASEAN) Human Rights Declaration adopted in Phnom Penh, Cambodia on 9 November 2012.

Barbanel, Dove (2021) No Remedy to Cholera in Haiti: How the UN Undermines Human Rights. *Journal of Human Rights Practice* 13(2): 386–406.

Bedjaoui, Mohammed (1991) The Right to Development. In: Mayor, F. and Bedjaoui, M. (eds) *International Law: Achievements and Prospects*. Leiden: Brill/Nijhoff.

Bretton Woods Project (2019) What are the Main Criticisms of the World Bank and IMF? Available at: https://www.brettonwoodsproject.org/wp-content/uploads/2019/06/Common-Criticisms-FINAL.pdf (consulted 17 September 2024).

Ceccarelli, Daniela et al (2011) Origin of Vibrio Cholerae in Haiti. *The Lancet Infectious Diseases* 11(4): 262.

Daugirdas, Kristina (2021) Member States' Due Diligence Obligations to Supervise International Organizations. In: Krieger, H.; Peters, A. and Kreuzer, L. (eds) *Due Diligence in the International Legal Order*. Oxford: Oxford University Press.

Daugirdas, Kristina (2019) Reputation and Accountability: Another Look at the United Nations' Response to the Cholera Epidemic in Haiti. *International Organizations Law Review* 16(1): 11–41.

Declaration on the Right to Development Resolution A/RES/41/128 adopted by UN General Assembly on 4 December 1986.

Draft Articles on the Responsibility of International Organisations 2011, adopted by the UN International Law Commission (ILC).

Draft International Covenant on the Right to Development—Report by the Chair-Rapporteur of the Working Group on the Right to Development, Zamir Akram (Pakistan) Human Rights Council A/HRC/54/50 54th Session, 6 October 2023.

Faix, Martin (2014) Are International Organisations Bound by International Human Rights Obligations. *Czech Yearbook of Public and Private International Law* 5: 267–290.

Freedman, Rosa (2014) UN Immunity or Impunity? A Human Rights Based Challenge. *European Journal of International Law* 25(1): 239–254.

Gladstone, Rick (2016) Cholera Deaths in Haiti Could Far Exceed Official Count. *New York Times*.

Harvard Law School International Human Rights Clinic, Institute for Justice and Democracy in Haiti, Bureau des Avocats Internationaux (2020) Violations of the Right to Effective Remedy: The UN's Responsibility for Cholera in Haiti. Available at: https://humanrightsclinic.law.harvard.edu/wp-content/uploads/2022/10/HLS-IHRC-IJDH-BAI-Submission-to-Special-Procedures_Cholera.pdf (consulted 25 April 2025).

Institute for Justice and Democracy in Haiti's Report (2020) Years on: A "New Approach"? The ongoing violation of victims' rights in the UN's response to cholera in Haiti.

Inter-American Democratic Charter adopted by Special Session of the General Assembly of the Organisation of American States in Lima, Peru on 1 September 2001.

International Covenant on Civil and Political Rights adopted by the UN General Assembly, Resolution 2200A (XXI) of 16 December 1966, 993 UNTS 3 UN Doc A/6316 (1966).

International Covenant on Economic, Social and Cultural Rights adopted by the UN General Assembly, Resolution 2200A (XXI) of 16 December 1966, 999 UNTS 171 UN Doc A/6316 (1966).

International Law Association (2004) Committee on Accountability of International Organisations, Berlin Conference Final Report. Available at: https://www.ila-hq.org/en_GB/documents/final-conference-report-berlin-2004-1 (consulted 26 August 2024).

International Monetary Fund (2022) The IMF and the World Bank. Available at: https://www.imf.org/en/About/Factsheets/Sheets/2022/IMF-World-Bank-New (consulted 17 September 2024).

Interpretation of the Agreement of 25 March 1951 Between the WHO and Egypt, Advisory Opinion, 1980 I.C.J. Rep. 73, pp. 89–90 (Dec. 20).

London School of Economics (2012) The World Bank and the Development Delusion. Available at: https://blogs.lse.ac.uk/africaatlse/2012/11/16/the-world-bank-and-the-development-delusion-2/ (consulted 18 September 2024).

London School of Economics (2015) The Ebola Crisis in West Africa and the Enduring Legacy of the Structural Adjustment Policies. Available at: https://eprints.lse.ac.uk/75575/1/Africa%20at%20LSE%20%E2%80%93%20The%20Ebola%20crisis%20in%20West%20Africa%20and%20the%20enduring%20legacy%20of%20the%20Structural%20Adjustment%20Policies.pdf (consulted 25 April 2025).

Luquero, Francisco et al (2016) Mortality Rates During Cholera Epidemic, Haiti, 2010–2011. *Emerging Infectious Diseases* 22(3): 410–416.

Marks, Stephen (2004) The Human Right to Development: Between Rhetoric and Reality. *Harvard Human Rights Journal* 17: 137–168.

Monterrey Consensus of the International Conference on Financing for Development, adopted by the United Nations in Monterrey, Mexico, 18–22 March 2002.

Neuman, Gerald (2019) International Organizations and Human Rights: The Need for Substance. *Research Working Paper Series Vol 9—HRP 19-001, Harvard Law School.*

Ngang, Carol Chi (2021) *The Right to Development in Africa.* Leiden/Boston: Brill Publishers.

Nwauche, E.S. and Nwobike, J.C. (2004) Implementing the Right to Development. *Sur—International Journal on Human Rights* 2(2): 93–112.

Platise, Mateja S. (d.n.a) Responsibility of International Organizations for Human Rights Violations. Available at: https://www.mpil.de/en/pub/research/areas/public

-international-law/ipa/responsibility-organizations.cfm#publications (consulted 27 August 2024).

Protocol to the African Charter on Human and Peoples' Rights on the Rights of Women in Africa adopted by the Assembly of Heads of States and Government in Maputo, Mozambique on 11 July 2003.

Reza, Mohammad (2015) Realization of the Right to Development: Prospects for Drafting a Convention on the Right to Development. *Journal of Human Rights* 14(6): 548–558.

Rio Declaration on Environment and Development adopted at the United Nations Conference on Environment and Development at Rio de Janeiro, Brazil, 3 to 14 June 1992.

Sarooshi, Dan (2007) Transfers of Powers to International Organizations. In: Sarooshi, Dan (ed) *International Organizations and their Exercise of Sovereign Powers*. London: Oxford University Press.

Schmitt, Pierre (2017) Setting the Scene: The Case of Individual Victims of Human Rights Violations. In: Schmitt, Pierre (ed) *Access to Justice and International Organizations*. London: Edward Elgar Publishing, 1–52.

Schmitt, Pierre (2017) *Access to Justice and International Organizations: The Case of Individual Victims of Human Rights Violations*. London: Edward Elgar Publishing.

UN Sustainable Development Group (2003) The Human Rights Based Approach to Development Cooperation Towards a Common Understanding Among UN Agencies. Available at: https://unsdg.un.org/sites/default/files/6959The_Human_Rights_Based_Approach_to_Development_Cooperation_Towards_a_Common_Understanding_among_UN.pdf (consulted 25 April 2025).

UNICEF (2023) Update on UNICEF Engagement with International Financial Institutions. Available at: https://www.unicef.org/executiveboard/media/14836/file/2023-EB7-Update_on_UNICEF_engagement_with_IFI-EN-2023.01.09.pdf (consulted 6 September 2024).

United Nations Declaration on the Rights of Indigenous Peoples, Resolution 61/295 adopted by the UN General Assembly on 13 September 2007.

United Nations Development Programme (2022) Strong Partnerships, Stronger Impact: Governments, International Financial Institutions and UNDP Working Together for Development Results. Available at: https://www.undp.org/sites/g/files/zskgke326/files/2022-03/Web-Tripartite%20Brochure.pdf (consulted 6 September 2024).

Vienna Declaration and Programme of Action adopted by the United Nations World Conference on Human Rights UN Doc. A/CONF.157/24, 25 June 1993.

Zagel, Gudrun (2018) International Organisations and Human Rights: The Role of the UN Covenants in Overcoming the Accountability Gap. *Nordic Journal of Human Rights* 36(1): 74–90.

CHAPTER 8

Development Financing in the Global South: an Analysis of Governance at the IMF and the World Bank

Daniel M. Walyemera

1 Introduction

The dawn of the post-colonial era led to calls from the formerly colonised territories for global policies that enable equitable development. This was because many independent states argued that they had only obtained political independence from the "white"[1] colonisers, but not economic independence.[2] The formerly colonised states argued that global economic policies were dominated by Western ideologies, which continued to perpetuate colonial power. It is argued that the Global North hegemony continues to perpetuate global inequities evidenced by the extreme differences in living standards that prevail globally. These inequalities have accelerated global poverty.[3]

The United Nations General Assembly (UNGA) adopted the Declaration on New International Economic Order (NIEO) in 1974.[4] The NIEO was and still remains the conceptual vehicle by which former colonised states have consistently sought to use in advocating for global balance and an equitable international economic order against neo-colonialism that sustains Western imperialism in formerly colonised states.[5] The NIEO aimed for equal and fair trade as well as favourable financial and economic terms for newly independent

---

1 Andersson, M. (2017) Race: A Contested and Traveling Concept. In: Leiulfsrud, H. and Sohlberg, P. (eds) *Concepts in Action: Conceptual Constructivism*. Leiden: Brill, 284–301.

2 Gardner, James A. (2013) The Myth of State Autonomy: Federalism, Political Parties, and the National Colonization of State Politics. *Journal of Law and Politics* 29: 1; see also Young, Crawford (2012) *The Postcolonial State in Africa: Fifty Years of Independence, 1960–2010*. Madison, Wisconsin: University of Wisconsin Press.

3 Milanovic, Branko (2012) Global Inequality: From Class to Location, From Proletarians to Migrants. *Global Policy* 3(2): 125–134.

4 Declaration on the Establishment of a New International Economic Order, Gen Ass Resolution A/RES/S-6/3201, adopted on 1 May 1974.

5 Salomon, Margot (2013) From NIEO to Now and the Unfinishable Story of Economic Justice. *International and Comparative Law Quarterly* 62(1): 31–54.

 | DOI:10.1163/9789004734357_009

states to deal with the global economic inequalities perpetuated by Western hegemony.[6] The NIEO influenced the birth of the right to development. The promoters of the NIEO embraced the right to development as a normative basis for their economic proposals to the world. Subsequent efforts within the United Nations (UN) acknowledged that this right to development advocated for by the Global South to enable a more equitable global economic order could be deduced from soft law and hard law instruments, which espoused international law values.[7] The NIEO was intended to facilitate the restructuring of a global economic order that enables "[...] developing societies of the South to participate more effectively in decision-making on international economic matters".[8] It also includes the Global South's sovereignty and control over its natural resources.[9] The protestations from the Global South about this exploitative and domineering economic order have led to little or no change. This can, for example, be evidenced by the governance structures of the International Monetary Fund (IMF) and the International Bank for Reconstruction and Development (World Bank). A discussion of the governances of these two global economic institutions follows hereunder.

The mandate of the IMF is prescribed under Article I of its Articles of Agreement. It provides that the purpose of the IMF is "To promote international monetary cooperation through a permanent institution which provides the machinery for consultation and collaboration on international monetary problems".[10] Article IV of the Articles of Agreement of the IMF further provides for the purpose of the international monetary system as follows:

> Recognizing that the essential purpose of the international monetary system is to provide a framework that facilitates the exchange of goods, services, and capital among countries, and that sustains sound economic growth, and that a principal objective is the continuing development of the orderly underlying conditions that are necessary for financial and

6 Declaration on the New International Economic Order, supra note 4, Para 4; Gilman, Nils (2015) The New International Economic Order: A Reintroduction. *Humanity: An International Journal of Human Rights, Humanitarianism, and Development* 6(1): 3.

7 Sengupta, Arjun (2000) Realizing the Right to Development. *Development and Change*, 31(3): 553–578.

8 Ibhawoh, Bonny (2011) The Right to Development: The Politics and Polemics of Power and Resistance. *Human Rights Quarterly* 33(1): 90.

9 Declaration on the New International Economic Order, supra note 4, Para 4.

10 Articles of Agreement of the International Monetary Fund Adopted at the United Nations Monetary and Financial Conference, Bretton Woods, New Hampshire, on 22 July 1944; entered into force on 27 December 1945, Art I(i).

> economic stability, each member undertakes to collaborate with the Fund and other members to assure orderly exchange arrangements and to promote a stable system of exchange rates.[11]

Two key functions can be deduced from the mandate of the IMF. The first is the supervision and regulation of exchange rates. Secondly, the IMF must also enable efficiency within the international payments and transfers system. The purpose of the World Bank is prescribed in Article I of the Articles of Agreement of the World Bank as follows:

> To assist in the reconstruction and development of territories of members by facilitating the investment of capital for productive purposes, including the restoration of economies destroyed or disrupted by war, the reconversion of productive facilities to peacetime needs, and the encouragement of the development of productive facilities and resources in less developed countries. To promote private foreign investment by means of guarantees or participations in loans and other investments made by private investors; and when private capital is not available on reasonable terms, to supplement private investment by providing, on suitable conditions, finance for productive purposes out of its own capital, funds raised by it and its other resources. To promote the long-range balanced growth of international trade and the maintenance of equilibrium in balances of payments by encouraging international investment for the development of the productive resources of members, thereby assisting in raising productivity, the standard of living, and conditions of labor in their territories. To arrange the loans made or guaranteed by it in relation to international loans through other channels so that the more useful and urgent projects, large and small alike, will be dealt with first. To conduct its operations with due regard to the effect of international investment on business conditions in the territories of members and, in the immediate post-war years, to assist in bringing about a smooth transition from a wartime to a peacetime economy.[12]

---

11 Ibid at Art IV(1).

12 International Bank for Reconstruction and Development (The World Bank) Articles of Agreement drawn up at the United Nations Monetary and Financial Conference, at Bretton Woods, New Hampshire, 1–22 July 1944; became effective on 27 December 1945 (As amended effective 27 June 2012), Art I(i), (ii), (iii), (iv), and (v).

The World Bank's mandate envisages the development and reconstruction of member states' infrastructure and provides financial facilities to both governments and certain private entities for productive purposes. The initial purpose of the World Bank was to provide finance for reconstruction projects after the effects of World War II. In recent decades, the World Bank's focus has moved to providing financing for infrastructure and development for member countries in the Global South.[13] For a country to be a member state of the World Bank, it must first attain membership in the IMF.[14]

The governance structure of the World Bank is like that of the IMF. The governance structure grants more powers to former colonial powers to dictate the internal and ultimately, external policies and programmes of the Bretton Woods Institutions, which has sustained undemocratic governance practices by the two institutions thus, perpetuating global economic inequalities. For example, the structural adjustment programmes proposed by the IMF and the World Bank in the mid-1980s, which enabled the privatisation of state enterprises, were disastrous economic policies for the Global South.[15] The privatisation of state enterprises to enable free market policies has eventually led some policymakers and scholars to argue for a return of the state to the market to correct the failures of a free market.[16]

This unfair global economic structure has further been perpetuated and sustained by several global economic institutions and systems. These institutions and systems are dominated by former colonial powers, who dictate their policies and operations. The most prominent of the global institutions

13 Orakhelashvili, Alexander (2022) *Akehurst's Modern Introduction to International Law*. London: Routledge, 227.

14 The World Bank Articles of Agreement, supra note 12, Art II(a).

15 Kwaghe, Zara Emmanuel and Odeh, Okpale Alfred (2020) A History of Privatisation: The Global Perspective. *International Journal of Humanitatis Theoreticus* 3(1): 141–152; Kempe, Ronald Hope (ed) (2019) *Structural Adjustment, Reconstruction, and Development in Africa*. London: Routledge; Reinsberg, Bernhard et al (2019) The World System and the Hollowing out of State Capacity: How Structural Adjustment Programs Affect Bureaucratic Quality in Developing Countries. *American Journal of Sociology* 124(4): 1222–1257; Reinsberg, Bernhard et al (2020) Bad Governance: How Privatization Increases Corruption in the Developing World. *Regulation and Governance* 14(4): 698–717; Herbst, Jeffrey (2019) Privatization in Africa. *The Political Economy of Public Sector Reform and Privatization*, 234.

16 Mbaku, J.M. (2018) A Balance Sheet of Structural Adjustment in Africa: Towards a Sustainable Development Agenda. In: Mbaku, J.M. (ed) *Preparing Africa for the Twenty-First Century: Strategies for Peaceful Coexistence and Sustainable Development*. London: Routledge, 119–149; Reinsberg, supra note 15, 698–717.

include the World Trade Organisation (WTO), the IMF, and the World Bank.[17] This chapter focuses on the IMF and the World Bank—international financial institutions—established at the United Nations Financial and Development Conference at Bretton Woods, New Hampshire in the United States of America (USA) in July 1944.[18] As a result, both economic organisations are referred to informally as the "Bretton Woods institutions".[19]

This chapter consists of eight sections. The introductory section provides context for the chapter. Section two reviews the theoretical concepts under which the study is situated. The justiciability of the right to development is explored in section three. The relationship between equitable development and sustainable development is discussed in section four. The undemocratic governance practices by the IMF and the World Bank and how it poses a challenge to equitable development in the Global South is detailed in section five. Section five juxtaposes the undemocratic government practices by the Bretton Woods Institutions with the obligations of international organisations. Section six discusses the possibility of democratic governance at the IMF and the World Bank, enabling equitable development in the Global South. The recommendations are suggested in section seven. Section eight concludes the chapter. The theoretical grounding of the chapter follows in the next section.

2 Theoretical Grounding

This chapter is grounded on several concepts to enable an adequate analysis of the key arguments. These include the concept of development financing, which has been associated with the World Bank since its establishment.[20] Development financing has numerous definitions. This is partly due to the lack of attention to it as a discipline in academia. For this chapter, "development financing" is defined as "an approach to funding developmental outcomes which covers strategies, principles/processes and instruments employed

17 Bernstein, E.M. (2015) The Making and Remaking of the Bretton Woods Institutions. In: Kirschner, O. (ed) *The Bretton Woods-GATT System: Retrospect and Prospects after Fifty Years*. New York: Routledge, 89–98.

18 Korten, D. (2014) The Failure of Bretton Woods. In: Goldsmith, E. and Mander, J. (eds) *The Case Against the Global Economy: And for a Turn towards Localisation*. London: Routledge, 35–44.

19 Bernstein, supra note 17.

20 Abdul, Latif Alhassan (2023) Development Finance: A Conceptual Definition. *Development Financing Agenda* 8(5): 16–18.

by multiple development stakeholders to mobilize and align finance for sustainability".[21] According to the United Nations Trade and Development Organisation, the "Global South" includes Oceania,[22] Asia,[23] Latin America, and Africa. These regions are characterised by a scarcity of resources and meagre income levels.[24]

The other key theory in this chapter is "equitable development", which is defined as "[…] a positive development strategy that ensures everyone participates in and benefits from the […] economic transformation—especially low-income residents, communities of colour, immigrants, and others at risk of being left behind."[25] Consequently, for equitable development to be realised, racial indignities must be eliminated by investing in social justice initiatives that provide equal economic, social, and political opportunities to everyone without discrimination.[26]

Another theoretical concept foregrounded in the chapter is "democratic governance," entailing first and foremost, an exploration of what "governance" means. There are varied conceptions of governance, which as Fukuyama notes is as old as human existence.[27] Consequently, there are varied definitions of what governance means. The World Bank defines "governance" as "the manner in which power exercised in the management of a country's economic and social resources for development".[28]

A renewed conceptualisation of governance is the idea of "democratic governance". Democratic governance espouses public participation in decision-making in optimally using resources for the benefit of everyone. The United Nations gave governance a new dimension when the theory was termed "democratic governance". The United Nations posits that "[…] democratic governance encompasses respecting people's human rights and freedom, say in decision making, which affects their lives and holding decision-makers accountable.

21 Ibid.

22 New Zealand and Australia are not included.

23 South Korea, Japan, and Israel are excluded.

24 Kowalski, A.M. (2021) Global South-Global North Differences. In: Filho, W.L. et al (eds) *No Poverty*. Cham: Springer International Publishing, 389–400.

25 Treuhart, Sara (2016) Equitable Development: The Path to All in Pittsburgh. *Policylink*. Available at: https://www.policylink.org/sites/default/files/summary_pittsburgh_FINAL_PDF.pdf (consulted 30 October 2024).

26 Ibid.

27 Fukuyama, Francis (2013) What is Governance? *Governance* 26(3): 347–368.

28 World Bank (2000) *Reforming Public Institutions and Strengthening Governance: A World Bank Strategy*. Washington DC: The World Bank; see also Khan, K.K. (2002) Good Governance: Concept and the Case of Bangladesh. In: Chowdhury, M.H. (ed) *Thirty Years of Bangladesh Politics: Essays in Memory of Dr Mahfuzul Huq*. Dhaka: University Press Limited, 63–76.

It attempts to make the economic and social policies more responsive to the people's needs".[29] The principles of democratic governance include inclusivity, equitability, participation, accountability, transparency, and consensus.[30] The theories are used to provide a theoretical frame for the chapter.

3 The Right to Development

Efforts to have the right to development recognised as a substantive human right, before 1986, were met with resistance by former colonial powers due to the ideological polarisation of the postcolonial world.[31] The UN General Assembly, however, eventually adopted the Declaration on the Right to Development on 4 December 1986, because this right could be deduced from prior soft and hard law instruments.[32] Several human rights instruments contained elements of the right to development. This is especially so for the economic, social, and cultural rights. These rights include the right to an adequate standard of living,[33] the right to healthcare, and the right to work, among many others.[34] Commentators have argued that although the UN General Assembly adopted the Declaration on the Right to Development, it hardly dealt with the concrete proposals of the NIEO to enable a balance of global economic power.[35] This is because, at the international level, the right to development is not binding.[36] The non-binding nature of this human right has, consequently, led to a discourse about its justiciability. Some scholars

29 United Nations (d.n.a.) Global Issues: Democracy. Available at: https://www.un.org/en/global-issues/democracy (Consulted 20 December 2024).

30 Gyong, J.E. (2014) Good Governance and Accountability in a Democracy. *European Scientific Journal* 7(26): 71–89.

31 Ngang, Carol Chi (2021) *The Right to Development in Africa*. Leiden/Boston: BRILL, 22–53.

32 Teshome, Roman Girma (2022) The Draft Convention on the Right to Development: A New Dawn to the Recognition of the Right to Development as a Human Right? *Human Rights Law Review* 22(2): 1.

33 International Covenant on Economic, Social and Cultural Rights adopted by the UN General Assembly, Resolution 2200A (XXI) of 16 December 1966, 999 UNTS 171 UN Doc A/6316 (1966) Art 11.

34 Ibid at Arts 6 and 12.

35 Fukuda-Parr, Sakiko (2012) The Right to Development: Reframing a New Discourse for the Twenty-First Century. *Human Rights and the Global Economy* 79(4): 839; Uvin, Peter (2007) From the Right to Development to the Rights-Based Approach: How "Human Rights" Entered Development. *Development in Practice* 17(4/5): 598.

36 This is apart from the Arab and African regions that have binding human rights treaties on the right to development.

argue that the right to development is not enforceable in the courts of law, which lessens its substantive ability to be called a human right.[37] The counterargument is that the normative value of any human right is not pegged to its enforcement as a human right in the courts of law because the existence of human rights precedes law and is derived from the concept of human dignity.[38] A prominent human rights scholar has argued that the inability of a human right to be justiciable does not make the right ineffective, because human rights can be made effective through social and political crusading.[39] It is important to note that the African Charter on Human and Peoples Rights (African Charter) and the Arab Charter on Human Rights enshrine binding provisions on the right to development.[40] Article 22 of the African Charter provides as follows:

1. All peoples shall have the right to their economic, social, and cultural development with due regard to their freedom and identity and in the equal enjoyment of the common heritage of mankind.
2. States shall have the duty, individually or collectively, to ensure the exercise of the right to development.[41]

Relatedly, Article 37 of the Arab Charter on Human Rights (Arab Charter) states that:

> The right to development is a fundamental human right, and all States are required to establish the development policies and to take the measures needed to guarantee this right. They have a duty to give effect to the values of solidarity and cooperation among them and at the international level with a view to eradicating poverty and achieving economic, social, cultural, and political development. By virtue of this right, every citizen has the right to participate in the realization of development and to enjoy the benefits and fruits thereof.

---

37 Teshome, supra note 32.

38 Ibid.

39 Sen, A. (2010) Human Rights and Development. In: Andreassen, B., and Marks, S. (eds) *Development as a Human Right: Legal, Political and Economic Dimensions*, 2nd Edn, Antwerp: Intersentia, 8.

40 African Charter on Human and Peoples' Rights adopted in Nairobi, Kenya on 27 June 1981 OAU Doc CAB/LEG/67/3 Rev.5 (1981), Art 22; and Arab Charter on Human Rights adopted in Cairo, Egypt on 15 September 1994, Art 37.

41 African Charter, supra note 40, Art 22(1)(2).

The African Commission on Human and Peoples Rights (African Commission) and the African Court on Human and Peoples Rights (African Court) have developed a robust jurisprudence on the justiciability of the right to development. In the *Centre for Minority Rights Development (Kenya) and Another v Republic of Kenya* case,[42] the African Commission held as follows:

> The African Commission is of the view that the right to development is a two-pronged test, that it is both constitutive and instrumental, or useful as both a means and an end. A violation of either the procedural or substantive element constitutes a violation of the right to development. Fulfilling only one of the two prongs will not satisfy the right to development. The African Commission notes the Complainants' arguments that recognising the right to development requires fulfilling five main criteria: it must be equitable, non-discriminatory, participatory, accountable, and transparent, with equity and choice as important, over-arching themes in the right to development.[43]
> […]
> The African Commission also states that the Respondent State bears the burden for creating conditions favourable to a people's development.[44]

The African Court has also weighed in on the justiciability of the right to development. In the *African Commission on Human and Peoples Rights v Republic of Kenya* case,[45] the Court held that:

> In the instant case, the Court recalls that the Ogieks have been continuously evicted from the Mau Forest by the Respondent, without being effectively consulted. The evictions have adversely impacted their economic, social, and cultural development. They have also not been actively involved in developing and determining health, housing, and other economic and social programmes affecting them. The Court therefore holds that the Respondent violated Article 22 of the Charter.[46]

The Arab human rights monitoring mechanisms are yet to interpret Article 37 of the Arab Charter. This is because the monitoring mechanisms, including the

42 *Centre for Minority Rights Development (Kenya) and Another v Republic of Kenya* ACHPR Comm No 276/03, 25 November 2009.

43 Ibid at Para 277.

44 Ibid at Para 298.

45 *African Commission on Human and Peoples Rights v Republic of Kenya* ACtPHR Application No 006/2012, 26 May 2017.

46 Ibid at Paras 210 and 211.

Arab Court on Human Rights are not fully operational.[47] Judgments[48] from numerous courts in national jurisdictions have also strengthened the justiciability of the right to development.[49] Despite these debates about the justiciability of the right to development, a considerable number of soft law instruments adopted by the United Nations General Assembly and other international bodies point to the undeniability of the right to development as a "[…] universal and inalienable right and an integral part of fundamental human rights".[50] These soft law instruments include the Cairo Declaration of the International Conference on Population and Development,[51] the Rio Declaration on Environment and Development,[52] and the Copenhagen Declaration of Social Development.[53] These soft-law instruments are proof that several UN member states are concerned about the glaring global economic inequalities that continue to be perpetuated by colonial powers through global economic institutions including the IMF and the World Bank as mentioned earlier.[54] Despite the perceived non-justiciability of the right to development, it has been argued that the right has attained *jus cogens* status and therefore, is part of customary international law and, consequently justiciable.[55]

---

47 Magliveras, Konstantinos and Naldi, Gino (2016) The Arab Court of Human Rights: A Study in Impotence. *Revue Québécoise de Droit International* 29(2): 147–172.

48 *Soobramoney v Minister of Health (KwaZulu-Natal)* Case No CCT32/97 1997 (12) BCLR 1696; Sentencia C-175/09, Colombia: Corte Constitucional, 18 March 2009; *Minister of Health v Treatment Action Campaign*, Case No CCT 8/02 2002 (10) BCLR 1033; *Republic of South Africa v. Grootboom*, Case No CCT 11/00 2000 (11) BCLR 1169.

49 The Courts in South Africa and Colombia have stated that the right to development is enforceable in their legal systems.

50 UN General Assembly, Vienna Declaration and Programme of Action A/CONF.157/2, adopted at the World Conference on Human Rights in Vienna, Austria, 14–25 June 1993, Para 1(10); see also UN General Assembly Resolution A/RES/64/172 of 18 December 2009; UN General Assembly Resolution A/RES/73/166 of 17 December 2018.

51 United Nations Population Fund, Cairo Declaration on Population and Development, adopted in Cairo, Egypt on 3–4 September 1994. Available at: https://www.unfpa.org/resources/cairo-declaration-population-development (consulted 20 December 2024); Brown, Win and Hardee, Karin (2024). Can the International Conference on Population and Development Programme of Action and Cairo Consensus Normalize the Discourse on Population? *Global Health: Science and Practice* 12(5): 1–14.

52 Rio Declaration on Environment and Development—Report of the United Nations Conference on Environment and Development A/CONF.151/26 (Vol. I) adopted at Rio de Janeiro, Brazil, 3–14 June 1992.

53 Copenhagen Declaration on Social Development A/CONF.166/9 Chapter I, Annex I—UN Documents adopted at the World Summit for Social Development in Copenhagen, Denmark, 14 March 1995.

54 Tashome, supra note 32.

55 Masum, Ahmad (2013) The Right to Development and its Corresponding Obligations on Developing Countries. *Journal of International Studies* 9: 33–45.

3.1 *Human Rights-Based Approach to Development*

There was initial resistance towards the interlinkage of human rights and development, given the ideological differences between the Global North and Global South.[56] Recent scholarship has increasingly warmed up to the idea that development and human rights are interlinked.[57] Consequently, the right to development and the human rights-based approach to development are concepts that arise out of this mutuality. The concept of a human rights-based approach to development envisages that human beings should be at the centre of any development policies and activities.[58] As a result, any development initiatives should have a human rights lens. The Charter of the United Nations (UN Charter) provides for the interdependence between human rights and development in Article 55, which states as follows:

> With a view to the creation of conditions of stability and well-being which are necessary for peaceful and friendly relations among nations based on respect for the principle of equal rights and self-determination of peoples, the United Nations shall promote: 1. higher standards of living, full employment, and conditions of economic and social progress and development; 2. solutions of international economic, social, health, and related problems; and international cultural and educational cooperation; and 3. universal respect for, and observance of, human rights and fundamental freedoms for all without distinction as to race, sex, language, or religion.

The human rights-based approach to development envisages that the values of public participation, transparency, access to information, and non-discrimination will be applied. The right to development equally promotes these principles. Public participation is a key value of the right to development. Meaningful public participation means that participation would have to influence the outcomes of decision-making. Without evidence of the people's influence on decisions taken, it would be difficult to prove that there was public participation in the decisions taken. Whatever the decision(s) taken, the decisions must, as a consequence, enable "[…] equality of opportunity for

---

56 Tashome, supra note 32.

57 Uvin, supra note 35, 597.

58 Vandenhole, W. and Gready, P. (2018) Failures and Successes of Human Rights-Based Approaches to Development: Towards a Change Perspective. In: Mustaniemi-Laakso, M. and Sano, H.O. (eds) *Human Rights-Based Change: The Institutionalisation of Economic and Social Rights*. London: Routledge, 15–54.

all in their access to basic resources, education, health services, food, housing, employment and the fair distribution of income".[59] The concept of equitable distribution of the "fruits" of development to all humanity including vulnerable groups has an association with social justice.[60] The concept of social justice envisages a world where everyone has access to equal political, social, and economic goods and services.[61] Social justice therefore involves equality and distributive justice. The discussion on equality means that no person will be discriminated against in the distribution of the benefits of development.[62] Equal access includes the opportunities available to everyone in a just world. Consequently, the benefits of development should be enjoyed by all citizens of the world regardless of their geographical location. These values of equal access to economic opportunities for all global citizens have been enshrined in United Nations instruments. Some of these values as discussed in the next section.

3.2 *Democratic Governance of Bretton Woods Institutions and the Self-Determination of Nations*

The Western ideology that informs the policies that govern the Bretton Woods Institutions on the management of the global economy violates the principle of sovereign equality among nations provided for by the United Nations Charter.[63] Article 2(1) of the United Nations Charter aims "To develop friendly relations among nations based on respect for the principle of equal rights and self-determination of peoples, and to take other appropriate measures to strengthen universal peace". The provision envisages that states have the sovereign right to choose economic policies that may facilitate a quicker realisation of development. This provision does not envisage a situation where institutions established based on Western capitalist ideologies should dictate what economic policies a state should implement. Article 2(2) of the UN Charter fortifies the autonomy of states' economic decision-making by prescribing the commitment "To achieve international cooperation in solving international problems of an economic, social, cultural, or humanitarian character, and

59 See the Declaration on the Right to Development Resolution A/RES/41/128 adopted by UN General Assembly on 4 December 1986, Art 8.

60 Rawls, John (1971) *A Theory of Justice*. Harvard: Harvard University Press, 302.

61 Everingham, Christine (2018) *Social Justice and the Politics of Community*. London: Routledge.

62 Rawls, supra note 60, 302.

63 Linarelli, John; Salomon, Margot, and Sornarajah, Muthucumaraswamy (2018) *The Misery of International Law: Confrontations with Injustice in the Global Economy*. Oxford: Oxford University Press.

in promoting and encouraging respect for human rights and for fundamental freedoms for all without distinction as to race, sex, language, or religion". The provision buttresses Article 2(1) of the UN Charter about the autonomy of states regarding the economic policies they should adopt and pursue to enable economic development. The cited provisions of the UN Charter reinforce the values of sovereign equality of states and self-determination, which are key concepts that support claims for an equal global economic order.

4 Sustainable Development

The preambular paragraphs of the 2030 Agenda for Sustainable Development state that it is "[…] a plan of action for people, planet and prosperity […] recognize that eradicating poverty in all its forms and dimensions, including extreme poverty, which is the greatest global challenge and an indispensable requirement for sustainable development".[64] The 2030 Agenda calls on "all countries and all stakeholders, acting in collaborative partnership" to ensure the realisation of all the goals of the plan.[65] The preambular paragraphs further provide that "[…] all countries and all stakeholders, acting in collaborative partnership, […] are resolved to free the human race from the tyranny of poverty and want and to heal and secure our planet".[66] Several of the goals of the 2030 Agenda obligate states and other stakeholders, including the IMF and the World Bank to "end poverty in all its forms everywhere".[67] The 2030 Agenda states in addition that, it will "Promote sustained, inclusive, and equitable quality education, economic growth and full and productive work for all",[68] as well as "reduce inequality within and among countries".[69] Goal 16 of the 2030 Agenda aspires to "Promote peaceful and inclusive societies for sustainable development, provide access to justice for all, and build effective, accountable and inclusive institutions at all levels".[70] Relatedly, the 2030 Agenda promises to "Strengthen the means of implementation and revitalize the global partnership for sustainable development".[71] These Goals reinforce and buttress

64 Transforming Our World: The 2030 Agenda for Sustainable Development Resolution A/RES/70/1 adopted by the United Nations General Assembly on 27 September 2015 (Sustainable Development Goals Framework), Preamble Para 1.

65 Ibid.

66 Ibid.

67 Ibid at Goal 1.

68 Ibid at Goal 8.

69 Ibid at Goal 10.

70 Ibid at Goal 16.

71 Ibid at Goal 16.

the concept of equitable development for all persons regardless of their geographical location.

4.1 *States' Duty to Co-operate*

One of the major challenges that enables and sustains the current global economic order is the unfair economic, financial, and trading terms between states in the Global North and the Global South. These unfair terms include; the over-representation of Western interests on global economic institutions, international payment systems pegged to Western currencies, and protectionist trade policies, among others.[72] Building on the values of previous international instruments in dealing with these economic inequalities, the draft Covenant on the Right to Development (draft Covenant) provides for the "duty to cooperate".[73] This duty to cooperate imposed on states to enable equitable development has continually been opposed by the Global North on the premise that it interferes with their capitalist ideologies.[74] Several bilateral and multilateral instruments signed by countries of the Global South continually urge economically powerful states of the Global North to accelerate international cooperation to deal with this issue.[75] This is to solve the glaring global economic inequalities that sustain subhuman living conditions for people in the Global South. Consequently, states in the Global South embrace the right to development as a means to deal with the injustices.[76]

4.2 *Instruments Recognising the Duty to Cooperate*

As indicated earlier, numerous soft and hard law instruments recognise states' duty to cooperate.[77] These instruments include the UN Charter and the

72 Benería, Lourdes; Berik, Günseli, and Floro, Maria (2015) *Gender, Development and Globalization: Economics as if all People Mattered.* New York/London: Routledge.

73 Draft International Covenant on the Right to Development—Report by the Chair-Rapporteur of the Working Group on the Right to Development, Zamir Akram (Pakistan) Human Rights Council A/HRC/54/50 54th Session, 6 October 2023, Art 13.

74 Tashome, supra note 32.

75 See for example, Declaration on the Right to Development, supra note 59; Declaration on the New International Economic Order, supra note 4; Charter of Economic Rights and Duties of States, UN General Assembly Resolution A/RES/39/163 3281 (XXIX) of 12 December 1974.

76 Ngang, C.C.; Kamga, S.D. and Gumede, V. (2018) Introduction: The Right to Development in Broad Perspectives. In: Ngang, C.C.; Kamga, S.D. and Gumede, V. (eds) *Perspectives on the Right to Development.* Pretoria: University of Pretoria Law Press, 2.

77 Cairo Declaration, supra note 51; Rio Declaration, supra note 52; Copenhagen Declaration, supra note 53; Charter of the United Nations and Statute of the International Court of Justice, adopted in San Francisco, United States of America on 26 June 1945; International Covenant on Civil and Political Rights adopted by the UN General Assembly,

Universal Declaration of Human Rights (UDHR), some of whose provisions have attained *jus cogens* status under international law.[78] Article 1(3) of the UN Charter provides as follows, "To achieve international cooperation in solving international problems of an economic, social, cultural, or humanitarian character, and in promoting and encouraging respect for human rights and for fundamental freedoms for all without distinction as to race, sex, language, or religion."[79] It is important to emphasise that Article 1(3) implores UN member states to cooperate in resolving international problems, which entails restructuring the global economic order. Additionally, Article 22 of the UDHR provides that

> Everyone, as a member of society, has the right to social security and is entitled to realization, through national effort and international cooperation and in accordance with the organization and resources of each State, of the economic, social, and cultural rights indispensable for his dignity and the free development of his personality.

The provision further implores states through national and international cooperation to ensure the economic dignity of every human being regardless of their geographical residence. The Article 22 provision of the UDHR envisages that states must individually and in cooperation with other states, ensure the full realisation of an equitable global economic order. One of the core duties to cooperate is mitigating global economic inequalities. It is interesting that the draft Covenant does not expressly provide for this major challenge to global development. The duty to cooperate is one of the provisions of the draft Covenant likely to enlist contestations between the Global North and the Global South due to the ideological differences over this issue.

5 Undemocratic Governance at the IMF and the World Bank—an Impediment to Development in the Global South

As opposed to several international institutions, such as the United Nations General Assembly where each state is entitled to one vote, the IMF and World

---

Resolution 2200A (XXI) of 16 December 1966, 993 UNTS 3 UN Doc A/6316 (1966) among others.

78 Özdan, S. (2022) Human Rights Recognised as Jus Cogens. In: Özdan, S. (ed) *The Human Rights Challenge to Immunity in International Law*. Cham: Springer International Publishing, 47–78.

79 See also UN Charter, supra note 77, Art 55.

Bank have different criteria for decision-making. This criterion is based on either a state's capital subscriptions to the World Bank or a quota system based on capital contributions to the IMF.[80]

5.1 *International Monetary Fund*

The constitutive instrument of the IMF provides rights and duties based on a weighted system of quotas. These quotas determine the capital contributions of a state to the IMF. Article XII (5) of the Articles of Agreement of the IMF prescribes as follows:

> The total votes of each member shall be equal to the sum of its basic votes and its quota-based votes. The basic votes of each member shall be the number of votes that results from the equal distribution among all [...] The quota-based votes of each member shall be the number of votes that results from the allocation of one vote for each part of its quota, equivalent to one hundred thousand special drawing rights. Whenever voting is required under Article V, Section 4 or 5, each member shall have the number of votes to which it is entitled under (*a*) above adjusted by the addition of one vote for the equivalent of each four hundred thousand special drawing rights of net sales of its currency from the general resources of the Fund up to the date when the vote is taken, or by the subtraction of one vote for the equivalent of each four hundred thousand special drawing rights of its net purchases under Article V, Section 3(*b*) and (*f*) up to the date when the vote is taken, provided that neither net purchases nor net sales shall be deemed at any time to exceed an amount equal to the quota of the member involved. Except as otherwise specifically provided, all decisions of the Fund shall be made by a majority of the votes cast.[81] (emphasis mine).

Member states with the five largest capital contributions appoint the board of directors.[82] The countries with the biggest capital contributions make the decisions that govern the IMF. Except for Japan, the other countries are former colonial powers.[83] The supreme decision-making organ of the IMF is the Board of Directors. Each member of the IMF has a right to appoint a representative to the IMF Board of Directors. The Board of Governors is assisted by the Executive

80 Orakhelashvili, supra note 13.
81 Articles of Agreement of the IMF, supra note 10, Art XII(5)(a)(b)(c).
82 Orakhelashvili, supra note 13.
83 The other countries are the United Kingdom, Germany, France, and the United States of America.

Board, which oversees the actual decision-making of the IMF. The members with the largest quotas have the onus of appointing directors to the Executive Board. The Executive Board appoints and disappoints the Managing Director of the Fund.[84] Almost all the Managing Directors of the IMF have been citizens of Western countries, with the largest quotas at the IMF.[85] All past and present Managing Director(s) of IMF have been and are citizens of European countries. A significant percentage of the Deputy Managing Directors of the IMF since it was established in 1944, have been citizens of the United States of America.[86] The Managing Director can hire and dismiss all IMF staff.[87] It is important to note that the IMF Managing Director, who is usually a citizen of a former colonial power, has significant control over the operations of the Bank. Attempts have been made to open up the leadership of the IMF.[88] In the past two decades, proposed candidates for the position of Managing Director of the IMF who are not European citizens have been shunned.[89] There has been significant advocacy to allow applications for the position of the Managing Director of the IMF to be open to all persons of member countries regardless of their citizenship, considering that the IMF passes off as a global economic institution.[90] The IMF Executive Board agreed to this position a decade ago, but there have been challenges with political buy-in of the idea.[91]

5.2 *The World Bank*

The governance structure of the World Bank is similar to that of the IMF. The World Bank member states with the largest share of financial contributions have more voting powers and influence over governance of the Bank. Article V(5)(b) of the Bank's Articles of Agreement provides as follows:

> *The voting power of each member shall be equal to the sum of its basic votes and share votes.* (i) The basic votes of each member shall be the number of votes that result from the equal distribution among all members of

84 Articles of Agreement of the IMF, supra note 10, Article XII (4)(a).

85 This is the excerpt from the current Managing Director, Kristalina Georgieva who is Bulgarian. She was the former Chief Executive Officer of the World Bank.

86 Walyemera, Daniel Masumba (2014) Post Washington Consensus: Have the 2010 Governance Reforms at the World Bank and IMF Addressed the Concerns of the Developing World? *Makerere Law Journal* 118.

87 Articles of Agreement of the IMF, supra note 10, Art XII(4)(b).

88 Walyemera, supra note 86, 118.

89 Ibid.

90 Walyemera, supra note 86.

91 Ibid at 119.

> 5.55 percent of the aggregate sum of the voting power of all the members, provided that there shall be no fractional basic votes. *The share votes of each member shall be the number of votes that results from the allocation of one vote for each share of stock held.* Except as otherwise specifically provided, all matters before the Bank shall be decided by a majority of the votes cast (emphasis added).

Article V of the Articles of Agreement provides for the governance structure of the Bank comprising a Board of Governors and the Executive Directors who select the President of the Bank. The Executive Directors can dismiss the President of the Bank when they deem it necessary.[92] The President oversees the day-to-day management of the Bank and has the power to appoint and dismiss Bank staff.[93] The United States of America which has the largest capital contribution to the World Bank, has always appointed a citizen of the USA as President of the Bank.[94]

Therefore, the decision-making within the IMF and the World Bank fosters unequal relations between states based on whether they are wealthy and can make significant capital contributions to the Bretton Woods Institutions. These undemocratic tendencies also extend to the hiring of senior staff within the institutions.[95] The failure of equal decision-making and participation in these global economic institutions has been cited by developing countries as one of the major reasons for unequal global development.[96] The unequal power in the governance of the IMF and the World Bank is premised on the capitalist theory of comparative advantage, which applies the market theory to international transactions.[97] Many countries that follow communist ideologies rejected membership in the IMF and the World Bank on the premise that the institutions promote capitalist ideologies that are exploitative of the masses.[98] In this regard, Article 13(4)(d) of the draft Covenant on the Right to Development states as follows:

---

92 Articles of Agreement of the World Bank, supra note 12, Art VI(5)(a).

93 Ibid.

94 Congressional Research Service (2023) Selecting the World Bank President. Available at: https://sgp.fas.org/crs/row/R42463.pdf (consulted 27 September 2024).

95 Articles of Agreement of the World Bank, supra note 12, Art VI(5)(a).

96 Egypt's submission in follow-up to HRC Resolution 15/25 "The Right to Development" on behalf of the Non-Aligned Movement (NAM).

97 Birdsall, N. (2004) Why it Matters Who Runs the IMF and the World Bank. In: Kosack, S.; Ranis, G., and Vreeland, J. (eds) *Globalization and the Nation State*. London: Routledge, 449–471.

98 Tashome, supra note 32.

> States Parties reaffirm and shall implement their duty to cooperate with each other, through joint and separate action, [...] States Parties recognize their duty to cooperate to create a social and international order conducive to the realization of the right to development by, inter alia: Ensuring enhanced representation and voice for developing countries, including least developed countries, in decision-making in all international economic and financial institutions, in order to deliver more effective, credible, accountable and legitimate institutions.

This provision explicitly indicates that the duty to cooperate is a key facility in the realisation of the right to development. It mirrors the values of the Sustainable Development Goals (SDGs) envisaged to be achieved by 2030.[99] These values include enabling an equitable, non-discriminatory, and universal multilateral trading system to prevent the effects of an unfair global economic structure. This unfair global economic order favours the trading interests of developed countries. Consequently, all states have a duty to cooperate to enable a fair global trading system that recognises the effects that the current multilateral trading system has occasioned on developing countries. The duty to cooperate includes facilitating programmes and activities that are intended to remedy the development challenges faced by developing countries. The draft Covenant provides for equitable participation of developing countries in global financial markets and institutions. Article 13(4)(c) thereof provides that "States Parties recognize their duty to cooperate to create a social and international order conducive to the realization of the right to development by, inter alia: *Improving the regulation and monitoring of global financial markets and institutions, and strengthening the implementation of such regulations*" (emphasis mine).

Article 13(4)(d) of the draft Covenant additionally envisages the effective participation of developing countries in the decision-making at these international financial institutions, which will enhance their credibility, legitimacy, and accountability. The international financial institutions referred to in Article 13(4)(c), include the IMF and the World Bank. The voting systems at these institutions have from inception, been unfair to developing countries that bear the brunt of the undemocratic decision-making.[100] As mentioned earlier, the voting system is based on the financial muscle of states and their ability to subscribe to share capital with financial institutions. The system of governance alienates developing countries and reinforces and sustains

99 Transforming Our World, supra note 64.
100 Walyemera, supra note 86.

colonial economic relationships between the Global North and the Global South. The undemocratic governance practices at the IMF and the World Bank relate to the economic strength of developed countries to make decisions that often, adversely affect countries of the Global South. The phenomenon perpetuates a superiority complex that enables developed countries within the Bretton Woods Institutions to dictate to developing countries how they should approach development.[101]

Former European colonisers have consistently opposed an equal global economic order. Consequently, there are doubts that these influential Western states would support any significant reform in these Bretton Woods Institutions to enable equal participation and decision-making by all states. Even when equal decision-making and participation are achieved at the IMF and World Bank, the international economic order would require restructuring because other global actors like the WTO have a key role to play in enabling an equal global economic order. Besides the WTO, other wealthy countries would have to buy into this quest for an equal economic and financial world structure. Overall, the duty to cooperate prescribed in the draft Covenant also requires wealthy states to facilitate the provision of financial and development assistance to developing states. Article 13(4)(e) states as follows:

> States Parties reaffirm and shall implement their duty to cooperate with each other, through joint and separate action, in order to: To mobilize appropriate technical, technological, financial, infrastructural and other necessary resources to enable States Parties, particularly in developing or least developed countries, to fulfil their obligations under the present Convention.

The provision not only vouches for development aid but also the transfer of technical skills and resources to the Global South. As indicated earlier, incorporating democratic governance at the IMF and the World Bank may not necessarily culminate in an equal international financial, trading, and economic order without the efforts of other key global economic players. Consequently, the duty to cooperate provides a normative global standard to aspire to by all key international financial, trade, and economic stakeholders to enable an equal global economic order.

101 Tashome, supra note 32.

5.3 *Obligations of International Organisations*

Article 2(b) of the International Law Commission (ILC) draft Articles on the Responsibility of International Organisations, 2011 defines an international organisation as "[…] an organization established by a treaty or other instrument governed by international law and possessing its own international legal personality. International organizations may include as members, in addition to States, other entities". This definition encompasses the IMF and the World Bank among international organisations that have international obligations. The draft Covenant on the Right to Development requires international organisations not to engage in activities that hinder the right to development.[102] Article 9 of the Draft Covenant provides that

> Without prejudice to the general duty contained in Article 7, States Parties agree that international organizations also have the obligation to refrain from conduct that aids, assists, directs, controls, or coerces, with knowledge of the circumstances of the act, a State or another international organization to breach any obligation that the State or the latter organization may have with regard to the right to development.[103]

Article 7 of the draft Covenant urges everyone to respect the right to development. State parties must abide by these international obligations and ensure that every natural and juristic person within their borders refrains from engaging in acts that violate the right to development. Juristic persons include international organisations like the IMF and the World Bank. There are numerous ways in which an international organisation may engage in an internationally wrongful act, including through aiding, assisting, directing, controlling, or coercing a state or another international organisation to commit such a wrongful act.[104]

There are still reservations about whether international organisations have an obligation to observe human rights. However, under customary international law, a case may be made for this legal position.[105] Consequently, an

---

102 Draft Covenant on the Right to Development, supra note 73, Art 9.

103 See Draft Articles on the Responsibility of International Organisations, adopted by the International Law Commission at its 63rd Session in 2011, Yearbook of the International Law Commission, 2011, vol. II, Part Two, Arts 14, 15, 16, 17, and 18. The draft articles inspired theses provision in the Draft Convention.

104 Ibid at Arts 14, 15, 16, 17, and 18.

105 Sarfaty, Garlit (2009) Why Culture Matters in International Institutions: The Marginality of Human Rights at the World Bank. *American Journal of International Law* 103: 657; Verdirame, Guglielmo (2011) *The UN and Human Rights: Who Guards the Guardians?* Cambridge: Cambridge University Press, 55.

argument can be made requiring the IMF and the World Bank to observe human rights in general and the right to development in particular, in the conduct of their business. In this regard, the right to development can be achieved with the effective participation of states in the Global South in the governance of the Bretton Woods institutions.

6 Can Democratic Governance at the IMF and World Bank Enable Equitable Development in the Global South?

The IMF and the World Bank have undergone several reforms since they were founded in 1944. The reforms, including the so-called "Voice Reforms" at the World Bank, have however, not resulted in any significant democratic governance changes at these institutions. The reforms at the World Bank were intended to give more voting powers to developing countries on the Bank's Board of Governors. Under the theme "New World, New World Bank", the Bank launched the most significant reforms since its establishment in 1944.[106] The "Voice Reforms" were inspired by the need for equal power between developing, transitional, and developed countries. This included the restructuring of the economic weight of member states to their voting shares. The other Bank reforms also included guarding against any loss of shares by developing member states. Relatedly, the IMF also embarked on reforms.[107] The IMF reforms included ensuring that fast-growing countries have more power over decision-making within the organisation. This inevitably translates into European countries having less power within the Executive Board of the IMF. These reforms, however, did not achieve much. Wealthy countries in the Global North still retain significant power in shaping the IMF and the World Bank's policies and operations.

7 Recommendations

Adoption of the International Covenant on the Right to Development will ensure that equitable development can be realised through the member states duty to cooperate, which is an international obligation that can enable democratic governance at the IMF and the World Bank. Other concepts provided for in the draft Convention on the Right to Development that can facilitate equitable development include sustainable development. The three pillars

106 Walyemera, supra note 86.
107 Ibid.

of sustainable development—economic, social, and environmental—will provide a normative standard in facilitating equitable development among countries in the Global North and those in the Global South. Another key normative standard prescribed in the draft Covenant on the Right to Development to enable equitable development is the obligation of international organisations to respect the right to development. The establishment of a monitoring mechanism under the Covenant on the Right to Development will enable the monitoring of states and international organisations to comply with the duty to cooperate enshrined in the Covenant. Incorporating such democratic governance practices into the operations of the Bretton Woods establishments will facilitate equitable development in the Global South and consequently, narrow the income inequalities between these two global regions.

Ratification of the Covenant on the Right to Development when it is eventually adopted by the UN General Assembly might not be enough to enable democratic governance within the IMF and the World Bank. It will simply reinforce the normative framework through which the Bretton Woods institutions can be held to greater accountability and enjoined to institute democratic governance in their operations. Accordingly, relevant reforms that need to be instituted include: First, the recruitment of senior management staff which should be made open to citizens from all member countries beyond the USA and European countries. Secondly, the key decision-making organs of both the IMF and the World Bank must have representation of all member countries in some significant capacity. Thirdly, the principle that equates vote share to voting power should be reformed to enable meaningful participation of developing member countries from the Global South in the affairs of the Bretton Woods institutions. The democratic governance reforms within the IMF and the World Bank will enable equitable development because the economic policies of these global economic institutions have a significant effect on standards of living for communities in the Global South.

8 Conclusion

The governance structures of the IMF and the World Bank do not meet the threshold of the principles of democratic governance.[108] Considering the Bretton Woods establishments' emphasis on good governance practices by its member states, it would be prudent for these global economic institutions to implement good governance practices internally for the sake of their

108 Strand, Jonathan and Retzl, Kenneth (2016) Did Recent Voice Reforms Improve Good Governance within the World Bank? *Development and Change* 47(3): 437.

legitimacy globally. The IMF and the World Bank have indicated in several official documents that transparent and participatory policies enable good governance.[109] One of the ways of enabling a culture of democracy in these powerful global economic institutions is by opening the staffing, representation, and decision-making to all member countries. This will enhance the legitimacy of the global financial institutions, not only in the Global South but internationally. Additionally, the historical ideological differences between the Global North and the Global South over the duty to cooperate will likely result in rigorous debates before the draft Covenant is adopted as a binding international instrument on the right to development.

References

Abdul, Latif Alhassan (2023) Development Finance: A Conceptual Definition. *Development Financing Agenda* 8(5): 16–18.

African Charter on Human and Peoples' Rights adopted in Nairobi, Kenya on 27 June 1981 OAU Doc CAB/LEG/67/3 Rev.5 (1981).

African Commission on Human and Peoples Rights v Republic of Kenya ACtPHR Application No 006/2012, 26 May 2017.

Andersson, M. (2017) Race: A Contested and Traveling Concept. In: Leiulfsrud, H. and Sohlberg, P. (eds) *Concepts in Action: Conceptual Constructivism*. Leiden: Brill, 284–301.

Arab Charter on Human Rights adopted in Cairo, Egypt on 15 September 1994.

Articles of Agreement of the International Monetary Fund Adopted at the United Nations Monetary and Financial Conference, Bretton Woods, New Hampshire, on 22 July 1944; entered into force on 27 December 1945.

Benería, Lourdes; Berik, Günseli, and Floro, Maria (2015) *Gender, Development and Globalization: Economics as if all People Mattered*. New York/London: Routledge.

Bernstein, E.M. (2015) The Making and Remaking of the Bretton Woods Institutions. In: Kirschner, O. (ed) *The Bretton Woods-GATT System: Retrospect and Prospects after Fifty Years*. New York: Routledge, 89–98.

Birdsall, N. (2004) Why it Matters Who Runs the IMF and the World Bank. In: Kosack, S.; Ranis, G., and Vreeland, J. (eds) *Globalization and the Nation State*. London: Routledge, 449–471.

Brown, Win and Hardee, Karin (2024). Can the International Conference on Population and Development Programme of Action and Cairo Consensus Normalize the Discourse on Population? *Global Health: Science and Practice* 12(5): 1–14.

109 Ibid.

Cairo Declaration of the International Conference on Population and Development.

Centre for Minority Rights Development (Kenya) and Another v Republic of Kenya ACHPR Comm No 276/03, 25 November 2009.

Charter of Economic Rights and Duties of States, UN General Assembly Resolution A/RES/39/163 3281 (XXIX) of 12 December 1974.

Charter of the United Nations and Statute of the International Court of Justice, adopted in San Francisco, United States of America on 26 June 1945.

Congressional Research Service (2023) Selecting the World Bank President. Available at: https://sgp.fas.org/crs/row/R42463.pdf (consulted 27 September 2024).

Copenhagen Declaration on Social Development A/CONF.166/9 Chapter I, Annex I—UN Documents adopted at the World Summit for Social Development in Copenhagen, Denmark, 14 March 1995.

Declaration on the Establishment of a New International Economic Order, Gen Ass Resolution A/RES/S-6/3201, adopted on 1 May 1974.

Declaration on the Right to Development Resolution A/RES/41/128 adopted by UN General Assembly on 4 December 1986.

Draft Articles on the Responsibility of International Organisations, adopted by the International Law Commission at its 63rd Session in 2011, Yearbook of the International Law Commission, 2011, vol. II, Part Two.

Draft International Covenant on the Right to Development—Report by the Chair-Rapporteur of the Working Group on the Right to Development, Zamir Akram (Pakistan) Human Rights Council A/HRC/54/50 54th Session, 6 October 2023.

Everingham, Christine (2018) *Social Justice and the Politics of Community*. London: Routledge.

Fukuda-Parr, Sakiko (2012) The Right to Development: Reframing a New Discourse for the Twenty-First Century. *Human Rights and the Global Economy* 79(4): 839–864.

Fukuyama, Francis (2013) What is Governance? *Governance* 26(3): 347–368.

Gardner, James A. (2013) The Myth of State Autonomy: Federalism, Political Parties, and the National Colonization of State Politics. *Journal of Law and Politics* 29: 1–68.

Gilman, Nils (2015) The New International Economic Order: A Reintroduction. *Humanity: An International Journal of Human Rights, Humanitarianism, and Development* 6(1): 1–16.

Gyong, J.E. (2014) Good Governance and Accountability in a Democracy. *European Scientific Journal* 7(26): 71–89.

Herbst, Jeffrey (2019) Privatization in Africa. *The Political Economy of Public Sector Reform and Privatization*.

Ibhawoh, Bonny (2011) The Right to Development: The Politics and Polemics of Power and Resistance. *Human Rights Quarterly* 33(1): 76–104.

International Bank for Reconstruction and Development (The World Bank) Articles of Agreement drawn up at the United Nations Monetary and Financial

Conference, at Bretton Woods, New Hampshire, 1–22 July 1944; became effective on 27 December 1945 (As amended effective 27 June 2012).

International Covenant on Civil and Political Rights adopted by the UN General Assembly, Resolution 2200A (XXI) of 16 December 1966, 993 UNTS 3 UN Doc A/6316 (1966).

International Covenant on Economic, Social and Cultural Rights adopted by the UN General Assembly, Resolution 2200A (XXI) of 16 December 1966, 999 UNTS 171 UN Doc A/6316 (1966).

Kempe, Ronald Hope (ed) (2019) *Structural Adjustment, Reconstruction, and Development in Africa*. London: Routledge.

Khan, K.K. (2002) Good Governance: Concept and the Case of Bangladesh. In: Chowdhury, M.H. (ed) *Thirty Years of Bangladesh Politics: Essays in Memory of Dr Mahfuzul Huq*. Dhaka: University Press Limited, 63–76.

Korten, D. (2014) The Failure of Bretton Woods. In: Goldsmith, E. and Mander, J. (eds) *The Case Against the Global Economy: And for a Turn towards Localisation*. London: Routledge, 35–44.

Kowalski, A.M. (2021) Global South-Global North Differences. In: Filho, W.L. et al (eds) *No Poverty*. Cham: Springer International Publishing, 389–400.

Kwaghe, Zara Emmanuel and Odeh, Okpale Alfred (2020) A History of Privatisation: The Global Perspective. *International Journal of Humanitatis Theoreticus* 3(1): 141–152.

Linarelli, John; Salomon, Margot, and Sornarajah, Muthucumaraswamy (2018) *The Misery of International Law: Confrontations with Injustice in the Global Economy*. Oxford: Oxford University Press.

Magliveras, Konstantinos and Naldi, Gino (2016) The Arab Court of Human Rights: A Study in Impotence. *Revue Québécoise de Droit International* 29(2): 147–172.

Masum, Ahmad (2013) The Right to Development and its Corresponding Obligations on Developing Countries. *Journal of International Studies* 9: 33–45.

Mbaku, J.M. (2018) A Balance Sheet of Structural Adjustment in Africa: Towards a Sustainable Development Agenda. In: Mbaku, J.M. (ed) *Preparing Africa for the Twenty-First Century: Strategies for Peaceful Coexistence and Sustainable Development*. London: Routledge, 119–149.

Milanovic, Branko (2012) Global Inequality: From Class to Location, from Proletarians to Migrants. *Global Policy* 3(2): 125–134.

Minister of Health v Treatment Action Campaign, Case No CCT 8/02 2002 (10) BCLR 1033.

Ngang, C.C.; Kamga, S.D. and Gumede, V. (2018) Introduction: The Right to Development in Broad Perspectives. In: Ngang, C.C.; Kamga, S.D. and Gumede, V. (eds) *Perspectives on the Right to Development*. Pretoria: University of Pretoria Law Press.

Ngang, Carol Chi (2021) *The Right to Development in Africa*. Leiden/Boston: BRILL.

Orakhelashvili, Alexander (2022) *Akehurst's Modern Introduction to International Law*. London: Routledge.

Özdan, S. (2022) Human Rights Recognised as Jus Cogens. In: Özdan, S. (ed) *The Human Rights Challenge to Immunity in International Law*. Cham: Springer International Publishing, 47–78.

Rawls, John (1971) *A Theory of Justice*. Harvard: Harvard University Press.

Reinsberg, Bernhard et al (2019) The World System and the Hollowing out of State Capacity: How Structural Adjustment Programs Affect Bureaucratic Quality in Developing Countries. *American Journal of Sociology* 124(4): 1222–1257.

Reinsberg, Bernhard et al (2020) Bad Governance: How Privatization Increases Corruption in the Developing World. *Regulation and Governance* 14(4): 698–717.

Republic of South Africa v Grootboom, Case No CCT 11/00 2000 (11) BCLR 1169.

Rio Declaration on Environment and Development—Report of the United Nations Conference on Environment and Development A/CONF.151/26 (Vol. I) adopted at Rio de Janeiro, Brazil, 3–14 June 1992.

Salomon, Margot (2013) From NIEO to Now and the Unfinishable Story of Economic Justice. *International and Comparative Law Quarterly* 62(1): 31–54.

Sarfaty, Garlit (2009) Why Culture Matters in International Institutions: The Marginality of Human Rights at the World Bank. *American Journal of International Law* 103: 647–683.

Sen, A. (2010) Human Rights and Development. In: Andreassen, B., and Marks, S. (eds) *Development as a Human Right: Legal, Political and Economic Dimensions*, 2nd Edn, Antwerp: Intersentia.

Sengupta, Arjun (2000) Realizing the Right to Development. *Development and Change*, 31(3): 553–578.

Sentencia C-175/09, Colombia: Corte Constitucional, 18 March 2009.

Soobramoney v Minister of Health (KwaZulu-Natal) Case No CCT32/97 1997 (12) BCLR 1696.

Strand, Jonathan and Retzl, Kenneth (2016) Did Recent Voice Reforms Improve Good Governance within the World Bank? *Development and Change* 47(3): 415–445.

Teshome, Roman Girma (2022) The Draft Convention on the Right to Development: A New Dawn to the Recognition of the Right to Development as a Human Right? *Human Rights Law Review* 22(2): 1–24.

Transforming Our World: The 2030 Agenda for Sustainable Development Resolution A/RES/70/1 adopted by the United Nations General Assembly on 27 September 2015 (Sustainable Development Goals Framework).

Treuhart, Sara (2016) Equitable Development: The Path to All in Pittsburgh. *Policylink*. Available at: https://www.policylink.org/sites/default/files/summary_pittsburgh_FINAL_PDF.pdf (consulted 30 October 2024).

United Nations General Assembly Resolution A/RES/64/172 of 18 December 2009.
United Nations General Assembly Resolution A/RES/73/166 of 17 December 2018.
UN General Assembly Vienna Declaration and Programme of Action A/CONF.157/2, adopted at the World Conference on Human Rights in Vienna, Austria, 14–25 June 1993.
United Nations (d.n.a.) Global Issues: Democracy. Available at: https://www.un.org/en/global-issues/democracy (Consulted 20 December 2024).
United Nations Population Fund, Cairo Declaration on Population and Development, adopted in Cairo, Egypt on 3–4 September 1994. Available at: https://www.unfpa.org/resources/cairo-declaration-population-development (consulted 20 December 2024).
Uvin, Peter (2007) From the Right to Development to the Rights-Based Approach: How "Human Rights" Entered Development. *Development in Practice* 17(4/5): 597–606.
Vandenhole, W. and Gready, P. (2018) Failures and Successes of Human Rights-Based Approaches to Development: Towards a Change Perspective. In: Mustaniemi-Laakso, M. and Sano, H.-O. (eds) *Human Rights-Based Change: The Institutionalisation of Economic and Social Rights*. London: Routledge, 15–54.
Verdirame, Guglielmo (2011) *The UN and Human Rights: Who Guards the Guardians?* Cambridge: Cambridge University Press.
Walyemera, Daniel Masumba (2014) Post Washington Consensus: Have the 2010 Governance Reforms at the World Bank and IMF Addressed the Concerns of the Developing World? *Makerere Law Journal* 118.
World Bank (2000) *Reforming Public Institutions and Strengthening Governance: A World Bank Strategy*. Washington DC: The World Bank.
Young, Crawford (2012) *The Postcolonial State in Africa: Fifty Years of Independence, 1960–2010*. Madison, Wisconsin: University of Wisconsin Press.

PART 3

Perspectives on Right to Development Justice

CHAPTER 9

Operationalising the Right to Development within the Context of the African Continental Free Trade Area: Some Gender Considerations

Rita Nkiruka Ozoemena

1 Introduction

It has been observed that intra-African trade is not big and so, economic integration on the continent suffers, resulting in poor economies for some countries across the continent. Operationalising the African Continental Free Trade Area (AfCFTA) with the launch of it in Niamey, Niger on 7 July 2019 counts as one of the biggest developmental projects of the African Union (AU) towards achieving the "Africa we want".[1] The idea that these two development plans are mutually reinforcing cannot be understated. Countries on the African continent are being drawn to introvert trading arrangements to grow the economies of the continent rather than the dominant extrovert plans post-independent of many African countries.

One of the guiding principles of the AfCFTA is welfare of countries in addition to economic growth. Basic elements of wellbeing as envisaged in the operationalisation of the AfCFTA would involve increased and sustained participation in trade amongst member states, access to markets, industrialisation, and the promotion of shared values, policies and prosperity. The right to development forms a formidable base for the realisation of this continental development agenda. This chapter engages with these developmental plans with a view to providing strong pillars for their realisation through projecting Africa as a capable, competitive, and consistent global player. In much the same way as poor economic trade between countries exist, so also is the limited participation of women in high end businesses and cross-border trade.

The only way to improve this trend is to ensure that there are consistent efforts to locate gender fairness in the development processes and practices. In the first place, this chapter examines the AfCFTA as a development agenda

1 Zongwe, Dunia (2024, Jan/Feb) The African Continental Free Trade Area: The Law, the Economics and the Research. Available at: https://www.nyulawglobal.org/globalex/afcfta html# (consulted 12 October 2024).

 | DOI:10.1163/9789004734357_010

to promote regional integration. Secondly, the chapter examines the gender dimensions of trade and development with the view to understanding the prospects and challenges of the AfCFTA in fostering sustainable development on the continent. Finally, the chapter discusses the right to development as a mechanism for the realisation of the Africa we want.

2 AfCFTA Overview and Strategic Plan for Regional Integration

The AfCFTA was established to harness the movement of goods and services within the African continent.[2] The recognition that African countries need to trade more with each other to boost what may be called "herd development" is critical to the growth and well-being of Africans and in fact, forms a formidable defence to any threat. Against that backdrop, in the last decade, there has been a shift in the way development is conceptualised on the African continent. Perhaps, it is instructive to go much farther to about over three decades ago when the African Charter on Human and Peoples' Rights (African Charter) was adopted. The Preamble to the African Charter, envisions and emphasises unity of the African continent through socio-economic development and regional integration. At the heart of this vision is the growth and well-being of the peoples. So, one of the founding pillars of the OAU was advocacy for the total emancipation of the African peoples; socially, economically, culturally and politically. With the transition of the OAU to the AU, it became vital for the latter to foster a development approach that is people-driven underscoring the critical role of the well-being of the people.

The establishment of the AfCFTA has a long history. It has even been compared to the African Economic Community formed more than three decades ago having similar objectives.[3] It is very clear that at the core of these continental development efforts is regional integration to try and change the narratives on Africa and position the continent as a competitive global player. The AfCFTA was then put forward as an African agreement at the 18th session of the AU in Ethiopia in 2012. It took 6 years later when about 44 Heads of State formally signed the agreement establishing the AfCFTA in Kigali on 21 March 2018, and it

2 Vhumbunu, C. (2023) Gender Equality and Women's Empowerment in the African Continental Free Trade Area: What Lessons can be Learnt from SADC. In: World Trade Organisation (ed) *Making Trade work for Women*, Geneva: World Trade Organisation, 122.

3 Erasmus, Gerard (2024, 29 February) Comparing the Abuja Treaty and African Continental Free Trade Area. Available at: https://www.tralac.org/blog/article/16331-comparing-the-abuja-treaty-and-the-afcfta-agreement.html (consulted 11 October 2024).

came into force on 30 May 2019.[4] Undoubtedly, the commitment to accelerate socio-economic development on the continent has been momentous, marked by the speediness in the ratification of the AfCFTA, which took only a year and ten days to garner the required 22 signatories to enter into force. The Gambia was the 22nd signatory, resulting in the official launch of the AfCFTA during the 12th Extra-ordinary Assembly of the AU in Niamey, Niger on 7 July 2019.[5] The OAU, predecessor to the AU, envisioned a consolidated effort to ensure that the socio-economic development and by implication, the right to development gained traction across the continent through boosting intra-African trade relations. This vision is provided for in Article 22 of the African Charter. To provide further clarity on intra-African economic relations after many false starts and realising that the "silo" approach to economic development has left the continent weaker at the regional and global levels, the AU developed the 50-year plan for African integration and development framework in the form of "Agenda 2063—The Africa We Want" launched in 2013. The AfCFTA is thus, one of the flagship projects of Agenda 2063—Africa's framework for development.[6] It has become imperative for the African continent to promote socio-economic development, achievable through boosting intra-African trade.

The main aim of the AfCFTA is to increase and enhance trade amongst African countries across all sectors of the economy as well as advance Africa's global trade position through, a common voice and policy direction. It is common knowledge that Africa struggles to have a say in global trade negotiations due to the very low level of trade among member countries on the continent. The Africa intra-trade ranks lowest at 18% compared to trade with Europe, which stands at 69% and with Asia where total trade stands at 59%.[7] The strategic plan of regional integration and more broadly, development would be greatly harnessed with the AfCFTA given the market share of 1.3 billion consumers with a combined gross domestic product of USD 3.5 trillion.[8] The value add to industrialisation and regional integration of the AfCFTA is enormous, and has the potential to engender sustainable, inclusive growth and development for the continent. In furtherance of the pan-African vision, the main objectives of the AfCFTA include:

---

4 Zongwe, supra note 1.

5 Marie, Daniel (2021, 16 August) The Development of the AFCFTA: Where did it Start? *Trade Unions and Trade in Africa*. Available at: https://www.tradeunionsinafcfta.org/the-development-of-the-afcfta-where-did-it-start/ (consulted 10 October 2024).

6 Zongwe, supra note 1.

7 Ibid.

8 Ibid.

- creation of a single market for good and services, movement of persons across the continent in accordance with the "integrated, prosperous and peaceful Africa" mission of Agenda 2063.
- Consolidating initiatives of Regional Economic Communities (RECs) and contributing to movement of natural resources and capital for investment initiatives by State Parties.
- Enhancing the competitiveness of State Parties with the continent and at the global market arena.
- Promote gender equality, structural transformation of State Parties and sustainable and inclusive socio-economic development.[9]

The institutions of the AfCFTA already established to ensure the operationalisation of this agreement, include the AfCFTA Secretariat located in Accra, Ghana which is responsible for coordination and implementation of the AfCFTA. The highest decision-making body of the AU is the Assembly of Heads of State and Government, which has the exclusive authority to adopt interpretation of the AfCFTA Agreement based on the recommendations of the Council of Ministers. It is the Council of Ministers comprising of Ministers of Trade of the state parties or their designated representatives who take decisions on all matters regarding the AfCFTA.[10] In addition to these institutional architecture, the Protocols that also came into force on 30 May 2019, such as the Protocol on Goods, the Protocol on Competition Policy, the Protocol on Services, and the Protocol on Intellectual Property which serve to ensure equity, inclusivity and growth within the system. By this, the AU has indeed, charted a great course for Africa's development and sustainable regional integration that is envisaged to stand the test of time.

One of the strong pillars of the AU regional architecture is the importance of gender equality. Gender equality has remained a consistent aspect of the vision and operations of the AU starting with Article 18(3) of the African Charter, which provides for the protection of women and the youth of Africa. Noting that women and men are key partners in the continent's development aspirations, the AU strives to promote inclusive gender participation in all sectors and projects. Although there is no explicit chapter on gender, trade and development in the AfCFTA agreement, the Preamble to the agreement recognises the vital need of creating equality of opportunity for women. The AfCFTA

9 AFCFTA Secretariat (2020, December) The Futures Report: Making AfCFTA Work for Women and Youth. African Union and the United Nations Development Programme. Available at: https://au.int/en/documents/20201202/making-afcfta-work-women-and-youth (consulted 12 October 2024), 11.

10 Zongwe, supra note 1.

agreement will enable women thrive as producers, cross-border traders and entrepreneurs through sectoral programmes in agriculture, added value chain in production and services.[11]

The promise of the AfCFTA on gender equality is laudable yet the position of the women in trade, industrialisation and development on the continent remains inadequate and fragile. Women contribute more than 80% of cross-border trade in Africa.[12] They produce farm goods like maize, cassava, rice and palm oil that are exported, making significant contribution to informal cross-border trade.[13] Despite women's increasing involvement in informal cross-border trade, there are significant constraints to their progress. Access to finance and credit remain a stumbling block for many women in small businesses and entrepreneurship.[14] Often, women face challenges with exporting their produce across borders due to regulatory constraints, access to networking and client base, funding and loans. Literacy and information technology contribute to the inadequacies experienced by many women traders on the continent. Notwithstanding the present situation of women, the potential of the AfCFTA in fostering gender equality, which is a key ingredient of the right to development remains promising for a majority of women across the continent.

3 The Cost of Gender Inequality in Africa

The African continent measures well below global indicators on the United Nations Development Programme (UNDP) human development index.[15] According to the report, the world has witnessed persistent inequalities across

11 United Nations Economic Commission for Africa (2020, February) Gender Mainstreaming in African Continental Free Trade Areas National Implementation Strategies: An Inclusive and Sustainable Pathways towards Gender Equality. *UNECA Working Paper*. Available at: https://repository.uneca.org/ds2/stream/?#/documents/0b9379be-8df3-46b4-a4cd-efe5f0a4acdc/page/4 (consulted 25 October 2024).

12 Ityavyar, S.D. (2013) Women Cross-Border Traders, Challenges, and Behaviour Change communications. In: Brenton, P.; Gamberoni, E. and Sear, C. (eds) *Women and Trade in Africa: Realising the Potential*, Washington DC: The World Bank, 60.

13 Brenton, P.; Gamberoni, E. and Sear, C. (2013) Introduction. In: Brenton, P.; Gamberoni, E. and Sear, C. (eds) *Women and Trade in Africa: Realising the Potential*. Washington DC: The World Bank, 1–3.

14 Ndumbe, L.N. (2013) Unshackling Women Traders: Cross-Border Trade of Eru from Cameroon to Nigeria. In: Brenton, P; Gamberoni, E. and Sears, C. (eds) *Women and Trade in Africa: Realising the Potential*, Washington DC: The World Bank, 43–58.

15 UNDP (2019) Beyond Income, Beyond Averages, Beyond Today: Inequalities in Human Development in the 21st Century. *Human Development Report 2019*, 116.

sectors such that it is no longer sufficient to reduce the issues as mere pernicious matters but rather as broader issues of society and the economy. Inequality thus, remains very high among African countries with Southern Africa as the most unequal.[16] This has become an intractable concern and remains a great cost to the continent. Clearly, in this kind of unequal environment, growth and development become distant resulting in a vicious cycle of poverty. In the different sectors of the economy, there are existing gender disparities that inhibit growth, and empowerment for many women. In recent times, issues such as climate change, COVID-19, conflict and violence have resulted in undermining any progress made previously. In almost all the sectors, persistent gaps exist between men and women.

According to the Africa Gender Index Report of 2019, which focused specifically on what gender inequality means for the continent whilst offering pathways to bridging the gender gap, it is concerning that the Africa Gender Index scorecard is at 48.6% at the scale of 0 to 1 (where close to 1 is less inequality and close to zero is more inequality).[17] The scorecard is indicative of how far Africa needs to go before gender inequality can be eliminated on the continent. Africa unfortunately, do not still perform better at the global gender inequality index with sub-Saharan Africa being the worst performer at 0.56% as opposed to 0.22% for Europe, East Asia and Pacific at 0.34 % , Latin America and the Caribbean at 0.39%.[18] Sub-Saharan Africa also has huge disparity in health. For example, the region accounts for about 70% of global maternal rate, a result of gender bias in the distribution of healthcare and healthcare services.

Women and girls are further burdened with domestic work and unpaid care work and consequently, are vulnerable and at risk of violence in public spaces as well as in the home. Despite the gloomy outlook, there is gender parity in basic education, which stands at 96% and in about 11 countries on the continent, women hold close to one third of the seats in parliament more than in Europe.[19] Notwithstanding the progress made in the education sector, it does not necessarily translate into work opportunities for women.

16 Ibid.

17 African Development Bank and United Nations Economic Commission for Africa (2020) What the 2019 Africa Gender Index Tells us About Gender Equality, and How Can it be Achieved. *Africa Gender Index Report 2019*, 16.

18 Yeboua, Kouassi (2024, 29 April) Gender Equality Matters for Africa's Development: Addressing the Gender Gap in Africa Promotes Growth and Reduces Poverty. *ISS-African Futures*. Available at: https://futures.issafrica.org/blog/2024/Gender-equality-matters-for-Africas-development (consulted 14 October 2024).

19 African Development Bank (2024) Gender Equality Index. Available at: https://www.afdb.org/en/topics-and-sectors/topics/quality-assurance-results/gender-equality-index (consulted 14 October 24).

In North Africa for example, women in the region face cultural and social norms that prohibit them from working in certain industries in Morocco, Egypt, and Tunisia according to the 2021 World Bank Women; Business and Law Report (WBL).[20] The widest gender gap is found in the representation and governance structures on the continent. Decision-making, representation in high-level senior management positions in the public and private sectors are still largely male-dominated with a gender gap value of about 23%.[21]

Aspiration to political office on the continent remains volatile and almost hostile to women participation in many areas such as high cost of forms, security challenges and poor electoral systems to manage the electoral process with fairness and accountability. In most countries on the continent, men are still substantially, the largest representatives in parliament with few exceptions in countries like Rwanda, Namibia, South Africa, Senegal and Mozambique which are among the top ten countries globally for female representation. Despite these exceptions, the position of women at the lowest entry level of politics at the local government council level is at an all-time low of only 21% of local government council positions held by women.[22] Undoubtedly, the continent has recorded significant progress in reducing gender inequality in education, for example. However, disproportionate gender biases weigh heavily against women. Several factors contribute to constraining the girl child such as poverty, early child marriage, teenage pregnancy and other social norms that increase vulnerabilities of the girl child.

Women participate in trade in many ways as producers, service providers and entrepreneurs and they are actively engaged in cross-border trade. In Southern Africa alone, women cross-border traders account for about 43% of the African population, generating about USD 20 billion as source of income.[23] This is a significant contribution that would add value to the growth of the economy and improvement in the lives of the people. Women in business and trade also face multitude of barriers preventing them from actively participating and contributing to the growth of the economy and well-being of the family. Access to finance is a major non-tariff barrier that contributes significantly to gender disparities in trade and business.[24] Intricately linked to lack of credit

20 World Bank Group (2021) Women Business and the Law 2021. *World Bank Group*. Available at: www.wbl.worldbank.org/content/dam/sites/wbl/documents/2021/WBL2021_eng_v2.pdf (consulted 02 November 2024).

21 Africa Development Bank and United Nations Economic Commission for Africa (2020, March) Africa Gender Index Report 2019. Available at: www.afdb.org/en/documents/africa-gender-index-report-2019-analytical-report (consulted 2 November 2024) 16.

22 Yeboua, supra note 18.

23 Brenton, Gamberoni and Sear, supra note 13, 2–4.

24 Ibid at 2.

is the ownership of land or property that are in most cases used as collateral for loans. The non-tariff barriers push many women involved in cross-border trade to the fringes of the formal sector where they do not have access to information, strong connections to assist them in improving their trade and/or productivity.[25] As a result, it is easier to find women borrow informally than through formal avenues due to stringent lending or borrowing requirements for such business transactions.

Another barrier that hampers women traders and entrepreneurs involves risks not only to their investments but to their person. The time devoted to business particularly cross-border trade hampers domestic relationships as many women spend lots of hours outside of their homes. Further, they face risks of gender-based violence from officials at the border. With the risks of violence and abuse, many women are prevented from engaging in these productive activities despite the gains. In the Great Lakes region for example, women involved in cross-border trade are exposed to corrupt practices by customs officials where about 80% of women traders resort to paying bribes to be able to freely conduct business.[26] Also, women involved in agriculture thus, contributing to food security, the well-being of the family and thereby, improving the socio-economic conditions of their families, equally face challenges and barriers to their agri-businesses and investments. These women deal mostly in perishable items that are usually at risk of destruction due to time-limiting factors.[27] Unlocking the capacity and capabilities of African women to contribute to Africa's development lies in removing the barriers to trade, investment and services.

The AfCFTA seeks to eliminate these barriers to growth and development on the continent through making gender equality a core focus of its operationalisation with a view to advancing the right to development. The AfCFTA holds great promises for women and youth who are core drivers of Africa's development agenda. As illustrated above where many productive activities are substantially in the hands of the male gender, it has become increasingly clear that an enabling environment must be created to harness the capabilities of women and young people. It is widely suggested that Africa's biggest resource is its youthful population. The role of these groups must shift from being vulnerable

---

25 Ibid at 2–4.

26 Elena, M.; Moru, G. and Roshan, S. (2013) Barriers, Risks, and Productive Potential for Small Scale Traders in the Great Lakes Region. In: Brenton, P.; Gamberoni, E. and Sear, C. (eds) *Women and Trade in Africa: Realising the Potentials*. Washington DC: World Bank Group, 27–42.

27 Brenton, Gamberoni and Sear, supra note 13.

to being strong and capable. The section that follows discusses the AfCFTA, its operationalisation and how it can effectively empower women.

4 The AfCFTA, Its Operationalisation and Shifting Paradigm

It is envisaged that the AfCFTA will shift the trade and regional integration pattern and by so doing, kickstart a new economic order for Africa. Consequently, the narrative on Africa is bound to change with the expansion of trade within Africa, the largest free trade area since the establishment of the World Trade Organisation.[28] The launch of the operational phase of the AfCFTA took place at the July 2019 Summit of the African Union held in Niamey, Niger. Several instruments relevant to the operational phase were unveiled such as:

a) Rules of origin: This is envisaged to govern the conditions for duty free trade across the continent.
b) Tariff concessions: Tariff concessions that would boost trade regionally and internationally over a limited period, including products that are termed "sensitive".
c) Online monitoring mechanism to monitor non-tariff barriers that hinder trade such as poor infrastructure and unethical administrative conduct of customs officials.
d) Pan-African Payment and Settlement System (PAPSS): This innovative system will be facilitated by Afrexim Bank to ensure speedy payment and boost confidence in the settlement of foreign exchanges within the trading system.
e) African trade observatory: This is an information portal to provide guidance on opportunities and hindrances to available opportunities, information on import and export as well as other relevant data provided by AU member states.[29]

As shown above, critical processes to ensure the success of this vital developmental project have been put in place to make certain that the economies of African countries grow. The trade liberalisation provides a pathway to ensure a level playing field for men and women producers and entrepreneurs, boosting

28 African Union (2024, 9 July) Operational Phase of the African Continental Free Trade Area launched. Available at: https://au.int/en/articles/operational-phase-african-continental-free-trade-area-launched (consulted 14 October 2024).

29 Ibid.

industrialisation.[30] It is important to note that it is for a limited period as the liberalisation could be harmful to businesses. Notwithstanding that trade liberalisation may assist in access to markets, it often works against women entrepreneurs whose businesses are of a small size, limiting their breakthrough into the export market. The online monitoring mechanism creates a platform to evaluate what is on offer in the marketplace and the observatory would act as a guide to locating the smallest businesses whose products are exportable.

The PAPSS, which is powered by Afrexim Bank is commendable.[31] Automated card systems in Africa for trade and services is a relatively new development in several African countries. The pan-African approach to trade, investment and industrialisation would bring confidence in global competitiveness of the African continent. It has now been four years since actual trading within the AfCFTA commenced from 1 July 2020. Some of the benefits expected are:

- strengthening the capacities of African companies to access global markets and trade competitively, develop regional value chains in the production of goods and services, manufacturing and agro processing,
- increase in intra-Africa trade to above the current level of less than 20 percent of trade; and
- Strengthen Africa's economic and commercial diplomacy.

Actual progress seems slow but according to the AfCFTA Secretary General, Wamkele Mene, in the four years of operation so far, Africa remains resolute in her resolve to pursue regional integration through trade because intra-African trade would double in the next five years.[32] In response to the issue of trading within the AfCFTA four years down the line, it was observed that back in 2022, seven countries introduced the customs system and gazetted the AfCFTA into their national laws. By the end of October 2024, it was expected that the number of countries ready for operations in terms of the AfCFTA will rise to thirty-seven.[33] Indeed, there is a shift in paradigm. The usual lacklustre political will to drive the development agenda has given way to consistent readiness to move forward. The institutions of the AU are the drivers of this programme

---

30 African Development Bank and United Nations Economic Commission for Africa, supra note at 21, 7–9.

31 African Union, supra note 28.

32 Lewis, Nell (2024, 7 October) Intra-African Trade Could Double in Next Five Years according to Wamkele Mene Secretary General of the African Continental Free Trade Area in an interview with CNN's Eleni Giokos on the programme "Connecting Africa". Available at: https://edition.cnn.com/2024/10/07/africa/afcfta-secretary-general-mene-interview-spc/index.html (consulted on 16 October 2024).

33 Ibid; Jardim, Sabrina "31 Nations set to initiate Trade under AFCFTA Agreement in 2024". Available at www.pacci.org (consulted on 02 May 2025).

as opposed to occasions where it is non-governmental or civil society organisations that push for the rules and its implementation. The progress made thus far, is commendable because at the level of states and entities, the framework is serving the purpose. However, specific gender considerations for implementation of the AfCFTA is vital and this contribution holds a bias in favour of women who are often disproportionately excluded from core business and productive activities.

5 Gender Considerations in the AfCFTA and the Protocol on Women and Youth in Trade

There is support in the AfCFTA for gender equality. Although no specific provisions exist in the agreement, the Preamble recognises the importance of gender equality alongside other core values for development such as human rights, the rule of law, democracy, and international security. To underscore the relevance and the vital role of women in trade, the Protocol on Women and Youth in Trade would act as a direct consequence of this aspiration.[34] Seemingly, the approach of the AfCFTA towards the socio-economic development of women is scattered in the several Protocols following the AfCFTA Agreement.[35] In the Protocol on Trade in Services, Article 27(2)(d) envisages to "improve export capacity of both formal and informal services with particular attention to micro, small and medium size ; women and youth service suppliers". This provision seeks to ensure an all-inclusive pathway to trade and services as also noted in proposed Article 3(e) of the Protocol on Women and Youth in Trade, which seeks "to promote socio-economic development that is inclusive and sustainable, promote gender equality and structural transformation of State Parties".[36] These provisions seem to strike at the critical issues that affect women and thus, must act to remove any form of restrictions on their full participation in trade, economic development and growth. Apparently, a critical understanding of these provisions would be that they are insufficient to get through to the underlying causes of gender inequality and by so doing, do not

34 The AFCFTA Agreement incorporates several Protocols. The Protocol on Women and Youth in Trade Falls under the Phase II of the AFCFTA Plan; AFCFTA website. Available at: https://www.au-afcfta.org/trade-areas/women-in-trade/ (consulted 2 November 2024); Klimke, Romy (2024, 21 March) Gender as a Trade Concern: On the African Protocol on Women and Youth in Trade. *Verfsfassungs on Matters Constitutional*. Available at: https://verfassungsblog.de/gender-as-a-trade-concern/ (consulted 14 October 2024).

35 Klimke, supra note 34.

36 Ibid.

accord genuine considerations to the socio-economic conditions of women. A cursory look at some gender considerations would include the following:

5.1 *Market Access*

Women entrepreneurs face unique barriers when accessing certain markets. For instance, the World Bank Enterprise Surveys of 2022 found that fully female-owned businesses had the greatest difficulty in accessing finance (28.52%) and electricity (18.19%).[37] This study also discovered that specific sectors, including retail, hospitality and tourism, textiles, garments and food showed elevated levels of female participation. This participation is not only reflected in female ownership, but full-time employment as well. Female owned businesses were also found to experience challenges such as corruption, lack of access to land and political instability even more intensely than their male counterparts.[38] A sectoral-focused dataset revealed that the overriding obstacle faced by female entrepreneurs is access to finance.[39] These barriers, which disproportionately affect female businesses will need to be addressed from the onset to ensure success of the AfCFTA.

5.2 *Employment Opportunities*

The United Nations Industrial Development Organisation (UNIDO) provided a dataset which revealed that female employment in Africa is labour-intensive in clothing, textiles and leather sectors especially in the least developed countries.[40] The same dataset reveals that countries which have large mining and fuel sectors, have lower female employment rates. This suggests that industries that are less capital-intensive will have a higher percentage of women participation. The World Bank Enterprise Surveys of 2022 also concluded that access to finance was one of the major obstacles encountered by women entrepreneurs.[41] Employment opportunities collectively with female-sensitive pol-

---

37 The World Bank Enterprise Surveys (2020) The African Continental Free Trade Area: New 2022 AfCFTA Report. Making the Most of the AfCFTA. Available at: https://www.worldbank.org/en/topic/trade/publication/the-african-continental-free-trade-area (consulted 7 August 2024).

38 Ibid.

39 Ibid.

40 UNIDO (2024) Data. Available at: https://www.unido.org//sites/default/files/unido-publications/2024-06/Industrial%20Development%20Report%202024.pdf (consulted 7 August 2024).

41 The World Bank Enterprise Surveys (2022) Available at: https://www.worldbank.org/en/topic/trade/publication/the-african-continental-free-trade-area (consulted 7 August 2024).

icies must be in place to guarantee that women are afforded access to new prospects under the AfCFTA.

5.3 *Policy Design and Implementation*

Surveys and studies such as those conducted by UNIDO, the World Bank Enterprise Surveys and the Trade Law Centre (TRALAC Gendered Enterprise Value Chains Survey) are essential in the design and implementation stages of policy development under the AfCFTA. These gender-sensitive studies have essentially set out for policy formulators, industry leaders and member states which industries are dominantly female, which sectors have overriding female employment, indicating the reasons why many women are unable to transcend the micro-enterprise ceiling. At the stage of policy design, gender considerations reflected in some of these surveys and studies guarantee that trade policies are equitable to women.

5.4 *Economic Impact*

The World Bank Enterprise Surveys of 2022 indicates that women contribute considerably to the African economy through their small enterprises, especially in the informal sector. Barriers such as lack of access to finance and electricity supply bar entry to larger sized enterprises. This suggests that the bigger the size of the enterprise, the lower the percentage of female ownership. Gender-sensitive and female empowering policies when implemented, will enhance the economic growth of women in trade.

5.5 *Capacity Building and Support*

Women in Africa are disproportionately affected by intensely rooted gender disparities and have faced numerous barriers in achieving economic empowerment. This is uncontested. Fostering and advocating for equity-based trade policies will allow all women traders, wherever on the continent they find themselves, to have access to resources specific to their own needs and circumstances. Providing finance of one million Kenyan shillings to each aspirant African female trader with a small business enterprise will not guarantee success to all of them. This is because a one-size-fits-all gender sensitive policy cannot possibly address the diverse needs and challenges of all African women. Country-support initiatives under the AfCFTA are necessary to help female businesses achieve their full potential.

Given the level of participation, inclusiveness and gender-responsiveness required for successful implementation of the AFCFTA, there is need for consolidated efforts at strengthening the linkages. In the first part of strengthening the linkages is a firm approach to giving force to the Protocol on Women and Youth in Trade. Key provisions of the Protocol speak directly to the issues of non-discrimination, participation and inclusion. Yet, women are excluded from the social protection that exists within the formal sector. The informal cross-border trade that is more accessible to women are not usually registered, do not pay taxes and are without social protection. To further strengthen the position of women, it is imperative that the assistance and protection they need in the informal sector are provided due to the significant contribution they make to the economy. Secondly, the protection of women in the sector where they mostly operate requires specific gender responsive mechanisms.

There must be concerted effort to give effect to the provisions in the Protocol. Article 22 of the Protocol on Women and Youth in Trade is a step in the right direction. In terms of Article 22, national gender and youth focal points would be established to ensure that gender mainstreaming and gender responsiveness are intricate parts of the operational mechanism. A case has been made by many development agencies for gender mainstreaming as the main tool to advance gender equality in the AfCFTA.[42] It has been argued in the United Nations Economic Commission for Africa (UNECA) Working Paper that countries must establish national policies and strategies to give effect to the provisions of the AfCFTA.[43] Gender mainstreaming refers to "the process of assessing the implications for women and men of any planned action, including legislation, policies or programmes, in all areas and at all levels".[44] The essence of gender mainstreaming is to ensure fairness in policies, opportunities and ultimately, the outcome of such processes.

Given the vision of the AfCFTA towards trade and development, gender mainstreaming at national level would clearly add to the success of the AfCFTA if embraced with the same political zeal with which countries adopted the AfCFTA agreement. Giving effect to this implementation strategy might be problematic on two fronts; on the one front, the status of the Protocol on Women and Youth in Trade is uncertain. It is an additional Protocol whose entry into force is unclear according to Article 23(4) of the AfCFTA Agreement, which stipulates that "for member states acceding to the Protocols on Investment, Intellectual Property Rights, Competition Policy and any other Instrument within the scope of this agreement deemed necessary shall enter into force on the date of the deposit of its instrument of accession".

---

42 UNECA (2020) Gender Mainstreaming in African Continental Free Trade Area national Implementation Strategies: An Inclusive and Sustainable Pathway towards Gender Equality in Africa. Addis Ababa: Ethiopia, 2–10.

43 Ibid at 1.

44 Ibid.

This provision portrays a choice to be made by countries as the Protocol on Gender and Youth falls through the cracks and was put as "*any other instrument within the scope of this agreement deemed necessary*" (emphasis mine). Consequently, South Africa has announced that she will only be bound by the Protocols it specifically ratified.[45] Accordingly, if for example, South Africa does not ratify the Protocol on Competition Policy, it would not be bound by any of its provisions. It follows therefore, that other countries could make such choices resulting in a distortion and/or division of the platform. Clearly, this would adversely affect the progressive and transformative featuring of gender equality in the AFCFTA and by implication, its implementation. Perhaps there is some benefit in operationalising the Protocols establishing the Agreement on AFCFTA in phases, however, the uncertainty regarding the status of the Protocol on Women and Youth in Trade poses significant risk to setting of normative standards for trade on gender equality and women empowerment.

It is important also to draw attention to the African Protocol on the Rights of Women in Africa (Maputo Protocol). This Protocol plays a central role in addressing gender discrimination in all its ramifications as well as the recognition of the role of women as key partners in development on the continent. In its preamble, the Maputo Protocol reaffirms the commitment to the promotion of gender equality by the African Union and its several agencies including the New Partnership for Africa's Development (NEPAD), a specialised agency of the African Union that was rebranded in July 2018 in pursuance of the development objectives of the African Union. The agency, now referred to as African Union Development Agency (AUDA) is mandated to "coordinate between specialised agencies, organs and other institutions to create an enabling and supportive environment for the achievement of the goals and priorities of Agenda 2063".[46] In alignment with the aspiration of people-driven development in Africa, the Maputo Protocol provides the basis for the advancement of gender equality and women empowerment. Article 19 of the Maputo Protocol provides that

> Women shall have the right to fully enjoy their right to sustainable development. In this connection, the States Parties shall take all appropriate measures to:
>
> a) Introduce the gender perspective in the national development planning procedures;

45 Ibid.

46 New Partnership for Africa's Development Platform. Available at: https://www.nepad.org/microsite/who-we-are-0#the_auda-nepad_journey (consulted 4 September 2024).

b) Ensure participation of women at all levels in the conceptualisation, decision-making, implementation and evaluation of development policies and programmes;
c) Promote women's access to and control over productive resources such as land and guarantee their right to property;
d) Promote women's access to credit, training, skills development and extension services at rural and urban levels in order to provide women with a higher quality of life and reduce the level of poverty among women;
e) Take into account indicators of human development specifically relating to women in the elaboration of development policies and programmes; and
f) Ensure that the negative effects of globalisation and any adverse effects of the implementation of trade and economic policies and programmes are reduced to the minimum for women.[47]

From the above provision, it is clear on the importance of the participation of women as co-partners in development and the need to remove any impediments from globalisation or trade and economic policies that would negatively impact women. On the African continent, it is common knowledge that the development trajectory of many countries is not on equal footing, but the shared values present an opportunity for them to collectively promote gender equality and women empowerment. It is therefore, important to strengthen the linkages through a multidimensional operationalisation approach that will consolidate the development strategies in the form of the right to development.

6 Operationalising the Right to Development in the AfCFTA

The AfCFTA Agreement recognises the vital role intra-African trade and investments play in regional integration. The AU development framework—Agenda 2063 is the broad stroke that encompasses these strategies, underscoring the realisation of the right to development (RTD) as enshrined in the African Charter. It must be stated from the onset that the RTD is not explicitly canvassed in the AfCFTA. Although the AfCFTA envisages people-centred development through trade and investments, it is a missed opportunity that the RTD is not raised in the agreement or debates before it

47 Protocol to the African Charter on Human and Peoples' Rights on the Rights of Women in Africa adopted by the AU Assembly of Heads of State and Government in Maputo, Mozambique on 11 July 2003, Art 19.

was signed by countries on the continent. The RTD is a fully justiciable right across the continent in terms of the African Charter on Human and Peoples' Rights (African Charter).[48] It is interesting to note that the right to development is explicitly provided for in the national constitution of a number of countries on the African continent, including Cameroon, Ethiopia, Malawi, the Democratic Republic of Congo, Benin, and Uganda while some other countries like Nigeria and Kenya implicitly make provision for domestic recognition of the RTD enshrined in the African Charter. The 1972 Constitution of Cameroon, which was the first legal instrument to give legal recognition of the RTD provides as following:

> RESOLVED to harness our natural resources in order to ensure the well-being of every citizen without discrimination, by raising living standards, proclaim our right to development as well as our determination to devote all our efforts to that end and declare our readiness to co-operate with all States desirous of participating in this national endeavour with due respect for our sovereignty and the independence of the Cameroonian State.[49]

While the above provision is contained in the Preamble, Article 65 of the Cameroon Constitution, affirms that the Preamble is an integral part of the Constitution and therefore, justiciable and has the same status as the binding provisions of the Constitution. So, the RTD is not just a mere ideal but actual justiciable right. Notably, there is a correlation between the utilisation of the wealth of Cameroon as a sovereign country and the living standards of its people. In other words, there is that determination to pursue economic development solely for the benefit of its people without compromise of their living standard. In Malawi, the RTD is provided for in Section 30 of the Constitution, which provides that:

1. All persons and people shall have a right to development and therefore to enjoyment of economic, social, cultural and political development and women, children and the disabled in particular shall be given special consideration in the application of this right.

---

48 African Charter on Human and Peoples' Rights adopted in Nairobi, Kenya on 27 June 1981 OAU Doc CAB/LEG/67/3 Rev.5 (1981), entered into force on 21 October 1986.

49 Constitution of the Republic of Cameroon, adopted on 20 May 1972, promulgated on 2 June 1972 and amended by Law No 75/1 of 9 May 1975; Law No 79/2 of 29 June 1979; Law No 83/10 of 21 July 1983; Law No 83/25 of 29 November 1984; Law No 84/1 of 4 February 1984. Preamble Para 3.

2. The state shall take all necessary measures for the realisation of the right to development. Such measures shall include, amongst other things, equality of opportunity for all in their access to basic resources, education, health services, food, shelter, employment and infrastructure.
3. The state shall take measures to introduce reforms aimed at eradicating social injustices and inequalities.
4. The state has the responsibility to respect the right to development and to justify its policies in accordance with this responsibility.

The formulation of the RTD in the Malawian Constitution is remarkable due to the clarity in the content, duty bearers and beneficiaries of the right. In addition, the accountability requirement contained therein is a testament of the force of the law in advancing the RTD guaranteed to the people of Malawi. The RTD as a justiciable entitlement is also enshrined in Article 43 of the Constitution of the Federal Republic of Ethiopia. Article 43(3) specifically guarantees that all peoples' and nation-states within Ethiopia have the right to improved living standards and the right to sustainable development. Although this formulation is different from those above, it is noted that sustainable development is viewed as a sub-set of RTD.[50] The sustainability aspect in the RTD underscores the need to eliminate structural inequalities that may hinder development.

The RTD is an all-encompassing human right that incorporates all other human rights. The key principles underlying the RTD include ideas of justice and equality; and integrates economic, social and cultural right with civil and political rights; it has the value addition in looking at programmes for development as a process of realisation of human rights; it envisages that true individual freedoms cannot exist without economic security and independence; it emphasises the active participation of women; upholds the fact that the human person is the central subject of the RTD; and most importantly that the state has the primary obligation for creating conditions necessary for the realisation of RTD.

These key principles represent critical issues that must be protected for the people of Africa, underscoring the importance of the RTD as a "composite right".[51] The nature and content of the RTD have been the source of much controversy on whether it is actually a right to be claimed by a human person or

50 Mekomen, Seid Demeke (2021) The Right to Sustainable Development in Art 43(3) of the Ethiopian Constitution, *African Human Rights Law Journal* 21(2): 1009–1035.

51 Browning, Rebecca (2011, August) The Right to Development in Africa, An Emerging Jurisprudence? *University of Cape Town*. Available at: www.kenyalaw.org/kl/index.php?id=1900 (consulted 18 October 2024).

not.[52] Mostly, the controversy stems from the understanding of a human right to development by countries in the Global North. This has resulted in the view that the RTD is largely defended by developing countries.[53] It is important to reiterate that the discourse has moved beyond the controversy following the increasing recognition of the RTD in various international instruments and commitments,[54] including the drafting of the International Covenant on the Right to Development driven by the UN Human Rights Council, which when eventually adopted by the UN General Assembly, will become a legally binding treaty at the global level.[55]

Notwithstanding the possibility that a legally binding treaty on the RTD will not completely address all the contestations and debates regarding the nature and content of the right, the draft Covenant on the Right to Development presents a great opportunity for normative standard-setting in international economic law discourses. Further, such a treaty provides a crucial step forward in building a shared foundation in the midst of the controversies that have constrained recognition of the RTD at the global level.[56] The United Nations Declaration on the Right to Development (UNDRTD) provides an incisive definition of the right to development in Article 1 which stipulates that "The right to development is an inalienable human right by virtue of which every human person and all peoples are entitled to participate in, contribute to, and enjoy economic, social, cultural and political development, in which all human rights and fundamental freedoms can be fully realized".[57]

In terms of the above definition, the RTD is regarded both as a group right and as a right to be claimed by individuals. Also, Article 4 of the Draft Covenant on the Right to Development builds on the UNDRTD, which stipulates as follows:

52 Vandenbogaerde, Arne (2013) The Right to Development in International Human Right Law: A Call for its Dissolution. *Netherlands Quarterly of Human Rights* 31(2): 196.

53 Hieronymi, Mortiz and Karimov, Danil (2023) The Right to Development: BRICS' Answer of the Rule-based Order. *International Journal of Law in Changing World* 2(2): 100–123.

54 Ngang, C.C. and Kamga, S.D. (2020) Introduction. In: Ngang, C.C. and Kamga, S.D. (eds) *Insights into Policies and Practices on the Right to Development.* New York: Rowman and Littlefield, 2.

55 Human Rights Council Working Group on the Right to Development, Twenty-Third Session 16–20 May 2022. Revised Draft Convention on the Right to Development A/HRC/WG.2/23/2.

56 Desierto, Diane (2023) The Human Rights to Development as a New Foundation for International Economic Law. *Tulane Journal of International and Comparative Law* 31(1): 57–73.

57 Declaration on the Right to Development Resolution A/RES/41/128 adopted by UN General Assembly on 4 December 1986.

1. Every human person and all peoples have the inalienable right to development, by virtue of which they are entitled to participate in, contribute to and enjoy civil, cultural, economic, political and social development that is indivisible from and interdependent and interrelated with all other human rights and fundamental freedoms.
2. Every human person and all peoples have the right to active, free and meaningful participation in development and in the fair distribution of benefits resulting therefrom.

Clearly, the binding treaty reaffirms and strengthens the contents and nature of the RTD provisions contained in the UNDRTD. On the part of the African continent, she is poised to fully utilise the RTD in pursuance of its development agenda and development framework such as Agenda 2063 and more importantly, the AfCFTA. The clear obligation imposed by the provisions of Article 22 should always act as a guide when the AU develops strategies for the African development agenda. Article 22 of the African Charter provides that

1. All peoples shall have the right to their economic, social and cultural development with regard to their freedom and identity and in the equal enjoyment of the common heritage of mankind.
2. States shall have the duty, individually or collectively, to ensure the exercise of the right to development.

It can be argued that the core elements of the Article 22 provision are contained in the AfCFTA, being the socio-economic development and enjoyment of the common heritage of the African people as denoted in the shared values of Agenda 2063 and the AfCFTA. It is common knowledge that Africa is enormously endowed with natural resources that can sustain intra-African trade, which could boost the economies of African countries if they are able to harness what they have been given by nature.[58] The understanding therefore, should be that proper recognition of the common entitlements to trade, compete positively and invest within them on the basis of the RTD should have been part of the formulation of the AfCFTA. Further, since the AfCFTA could be highlighted as a pan-African agenda bearing the aspirations of all Africans, the RTD would be a natural gravitation towards the collective effort that is highlighted in the AfCFTA and its operationalisation. I argue that without explicit recognition of the RTD in the operationalisation of the AfCFTA, the perceived promises may ring hollow.

---

58 Ngang, Carol Chi (2020) Right to Development in Africa and the Common Heritage Entitlement. *Journal of Juridical Science—Special Issue* 45(1).

According to Kamga, law making is by international agreement.[59] Although the debates on whether the law is "soft" or "hard" indicating its binding effect on the parties, it is the nature of the organisation that makes the treaty or agreement matter the most. In this instance, the AfCFTA has been hailed as the largest trade framework in recent history and the agreement establishing it affirms its status as a binding instrument (hard law). In its conceptualisation, the RTD envisages a people-oriented development approach that will progressively contribute to the improvement and the well-being and the living standard of the human person.[60] The principal element of the RTD is participation, where the realisation of the RTD itself is envisaged to ensure the "active, free and meaningful participation in development and in the fair distribution of the benefits therefrom".[61] The crux of the realisation of the RTD makes no distinction on active, free and meaningful participation. It enjoins all to be part of the process of development and to benefit from it. From these conceptualisations of the RTD, there is a correlation to the objectives of the AfCFTA in creating a platform for trade for all Africans. Moreso, where women are key drivers of development, the impetus for gender considerations in the AFCTFA cannot be over-emphasised. Women often face exclusions from being active participants in political, economic and social activities. The RTD, therefore, with its emancipatory rights presents an appropriate mechanism for AFCFTA to drive its development agenda with the full complement of development actors, partners and beneficiaries. The human person is the central subject of development[62] and so, the freedom and opportunities created must not exclude anyone especially women. In other words, both the AFCFTA and the RTD have implications for gender equality at their core hence, there is a need to stress the gender considerations that the AfCFTA would need to adopt to give effect to the RTD of all peoples of the continent. There must be a development-oriented trade framework, which needs to be part of the AU development architecture.

59 Kamga, S.D. (2020) Contemporary International Law and the Realisation of the Right to Development. In: Ngang, C.C. and Kamga, S.D. (eds) *Insights into the Policies and Practices of the Right to Development.* New York: Rowman and Littlefield, 255.

60 Declaration on the Right to Development, note 57.

61 Ibid.

62 Piovesan, Flavia and Fanchi, Melina (2018) *Gender Equality, the Right to Development and the 2020 Agenda for Sustainable Development. Operationalising the Right to development in the Implementing the Sustainable Development Goals.* Geneva/Cudad Colon/Kuala Lumpur: OHCHR, UPEACE and UNU-IIGR.

7 Conclusion

The African continent has woken up to its potential and the critical role it could play at the global level if it can effectively harness its natural resources and human capabilities. The AfCFTA is a step in the right direction through its main objectives of boosting intra-African trade but also ensuring that its policies on services, investments, competition and intellectual property are adequately protected as noted in the Protocols establishing these key areas of trade. The specific provision in the agreement seeking to protect gender equality is commendable and the Protocol on Women and Youth in trade is a clear recognition of the main drivers of development on the continent especially, regarding informal trade. The gender considerations are not extensive in its composition and areas of coverage. There are gaps that must be filled such as a meaningful way of incorporating informal trade, the sector wherein majority of African women operate. It is the finding of this contribution that the RTD presents a valuable tool in achieving the goals of AfCFTA maximally through development-oriented trade policies. Above all, states must take their obligations seriously to collectively ensure that all Africans benefit from the AfCFTA trade framework for the benefit of its overall human rights architecture in the 21st Century development agenda.

References

Africa Development Bank and United Nations Economic Commission for Africa (2020, March) Africa Gender Index Report 2019. Available at: https://www.afdb.org/en/documents/africa-gender-index-report-2019-analytical-report (consulted 02 November 2024).

African Charter on Human and Peoples' Rights adopted in Nairobi, Kenya on 27 June 1981 OAU Doc CAB/LEG/67/3 Rev.5 (1981), entered into force on 21 October 1986.

African Development Bank and United Nations Economic Commission for Africa (2020) What the 2019 Africa Gender Index Tells us About Gender Equality, and How Can it be Achieved. *Africa Gender Index Report 2019*.

African Union (2024, 9 July) Operational Phase of the African Continental Free Trade Area launched. Available at: https://au.int/en/articles/operational-phase-african-continental-free-trade-area-launched (consulted 14 October 2024).

Brenton, P.; Gamberoni, E. and Sear, C. (2013) Introduction. In: Brenton, P.; Gamberoni, E. and Sear, C. (eds) *Women and Trade in Africa: Realising the Potential*. Washington DC: The World Bank.

Browning, Rebecca (2011, August) The Right to Development in Africa, An Emerging Jurisprudence? University of Cape Town. Available at: https://www.kenyalaw.org/kl/index.php?id=1900 (consulted 18 October 2024).

Constitution of the Republic of Cameroon, adopted on 20 May 1972, promulgated on 2 June 1972 and amended by Law No 75/1 of 9 May 1975; Law No 79/2 of 29 June 1979; Law No 83/10 of 21 July 1983; Law No 83/25 of 29 November 1984; Law No 84/1 of 4 February 1984.

Declaration on the Right to Development Resolution A/RES/41/128 adopted by UN General Assembly on 4 December 1986.

Desierto, Diane (2023) The Human Rights to Development as a New Foundation for International Economic Law. *Tulane Journal of International and Comparative Law* 31(1): 57–73.

Draft International Covenant on the Right to Development—Report by the Chair-Rapporteur of the Working Group on the Right to Development, Zamir Akram (Pakistan) Human Rights Council A/HRC/54/50 54th Session, 6 October 2023.

Elena, M.; Moru, G. and Roshan, S. (2013) Barriers, Risks, and Productive Potential for Small Scale Traders in the Great Lakes Region. In: Brenton, P.; Gamberoni, E. and Sear, C. (eds) *Women and Trade in Africa: Realising the Potentials*. Washington DC: World Bank Group, 27–42.

Erasmus, Gerard (2024, 29 February) Comparing Abuja Treaty and African Continental Free Trade Area. Available at: https://www.tralac.org/blog/article/16331-comparing-the-abuja-treaty-and-the-afcfta-agreement.html (consulted 11 October 2024).

Hieronymi, Mortiz and Karimov, Danil (2023) The Right to Development: BRICS' Understanding of the Human Rights. *International Journal of Law in Changing World* 2(2): 100–123.

Human Rights Council Working Group on the Right to Development, Twenty-Third Session 16–20 May 2022. Revised Draft Convention on the Right to Development A/HRC/WG.2/23/2.

Ityavyar, S.D. (2013) Women Cross-Border Traders, Challenges, and Behaviour Change Communications. In: Brenton, P.; Gamberoni, E. and Sear, C. (eds) *Women and Trade in Africa: Realising the Potential*, Washington DC: The World Bank.

Kamga, S.D. (2020) Contemporary International Law and the Realisation of the Right to Development. In: Ngang, C.C. and Kamga, S.D. (eds) *Insights into the Policies and Practices of the Right to Development*. New York: Rowman and Littlefield.

Klimke, Romy (2024, 21 March) Gender as a Trade Concern: On the African Protocol on Women and Youth in Trade. *Verfsfassungs on Matters Constitutional*. Available at: https://verfassungsblog.de/gender-as-a-trade-concern/ (consulted 14 October 2024).

Lewis, Nell (2024, 7 October) Intra-African Trade Could Double in Next Five Years according to Wamkele Mene Secretary General of the African Continental Free

Trade Area in an interview with CNN's Eleni Giokos on the Programme "Connecting Africa". Available at: https://edition.cnn.com/2024/10/07/africa/afcfta-secretary-general-mene-interview-spc/index.html (consulted on 16 October 2024).

Marie, Daniel (2021, 16 August) The Development of the AFCFTA: Where did it Start? *Trade Unions and Trade in Africa*. Available at: https://www.tradeunionsinafcfta.org/the-development-of-the-afcfta-where-did-it-start/ (consulted 10 October 2024).

Mekomen, Seid Demeke (2021) The Right to Sustainable Development in Art 43(3) of the Ethiopian Constitution, *African Human Rights Law Journal* 21(2): 1009–1035.

Ndumbe, L.N. (2013) Unshackling Women Traders: Cross-Border Trade of Eru from Cameroon to Nigeria. In: Brenton, P; Gamberoni, E. and Sears, C. (eds) *Women and Trade in Africa: Realising the Potential*, Washington DC: The World Bank, 43–58.

New Partnership for Africa's Development Platform. Available at: https://www.nepad.org/microsite/who-we-are-0#the_auda-nepad_journey (consulted 4 September 2024).

Ngang, C.C. and Kamga, S.D (2020) Introduction. In: Ngang, C.C. and Kamga, S.D. (eds) *Insights into Policies and Practices on the Right to Development*. New York: Rowman and Littlefield.

Ngang, Carol Chi (2020) Right to Development in Africa and the Common Heritage Entitlement. *Journal of Juridical Science—Special Issue* 45(1): 28–50.

Piovesan, Flavia and Fanchi, Melina (2018) *Gender Equality, the Right to Development and the 2020 Agenda for Sustainable Development: Operationalising the Right to Development in the Implementing the Sustainable Development Goals*. Geneva/Cudad Colon/Kuala Lumpur: OHCHR, UPEACE and UNU-IIGR.

Protocol to the African Charter on Human and Peoples' Rights on the Rights of Women in Africa adopted by the AU Assembly of Heads of State and Government in Maputo, Mozambique on 11 July 2003.

The AFCFTA Secretariat the Futures Report: Making AfCFTA Work for Women and Youth (December 2020) African Union and the United Nations Development Programme. Available at: https://au.int/en/documents/20201202/making-afcfta-work-women-and-youth (consulted 12 October 2024).

The World Bank Enterprise Surveys (2020) The African Continental Free Trade Area: New 2022 AfCFTA Report. Making the Most of the AfCFTA. Available at: https://www.worldbank.org/en/topic/trade/publication/the-african-continental-free-trade-area (consulted 7 August 2024).

The World Bank Enterprise Surveys (2022) Available at: https://www.worldbank.org/en/topic/trade/publication/the-african-continental-free-trade-area (consulted 7 August 2024).

United Nation Development Programme (2019) Beyond Income, Beyond Averages, Beyond Today: Inequalities in Human Development in the 21st Century. *Human Development Report 2019*.

United Nations Economic Commission for Africa (2020) Gender Mainstreaming in African Continental Free Trade Area national Implementation Strategies: An Inclusive and Sustainable Pathway towards Gender Equality in Africa. Addis Ababa: Ethiopia, 2–10.

United Nations Economic Commission for Africa (2020, February) Gender Mainstreaming in African Continental Free Trade Areas National Implementation Strategies: An Inclusive and Sustainable Pathways towards Gender Equality. *UNECA Working Paper*. Available at: https://repository.uneca.org/ds2/stream/?#/documents/0b9379be-8df3-46b4-a4cd-efe5f0a4acdc/page/4 (consulted 25 October 2024).

United Nations Industrial Development Organisation (2024) Data. Available at: https://www.unido.org//sites/default/files/unido-publications/2024-06/Industrial%20Development%20Report%202024.pdf (consulted 07 August 2024).

Vandenbogaerde, Arne (2013) The Right to Development in Internation Human Right Law: A Call for its Dissolution. *Netherlands Quarterly of Human Rights* 31(2): 187–209.

Vhumbunu, Clayton (2023) Gender Equality and Women's Empowerment in the African Continental Free Trade Area: What Lessons can be Learnt from SADC. In: World Trade Organisation (ed) *Making Trade work for Women*, Geneva: World Trade Organisation, 120–141.

World Bank Group (2021) Women Business and the Law 2021. *World Bank Group*. Available at: https://wbl.worldbank.org/content/dam/sites/wbl/documents/2021/02/WBL2021_ENG_v2.pdf (consulted 2 November 2024).

Yeboua, Kouassi (2024, 29 April) Gender Equality Matters for Africa's Development: Addressing the Gender Gap in Africa Promotes Growth and Reduces Poverty. *ISS-African Futures*. Available at: https://futures.issafrica.org/blog/2024/Gender-equality-matters-for-Africas-development (consulted 14 October 2024).

Zongwe, Dunia (2024, Jan/Feb) The African Continental Free Trade Area: The Law, the Economics and the Research. Available at: https://www.nyulawglobal.org/globalex/afcfta.html# (consulted 12 October 2024).

CHAPTER 10

Bridging the Divide: the Impact of Digital Technological Advancements on the Right to Development in Africa

Dorcas Basimanyane

1 Introduction

Mobile technology has emerged as a driving force in Africa's socio-economic transformation, offering unprecedented opportunities to accelerate the realisation of human rights, including the right to development.[1] By offering innovative solutions that reach underserved and marginalised communities, mobile technology has the potential to reduce inequalities, empower individuals and contribute to more equitable and sustainable development.[2] Despite these promises, the uneven distribution of mobile internet technologies coupled with other global, regional and national barriers, hinder the full realisation of the potential of these technologies.

While Africa's exponential mobile connectivity growth has become more evident in the current times, many structural barriers persist, including underdeveloped infrastructure. This is largely due to political reasons, lack of resources, digital skills gap, regulatory and policy barriers, corruption and the failure of developed countries to support technology transfer in a way that aligns with the principles of the right to development (RTD).[3] Intellectual property regimes, restrictive trade practices, and insufficient financial and technical support from the global community continue to impede Africa's ability to

1 Toppan Digital Language (2024) How Mobile Technology is Transforming Africa. Available at: https://toppandigital.com/translation-blog/mobile-technology-transforming-africa/ (consulted 28 October 2024).

2 UNDP (2024) From Access to Empowerment: Digital Inclusion in a Dynamic World. Singapore: UNDP Policy Centre. Available at: https://www.undp.org/sites/g/files/zskgke326/files/2024-05/undp_digital_inclusion_in_a_dynamic_world.pdf (consulted 28 October 2024).

3 ICT Works (2024, 24 July) 6 Barriers to the Fourth Industrial Revolution in African Countries. Available at: https://www.ictworks.org/barriers-fourth-industrial-revolution-africa/ (consulted 28 October 2024).

 | DOI:10.1163/9789004734357_011

fully leverage mobile internet technology for development on the continent.[4] However, while the failures of the past technology transfer initiatives emanating from international trade, climate change, biotechnology and intellectual property debates are well documented,[5] Article 13 of the draft Covenant on the Right to Development brings hope to developing countries. In other words, the provision seeks to resuscitate the dying horse of technology transfer using human rights-based approaches.

Article 13 calls for greater technology transfer and international cooperation to enable developing countries to leverage technological advancements for development and the well-being of their peoples. It re-envisions a world where developing countries can fully harness technological advancements through equitable access to new technologies facilitated by robust global partnerships and cooperation as a matter of human right.[6] The shift in dynamics now prioritises equitable access to technology as a matter of global justice not just as a commercial transaction or charity. The draft Convention will upon adoption, add a moral and legal weight to the obligations on developed countries, imposing technology transfer as a legal duty necessitating accountability on the part of developed states if they fail to comply.

Further, in this mobile internet era, the human RTD assumes new relevance, prompting a re-evaluation of its principles in the context of rapid digital transformation. This chapter investigates what the principles of the RTD such as comprehensive development, participatory processes, social justice, and equity mean in a world which is increasingly driven by digital connectivity. How do these principles manifest in the context of mobile internet, and how does technological advancement impact self-determination, sovereignty and international cooperation?

---

4 Maskus, Keith (2004) Encouraging International Technology Transfer. *UNCTAD-ICTSD Project on IPRs and Sustainable Development*, 22–31.

5 Hope, Kempe (1983) Basic Needs and Technology Transfer Issues in the "New International Economic Order". *The American Journal of Economics and Sociology* 42(4): 393–403; see also, Dos Santos, Fernando (2020) Levelling the Playing Field to Promote Technology Transfer and Innovation in African Least Developed Countries. *South African Intellectual Property Law Journal* 8(1): 35–55.

6 Draft International Covenant on the Right to Development—Report by the Chair-Rapporteur of the Working Group on the Right to Development, Zamir Akram (Pakistan) Human Rights Council A/HRC/54/50 54th Session, 6 October 2023, Art 13.

2 Context and Significance of the Right to Development—Legal and Theoretical Framework

On the 4 December 1986, with 147 votes in favour, 6 abstentions and 1 opposing vote by the United States of America (USA),[7] the United Nations broke a new ground in the universal struggle for greater human dignity, freedom, equality, non-discrimination, participation, transparency, accountability, and social justice.[8] The Declaration on the Right to Development (DRTD) was adopted, which officially introduce the composite and fundamental human right to development (RTD) into the international human rights system. According to Aguirre, adoption of the DRTD was a furtherance of Article 28 of the Universal Declaration of Human Rights (UDHR) which entitles everyone to an enabling social and international order necessary for the full realisation of their protected fundamental rights.[9] This signifies that though it was initially not explicit, the spirit and purpose of the RTD has always been at the heart of the purpose and objectives of the United Nations.

2.1 *Contents and Obligations on the Right to Development*

The right to development is defined in Article 1 of the DRTD as "[…] an inalienable human right by virtue of which every human person and all peoples are entitled to participate in, contribute to, and enjoy economic, social, cultural and political development, in which all human rights and fundamental freedoms can be fully realized".[10] Further, the RTD implies the full realisation of the right of peoples to self-determination, which includes, subject to the relevant provisions of both International Covenants on Human Rights, the exercise of their inalienable right to full sovereignty over all their natural wealth and resources.[11] The DRDT envisages friendly relations between states, international solidarity, cooperation and assistance in areas of concern to developing countries, including technology transfer, access to essential medicines, debt sustainability, development aid, international trade and policy space in decision-making.[12]

7 Declaration on the Right to Development Resolution A/RES/41/128 adopted by UN General Assembly on 4 December 1986.

8 Declaration on the Right to Development: Speech by the Office of the High Commissioner. Available at: https://www.ohchr.org/ (consulted 15 October 2024).

9 Aguirre, Daniel (2008) *The Human Right to Development in a Globalizing World*. London: Routledge, 70.

10 Declaration on the Right to Development, supra note 7, Art 1.

11 Ibid at Art 1(b).

12 Declaration on the Right to Development, supra note 7, Art 3; see also, Sengupta, Ranja (2016) International Trade and the 2030 Agenda for Sustainable Development. *Third*

2.2 *Contestations over the Right to Development*

The RTD has remained a subject of serious contestations in and outside of United Nations platforms even after over three (3) decades following the adoption of the DRTD.[13] From inception, the idea of a RTD has been dragged through conceptual mud and political quicksand.[14] The contestations stemmed from its contents, nature, and status as a human right and thus, whether the RTD is indeed, a legally enforceable human right with binding obligations on states and the international community.[15] Its collective nature is perceived to be vague and therefore, antipodal to the doctrines of natural rights, specifically the views that human rights are inherent in humans and not a product of social cooperation, and therefore, they should be conceptualised in a clear and unambiguous manner.[16]

Sakiko Fukuda-Parr recalls that the UNDRTD has widely been criticised for being poorly written, containing too much ambiguity over basic issues such as whether this is a collective or an individual right, to provide a basis for defining a conceptually robust human right that would have significant meaning for improving human welfare.[17] In response to this argument, the office of the UN High Commissioner for Human Rights (OHCHR) has explicitly stated that the RTD is a fundamental human right and should be placed on the same status of other human rights.[18] The excuses over the vagueness of the RTD were further addressed in 2006 through the OHCHR resolution reaffirming their commitment to reinforce the UN human rights machinery, to ensure the effective enjoyment by all human persons, whether civil, political, economic, social and cultural rights as well as RTD.[19] The resolution highlighted that the

World Network 130–139; see also Reports of the Secretary-General and the High Commissioner on International Cooperation in the Field of Human Rights A/74/351 and A/HRC/44/28.

13 United Nations Office of the High Commissioner (2013) *Realizing the Right to Development: Essays in Commemoration of 25 Years of the United Nations Declaration on the Right to Development*. Geneva/New York: United Nations Publishing, iii.

14 Arts, Karin and Tamo, Atabongawung (2016) The Right to Development in International Law: New Momentum Thirty Years Down the Line? *Netherlands International Law Review* 63: 221–249.

15 Teshome, Roman Girma (2022) The Draft Convention on the Right to Development: A New Dawn to the Recognition of the Right to Development as a Human Right? *Human Rights Law Review* 22: 1–24.

16 Teshome, supra note 15, 2.

17 Fukuda-Parr, Sakiko (2012) The Right to Development: Reframing a New Discourse for the Twenty-First Century Social Research. *Human Rights and the Global Economy* 79(4): 845.

18 Summary of the Open-ended Informal Consultations held by the Commission on Human Rights pursuant to Economic and Social Council Decisions 2005/217 Para 18; UN Doc. A/59/847-E/2005/73 Paras 18, 42, 68.

19 The UN Doc. A/RES/60/251(2006) Preamble.

OHCHR's work reflects the interdependence of all human rights, including the RTD.[20]

The RTD has subsequently, been affirmed by the United Nations and its various agencies as a universal and inalienable human right and integral to the universal human rights regime. It was recognised for instance, at the Vienna World Summit on Human Rights and incorporated in Declaration and Programme of Action adopted at the summit in Vienna in 1993,[21] followed by the 2000 Millennium Declaration,[22] the 2002 Durban Declaration and Programme of Action, the 2005 World Summit Outcome Document[23] and the Declaration on the Rights of Indigenous Peoples.[24]

Another criticism against the RTD by Western states rests on the none-binding nature of the DRDT and therefore, incapable of imposing legal and enforceable obligations on states and the international community. Thus, developed communities can only assist the developing communities based on their free moral will and charity which is exercised in accordance with their capabilities and terms.[25] Despite extensive academic literature on the definition of the RTD, developed countries such as the USA continue to contest that the RTD has not yet attained an internationally accepted legal definition.[26] Thus, it cannot impose any legal obligations on the developed communities to provide development assistance to the poor and economically struggling states. They argue that the DRTD in its legal nature as a declaration does not have any binding legal force to compel them to abide by it.[27] Rather, they hold an unwavering view that the RTD should be an individual national priority.[28]

20 Ibid at Para 4.

21 Vienna Declaration and Programme of Action, adopted by the World Conference on Human Rights on 25 June 1993, UN Doc. A/CONF.157/23, 12 July 1993; see also, Arts and Tamo, supra note 9.

22 Appointed by the Commission on Human Rights, held by Arjun K. Sengupta from India between 1999 and 2004. Available at: http://www.ohchr.org/EN/Issues/Poverty/Pages/ASengupta.aspx (consulted 15 October 2024).

23 Resolution adopted by the General Assembly on 16 September 2005, Resolution 60/1. 2005 World Summit Outcome.

24 United Nations Declaration on the Rights of Indigenous Peoples (2007), United Nations A/RES/61/295.

25 Alston, Philip (2005) Ships Passing in the Night: The Current State of the Human Rights and Development Debate Seen Through the Lens of the Millennium Development Goals. *Human Rights Quarterly* 27(3): 755–829.

26 Danies, Joel (2003) US Representative to the UN HRC Summary Record of the 63rd Meeting. 59th Session, UN Doc, E/CN.4/2003/SR.63. Paras 5 and 15.

27 Salomon, Margot and Sengupta, Arjun (2023) The Right to Development: Obligations of States and the Rights of Minorities and Indigenous Peoples. *Minority Group International—Issues Papers*, 7–8.

28 Secretary General, Report on the Right to Development (2003) UN Doc. A/58/276, Para 11.

While there is some truth to the above from a legal standpoint, the obligations on developed states as envisaged in the DRTD cannot be considered merely voluntary and charitable.[29] This is because these obligations have been there under other binding international agreements and developed countries have constantly failed to implement them. This includes obligations under the United Nations Charter, International Covenant on Civil and Political Rights (ICCPR) and the International Covenant on Economic, Social and Cultural Rights (ICESCR), which have all been ratified by developed countries and developing countries alike. The DRTD recognises that development only happens when all human rights protected by these instruments are realised without exception,[30] and it repeatedly refers to the UN Charter, UDHR, ICCPR, and ICESCR. The fact that the DRDT also reaffirms the values of universality, interdependence, and indivisibility of human rights should to some extent, grant the RTD some recognisable value of prominence.[31] Moreover, the RTD remains a prominent source of international law as it addresses the link between economic globalisation, development, and fundamental human rights law. Further, it irrevocably establishes a rights-based framework for development processes which should guide state's actions, and it strives to promote accountability through international cooperation.[32]

In addition, the DRTD remains a source of international law, and it can be used to codify international law or influence its development.[33] While it has arguably not yet attained customary international law standard, it can influence the formation of other treaties just like the UDHR resulted in the birth of the ICCPR and the ICESCR. Further, despite the non-binding nature of the DRTD, it remains an important instrument of the United Nations legal system, and like other General Assembly declarations, DRDT should give rise to some expectations which have both political and moral implications on the member states.[34]

---

29 Kanade, Mihir (2023) The Right to Development and the 2030 Agenda for Sustainable Development. e-learning Chapter 3 Module on Operationalizing the Right to Development in Implementing the Sustainable Development Goals. University for Peace—UN Mandate.

30 Declaration on the Right to Development, supra note 7, Preamble Para 10.

31 Hansungule, Michelo (2005) The Right to Development, Paper presented at the International Human Rights Academy jointly organised by University of Western Cape, Utrecht University, Ghent University, American University; October 2005, Sea Point, Cape Town, South Africa, 18.

32 Declaration on the Right to Development, supra note 7, Preamble Para 1 and Art 4(2).

33 Art and Tamo, supra note 14.

34 Subedi, Surya (2021) Declaration on The Right to Development. *United Nations Audiovisual Library of International Law*, 1–9.

Due to rejection of the RTD based on the above arguments advanced by developed countries, the RTD has to date, not effectively been implemented by them. However, this has not stopped the evolution and continuous development of the concept of the RTD. In 1998, the idea of a legally binding RTD treaty emerged during a summit of the movement of non-aligned countries in Durban, South Africa, under the leadership of then President Nelson Mandela.[35] This led to the establishment of the Open-ended Intergovernmental Group of the UN Human Rights Council tasked to monitor and review progress made in the promotion and implementation of the RTD as elaborated in the DRTD.[36] In 2015, Mr Zamir Akram, Chair-Rapporteur of the Intergovernmental Working Group on the Right to Development (IGWG) was appointed.[37] Prof Mihir Kanade was also appointed in 2018 to chair the committee drafting the International Convention on the RTD.[38] The USA has remained a strong opponent to the RTD and consistently voted against several intergovernmental resolutions on the RTD.[39] Japan expressed its opposition to the treaty drafting whilst the European Union, though still a participant, opposes aligning the Sustainable Development Goals to the RTD and other issues.[40]

The drafting of the Convention has however, proceeded unabated and the text of the first draft Convention on the RTD was ready by January 2020.[41] The 17–21 May 2021 marked the 21st session of the Working Group on the RTD where interactive dialogues with the Chair of the Expert Mechanism on the RTD, and the Special Rapporteur on RTD were held as well as consideration of contributions made by states and stakeholders towards implementation of the RTD and progress on the SDGs at national level.[42] As of 12 October 2023, the Human Rights Council submitted to the General Assembly the draft

35 United Nations (2023, 11 May) Right to Development: New Treaty would Codify Right to Development. Available at: https://www.ohchr.org/en/stories/2023/05/new-treaty-would-codify-right-development (consulted 28 October 2024).

36 The Right to Development Commission on Human Rights Resolution 1998/72.

37 United Nations (1996–2024) Ambassador Zamir Akram, Working group on the Right to Development. Available at: https://www.ohchr.org/en/hrc-subsidiaries/iwg-on-development/ambassador-zamir-akram (consulted 25 October 2024).

38 Ibid.

39 Li, Yuefen; Uribe Daniele and Danish (2022) The International Discourse on the Right to Development and the Need to Reinvigorate its Implementation. *The South Centre.*

40 Ibid.

41 United Nations, supra note 35.

42 United Nations (2021, 17–21 May) Working Group on the Right to Development: 21st Session. Available at: https://www.ohchr.org/EN/Issues/Development/Pages/21stSession.aspx (consulted 13 October 2024).

International Covenant on the Right to Development for its consideration, negotiation and subsequent adoption.[43]

While this is an initiative spearheaded by developing countries that are hopeful to benefit from a binding treaty on the RTD, the whole division and lack of involvement of the world economic giants in the drafting processes has left the world puzzled. What will happen after the adoption of the Covenant remains unknown. In the meantime, the RTD had also gained ground in some regional and interregional legal instruments. The most prominent expression at a regional level is Article 22 of the 1981 African Charter on Human and Peoples' Rights.[44] To date, the African Charter remains the only hard law document bestowing an individual and collective RTD with binding and enforceable obligations imposed on state parties.

3 The Right to Development and Technology Advancement

Against the foregoing, there is a great potential for development in Africa and other developing countries through the opportunities that come along with the fourth industrial revolution (4IR), offering a beacon of hope for transformative progress across the continent.[45] Unlike in the past when only a handful of people could read and write, and only the rich had access to technology and the technical knowhow, in the present, Africans have become increasingly literate, including in the use of advanced technologies.[46] As of 2019, for instance, at least 34% of the African population possessed basic information communications skills.[47] The International Telecommunications Union (ITU),[48] reports that between 2005 and 2019, African mobile subscriptions soared from 73.5 to

43 United Nations (2023, 12 October) Human Rights Council Adopts Five Resolutions, Submits to General Assembly Draft International Covenant on the Right to Development for its Negotiation and Adoption, and Extends Mandate on Burundi. Available at: https://www.ohchr.org/en/news/2023/10/human-rights-council-adopts-five-resolutions-submits-general-assembly-draft (consulted 28 October 2024).

44 African Charter on Human and Peoples' Rights adopted in Nairobi, Kenya on 27 June 1981 OAU Doc CAB/LEG/67/3 Rev.5 (1981), Art 22.

45 Brown, Edward (2020, 9 March) The Fourth Industrial Revolution Will Africa be Ready? African Centre for economic transformation. *African Centre for Economic Transformation.*

46 Broadband Commission (2019, 31 September) The State of Broad Band 2019: Broadband as a Foundation of Sustainable Development. *ITU/UNESCO*. Available at: file:///F:/chapter%203/S-POL-BROADBAND.20-2019-PDF-E.pdf (consulted 15 October 2024).

47 Ibid.

48 A specialised agency of the United Nations.

80.1 per 100 people[49] while the broadband subscriptions grew nearly double fold, from 17.4 per 100 people to 34.0.[50] To date, according to internet stats, about 39.8% of Africa's 1.3 billion population can go online, using mobile technologies such as cell phones and laptops.[51]

The use of mobile and internet technology is aiding the continent to leapfrog the challenges of infrastructure deficit and other forms of underdevelopment. Precisely, the unreliable and expensive postal and telephone services, which are now becoming obsolete artifacts of the past.[52] Mobile technology and the internet have become a tool for productivity, efficiency and problem solving in various sectors such as communication, education, economics, healthcare, infrastructure, agriculture, governance, and finance among others. Nowadays, there is no need to physically approach government departments to report issues or lay a complaint, it is becoming increasingly possible to do so through internet and mobile technology. Important social justice related measures as well as service deliveries by government to the people have become easier and more efficient through the use of digital technologies.[53] With the average technical knowledge many African societies now possess, the citizenry is increasingly able to establish digital platforms through which they can participate in public debates aimed towards alleviating the challenges of under-development, poverty and empowerment for the people.[54] These technologies foster public participation in decision making and thus, empower citizens to contribute to social and economic development.[55] Similarly, the technologies also improve transparency and accountability and hence also promotes good governance, which is a major pillar of the right to development.[56]

---

49 Bogdan-Martin, Doreen (2019) Measuring Digital Development: Facts and Figures. *ITU Publications*. Available at: https://www.itu.int/en/ITU-D/Statistics/Documents/facts/FactsFigures2019.pdf 5 (consulted 15 October 2024).

50 Ibid.

51 Broadband Commission (2019, 31 September) The State of Broad Band 2019: Broadband as a Foundation of Sustainable Development. *ITU/UNESCO*. Available at: file:///F:/chapter%203/S-POL-BROADBAND.20-2019-PDF-E.pdf (consulted 15 October 2014).

52 UNDP (2016) The Africa Data Revolution Report 2016 Highlighting Developments in African Data Ecosystems. Available at: https://www.africa.undp.org/content/rba/en/home/library/reports/the_africa_data_revolution_report_2016.html (consulted 15 October 2024).

53 Ye, Lisha and Yang, Huiqin (2020) From Digital Divide to Social Inclusion: A Tale of Mobile Platform Empowerment in Rural Areas. *Sustainability* 12(6): 2424.

54 Ibid.

55 Horner, Lisa (2011) Human Rights Approach to the Mobile Internet. *Association for Progressive Communications*.

56 Ibid.

Indeed, one of the contemporary advancements that has been a major enabler of almost all fundamental human rights in Africa is the internet and mobile technologies. They enhance access to and the free flow of information and communications especially, through modern forms of social interactions on social media.[57] Human rights such as access to information, freedom of expression, democratic participation, the right to education, all embodied in the right to development, are made possible these days by the combination of mobile and internet technologies.[58] As Castells postulates:

> The internet is not just a technology; it is the technological tool and organisational form that distributes information power, knowledge generation and networking capacity in all realms of activity. Without an internet-based economy and management system, there is little chance for any country to generate resources to cover its developmental needs, on a sustainable ground, economically, socially and environmentally.[59]

Mobile and internet technologies have spurred a tremendous cultural, social, political, and economic revolution in Africa.[60] The mobile and internet "miracle", encompassing artificial intelligence, 5Gs networks, the internet of things, robotics, blockchains, open data, big data and other advanced technologies has brought hope for regional integration and development in Africa.[61] Most African governments are gradually developing an unquenchable thirst to transform their national economies into digital economies for economic advancements, as highlighted in the African Union Agenda 2063.[62]

In 2018, the Global System for Mobile Association, accelerator recorded about 314 active technology hubs in 93 cities of 43 African countries.[63] South Africa, Ghana, Kenya and Nigeria have indeed, digitised some of their main cities, also known as "smart cities".[64] Smart cities refer to cities comprising of

---

57 Ye and Lang, supra note 53.

58 Ojo, Adegboyega et al (2013) Enabling Development Through Governance and Mobile Technology. *Government Information Quarterly* 30(1): 34.

59 Castells, Manuel (2001) *The Internet Galaxy: Reflections on the Internet, Business and Society*. Oxford: Oxford University Press, 269.

60 The Africa Data Revolution Report (2016) Highlighting Developments in African Data Ecosystems. *UNDP*.

61 Ibid.

62 Agenda 2063: African Union.

63 International Trade Centre (2024) *Tech Hubs in Africa: Accelerating Start-Ups for Resilient Growth*. 3rd Edn, Geneva: ITC, 2.

64 AFR-IX Telecom. Available at: https://afr-ix.com/2019/05/15/smart-cities-in-africa/last (consulted 15 October 2024).

a smart economy, smart mobility, smart environment, smart people, smart energy, smart transportation, smart health care and a smart lifestyle.[65] They are mainly driven by data collecting technologies, modern infrastructure and the internet of things intended to provide efficiency, flexibility and sustainability in services delivery to the citizens. The key enabling factor for smart cities is information communications technology (ICT) facilitated by the internet and mobile smart phones.

These modern developments confirm the prophecies of the "construction theory" of innovation by Joseph Schumpeter,[66] as well as Marshall McLuhan's *global village*.[67] Schumpeter envisioned a futuristic economy upon which the entrepreneur as "the pivot around which everything turns," who, driven by competition, pushes for new innovation, as a result of advanced innovation, the capitalist experience rapid economic advancement.[68] McLuhan had a revelation of the world becoming knitted together into a single unit by rapid innovation and technological developments. Where, notwithstanding the status of whether poor, rich, old or young, no one would be excluded from the orbit. All the spheres of life will be operating under a one stop shop setting, within a "global village".[69] This is what the world is currently facing in the contemporary times of the industrial revolution. The world is now seamlessly interconnected despite existing divides. However, this means that only those fully equipped will be able to benefit from these developments.

It can accordingly, be deduced that the relationship between the right to development and mobile internet technology is symbiotic. This is because currently, there can be no development without technology, and no effective realisation of human rights without technology. Therefore, the need for technological advancement and transfer to developing states can no longer be ignored but should be enabled through adopting rights-based policies and regulatory frameworks. This is what Article 13 of the draft Covenant on the RTD seeks to resuscitate. The potential for development driven by mobile and internet technology calls for a rethinking of the concepts, policies, developments strategies.

---

65 Mohanty, Saraju *et al* (2016) Everything You Wanted to Know About Smart Cities: The Internet of Things is the Backbone. *IEEE Consumer Electronics Magazine* 5(3): 60–70.

66 MacCraw, Thomas (2007) *Prophet of Innovation; Joseph Schumpeter and Creative Destruction*. Harvard: Harvard University Press, 3–9.

67 Kohl, Uta (2007) *Jurisdiction and the Internet: Regulatory Competence Over Online Activity*. Cambridge: Cambridge University Press, 3.

68 Ibid.

69 Kohl, supra note 67, 3–4.

4 Redefining the RTD in the Context of Technological Advancement

4.1 *Comprehensive, People-Centred and Rights-Based Development*

The DRTD defines development as more than a growth and for-profit focus but as recognising the limits of the current international economic framework and apprehending the participatory equality of all people.[70] It recognises that development should be comprehensive, which implies social, economic, cultural and political development of every individual and all peoples on the basis of their active and meaningful participation in the development process.[71] Rights-based as the wording suggests, means that development or the enablement of technologies in societies must be conducted in a way that respects and protects human rights. It must be born in mind that while technological advancement is designed and intended to be used by people, it often also affects people adversely. Therefore, in accordance with the DRTD, and the draft Covenant on the RTD, the human person must meaningfully participate in its development processes, and it must only be developed in accordance with human rights standards.

Emphasis on the rights-based approach is for the reason that in the digital world, the "human person" is both the beneficiary and the consumer. Therefore, human rights considerations must be integrated in the development and governance of the technological sector. They must have a say on the development and governance issues relating to digital technology and must be granted adequate protection of their rights in the digital world in the same way they enjoy the protections in the analogue world.[72] Mobile internet technologies are also the modern enablers of fundamental human rights, including the right to development which encapsulates other rights such as the right of access to information, freedom of expression, democratic participation, healthcare and education among others.[73]

The need to promote and enable the development of mobile technology and internet on the African continent in a manner that is people-centred and human rights based is imperative. It implies that the development of mobile and internet technology should be done in a manner that promotes people's interest such as enabling easy and secure access to technology for purposes of

70 Declaration on the Right to Development, supra note 7, Preamble Para 16 and Art 3.

71 Ibid at Preamble Para 2, Art 2(3) and Art 8(2).

72 United Nations General Assembly (2016, 27 June) The Promotion, Protection and Enjoyment of Human Rights on the Internet, Resolution A/HRC/32/L.20. Available at: https://digitallibrary.un.org/record/845728?ln=en&v=pdf (consulted 28 October 2024).

73 The UN declared that it considers the internet to be a human right.

voting, doing business online, engaging in political debates, having access to information, and social services. In this regard, technology should be promoted because it enhances people's capabilities, autonomy and their decision-making power. Technology is indeed, a tool for empowerment.

African state governments must accordingly, promulgate the necessary electronic communications and transactions, cybercrimes and security as well as data protection privacies and laws to enable the use and enjoyment and most importantly, the protection of human rights online.[74] In the same way, the continent should protect consumers against unfair trading on the digital space through robust consumer protection laws. Consumers must be assured that the same way their rights are protected in manual transactions they will receive the same protection, if not better protection, in the digital settings.[75] This will dispel fears of using online facilities and technology and hence, boost the e-commerce sector.

As per Article 7 of the draft Covenant on the RTD, states must refrain from actions that may hinder the enjoyment of human rights online, as well as repeal laws that may have the effect of deterring the use, access, and development of the sector.[76] Technologies are a source of empowerment for the marginalised and underprivileged groups in societies and therefore, they must equally be allowed access rights. The draft Covenant envisions adopting policies that promote affordable access to mobile technology and fostering partnerships to enhance knowledge-sharing and technological development.[77]

Alemneh and Hastings note that the internet is the source of information, which is the light for scholarship.[78] By inference, power and wealth are derived from the ability to access information, obtain and use that information effectively for development. However, due to lack of development, Africa has not been able to fully exploit this opportunity, and therefore, has remained behind.[79] Until Africa stands firm and becomes a full actor in the global

74 Litan, Robert and Niskanen, Willia (1998) *Going Digital!: A Guide to Policy in the Digital Age*. Washington DC: Brookings Institute Press, 1–3.

75 Conteanu, Christina (2005) *Cyber Consumer Law and Unfair Trading Practices*. New York: Routledge, 31.

76 Draft Covenant on the Right to Development, supra note 6, Art 7.

77 Draft Covenant on the Right to Development, supra note 6, Art 13(2)(c)(d)(e) and Art 13(4).

78 Alemneh, Daniel Gelaw and Hastings, Samantha Kelly (2006) Developing the ICT Infrastructure for Africa: Overview of Barriers to Harnessing the Full Power of the Internet. *Journal of Education for Library and Information Science* 47(1): 1.

79 Ibid.

information revolution, the digital gap will not cease to exist.[80] ICT is an inevitable tool for development in the sense that it has the potential to reduce poverty, build capacities and capabilities, enrich skills and inspire new approaches to governance.[81]

Access to the internet and mobile technology is thus, essential for the effective realisation of the Right to Development (RTD). The Preamble to the draft Covenant on the RTD reaffirms this assertion and envisages promoting a holistic view of development where progress should be made on multiple fronts simultaneously. The emphasis on providing assistance to marginalised and vulnerable communities clearly aligns with the people-centred approach to development, including within the technology sector. Thus, technological advancement, as any form of development should be inclusive and accessible to all as a means of empowering marginalised communities and in turn, addressing societal inequalities and poverty.[82] This calls for international cooperation and promotion of solidarity rights.

4.2 *International Cooperation and the Right to Self-Determination on Matters of Mobile and Internet Technology Development*

Due to its nature as an ubiquitous, interactive, multimodal, communication medium, able to transcend between traditional national borders, mobile internet technology has become increasingly sophisticated and multifaceted. As the fifth domain of human activity,[83] aided by the proliferation of mobile smart technology, it has emerged as a repository of numerous threats and vulnerabilities for the global community, which threaten even international peace and security.[84] Despite the benefits of digital technologies across various aspects of life, they have their dark side, providing target-rich environments for certain individuals, governments, and non-governmental actors to engage in malicious activities.

The vast quantity of information and the communications residing within these domains, coupled with the speed and anonymity they afford, makes them susceptible to cyber hacktivism, cyber vandalism, cybercrime, cyber

80 Ibid.

81 Ibid.

82 Draft Covenant on the Right to Development, supra note 6, Preamble.

83 The Netherlands Ministry of Defence (2012) The Defence Cyber Strategy. Available at: www.ccdddcoe.org/strategies/Defence_cyberstrategy_ndl.pdf 4 (consulted 20 October 2024).

84 UN Secretary General, Foreword Group of Governmental Experts on Developments in the Fields of Information and Telecommunication in the Context of International Security, UN Doc A/70/174, 22 July 2015.

terrorism, cyberwars, and cyber espionage.[85] These illicit cyber activities are of global nature, affecting individual states, of course in a disproportionate manner. They also have serious negative implications on digital rights, and on economic, political, and social development necessitating global solutions in the form of treaties and other mechanisms for collective interventions. They call for international cooperation, unity and the spirit of solidarity among states to foster enabling and safe national and international environments for technological advancement. This is supported by the provisions of Article 3 and Article 13 of the draft Covenant on the RTD, which impose the duty to cooperate and a spirit of solidarity in resolving international problems of an economic, social, cultural, political, environmental, health-related, educational, technological or humanitarian character.[86]

Article 23 also obligates state parties to promote international peace and security as well as inclusive societies within their territories. Therefore, states must undertake to pursue collective measures necessary to ensure that the world's human, ecological, economic, and technological resources can be used for the full realisation of the right to development for all, and not to cause harm.[87] As serious as matters of technology are at the moment, there are still no international treaties in place to regulate the rapidly growing sector of technology advancement.

4.2.1 Lack of Global Treaties on Cyber Espionage

Taking cyber espionage as an example, it can be described as unauthorised acts by state or non-state actors aimed at harvesting confidential information on political, military and security affairs, as well as sensitive economic information, and policy developments to gain strategic advantage.[88] This is mostly conducted through national intelligence centres using intrusive surveillance tools adept for this purpose, a practice known as extraterritorial surveillance.[89] Clearly, this breaches the rights to equal sovereignty as a foundational value of the international order and hence, contravenes Article 5 of the draft Covenant on the RTD.

Cyber espionage also threatens the customary international law principle of territorial sovereignty,[90] which accords every state the right to independence,

85 Buchan, Russel (2018) *Cyber Espionage and International Law*. Bloomsbury Academic, 2.
86 Draft Covenant on the Right to Development, supra note 6, Art 13.
87 Draft Covenant on the Right to Development, supra note 6, Art 23.
88 Buchan, supra note 85.
89 Ibid.
90 Schmid, Michael N and Vihul, Liis (2017) Respect for Sovereignty in Cyber Space. *Texas Law Review* 95(7): 1639.

control over access to its territory,[91] and the ability to perform governmental duties without external interference. Cyber espionage has the capacity to cripple the economies of fragile states especially those in the developing regions of the world. While governments are not the only perpetrators of cyber illicit activities, it remains a customary international law obligation for host countries to enact laws that curb the practices and suppress the conduct of the non-state actors that operate within their territories.[92] Cyber espionage in itself constitutes a breach of the right to development for the victim states.

Acts of cyber espionage have the capacity to cripple other states economically as well as destabilise the international order. Where trade secrets of a company located under one state jurisdiction are stolen and utilised by a competitor company in another state to produce the same products at relatively lowest prices, it can severely undermine the competitive edge of the original company.[93] Articles 7 and 9 of the draft Covenant on the RTD make provisions on how to resolve the problem by imposing duties on states and non-state actors to respect the RTD.[94]

In 2013, the Edward Snowden leaks revealed that for a long time the world giants like the USA and the United Kingdom (UK) through the US National Security Agency, were harvesting information from across the globe, including the trade secrets of other countries which made them able to compete at an international level and protect their domestic businesses from competition as well as political secrets of other states.[95] This dynamic has contributed to the sustained economic power of the western countries over developing nations, as it enables them to gain insights in to the intentions and the capacities of developing countries, leaving the latter at a perpetual disadvantage.. The draft Covenant seeks to restore equity and address the disproportionate relations and the imbalanced bargaining powers resulting from the technological privileges held by developed countries. These acts were expressly rejected by many of the victims of cyber espionage like Argentina, Bolivia, Brazil, Uruguay and Venezuela based on the violation of the territorial sovereignty principle.

91 Von Heinegg, Wolff Heintschel (2013) Territorial Sovereignty and Neutrality in Cyber Space. *International Law Studies* 89: 123–124.

92 Corfu Channel (1949) *United Kingdom of Great Britain and Northern Ireland v Albania*. ICJ Judgments on Merits.

93 Pehlivan, Oğuz Kaan (2020) *Confronting Cyber Espionage Under International Law*. New York: Routledge, 1.

94 Draft Covenant on the Right to Development, supra note 6, Arts 7 and 9, including international organisations.

95 The Guardian (2013, 9 June) Edward Snowden: The Whistleblower Behind the NSA Surveillance Revelations. Available at: https://www.theguardian.com/world/2013/jun/09/edward-snowden-nsa-whistleblower-surveillance (consulted 28 October 2024).

The USA also acknowledged that the acts of cyber espionage contravene the rules of international order and threaten international peace and security due to their negative impacts to the economy.[96]

In 2013, it was recorded that the cyber espionage enable theft of intellectual property valued at over USD 300 billion annually .[97] The USA however, also points a finger at China for their rigorous espionage operations, which continue to encroach upon its economic developments, costing the USA USD 10 billion annually. This was revealed by the Mandiant[98] company in 2013, which attest that China has been stealing a large volume of valuable intellectual property, including blueprints, trade secrets, business plans, proprietary manufacturing processes, partnership agreements, emails and contact list of powerful people around the world. In spite of that, even after experiencing the cyber espionage effects on their economies, the international community still refuse to accept that unauthorised collection of confidential information amounts to interference with the exercise of governmental functions.[99] For instance, the UK arguably stated that they do not believe that the rule of territorial sovereignty applies over the internet space.[100]

Moreover, the above explains the Chinese influence over Africa where, thus; nothing of African origin at the moment exist that is not manufactured in China and sold at a cheaper price. The situation is exacerbated by poor policies on the protection of intellectual property and indigenous knowledge in Africa, which causes a strain to the local content, and local markets.[101] There is no market for locally produced goods as Chinese retailers have taken over with cheaper prices despite not the best quality. Misappropriated trade secrets of other countries are passed on to non-state actors such as companies and

96 Von Heinegg, supra note 91, 124.

97 Blair, Denis and Huntsman, John Jr. (2013) The IP Commission Report: The Report of the Commission on the Theft of American Intellectual Property. Available at: www.ipcommision.org/report/ip_commission_report052213.pdf (consulted 15 October 2024).

98 Mandiant (2013) Exposing one of China's Cyber Espionage Units. Available at: https://nsarchive2.gwu.edu/NSAEBB/NSAEBB424/docs/Cyber-083.pdf (consulted 15 October 2024).

99 Buchan, supra note 85, 69.

100 Wright, Jeremy (2018, 22 May) Cyber and International Law in the 21st Century. Available at: https://www.gov.uk/government/speeches/cyber-and-international-law-in-the-21st-century (consulted 15 October 2024); see also, Corn, Gary and Taylor, Robert (2017) Sovereignty in the Cyber Space in the Age of Cyber. *American Journal of International Law* 111: 207.

101 Ncube, Caroline (2013) Harnessing Intellectual Property for Development: Some Thoughts on an Appropriate Theoretical Framework. *Potchefstroom Electronic Law Journal* 16(4): 1–30.

local businesses often subsidised by the government to maintain the highest competitive level in the global trading sphere.[102] This cripples a lot of African developing economies. Upon adoption of the Covenant on the RTD, many obligations curbing these practices will be created and therefore, allow victim states to seek legal accountability and redress.

China financed construction of the African Union headquarters building in Ethiopia, and thereafter, it was revealed that they planted a powerful surveillance system in the building to enable them access African development plans and secrets.[103] In addition to encroaching on state's sovereignty rights and hindering development, acts of cyberespionage also pose a threat to international peace and order. Yet no international treaties on cyber espionage at a global level exist to address these issues.

4.2.2 International Developments in Digital Technology, Cyber Security, and Data Protection

Similarly, there is also no international treaty specifically governing internet and mobile technology advancement. However, there have been several model laws developed to guide global electronic transactions such as the United Nations Commission on International Trade Law model laws on e-commerce.[104] These model laws were harmonised into an international treaty in 2005, dubbed the United Nations Convention on the Use of Electronic Communications in International Contracts, which has played a significant role in facilitating electronic communications and transactions over the years. In addition, the World Trade Organisation has continued to join hands with other stakeholders and states in finding ways to tackle the persisting problems in the e-commerce sector primarily; security enhancing measures, consumer protection, liberalisation, and development of the sector.[105] During the 11th Ministerial Conference held in December 2017, as the community gathered

102 Ibid.

103 Solomon, Salem (2021, 5 January) Experts: Report of China Hacking African Union HQ Fits Larger Pattern. Available at: https://www.voanews.com/a/east-asia-pacific_voa-news-china_experts-report-china-hacking-african-union-hq-fits-larger-pattern/6200356.html (consulted 23 October 2024).

104 Model laws on Electronic Commerce 1996 and Model Law on Electronic Signature, 2001.

105 Pittet, Faith Tigere (2022) African Participation in WTO e-Commerce Negotiations: Policy Positions and Development Issues. *African Perspectives, Global Insights—South African Institute of International Affairs* 131: 2.

to continue negotiating the rules to govern the sector, African states signalled a resistance to the proposed negotiations on cross-border e-commerce rules.[106]

Given the potential of the sector for Africa as elaborated above, the lack of interest in this important global rule making processes for the ICT sector put the continent in a disadvantaged position. As one of the rapidly developing continents, and the most populous,[107] Africa stands to benefit more from negotiating the rules than other regions of the world which are already advanced in technology. Whilst there are multifaceted limiting factors in developing the technology sector in Africa, such as building appropriate infrastructure, technology transfer, and technical ICT expertise, the sector cannot progress without legal enablement. The law remains an engine for driving development. Despite the rapid penetration of the 4IR on the continent, they mostly preceded the law and therefore, need to be regulated. Adequate regulation dispels issues of distrust and enables the use and enjoyment of technology in a rights-based manner. It also has potential to open great doors for local markets and stimulate foreign direct investments. As emphasised in Article 3 of the draft Covenant on the RTD, national and international solidarity is necessary for the realisation of the right to development. Similarly, advancement in technology requires an enabling national and international environment created through a spirit of cooperation and unity among individuals, peoples, states and international organisations.[108] This principle includes the duty to cooperate with full respect for the principles of international law.

International cooperation and participation on international fora for ICT developments will enable Africa to acquire the relevant knowledge and draw lessons on the best practices in regulating the sector as well as its infrastructural development. Moreover, partaking in the global rule-making processes for cross-border e-commerce will yield long-term benefits for sustainable development rather than concentrating on seeking development donations which are hardly accounted for. Although there is great potential for Africa, it will take time and committed efforts to unleash it into tangible sustainable developments. Africa must aim for sustainable technological advancement to be able to achieve long lasting development on the continent. Like China, Africa has the potential and is capable of manufacturing its own technologies. It needs self-empowerment as well as international cooperation to achieve

106 Trade Law Centre (2018, 19 January) Africa and WTO's e-Commerce Agenda. Available at: https://www.tralac.org (consulted 20 October 2024).

107 African Development Bank (2013, 11 July) Africa is Now the Fastest Growing Continent in the World. Available at: https://www.afdb.org/fr/news-and-events/africa-is-now-the-fastest-growing-continent-in-the-world-12107 (consulted 28 October 2024).

108 Draft Covenant on the Right to Development, supra note 6, Art 3.

this. For instance, Africa needs to focus more on investing in ICT education and skills development, research and development, infrastructure development, ICT policy formulation, regional collaborations, public-private partnerships, promoting local solutions, promoting endogenous innovations, seeking international technical assistance and expertise where necessary. It will be overly ambitious of Africa to expect rapid advancement in the field of digital technology comparable to Europe or China in one day given the continent's historical background of dispossession and systemic disadvantages. However, long term progress is possible if Africa can prioritise investments in the digital technology sector. Without such commitments sustainable technological advancement will be out of reach and the existing digital divide will persist.

4.2.3 Challenge Posed by of the Lack of International Treaties on Cybercrime, Data Protection, Cyberwarfare and Cyberterrorism

Currently there is no global treaty on data protection, cybercrime, cyber terrorism or cyber warfare despite the growing need to effectively regulate these fields amid rapid technological advancements. The EU contrived the landmark General Data Protection Regulation (GDPR) in 2018,[109] which has been recognised as the best standard for the protection of digital rights globally and hence, is gradually and strategically being imposed on the rest of the world, including Africa by virtue of its extraterritorial applicability.[110] Through this legal development, the EU threatens to cut ties with countries that do business with them if the laws of those countries do not incorporate standards equating to those of the GDPR. This is no doubt a tactical way of imposing the GDPR on developing countries. While it is unlikely that developing countries would want to lose business opportunities with the EU, particularly the consultancy services that significantly boost economic development, the EU'S conditionality is no justifiable excuse to blindly cut and paste the GDPR into domestic laws.

The strategy of imposing cyber laws on developing countries also happened with the Council of Europe, Convention on Cybercrime (Budapest Convention),[111] which was made open for accession by other countries outside of Europe, including African Countries. Suggestions later emerged that the Budapest Convention be declared an international treaty on cybercrime.[112]

109 EU General Data Protection Regulations, 2018.

110 Art 3 of the EU GDPR.

111 Convention on Cybercrime (Budapest Convention, ETS No 185) and its Protocols.

112 Daskal, Jennifer and Kennedy-Mayo (2020) Budapest Convention: What is it and How is it Being Updated? Available at: https://www.crossborderdataforum.org/budapest-convention-what-is-it-and-how-is-it-being-updated/ (consulted 2 July 2020); Peters, Allison (2019) Russia and China are Trying to Set the UN's Rules on Cybercrime. *Foreign Policy*.

While these EU cyber law instruments are undoubtedly ground-breaking, imposing them on developing countries is problematic and contradict the principles of international cooperation, solidarity and self-determination discussed earlier.

What works for the EU may not necessarily work for Africa and vice versa. Advancements in technology affect countries to differing degrees, and these technologies have penetrated the different regions of the world at different pace. There are issues of cultural patterns of life, indigenous languages and other societal needs that are only uniquely common to the African region, which must be considered in developing the African digital technology sector regulation. Further, by reason that other continents had not participated in the drafting of the EU standards, put them in a disproportionately unfair position.

Despite the political debates around issues of sovereignty over the internet and regulating cybercrimes particularly led by China and Russia, the UN has recognised the need to draft an alternative international treaty on cybercrimes which is currently underway.[113] Notwithstanding this, it is noteworthy to recognise the AU efforts in adopting a regional Convention on Cyber Security and Personal Data Protection in 2014, which came into effect in 2023.[114] Despite significant criticisms on its structure among other things, the AU Convention stands out as an endogenous landmark legal development requiring state parties to contrive the digital space laws at the national level. It addresses issues relating to electronic transactions and communications, cybercrimes and data protection in Africa.

4.3 *Global Institutions on ICT Development*

Institutionally, the organisation entrusted with spearheading advancements in global information technological advancement is the International Telecommunications Union, an agency of the UN, established to focus on development of the internet and governance.[115] The Telecommunications Union, with its 193-member states, 900 companies, universities and regional organisations, has continued to drive innovation in the ICT sector globally.

Available at: https://foreignpolicy.com/2019/09/16/russia-and-china-are-trying-to-set-the-u-n-s-rules-on-cybercrime/ (consulted 16 September 2019).

113 United Nations (2024, 9 August) United Nations: Member States Finalize a New Cybercrime Convention. Available at: https://www.unodc.org/unodc/en/frontpage/2024/August/united-nations_-member-states-finalize-a-new-cybercrime-convention.html (consulted 8 October 2024).

114 African Union Convention on Cyber Security and Personal Data Protection, 2014.

115 International Telecommunication Union. Available at: http://www.itu.int/ last (consulted 20 February 2020).

It also helps with allocating the global radio spectrum, satellite orbits, and in establishing technical standards to ensure that networks and technologies interconnect seamlessly. They also strive to improve access to ICTs in marginalised communities worldwide.[116]

In light of the above, the RTD within the context of technological advancements compels the entire international community to work collectively in creating a safe and development-friendly internet space. There is a need for strong international solidarity in technological progress particularly, in safeguarding human rights online. The international community and local regulators especially in Africa, can no longer ignore the increasingly adverse impacts of the rapidly evolving digital technologies on societies, as these developments affects the RTD which is guaranteed to every individual and to all peoples worldwide.

4.4 *The Question of Technology Transfer*

The quest for technology transfer has been an integral component of several international treaties, including for instance, Articles 7 and 66.5 of the Agreement on Trade-Related Aspects of Intellectual Property Rights (TRIPS) and other international agreements such as the UN Framework Convention on Climate Change (UNFCCC).[117] This principle is also embedded in Target 17 of the 2030 agenda on the Sustainable Development Goals (SDGs), which envisages technology and innovation cooperation, knowledge sharing, and access to science. It also envisages the development, transfer, dissemination, and diffusion of environmentally sound technologies to developing countries on favourable terms.[118] However, for political reasons these provisions have never been implemented, leaving little to show in terms of tangible outcomes. As a result developing countries remain largely underdeveloped and impoverished partly due to the lack of effective technology transfer.[119]

Moreover, Article 13 of the draft Covenant on the RTD reaffirms the question of technology transfer as a right integral to the RTD for developing countries. It envisions legally binding obligations on developed countries to ensure that developing states have equitable access to technology, technical assistance and

116 International Telecommunication Union (2024) Committed to Connecting the World. Available at: http://www.itu.int/ (consulted 20 February 2020).

117 Dos Santos, supra note 5, 39.

118 Target 17.6 and 17.7 of SDGs.

119 Fox, David (2019) Technology Transfer and the TRIPS Agreement are Developed Countries Meeting their end of the Bargain? *Hastings Science and Technology Law Journal* 10(1): 1–32.

technology transfer as a matter of justice, rather than charity or commercial exchange. The draft Covenant mandates international cooperation to facilitate access to technology by developing countries. Article 13 encourages removing the barriers to access, including those arising from intellectual property laws that hinder developing countries from accessing requisite technologies for their development. By incorporating technology transfer as a right integral to the RTD, the draft Covenant adds moral and legal weight to the obligations on developed countries. To ensure effective implementation of the Covenant when it is adopted and comes into force, a treaty monitoring body similar to those for other human rights treaties will need to be put in place to ensure compliance and promote accountability.

Africa has established partnerships that include aspects of technology transfer such as the Forum on China-Africa Cooperation which have however largely remained on paper.[120] Except for the mobile technologies that infiltrated the continent at an alarming rate, there is little evidence on the ground on technology transfer, technical assistance, the sharing of technological knowhow, innovation, technological adoption and assimilation for sustainability. This raises questions on the effectiveness and implementation of these initiatives.

In the last decade, the world witnessed China's economic boom, due to their massive investments in technology and innovation. To date China is a leading champion in access to fibre optic broadband. They also have the largest e-commerce market in the world, which is predicted to be the size of the US and EU combined.[121] According to the World Bank, between 2000 and 2010, China's mobile subscriptions (per 100 people) rose from 6.3 to 63.2 whereas the export of high technology manufactured goods soared from 19% to 28%.[122] GDP per capita also arose from USD 1,211.35 billion to USD 6,100.62 billion within the same timelines.[123] On the other hand, Africa has remained overly dependent on donations accompanied by the now unending development loans from China, which continue to impoverish the continent.[124] Despite the comparative

120 Mlambo, Courage; Kushamba, Audrey and Simawu, More Blessing (2016) China-Africa Relations: What Lies Beneath? *The Chinese Economy* 49(4): 257–276.

121 McKinsey and Company (2017, 3 August) China's Digital Economic Force: A Leading Global Force. Available at: https://www.mckinsey.com/featured-insights/china/chinas-digital-economy-a-leading-global-force (consulted 28 October 2024).

122 World Bank Group (2024) Statistics per Country. Available at: https://databank.worldbank.org/ (consulted 28 October 2024).

123 Ibid.

124 Adem, Seifudein and Babagana, Waziri Babagana (2023) Is Africa China's Neo-Dependency in the Making? *Third World Quarterly* 44(7): 1363–1379.

advantages that Africa possesses,[125] and the capabilities to sustainably develop the continent including, through endogenous technologies, Africa has remained a sleeping giant waiting to be fed.

Although the law reiterates the need for technology transfer as an obligation for economic advancement of developing countries, a valuable lesson to draw from China is that rather than waiting endlessly, developing states should empower themselves by leveraging the existing resources to locally develop their technology sectors, and invest in infrastructure. If a once poor developing country China made it, then Africa as a continent can do even better.

5 Conclusion

The conclusion drawn in this chapter is that digital technologies have the potential to enable realisation of the RTD, but this potential is hindered by persisting factors generated within the digital context . Africa and other developing countries need to work collaboratively and commit to the development of the technology sector. This, entails engaging in international cooperation and establishing ICT institutional mechanisms while seeking opportunities for sustainable technology transfer. It is noted that Africa has also been lagging in regulating the technology sector despite their reluctance to participate in the international negotiations on the rules governing the sector where valuable lessons could be learnt and best practices in the field adopted.

Africa needs to ensure that developments in the sector of ICT just like other forms of development should be people-centred and human rights-based. The draft Covenant on the RTD offers hope for sustainable technology advancement for developing countries particularly those in Africa. The chapter concludes that by fulfilling the obligations under Article 13 of the draft Covenant, developed countries can play a pivotal role in dismantling the barriers that hinder technology transfer to developing countries. This will ensure that advancements in digital technology translate into tangible socio-economic benefits for developing countries. Finally, governments, international organisations, and the private sector must work together in overcoming the barriers and fully realise the potential of digital technologies in advancing the RTD.

125 UNCTAD's Economic Development in Africa Report (2023) The Potential of Africa to Capture Technology—Intensive Global Supply Chains.

References

Adem, Seifudein and Babagana, Waziri Babagana (2023) Is Africa China's Neo-Dependency in the Making? *Third World Quarterly* 44(7): 1363–1379.

African Charter on Human and Peoples' Rights adopted in Nairobi, Kenya on 27 June 1981 OAU Doc CAB/LEG/67/3 Rev.5 (1981).

African Development Bank (2013, 11 July) Africa is Now the Fastest Growing Continent in the World. Available at: https://www.afdb.org/fr/news-and-events/africa-is-now-the-fastest-growing-continent-in-the-world-12107 (consulted 28 October 2024).

African Union Convention on Cyber Security and Personal Data Protection, 2014.

AFR-IX Telecom. Available at: https://afr-ix.com/2019/05/15/smart-cities-in-africa/ (consulted 15 October 2024).

Aguirre, Daniel (2008) *The Human Right to Development in A Globalizing World.* London: Routledge.

Alemneh, Daniel Gelaw and Hastings, Samantha Kelly (2006) Developing the ICT Infrastructure for Africa: Overview of Barriers to Harnessing the Full Power of the Internet. *Journal of Education for Library and Information Science* 47(1): 4–16.

Alston, Philip (2005) Ships Passing in the Night: The Current State of the Human Rights and Development Debate Seen Through the Lens of the Millennium Development Goals. *Human Rights Quarterly* 27(3): 755–829.

Appointed by the Commission on Human Rights, Held by Arjun K. Sengupta from India Between 1999 and 2004. Available at: http://www.ohchr.org/en/issues/poverty/pages/asengupta.aspx (consulted 15 October 2024).

Arts, Karin and Tamo, Atabongawung (2016) The Right to Development in International Law: New Momentum Thirty Years Down the Line? *Netherlands International Law Review* 63: 221–249.

Blair, Denis and Huntsman, John Jr. (2013) The IP Commission Report: The Report of the Commission on the Theft of American Intellectual Property. Available at: www.ipcommision.org/report/ip_commission_report052213.pdf (consulted 15 October 2024).

Bogdan-Martin, Doreen (2019) Measuring Digital Development: Facts and Figures. *ITU Publications.* Available At: https://www.itu.int/en/itu-d/statistics/documents/facts/factsfigures2019.pdf5 (consulted 15 October 2024).

Broadband Commission (2019, 31 September) The State of Broad Band 2019: Broadband as a Foundation of Sustainable Development. *ITU/UNESCO*. Available At: file:///f:/chapter%203/s-pol-broadband.20-2019-pdf-e.pdf (consulted 15 October 2024).

Broadband Commission (2019, 31 September) The State of Broad Band 2019: Broadband as a Foundation of Sustainable Development. *ITU/UNESCO*. Available at: file:///f:/chapter%203/s-pol-broadband.20-2019-pdf-e.pdf (consulted 15 October 2014).

Brown, Edward K. (2020, 9 March) The Fourth Industrial Revolution Will Africa be Ready? African Centre for Economic Transformation. *African Centre for Economic Transformation*.

Buchan, Russel (2018) *Cyber Espionage and International Law*. Blombery Academic.

Castells, Manuel (2001) *The Internet Galaxy: Reflections on the Internet, Business and Society*. Oxford: Oxford University Press.

Conteanu, Christina (2005) *Cyber Consumer Law and Unfair Trading Practices*. New York: Routledge.

Convention on Cybercrime (Budapest Convention, ETS No 185) and its Protocols.

Corfu Channel (1949) *United Kingdom of Great Britain and Northern Ireland v Albania*. ICJ Judgments on Merits.

Corn, Gary and Taylor, Robert (2017) Sovereignty in the Cyber Space in the Age of Cyber. *American Journal of International Law* 111: 207–212.

Danies, Joel (2003) US Representative to the UN HRC Summary Record of the 63rd Meeting. 59th Session, UN Doc, E/CN.4/2003/SR.63.

Declaration on the Right to Development Resolution A/Res/41/128 Adopted by the UN General Assembly on 4 December 1986.

Declaration on the Right to Development: Speech by the Office of the High Commissioner. Available At: https://www.ohchr.org/ (consulted 15 October 2024).

Dos Santos, Fernando (2020) Levelling the Playing Field to Promote Technology Transfer and Innovation in African Least Developed Countries. *South African Intellectual Property Law Journal* 8(1): 35–55.

Dos Santos, Fernando (2020) Levelling the Playing Field to Promote Technology Transfer and Innovation in African Least Developed Countries. *South African Intellectual Property Law Journal* 35(8): 35–55.

Draft International Covenant on the Right to Development—Report by the Chair-Rapporteur of the Working Group on the Right to Development, Zamir Akram (Pakistan) Human Rights Council A/HRC/54/50 54th Session, 6 October 2023.

Fox, David (2019) Technology Transfer and the TRIPS Agreement are Developed Countries Meeting their End of the Bargain? *Hastings Science and Technology Law Journal* 10(1): 1–32.

Fukuda-Parr, Sakiko (2012) The Right to Development: Reframing a New Discourse for the Twenty-First Century Social Research. *Human Rights and the Global Economy* 79(4): 839–864.

Hansungule, Michelo (2005) The Right to Development. Paper Presented at the International Human Rights Academy Jointly Organised by University of Western Cape, Utrecht University, Ghent University, American University; October 2005, Sea Point, Cape Town, South Africa.

Hope, Kempe (1983) Basic Needs and Technology Transfer Issues in the 'New International Economic Order'. *The American Journal of Economics and Sociology* 42(4): 393–403.

Horner, Lisa (2011) Human Rights Approach to the Mobile Internet. *Association For Progressive Communications.*

ICT Works (2024, 24 July) 6 Barriers to the Fourth Industrial Revolution in African Countries. Available at: https://www.ictworks.org/barriers-fourth-industrial-revolution-africa/ (consulted 28 October 2024).

International Telecommunication Union (2024) Committed to Connecting the World. Available at: http://www.itu.int/ (consulted 20 February 2020).

International Trade Centre (2024) *Tech Hubs in Africa: Accelerating Start-Ups for Resilient Growth.* 3rd Edn, Geneva: ITC.

Jennifer And Kennedy-Mayo (2020) Budapest Convention: What is it and How is it Being Updated? Available at: https://www.crossborderdataforum.org/budapest-convention-what-is-it-and-how-is-it-being-updated/ (consulted 2 July 2020).

Kanade, Mihir (2023) The Right to Development and the 2030 Agenda for Sustainable Development. E-Learning Chapter 3 Module on Operationalising the Right to Development in Implementing the Sustainable Development Goals. University for Peace—UN Mandate.

Kohl, Uta (2007) *Jurisdiction and The Internet: Regulatory Competence Over Online Activity.* Cambridge: Cambridge University Press.

Li, Yuefen; Uribe, Daniele and Danish (2022) The International Discourse on the Right to Development and the Need to Reinvigorate its Implementation. *The South Centre.*

Litan, Robert and Niskanen, Willia (1998) *Going Digital!: A Guide to Policy in the Digital Age.* Washington DC: Brookings Institute Press.

Maccraw, Thomas (2007) *Prophet of Innovation; Joseph Schumpeter and Creative Destruction.* Harvard: Harvard University Press.

Mandiant (2013) Exposing One of China's Cyber Espionage Units. Available at: https://nsarchive2.gwu.edu/nsaebb/nsaebb424/docs/cyber-083.pdf (consulted 15 October 2024).

Maskus, Keith E (2004) Encouraging International Technology Transfer. *UNCTAD-ICTSD Project on IPRs and Sustainable Development*, 22–31.

McKinsey and Company (2017, 3 August) China's Digital Economic Force: A Leading Global Force. Available at: https://www.mckinsey.com/featured-insights/china/chinas-digital-economy-a-leading-global-force (consulted 28 October 2024).

Mlambo, Courage; Kushamba, Audrey and Simawu, More Blessing (2016) China-Africa Relations: What Lies Beneath? *The Chinese Economy* 49(4): 257–276.

Model Laws on Electronic Commerce 1996 and Model Law on Electronic Signature, 2001.

Mohanty, Saraju et al (2016) Everything You Wanted to Know About Smart Cities: The Internet of Things is the Backbone. *IEEE Consumer Electronics Magazine* 5(3): 60–70.

Ncube, Caroline (2013) Harnessing Intellectual Property for Development: Some Thoughts on an Appropriate Theoretical Framework. *Potchefstroom Electronic Law Journal* 16(4): 1–30.

Ojo, Adegboyega et al (2013) Enabling Development Through Governance and Mobile Technology. *Government Information Quarterly* 30(1): 32–45.

Pehlivan, Oğuz Kaan (2020) *Confronting Cyber Espionage Under International Law*. New York: Routledge.

Peters, Allison (2019) Russia and China are Trying to Set the UN's Rules on Cybercrime. *Foreign Policy*. Available at: https://foreignpolicy.com/2019/09/16/russia-and-china-are-trying-to-set-the-u-n-s-rules-on-cybercrime/ (consulted 16 September 2019).

Pittet, Faith Tigere (2022) African Participation in WTO e-Commerce Negotiations: Policy Positions and Development Issues. *African Perspectives, Global Insights—South African Institute of International Affairs* 131: 1–18.

Reports of the Secretary-General and the High Commissioner on International Cooperation in the Field of Human Rights A/74/351 And A/HRC/44/28.

Resolution Adopted by the General Assembly On 16 September 2005, Resolution 60/1. 2005 World Summit Outcome.

Salomon, Margot and Sengupta, Arjun (2023) The Right to Development: Obligations of States and the Rights of Minorities and Indigenous Peoples. *Minority Group International—Issues Papers*.

Schmid, Michael and Vihul, Liis (2017) Respect for Sovereignty in Cyber Space. *Texas Law Review* 95(7): 1639–1670.

Secretary General, Report on the Right to Development (2003) UN Doc. A/58/276.

Sengupta, Ranja (2016) International Trade and the 2030 Agenda for Sustainable Development. *Third World Network—Spotlight on the SDGs* 2(17): 130–139.

Solomon, Salem (2021, 5 January) Experts: Report of China Hacking African Union HQ Fits Larger Pattern. Available at: https://www.voanews.com/a/east-asia-pacific_voa-news-china_experts-report-china-hacking-african-union-hq-fits-larger-pattern/6200356.html (consulted 23 October 2024).

Subedi, Surya (2021) Declaration on the Right to Development. *United Nations Audiovisual Library of International Law*, 1–9.

Summary of the Open-Ended Informal Consultations Held by the Commission on Human Rights Pursuant to Economic and Social Council Decisions 2005/217 Para 18; UN Doc. A/59/847-E/2005/73.

Teshome, Roman Girma (2022) The Draft Convention on the Right to Development: A New Dawn to the Recognition of the Right to Development as a Human Right? *Human Rights Law Review* 22(2): 1–24.

The Africa Data Revolution Report (2016) Highlighting Developments in African Data Ecosystems. *United Nations Development Programme*.

The Guardian (2013, 9 June) Edward Snowden: The Whistleblower Behind the NSA Surveillance Revelations. Available at: https://www.theguardian.com/world/2013/jun/09/edward-snowden-nsa-whistleblower-surveillance (consulted 28 October 2024).

The Netherlands Ministry of Defence (2012) The Defence Cyber Strategy. Available at: www.ccdddcoe.org/strategies/defence_cyberstrategy_ndl.pdf 4 (consulted 20 October 2024).

Toppan How Mobile Technology is Transforming Africa. Available at: Https://Toppandigital.Com/Translation-Blog/Mobile-Technology-Transforming-Africa/ (Consulted 28 October 2024).

Trade Law Centre (2018, 19 January) Africa and WTO's E-Commerce Agenda. Available At: Https://Www.Tralac.Org (Consulted 20 October 2024).

UNCTAD's Economic Development in Africa Report (2023) The Potential of Africa to Capture Technology—Intensive Global Supply Chains.

UNDP (2024) From Access to Empowerment: Digital Inclusion in a Dynamic World. Singapore: UNDP Policy Centre. Available at: https://www.undp.org/sites/g/files/zskgke326/files/2024-05/undp_digital_inclusion_in_a_dynamic_world.pdf (consulted 28 October 2024).

United Nations (1996–2024) Ambassador Zamir Akram, Working Group on the Right to Development. Available at: https://www.ohchr.org/en/hrc-subsidiaries/iwg-on-development/ambassador-zamir-akram (consulted 25 October 2024).

United Nations (2021, 17–21 May) Working Group on the Right to Development: 21st Session. Available at: https://www.ohchr.org/en/issues/development/pages/21stsession.aspx (consulted 13 October 2024).

United Nations (2023, 11 May) Right to Development: New Treaty Would Codify Right to Development. Available at: https://www.ohchr.org/en/stories/2023/05/new-treaty-would-codify-right-development (consulted 28 October 2024).

United Nations (2023, 12 October) Human Rights Council Adopts Five Resolutions, Submits to General Assembly Draft International Covenant on the Right to Development for its Negotiation and Adoption, and Extends Mandate on Burundi. Available at: https://www.ohchr.org/en/news/2023/10/human-rights-council-adopts-five-resolutions-submits-general-assembly-draft (consulted 28 October 2024).

United Nations (2024, 9 August) United Nations: Member States Finalize a New Cybercrime Convention. Available at: https://www.unodc.org/unodc/en/frontpage/2024/august/united-nations-member-states-finalize-a-new-cybercrime-convention.html (consulted 8 October 2024).

United Nations Declaration on the Rights of Indigenous Peoples (2007), United Nations A/RES/61/295.

United Nations Development Programme (2016) The Africa Data Revolution Report 2016 Highlighting Developments in African Data Ecosystems. Available at: https://

www.africa.undp.org/content/rba/en/home/library/reports/the_africa_data_revolution_report_2016.html (consulted 15 October 2024).

United Nations General Assembly (2016, 27 June) The Promotion, Protection and Enjoyment of Human Rights on the Internet, Resolution A/HRC/32/L.20. Available at: https://digitallibrary.un.org/record/845728?ln=en&v=pdf (consulted 28 October 2024).

United Nations Office of the High Commissioner (2013) *Realizing the Right to Development: Essays in Commemoration of 25 Years of the United Nations Declaration on the Right to Development*. Geneva/New York: United Nations Publishing.

United Nations Secretary General, Foreword Group of Governmental Experts on Developments in the Fields of Information and Telecommunication in the Context of International Security, UN Doc A/70/174, 22 July 2015.

Vienna Declaration and Programme of Action, adopted by the World Conference on Human Rights on 25 June 1993, UN Doc. A/CONF.157/23, 12 July 1993.

Von Heinegg, Wolff Heintschel (2013) Territorial Sovereignty and Neutrality in Cyber Space. *International Law Studies* 89: 123–124.

World Bank Group (2024) Statistics per Country. Available at: https://databank.worldbank.org/ (Consulted 28 October 2024).

Wright, Jeremy (2018, 22 May) Cyber and International Law in the 21st Century. Available at: https://www.gov.uk/government/speeches/cyber-and-international-law-in-the-21st-century (consulted 15 October 2024).

Ye, Lisha and Yang, Huiqin (2020) From Digital Divide to Social Inclusion: A Tale of Mobile Platform Empowerment in Rural Areas. *Sustainability* 12(6): 1–16.

CHAPTER 11

South Africa's Constitutional Remedies in the Practice of the Right to Development

Mofihli Teleki

1 Introduction

South Africa is state party to the African Charter on Human and Peoples' Rights, which makes provision for the right to development.[1] In addition, South Africa also adheres to the United Nations Declaration to the Right to Development (UNDRTD), which is being transformed into the International Covenant on the Right to Development.[2] These two instruments enshrine aspirations where development is not only concerned with economic growth but considers a holistic approach that incorporates social, cultural political elements in ensuring that citizens of South Africa are involved in their own self development and become beneficiaries of that development.[3]

The Constitution of South Africa provides a legal framework that encapsulates the notions of dignity, equality before the law and social justice in seeking to foster the development of the cultural, social and political elements that are important within a democratic setting.[4] The Constitution emphasises the notion of human rights in redressing the injustices of the past, especially those that arise from the legacy of apartheid.[5]

Even though the country is party to the African Charter and adheres to the UNDRTD, South Africa did not include the right to development in its

1 African Charter on Human and Peoples' Rights adopted in Nairobi, Kenya on 27 June 1981 OAU Doc CAB/LEG/67/3 Rev.5 (1981), Art 22.

2 United Nations (2023) Third Committee Underscores Need for Legally Binding Tool to Enforce the Right to Development, Unrealized by Millions Worldwide, Directed Also at Businesses. Meetings, Coverage and Press Releases Seventy-eighth Session, 20th and 21st Meeting (AM & PM) GA/SHC/4383, 13 October 2023. *United Nations*. Available at: https://press.un.org/en/2023/gashc4383.doc.htm (consulted 5 October 2024).

3 Hawksley, C. and Georgeou, N. (2021) Right to Development: Theory, Practice, and Articulation with SDGs. In: Filho, W.L. et al (eds) *No Poverty*. Cham: Springer International Publishing, 818.

4 Khan, Fatima (2020) Does the Right to Dignity Extend Equally to Refugees in South Africa? *African Human Rights Law Journal* 20(1): 282.

5 Albertyn, Catherine (2019) (In)equality and the South African Constitution. *Development Southern Africa* 36(6): 756.

 | DOI:10.1163/9789004734357_012

Constitution, even though the Constitution embraces elements of the right to development in Chapter 2 on the Bill of Rights. In other words, the right to development is implied in the Bill of Rights, as per the Constitution.[6] This means that the right to development exist in the context of the Bill of Rights. There has been a debate about the positionality of the right to development in that, while there is no inscription of it in the Constitution, the socio-economic rights enshrined in the Bill of Rights are read to give prominence to the right to development.

This chapter focuses on the tools available in obliging South Africa to adhere to the principles of the right to development even though they may not explicitly be enshrined in the Constitution. The solutions for remedial actions may be more important in enhancing the right to development. In essence, the chapter looks into aspects of the Constitution that may enhance remedies for potential lack of implementation of the right to development as envisaged by the draft Covenant on the Right to Development and other legally binding instruments like the African Charter. In addition to the African Charter, if South Africa eventually becomes state party to the International Covenant on the Right to Development, the latter will amplify the binding obligations on accountability relating to adherence to the right to development which the government must adhere to.

Accountability in this instance refers to the capacity of the state to enforce the socio-economic rights that are contained in the Bill of Rights. With accountability, partly follows the notion of remedies, which should apply within the domestic setting, with the involvement of the state, non-state actors and, or citizens. The involvement of role players include, raising voices of concern over the remedial actions and the potential outcome thereof. In academia, scholars have voiced concerns over the Constitution's implicit articulation of the right to development.[7] This indirect approach to fulfilling the right to development might pose a challenge to accountability because it may be difficult to hold the state liable for failing in its development-related obligations that are not explicitly defined, but rather left to varied interpretations that could be diametrically opposed.[8]

---

6 Shai, I. and Kamga, S.D. (2021) Challenges and Prospects in Attaining Development Within and Through the Rule of Law in South Africa. In: Kamga, S.D. (ed) *The Right to Development in Africa: Issues, Constraints*. Austin: Pan African University Press, 38.

7 Ngang, Carol Chi (2019) Radical Transformation and a Reading of the Right to Development in the South African Constitutional Order. *South African Journal on Human Rights* 35(1): 43; Teleki, Mofihli (2017) Framing of the Right to Development Policy in the Context of South Africa. *Africa Insight* 47(3): 78.

8 Teleki, supra note 7, 78.

Individuals and communities may find it difficult to seek redress when their developmental needs go unfulfilled due to the absence of specific enforceable rights that are accompanied by a policy framework which directly addresses the right to development. The situation raises questions about the effectiveness of existing measures in ensuring that citizens directly benefit from the right to development. Without proper accountability and remedial mechanisms, ineffective implementation of the right to development may lead South Africa into deeper cycles of poverty and socio-economic marginalisation, and for that reason it is important to ensure that the rights are guaranteed under a policy framework that clearly makes provision for the right to development. In this instance, accountability should not be viewed as a means to bureaucracy but as a tool for guaranteeing that development efforts meet the needs of society.[9] Remedial measures should provide communities with the tools in accessing justice in cases where citizens' right are infringed.[10]

It is important to assess South African constitutionalism, considering the above aspects, where practices of remedies and accountability on the right to development have been advanced by the courts. South Africa is often faced with challenge of implementing the Bill of Rights (an embodiment of the right to development) and for this reason, other provisions in the Constitution could potentially offer remedies.[11] The constitutional provisions on participation in decision-making processes and the right to fair administrative action can help to improve the right to development framework on accountability and remedial action. The chapter identifies domestic rather than global solutions and therefore, critically analyses South Africa's constitutionalism regarding the right to development and the opportunity to use existing constitutional provisions for remedial action in the event of non-compliance.

2 South African Context and the Right to Development

Fundamental human rights are contained in the South African Constitution of 1996, which allows for progressive prioritisation of those rights, instruments of democracy and the means to social justice.[12] South African constitutionalism

9 Okafor, Obiora Chinedu and Ngwaba, Uchechukwu (2020) International Accountability in the Implementation of the Right to Development and the "Wonderful Artificiality" of Law: An African Perspective. *Transnational Human Rights Review* 7(1): 20.

10 Schormair, Maximilian and Gerlach, Lara (2020) Corporate Remediation of Human Rights Violations: A Restorative Justice Framework. *Journal of Business Ethics* 167(3): 477.

11 Ally, Nurina and Linde, Daniel (2021) Pridwin: Private School Contracts, the Bill of Rights and a Missed Opportunity. *Constitutional Court Review* 11(1): 10.

12 Francis, David and Webster, Edward (2019) Poverty and Inequality in South Africa: Critical Reflections. *Development Southern Africa* 36(6): 788.

is aligned to the United Nations International Covenant on the Right to Development in the sense that socio-economic rights are incorporated in the Constitution, which together with the civil and political rights, are interpreted to imply a constitutional right to development.[13]

The existence of these rights in the South Africa Constitution does not in any way suggest that South Africans are in a better position compared to other states that explicitly enshrine and adhere to the right to development because as noted above, enforcement and access to these rights remains a challenge. The South Africa Bill of Rights, despite enshrining socio-economic rights, has limitations, relating to instances where legislation or actions may affect the conduct or interests protected by the Constitution.[14] Other factors that influence adequate enforcement or implementation of the right to development relate to the capacity of the state in terms of resource availability. South Africans have over the years responded to the lack or poor implementation of some aspects of the Bill of Rights, which emphasises access to socio-economic rights.

This has been witnessed through violent service delivery protests, indicating growing citizen dissatisfaction with the government's ability to provide essential needs and protect rights.[15] The demonstrations often arise from discontent resulting from inadequate access to essential services such as water, electricity, healthcare, and education among others. The frequency and intensity of the demonstrations highlight a major gap between the constitutional guarantees of dignity, socioeconomic rights, and equality and the lived reality of many South Africans.[16] The disparate situation in South Africa remains a significant obstacle in the fulfilment of the right to development, which fundamentally entails improving quality of life for every individual and all peoples and ensuring equitable access to resources and opportunities.

The Marikana Massacre that occurred in August 2012, is one of the most tragic episodes that piqued provisions of the Bill of Rights.[17] The massacre happened when mine workers, campaigning for increment in wages and better

13 Shai and Kamga, supra note 6, 48; Ngang 2019, supra note 7, 25–49.

14 Rautenbach, I.M. (2014) Proportionality and the Limitation Clauses of the South African Bill of Rights. *Potchefstroom Electronic Law Journal* 17(6): 2231.

15 Ngcamu, Bethuel (2019) Exploring Service Delivery Protests in Post-Apartheid South African Municipalities: A Literature Review. *Journal for Transdisciplinary Research in Southern Africa* 15(1): 02.

16 Breakfast, Ntsikelelo; Bradshaw, Gavin and Nomarwayi, Thandolwethu (2019) Violent Service Delivery Protests in Post-Apartheid South Africa, 1994–2017: A Conflict Resolution Perspective. *African Journal of Public Affairs* 11(1): 107.

17 Nodangala, Norless Zibele and Masumbe, Paul (2023) A Narrative of Marikana Tragedy against Right to Life and Right to Human Dignity under the South African Constitution. *E-Journal of Humanities, Arts and Social Sciences* 4(10): 1299.

working conditions, clashed violently with law enforcement services, culminating in the death of 34 miners, provoking extensive national condemnation.[18] The Marikana tragedy was indicative of the dire socio-economic conditions faced by mine workers in South Africa, which raised important questions about government's commitment to protecting the constitutional rights of the citizens, particularly those in vulnerable circumstances.[19] The massacre underscored the urgent need for the government to address systemic inequalities and ensure that the right to development is a tangible reality for all South Africans rather than only a theoretical concept.[20] The socio-economic rights and by inference, the right to development for the mine workers were not only denied, their right to assert entitlement to the rights guaranteed to them in the Constitution was also brutally suppressed.

The "Jeppestown fire" is another incident that highlights the difficulties associated with realising the right to development in South Africa. In this case, residents of a dilapidated building in Johannesburg sought governmental assistance for relocation to a safer setting, as their living conditions posed significant health and safety risks.[21] Regrettably, disregard for their appeals for governmental assistance led to the structure being engulfed in flames, resulting in casualties and displacement. This episode also emphasised critical concerns regarding the right to adequate housing, an essential component of the right to development.[22] It illustrates the state's failure to provide safe and secure living conditions for its citizens, particularly, the marginalised groups who often bear the brunt of inadequate housing policies.

The Marikana Massacre and the Jeppestown fire illustrate the discrepancy between South Africa's constitutional provisions, which guarantee the rights to dignity, socio-economic well-being and equality, and the harsh realities many citizens are confronted with daily. Both incidents demonstrate a systemic failure to translate constitutional concepts into concrete outcomes in enhancing quality of life for rights holders. In many instances, the interests of rights holders have been promoted by civil society organisations that have relentlessly pushed the South African government to adhere to the principles of the Bill

18 Tinsley, Meghan (2019) Constructing and Contesting the Post-apartheid State: Political Discourse and the Marikana Strike. *Language, Discourse and Society* 7(2): 16.

19 Nodangala and Masumbe, supra note 17, 1299.

20 Mfete, Tabiso (2020) Neoliberalism and Inequality in Post-Apartheid South Africa. *Pretoria Student Law Review* 14(1): 271.

21 Ngcobo, Khanyile (2024) Four Dead, Three Injured in Jeppestown Fire. Available at https://www.timeslive.co.za/news/south-africa/2024-08-25-three-dead-in-jeppestown-fire/ (consulted 30 November 2024).

22 Ibid.

of Rights, which embody the right to development.[23] Debate surrounds the extent to which civil society organisations promote the right to development, aiming to ensure state obligation for its realisation. To ensure effective realisation of the right to development, it is critical to first and foremost, recognise its indivisibility, as Subedi Surya notes that all rights are interrelated.[24] For instance, because of the interrelatedness between human rights like the rights to housing, education and sustainable livelihood, a claim to sustainable human settlement requires access to essential services like water, economic opportunities, healthcare, and educational facilities.

3 Constitutionalism and the Right to Development in South Africa

3.1 *Dynamics of Constitutionalism and the Covenant on the Right to Development*

The concept of constitutionalism shapes the structure of governance in many modern democratic states, showing the constitution's supremacy as a legal tool that ought to regulate fundamental rights and political authority.[25] The constitutional framework of South Africa, established in 1996, functions as a progressive instrument prioritising human rights, democracy, and social justice.[26] The right to development, not explicitly defined as a separate right but implicitly included under other socio-economic rights provisions, is one of the rights it encompasses.[27] South African constitutionalism is thus, consistent with international human rights norms, including the provisions on the right to development contained in the draft International Covenant on the Right to Development.

The Bill of Rights in the Constitution explicitly recognise socio-economic rights, including (for example) the right to housing (Section 26), health care (Section 27), and education (Section 29), which collectively support realisation of the right to development. Bilchitz states that the South African constitutional framework promotes a connection between socio-economic rights

23 Ndinga-Kanga, Masana; Van der Merwe, Hugo and Hartford, Daniel (2020) Forging a Resilient Social Contract in South Africa: States and Societies Sustaining Peace in the Post-Apartheid Era. *Journal of Intervention and Statebuilding* 14(1): 22.

24 Subedi, Surya (2021) Declaration on the Right to Development. *Legal UN*. Available at: https://legal.un.org/avl/pdf/ha/drd/drd_e.pdf (consulted 30 September 2024).

25 Tully, James et al (2016) Introducing Global Integral Constitutionalism. *Global Constitutionalism* 5(1): 1–15.

26 Francis and Webster, supra note 12, 788.

27 Shai and Kamga, supra note 6, 48.

and development, with the intention to eliminate poverty and the inequalities inherited from apartheid.[28] Despite the recognition and protection of these rights, challenges remain in their fulfilment, which raises concerns regarding the state's commitment in advancing the right to development.

The right to development, as it is articulated in the draft Covenant on the Right to Development, highlights several aspects that are relevant to individuals, communities, state parties and international stakeholders in incorporating economic advancement and the enhancement of freedoms.[29] South Africa's compliance with international human rights instruments, including in particular the African Charter on Human and Peoples' Rights, which it ratified in July 1996 and is accordingly bound by, obligates adherence to the right to development enshrined in Article 22.

Article 15 of the Covenant on the Right to Development is important for enacting necessary corrective measures in addressing deficiencies in the realisation of the right to development. It should be recognised that marginalised and vulnerable groups within the population, may face unique obstacles that hinder their ability to fully enjoy their rights. Article 15(1) emphasises the imperative of implementing specific measures designed to accelerate the fulfilment of the right to development for specific population groupings. Article 15 of the Covenant also calls for the implementation of "specific and remedial measures".[30] These measures are intended to be proactive and tailored to the needs of marginalised populations, facilitating their involvement in developmental efforts. It is essential to guarantee the active and meaningful involvement of individuals, groups, and communities in decision-making processes on issues of concern to them. It is critical to engage marginalised voices and incorporate their perspectives and needs into the formulation of development programmes and policies that have a direct impact on their lives.

The Covenant underscores the necessity of creating an environment that allows these groups to engage meaningfully in discussions and decisions that impact their equitable and holistic enjoyment of the right to development. It entails that their engagement must be conceived to remove any structural, environmental, or institutional obstacles that might impede their participation. The Covenant seeks to tackle these challenges by promoting an inclusive

---

28 Bilchitz, David (2007) *Poverty and Fundamental Rights: The Justification and Execution of Socio-Economic Rights*. Oxford: Oxford University Press.

29 Draft International Covenant on the Right to Development—Report by the Chair-Rapporteur of the Working Group on the Right to Development, Zamir Akram (Pakistan) Human Rights Council A/HRC/54/50 54th Session, 6 October 2023.

30 United Nations, supra note 2.

development strategy that acknowledges and appreciates the contributions of all social groups, especially those that have faced historical marginalisation.

Article 15 of the Covenant establishes a vital basis for executing remedial actions that support marginalised and disadvantaged populations in realising their right to development. The Covenant accordingly, seeks to create an equitable society by implementing specific measures that foster active participation in decision-making, allowing all individuals to thrive and fully enjoy their rights. Sections 59(1)(a) and 72(1)(a) of the South African Constitution underscore the imperative of "facilitation of involvement", emphasising the requirement for inclusive governance. In South Africa, the terms "involvement" and "participation" are frequently used interchangeably, reflecting a shared acknowledgement of the need for everyone to engage actively in the democratic process.

Public participation should be understood as a multifaceted endeavour, which should be driven by civil society organisations with vested interests in policy reforms on behalf of and to the benefit of the impoverished.[31] For the engagements to be meaningful, issues of responsiveness, community exigencies and transparency become important. Effective public engagement mechanisms should include multiple viewpoints intended at improving the decision-making processes.[32] This will enable the active participation of communities with the aim of making valuable inputs into the development process where there is an exchange of views. By allowing communities to participate in the decision-making processes, it is highly likely that those decisions will be made with a clearer understanding of the potential disadvantages of the policy choices and the decisions made.[33]

Civil society organisations in South Africa are given an oversight role in monitoring governmental and parliamentary decisions, as well as the distribution of resources for the public good.[34] In addition, enabling public participation

---

31 Gorwa, R. and Ash, T.G. (2020) Democratic Transparency in the Platform Society. In: Persily, N. and Tucker, J.A. (eds) *Social Media and Democracy: The State of the Field and Prospects for Reform*, Cambridge University Press, 286.

32 Hügel, Stephan and Davies, Anna (2020) Public Participation, Engagement, and Climate Change Adaptation: A Review of the Research Literature. *Wiley Interdisciplinary Reviews: Climate Change* 11(4): 1–20.

33 Fraussen, Bert; Albareda, Adrià and Braun, Celesta (2020) Conceptualizing Consultation Approaches: Identifying Combinations of Consultation Tools and Analysing their Implications for Stakeholder Diversity. *Policy Sciences* 53(3): 475.

34 Parliament of South Africa (1996) Democracy Works Foundation Public Participation Toolkit. Available at: https://www.parliament.gov.za/storage/app/media/Pages/2023/21-08-2023_NCOP_Co-ordination_Co-operation_and_Consultation_Workshop/Commiss

strengthens the connection between the state and the citizens, while enhancing trust and increasing the legitimacy of public institutions. When citizens are part of the process of development, they appreciate the fact that their opinions will be valued, and they are likely to embrace the process and take ownership of the final decisions.

Malan emphasises the limitations of traditional enforcement mechanisms in effectively addressing human rights violations, particularly concerning socio-economic rights.[35] This limitation is indicative of the need for the active participation of non-state players, such as civil society organisations, community groups, and the private sector in the execution of socio-economic rights.

Liebenberg and Goldblatt clarify the point by highlighting the intrinsic link between the principle of equality enshrined in the South African Constitution and the realisation of socio-economic rights.[36] They assert that the link should be intentionally used to enhance the legal framework response to the pressing issues of poverty and inequality that persist in South Africa.[37] Recognising the relationship between equality and socio-economic rights enables legal professionals and politicians to devise more effective strategies in addressing the structural inequities and promote social equity.

Civil society organisations are thus, instrumental in that they advocate for the realisation of socio-economic rights and serve as monitors in ensuring state accountability. Their role in monitoring government plans, implementation and accountability is essential for fostering transparency and responsiveness in the implementation of socio-economic initiatives for the benefit of society. These organisations have the power to galvanise and mobilise communities, raise awareness on constitutional rights, and provide legal assistance, thereby empowering citizens to claim their socio-economic rights. The connection between traditional enforcement mechanisms, the principle of equality, and the role of civil society organisations underscores the complexity in addressing socio-economic rights in South Africa. A comprehensive plan involving non-state actors is essential in rectifying the deficiencies of existing frameworks and in ensuring the realisation of socio-economic rights for every individual.

---

ion_2/Democracy_Works_Foundation_Public_Participation_Toolkit_compressed.pdf (consulted 30 September 2024); Constitution of South Africa 1996.

35 Malan, Naude (2008) Rights, the Populace, and the South African Constitution: Civil Society and the Implementation of Rights. *Anthropology Southern Africa* 31(1–2): 60.

36 Liebenberg, Sandra and Goldblatt, Beth (2007) The Relationship Between Equality and Socio-Economic Rights Under South Africa's Transformative Constitution. *South African Journal of Human Rights* 23(2): 335.

37 Ibid.

3.2 *Application of Constitutionalism through Practice*

The South African social, political and legal landscape has made it possible for constitutionalism since the dawn of a democratic state in 1994. In essence, South Africa is no different from most African states that espouse constitutionalism by upholding the rule of law, democracy, political accountability, human rights, equality and social justice.[38] The nuances of democracy in South Africa therefore follows a historical legacy where change from abuse of power during the apartheid period was to be effected during the current era of democracy.[39] Democracy in this instance becomes an enabler for justice, fairness, human rights and equality. This is why Klaasen[40] opines that South Africa's constitutionalism exists within the context of liberal democracy which seems to protect and the rule of law through the functions of the state and non-state institutions in a situation of stark social inequalities and socio-economic challenges.

Constitutionalism refers to the ideas of governance, which delineates an assortment of rights, values, norms, principles and rules that help to contain state power by limiting the powers of government, compliance with the rule of law and the protection of fundamental rights in the Constitution.[41] This means that constitutionalism is a mixture of judicial review and an instrument for the enforcement of accountability.[42]

In an effort to establish whether the ideals of constitutionalism are adequately upheld depends on whether institutions founded on promoting democracy have performed their roles through governance.[43] This has certainly been the case in the South African scenario in the sense that Chapter 9 Institutions were created to ensure that they promote human rights, and in addition that they play a role of a watchdog for possible infringement of rights, with an impartial approach to in their quest to protect the rights of citizens.

38 Udombana, Nsongurua (2024) Reflections on Constitutionalism and Democratic Governance in Africa. *Journal of African Law* 68(2): 137.

39 Graybill, Lyn (2000) Lingering Legacy: Apartheid and the South African Press. *Current History* 99(637): 228.

40 Klaasen, Abraham (2020) The Quest for Socio-Economic Rights: The Rule of Law and Violent Protest in South Africa. *Sustainable Development* 28(3): 479.

41 Acton, Helen (2022) Lawfare: How to Approach it in South Africa's Constitutional Democracy. *The Africa Governance Papers* 1(2): 51.

42 Mcineka, A. and Nomthandazo, N. (2019) A Perspective on the Principle of "Constitutionalism" in Relation to Executive and Legislative Accountability in South Africa. In: Fagbadebo, O. and Ruffin, F. (eds) *Perspectives on the Legislature and the Prospects of Accountability in Nigeria and South Africa*. Cham, Switzerland: Springer: 46.

43 Udombana, supra note 39, 138.

Constitutionalism is given impetus in Section 1 of the Constitution of South Africa, which provides for supremacy of the Constitution, and a multiparty political system that adheres to the rule of law in ensuring that there is transparency, accountability and openness in the governance systems of the state.[44] In addition, Section 38 of the Constitution makes provision for ordinary citizens to approach the courts when they believe that the Bill of Rights has been infringed, where organisations with resources can act on behalf of the marginalised poor and also encourages legal mobilization amongst citizens to protect the rights.[45]

Although the right to development is infused in the Bill of Rights, it does not mean that South Africa is in a better position than countries that have not enshrined the right to development. South Africa has been riddled with governance challenges which make it possible for corruption, maladministration, financial malfeasance, and cronyism which hamper the implementation of socio-economic rights.[46] Part of the reason why South Africa finds itself in a challenge to advance socio-economic rights is due to bad governance, which leads to corruption, and lack of accountability.[47] The violations of the Bill of Rights are as a result of the political hindrances occurring in public institutions, which fail to meet their constitutional obligations, culminating in lack of access to socio-economic rights.[48] The challenge in accessing socio-economic rights often translate into service delivery protests which become violent.[49]

Socio-economic rights are costly to maintain and the Constitution of South Africa states that these rights may be afforded in line with the availability of resources, which presents limitation in the affordance of the rights.[50] Constitutionalism in South Africa is being tested because of the lack of ethical

---

44 Maganoe, Shadi (2023) Legislative Oversight and Executive Accountability in South Africa. *Potchefstroom Electronic Law Journal* 26(1): 2.

45 Tait, Kira, and Taylor, Witney (2023) The Possibility of Rights Claims-Making in Court: Looking Back on Twenty-Five Years of Social Rights Constitutionalism in South Africa. *Law and Social Inquiry* 48(3): 1028.

46 Maganoe, supra note 44, 1.

47 Ibid.

48 Liebenberg, Sandra (2022) The Art of the (Im)possible? Justice Froneman's Contribution to Designing Remedies for Structural Human Rights Violations. *Constitutional Court Review* 12(1): 139.

49 Klaasen, Abraham (2020) The Quest for Socio-Economic Rights: The Rule of Law and Violent Protest in South Africa. *Sustainable Development* 28(3): 479.

50 Mcineka and Nomthandazo, supra note 42, 46.

and moral leadership in regulating the authority of the state within particular norms and standards.[51]

Since the dawn of democracy in South Africa, the public has often relied on legal channels to have their grievances on service delivery resolved.[52] The violations of socio-economic rights are complex, and often linked to the abuse of power and it is often difficult to devise remedies that seek to address such violations.[53] Part of the complexity is seen in how the courts in South Africa often avoid a prescriptive approach in the enforcement of socio-economic rights as they often moderate their conclusions and remedial orders deferring to respondents and government, the result of which impact claims of socio-economic rights which are neutral.[54] In addition to this, court cases related to socio-economic rights are often complex and costly because by their nature, courts do not have the political leverage to engineer structural change and cannot reallocate resources for development.[55]

The course for accessing socio-economic rights in South Africa has provided adequate protections in case law and in this instance, the courts are often used for framing the issues, setting the agenda, brokering negotiations, provide the rallying points for political and social pressure.[56] Municipalities have the constitutional obligations to promote respect for the Bill of Rights in South Africa's Constitution which encapsulates socio-economic rights. In addition, the municipalities have an obligation to make accessible the right to housing, education, healthcare, and water to communities.[57]

Due to the prevailing constitutionalism in South Africa municipalities have become creatures of statutes, which create the space for governance systems that are intended to fulfil socio-economic rights.[58] The Constitution of South Africa is referred to as the pinnacle of the rule of law, regarded as the supreme law of the country and it presents the means to provide access to the Bill of Rights in a redistributive manner.[59] It is common cause that South

51 Ibid.

52 Tait and Taylor, supra note 45, 1029.

53 Liebenberg, supra note 48, 140.

54 Langford, Malcolm (2021) The Impact of Public Interest Litigation: The Case of Socio-Economic Rights. *Australian Journal of Human Rights* 27(3): 510.

55 Ibid.

56 David and Webster, supra note 12, 797.

57 Pieterse, Marius (2023) Rule of Law Through the 'Urban Turn' in South African Constitutionalism. *Hague Journal on the Rule of Law* 15(2): 307.

58 Ibid at 308.

59 Ibid at 306.

Africa has an ongoing practice of holding the government accountable for socio-economic policies, and in doing so the courts have the power to promote the values of equality, dignity and freedom, in an effort to increase participation of citizens and advance accountability.[60] It should be noted that in this instance, the courts may encourage, influence and promote particular values that are enshrined in the Constitution in a neutral manner.

In addition, the courts may also point out potential remedies that ought to be prescribed by oversight institutions (on human rights) such as those that fall under Chapter 9 of the Constitution. For example, in a recent court matter of the Economic Freedom Fighters (political party), the court ruled that the remedial action prescribed by a Chapter 9 Institution such as the Office of the Public Protector ought to be binding even in the context where the sitting President of South Africa is accused of corruption.[61] The court also found that the recommendations for remedial action cannot be ignored but should be binding.[62]

There are some scholars who caution that even the Constitutional Court as the apex court of South Africa should also be mindful of the notion of overreach where rulings are made.[63] Therefore, the notion of separation of powers plays a role in making sure that the courts are seen to be impartial and avoid overreach. This is the reason why in certain court matters, the courts have avoided prescribing the details that should be applied by government, because it is government that ought to apply appropriate remedies regarding resources that are at the disposal of government.[64]

The Constitutional Court of South Africa has often issued remedies that are prospective and where there is a flexible dialogic approach in the interaction between the judiciary and government, together with civil society.[65] In light of the discussions above, it is clear that South Africa faces challenges in the advancement of the right to development through socio-economic rights, which result in violent protests. While this remains the case, several events

60 Liebenberg, supra note 48, 190.

61 Wolf, Loammi (2017) The Remedial Action of the "State of Capture" Report in Perspective. *Potchefstroom Electronic Law Journal* 20(1): 8.

62 Ibid.

63 Steytler, N. (2017) The Constitutional Court of South Africa: Reinforcing an Hourglass System of Multi-level government. In: Aroney, N. and Kincaid, J. (eds) *Courts in Federal Countries: Federalists or Unitarists*. Toronto: University of Toronto Press, 342.

64 Chilton, Adam S., and Versteeg, Mila (2018) Courts' Limited Ability to Protect Constitutional Rights. *The University of Chicago Law Review* 85(2): 322.

65 Leckey, Robert (2016) The Harms of Remedial Discretion. *International Journal of Constitutional Law* 14(3): 586.

have occurred where the public, and institutions that support democracy have used the ideas of constitutionalism in ensuring that government is forced to comply with policies that promote socio-economic rights. This has happened with limitations of power by either government or the courts, thereby upholding the notion of separation of powers and the rule of law.

The discussions above explain that South Africa has institutions and tools that help shape constitutionalism. As explained, socio-economic rights ought to be realised by institutions, including local government in ensuring that citizens benefit from accessing those rights guaranteed to them in the Constitution. The practice of affording the rights is subject to oversight from Chapter 9 Institutions. The practice of testing constitutionalism by applying remedies, puts South Africa at an advantage in advancing Article 15 of the draft Convention on the Right to Development which states that "Specific and remedial measures can include, among others, enabling the full, effective, appropriate and dignified participation of such human persons, groups, and peoples in decision-making processes, programmes and policymaking that affect their full and equal enjoyment of the right to development, without subjecting them to structural, environmental or institutional constraints or barriers".[66]

4 Role of Civil Society Organisations in Monitoring Remedial Action

Civil society organisations have consistently played a major role in pushing the South African government to adhere to the principles of the right to development.[67] This trend indicates a growing recognition of the need for a holistic approach to human rights, viewing development not only as an economic issue but as a fundamental human right that incorporates the social, cultural, and economic dimensions. Civil society organisations in South Africa have proven that they have an important role in the monitoring of the right to development and need to use their powers to hold government accountable. Some of the civil society organisations have progressed in integrating the right to development into their advocacy efforts, underscoring its importance in policy design and implementation.[68]

66 United Nations, supra note 2.

67 Mamokhere, John; Mavhungu, Elias and Mmbengeni, Victor (2022) The Implementation of the Basic Values and Principles Governing Public Administration and Service Delivery in South Africa. *Journal of Public Affairs* 22(4): 2627.

68 Lidström, Anders; Sellers, Jeffrey and Bae, Yooil (2020) *Multilevel Democracy: How Local Institutions and Civil Society Shape the Modern State.* Cambridge: Cambridge University Press, 4.

To effectively address the question of remedial actions on the right to development, it is critical to recognise its indivisibility, since all human rights are interrelated. The interconnectedness indicates that the realisation of one right is often dependent on the fulfilment of other rights. As earlier noted, fundamental links exist between the right to housing and the right to education. Insufficient housing may impede families from creating a stable atmosphere crucial for learning, thereby affecting children's educational achievements. Similarly, thriving human communities need access to essential utilities such as water, economic opportunities, healthcare, and educational institutions. The absence of service delivery perpetuates cycles of poverty and inequality, undermining the foundation of progress,[69] which impacts on the right to development.

The right to development encompasses not only the right of access to essential services but also the empowerment of individuals and communities to participate in decision-making processes that affect their lives.[70] The participatory component is crucial for ensuring that development programmes are inclusive and responsive to the needs of marginalised communities. Civil society organisations are essential in advocating for participatory approaches in influencing policies that prioritise the viewpoints of people most affected by developmental issues.

Article 3(c) of the Covenant on the Right to Development emphasises the need for a comprehensive understanding of rights as interconnected and interdependent.[71] Fostering a collaborative environment among civil society organisations, government entities, and communities enable the creation of an equitable and just society that embodies development as an intrinsic human right. This is possible to achieve given South Africa's history of civil society actions. It should be noted that civil society organisation in South Africa have a legacy of galvanising and mobilising communities in resolving complex issues that arise from the history of apartheid and to advance social justice.[72] Over the decades, South African civil society organisations have operated in close proximity with communities, and played a significant role in promoting the rights

69 De Kadt, Daniel and Lieberman, Evan (2020) Nuanced Accountability: Voter Responses to Service delivery in southern Africa. *British Journal of Political Science* 50(1): 185.

70 Mohammad, N. and Farjana, Y. (2018) Participation as a Human Right: A Rights-Based Approach to Development. In: *Stakeholders, Governance and Responsibility* (*Developments in Corporate Governance and Responsibility, Vol 14*). Leeds: Emerald Publishing Limited, 34.

71 United Nations, supra note 2.

72 Plagerson, Sophie et al (2019) Social Policy in South Africa: Navigating the Route to Social Development. *World Development* 113(c): 04.

of those communities in raising issues that pertain to systemic inequalities.[73] Some of these organisations, have over the decades, tackled issues pertaining the right of access to education, healthcare, water and sanitation, economic opportunities and actively participated in processes of policy reform.[74]

Given South Africa's history of apartheid which excluded the majority of the population from enjoying human rights, the Covenant on the Right to Development presents the opportunity for corrective measures through remedial action for the realisation of the right to development. The vibrant nature of the civil society movement in South Africa makes it possible for advancing the right to development among the communities in the country. Despite this potential, there is a considerable absence of a dedicated social movement in South Africa that explicitly advocates for the right to development. Despite the existence of similar issues addressed by other organisations and groups, there is no specific coordinated effort in monitoring government's progress in upholding the right to development.

The draft Covenant on the Right to Development offers new ideas in addressing the socio-economic challenges in South Africa, which has one of the highest unemployment rates in the world with the youth population most affected, a situation that is exacerbated by stark inequalities. By establishing a framework for advancing the right to development, the Covenant may eventually facilitate the integration of civil society organisations, interest groups, and social movements towards a common goal of improved human well-being. This collaborative approach would improve accountability mechanisms, allowing for more effective scrutiny of governmental policies and development processes.

The Preamble to the UNDRTD provides that state parties should take into account, the fundamental values of human rights and liberties, irrespective of race, colour, religion, language or status and that state parties ought to assert these values for the full enjoyment of the liberties.[75] This points to the notion of social inclusion in advancing the right to development, which may in turn, create a conducive environment where communities can be actively involved in the development process, recognising the importance of community participation.

---

73 Handmaker, Jeff and Tandiwe, Matthews (2019) Analysing Legal Mobilisation's Potential to Secure Equal Access to Socioeconomic Justice in South Africa. *Development Southern Africa* 36(6): 886.

74 Ibid.

75 Declaration on the Right to Development Resolution A/RES/41/128 adopted by UN General Assembly on 4 December 1986.

5 Potential Aspects for Remedial Actions

5.1 *Recent Issues Remedied by Individuals and Civil Society*

South African courts have over the three decades since the dawn of democracy, played a significant role as arbiters in matters pertaining to socio-economic rights. To date, the courts have made landmark rulings, including amongst others, *Government of the Republic of South Africa v. Grootboom* (2001) and *Minister of Health v. Treatment Action Campaign* (2002).[76] The courts have often ruled in these cases in favour an obligation imposed on the state to implement the relevant socio-economic rights, which should happen within available resources.[77] This is connected to the spirit of the right to development, which encourages state parties to undertake development processes aimed at enhancing the well-being of citizens.[78]

Despite these advancements, several challenges continue to hinder the full realisation of the right to development in South Africa. These include structural issues such as bureaucracy, corruption, and socio-economic inequality, which hinder the state's ability to fulfil its constitutional obligations. Liebenberg contends that while the South African Constitution provides a robust framework for socio-economic rights, their implementation and enforcement often fails due to political, economic, and institutional impediments.[79] This points out the need for remedial actions for purposes of improving accountability and promoting effectiveness in the achievement of developmental goals to the benefit of citizens.

The South African experience exemplifies a scenario where citizens have often had to assert the right to development through violent service delivery protests. This is however, not unique to South Africa but is a phenomenon that is prevalent globally. Hence, Andreassen and Marks opine that the UNDRTD establishes development as an enforceable right yet, the lack of commitment by state governments in realising this right remains a serious problem.[80]

---

76 *Government of the Republic of South Africa v Grootboom* (2001); *Minister of Health v Treatment Action Campaign* (2002).

77 Ibid.

78 Declaration on the Right to Development, supra note 75.

79 Liebenberg, Sandra (2010) *Socio-Economic Rights: Juridical Interpretation under a Transformative Constitution*. Claremont: Juta and Company Ltd.

80 Andreassen, Bart Andreas and Marks, Stephen (2006) *Development as an Essential Human Right: Legal, Political, and Economic Dimensions*. Cambridge/Massachusetts: Harvard University Press.

6 Remedial Actions by Civil Society

The notion of remedial action and the involvement of civil society in a manner that has been described in the preceding sections of this chapter should be viewed as potential indicators for a framework on issues of importance in the accountability process. Key to this is the need to ensure that principles of the right to development under Article 8 of the Covenant on the Right to Development, place emphasis on the fact that the obligation of states to respect provisions of the Covenant ought to be monitored. It is also worth monitoring whether the state contravenes aspects of the right to development, as a requirement of Article 8 of the Covenant. This means that tools for monitoring should include a determination on whether the state has not avoided implementation of the right to development wilfully or otherwise. Section 38(a) of the Constitution of South Africa raises the importance of protecting socio-economic rights if they are under threat thus, necessitating corrective measures by the courts against their possible contravention. This constitutional clause aligns with Article 8 of the Covenant, which places emphasis on the removal of all obstacles that threaten implementation of the right to development.

Article 13 on the duty to cooperate, underscores the necessity for a comprehensive assessment of international legal frameworks, laws, and practices that may hinder progress in advancing the right to development. It requires a comprehensive examination of existing frameworks to identify and remove barriers that prevent individuals and communities from achieving the right to development. It provides an atmosphere where growth is not only a possibility but an assured entitlement for all, ensuring that every individual can participate in and reap the benefits of economic, social, cultural, and political development. Article 13 of the Covenant places emphasis on the need to review any policy, legislation, and practices that may be an obstacle in the implementation of the right to development, encouraging an enabling environment where development is a practical reality and beneficiation of citizens occur through participation in the social, economic, cultural and political processes.

The interconnection of these clauses of the Constitution and the Covenant creates obligations for state parties, including South Africa to adopt measures in safeguarding right to development. It requires a concerted effort in implementing policies that protect human rights while offering the necessary support and assistance in enabling communities experience the impact of the rights. This approach is essential for fostering an inclusive development process that upholds and protects the dignity and rights of all citizens. Self-determination within the domestic setting as a crucial element highlighted in the Covenant, aims at empowering individuals to achieve their full potential through particular rights, including access to education, housing, and healthcare. This perspective aligns with Amartya Sen's concept of self-capability, suggesting that self-capability is a fundamental component of self-determination.[81]

Sen argues that freedom includes not only the absence of constraints to development but also the presence of opportunities that enable individuals to realise their unique goals and aspirations.[82] In this instance, self-determination is important for understanding how individuals navigate their complex social and economic conditions, which necessitates making choices that promote self-development.[83] The outcome in the implementation of the Bill of Rights, if the rights were implemented adequately, could promote self-determination. Despite the South African government's efforts in enhancing healthcare, education, and housing, other challenges persist. These concerns often result in community dissatisfaction, particularly when government-funded housing initiatives are implemented with substandard quality.[84] Multiple instances of poorly constructed dwellings without fundamental amenities or infrastructure, highlight the problems associated with inferior quality in service delivery.[85] Instances of leaking roofs, inadequate sanitation, and limited access to clean water in newly constructed housing developments illustrate the gap between statutory objectives and real outcomes.[86] These challenges compromise the right to dignity which is an important feature in the Bill of Rights in the South African Constitution.

The quality of service delivery has a significant impact on human well-being. Individuals may compromise their ability for self-determination when there is no access to adequate healthcare, quality education, or decent housing. Lack of access to these entitlements can sustain the cycle of poverty and marginalisation, leaving citizens with no power to change their circumstances. Consequently, South Africa must undertake remedial measures that emphasise self-determination, responsibility, and improved quality of service delivery. To

81 Sen, A. (1993) Capability and Well-Being. In: Nussbaum, M. and Sen, A. (eds) *The Quality of Life*. Caledon Press, 271.

82 Ibid.

83 Ibid.

84 Manomano, Tatenda; Tanga, Pius and Tanyi, Perpetua (2016) Housing Problems and Programs in South Africa: A Literature Review. *Journal of Sociology and Social Anthropology* 7(2): 114.

85 Aigbavboa, C. et al (2019) Quality of Low-income Housing Projects in South Africa. *IOP Conference Series: Materials Science and Engineering* 640(1): 07.

86 Manomano, Tanga and Tanyi, supra note 84, 114.

address these issues, the government must prioritise implementing quality control measures in public service delivery.

7 Conclusion

The above analysis is indicative of how the right to development can become part of the mandate of civil society as well as the government, which ought to take the rights and interests of South Africa citizens seriously. Despite the apparent gaps in the realisation of the right to development implied in the South Africa Constitution, this chapter has shown how the Constitution could be read more expansively in holding the government accountable. If South Africa eventually ratifies the Covenant on the Right to Development when it is adopted, it will be crucial to consider the following factors as corrective measures for accountability:

- Establish a framework for civil society organisations to oversee the implementation of the right to development. In this instance, the civil society organisations will play a key role in coordinating engagement between communities and the government.
- The use of case law in tackling similar issues in the future.
- Continuous research should be used in strengthening accountability on the right to development, ensuring that this happens in an indivisible manner.
- Civil society organisations must continue advocating for, and educating citizens on the right to development, and endeavour to integrate it into the public conversation as a means of enabling citizens to hold the government responsible and accordingly, promote the related aspect of citizens' self-determination.

In assessing South Africa's constitutionalism in relation to the right to development, it is clear as illustrated in this chapter that the country's constitutional framework aligns with the provisions on the right to development articulated in the International Covenant on the Right to Development. Nevertheless, several challenges persist in the effective implementation of fundamental rights, necessitating remedial actions for effective enforcement and accountability. The South African context emphasises the need for a holistic approach in remedying the challenges that arise from the shortfalls in implementing the right to development. It is possible to achieve this even without formal recognition and protection or the adoption of a relevant policy on the right to development. It is important to note that South Africa stands in an opportune situation where a strong human rights culture and the culture of holding the state accountable prevails, and case law on matters pertaining to the rights enshrined in the Bill of Rights provides an opportunity for remedial action.

It is important to note that constitutionalism as part of the focus of this chapter has been explored to illustrate the means to which remedies arise. The point has been made that sections of the Constitution emphasise the need for the rule of law to exist in the context of separation of powers. In the same vein, the courts are also cautioned not to overreach while remaining impartial. These factors which are found in the Constitution of South Africa have been tested and ventilated in the courts, leaving a trail of case law that ought to be followed. This then places civil society organisations in good stead to play the bigger role of monitoring the remedial actions.

References

Acton, Helen (2022) Lawfare: How to Approach it in South Africa's Constitutional Democracy. *The Africa Governance Papers* 1(2): 48–75.

Aigbavboa, C. et al (2019) Quality of Low-income Housing Projects in South Africa. *IOP Conference Series: Materials Science and Engineering* 640(1): 1–7.

Albertyn, Catherine (2019) (In)equality and the South African Constitution. *Development Southern Africa* 36(6): 751–766.

Ally, Nurina and Linde, Daniel (2021) Pridwin: Private School Contracts, the Bill of Rights and a Missed Opportunity. *Constitutional Court Review* 11(1): 1–26.

Andreassen, Bart Andreas and Marks, Stephen (2006) *Development as an Essential Human Right: Legal, Political, and Economic Dimensions*. Cambridge/Massachusetts: Harvard University Press.

Bilchitz, David (2007) *Poverty and Fundamental Rights: The Justification and Execution of Socio-Economic Rights*. Oxford: Oxford University Press.

Breakfast, Ntsikelelo, Bradshaw Gavin and Nomarwayi, Thandolwethu (2019) Violent Service Delivery Protests in Post-Apartheid South Africa, 1994–2017: A Conflict Resolution Perspective. *African Journal of Public Affairs* 11(1): 107–126.

Chilton, Adam and Versteeg, Mila (2018) Courts' Limited Ability to Protect Constitutional Rights. *The University of Chicago Law Review* 85(2): 293–235.

De Kadt, Daniel and Lieberman, Evan (2020) Nuanced Accountability: Voter Responses to Service Delivery in Southern Africa. *British Journal of Political Science* 50(1): 185–215.

Declaration on the Right to Development Resolution A/RES/41/128 adopted by UN General Assembly on 4 December 1986.

Draft International Covenant on the Right to Development—Report by the Chair-Rapporteur of the Working Group on the Right to Development, Zamir Akram (Pakistan) Human Rights Council A/HRC/54/50 54th Session, 6 October 2023.

Francis, David and Webster, Edward (2019) Poverty and Inequality in South Africa: Critical Reflections. *Development Southern Africa* 36(6): 788–802.

Fraussen, Bert; Albareda, Adrià and Braun, Celesta (2020) Conceptualizing Consultation Approaches: Identifying Combinations of Consultation Tools and Analysing their Implications for Stakeholder Diversity. *Policy Sciences* 53(3): 473–493.

Gorwa, R. and Ash, T.G. (2020) Democratic Transparency in the Platform Society. In: Persily, N. and Tucker, J.A. (eds) *Social Media and Democracy: The State of the Field and Prospects for Reform*, Cambridge University Press, 286–312.

Government of the Republic of South Africa v Grootboom 2001 (1) SA 46 (CC).

Government of the Republic of South Africa, 1996. Available at: https://www.justice.gov.za/constitution/SAConstitution-web-eng.pdf (consulted 30 September 2024).

Graybill, Lyn (2000) Lingering Legacy: Apartheid and the South African Press. *Current History* 99(637): 227–230.

Handmaker, Jeff and Tandiwe, Matthews (2019) Analysing Legal Mobilisation's Potential to Secure Equal Access to Socioeconomic Justice in South Africa. *Development Southern Africa* 36(6): 889–904.

Hawksley, C. and Georgeou, N. (2021) Right to Development: Theory, Practice, and Articulation with SDGs. In: Filho, W.L. et al (eds) *No Poverty*. Cham: Springer, 815–825.

Hügel, Stephan and Davies, Anna (2020) Public Participation, Engagement, and Climate Change Adaptation: A Review of the Research Literature. *Wiley Interdisciplinary Reviews: Climate Change* 11(4): 1–20.

Khan, Fatima (2020) Does the Right to Dignity Extend Equally to Refugees in South Africa? *African Human Rights Law Journal* 20(1): 261–284.

Klaasen, Abraham (2020) The Quest for Socio-Economic Rights: The Rule of Law and Violent Protest in South Africa. *Sustainable Development* 28(3): 478–484.

Langford, Malcolm (2021) The Impact of Public Interest Litigation: The Case of Socio-Economic Rights. *Australian Journal of Human Rights* 27(3): 505–531.

Leckey, Robert (2016) The Harms of Remedial Discretion. *International Journal of Constitutional Law* 14(3): 584–607.

Lidström, Anders; Sellers, Jeffrey and Bae, Yooil (2020) *Multilevel Democracy: How Local Institutions and Civil Society Shape the Modern State*. Cambridge: Cambridge University Press.

Liebenberg, Sandra (2010) *Socio-Economic Rights: Juridical Interpretation under a Transformative Constitution*. Claremont: Juta and Company Ltd.

Liebenberg, Sandra (2022) The Art of the (Im)possible? Justice Froneman's Contribution to Designing Remedies for Structural Human Rights Violations. *Constitutional Court Review* 12(1): 138–170.

Liebenberg, Sandra and Goldblatt, Beth (2007) The Relationship Between Equality and Socio-Economic Rights Under South Africa's Transformative Constitution. *South African Journal of Human Rights* 23(2): 335–361.

Maganoe, Shadi (2023) Legislative Oversight and Executive Accountability in South Africa. *Potchefstroom Electronic Law Journal* 26(1): 1–34.

Malan, Naude (2008) Rights, the Populace, and the South African Constitution: Civil Society and the Implementation of Rights. *Anthropology Southern Africa* 31(1–2): 58–69.

Manomano, Tatenda; Tanga, Pius and Tanyi, Perpetua (2016) Housing Problems and Programs in South Africa: A Literature Review. *Journal of Sociology and Social Anthropology* 7(2): 111–117.

Mcineka, A. and Nomthandazo, N. (2019) A Perspective on the Principle of "Constitutionalism" in Relation to Executive and Legislative Accountability in South Africa. In: Fagbadebo, O. and Ruffin, F. (eds) *Perspectives on the Legislature and the Prospects of Accountability in Nigeria and South Africa*. Cham, Switzerland: Springer, 45–61.

Mfete, Tabiso (2020) Neoliberalism and Inequality in Post-Apartheid South Africa. *Pretoria Student Law Review* 14(1): 270–297.

Minister of Health v. Treatment Action Campaign, 2002 (5) SA 721 (CC).

Mohammad, N. and Farjana, Y. (2018) Participation as a Human Right: A Rights-Based Approach to Development. In: *Stakeholders, Governance and Responsibility* (*Developments in Corporate Governance and Responsibility, Vol 14*). Leeds: Emerald Publishing Limited, 33–45.

Ndinga-Kanga, Masana; Van der Merwe, Hugo and Hartford, Daniel (2020) Forging a Resilient Social Contract in South Africa: States and Societies Sustaining Peace in the Post-Apartheid Era. *Journal of Intervention and Statebuilding* 14(1): 22–41.

Ngang, Carol Chi (2019) Radical Transformation and a Reading of the Right to Development in the South African Constitutional Order. *South African Journal on Human Rights* 35(1): 25–49.

Ngcamu, Bethuel (2019) Exploring Service Delivery Protests in Post-Apartheid South African Municipalities: A Literature Review. *Journal for Transdisciplinary Research in Southern Africa* 15(1): 1–9.

Ngcobo, Khanyile (2024) Four Dead, Three Injured in Jeppestown Fire. Available at: https://www.timeslive.co.za/news/south-africa/2024-08-25-three-dead-in-jeppestown-fire/ (consulted 30 November 2024).

Nodangala, Norless Zibele and Masumbe, Paul (2023) A Narrative of Marikana Tragedy against Right to Life and Right to Human Dignity under the South African Constitution. *E-Journal of Humanities, Arts and Social Sciences* 4(10): 1297–1306.

Okafor, Obiora Chinedu and Ngwaba, Uchechukwu (2020) International Accountability in the Implementation of the Right to Development and the "Wonderful Artificiality" of Law: An African Perspective. *Transnational Human Rights Review* 7(1): 40–74.

Parliament of South Africa (1996) Democracy Works Foundation Public Participation Toolkit. Available at: https://www.parliament.gov.za/storage/app/media/Pages/2023/21-08-2023_NCOP_Co-ordination_Co-operation_and_Consultation_Workshop/Commission_2/Democracy_Works_Foundation_Public_Participation_Toolkit_compressed.pdf (consulted 30 September 2024).

Pieterse, Marius (2023) Rule of Law Through the "Urban Turn" in South Africa constitutionalism. *Hague Journal on the Rule of Law* 15(2): 305–328.

Plagerson, Sophie et al (2019) Social Policy in South Africa: Navigating the Route to Social Development. *World Development* 113: 1–9.

Rautenbach, I.M. (2014) Proportionality and the Limitation Clauses of the South African Bill of Rights. *Potchefstroom Electronic Law Journal* 17(6): 2228–2267

Schormair, Maximilian J. and Gerlach, Lara M. (2020) Corporate Remediation of Human Rights Violations: A Restorative Justice Framework. *Journal of Business Ethics* 167(3): 475–493.

Sen, Amartya (1993) Capability and Well-Being. In: Nussbaum, M. and Sen, A. (eds) *The Quality of Life*. Caledon Press, 270–293.

Shai, I. and Kamga, S.D. (2021) Challenges and Prospects in Attaining Development Within and Through the Rule of Law in South Africa. In: Kamga, S.D. (ed) *The Right to Development in Africa: Issues, Constraints*. Austin: Pan African University Press, 37–52.

Steytler, N. (2017) The Constitutional Court of South Africa: Reinforcing an Hourglass System of Multi-Level Government. In: Aroney, N. and Kincaid, J. (eds) *Courts in Federal Countries: Federalists or Unitarists*. Toronto: University of Toronto Press.

Subedi, Surya (2021) Declaration on the Right to Development. *Legal UN*. Available at: https://legal.un.org/avl/pdf/ha/drd/drd_e.pdf (consulted 30 September 2024).

Tait, Kira, and Whitney Taylor (2023) The Possibility of Rights Claims-Making in Court: Looking Back on Twenty-Five Years of Social Rights Constitutionalism in South Africa. *Law and Social Inquiry* 48(3): 1023–1052.

Teleki, Mofihli (2017) Framing of the Right to Development Policy in the Context of South Africa. *Africa Insight* 47(3): 78–94.

Tinsley, Meghan (2019) Constructing and Contesting the Post-apartheid State: Political Discourse and the Marikana Strike. *Language, Discourse and Society* 7(2): 15–33.

Tully, James et al (2016) Introducing Global Integral Constitutionalism. *Global Constitutionalism* 5(1): 1–15.

Udombana, Nsongurua (2024) Reflections on Constitutionalism and Democratic Governance in Africa. *Journal of African Law* 68(2): 137–156.

United Nations Organisation (2017) *The Right to Development and Economic Progress: Achievements and Future Outlook*. New York: United Nations.

Wolf, Loammi (2017) The Remedial Action of the "State of Capture" Report in Perspective. *Potchefstroom Electronic Law Journal* 20(1): 1–46.

CHAPTER 12

Advancing Youth Right to Development: Challenges and Prospects

Bamisaye Olutola

1 Introduction

The human right to development (RTD) cannot be achieved in isolation without consideration of those who are its beneficiaries or rights holders. Therefore, any conversation around human rights generally and the RTD in particular, without considering who are their beneficiaries is not only meaningless but a complete exercise in futility. One of the criticisms that have been levelled against the RTD is the vagueness of its contents and the uncertainty around who are its beneficiaries or right holders.[1] However, it has been argued that the RTD was originally conceived not as an individual right that a person can claim against his/her state but as a right that belongs to peoples.[2] That is to say, at the embryonic stage of the RTD, peoples rather than individuals were the rights holders. It is pertinent to state from the outset that there is no one view of what amounts to the content and contour of the RTD. The RTD has remained hotly contested and highly debated among scholars, notwithstanding its important status among the family of rights.[3] Despite the various controversies around its status, it is noted as a general fact that the RTD is both an individual as well as a collective right.[4] By implication, it is a right that is claimable by an individual against his or her state, and it can also be claimed by peoples against their state.

It is incontestably true to state that various efforts at fashioning the RTD have deep roots. However, the ancestry of the RTD in contemporary international law has been argued to be implicitly traceable to the adoption of the Universal

1 Bunn, Isabella (2000) The Right to Development: Implications for International Economic Law. *American International Law Review* 15(6): 1434.

2 Ngang, Carol Chi (2021) *The Right to Development in* Africa. Leiden: Brill, 63–65; Villaroman, Noel (2010) The Right to Development: Exploring the Basis of Supernorm. *Florida Journal of International Law* 22(2): 300.

3 Kamga, Serges Djoyou and Fombad, Charles Manga (2013) A Critical Review of the Jurisprudence of the African Commission on Right to Development. *Journal of African Law* 57(2): 196.

4 Ibid.

 | DOI:10.1163/9789004734357_013

Declaration of Human Rights (UDHR) and the United Nations (UN) Charter.[5] In specific terms, the global recognition of the RTD can be traced to the adoption of the UN Declaration on the RTD (UNDRTD) by the General Assembly in 1986. The UNDRTD is not only revolutionary in terms of the articulation of the RTD, but pivotal because it is the first formal document on the RTD adopted by in the UN General Assembly.[6] Unfortunately, the UNDRTD is a non-binding instrument in which states are not under any international obligation to be bound by its provision.

Though a legal foundation for the RTD has not firmly been established at the global level in terms of having a binding framework on it, recognition of the existence of such a right is largely not in doubt. The RTD is a recognisable legal right under the African Charter on Human and Peoples' Rights (African Charter).[7] States parties to the African Charter are expected to fulfil their obligations on the RTD just like every other right under the Charter.[8] One of the unique features of the RTD is that it has the goal of empowering its rights holders whether as individuals or groups.[9] If indeed, the RTD has the capacity or the goal of empowering its rights-holders, ensuring its realisation for every individual or group globally, it should be a worthy mission to pursue vigorously.

It is this mission of pursuing the realisation of the RTD that this chapter sets out to achieve. Since it has been established that the RTD is both an individual and a collective right, the youth as a group, is therefore, entitled to claim it. Youth are victims of human rights violations globally. Often, the violation of their rights remains unaccounted for largely, due to the challenge around what groups of persons within society can be regarded as youth. Notwithstanding the existence of this challenge, there is indeed, a group of persons recognised as youth both under the UN and other regional frameworks. The crux of this chapter is therefore, to interrogate how the youth's RTD can be litigated in the event of its violation.

The chapter is founded on the premise that rights that cannot successfully be litigated in the event of a violation amount to an empty promise or no rights at all. Therefore, the RTD will amount to a meaningless right to the youth, if there are no available avenues to seek remedy when it is violated. In a bid to do

5 Acharya, Upendra (2007) Is Development a Lost Paradise? Trade, Environment and Development: A Triadic Dream of International Law. *Alberta Law Review* 45(2): 416.

6 Ibid.

7 African Charter on Human and Peoples' Rights adopted in Nairobi, Kenya on 27 June 1981 OAU Doc CAB/LEG/67/3 Rev.5 (1981), Art 22.

8 Kamga and Fombad, supra note 3, 203.

9 Ibid at 202.

justice to the goal of this chapter, it has been divided into five parts. Part one is the general introduction, which establishes the background to the discussion. It interrogates the meaning of the RTD and other connected issues. It sets the tone for the analysis in the entire chapter.

Part two focuses on the human rights of the youth under the UN human rights architecture. It interrogates the existence or otherwise of a group known as the youth under the UN human rights system. It further engages the various documents of the UN that expressly or/and impliedly guarantee the rights of the youth in general and their RTD in particular. Part three interrogates the various regional efforts aimed at recognising the human rights of the youth. It primarily focuses on the African Youth Charter (AYC), which is the fundamental regional instrument on youth rights. It considers some of the rights and ascertains whether the RTD is part of the rights guaranteed to youth under the AYC. Part four considers the pathways in litigating youth RTD both under the UN human rights system and regional human rights systems. It analyses the prospects and challenges in litigating youth RTD both at the global and regional levels.

Part five, which is the final section focuses on recommendations for strengthening the RTD for the youth both at the global and regional levels. It considers the existing gaps in both laws and institutions that can jeopardise the chances of the youth enjoying the RTD on equal footing with others in society. It offers ways through which these challenges can be surmounted and how the rights of the youth in general and their RTD, in particular, can be respected and protected under various human rights regimes.

2 Youth Rights under the Global Human Rights Regime

The global human rights regime as used in this chapter, refer to the human rights architecture of the UN. The UN has, both in the past and in recent times, continued to make advancements in the protection of human rights, including that of the youth at the global stage. However, before the establishment of the UN, the issue of human rights of the youth was already being discussed at the global level.[10] The UN has however, taken some giant steps towards ensuring that its members states do not pay lip service to recognition, guarantee, and

10 See generally Angel, William (2015) *The International Law of Youth Rights*. Leiden: Brill, 1–39.

respect of the rights of the youth in their respective states.[11] Some of these efforts are considered and interrogated further in this chapter.

The very first UN declaration on issues relating to youth rights was in 1965 when the General Assembly (GA) passed Resolution 2037 on the promotion of the ideals of peace, mutual respect, and understanding between people.[12] The central point of this Resolution is the undeniably, pivotal roles the youth can play in ensuring peaceful development on the global stage.[13] The resolution expansively speaks on the need to engage the youth and respect their rights globally but does not specify what categories of persons are regarded as youth under the UN human rights architecture. This obvious omission was later corrected by the UNGA in Resolution 36/28 in 1981, where it declared that for statistical purposes, the youth are persons between the ages of 15 to 24 years.[14]

In acknowledging the fact that despite the above resolutions, issues of youth rights have not fully been implemented by member states, the UN in 1995, declared a World Programme of Action for Youth to the Year 2000 and Beyond, popularly referred to as the WPAY Declaration.[15] In order not to keep any member state in doubt about the purport and the purpose of the WPAY Declaration, it "affirms the full and effective participation of youths in society and decision-making as one of its 10 priority areas of action".[16]

Despite the existence of the WPAY Declaration, in ensuring that the human rights of the youth are brought to the front burner on the global stage, another declaration known as the Braga Youth Action Plan (BYAP) was adopted by the Third World Youth Forum in Braga, Portugal in 1998. The BYAP underscores the importance of ensuring that the youth are recognised as critical players in proffering solutions to the myriads of issues bedevilling the world. It declares that for the youth to effectively play this critical role as solution providers,

---

11 Olutola, Bamisaye Olawaye (2020) Youth Right to Political Participation under International Human Rights Law. *Kabarak Journal of Law and Ethics* 5(1): 128–146.

12 Declaration on the Promotion among Youth of the Ideals of Peace, Mutual Respect and Understanding between Peoples, Proclaimed by the General Assembly, Resolution 2037 (XX), A/RES/20/2037, on 7 December 1965.

13 Mahidi, Mourad (2010) The Young and the Rightless? The Protection of Youth Rights in Europe. Unpublished Master Dissertation, Åbo Akademi University, 31.

14 International Youth Year: Participation, Development, Peace, UN General Assembly 36th Session Resolution 36/28 of 13 November 1981; see also, Policies and programmes involving youth, UN General Assembly 56th Session Resolution A/RES/56/117 of 18 January 2002.

15 World Programme of Action for Youth (2010, June) United Nations Declaration of Intent on Youth: Problems and Potentials. Available at: https://www.un.org/esa/socdev/unyin/documents/wpay2010.pdf (consulted 28 November 2024.

16 World Youth Report (2003) *The Global Situation of Young People*. United Nations, 271.

respect of their human rights to full and effective political participation in decision-making is non-negotiable.[17] In particular, it declares that they "should participate in the decisions taken today about the resources of tomorrow".[18]

In addition to the above, the year 2010 was proclaimed as the International Year of Youth: Dialogue and Mutual Understanding by the UNGA in its 2009 Resolution in a bid to ensure that its efforts in recognising youth rights are further crystallised.[19] The Resolution declares that the economic, and social conditions and future generations' wellbeing and livelihood will be ineluctably impacted by the way the human rights and issues of the youth are treated today.[20] It implies that UN member states cannot afford to handle the issues and rights of the youth with levity because they have the potential to affect future generations either positively or negatively.

To ensure that the human rights of youth are respected globally, the UNGA, on 25 August 2011, adopted a Resolution advising member states to ensure that they take targeted actions to promote the best interest of the youth.[21] The Resolution further states that to ensure that the human rights of the youth are respected, member states are expected to cascade "further efforts to promote the interests of youths, including the full enjoyment of their human rights, inter alia, by supporting young people in developing their potential and talents and tackling obstacles facing youth".[22] It is submitted that the UNGA adopted this declaration because without all the steps taken by member states, the human rights of the youth would be nothing but a pipedream.

Notwithstanding, the various efforts by the UN in recognising and calling for respect of the human rights of the youth globally, there is no enforceable UN mechanism specifically on youth rights. However, the statistical definition of youth by the UN, which as indicated earlier, is between 15 to 24 years, implies that their rights are nevertheless, secured under the general UN human rights instruments,[23] including the UN Convention on the Rights of

---

17 See the Braga Youth Action Plan (BYAP). Available at: http://www.youthpolicy.org/library/wp-content/uploads/library/1998_WYF_Braga_Eng.pdf (consulted 17 September 2024).

18 Ibid at 271.

19 Proclamation of 2010 as the International Year of Youth: Dialogue and Mutual Understanding, UN General Assembly 64th Session Resolution A/RES/64/134 of 1 February 2010.

20 Ibid.

21 United Nations A/RES/65/312 Outcome Document of the High-Level Meeting of the General Assembly on Youth: Dialogue and Mutual Understanding, Para 4.

22 Ibid at Para 7.

23 For example, International Covenant on Civil and Political Rights adopted by the UN General Assembly, Resolution 2200A (XXI) of 16 December 1966, 993 UNTS 3 UN Doc A/6316 (1966); International Covenant on Economic, Social and Cultural Rights adopted by the

the Child (CRC).[24] Thus, except for these human rights instruments, the youth do not have any additional protection for their rights under the UN human rights architecture.

The implication of the absence of a specific UN instrument on youth rights which does not fall within the age bracket of those covered by the CRC (0–17 years), is that they can only enforce their rights through general international human rights instruments applicable under the UN human rights system. Therefore, in the event of an encroachment on their rights, they are only able to ventilate a claim through the UN human rights enforcement mechanisms and nothing more. This of course, makes the youth less protected under the UN, unlike children who are eligible to enjoy the rights provided for them in the general international human rights instrument and the CRC.

3 Youth Rights under the Regional Human Rights System

Globally, various regional human rights regimes have put in place human rights norms that are binding on states within such regions. Three regional human rights regimes are quite popular, they are respectively established in Africa, Europe, and the Americas.[25] It is pertinent to note here that although these regimes are established as political or inter-governmental organisations, they do have human rights as part of their objectives.[26] More often than not, these regional human rights systems have succeeded over time in supplementing various global efforts to ensure that the culture of human rights is entrenched in these various regions.

However, youth rights have not found the full and well-deserved attention at all the various regional human rights regimes. Nevertheless, youth rights have found expression in the human rights instruments of some of these regional human rights regimes. For example, there are basically two regional human rights instruments globally that specifically, provide for the rights of the youth. These are the Ibero-American Convention on Young People's Rights

UN General Assembly, Resolution 2200A (XXI) of 16 December 1966, 999 UNTS 171 UN Doc A/6316 (1966).

24 Convention on the Rights of the Child, adopted by UN General Assembly Resolution 44/25, UN Treaty Series, vol. 1577, p. 3, of 20 November 1989.

25 Viljoen, Frans (2012) *International Human Rights Law in Africa*. 2nd Edn, Oxford: Oxford University Press, 11.

26 Ibid at 12.

(IACYR),[27] and the African Youth Charter (AYC).[28] The nature of the rights enshrined in these instruments and their implication for the youth's RTD will be considered *seriatim*.

The IACYR, which was established for the purpose of ensuring that the rights of the youth are respected, came into force on 1 March 2008. Its enactment was quite revolutionary in human rights history because it became the first international legally binding human rights treaty for the youth. It contains various human rights that speak to the challenges the youth are confronted with globally. These rights are incorporated in the 44 articles that are grouped into the five chapters that make up the IACYR. The rights range from sexual and reproductive rights to the right to political participation among others. Although the IACYR is principally applicable to some countries in the Americas, it equally has the force of law in Europe, due to some European countries haven subscribed to it.[29]

The rationale for adopting the IACYR is to secure the specific human rights of the youth. The drafters recognise the fact that the youth, who constitute an instrumental sector in society, often do encounter myriads of challenges that impact on the enjoyment of their human rights. This motivated the need to put in place a legally binding instrument that will delineate the nature and the contents of the human rights that are particularly, relevant to the youth. Just like in UNGA Resolution A/Res/50/8, the IACYR defines youth as persons between the ages of 15 and 24 years. Article 21 of the IACYR guarantees to the youth, the right to political participation.

The IACYR does not guarantee the RTD to the youth, which has remained one of the major drawbacks of the Convention. Guaranteeing the RTD to the youth would certainly have positive implications on the realisation of the full range of all other human rights that they are entitled to. Since the RTD is a composite right, it can be used as a tool for securing the enjoyment of other rights that are not explicitly guaranteed.[30] Another major drawback to the IACYR is the absence of any supervisory or monitoring mechanism. It means that persons whose rights are violated under the Charter have to seek alternative routes for redress rather than through the IACYR. The obvious implication of this is that many rights under the IACYR are likely not to be redressed in instances of their violation.

---

27 Ibero-American Convention on Young People's Rights. (2005, October). Regional Treaties, Agreements, Declarations and Related. Available at: http://www.refworld.org/docid/4b28eefe2.html (consulted 18 August 2018).

28 African Youth Charter adopted by the 7th Ordinary Session of the AU Assembly of Heads of State and Government in Banjul, the Gambia on 2 July 2006.

29 For example, Spain and Portugal are parties to the IACYR.

30 Kamga and Fombad supra note 3, 196.

The AYC remains the seminal regional treaty, which not only provides for the specific rights of the youth on the African continent but importantly also, recognises and protects their RTD in Article 10. The Preamble to the AYC gives an account of the reasons why it was adopted. It stipulates that the African youth remain the greatest resources of Africa, and the difficulties that lie ahead can only be conquered through the active and full participation of the youth in all spheres of society.[31] Similarly, the drafters of the AYC acknowledge that many youth in Africa are "marginalised from mainstream society through inequalities in income, wealth and power, [...]"[32] The drafters equally assert that the youth are "partners, assets and a prerequisite for sustainable development and for the peace and prosperity of Africa with a unique contribution to make to the present and to the future development".[33]

The AYC contains several human rights that are targeted at ensuring that the youth are not marginalised and consequently, that their human rights are respected. These rights are contained in the 31 articles that make up the AYC. To underscore the need for non-marginalisation of the youth in Africa, the first right guaranteed by the AYC is the right to freedom from discrimination.[34] It imposes an obligation on state parties to the AYC, to ensure that all appropriate measures are taken to protect the youth against all forms of discrimination.[35] It means that any state party that does not respect the human rights guaranteed to the youth, would be in clear violation of their obligations under the AYC. Unlike in UNGA Resolution A/Res/50/8 and the IACYR, the AYC defines youth as persons between the ages of 15 and 35 years.[36]

The AYC contains a broad range of rights that are ordinarily available in other human rights instruments. Reiterating them in the AYC emphasises the fact that the youth of Africa are entitled to and should not be denied the rights guaranteed to them. Some of these rights include the right to movement, right to property,[37] freedom of expression,[38] freedom of association,[39] and freedom of religion[40] among others. In addition to these range of rights, the AYC

31 African Youth Charter, supra note 27, Preamble.
32 Ibid.
33 Ibid.
34 Ibid at Art 2.
35 Ibid at Art 2(2).
36 African Youth Charter, supra note 27, Definition Section.
37 African Youth Charter, supra note 27, Art 9.
38 Ibid at Art 4.
39 Ibid at Art 5.
40 Ibid at Art 6.

guarantees the RTD to the youth in a very expansive manner.[41] It provides thus, "Every young person shall have the right to social, economic, political and cultural development with due regard to their freedom and identity and in the equal enjoyment of the common heritage of mankind".[42]

The above provision is elaborate and has several tentacles that encapsulate the broad nature of the RTD. Therefore, a state party may be liable to have violated this provision where any of its policies are inconsistent with an aspect of the right. That is to say, where any action or policy of a state party affects the social, economic, political and cultural development of the youth in their respective states, the Article 10 provision can be invoked and adjudged to be in violation. The RTD in the AYC is therefore, broad enough to cover several aspects of governmental policies and be a veritable lens through which adherence to the realisation of youth rights can be viewed. It is obligatory for state parties under the AYC, to ensure that the RTD is exercised by the youth.[43]

The provision on the RTD under the AYC is further fortified by the provision on the right to participation of the youth, which is a fundamental component for the realisation of the RTD. The controlling phrase in the right to participation under the AYC is "all spheres of society".[44] That is to say, the youth have the right to participate in all spheres of society and consequently, state parties are mandated to take targeted steps and measures to ensure the realisation of this right.[45] Part of the steps that are required of state parties in ensuring realisation of the right to participation includes, the guarantee of participation by the youth in parliament and various decision-making platforms.[46]

It is however, pertinent to note here that besides rights guaranteed under the AYC, youth in Africa are equally able to claim some rights in other African human rights instruments. For instance, they are entitled to the RTD which is guaranteed under Article 22 of the African Charter. Similarly, they can equally claim various rights which are applicable to young girls under the Protocol to the African Charter on Women's Rights (Maputo Protocol).[47]

State parties to the AYC are expected to recognised all the rights, freedom, and duties which are guaranteed in the Charter.[48] More importantly, they are

41 Ibid at Art 10.
42 Ibid at Art 10(1).
43 Ibid at Art 10(2).
44 Ibid at Art 11(1).
45 Ibid at Art 11(2).
46 Ibid at Art 11(2)(a).
47 Protocol to the African Charter on Human and Peoples' Rights on the Rights of Women in Africa adopted in Maputo, Mozambique on 11 July 2003.
48 African Youth Charter, supra note 27, Art 1(1).

expected to take necessary steps and measures in bringing their national laws in conformity with the provisions of the AYC so as to make its provisions effective at the domestic level.[49] These provisions are extremely necessary if the rights guaranteed to the youth in the AYC are not to be rendered illusory. It must be pointed out here that the AYC cannot be used by state parties to minimise existing higher human rights standards contained in other human rights instruments that state parties have subscribed to or those that are contained in their national laws and policies.[50]

It is arguable that despite the various human rights provisions of the AYC, which are capable of advancing the RTD for the youth in Africa, the Charter is silent on its monitoring or supervisory mechanism. This of course, makes the AYC capable of being violated without dire consequences on the part of state parties under the Charter.[51] The AYC only provides that the African Union Commission shall ensure that state parties respect and fulfil their obligations under the Charter.[52] Some scholars have argued that the absence of a monitoring mechanism under the AYC is not fatal as the mandates of other African Union (AU) human rights enforcement mechanisms can be extended to cover it.[53] Others have argued that otherwise, if the drafters wanted such institutions to entertain matters with respect to the AYC or other similar instruments, they would have expressly made provision for such.[54] The arguments notwithstanding, it is worth reiterating that the AYC lacks a monitoring mechanism.[55]

4 Prospects for Litigating Youth Right to Development

The RTD as guaranteed in various global and regional human rights instruments undoubtedly include the youth.[56] Therefore, litigating youth RTD should not ordinarily be a challenging exercise. However, what this chapter

49 Ibid at Art 1(2).
50 Ibid at Art 29.
51 Tomuschat, Christian (2014) *Human Rights: Between Idealism and Realism*. 3rd Edn, Oxford: Oxford University Press, 13.
52 African Youth Charter, supra note 27, Art 28.
53 Adeola, Ramola (2015, 6 July) The African Youth Charter and the Role of Regional Institutions in an Age of Africa Rising. *AfricLaw*. Available at: https://africlaw.com/2015/07/06/the-african-youth-charter-and-the-role-of-regional-institutions-in-an-age-of-africa-rising/ (consulted 16 October 2024).
54 Viljoen, supra note 25, 312.
55 Mahidi, supra note 10, 52.
56 African Charter, supra note 7, Art 22.

sets out to examine is to interrogate whether there are specific enforcement or supervisory mechanisms through which persons who are youth can bring their claims and get redress under international human rights law. It entails asking what the possibilities are under international human rights law for the youth to litigate violations of their RTD?

At the global level, litigating youth rights is a bit challenging due basically to two reasons. The first reason is due to the absence of a specific global human rights instrument on youth rights, and the second is due to the absence of any enforceable human rights instruments on the RTD except within the context of the African human rights system where enforcement of youth rights is possible and achievable through the African Commission on Human and Peoples' Rights and the African Court on Human and Peoples' Rights. Therefore, to ensure litigation of the RTD for the youth at the global level, such complaint must be brought through other enforceable human rights instruments that enshrine rights that are ancillary to the RTD.[57] Also, since based on the UN categorisation, some children are captured in the youth grouping (15–35), a violation of the RTD of these youth can be brought to the Committee of the CRC.[58]

However, at the regional levels, there are possibilities for litigating youth's RTD. This is principally because there are specific binding human rights instruments that speak directly to specific rights of the youth. Under the IACYR, since there is no specific RTD guaranteed to the youth, and no available supervisory mechanism under the Charter, litigating youth's RTD may not be achievable. Therefore, based on this fact, attention is focused on litigating youth's RTD under the African human rights system on the basis that the RTD is protected under the African Charter, the AYC and the Protocol on the Rights of Women in Africa, which is applicable to young girls.[59]

The first route of litigating youth RTD under the African human rights system is to submit such a complaint to the African Committee of Experts on the Rights and Welfare of the Child (African Children's Committee).[60] Though the mandate of the African Children's Committee is to ensure that rights guaranteed under the African Children's Charter are protected, it should nevertheless

57 For example, under the International Covenant on Economic, Social, and Cultural Rights (ICESCR) several articles speak to the RTD.

58 Convention on the Rights of the Child, supra note 24, Art 43.

59 African Youth Charter, supra note 27, Art 10; African Charter, supra note 7, Art 22; Protocol on the Rights of Women in Africa, supra note 47, Art 19.

60 African Charter on the Rights and Welfare of the Child adopted by the 26th Ordinary Session of the Assembly of Heads of State and Government of the OAU in Addis Ababa, Ethiopia, July 1990, Art 32.

be capable of entertaining matters that concern children generally.[61] Since children are defined by the African Children's Charter as persons under the age of 18,[62] and the AYC defines youth as persons between the ages of 15 and 35 years, it follows that the rights of some children are covered by the AYC.[63]

Therefore, children (also regarded as youth under the AYC) from ages 15 and 17 years should be able to enforce their RTD through the African Children's Committee. It is important to note that the African Children's Charter also guarantees children the right to survival and development.[64] Therefore, the youth whose RTD have been violated by their respective state can bring their complaint to the African Children's Committee using both the African Children's Charter and the AYC as the instruments which have been violated. This route will only be available to the youth who are below 18 years because the African Children's Committee may not be allowed by the instrument that creates it to entertain matters whose victims are not children.

The second route through which the RTD of youth can be litigated under the African human rights system is through the African Commission on Human and Peoples' Rights (African Commission).[65] Violation of the youth RTD can be brought to the African Commission for redress because its general mandate is the protection of human rights in Africa.[66] Since the RTD is protected under the African Charter and also the AYC, it is thus, within the promotional and protective mandate of the African Commission to entertain such a matter. Furthermore, notwithstanding the fact that the protective mandate of the African Commission is limited to the African human rights instruments,[67] it is nevertheless, encouraged to draw inspiration from other international human rights instruments.[68] Therefore, parties that are eligible to bring matters before the African Commission can validly seek redress for the violation of the RTD of the youth before it. Such a complaint though centred on the RTD of the youth is nevertheless, competent to be brought before the African Commission because it is based on the violation of the relevant provisions of the African Charter, the AYC or the Protocol on the Rights of Women in Africa to the extent that it is applicable to young women.[69]

---

61 Ibid at Art 42.

62 Ibid at Art 2.

63 African Youth Charter, supra note 27, Definition Section.

64 African Children's Charter, supra note 60, Art 5.

65 Africa Charter, supra note 7, Art 30.

66 Ibid.

67 African Charter, supra note 7, Art 45(2).

68 Ibid at Art 60.

69 Ibid at Art 56.

The third route through which violations of the RTD of the youth could be redressed under the African human rights system is through the African Court on Human and Peoples' Rights (African Court).[70] The jurisdictional powers of the African Court are wide and grossly extensive. This is because its powers extend across the African human rights system and therefore, covers all human rights instruments that have been ratified by the state parties that may be brought before the Court.[71] It therefore, means that competent parties can bring their complaints based on a violation of the RTD either solely on the provision of the AYC or both the AYC and the African Charter.[72] Therefore, the youth whose RTD has been violated can successfully litigate their claim before the African Court after meeting all the other jurisdictional and access conditions.[73]

The above are the three main routes through which the RTD of the youth could be litigated under the African human rights system. However, a violation of the RTD can also be litigated at the sub-regional levels, where the mandates of sub-regional courts has been extended to entertain human rights cases. For example, a sub-regional court like the ECOWAS Court of Justice has a human rights mandate and may be able to entertain cases relating to violations of the RTD.[74]

5 Recommendations and Conclusion

Actualisation of the RTD for many people around the world remains a pipe dream, due to the various controversies around its contents and contours. The global efforts at concretising the RTD have not yielded much result due to the absence of a binding instrument on it at the global level. More troubling is the realisation of the RTD for the youth at the international level where they

70 Viljoen, supra note 25, 400–444.

71 Protocol to the African Charter on Human and Peoples' Rights on the Establishment of an African Court on Human and Peoples' Rights adopted in Addis Ababa, Ethiopia on 10 June 1998 and entered into force on 25 January 2004, Art 3(1) provides that "The jurisdiction of the Court shall extend to all cases and disputes submitted to it concerning the interpretation and application of the Charter, this Protocol and *any other relevant human rights instruments ratified* by the states concerned" (my emphasis).

72 Ibid at Art 5 on Access to the Court.

73 Art 34(6) allows for direct access to the Court by NGOs with observer status before the African Commission and individuals; see Art 5(3) for a better understanding.

74 Protocol on the Community Court of Justice, amended by the Supplementary Protocol Amending the Protocol Relating to the Community Court of Justice, ECOWAS Doc A/SP.1/01/05, 19 January 2005, specifically Arts 9(4) and 10(d).

are confronted with two "evils", the first being the absence of a binding instrument on youth rights, and the second being, the lack of a legally binding instrument on the RTD. It appears like a near-to-no-hope situation for the youth as far as their RTD is concerned at the global level.

At the regional level, the existence of two binding human rights instruments on youth rights and the existence of the RTD in one of the major regional human rights instruments (the AYC) is quite gratifying. However, the conflation of the youth and children in these regional instruments on the youth remains an issue of concern. This is because such instruments can generate controversies around the appropriate grouping of the youth and this remains unsettled. Human rights instruments that are established for a particular group, should reflect a single grouping and a particular set of persons to be protected if the goals of such instruments are to be achieved.

Despite the drawbacks around the regional instruments that guarantee youth rights, their existence largely makes litigating the RTD for the youth possible and achievable especially at the African regional level where the youth's RTD is explicitly protected. Otherwise, advocating for the rights of the youth in general and their RTD in particular, would have been a daunting, if not an impossible task. The existence of the AYC which enshrines the RTD is certainly a step in the right direction toward ensuring that the rights of the youth in Africa is at the minimum, respected, protected, and fulfilled by state parties to the relevant treaties that recognised and guarantee to them sufficient protection. Therefore, in confronting the challenges bedevilling litigation for the youth's RTD both at the global and regional levels, the following recommendations are proffered.

First, the UN must take the decisive step of making a legally binding treaty on the human rights of the youth akin to instruments like the CRC and the Convention on the Elimination of all Forms of Discrimination against Women, which are dedicated to international protection of the rights of children and of women respectively. Such a specific treaty on youth rights must ensure that the age bracket for the youth does not overlap with other groupings like children. It must be a treaty specifically, for youth rights, which should be different from other groupings whose rights have been guaranteed protection in legally binding international treaties under the UN human rights architecture. Furthermore, such a treaty should, as a matter of necessity, enshrine all the categories of human rights, which the youth around the world must equally exercise and enjoy.

Second, the UN should equally begin the process of adopting an Additional Protocol to the draft Covenant on the RTD relating particularly to the youth, which will cater for the peculiar challenges facing them. This of course will assist in the realisation of the RTD of youth. After all, the youth are invariably part of the adults in society, so they are likely going to benefit from the existence of such a binding treaty. Article 27 of the draft Covenant on the RTD gives room for the adoption of additional protocols under it.

Third, at the regional level, the human rights instruments specific to youth rights should be redrawn to make them youth-only instruments. Youth in this context means those persons who are 18 years and above. Once this is achieved, the advocacy for youth rights in general and the RTD will record some level of success at the regional level. On the other hand, regions that have not adopted any youth-specific treaties should begin the process. Adopting a youth rights-specific treaty is in the interest of everyone and of society at large. More importantly, such a treaty must have its monitoring and enforcement mechanism.

In conclusion, the discussion in this chapter has shown that litigating the youth's RTD remains a challenge globally. That notwithstanding, prospects for doing so have been identified. It is hoped that these recommendations if implemented faithfully, and timeously, will redress and transform the existing human rights challenges which the youth are confronted with into opportunities.

References

Acharya, Upendra (2007) Is Development a Lost Paradise? Trade, Environment and Development: A Triadic Dream of International Law. *Alberta Law Review* 45(2): 401–420.

Adeola, Ramola (2015, 6 July) The African Youth Charter and the Role of Regional Institutions in an Age of Africa Rising. *AfricLaw*. Available at: https://africlaw.com/2015/07/06/the-african-youth-charter-and-the-role-of-regional-institutions-in-an-age-of-africa-rising/ (consulted 28 November 2024).

African Charter on Human and Peoples' Rights adopted in Nairobi, Kenya on 27 June 1981 OAU Doc CAB/LEG/67/3 Rev.5 (1981).

African Charter on the Rights and Welfare of the Child adopted by the 26th Ordinary Session of the Assembly of Heads of State and Government of the OAU in Addis Ababa, Ethiopia, July 1990.

African Youth Charter adopted by the 7th Ordinary Session of the AU Assembly of Heads of State and Government in Banjul, the Gambia on 2 July 2006.

Angel, William (2015) *The International Law of Youth Rights*. Leiden: Brill.

Braga Youth Action Plan (BYAP). Available at: http://www.youthpolicy.org/library/wp-content/uploads/library/1998_WYF_Braga_Eng.pdf (consulted 28 November 2024).

Bunn, Isabella (2000) The Right to Development: Implications for International Economic Law. *American International Law Review* 15(6): 1425–1467.
Convention on the Rights of the Child, adopted by UN General Assembly Resolution 44/25, UN Treaty Series, vol. 1577, p. 3, of 20 November 1989.
Declaration on the Promotion among Youth of the Ideals of Peace, Mutual Respect and Understanding between Peoples, Proclaimed by the General Assembly, Resolution 2037 (XX), A/RES/20/2037, on 7 December 1965.
Ibero-American Convention on Young People's Rights. (2005, October). Regional Treaties, Agreements, Declarations and Related. Available at: http://www.refworld.org/docid/4b28eefe2.html (consulted 18 August 2018).
International Covenant on Civil and Political Rights adopted by the UN General Assembly, Resolution 2200A (XXI) of 16 December 1966, 993 UNTS 3 UN Doc A/6316 (1966).
International Covenant on Economic, Social and Cultural Rights adopted by the UN General Assembly, Resolution 2200A (XXI) of 16 December 1966, 999 UNTS 171 UN Doc A/6316 (1966).
International Youth Year: Participation, Development, Peace, UN General Assembly 36th Session Resolution 36/28 of 13 November 1981.
Kamga, Serges Alain Djoyou and Fombad, Charles Manga (2013) A Critical Review of the Jurisprudence of the African Commission on Right to Development. *Journal of African Law* 57(2): 1–19.
Mahidi, M (2010) The Young and the Rightless? The Protection of Youth Rights in Europe. Unpublished Master Dissertation, Åbo Akademi University.
Ngang, Carol Chi (2021) *The Right to Development in Africa*. Leiden/Boston: Brill.
Olutola, Bamisaye Olawaye (2020) Youth Right to Political Participation under International Human Rights Law. *Kabarak Journal of Law and Ethics* 5(1): 127–146.
Outcome Document of the High-Level Meeting of the General Assembly on Youth: Dialogue and Mutual Understanding, UN General Assembly 65th Session Resolution A/RES/65/312 of 13 July 2011.
Policies and programmes involving youth, UN General Assembly 56th Session Resolution A/RES/56/117 of 18 January 2002.
Proclamation of 2010 as the International Year of Youth: Dialogue and Mutual Understanding, UN General Assembly 64th Session Resolution A/RES/64/134 of 1 February 2010.
Protocol on the Community Court of Justice, amended by the Supplementary Protocol Amending the Protocol Relating to the Community Court of Justice, ECOWAS Doc A/SP.1/01/05, 19 January 2005.
Protocol to the African Charter on Human and Peoples' Rights on the Rights of Women in Africa adopted in Maputo, Mozambique on 11 July 2003.

Protocol to the African Charter on Human and Peoples' Rights on the Establishment of an African Court on Human and Peoples' Rights adopted in Addis Ababa, Ethiopia on 10 June 1998.

Tomuschat, Christian (2014) *Human Rights: Between Idealism and Realism*. 3rd Edn, Oxford: Oxford University Press.

Viljoen, Frans (2012) *International Human Rights Law in Africa*. 2nd Edn, Oxford: Oxford University Press.

Villaroman, Noel (2010) The Right to Development: Exploring the Basis of Supernorm. *Florida Journal of International Law* 22(2): 299–332.

World Programme of Action for Youth (2010, June) United Nations Declaration of Intent on Youth: Problems and Potentials. Available at: https://www.un.org/esa/socdev/unyin/documents/wpay2010.pdf (consulted 28 November 2024.

World Youth Report (2003) *The Global Situation of Young People*. United Nations.

PART 4

Systemic Impediments to Realising the Right to Development

CHAPTER 13

African Responses to the Crisis of Illicit Financial Flows and the Draft Covenant on the Right to Development

Serges Djoyou Kamga

1 Introduction

While the right to development (RTD) is controversial at the global level, it is recognised as a justiciable and enforceable human right in the African human rights system. In this vein, it is well provided for by the African Charter on Human Peoples' Rights in its Article 22. To enhance the prospects for its realisation, the African Charter also guarantees the right to wealth and natural resources that can be tapped into.[1] However, the proceeds from the natural resources are often stolen through illicit financial flows (IFFs), which is defined as "illegal movements of money or capital from one country to another".[2]

Noting the adverse effects of IFFs to development on the African continent, initiatives have increasingly been taken to protect the continent from the scourge of IFFs and foster enjoyment the RTD guaranteed in the African Charter. At the same time, interestingly, the international community has adopted a draft International Covenant on the Right to Development (draft Covenant). This instrument not only urges states parties to curb IFFs,[3] but also to address corruption.[4] This development begs the question to understand the extent to which the draft Covenant (when into force) can be impactful in the fight against IFFs in Africa.

On this backdrop, the chapter examines the measures taken by African institutions to safeguard the continent against IFFs and interrogates the

1 African Charter on Human and Peoples' Rights adopted in Nairobi, Kenya on 27 June 1981 OAU Doc CAB/LEG/67/3 Rev.5 (1981), Art 21.

2 Global Financial Integrity (2024) Illicit Financial Flows. Available at: https://gfintegrity.org/issue/illicit-financial-flows/ (consulted 11 October 2024).

3 Draft International Covenant on the Right to Development—Report by the Chair-Rapporteur of the Working Group on the Right to Development, Zamir Akram (Pakistan) Human Rights Council A/HRC/54/50 54th Session, 6 October 2023, Art 13(4)(j).

4 Ibid at Art 19.

 | DOI:10.1163/9789004734357_014

implications of the draft Covenant for Africa when it eventually becomes an enforceable instrument of international law. The chapter is divided into six parts, including this introduction. The second part explores the taxonomy of IFFs, the third part demonstrates their impact on the enjoyment of the RTD, the fourth part examines African responses, the fifth part explores the potential significance of the draft Covenant on the fight against IFFs in Africa and the sixth part provides concluding remarks.

2 Categorisation of Illicit Financial Flows

While there is no clear-cut accepted definition of IFFs, they often refer to monies illegally or immorally acquired, transferred or used. The African High Level Panel Report describes IFFs as:

> [m]oney that is illegally earned, transferred or utilised. These funds typically originate from three sources: Commercial tax evasion, trade mis-invoicing and abusive transfer pricing; criminal activities, including the drug trade, human trafficking, illegal arms dealing, and smuggling of contraband; and bribery and theft by corrupt government officials.[5]

In this vein, the categorisation of IFFs includes tax evasion, tax avoidance, bribery, money laundering, contraband goods, and corruption. These IFFs, which are the result of commercial activities, are often orchestrated by the desire to hide wealth, avoid tax, and dodge customs duties as well as domestic tariffs.[6]

2.1 *Tax Evasion*

Tax evasion, which is an obvious violation of a nation's tax laws, is generally orchestrated through trade mis-invoicing, which result in falsifying trade documents. This can be done through under-invoicing exports or over-invoicing imports, which allows tax evaders to avoid paying a fair share of taxes applicable to their goods, and shifting the proceeds of their crime to secret bank

5 African Union/Economic Commission for Africa (2015) Illicit Financial Flows: Report of the High Level Panel on Illicit Financial Flows from Africa 9; see also, Muchhala, Bhumika (2018, 18 April) The Right to Development and Illicit Financial Flows: Realizing the Sustainable Development Goals and Financing for Development. Human Rights Council Working Group on the Right to Development, Nineteenth Session, Geneva, 23–27 April 2018, Para 8.

6 African Union/Economic Commission for Africa Report 2015, supra note 3, 24.

accounts or shelf companies in tax havens or secrecy jurisdictions.[7] In addition, distortion of the quality or price of imports or exports can also be engineered through "re-invoicing", which often happens when "the goods are exported under one invoice, and the latter is then transferred to another jurisdiction, or possible tax haven, where the price is altered, and finally, the revised invoice is sent to the importing country for clearing and payment".[8]

2.2 *Tax Avoidance*

Tax avoidance can be defined as "profit-shifting, where transnational corporations take advantage of tax rate differentials across jurisdictions and shift taxable income and assets away from source countries".[9] While not truly illegal, but morally wrong, it is "tax planning" by transnational companies that seek to reduce their tax responsibilities.[10] It involves shifting taxable incomes and assets from the source countries where the business activities take place to a different jurisdiction(s), with favourable tax rates often perceived as tax havens, where there is an associated company or companies with no tangible staff members or business activities.[11] The so-called tax planning consists of "taking advantage of the technicalities of a tax system or of mismatches between two or more tax systems for the purpose of reducing tax liability".[12] This activity is harmful to societies where transnational companies avoid paying a "fair share" of the tax burden through profit shifting.[13] It is a well know

7 Human Rights Council (2016) Final Study on Illicit Financial Flows, Human Rights and the 2030 Agenda for Sustainable Development of the Independent Expert on the Effects of Foreign Debt and other related International Financial Obligations of States on the Full Enjoyment of all Human Rights, Particularly Economic, Social, and Cultural Rights; General Assembly A/HRC/31/61, Para 14; see also African Development Bank and Global Financial Integrity Report (2013) Illicit Financial Flows and the Problem of Net Resource Transfers from Africa: 1980–2009. Available at: https://www.afdb.org/fileadmin/uploads/afdb/Documents/Publications/Illicit%20Financial%20Flows%20and%20the%20Problem%20of%20Net%20Resource%20Transfers%20from%20Africa%201980-2009.pdf (consulted 7 December 2024), 22.

8 African Development Bank/Global Financial Integrity Report 2013, supra note 7, 14.

9 Human Rights Council, supra note 7, Para 17.

10 Shubert, Esther (2015, 9 October) Illicit Financial Flows, Tax and Human Rights. *Background Paper*. Available at: https://www.ohchr.org/Documents/Issues/IEDebt/IllicitFinancialFlowsConsultation/BackgroundPaperFinal.pdf (consulted 4 October 2024), 10.

11 Action Aid (2013) How Tax Havens Plunder the Poor. Available at https://actionaid.org/publications/2013/how-tax-havens-plunder-poor (consulted 4 October 2024).

12 European Commission (2017) Aggressive Tax Planning Indicators: Final Report. *Taxation Papers No 71-2017*. Available at: https://ec.europa.eu/taxation_customs/sites/default/files/taxation_papers_71_atp_.pdf (consulted 4 October 2024), 23.

13 Shubert, supra note 10.

reality that almost one-third of international investments cross through tax havens before attaining their envisioned destinations as productive assets.[14] In other words, local communities are deprived from the benefits of international investments which are all taken away through tax avoidance.

2.3 *Criminal Activities*

Criminal activities are often used as vehicles to conceal irregular transactions and stolen funds from public authorities, the justice system, and fiscal agencies. They are often in the form of human and drug trafficking, firearm smuggling, and counterfeit dealings in the financial sector, including unlawful loans, money laundering, stock market manipulations, and absolute fraud.[15]

Corruption, which is associated with money laundering, is another criminal activity. In this context, the public and private sectors are infested by corrupt officials who manipulate the government systems for their own gain. Both sectors "capture" the state for their own benefit.[16] Corruption often takes place when a "tax administration official gets a kickback to either make a "favourable" interpretation of tax regulations that lower a person's/company's tax burden, or to turn a blind eye to straightforward tax evasion".[17] Corruption and money laundering are two sides of the same coin, which is the path used by masters of IFFs. Chaikin and Sharman, write:

> Corruption and money laundering are symbiotic: not only do they tend to co-occur, but more importantly the presence of one tends to create and reciprocally reinforce the incidence of the other. Corruption produces enormous profits to be laundered, estimated at more than $1 trillion of illicit funds annually, funds that are increasingly laundered in the international system. At the same time, bribery, trading in influence, and embezzlement can compromise the working of anti-money laundering systems.[18]

Also linked to corruption is the concept of secrecy jurisdictions. Distinct from tax havens, which enable tax planners to exploit the difference in tax rates

14 Ibid.

15 African Union/Economic Commission for Africa Report 2015, supra note 5, 24.

16 Matshiqi, Aubrey (2012, 16 April) Rise of Deep State Has Me Ducking for the Duvet. *Business Day*.

17 Reed, Quentin and Fontana, Alessandra (2011) Corruption and Illicit Financial Flows: The Limits and Possibilities of Current Approaches. *U4 Issue*. Available at: https://www.cmi.no/publications/3935-corruption-and-illicit-financial-flows (consulted 08 October 2024), 19.

18 Chaikin, David and Sharman, Campbell Jason (2009) *Corruption and Money Laundering: A Symbiotic Relationship*. New York: Palgrave Macmillan, 1.

amongst jurisdictions discussed earlier, secrecy jurisdictions received all financial resources, irrespective of their provenance or source. Some noteworthy examples of secrecy jurisdictions were described in the Panama Papers which exposed how illegally acquired wealth by powerful individuals were safeguarded without any queries.[19] These Papers clearly illustrated the functioning secrecy jurisdictions that accept illegally and/or immorally acquired monies without questioning their origins. Secrecy jurisdictions are truly the sanctuary of IFFs operatives in the execution of their criminal activities.

In sum, the strategies used by IFFs operatives include tax evasion, tax avoidance, bribery, money laundering, contraband goods, and numerous criminal activities such as corruption and its related attributes. Over the years, these criminal activities have been influential in ensuring that IFFs frustrate realisation of the RTD in Africa.

3 Impact of Illicit Financial Flows on the Right to Development in Africa

Enjoyment of the RTD cannot happen without a legal foundation. In this respect, under international human rights law, the state is compelled to adopt laws and policies as well as programmes to advance the implementation of human rights. To this end, states have the fundamental duty to deploy "the maximum available resources" to ensure that their populations enjoy to the fullest, the human rights guaranteed to them. Consequently, the availability of resources is critical for the enjoyment of the RTD. However, the Global South in general and African countries in particular, loses enormous resources to IFFs. The data is alarming. In evaluating the IFF crisis in the developing world, Global Financial Integrity (GFI) finds that 80% of all IFFs in developing countries is engineered by corporations, or roughly USD 4.7 trillion between 2002 and 2011 and USD 760 billion in the year 2011.[20] As accurately noted by the GFI, "this is five or six times the total of development assistance flowing into these countries during the same period".[21]

---

19 For more on this, see International Consortium of Investigative Journalists (2024) The Panama Papers: Exposing the Rogue Offshore Finance Industry. Available at: https://www.icij.org/investigations/panama-papers/ (consulted 4 October 2024).

20 Kar, Dev and LeBlanch, Brian (2013, December) Illicit Financial Flows from Developing Countries: 2002–2011. *Global Financial Integrity Report*. Available at: https://gfintegrity.org/report/2013-global-report-illicit-financial-flows-from-developing-countries-2002-2011/ (consulted 25 November 2024).

21 Ibid.

Similarly, a GFI 2017 report shows that countries in the developing world lost between USD 1.4 and USD 2.5 trillion in net resource transfers out of the continent between 2005 and 2014, with USD 970 billion of IFFs in 2014 alone.[22] The same report also unveils that IFFs amount to between 14.1% and 24% of total developing country trade, on average, with outflows estimated at between 4.6% and 7.2% of total trade and inflows between 9.5% and 16.8%.[23] As far as data on Africa is concerned, the numbers are equally shocking In 2015, a report by the High-Level Panel on Illicit Financial Flows from Africa revealed that the African continent loses an average of USD 50 billion annually through IFFs.[24] According to GFI calculations, this figure has been increasing at a frightening rate of 20.2% per year between 2002 and 2011.[25]

Prior to the High-Level Panel findings, a 2013 GFI report, co-authored with the African Development Bank, estimated that between 1980 and 2009, countries in Africa lost between USD 597 billion and USD 1.4 trillion in net resource transfers out of the continent.[26] An analysis of the revenues lost by some African countries to IFFs between 2002 and 2011 reveals the following: Tanzania's gross financial illicit flows were USD 1.87 billion yearly, amounting to more than USD 8 billion in domestic capital drained out of the economy illegally between 2002 and 2011; Kenya's gross financial illicit flows were USD 1.51 billion yearly, which meant about USD 13.58 billion left the country between 2002 and 2010; Mozambique's gross financial illicit flows were USD 585 million which amounts to USD 5.27 billion over the nine-year period between 2002 and 2010; Ghana's gross financial illicit flows were USD 1.44 billion and Uganda's USD 884 million between 2002 and 2010.[27] The GFI report stated that between 2003 and 2012, South Africa suffered illicit financial outflows totalling more than an unbelievable USD 122 billion.[28]

Based on the massive negative impact of IFFs on the enjoyment of the RTD in Africa, this chapter argues that IFFs are a curse on the continent. In this perspective, because of IFFs, Africans are unable to finance the delivery of social

22 Global Financial Integrity Report (2017, April) Illicit Financial Flows to and from Developing Countries: 2005–2014. Available at: https://gfintegrity.org/wp-content/uploads/2017/05/GFI-IFF-Report-2017_final.pdf (consulted 25 November 2024).

23 Ibid.

24 African Union/Economic Commission for Africa Report 2015, supra note 5.

25 Kar and LeBlanch, supra note 20.

26 Global Financial Integrity/African Development Bank Report 2013, supra note 7.

27 Spanjer, Joseph and Kar, Dev (2014, 16 December) Illicit Financial Flows from Developing Countries: 2003–2012. *Global Financial Integrity Report.* Available at: https://gfintegrity.org/report/2014-global-report-illicit-financial-flows-from-developing-countries-2003-2012/ (consulted 25 November 2024).

28 Ibid.

services, education, healthcare, and the construction of infrastructure, which are essential to operationalise the RTD. The African Economic Outlook Report of 2012 explains as follows:

> Capital flight out of Africa is undermining the continent's efforts to reduce poverty. If the lack of financial resources was the only constraint to human development, investing flight capital from Africa with the same efficiency that has characterized real investment would have reduced headcount poverty by an additional 4 to 6 percentage points [...] Using flight capital could also help African countries make substantial progress on improving education, and health infrastructure.[29]

In a similar perspective, Owens and McDonell contend that "the amount of illicit financial outflows from Africa per year is enough to pay for healthcare that could save the lives of four million children, and to employ enough teachers for every African child to receive education".[30] IFFs obviously hinder the enjoyment of economic, social, and cultural rights which are considerable elements of the RTD. The state's obligation to give effect to economic, social, and cultural rights is dependent on the "availability of resources" and "progressive realisation".[31] Therefore, depriving the state of its funds through IFFs or other means "not only take[s] away the resources needed for the operationalisation of the rights, it also delays their realisation".[32]

Besides blocking states' ability to give effect to socio-economic rights, IFFs also prevent governments' capacity to implement civil and political rights. In this respect, they take away for example, the funds needed to train judges to advance fair trials, protect freedom of association, empower and train police officers to avoid misuse of power, finance access to courts, and foster other civil and political rights.[33] The International Council on Human Rights Policy clarifies how IFFs undermine the justice system among others:

---

29 Organisation for Economic Cooperation and Development (2012) African Economic Outlook Issue: Promoting Youth Employment. 77 (on file with author) xz.

30 Owens, J. and McDonell R. (2017) Inter-agency Cooperation and Good Tax Governance in Africa: An Overview. In: Owens, J. et al (eds) *Inter-agency Cooperation and Good Tax Governance in Africa*. Pretoria: Pretoria University Law Press.

31 Moyo, Khulekani (2017) An Analysis of the Impact of Corruption on the Realisation of the Right to Development. *South African Journal of Human Rights* 33(2): 180.

32 Ibid.

33 Kamga, Serges Djoyou (2020) The Special Criminal Court in the Fight against Illicit Flows of Wealth and the Realisation of the Right to Development in Cameroon: Prospects and Challenges. *Journal for Juridical Science* 45(1): 143.

> Embezzlement or misappropriation of assets may also affect the right to a fair trial and to an effective remedy.[34] Embezzlement deprives the justice system of resources and hence, affects the quality and effectiveness of the legal services rendered and therefore also compromises the rule of law. The same lack of resources may mean that insufficient staff are employed, which in turn may create a backlog of cases and slow procedures, infringing the right to be tried without undue delay as provided under article 14(3)(c) of the ICCPR and consequently violating the right to a fair trial and an effective remedy.[35]

IFFs violate both civil and political rights as well as socio-economic rights which are composite elements of the RTD. Discussing the effects of IFFs on economic, social, cultural, civil, and political rights, the Independent Expert on IFFs writes: "Illicit financial outflows deprive Governments first and foremost of resources required to realize progressively economic, social and cultural rights. They also undermine efforts to build up effective institutions to uphold civil and political rights and the rule of law in the countries of origin".[36]

Actualising the RTD depends on states' capacity to raise adequate funding. Moyo writes: "Linking the realisation of the RTD to resource mobilisation including asset recovery is not a mere assumption, as no state can function without resources".[37] Put differently, the states' duty to implement human rights cannot be complied within the context where IFFs are an impediment to resource mobilisation. The right to equality and non-discrimination which is another critical element of the RTD is also hindered by IFFs. In this respect, the theft of money deprives the poor from the opportunity to access the public good and enjoy a decent standard of living as a result of the funds being misappropriated by corrupt individuals.[38] The poor are therefore, relegated to the bottom of the pyramid of standard of living, where they suffer marginalisation

---

34 International Covenant on Civil and Political Rights adopted by the UN General Assembly, Resolution 2200 A (XXI) of 16 December 1966, 993 UNTS 3 UN Doc A/6316 (1966) Arts 14 and 2(3).

35 International Council on Human Rights Policy (2009) Corruption and Human Rights: Making the Connection. Available at: https://assets.publishing.service.gov.uk/media/57a08b6540f0b64974000b10/humanrights-corruption.pdf (consulted 4 October 2024).

36 Human Rights Council, 28th Session, Illicit Financial Flows, Human Rights and the Post-2015 Development Agenda: Interim Study by the Independent Expert on the Effects of Foreign Debt and other Related International Financial Obligations of States on the Full Enjoyment of all Human Rights, Particularly Economic, Social and Cultural Rights, Juan Pablo Bohoslavsky UN Doc. A/HRC/28/60, Para 22.

37 Moyo, supra note 31, 212.

38 Ibid.

caused by corruption plotted by IFFs' operatives. In this context, the siphoning of tax revenues compels the poor and the most vulnerable to endure a higher tax burden. The former Special Rapporteur on Extreme Poverty and Human Rights, Magdalena Sepúlveda Carmona writes: "Tax abuse by corporations and high net-worth individuals forces Governments to raise revenue from other sources: often regressive taxes, the burden of which falls hardest on the poor".[39] Put differently, when a regressive tax applies, it does so across the board without consideration of incomes, with the rich and the poor paying the same amount. This further impoverishes the poor who end up paying for social programmes that were intended to take them out of poverty and advance their RTD.[40] The Independent Expert on IFFs observes that "Tax abuse has additional implications for the rights of equality and non-discrimination, and it perpetuates and exacerbates income inequality, which has further human rights impacts".[41]

It could be argued that corrupt government officials who embezzle state funds and channel them to safe tax havens are the problem, and not IFFs (by corporations). However, while corruption by government officials' is very problematic and should be condemned without reservation, it is noteworthy that such acts amount to only 5% of looted[42] African resources, while most of the IFFs are orchestrated by multinational companies through commercial activities.

In a nutshell, from a legal and moral standpoint, IFFs hamper states' ability to comply with their human rights obligations under international law. The Independent Expert on the Effects of Foreign Debt and Other Related International Financial Obligations of States on the Full Enjoyment of All Human Rights, Particularly Economic, Social and Cultural Rights, sums it up as follows: "Illicit financial flows divert resources away from activities that are critical for poverty eradication and sustainable economic and social development, as well as for realizing economic, social, cultural, civil and political

39 Human Rights Council, 28th Session, supra note 36, Para 60.

40 Pogge, Thomas (2015) How are Human Rights and Financial Transparency Connected? Keynote Address Delivered on 18 May 2015 at the Conference on "Financial Transparency and Human Rights in Africa: Fostering Greater National and Regional Economic Opportunity in Africa through Human Rights and Financial Transparency" co-hosted by Global Financial Integrity, the Friedrich-Ebert-Stiftung, and the International Bar Association's Human Rights Institute at the University of Johannesburg, South Africa. Available at: https://gfintegrity.org/press-release/thomas-pogge-how-are-human-rights-and-financial-transparency-connected/ (consulted 4 July 2021).

41 Human Rights Council, 28th Session, supra note 36, Para 22.

42 African Union/Economic Commission for Africa Report 2015, supra note 5, 24.

rights and the right to development".[43] Consequently, it is vital to address IFFs decisively, to enhance prospects for the enjoyment of the RTD. Failure to do so, keeps Africans entrapped in abject poverty and development as human right will not be achieved. Several initiatives have indeed, been adopted at the global and African regional levels to tackle IFFs. However, although the discussion here cannot be exhaustive, the following section explores what has been done at the African regional level to defeat IFFs.

4 Initiatives to Address IFFs at the African Regional Level

Initiatives that have been undertaken by Africa in addressing IFFs include normative standards adopted by the African Commission on Human and Peoples' Rights (the African Commission), establishment of the High-Level Panel on Illicit Financial Flows (HLP)[44] referred to earlier, the African Tax Administration Forum (ATAF),[45] and the African Union Convention on Preventing and Combating Corruption.[46]

4.1 *The African Commission on Human and Peoples' Rights Initiatives*

Article 45 of the African Charter empowers the African Commission to promote, protect, and interpret provisions of the African Charter. Relying on this provision, in 2013, the African Commission passed Resolution 236[47] in which it clarifies the nexus between "capital flight, tax evasion, and human rights" and recommended that member states should examine their legal and policy

43 Human Rights Council, Final study on illicit financial flows, human rights and the 2030 Agenda for Sustainable Development of the Independent Expert on the effects of foreign debt and other related international financial obligations of States on the full enjoyment of all human rights, particularly economic, social and cultural rights A/HRC/31/61, Para 2.

44 The High-Level Panel on Illicit Financial Flows from Africa was established in February 2012 following Resolution 896 (XLIV) of the Fifth Joint Annual Meeting of the Economic Commission for Africa Conference of African Ministers of Finance, Planning and Economic Development and the African Union Conference of Ministers of Economy and Finance.

45 African Tax Administration Forum Agreement, 20 November 2009 in Kampala, Uganda. Available at: https://irp-cdn.multiscreensite.com/a521d626/files/uploaded/ataf_agreement_9%20FEB.pdf (consulted 22 June 2024), Art 3.

46 African Union, African Union Convention on Preventing and Combating Corruption, adopted at the 2nd Ordinary Session of the African Union Assembly of Heads of State and Government in Maputo, Mozambique on 11 July 2003.

47 African Commission on Human and Peoples' Rights Resolution 236 on Illicit Capital Flight from Africa (2013). Available at: http://www.achpr.org/sessions/53rd/resolutions/236/ (consulted 20 June 2024).

frameworks to address IFFs. Furthermore, in reaction to the publication of the Paradise Papers in 2017, in which some African countries (Mauritius and Seychelles) were described as tax havens, the African Commission urged all state parties to the African Charter to review their national policies and legislation, and amend them in order to address IFFs and their harmful impact on other state parties.[48] Additionally, during its 60th Ordinary Session,[49] the African Commission adopted Resolution 367,[50] which amongst others, call on state to establish regional mechanisms for "fighting illicit financial flights common in the extractive industries".[51]

Moreover, in 2018, the African Commission adopted State Reporting Guidelines and Principles on Articles 21 and 24 of the African Charter Relating to Extractive Industries, Human Rights, and the Environment on Article 21[52] and 24[53] (State Reporting Guidelines). The Guidelines request states to include in their periodic reports, "steps taken to address illicit financial flows through amendments to national tax laws and policies, rules on related party transactions, company laws and policies, banking laws and policies and laws and policies governing the financial services sector"[54] under Article 21. In addition, states are requested to "develop and implement robust and efficient tax collection systems in order to address the challenge of illicit financial flows".[55] In summary, the African Commission has shown a commendable commitment to eradicate IFFs from Africa, even though the transgression is still rampant.

4.2 *The African Union High-Level Panel*

The 4th Joint African Union Commission and United Nations Economic Commission for Africa (AUC/ECA) Conference of African Ministers of Finance,

---

48 Statement of the African Commission on Human and Peoples' Rights on Illicit Financial Flight and Other Concerns Arising out of the Paradise Papers (2017). Available at: http://www.achpr.org/press/2017/12/d380/ (consulted 20 June 2024).

49 Held from 8 to 22 May 2017 in Niamey, Republic of Niger.

50 African Commission on Human and Peoples' Rights Resolution 367 on the Niamey Declaration on Ensuring the Upholding of the African Charter in the Extractive Industries Sector ACHPR/Res. 367 (LX), 2017.

51 Ibid at Para 5(d).

52 African Charter, "Right to freely dispose of wealth and natural resources".

53 African Charter, "Right to a General Satisfactory Environment".

54 African Commission on Human and Peoples' Rights (2017) State Reporting Guidelines and Principles on Articles 21 And 24 of the African Charter Relating to Extractive Industries, Human Rights and the Environment, Para 15. Available at: https://www.achpr.org/public/Document/file/English/Articles%2021%20&%2024%20State%20Reporting%20Guidelines.pdf (consulted 17 July 2024).

55 Ibid at Paras 33 and 46.

Planning and Economic Development was held in 2011. Under this initiative, the Economic Commission for Africa was mandated to establish the High-Level Panel on Illicit Financial Flows from Africa. This commitment was imperative to guide the continent on the path of self-reliance for its development.[56] It is against this backdrop that the High-Level Panel chaired by the former South African President, Thabo Mbeki, was established and mandated to determine the nature and patterns of IFFs from the continent, examine their extended impacts on Africa's development, bring them to the attention of the public and the international community and "suggest policies and mobilise support for practices that would reverse such illicit financial outflows".[57]

Among others, as indicated earlier, the High-Level Panel found that Africa loses more than USD 50 billion dollars annually to IFFs and has become as such a creditor to the world.[58] While pointing out the global efforts to curb IFFs,[59] it also underlined the challenges in dealing with the problem at the national and regional levels, which include insufficiency of "adequate regulatory frameworks, information and telecommunication facilities, transportation and other relevant infrastructure, adequate funding and reliance on unpredictable foreign assistance, technical and human capacity to deal with crime, and the participation in corruption of top government officials operating at different levels of governance".[60]

Among its recommendations, the High-Level Panel called on African states to demonstrate the political will to deal with the problem, to be transparent in addressing IFFs, to monitor commercial routes and pay attention to trade mispricing, transfer pricing, base erosion, and profit shifting and build effective institutions to deal with these challenges.[61] African countries should pay attention to criminal components of IFFs, which include poaching, drugs, arms and human trafficking, oil and mineral theft, and money laundering among others. This involves, among other initiatives, the sharing of information on the continent and the strengthening of national and regional capacities to tackle IFFs; to ensure that tax incentives are informed by cost-benefit analyses; to supplement the global architecture for tackling IFFs; and to scrutinise financial secrecy jurisdictions and urge development partners to play

56 Mbeki, Thabo (2015) Foreword in Illicit Financial Flows—Report of the High-Level Panel on Illicit Financial Flows from Africa, commissioned by the AU/ECA Conference of Ministers of Finance, Planning and Economic Development, 3.

57 African Union/Economic Commission for Africa Report 2015, supra note 5, 15.

58 Ibid.

59 To be discussed later in this section.

60 African Union/Economic Commission for Africa Report 2015, supra note 5, 43.

61 Ibid at 82.

their critical role in curbing IFFs across Africa.[62] In addition, the High-Level Panel called on African states to be at the forefront of raising money and other supplies to combat IFFs on the continent.[63] In this perspective, IFFs should be mainstreamed in the African Peer Review Mechanism, which is a process to enhance good governance in Africa.[64] The other initiative prescribed by the High-Level Panel is the need to conduct research on reducing complexity on taxation in Africa and globally with the aim to ease tax compliance by transnational companies operating on the continent.[65]

On the cooperation front, in its recommendations to the international community, the High-Level Panel highlighted the need to take all measures possible to close down secrecy jurisdictions, introduce transparency in financial transfers, deal with money laundering, and foster greater transparency in the international banking system. It explicitly calls on the African Union, the G20 (Group of 20), the International Monetary Fund (IMF), and the Organisation for Economic Co-operation and Development (OECD) to provide the much-needed leadership in these initiatives and to this end, underlined the need for strong cooperation between industrialised countries.[66]

The High-Level Panel has also been unequivocal in calling for the collection and dissemination of detailed data and the publication of country-specific transnational companies' financial reports. Added to this, they stressed the importance of collaboration between the African Union and partner institutions to adopt a global governance framework to define the conditions under which stolen assets should be frozen, managed, and repatriated. They also recommend that global institutions such as the IMF, the United Nations, and the World Bank should lead the fight against IFFs and ensure its global reach.

To its credit, the High-Level Panel clearly calls on the international community to reflect on the significance of IFFs for the achievement of the Sustainable Development Goals (SDGs) in the post-2015 agenda,[67] and this was done with the inclusion of IFFs in Target 4 of Goal 16, which seeks to secure, peace, justice, and strong institutions on the list of the SDGs. The need to address IFFs for the achievement of the SDGs is reiterated in Target 1 of Goal 17, according to which states commit themselves to reinforcing national resource mobilisation whilst relying on international cooperation, and capacity building for tax and other revenue collection.

---

62 Ibid at 63.
63 Ibid at 79.
64 Ibid.
65 Ibid.
66 Ibid.
67 Ibid.

4.3 *The African Tax Administration Forum*

The African continent also established the ATAF, which was launched in Kampala on 8 November 2009. It seeks to promote cooperation among African revenue services. Ultimately, as per its vision, the ATAF seeks to "promote efficient and effective tax administration to improve the living standards of the people in Africa".[68] The ATAF was instrumental for the emergence of harmonised trade regulations adapted to the continental context.[69] Among others, the ATAF has, over the years, provided technical assistance through 20 country programmes in Africa (12 on cross border taxation, and 8 on exchange of information).[70]

The ATAF has also enhanced the capacity of African tax administrations across the continent, cooperated with international partners and played an active role in the global tax agenda. It has also initiated its African Tax Outlook in 2015, which is now an important reference point on the continental tax data, providing valuable practical and relevant descriptive and analytical work on tax issues. In the fields of education and capacity-building, the ATAF launched an Executive Masters Programme in Taxation in 2014 to strengthen the skills of tax officials, tax policy makers, and tax practitioners from across Africa. Notwithstanding the fact that African countries still face challenges in tax cooperation, the ATAF provides some hope as it seeks to offer some constructive responses to the problem with special attention to the regional context.

4.4 *African Union Convention on Preventing and Combating Corruption*

The African Union adopted the African Union Convention on Preventing and Combating Corruption (AUCPCC) in July 2003.[71] With special attention to IFFs and related issues, it calls on African states to criminalise money laundering at the national level,[72] while defining illicit enrichment as the "significant increase in the assets of a public official or any other person which he or she cannot reasonably explain in relation to his or her income".[73] In the same vein, states parties are compelled to "adopt legislative measures as to enable the confiscation and seizure of the proceeds and instrumentalities of corruption,

68 African Tax Administration Forum Agreement, supra note 45, Art 3.

69 Muchhala, supra note 5, Para 90.

70 The African Tax Administration Forum. Available at: https://www.ataftax.org/overview (consulted 22 June 2024).

71 African Union Convention on Preventing and Combating Corruption, adopted by the 2nd Ordinary Session of the Assembly of Heads of State and Government in Maputo, Mozambique on 11 July 2003.

72 Ibid at Art 6.

73 Ibid at Art 1(1).

and this includes the repatriation of stolen assets or proceeds of corruption".[74] Under Article 17 on bank secrecy rule, states are obliged to equip the courts with the powers to by-pass the bank secrecy rule, an impediment to the implementation of Article 16 which provides for the confiscation and seizure of the proceeds of corruption.

The other positive development in the AUCPCC is the establishment of an advisory Board on Corruption within the African Union called the African Union Advisory Board on Corruption, which was inaugurated on 26 May 2009.[75] These initiatives are supported by numerous national anti-corruption legislative measures and institutions that show their commitment to address IFFs.[76] However, notwithstanding these normative provisions, the AUCPCC is not focused on combating IFFs *per se*, only some of their components are listed. Hence, the recommendation of the High Level Panel (HLP) underlines the need to integrate IFFs as a "specific component in the African Union Convention on Preventing and Combating Corruption. This will immediately bring IFFs into the Strategy of the Advisory Board of the Convention. The association of civil society and media, as required of governments under Article 12 of the Convention, will become accepted standard practice".[77]

In this register, the HLP also calls (correctly in my view) for the extension of the functions of the Advisory Board to "develop methodologies for analysing the nature and extent of illicit financial flows from Africa and disseminate information and sensitize the public on the negative effects of illicit financial flows from Africa".[78] Implementing this recommendation will enhance the prospects of success of the Advisory Board.

Another major challenge facing the Advisory Board is that although 44 of the 55 African Union member states have ratified the AUCPCC, it is very difficult to find information on the extent to which the treaty is being implemented. Although mandated to monitor countries' progress in implementing the Convention, the Board has only received 13 progress reports as of 2020, and these are concealed to the public.[79] Such deficiency led Olaniyan to argue

74 Ibid at Art 16(c).

75 Ibid at Art 22.

76 African Union and Economic Commission for Africa (2017, 2 June) Report of the High Level Panel on Illicit Financial Flows from Africa, Addis Ababa. Available at: https://www.uneca.org/sites/default/files/PublicationFiles/iff_main_report_26feb_en.pdf (consulted 18 October 2024), 32.

77 African Union/Economic Commission for Africa Report 2015, supra note 5, 83.

78 Ibid at 84.

79 Transparency International (2020) Implementing and Enforcing the African Union Convention on Preventing and Combating Corruption. Available at: https://images.trans

that the AUCPCC "lacks a serious and effective mechanism for holding states accountable".[80] It is, therefore, imperative to ensure that member states report on their operationalisation of the AUCPCC, and this report should be made available to the public.

Despite the lack of explicit reference to IFFs by the AUCPCC, and challenges to its implementation, this instrument is a good start because it is a credible normative contribution to the fight against some core components of IFFs. However, these normative commitments are often damaged by poor governance, weak institutions, massive corruption, and conflicts which do not ease the fight against transnational crimes, including IFFs. Due to some of these challenges; the continent continues to experience a high level of IFFs as discussed in the introductory section of this chapter. Moreover, given the magnitude and complexity of the IFFs which need more than a regional or national response, the continent has yet to reap the fruits of its efforts to eradicate this development challenge. To achieve this objective and foster the RTD, there is a need to improve not only national and regional financial integrity, but also global financial transparency.

5 Implications of the Draft Covenant on the Right to Development in Africa

As alluded to earlier, the draft International Covenant on the Right to Development is currently undergoing intergovernmental negotiations for eventual adoption by the UN General Assembly.[81] The Covenant originated from the UN Human Rights Council, drafted in accordance with Resolution A/HRC/RES/39/9 dating back to 2018 when the Human Rights Council tasked the Open-ended Working Group on the Right to Development to engage in discussions for the drafting of a legally binding instrument (convention) on the right to development.[82] It was initially named as the Draft Convention on the

parencycdn.org/images/2020_Report_AU-Convention-Review_English.pdf (consulted 2 July 2024), 5.

80 Olaniyan, Kolawole (2004) The African Union Convention on Preventing and Combating Corruption: A Critical Appraisal. *African Human Rights Law Journal* 4(1): 74.

81 Draft Convention on the Right to Development (the Draft Convention), 17 January 2020, A/HRC/WG.2/21/2; Draft Convention on the Right to Development with Commentaries, 20 January 2020, A/HRC/WG.2/21/2/Add.1.

82 Human Rights Council Resolution A/HRC/RES/39/9 on the Right to Development adopted at the 39th Session on 27 September 2018.

Right to Development and eventually renamed, Draft International Covenant on the Right to Development. It contains three parts: The first part covers its objectives, general principles and definitions of terms used (Articles 1–3). The second part explains the RTD, and its nexus with other obligations under international law, and sheds light on the rights holders (Articles 4–7). The last part describes obligations under the RTD and explains who the duty-bearers of the RTD are (Articles 8–23). While the drafters recognises that no concepts, norms, rights or obligations have been created *de novo*,[83] the draft Covenant is instrumental in stressing and strengthening the interdependence of human rights and development,[84] as well as giving prominence to IFFs as a constraint to the enjoyment of this right.[85]

Very importantly, in line with the Universal Declaration of Human Rights,[86] which calls on states to collaborate to establish a "social and international order" conducive to a better life for all, the draft Covenant also emphasises the need for international collaboration in the spirit of international solidarity to set up an international dispensation that will lead to the enjoyment of the RTD.[87] This is a precise call to the international community to effectively regulate the international space to protect it against international crimes, including the practice of IFFs.

More clearly and in direct link with IFFs, the draft Covenant imposes on states parties, the obligation of "eliminating illicit financial flows by combating tax evasion and corruption, reducing opportunities for tax avoidance, enhancing disclosure and transparency in financial and property transactions in both source and destination countries and strengthening the recovery and return of stolen assets".[88] Put differently, the draft Covenant explicitly highlights the duties and responsibilities of state holders to combat IFFs and foster global governance and more so, obliges the return of stolen assets as a means to ensure that the RTD becomes a reality. In the same vein, the draft Covenant also prohibits corruption and obliges state parties to stand together against corruption, which is a "serious obstacle" to the enjoyment of the RTD.[89]

83 Draft Convention on the Right to Development, supra note 81, 2.

84 Teshome, Roman Girma (2022) The Draft Convention on the Right to Development: A New Dawn to the Recognition of the Right to Development as a Human Right? *Human Rights Law Review* 22(2): 2.

85 Draft Covenant, supra note 3, Art 13.

86 Art 28.

87 Draft Covenant, supra note 3, Preamble Para 11 and Art 13(2).

88 Ibid.

89 Draft Covenant, supra note 3, Art 19.

Similarly, states should collaborate to enhance "the regulation and monitoring of global financial markets and institutions and their implementation".[90]

The significance of this development for the fight against IFFs from Africa is massive. In this regard, the draft Covenant clearly demonstrates that while Africa is taking initiatives to address IFFs, the latter cannot be defeated without cooperation and collaboration at the global level. In other words, the African initiatives to deal with IFFs cannot yield expected outcomes if members of the international community do not adopt global policies in support of initiatives from the continent. The draft Covenant adds to the normative value of the RTD and explicitly highlights that IFFs are an impediment to this right. When adopted, the draft Covenant will become binding on state parties. In other words, the draft Covenant is perceived as "a game changer" in its recognition of IFFs as obstacles to the enjoyment of the RTD. In highlighting the importance of a legally binding instrument on the RTD, Teshome writes: "the draft is a momentous step in the recognition of the right to development as a human right not only because it is binding, if adopted, but also contains concrete, detailed and implementable norms, [including addressing IFFs]".[91]

Under the draft Covenant, states (as subjects of international law), are traditionally obliged to respect the RTD implying that among other obligations, they are enjoined to refrain from any actions or inactions that can violate the RTD. It entails for example, for state parties to refrain from becoming a save heaven for IFFs as, this would amount to violation of the RTD. While relying on the established initiatives and response mechanisms in addressing IFFs, African states will also rely on the guidance and spirit of the draft Covenant which describes the "legal implications for violations" with the involvement of monitoring by the Conference of the States Parties[92] and an implementation mechanism comprising of experts.[93] The monitoring mechanism moves away from relying on treaty monitoring bodies. To its benefit, among others it provides a platform for experts to assist in deliberations. This is important in the fight against IFFs where specific expertise is needed to deal with taxation, tax evasion or avoidance and their impact on the RTD.

In sum, the coming into force of the draft Covenant will enable African states to legitimately oblige the international community to take its responsibility seriously in preventing IFFs, which has been a nemesis to the enjoyment of the RTD in Africa. When adopted, the International Covenant will not only

90 Ibid at Art 13(4)(c).

91 Teshome, supra note 84, 1.

92 Draft Covenant, supra note 3, Art 24.

93 Ibid at Art 26.

help in and facilitate the combatting of IFFs, but also boost implementation and enforcement of the RTD, which has since 1981, been guaranteed recognition and protection in the African Charter on Human and Peoples' Rights as a legally binding and justiciable entitlement.

6 Conclusion

This chapter has explored the extent to which African responses in addressing the increasingly problematic phenomenon of IFFs, which has become a nemesis for the enjoyment of the RTD across the continent. It also explores whether the draft International Covenant on the Right to Development can be impactful in enhancing African initiatives in the fight against IFFs. In setting the scene, the chapter looks at various ways by which IFFs manifest in the form of tax evasion, tax avoidance, criminal activities and corruption that has to a large extent, frustrated the RTD in Africa over the decades. To this end, the chapter demonstrates that IFF practices hinder states' ability to effectively engage in development and as such frustrate enjoyment of the RTD on the continent.

At the centre of the discussion in this chapter, is the question whether, given the magnitude of IFFs and their negative impact on the RTD, existing African responses are adequate in redressing the problem. The chapter finds that firstly, the African Commission on Human and Peoples' Rights has been hard at work in seeking to eradicate IFFs from the continent. Secondly, the chapter finds that besides the African Commission having adopted guidelines for state reporting on IFFs and voted a resolution to that effect, the African Union HLP has been unequivocal in calling on the international community to engage in the fight against IFFs. The HLP has also urged African governments to be proactive and demonstrate strong political will in tackling IFFs. In the same vein, it is noted that the African Tax Administration Forum has been committed in sanitising the tax landscape, calling on tax officials across the continent to work together and share information on the best ways in effectively and efficiently responding to IFFs.

In other words, the African Union has taken many initiatives to address IFFs. However, given the transnational character of the problem, without joint efforts with other countries around the world that are complicit in the practice, it is impossible to eliminate this curse that hinders the enjoyment of the RTD in Africa. The obligation of Western countries is well captured in the draft Covenant that compels all members of the international community to work together through international cooperation mechanisms to address IFFs globally. The chapter finds that all states parties have an absolute obligation to refrain from enabling IFFs, which amounts to a violation of the RTD. The chapter ultimately notes that when the draft Covenant is eventually adopted and comes into force, it will be instrumental in strengthening the existing African initiatives, which are envisaged to then become binding and applicable at the global level in accordance with the provisions of the Covenant and thus, enhance prospects for the enjoyment of the RTD in Africa.

References

Action Aid (2013) How Tax Havens Plunder the Poor. Available at https://actionaid.org/publications/2013/how-tax-havens-plunder-poor (consulted 4 October 2024).

African Charter on Human and Peoples' Rights adopted in Nairobi, Kenya on 27 June 1981 OAU Doc CAB/LEG/67/3 Rev.5 (1981).

African Commission on Human and Peoples' Rights (2017) State Reporting Guidelines and Principles on Articles 21 And 24 of the African Charter Relating to Extractive Industries, Human Rights and the Environment. Available at: https://www.achpr.org/public/Document/file/English/Articles%2021%20&%2024%20State%20Reporting%20Guidelines.pdf (consulted 17 July 2024).

African Commission on Human and Peoples' Rights Resolution 236 on Illicit Capital Flight from Africa (2013). Available at: http://www.achpr.org/sessions/53rd/resolutions/236/ (consulted 20 June 2024).

African Commission on Human and Peoples' Rights Resolution 367 on the Niamey Declaration on Ensuring the Upholding of the African Charter in the Extractive Industries Sector ACHPR/Res. 367(LX), 2017.

African Development Bank and Global Financial Integrity Report (2013) Illicit Financial Flows and the Problem of Net Resource Transfers from Africa: 1980–2009. Available at: https://www.afdb.org/fileadmin/uploads/afdb/Documents/Publications/Illicit%20Financial%20Flows%20and%20the%20Problem%20of%20Net%20Resource%20Transfers%20from%20Africa%201980-2009.pdf (consulted 7 December 2024).

African Tax Administration Forum Agreement, 20 November 2009 in Kampala, Uganda. Available at: https://irp-cdn.multiscreensite.com/a521d626/files/uploaded/ataf_agreement_9%20FEB.pdf (consulted 22 June 2024).

African Tax Administration Forum Agreement, 20 November 2009 in Kampala, Uganda. Available at: https://irp-cdn.multiscreensite.com/a521d626/files/uploaded/ataf_agreement_9%20FEB.pdf (consulted 22 June 2024).

African Tax Administration Forum. Available at: https://www.ataftax.org/overview (consulted 22 June 2024).

African Union and Economic Commission for Africa (2017, 2 June) Report of the High Level Panel on Illicit Financial Flows from Africa, Addis Ababa. Available at: https://www.uneca.org/sites/default/files/PublicationFiles/iff_main_report_26feb_en.pdf (consulted 18 October 2024).

African Union Convention on Preventing and Combating Corruption, adopted by the 2nd Ordinary Session of the Assembly of Heads of State and Government in Maputo, Mozambique on 11 July 2003.

African Union, African Union Convention on Preventing and Combating Corruption, adopted at the 2nd Ordinary Session of the African Union Assembly of Heads of State and Government in Maputo, Mozambique on 11 July 2003.

African Union/Economic Commission for Africa (2015) Illicit Financial Flows: Report of the High Level Panel on Illicit Financial Flows from Africa.

Chaikin, David and Sharman, Jason Campbell. (2009) *Corruption and Money Laundering: A Symbiotic Relationship*. New York: Palgrave Macmillan.

Draft Convention on the Right to Development (the Draft Convention), 17 January 2020, A/HRC/WG.2/21/2; Draft Convention on the Right to Development with Commentaries, 20 January 2020, A/HRC/WG.2/21/2/Add.1.

Draft International Covenant on the Right to Development—Report by the Chair-Rapporteur of the Working Group on the Right to Development, Zamir Akram (Pakistan) Human Rights Council A/HRC/54/50 54th Session, 6 October 2023.

European Commission (2017) Aggressive Tax Planning Indicators: Final Report. *Taxation Papers No 71-2017*. Available at: https://ec.europa.eu/taxation_customs/sites/default/files/taxation_papers_71_atp_.pdf (consulted 4 October 2024).

Global Financial Integrity (2024) Illicit Financial Flows. Available at: https://gfintegrity.org/issue/illicit-financial-flows/ (consulted 11 October 2024).

Global Financial Integrity Report (2017, April) Illicit Financial Flows to and from Developing Countries: 2005–2014. Available at: https://gfintegrity.org/wp-content/uploads/2017/05/GFI-IFF-Report-2017_final.pdf (consulted 25 November 2024).

Human Rights Council Resolution A/HRC/RES/39/9 on the Right to Development adopted at the 39th Session on 27 September 2018.

Human Rights Council (2016) Final Study on Illicit Financial Flows, Human Rights and the 2030 Agenda for Sustainable Development of the Independent Expert on the Effects of Foreign Debt and other related International Financial Obligations of States on the Full Enjoyment of all Human Rights, Particularly Economic, Social, and Cultural Rights; General Assembly A/HRC/31/61.

Human Rights Council, 28th Session, Illicit Financial Flows, Human Rights and the Post-2015 Development Agenda: Interim Study by the Independent Expert on the Effects of Foreign Debt and other Related International Financial Obligations of States on the Full Enjoyment of all Human Rights, Particularly Economic, Social and Cultural Rights, Juan Pablo Bohoslavsky UN doc. A/HRC/28/60.

International Consortium of Investigative Journalists (2024) The Panama Papers: Exposing the Rogue Offshore Finance Industry. Available at: https://www.icij.org/investigations/panama-papers/ (consulted 4 October 2024).

International Council on Human Rights Policy (2009) Corruption and Human Rights: Making the Connection. Available at: https://assets.publishing.service.gov.uk/media/57a08b6540f0b64974000b10/humanrights-corruption.pdf (consulted 4 October 2024).

International Covenant on Civil and Political Rights adopted by the UN General Assembly, Resolution 2200A (XXI) of 16 December 1966, 993 UNTS 3 UN Doc A/6316 (1966).

Kamga, Serges Djoyou (2020) The Special Criminal Court in the Fight against Illicit Flows of Wealth and the Realisation of the Right to Development in Cameroon: Prospects and Challenges. *Journal for Juridical Science* 45(1): 141–160.

Kar, Dev and LeBlanch, Brian (2013, December) Illicit Financial Flows from Developing Countries: 2002–2011. *Global Financial Integrity Report.* Available at: https://gfintegrity.org/report/2013-global-report-illicit-financial-flows-from-developing-countries-2002-2011/ (consulted 25 November 2024).

Matshiqi, Aubrey (2012, 16 April) Rise of Deep State Has Me Ducking for the Duvet. *Business Day.*

Mbeki, Thabo (2015) Foreword in Illicit Financial Flows—Report of the High-Level Panel on Illicit Financial Flows from Africa, commissioned by the AU/ECA Conference of Ministers of Finance, Planning and Economic Development.

Moyo, Khulekani (2017) An Analysis of the Impact of Corruption on the Realisation of the Right to Development. *South African Journal of Human Rights* 33(2): 193–213.

Muchhala, Bhumika (2018, 18 April) The Right to Development and Illicit Financial Flows: Realizing the Sustainable Development Goals and Financing for Development. Human Rights Council Working Group on the Right to Development, Nineteenth Session, Geneva, 23–27 April 2018.

Olaniyan, Kolawole (2004) The African Union Convention on Preventing and Combating Corruption: A Critical Appraisal. *African Human Rights Law Journal* 4(1): 74–92.

Organisation for Economic Cooperation and Development (2012) Development Centre—African Economic Outlook Issue (2012) Promoting Youth Employment.

Owens, J. and McDonell R. (2017) Inter-agency Cooperation and Good Tax Governance in Africa: An Overview. In: Owens, J. et al (eds) *Inter-agency Cooperation and Good Tax Governance in Africa.* Pretoria: Pretoria University Law Press.

Pogge, Thomas (2015) How are Human Rights and Financial Transparency Connected? Keynote Address Delivered on 18 May 2015 at the Conference on "Financial Transparency and Human Rights in Africa: Fostering Greater National and Regional Economic Opportunity in Africa through Human Rights and Financial Transparency". University of Johannesburg, South Africa. Available at: https://gf

integrity.org/press-release/thomas-pogge-how-are-human-rights-and-financial-transparency-connected/ (consulted 4 July 2021).

Reed, Quentin and Fontana, Alessandra (2011) Corruption and Illicit Financial Flows: The Limits and Possibilities of Current Approaches. *U4 Issue*. Available at: https://www.cmi.no/publications/3935-corruption-and-illicit-financial-flows (consulted 8 October 2024).

Shubert, Esther (2015, 9 October) 'Illicit Financial Flows, Tax and Human Rights. *Background Paper*. Available at: https://www.ohchr.org/Documents/Issues/IEDebt/IllicitFinancialFlowsConsultation/BackgroundPaperFinal.pdf (consulted 4 October 2024).

Spanjer, Joseph and Kar, Dev (2014, 16 December) Illicit Financial Flows from Developing Countries: 2003–2012. *Global Financial Integrity Report*. Available at: https://gfintegrity.org/report/2014-global-report-illicit-financial-flows-from-developing-countries-2003-2012/ (consulted 25 November 2024).

Statement of the African Commission on Human and Peoples' Rights on Illicit Financial Flight and Other Concerns Arising out of the Paradise Papers (2017) Available at: http://www.achpr.org/press/2017/12/d380/ (consulted 20 June 2024).

Teshome, Roman Girma (2022) The Draft Convention on the Right to Development: A New Dawn to the Recognition of the Right to Development as a Human Right? *Human Rights Law Review* 22(2): 1–24.

The High-Level Panel on Illicit Financial Flows from Africa was established in February 2012 following Resolution 896 (XLIV) of the Fifth Joint Annual Meeting of the Economic Commission for Africa Conference of African Ministers of Finance, Planning and Economic Development and the African Union Conference of Ministers of Economy and Finance.

Transparency International (2020) Implementing and Enforcing the African Union Convention on Preventing and Combating Corruption. Available at: https://images.transparencycdn.org/images/2020_Report_AU-Convention-Review_English.pdf (consulted 2 July 2024).

CHAPTER 14

International Trade Restrictions for Developing Countries: a Critique of Trade Policies

Denis Nfor Yuni

1 Overview of International Trade Rules on Trade Restrictions

Trade restrictions stem back to the mercantilist era of the 16th–18th centuries. This era was characterised by national laws that simply promoted exports and prevented imports, driven by the zero-sum game principle. The mercantilist era emphasised accumulation of wealth, protectionism, navigation and maritime dominance, colonial exploitation, restricted trade agreements, and employed state intervention measures in trade to ensure export promotion at all cost. At the time, trade was perceived as an *all or nothing game* (winner takes it all)—zero-sum game. This premise is particularly important because it is key to the rationale for trade restrictions and the global agreements that have taken place overtime to manage trade restrictions amongst countries.

Since the mercantilist era, trade restrictions have evolved in form, scope and types, leading to a plethora of different types. Some of the trade restrictions include tariffs, quotas, import licensing, export licensing, subsidies, voluntary export restraints, imposition of technical standards and regulations, anti-dumping duties, countervailing duties, embargoes as well as administrative and procedural custom requirements. Evidently, increasing trade restrictions only minimise global trade, which erodes benefits such as reduction in costs, access to efficient products, transfer of technology, specialisation, and access to products not produced locally; hence the need for a regulatory Multilateral Trade System (MTS).

The first attempt to have a MTS was established in 1947, with the General Agreement on Tariffs and Trade (GATT). After World War II, the international community sought to manage international cooperation which led to the establishment of the International Monetary Fund, the (now) World Bank and the GATT.[1] Poised with different objectives, the GATT sought to establish an

1 Van Grasstek, Craig (2013) *The History and Future of the World Trade Organization*. Lausane: World Trade Organisation.

 | DOI:10.1163/9789004734357_015

international trade organisation to reduce discriminatory practices and excessive trade barriers in international economic intercourse.[2]

Since its establishment, the GATT recorded several trade agreements that ultimately metamorphosed into the World Trade Organisation (WTO). Today, the WTO is the only international organisation dealing with global trade rules aimed at raising living standards, creating jobs and improving lives. The WTO currently consists of 165 members, and 24 observer members (countries undergoing the process of becoming members),[3] constituting about 97% of all countries. The legal framework of the WTO stems back to the GATT rules and its several revisions and additions. By its nature, the agreements have been done over the years via interest-driven strategic negotiations, which should naturally lean in favour of those with higher bargaining power. This naturally provokes inquiries on the extent to which these global trade rules benefit developing countries, who generally have lower industrial capacities but have the desired markets.

The trend is bleak for developing countries that are part of the WTO. Between 1995 (when the WTO took effect) and 2023, 35 of the 46 African countries—constituting 76% that are member states of the WTO with data records, have a negative average net trade in goods and services.[4] Similarly, 17 of the 32 Asian countries—constituting 53% that are part of the WTO with data records, have a negative average net trade in goods and services, according to the World Bank.[5] This outcome is true even for some of the 23 original countries who signed the GATT. In the last 5 decades, developing countries like Dominica and Haiti who signed the GATT have consistently recorded negative net trade in goods and services without a single year being positive. Meanwhile, developed countries such as The Netherlands and Norway that were also part of the initial signing, have mostly recorded positive net trade in goods and services, with incredible growth during the period.

It is on this premise that this study interrogates the existing global trade rules on restrictions and the effect on developing countries, with particular focus on some African countries, within the context of the universal right to development. The chapter first highlights the theories that pertain to trade

2 Hexner, Ervin (1951) The General Agreement on Tariffs and Trade and the Monetary Fund. *International Monetary Fund Staff Papers* 1(3): 432–464.

3 World Trade Organisation (2024) Members and Observers. Available at: https://www.wto.org/english/thewto_e/whatis_e/tif_e/org6_e.htm (consulted 16 June 2024).

4 World Bank (2024) World Development Indicators: Available at: https://data.worldbank.org/indicator/[indicator-code] (consulted 28 August 2024).

5 Ibid.

restrictions and then delves into key global rules on trade restrictions, before closing with a robust synthesis of the issues discussed.

2 Theoretical Foundations and Economic Rationale Supporting Trade Restrictions

There exists several theoretical justifications by economists for instituting and/or promoting trade restrictions. Some of the fundamental justifications include the protection of infant industries, support for strategic industries, prevention of dumping and unfair trade practices, national security concerns, and balance of payments stability. Interestingly, these theoretical justifications have been used in arguing for and/or against trade restrictions, which ultimately advocates for the promotion or protection of local firms, systems and the economy.

The infant industry argument is credited to List, who posits that the protection of infant industry is necessary for countries at the early stages of industrialisation due to the gap that exists between countries in terms of manufacturing.[6] The protection of infant industries is meant to guard against the economies of scale that larger firms, especially from abroad, enjoy. In the interest of "universal association", List supports international trade and export expansion, but also argues for the protection of infant industries for "national interest" and sustainable growth.[7] Contrary to popular opinion, List does not completely negate free international trade, he rather argues that selective infant industry protection is necessary in the short run to boost production and strengthen local firms, after which liberalisation could be promoted selectively and progressively until such time when all nations would have reached the same level of development.[8] Shafaeddin supports the infant industry argument and its ability to develop small industries if properly applied. Meanwhile, Meiltz argues that infant industry protection is not always an optimal decision and should depend on the industry's learning potential, the shape of the learning curve, and the degree of substitutability between domestic and foreign goods.[9]

6 List, Friedrich (1856) *The National System of Political Economy*. Philadelphia: JB Lippincott and Co.

7 Ibid.

8 Shafaeddin, Medhi (2000) What did Frederick List Actually Say? Some Clarifications on the Infant Industry Argument. *UNCTAD Discussion Papers No 149*. Available at: https://unctad.org/system/files/official-document/dp_149.en.pdf consulted 20 June 2024).

9 Melitz, Marc (2005) When and How Should Infant Industries Be Protected? *Journal of International Economics* 66(1): 177–196.

A similar argument to protecting infant industries is that of supporting strategic industries. This postulation is often associated to Brander and Spencer who argue that for the sake of protecting oligopolistic competition, nations could initiate strategic trade policy that will potentially lead to national advantages in international trade.[10] This argument is now used in restricting trade in certain industries or sectors that are strategically important for the economy for a broader set of reasons. They include national security, employment protection, and environmental protection, countering unfair trade practices, political considerations, gaining competitive advantage, self-sufficiency and preserving critical supply chains. Interestingly, such examples abound across the globe. In March 2018, the United States (US) imposed tariffs on steel and aluminium imports set at 25% on steel imports and 10% on aluminium imports to protect the US steel, aluminium, and shipbuilding industries from unfair trade practices by China.[11] Such trade restrictions for the prevention of dumping and unfair trade practices is as old as international trade itself, dating back to the mercantilist era. Also, the European Union (EU) imposes tariff-rate quotas via regulatory frameworks like the Regulation (EU) No 1308/2013 (Common Market Organisation Regulation), and Regulation (EU) No 374/2014 (Autonomous Trade Preferences) for specific agricultural products.

The argument for upholding trade restrictions for the sake of *national security* could again be traced to List in his *magnus opus*, "the National System of Political Economy" in which he critiques the idea of free international trade propounded by classical economists like Adam Smith, David Ricardo and Say.[12] He posits that the argument of free international trade infers a promotion of universal or individual wellbeing, meanwhile countries and economies are guided by national lines and vested interest to develop respective national territories. To do so, there is need to develop sophisticated industry requiring prudently designed and sequentially planned policies, interventions and programmes. List postulates that free competition between two countries can only be mutually beneficial if they are both almost at the same level of industrial development, and so countries with lower development strides should first grow to such heights before considering free trade. This assertion is supported by Mastanduno and Norris who argue that trade restrictions could be

10 Brander, Jame and Spencer, Barbara (1985) Export Subsidies and International Market Share Rivalry. *Journal of International Economics* 18(1–2): 83–100.

11 The Guardian (2018, 1 March) Trump to Impose Tariffs on Steel and Aluminium Imports in Bold Trade Move. Available at: https://www.theguardian.com/business/2018/mar/01/trump-to-impose-tariffs-on-steel-and-aluminum-imports-in-bold-trade-move (consulted 12 December 2024).

12 List, supra note 6.

employed in the face of national security threats and to minimise precarious dependence on foreign powers that could compromise national security.[13]

Another critical justification for trade restriction is for balance of payments stability. In particular, the balance of payment deficits that reflect lower exports than imports, have the potential to trigger persistent dire economic consequences such as currency depreciation, depletion of foreign exchange reserves, loss of investor confidence, and foreign aid dependence amongst others. These may translate to the loss of jobs, imported inflation, high exposure to external shocks, low revenue, and ultimately economic slowdown with the potential for severe austerity measures. Keynes' "The General Theory of Employment, Interest, and Money" promotes trade restrictions in the form of tariffs and quotas for balance of payment stability.[14] He postulates that in some cases, particularly during economic downturns or when confronted with a persistent trade deficit, countries may need to adopt trade restrictions to fix imbalances and protect domestic jobs.[15]

These theoretical justifications for trade restrictions are in direct contrast to the views of revered economists like Adam Smith, David Ricardo, Milton Friedman, Paul Krugman and Jagdish Bhagwati. These authors largely show how free trade is more beneficial to the combined trade between countries than individual trade gains. They argue that free trade fosters competition, innovation, efficiency, access to more goods, economies of scale and expertise via specialisation. Bhagwati posits that free trade promotes economic growth, reduces poverty, and enhances global welfare.[16] Meanwhile, Krugman and Irwin argue that trade restrictions could lead to economic inefficiencies that could be counterproductive if it deteriorates to trade wars, potentially harming global economic welfare.[17]

It is however, worth noting that there exists no country that does not practice one form of trade restriction or the other. The extent to which country policies impose trade restrictions vary from more liberal to extreme protectionists. Singapore and Hong Kong for example, practice more liberal trade

---

13 Mastanduno, Michael (1998) Economics and Security in Statecraft and Scholarship. *International Organization* 52(4): 825–854; Norris, William (2016) *Chinese Economic Statecraft: Commercial Actors, Grand Strategy, and State Control*. Ithaca/London: Cornell University Press.

14 Keynes, John Maynard (1936) *The General Theory of Employment, Interest, and Money*. Zurich: International Relations and Security Network.

15 Ibid.

16 Bhagwati, Jagdish (2002) *Free Trade Today*. Princeton: Princeton University Press.

17 Krugman, Paul (1993) The Narrow and Broad Arguments for Free Trade. *American Economic Review* 83(2): 362–366; Irwin, Douglas (2009) *Free Trade Under Fire*. Princeston: Princeton University.

restrictions with relatively low tariffs, yet Singapore enforces regulations for health and security reasons while Hong Kong is still subject to the trade restriction policies of China. Hence, the practice validates the theoretical justification for trade restrictions. Conversely, countries like Cuba and Venezuela have retained strict trade controls, while North Korea, Iran and Syria have some of the most isolated trade environments due to international trade sanctions. Free trade is largely practiced at different levels of openness, and although it mostly reduces/eliminates tariffs and trade barriers for the free trade unions, it imposes trade restrictions to those outside the union.

3 Restrictions in Global Trade Agreements and Their Implications on Developing Countries

There exists a plethora of global trade policies, which directly or indirectly define how developing countries practice international trade and the extent to which they can impose trade restrictions. Most of them are additions or contributions to the General Agreement on Tariffs and Trade (GATT) of 1947. Some of them include the GATT, Generalised System of Preferences (GSP) (1971, Agreement on Technical Barriers to Trade (TBT) (1979), Agreement on Trade-Related Investment Measures (TRIMs) (1995), Agreement on Trade-Related Aspects of Intellectual Property Rights (TRIPS) (1995), Agreement on the Application of Sanitary and Phytosanitary Measures (SPS) (1995), Agreement on Subsidies and Countervailing Measures (SCM) (1995), the Special and Differential Treatment (SDT) Provisions (Various Years), Trade Facilitation Agreement (TFA) (2017). For interrogating the global trade rules with controversial provisions for trade restrictions and highlighting its implications for developing countries, the study discusses the provisions of the initial GATT framework, the Tokyo, Uruguay and Doha Rounds of multilateral trade negotiations.

3.1 *General Agreement on Tariffs and Trade*

The GATT was originally signed by 23 founding member countries on 30 October 1947, in Geneva, Switzerland, with the primary aim of promoting international trade by reducing or eliminating trade barriers such as tariffs or quotas. These countries represented a diverse group of both developed and developing nations. The agreement came into effect on 1 January 1948. Membership of the GATT framework increased to 128 countries in 1995 when it metamorphosed into the WTO. The GATT generally prohibits trade restrictions (such as tariffs and quotas) but provides exceptions in Articles XI, XX and XVII that favour developing countries. The GATT recognised the need to protect infant industries and thus, allows developing countries to implement some trade restrictions for economic development. Article XVIII of the GATT, titled Governmental Assistance to Economic Development, states in subsection 2 that:

> The contracting parties recognize further that it may be necessary for those contracting parties, in order to implement programmes and policies of economic development designed to raise the general standard of living of their people, to take protective or other measures affecting imports, and that such measures are justified in so far as they facilitate the attainment of the objectives of this Agreement. They agree, therefore, that those contracting parties should enjoy additional facilities to enable them (a) to maintain sufficient flexibility in their tariff structure to be able to grant the tariff protection required for the establishment of a particular industry and (b) to apply quantitative restrictions for balance of payments purposes in a manner which takes full account of the continued high level of demand for imports likely to be generated by their programmes of economic development.[18]

This article justifies the need for trade restrictions to protect infant industries or for balance of payment stability. Article XX of the GATT includes additional specific circumstances, such as protecting public morals, human, animal, or plant life, and conserving exhaustible natural resources, as reasons for trade restrictions, on the condition that these measures are not applied in a discriminatory manner.

The argument for preferential treatment for developing countries to impose trade restrictions in some specific conditions have been largely supported in the literature and justified by the theoretical justifications discussed above.[19] By allowing trade restrictions, for developing countries, the GATT envisaged the protection of domestic infant industries and employment in developing countries until such a time that they can compete at the global stage. It also provided some degree of flexibility that could permit developing countries to grow to implement policies that are tailored to their unique economic challenges and that align with their national development goals. Meanwhile, the critics of Article XVIII and the related articles cited above, argue that such

18 World Trade Organisation (1986) The General Agreement on Tariffs and Trade. Available at: https://www.wto.org/english/docs_e/legal_e/gatt47.pdf (consulted 8 December 2024).

19 Hoekman, B. (2014) Trade Agreements and Trade Policy Spillovers. Available at: https://doi.org/10.2139/ssrn.2550550 (consulted 19 October 2024).

flexibility could lead to the inefficiencies in the domestic industries and rent seeking behaviour where industries lobby for continued protection rather than striving for competitiveness.[20]

Although the GATT is celebrated for its flexibility toward developing countries in protecting infant industries for economic development, it has often come under heavy criticism for its discriminatory stands in favour of developed countries on three fronts. First, implementation of the GATT policies are perceived to be in favour of developed countries that have found ways of flouting the policies. In practice, most developed countries charge higher tariffs on processed goods from developing countries, and/or impose non-tariff barriers (such as stringent health and safety standards) that ultimately constitute trade restrictions to developing countries, which weakens growth in industrialisation.[21] Also, the GATT rules, though developed through the years, is still perceived as complex and the dispute resolution mechanism often favours developed nations.[22] Although the WTO now provides for the SDT for developing countries in dispute resolutions, the practical enforcement is often limited, inconsistent and ineffective in supporting developing countries during disputes or undermines their ability to effectively invoke SDT provisions at all stages of the WTO dispute settlement process.[23] In particular, the Dispute Settlement Understandings suffers from ambiguity and practical inefficacy, which undermines the ability of developing countries to effectively invoke SDT provisions at all stages of the WTO dispute settlement process.

Second, the GATT restricts primary products exporting countries from offering substantial subsidies to their farmers, making it difficult for developing countries to compete. Sub-sections 3 of Article XVI of the GATT states that:

> contracting parties should seek to avoid the use of subsidies on the export of primary products. If, however, a contracting party grants

20 Grossman, Gene and Helpman, Elhanan (1994) Protection for Sale. *The American Economic Review* 84(4): 833–850; Krueger, Anne (1997) Trade Policy and Economic Development: How we Learn. *The American Economic Review* 87(1): 1–22.

21 Cline, William (2004) *Trade Policy and Global Poverty*. Washington DC: Center for Global Development and Institute for International Economics; Baldwin, Robert (1984) Trade Policies in Developed Countries. *Handbook of Development Economics* 1: 453–529.

22 Finger, Michael and Nogués, Julio (2001) The Unbalanced Uruguay Round Outcome: The New Areas in Future WTO Negotiations. *The World Economy* 24(9): 1131–1161.

23 Lee, Hyo Won and Kim, Youngwan (2022) Who Uses the Special and Differential Treatment Provisions of the WTO? *Journal of World Trade* 56(1): 141–164; Tania, Sharmin et al (2024) Reimagining the Special and Differential Treatment Provisions in the WTO's Dispute Settlement Understanding. *Asian Journal of International Law* 14(1): 123–153.

> directly or indirectly any form of subsidy which operates to increase the export of any primary product from its territory, such subsidy shall not be applied in a manner which results in that contracting party having more than an equitable share of world export trade in that product, account being taken of the shares of the contracting parties in such trade in the product during a previous representative period, and any special factors which may have affected or may be affecting such trade in the product.

Although not specifically attributed to developing countries, sub-sections 3 of Article XVI of the GATT limits the ability to give subsidies to the export of primary products generally associated to developing countries and does not restrict subsidies on the exportation of semi-finished and finished agricultural products. This imbalance has been highlighted by several authors who opined that this provision perpetuates inequalities in the global agricultural market, with developed countries benefiting disproportionately.[24] The GATT's recognition of the peculiarities of developing countries on protection for industries is not explicit about subsidies.

Third, the provisions of Article XXIV of the GATT enables the formation of customs unions and free trade areas which promotes trade among members of a particular free trade zone. Although the primary intention of this provision may have been to facilitate trade liberalisation amongst group of countries, the fundamental nature of customs unions and free trade areas is that it offers higher privileges to member countries within the network, compared to those outside. Custom unions like the EU and free trade areas such as the North American Free Trade Agreement, European Free Trade Association, Australia-New Zealand Closer Economic Relations Trade Agreement and the European Economic Area, improved trade amongst members, while to an extent, restricting trade to developing countries. Custom unions and free trade areas could restrict trade to non-members by promoting trade diversion from more efficient outside suppliers to less efficient member states while, non-member states are excluded from the lower tariffs or in some cases tariff-free agreements enjoyed by member states.

---

24 Lal Das, Balgirath (1998) *The WTO Agreements: Deficiencies, Imbalances, and Required Changes*. London/New York: Zed Books Ltd and Penang: Third World Network; Obida, Idibia Daniel (2018) African Trade Growth or Trade Deficit: GATT/WTO Rules as Trojan Horse on African Trade Development. *World Journal of Research and Review* 6(2): 70–89.

3.2 *Tokyo Round of Multilateral Trade Negotiations (1973–1979)*

The Tokyo Round of trade agreements was the seventh and a significant round of agreements because there was a major attempt to address non-tariff barriers. The round started in 1973 and the agreements reached in 1979. The agreements from the Tokyo Round known as the TBT, was incorporated into the WTO framework after establishment. The Tokyo Round was however, less impactful and had a smaller scope than the GATT and the Uruguay rounds. Like the GATT, the Tokyo Round did not solve the problem of unequal trade systems identified with the GATT.

The Tokyo Round was not binding to all and so generated a dual system made up of those who signed (mostly developed countries) and those who did not (mostly developing countries) who were mostly side-lined, causing disparities in the application of trade rules, thereby fortifying existing inequalities in the global trade structure.[25] Meanwhile, the Subsidies Code of the Tokyo Round predominantly benefited developed countries, giving them advantage in maintaining certain subsidies as oppose to developing countries.[26] Developing countries argued that levying higher tariffs on exports of processed raw materials than when they are exported in unprocessed form meant that the Tokyo Round gave high "effective" protection to processing firms in the importing country and discouraged developing countries from establishing their own processing industries.[27]

In 1980, the World Bank cited other concerns from developing countries about the negotiations, including the inability to liberalise quantitative restrictions or measures that have detrimental effects in the fields of agriculture, textiles and leather goods, continuous trade barriers on tropical products by developed countries, the importance of export and other subsidies for achieving social and economic objectives, and that the concept of "graduation" introduced into the negotiations by developed countries would allow them to discriminate among developing countries arbitrarily.[28] Also, the use of voluntary codes for non-tariff barriers to reflect the interest of the main trading

---

25 Bhala, Raj (2011) Doha Round Schisms: Numerous, Technical, and Deep. *Loyola University Chicago International Law Review* 6(1): 1–18.

26 Hoekman, Bernard (2014) The Bali Trade Facilitation Agreement and Rulemaking in the WTO: Milestone, Mistake, or Mirage? *European University Institute—Robert Schuman Centre for Advanced Studies Research Paper No 2014/102.*

27 Overseas Development Institute (1977) The Tokyo Round and the Developing Countries. Available at: https://odi.cdn.ngo/media/documents/6612.pdf (consulted 28 July 2024).

28 Kemper, Ria (1980) The Tokyo Round: Results and Implications for Developing Countries. *World Bank Staff Working Paper No 372*, 1–49.

partners marginalise developing countries. This led to the Uruguay Round of trade agreement which gave birth to the World Trade Organisation that we have today.

3.3 *Uruguay Round of Multilateral Trade Negotiations (1986–1994)*

To further reform and operationalise the GATT framework, the Uruguay Round of trade agreements was instituted. The Uruguay Round of Multilateral Trade Negotiations has a landmark impact in the history of international trade agreements as it delivered several agreements among which is the TRIPS, TRIMS, Agreement on Agriculture (AoA), the SCM, and the General Agreement on Trade in Services (GATS) were established. The Uruguay Round is credited for instituting a more robust dispute resolution mechanism, increasing the scope of trade rules to incorporate other areas such as trade in services, and intellectual property rights and significant tariff cuts globally.

Although the goal of these agreements is in part, to reduce the inequalities faced by developing countries, they have countlessly been criticised for allowing developed countries to continue providing significant subsidies, particularly in the agricultural sector, while placing stricter limits on developing countries.[29] For example, Abreu posits that "since 1959, successive arrangements in the GATT have de facto legitimized textile and clothing protection, allowing industrial countries to impose quantitative restrictions on an increasing range of such exports from developing countries".[30] According to Makong, "[t]he outcome of the Uruguay round has been deemed by African countries as having created an unfair MTS that take into account the economic needs of developed and advanced members to the neglect of developing countries".[31] To shed light on these claims, I proceed to discuss the agreements that arose from the Uruguay Round.

Articles 22–24, 27, 31, and 39.3 of the TRIPS have been highlighted as controversial provisions in the literature that may widen the inequality in MTS. Article 22–24 of the TRIPS offer protection for geographical indicators, requiring that suppliers specify the origins of the productions on the products.

---

29 Abreu, Marcelo de Paiva (1990) Developing Countries and the Uruguay Round of Trade Negotiations. The International Bank for Reconstruction and Development/The World Bank—Proceedings of the World Bank Annual Conference on Development Economics 1989. Available at: https://documents1.worldbank.org/curated/en/528281468765615536/pdf/multi-page.pdf (consulted 4 August 2024).

30 Ibid.

31 Makong, Tsotetsi (2023) Extract of Keynote Paper: The Political Economy of Regional Integration and International Trade in Africa. Available at: nulwtochair.org.ls/wp-content/uploads/2023/12/Conference-Proceedings-1.pdf (consulted 4 August 2024).

Rangnekar argues that such requirements may restrict trade from countries that may not have a brand name in specific products.[32] Article 27 of the TRIPS enforces the adoption of trade patents for all inventions and products which disproportionately profits developed countries where most patent holders reside.[33] Article 31(f) restricts the application of mandatory licencing to the primary domestic market, making it more difficult for nations with low manufacturing capability to import generics from other nations.[34] Article 39.3 then provides that undisclosed test data submitted to governments for the approval of pharmaceutical or agricultural chemical products must be protected against unfair commercial use. However, this gives the producers the advantage to enjoy a period of data exclusivity during which producers cannot rely on the original data to obtain marketing approval.[35]

Criticisms of the TRIMs have largely been on Article 2 and the Annex, especially in the prohibition of local content requirements, elimination of trade-balancing requirements, and the restrictions on performance requirements. The prohibition of local content requirements by TRIMs is in direct contrast to the need for developing countries to protect local industries and consequently the inability to promote local industries. Similarly, TRIMs eliminates trade-balancing requirements which prevents firms or countries from putting in place mechanisms to prevent trade deficits or balancing imports and exports. This particular provision grossly disadvantages many developing countries that consistently record trade deficits due to higher imports than exports. Countries with higher exports generate more revenue, increase foreign reserves, create jobs, and reduce poverty among others. The prohibition of performance requirements under the TRIMs could be seen as permitting multinational corporations from developed countries operating in developing countries to function without meeting development commitments such as

---

32 Rangnekar, Dwijen (2004) The Socioeconomics of Geographical Indications: A Review of Empirical Evidence from Europe. *UNCTAD-ICTSD Project on IPRs and Sustainable Development.*

33 Correa, Carlos Maria (2000) *Intellectual Property Rights, the WTO and Developing Countries: The TRIPS Agreement and Policy Options.* London/New York: Zed Books Ltd and Penang: Third World Network.

34 Reichman, Jerome and Hasenzahl, Catherine (2003) Non-Voluntary Licensing of Patented Inventions: Historical Perspective, Legal Framework under TRIPS, and an Overview of the Practice in Canada and the USA. *UNCTAD-ICTSD Project on IPRs and Sustainable Development.*

35 Shaffer, Gregory and Brenner, Susan (2009) A Trade War with New Tools: Rethinking Embedded Liberalism in the Context of TRIPS. *Minnesota Journal of International Law* 18(2): 274–319.

technology transfer, efficiency and industrial development.[36] The TRIMs focus on promoting short-term gains from trade liberalisation rather than allowing developing countries to put in place strategic policies that ensure sustainable development in the middle and long-run.[37]

The controversies in the AoA could be grouped into two; there were provisions that sought to address the concerns from developing countries and those that out-rightly left developing countries worse-off in terms of MTS Inequalities. For example, the AoA categorised domestic support into different categories, which include the "amber box" (trade-distorting subsidies), "blue box" (subsidies that are partially trade-distorting but are linked to production-limiting programs), and the "green box" (non-trade-distorting subsidies that are permitted without limits). This led to increasing inequalities in MTS, wherein developed countries were allowed to retain greater levels of trade-distorting subsidies under the "amber box", whereas developing countries were constrained from providing similar domestic support. Evidence shows that the continuous offer of domestic support by developed countries have increasingly up scaled the uneven playing field of the MTS.[38]

The AoA also discourage the use of non-tariff barriers, recommending that it be replaced with tariffs, which ought to reduce overtime for developing countries unlike for developed countries. While developing countries face greater pressure to liberalise, thereby succumbing to global competition, developed countries protect sensitive agricultural products such as dairy, sugar, and cereals, with high tariffs, and quotas.[39] On the third and final pillar of the AoA—reduction of export subsidies—developed countries are allowed to reduce their export subsidies only slightly, relative to the base year, meanwhile developing countries with relatively limited or no export subsidies, are required to reduce or eliminate them. The reductions were expected to be as follows:

---

36 Wade, Robert Hunter (2003) What Strategies are Viable for Developing Countries Today? The World Trade Organization and the Shrinking of "Development Space". *Review of International Political Economy* 10(4): 621–644.

37 Akyüz, Yilmaz (2005) WTO Negotiations on Industrial Tariffs: What is at Stake for Developing Countries? *Economic and Political Weekly* 40(10): 4827–4836.

38 Murphy, Sophia; Lilliston, Ben and Lake, Mary (2005, February) WTO Agreement on Agriculture: A Decade of Dumping. Institute for Agriculture and Trade Policy. Available at: https://www.iatp.org/documents/wto-agreement-agriculture-decade-dumping (consulted 12 December 20224).

39 Clapp, Jennifer (2006) WTO Agriculture Negotiations: Implications for the Global South. *Third World Quarterly* 27(4): 563–577.

It implies that least developed countries are not expected to reduce these trade restrictions while developing and developed countries are expected to do so as shown in Table 14.1. In relative terms, it implies a huge difference between developed and developing countries, especially because of the differences that already existed in the base year. This is evident with prevailing statistics as shown in Figure 14.1. In 2022 for example, the agricultural export subsidies, for key continents show how the export subsidies from developed countries could almost mirror that of the globe, meanwhile agricultural export subsidies from sub-Saharan Africa and Asia are negligible. It is worth noting that the argument made in the literature on the ability to afford agricultural export subsidies by developing countries should not justify the limitation of developing countries. The social conditioning of ceilings, especially when discriminatory, could be far-reaching.

TABLE 14.1 Reduction rates required in the Agriculture Agreement (%)

Description	Reformed areas	Developed	Developing	Least developed
Market access	Simple average tariff	36	24	0
	Minimum reduction per tariff line	15	10	0
Domestic support	Total Aggregate Measurement of Support (AMS)	20	13.3	0
Export subsidy	Value of expenditure on subsidies	36	24	0
	Quantity of subsidised exports	21	14	0

SOURCE: FOOD AND AGRICULTURAL ORGANISATION (D.N.A.)

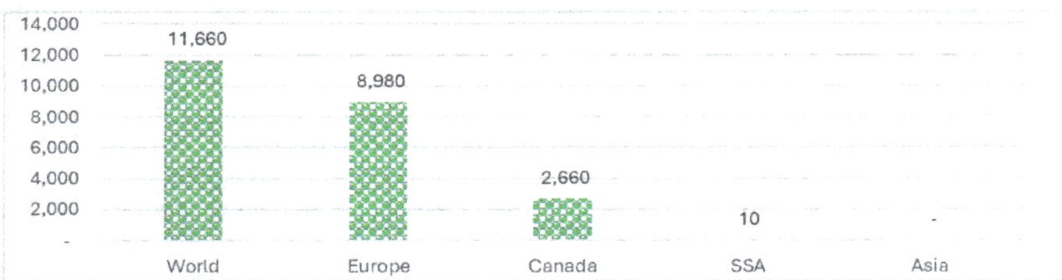

FIGURE 14.1 Agricultural export subsidies, (Thousands of USD)
SOURCE: WORLD TRADE ORGANISATION (2024)

The Agreement on SCM constitutes the legal frameworks that expanded the coverage on subsidies and countervailing measures in MTS. Article 2 of the SCM prohibits subsidies that aim to promote domestic over imported goods. Article 3 of the SCM states that:

> Except as provided in the Agreement on Agriculture, the following subsidies, within the meaning of Article 1, shall be prohibited: (a) subsidies contingent, in law or in fact, whether solely or as one of several other conditions, upon export performance, including those illustrated in Annex I; (b) subsidies contingent, whether solely or as one of several other conditions, upon the use of domestic over imported goods.

This simply prevents developing countries from protecting their local industries or promoting local firms via subsidies, especially, in the face of high dumping occurrences from well-established industries or industrial countries, whose aim is to reduce price as much as possible to frustrate domestic firms and force them out of the market for the sake of domination. More importantly, like Chang argues in his famous book, "Kicking Away the Ladder: Development Strategy in Historical Perspective", by instituting such policies now, developed countries are effectively *kicking away the ladder* that they themselves used to become developed countries.[40] Other provisions of the SCM such as Articles, 5, 6, 10, 11 and 27 either require huge legal and financial resources, or are complex with temporary exemptions (Article 27), making it difficult for developing countries to effectively utilise the "differential treatment" that it seeks to address. This assertion is supported by Shaffer and Meléndez-Ortiz who posit that,

> the requirements imposed by Articles 5 and 6 of the SCM Agreement disproportionately affect developing countries, as they lack the legal and financial resources to defend their subsidies or challenge those of developed countries effectively. The burden of proof for demonstrating "serious prejudice" is high, creating a significant barrier for developing countries.[41]

---

40 Chang, Ha-Joon (2003) *Kicking Away the Ladder: Development Strategy in Historical Perspective*. London: Anthem Press.

41 Shaffer, Gregory and Meléndez-Ortiz, Ricardo (2010) *Dispute Settlement at the WTO: The Developing Country Experience*. Cambridge: Cambridge University Press, 175.

Gallagher also argues that

> although Article 27 offers some concessions to developing countries, these are often seen as insufficient. The temporary nature of the exemptions, coupled with the stringent conditions for their application, limits the effectiveness of these provisions. Developing countries are pressured to phase out subsidies before they have fully achieved their development goals.[42]

The GATS provides more detailed trade regulations which focuses on trade in services but has also come under heavy criticism for disproportionately favouring developed countries. Article VI of the GATS that addresses the need for transparency and barrier-free domestic regulation to trade, sub-section 1, states that, "Measures by Members affecting trade in services shall not be more burdensome than necessary to ensure the quality of the service". However, developing countries often lack the regulatory infrastructure and resources to comply with stringent standards imposed by developed countries, which can act as a non-tariff barrier. The South Centre observes that "[s]trict disciplines on licensing procedures can be quite harmful for developing countries particularly given their low level of technological development and sophistication of regulatory bodies and frameworks".[43]

Similarly, Article XIV provides exceptions to the GATS rules for the protection of public morals, human life and public health. But these require financial recourses and advanced institutional systems to effectively categorise these exceptions and manage the implementations that developing countries may not have. This competitive disadvantage could also be highlighted in the provisions of Article XVII on market access. Furthermore, the most-favoured-nation principle in Article II intends to be fair but could increase inequalities in the MTS due to the already developed physical and technological infrastructure that is enjoyed by the developed countries.[44]

---

42 Gallagher, Kevin (2005) *Putting Development First: The Importance of Policy Space in the WTO and IFIs*. London/New York: Zed Books, 96.

43 South Centre (2026, August). The Development Dimension of the GATS Domestic Regulation Negotiations SC/AN/TDP/SV/11. Analytical Note. Available at: https://www.southcentre.int/wp-content/uploads/2013/08/AN_SV11_The-Development-Dimension-of-the-GATS-Domestic-Regulations_EN.pdf (consulted 12 December 2024).

44 Petersmann, Ernst-Ulrich (2003) The Role of the GATS in the Global Trade System. *European Journal of International Law* 14(2): 39–58.

3.4 *Doha Development Round of Multilateral Trade Negotiations (2001–to Date)*

The Fourth Ministerial Conference in Doha, Qatar, tagged the "Doha Development Round" of multilateral trade negotiations was launched in 2001 and it is still not formally concluded. It ambitiously intended to address many of the concerns especially, those raised by developing countries as discussed above, but have been stalled for years with many unresolved issues. In Doha, the Ministerial Conference "agreed to adopt around 50 decisions clarifying the obligations of developing country member governments with respect to issues including agriculture, subsidies, textiles and clothing, technical barriers to trade, trade-related investment measures and rules of origin".[45] Since 2001, the Doha Round recorded high points of agreements in 2005, 2008 and most especially in 2013 and 2015. Three notable attempts at reducing the inequality in MTS for developing countries are credited to the Doha Round.

First, is the export subsidies and domestic support for agriculture, which disproportionately benefited developed countries. The revised draft modalities of July 2008 shows specific reductions in trade distorting subsidies in the amber and blue boxes for developed countries and the agreement to eliminate export subsidies by end of 2013 for developed countries while giving a longer time for developing countries. The reality is however, not reflective of the agreement. The implementation of the 2008 revised draft modalities has been largely ineffective, with developed countries continuing to shield key sectors through various loopholes in the agreement. The Doha Round's ambition to significantly cut trade-distorting subsidies has been thwarted by domestic pressures within developed countries, leading to only marginal reductions in actual subsidy levels.[46]

The second key attempt is the Bali Ministerial Conference of 2013 via the TFA, which expedited the movement, release, and clearance of goods across borders. This is largely perceived to be more successful in reducing trade costs and trade competitiveness for developing countries. In fact, the WTO Director-General at the time, Roberto Azevêdo said that "for the first time in our history: the WTO has truly delivered".[47] These sentiments are shared by other authors who consider the decision to be a landmark achievement in the

45 World Trade Organisation (2024) The Doha Round. Available at: https://www.wto.org/english/tratop_e/dda_e/dda_e.htm (consulted 14 August 2024).

46 Hoekman 2014, supra note 23.

47 World Trade Organisation (2013) Round-the-clock Consultations Produce "Bali Package". *News Items*. Available at: https://www.wto.org/english/news_e/news13_e/mc9sum_07dec13_e.htm (consulted 19 August 2024).

WTO.[48] However, other authors have been more cautious about the extent of implementation based on the technical and capacity requirements needed to fully take advantage of this.[49]

Ultimately, the Doha Round has been characterised by the SDT, which aims to benefit developing countries. The SDT acknowledges that countries are not equal and so, special considerations should be given to countries with special needs, intended to reduce global inequalities. This include giving longer deadlines for developing countries and higher cuts in trade distorting subsidies for developed countries amongst others. The SDT have been instrumental in generating the necessary flexibility, support and trust for developing countries to engage in trade liberalization. The WTO posits that the "S&DT has allowed developing countries to protect sensitive sectors, gain time for adjustment, and receive technical assistance, which are all crucial for building their capacity to trade competitively on the global stage".[50] However, critiques argue that the provisions of the SDT have limited substantive impact due to the use of vague language and lack of enforceability and the reluctance of developed countries to offer meaningful concessions.[51]

Another important argument is that the SDT acknowledges the needs of developing countries but fails to further recognise that even developing countries differ from each other. Stevens states that, "the 'one-size-fits-all' approach in the form of the SDT is not suitable for addressing and actualising the development needs of these states [all developing countries]".[52] This

48 Evdokia, Moïsé and Sorescu, Silvia. (2013) Trade Facilitation Indicators: The Potential Impact of Trade Facilitation on Developing Countries' Trade. *OECD Trade Policy Papers No 144*. Neufeld, Nora (2014) The Long and Winding Road: How WTO Members Finally Reached a Trade Facilitation Agreement. *WTO Staff Working Paper ERSD-2014-06*. Available at: https://www.wto.org/english/res_e/reser_e/ersd201406_e.htm (consulted 23 August 2024).

49 Finger and Nogués, supra note 19, 1131–1161.

50 World Trade Organisation (2013) Special and Differential Treatment Provisions. Available at: https://www.wto.org/english/tratop_e/devel_e/dev_special_differential_provisions_e.htm (consulted 3 September 2024).

51 Stevens, Clydenia (2002) The Future of Special and Differential Treatment (S&DT) for Developing Countries in the WTO. *Institute of Development Studies Working Paper 163*. Available at: https://opendocs.ids.ac.uk/opendocs/handle/20.500.12413/3307 (consulted 5 September 2024); Keck, Alexander and Low, Patrick (2004) Special and Differential Treatment in the WTO: Why, When and How? *WTO Staff Working Paper ERSD-2004-03*. Available at: https://www.wto.org/english/res_e/reser_e/ersd200403_e.htm (consulted 5 September 2024).

52 Stevens, Clydenia (2019) Reviving the Right to Development Within the Multilateral Trade Framework Affecting (African) Countries to Actualise Agenda 2063. *African Human Rights Law Journal* 19(2): 470–493.

is justified by the argument that global development paradigms cannot and should not apply uniformly, especially in addressing issues relating to poverty, and socio-economic development, which have peculiar features in developing countries, though perceived as global concerns.[53]

4 Conclusion: Political Dynamics of Global Trade Rules on Trade Restrictions and the Right to Development

At face value, the global trade rules discussed above, seek to appreciate and to some extent, promote development via the trade argument. However, an in-depth analysis of some of the provisions of the trade rules show a systematic, and in some cases, an intentional endeavour to retain trade gain advantage for developed countries at best or buffer the inequalities that exists in the MTS at worst; what Chang refers to as "kicking away the ladder".[54] Although the Doha Round breathes a wind of change in bridging this gap, the statistics, show that in spite of the several agreements on international trade rules from the inception of the GATT in 1947, majority of the developing countries have continued to record negative net trade in goods and services. This therefore raises concerns on the effect of the trade rules on developing countries and by extension, begs the question of the most appropriate development stage a country needs to join the MTS.

China seems to have understood this early enough. Though China was one of the 23 countries to sign the GATT, it only joined the WTO in 2001. Between the late 1970s and early 1980s, China focused on reforming its domestic economy while maintaining significant control over foreign trade and investment. For example, the government introduced special economic zones that encouraged foreign investment under controlled conditions and allowed for transfer of technology while protecting domestic industries.[55] By the mid-1980s and 1990s, when China had established production networks and supply chains, it then gradually and strategically began to liberalise. It only joined the WTO in 2001 wherein it still carefully negotiated for special provisions to protect

53 Ngang, Carol Chi (2017) Differentiated Responsibilities Under International Law and the Right to Development Paradigm for Developing Countries. *Human Rights and International Legal Discourse* 11(2): 287.

54 Chang, supra note 37.

55 Naughton, Barry (2007) *The Chinese Economy: Transitions and Growth*. Massachusetts: The MIT Press.

sensitive industries.[56] Prior to joining the WTO, the Chinese government provided subsidies to state-owned enterprises to protect them from foreign competition and acquired advanced technologies through foreign direct investment, and strategic partnerships.[57]

Majority of the WTO's 165 member states are developing countries that have consistently raised concerns about the disproportionate advantage that the existing trade rules give developed countries. Beyond the trade rules that are already polarised, the practice of these rules further worsen the expectations of the trade rules. For example, the Doha Round agreement of 2008 envisaged the elimination of export subsidies for developing countries by 2013. However, as recent as 2021 (over 8 years after the deadline), the EU introduced the Common Agricultural Policy, which includes direct payments to farmers and other market support measures that could indirectly support exports.[58] Additionally, the US Government Accountability Office posits that "while overt export subsidies have been largely eliminated, programs like the Export Credit Guarantee Program (GSM-102) provide subsidies that effectively lower the cost of U.S. exports".[59] In Canada, the International Trade Centre notes that, "Canada's Class 7 pricing has been viewed by trading partners as a form of export subsidy, as it allows Canadian processors to sell milk protein at below-market rates, thereby supporting exports".[60] There is no better way to put this than reference the Nobel Prize winner, Joseph Stiglitz, who said "I found myself in the uncomfortable position of an American saying 'do as we say, not as we do'".[61]

56 Scott, Robert and Jorgensen, Hilary (2015) China's Accession to the WTO: U.S. Trade Deficits, Jobs, and Industries Affected. *Economic Policy Institute*. Available at: https://www.epi.org/publication/chinas-accession-to-the-wto-u-s-trade-deficits-jobs-and-industries-affected/ (consulted 18 September 2024).

57 Huang, Yasheng (2003) *Selling China: Foreign Direct Investment During the Reform Era*. Cambridge: Cambridge University Press; Naughton, Barry (2018) *The Chinese Economy: Adaptation and Growth*. Massachusetts: The MIT Press.

58 OECD (2021, June) Agricultural Policy Monitoring and Evaluation 2021: Addressing the Challenges Facing Food Systems. *OECD Publishing*. https://doi.org/10.1787/2d810e01-en (consulted 18 September 2024).

59 US Government Accountability Office (2020) Agricultural Export Credit Programs: Opportunities to Reduce Redundancy and Improve Efficiencies. Available at: https://www.gao.gov/products/gao-20-35 (consulted 5 October 2024).

60 International Trade Centre (2021) Trade Map: Canadian Dairy Export Subsidies. *International Trade Centre*. Available at: https://www.intracen.org/ (consulted 17 October 2024).

61 Reinert, E. (2000) The Global Economy and the Developing Countries: An Overview of Trade, Development and Globalization. In: Jomo, K.S and Nagaraj, S. (eds) *Globalization Versus Development*. Cham, Switzerland: Palgrave Macmillan, 73–94.

The United Nations Declaration on the Right to Development Resolution 41/128 of 1986, is premised on the idea that all peoples have the inalienable right to participate in, contribute to, and enjoy economic, social, cultural and political development and that the right to development is recognised both as an individual and a collective right[62] because it is a universal and inalienable human right.[63] Although the right to development has been recognised at the highest levels in various international instruments, there seem to be a higher focus on the collective rights, much more than the individual rights. The right to development does not only recognise the human person as the focal point of the development process, it infers that development policies should make the human being the main participant and beneficiary of development.[64] It is safe to state that the right to development is denied, or at best infringed, when international instruments like the WTO international trade rules operate in ways that impede individual and collective socio-economic development.

In the context of international trade, the right to development infers that trade rules must not only focus on or be driven by market access and economic growth but also ensures that trade contributes to poverty reduction, food security, and access to essential services. This can only be achieved with an enabling environment that truly understands the need for SDT and, is driven by the political will to implement same. Trade liberalisation must not only be preached as being good for developing countries whereas, they evidently also need to protect strategic local industries for sustainable growth.

Although international trade is not the only determinant of development, it directly affects key components of the national income identity, which is the backbone for computing gross domestic product, and it has the potential to significantly improve socio-economic, political and cultural development. If MTS are governed with the firm believe and practical implementation of the right to development, international trade restrictions in particular and trade rules in general, will be modelled in ways that prioritise individual and

62 Stevens 2019, supra note 49; Declaration on the Right to Development, Resolution A/RES/41/128, Adopted by the UN General Assembly on 4 December 1986, Art 1(1).

63 Piron, Laure-Helen (2002) The Right to Development: A Review of the Current State of the Debate for the Department of International Development. *Overseas Development Institute*. Available at: https://www.odi.org/sites/odi.org.uk/files/odi-assets/publications-opinion-files/2317.pdf (consulted 8 December 2024), 9.

64 Declaration on the Right to Development, supra note 62, Preamble Paras 12 and 13; Oppong, Richard Frimpong (2006) Trade and Human Rights: A Perspective for Agents of Trade Policy Using a Rights-Based Approach to Development. *African Human Rights Law Journal* 6(1): 126–127.

collective entitlements to development in developing and least developed countries. This will give effective meaning to the commitment under the Millennium Declaration, which stipulates that "[w]e are committed to making the right to development a reality for everyone and to freeing the entire human race from want".[65]

In conclusion, the words of Stiglitz still echoes true today to the effect that "Globalization can be reshaped, and when it is, when it is properly, fairly run, with all countries having a voice in policies affecting them, there is a possibility that it will help create a new global economy in which growth is not only more sustainable and less volatile but the fruits of this growth are more equitable".[66] The delays in concluding the Doha Round of Trade Restrictions is evidently largely based on its SDT provisions, which are apparently not beneficial to developed countries. The right to development requires that trade rules in general, and especially on trade restrictions be fair and sensitive to equitable economic, social, cultural and political development for all nations.

References

Abreu, Marcelo de Paiva (1990) Developing Countries and the Uruguay Round of Trade Negotiations. The International Bank for Reconstruction and Development/ The World Bank—Proceedings of the World Bank Annual Conference on Development Economics 1989. Available at: https://documents1.worldbank.org/curated/en/528281468765615536/pdf/multi-page.pdf (consulted 4 August 2024).

Akyüz, Yilmaz (2005) WTO Negotiations on Industrial Tariffs: What is at Stake for Developing Countries? *Economic and Political Weekly* 40(10): 4827–4836.

Baldwin, Robert (1984) Trade Policies in Developed Countries. *Handbook of Development Economics* 1: 453–529.

Bhagwati, Jagdish (2002) *Free Trade Today*. Princeton: Princeton University Press.

Bhala Raj (2011) Doha Round Schisms: Numerous, Technical, and Deep. *Loyola University Chicago International Law Review* 6(1): 1–188.

Brander, Jame and Spencer, Barbara (1985) Export Subsidies and International Market Share Rivalry. *Journal of International Economics* 18(1–2): 83–100.

65 United Nations Millennium Declaration Resolution A/RES/55/2 18 adopted by the General Assembly on 8 September 2000, Para 11.

66 Stiglitz, Joseph (2002) *Globalization and its Discontents*. New York: W.W. Norton and Company, Inc.

Chang, Ha-Joon (2003) *Kicking Away the Ladder: Development Strategy in Historical Perspective*. London: Anthem Press.

Clapp, Jennifer (2006) WTO Agriculture Negotiations: Implications for the Global South. *Third World Quarterly* 27(4): 563–577.

Cline, William (2004) *Trade Policy and Global Poverty*. Washington DC: Center for Global Development and Institute for International Economics.

Correa, Carlos Maria (2000) *Intellectual Property Rights, the WTO and Developing Countries: The TRIPS Agreement and Policy Options*. London/New York: Zed Books Ltd and Penang: Third World Network.

Declaration on the Right to Development Resolution A/RES/41/128 adopted by UN General Assembly on 4 December 1986.

Evdokia, Moïsé and Sorescu, Silvia (2013) Trade Facilitation Indicators: The Potential Impact of Trade Facilitation on Developing Countries' Trade. *OECD Trade Policy Papers No 144*.

Finger, Michael and Nogués, Julio (2001) The Unbalanced Uruguay Round Outcome: The New Areas in Future WTO Negotiations. *The World Economy* 24(9): 1131–1161.

Gallagher, Kevin (2005) *Putting Development First: The Importance of Policy Space in the WTO and IFIs*. London/New York: Zed Books.

Grossman, Gene and Helpman, Elhanan (1994) Protection for Sale. *The American Economic Review* 84(4): 833–850.

Hexner, Ervin (1951) The General Agreement on Tariffs and Trade and the Monetary Fund. *International Monetary Fund Staff Papers* 1(3): 432–464.

Hoekman, B. (2014) Trade Agreements and Trade Policy Spillovers. Available at: https://doi.org/10.2139/ssrn.2550550 (consulted 19 October 2024).

Hoekman, Bernard (2014) The Bali Trade Facilitation Agreement and Rulemaking in the WTO: Milestone, Mistake, or Mirage? *European University Institute—Robert Schuman Centre for Advanced Studies Research Paper No 2014/102*.

Huang, Yasheng (2003) *Selling China: Foreign Direct Investment During the Reform Era*. Cambridge: Cambridge University Press.

International Trade Centre (2021) Trade Map: Canadian Dairy Export Subsidies. *International Trade Centre*. Available at: https://www.intracen.org/ (consulted 17 October 2024).

Irwin, Douglas (2009) *Free Trade Under Fire*. Princeton: Princeton University.

Keck, Alexander and Low, Patrick (2004) Special and Differential Treatment in the WTO: Why, When and How? *WTO Staff Working Paper ERSD-2004-03*. Available at: https://www.wto.org/english/res_e/reser_e/ersd200403_e.htm (consulted 5 September 2024).

Kemper, Ria (1980) The Tokyo Round: Results and Implications for Developing Countries. *World Bank Staff Working Paper No 372*, 1–49.

Keynes, John Maynard (1936) *The General Theory of Employment, Interest, and Money*. Zurich: International Relations and Security Network.

Krueger, Anne (1997) Trade Policy and Economic Development: How we Learn. *The American Economic Review* 87(1): 1–22.

Krugman, Paul (1993) The Narrow and Broad Arguments for Free Trade. *American Economic Review* 83(2): 362–366.

Lal Das, Balgirath (1998) *The WTO Agreements: Deficiencies, Imbalances, and Required Changes*. London/New York: Zed Books Ltd and Penang: Third World Network.

Lee, Hyo Won and Kim, Youngwan (2022) Who Uses the Special and Differential Treatment Provisions of the WTO? *Journal of World Trade* 56(1): 141–164.

List, Friedrich (1856) *The National System of Political Economy*. Philadelphia: JB Lippincott and Co.

Makong, Tsotetsi (2023) Extract of Keynote Paper: The Political Economy of Regional Integration and International Trade in Africa. Available at: nulwtochair.org.ls/wp-content/uploads/2023/12/Conference-Proceedings-1.pdf (consulted 4 August 2024).

Mastanduno, Michael (1998) Economics and Security in Statecraft and Scholarship. *International Organization* 52(4): 825–854.

Melitz, Marc (2005) When and How Should Infant Industries be Protected? *Journal of International Economics* 66(1): 177–196.

Murphy, Sophia; Lilliston, Ben and Lake, Mary (2005, February) WTO Agreement on Agriculture: A Decade of Dumping. Institute for Agriculture and Trade Policy. Available at: https://www.iatp.org/documents/wto-agreement-agriculture-decade-dumping (consulted 12 December 20224).

Naughton, Barry (2007) *The Chinese Economy: Transitions and Growth*. Massachusetts: The MIT Press.

Naughton, Barry (2018) *The Chinese Economy: Adaptation and Growth*. Massachusetts: The MIT Press.

Neufeld, Nora (2014) The Long and Winding Road: How WTO Members Finally Reached a Trade Facilitation Agreement. *WTO Staff Working Paper ERSD-2014-06*. Available at: https://www.wto.org/english/res_e/reser_e/ersd201406_e.htm (consulted 23 August 2024).

Ngang, Carol Chi (2017) Differentiated Responsibilities Under International Law and the Right to Development Paradigm for Developing Countries. *Human Rights and International Legal Discourse* 11(2): 265–288.

Norris, William (2016) *Chinese Economic Statecraft: Commercial Actors, Grand Strategy, and State Control*. Ithaca/London: Cornell University Press.

Obida, Idibia Daniel (2018) African Trade Growth or Trade Deficit: GATT/WTO Rules as Trojan Horse on African Trade Development. *World Journal of Research and Review* 6(2): 70–89.

Oppong, Richard Frimpong (2006) Trade and Human Rights: A Perspective for Agents of Trade Policy Using a Rights-Based Approach to Development. *African Human Rights Law Journal* 6(1): 126–127.

Organisation for Economic Cooperation and Development (2021, June) Agricultural Policy Monitoring and Evaluation 2021: Addressing the Challenges Facing Food Systems. *OECD Publishing*. https://doi.org/10.1787/2d810e01-en (consulted 18 September 2024).

Overseas Development Institute (1977) The Tokyo Round and the Developing Countries. Available at: https://odi.cdn.ngo/media/documents/6612.pdf (consulted 28 July 2024).

Petersmann, Ernst-Ulrich (2003) The Role of the GATS in the Global Trade System. *European Journal of International Law* 14(2): 39–58.

Piron, Laure-Helen (2002) The Right to Development: A Review of the Current State of the Debate for the Department of International Development. *Overseas Development Institute*. Available at: https://www.odi.org/sites/odi.org.uk/files/odi-assets/publications-opinion-files/2317.pdf (consulted 8 December 2024).

Rangnekar, Dwijen (2004) The Socio-Economics of Geographical Indications: A Review of Empirical Evidence from Europe. *UNCTAD-ICTSD Project on IPRs and Sustainable Development—Issue Paper No 8*.

Reichman, Jerome and Hasenzahl, Catherine (2003) Non-Voluntary Licensing of Patented Inventions: Historical Perspective, Legal Framework under TRIPS, and an Overview of the Practice in Canada and the USA. *UNCTAD-ICTSD Project on IPRs and Sustainable Development*.

Reinert, E. (2000) The Global Economy and the Developing Countries: An Overview of Trade, Development and Globalization. In: Jomo, K.S. and Nagaraj, S. (eds) *Globalization Versus Development*. Cham, Switzerland: Palgrave Macmillan, 73–94.

Scott, Robert and Jorgensen, Hilary (2015) China's Accession to the WTO: U.S. Trade Deficits, Jobs, and Industries Affected. *Economic Policy Institute*. Available at: https://www.epi.org/publication/chinas-accession-to-the-wto-u-s-trade-deficits-jobs-and-industries-affected/ (consulted 18 September 2024).

Shafaeddin, Medhi (2000) What did Frederick List Actually Say? Some Clarifications on the Infant Industry Argument. *UNCTAD Discussion Papers No 149*. Available at: https://unctad.org/system/files/official-document/dp_149.en.pdf (consulted 20 June 2024).

Shaffer, Gregory and Meléndez-Ortiz, Ricardo (2010) *Dispute Settlement at the WTO: The Developing Country Experience*. Cambridge: Cambridge University Press.

Shaffer, Gregory and Brenner, Susan (2009) A Trade War with New Tools: Rethinking Embedded Liberalism in the Context of TRIPS. *Minnesota Journal of International Law* 18(2): 274–319.

South Centre (2026, August) The Development Dimension of the GATS Domestic Regulation Negotiations SC/AN/TDP/SV/11. Analytical Note. Available at: https://www.southcentre.int/wp-content/uploads/2013/08/AN_SV11_The-Development-Dimension-of-the-GATS-Domestic-Regulations_EN.pdf (consulted 12 December 2024).

Stevens, Clydenia (2002) The Future of Special and Differential Treatment (S&DT) for Developing Countries in the WTO. *Institute of Development Studies Working Paper 163*. Available at: https://opendocs.ids.ac.uk/opendocs/handle/20.500.12413/3307 (consulted 5 September 2024).

Stevens, Clydenia (2019) Reviving the Right to Development Within the Multilateral Trade Framework Affecting (African) Countries to Actualise Agenda 2063. *African Human Rights Law Journal* 19(2): 470–493.

Stiglitz, Joseph (2002) *Globalization and its Discontents*. New York: W.W. Norton and Company, Inc.

Tania, Sharmin et al (2024) Reimagining the Special and Differential Treatment Provisions in the WTO's Dispute Settlement Understanding. *Asian Journal of International Law* 14(1): 123–153.

The Guardian (2018, 1 March) Trump to Impose Tariffs on Steel and Aluminium Imports in Bold Trade Move. Available at: https://www.theguardian.com/business/2018/mar/01/trump-to-impose-tariffs-on-steel-and-aluminum-imports-in-bold-trade-move (consulted 12 December 2024).

United Nations Millennium Declaration Resolution A/RES/55/2 18 adopted by the General Assembly on 8 September 2000.

United States Government Accountability Office (2020) Agricultural Export Credit Programs: Opportunities to Reduce Redundancy and Improve Efficiencies. Available at: https://www.gao.gov/products/gao-20-35 (consulted 5 October 2024).

Van Grasstek, Craig (2013) *The History and Future of the World Trade Organization*. Lausane: World Trade Organisation.

Wade, Robert Hunter (2003) What Strategies are Viable for Developing Countries Today? The World Trade Organization and the Shrinking of "Development Space". *Review of International Political Economy* 10(4): 621–644.

World Bank (2024) World Development Indicators: Available at: https://data.worldbank.org/indicator/[indicator-code] (consulted 28 August 2024).

World Trade Organisation (1986) The General Agreement on Tariffs and Trade. Available at: https://www.wto.org/english/docs_e/legal_e/gatt47.pdf (consulted 8 December 2024).

World Trade Organisation (2013) Round-the-clock Consultations Produce "Bali Package". *News Items*. Available at: https://www.wto.org/english/news_e/news13_e/mcgsum_07dec13_e.htm (consulted 19 August 2024).

World Trade Organisation (2013) Special and Differential Treatment Provisions. Available at: https://www.wto.org/english/tratop_e/devel_e/dev_special_differential_provisions_e.htm (consulted 3 September 2024).

World Trade Organisation (2024) Members and Observers. Available at: https://www.wto.org/english/thewto_e/whatis_e/tif_e/org6_e.htm (consulted 16 June 2024).

World Trade Organisation (2024) The Doha Round. Available at: https://www.wto.org/english/tratop_e/dda_e/dda_e.htm (consulted 14 August 2024).

CHAPTER 15

The Impact of Corruption on Social and Redistributive Justice and the Right to Development in Africa

Munyai Anzanilufuno

1 Introduction

Justice is distributive and procedural. In the social sciences, justice refers mostly to material wealth.[1] Thus, with consideration of the distribution of wealth, emphasis is on the enhancement of growth and the improvement of livelihood. Additionally, emphasis is on the intertwined relationship between the distribution of wealth and growth. This emphasis grounds the draft International Covenant on the Right to Development (draft Covenant) as it concerns participation and equity. The Cambridge dictionary defines distributive justice as the sharing of resources, goods or opportunities among members of society in a manner that is fair.[2] Considering that distributive justice aims to ensure that diverse members of society share equitably in benefits and burdens, the goal of distributive justice is to ensure the alleviation of economic deprivation and social reform.[3] The crucial question is, how and who ought to conduct the distribution?

As per the above definition, the "how" part of the question can be answered by the fairness approach. Fairness is treating people equally or in a way that is right or reasonable.[4] From this perspective, although often argued to be different, fairness cannot be completely separated from justice and equality as justice denotes the quality of being fair and reasonable.[5] Whereas, equality

1 Iqbal, Munawar; Ali, Salman Syed and Muljawan, Dadang (2007) Advances in Islamic Economics and Finance. *Proceedings of 6th International Conference on Islamic Economic and Finance* 1: 45.

2 Distributive Justice. *Cambridge Dictionary*. Available at: https://dictionary.cambridge.org/dictionary/english/distributive-justice#google_vignette (consulted 29 July 2024).

3 Saban, Liza Ireni (2016) *International Disaster Management Ethics*. New York: State University of New York Press, 40.

4 Rosen, Michael and Young, Annemarie (2018) *What is Right and Wrong? Who Decides? Where Do Values Come From? And Other Big Questions*. London: Hachette Children's Group, 18.

5 Ibid.

 | DOI:10.1163/9789004734357_016

may be understood as treating people in the same way or allowing everyone the same opportunities.[6] Put together, it may be argued that these concepts denote social justice, which is understood "as the fair and equitable distribution of power, resources, and obligations in society of all people, regardless of race, gender, ability status, sexual orientation, and religious or spiritual background".[7]

In a democratic society, social justice reflects inclusion, collaboration, cooperation, equal access and opportunity.[8] For some scholars, social justice accompanies economic justice thus, influencing individual and the social order. In this sense, principles of economic justice involve distributive, participative and social justice.[9] Distributive justice constitutes the foundational component of redistributive justice in that it denotes an approach to make right or remedy the skewed distribution of resources that may impact the wellbeing of society. In other words, redistributive justice is often associated with transitional justice and development.[10] Given the above, the distinction between the social justice approach on societal equality and the redistributive justice premise on resource distribution will be evident in the following discussions.

In light of the definition of the right to development (RTD) in Article 1 of the Declaration on the Right to Development,[11] this chapter articulates three arguments concerning the right to development: First, that the RTD seeks to achieve social justice; second, that the RTD is closely linked to redistributive justice and last, that corruption hampers the attainment of social and redistributive justice and realisation of the RTD. Taking a desktop approach, the arguments presented are laid out from an African perspective. What follows is the introductory remarks on the conceptual framework of social and distributive justice. Thereafter, the chapter delves into the understanding of redistributive justice. Following the conceptual framing, the chapter proceeds to

---

6 Combley, Roz (2011) *Cambridge Business English Dictionary*. Cambridge: Cambridge University Press, 292.

7 Hage, S.M.; Mason, M. and Kim, J. (2011) A Social Justice Approach to Group Counselling. In: Conye, R.K. (ed) *The Oxford Handbook of Group Counselling*. Oxford: Oxford University Press, 103.

8 Ibid.

9 Bhugra, Dinesh; Tribe, Rachel and Poulter, Daniel (2022) Social Justice, Health Equity, and Mental Health. *South African Journal of Psychology* 52(1): 4.

10 See Yusuf, Hakeem and van der Merwe, Hugo (2021) (eds) *Transitional Justice: Theories, Mechanisms and Debates*. New York: Taylor and Francis.

11 The right to development is an inalienable human right by virtue of which every human person and all people are entitled to participate in, contribute to, and enjoy economic, social, cultural and political development, in which all human rights and fundamental freedoms can be fully realised.

set out the essence of the RTD and presents the argument that the right is grounded on social and redistributive justice. Thereafter, corruption and its impact on development in Africa is explored. This is then followed by a synopsis of examples of social and redistributive efforts in selected countries and how they embody the RTD.

2 Conceptual Framework on Social and Distributive Justice

Social justice may be understood as equitable distribution of resources, opportunities, and privileges within society to ensure that all members of society have equal rights and access to basic necessities such as education, healthcare and employment. Social justice is premised on the principle of justice, which supports the maximisation of the welfare of the worst-off people in society. The principle emerged from the doctrine of the social contract established by members of society in order to establish a state or government under conditions of impartiality.[12] For example, the Convention of a Democratic South Africa was a series of negotiations by political parties representing South Africans calling for the establishment of a democratic society.[13]

John Rawls' theory of justice,[14] sets forth the original position, a hypothetical scenario that is used to establish principles of justice.[15] In this position, the veil of ignorance is a moral reasoning device aimed at promoting impartial decisions and denies decision makers potentially using bias information about who will benefit most or least.[16] In other words, factual knowledge about a society's economic and political situation, level of civilisation and culture and the generation of contracting parties' are suspended.[17] In these instances, decisions are made behind the veil of ignorance thus, concealing the current and future social position, abilities, preference and life plans of the contracting parties, which according to Lissowski et al, ensures impartiality.[18] However,

---

12 Lissowski, Grzegorz; Tyszka, Tadeusz and Okrasa, Wlodzimierz (1991) Principles of Distributive Justice: Experiments in Poland and American. *The Journal of Conflict Resolution* 35(1): 99–100.

13 Picard, Louis; Mogale, Thomas and Corrigan, Caitlin (2024) *The South Africa State Transformed? Sanctions, Negotiations, and Elite Pacts 1975–2018*. Cape Town: UCT Press 132–133.

14 See Rawls, John (1971) *Theory of Justice*. Cambridge: Harvard University Press.

15 Lissowski, Tyszka, and Okrasa, supra note 12, 99–100.

16 Huang, Karen; Greene, Joshua and Bazerman, Max (2019) Veil-of-Ignorance Reasoning Favors the Greater Good. *PNAS—Psychological and Cognitive Sciences* 116(48): 23989.

17 Lissowski, Tyszka, and Okrasa, supra note 12, 99–100.

18 Ibid.

"individuals in the original position are allowed general knowledge about human nature, psychology, social life, and the relationship between them".[19] In theory, Rwanda's efforts towards the implementation of policies on unity and reconciliation can be attributed to the promoting equality so as to prevent ethnic discrimination.[20]

Theoretically, social justice can be perceived as being closely associated with equity and distributive justice. Be it that as it may, the two are different. Equity may be understood as an ethical value denoting fairness or justice on how people should be treated.[21] Contextualised within social settings, social equity is also grounded on justice and fairness, but it is more concerned with social policies.[22] In other words, it requires ethical content or foundation to be effective.[23] Distributive justice on its part, is concerned with fairness in allocations. These words are often utilised in the context of justice.[24] Ultimately, these concepts relate to the allocation of resources and the participants involved in the exchange or allocation process.[25]

Social justice is interconnected to distributive and redistributive justice (discussed in the next section). For Nameda et al, there are three principles attributed to distributive justice, which are equality, equity and need.[26] The principle of equity has to do with the allocation of resources to those who contributed more; whereas, the need principle is concerned with the fair allocating of resources to those who need them more.[27] The principle of equality ensures fairness in the division of resources in equal amounts.[28] Considering that the component of fairness denotes equal opportunity, the consideration

19 Ibid.

20 See Republic of Rwanda National Policy of Unity and Reconciliation.

21 Braveman, P. (2016) Health Difference, Disparity, Inequality, or Inequity—What Difference Does it Make What we Call It: An Approach to Conceptualizing and Measuring Health Inequalities and Health Equity. In: Buchbinder, M.; Rivkin-Fish, M. and Walker, R.L. (eds) *Understanding Health Inequalities and Justice: New Conversations Across the Disciples*. Chapel Hill: University of North Carolina Press, 37.

22 Dutta, Subha Deep (2020) *Company Law: Based on Company Act 2013, Including Company Amendment Act* 2020. Uttar Pradesh: Shree Vinayak Publication, 26.

23 Hart, David, (1974) Social Equity, Justice and the Equitable Administrator. *Public Administration Review* 34(1): 3.

24 Cook, Karen and Hegtvedt, Karen (1983) Distributive Justice, Equity, and Equality. *Annual Review of Sociology* 9: 218.

25 Ibid at 219.

26 Nameda, Akinobu et al (2023) Distributive Justice and Development: Toward an Integrative Understanding of Reward and Responsibility Distributions. *Journal of Moral Education* 52(4): 436.

27 Ibid.

28 Ibid.

of equality of opportunity is very difficult to achieve or apply because of the complex nature of the term "opportunity" and the historical legacies of inequality. In these instances, distributive justice arises with the context of affirmative action and often racial integration policies.[29] For Africans, the African Union has undertaken initiatives towards equality and social justice through for example, the African Union Strategy for Gender Equality and Women's Empowerment 2018–2028; and Agenda 2063: The Africa We Want.

Society thrives by sharing available resources. In instances where the distribution of resources is unfair, it could lead to conflict. In other words, a peaceful society exists where there is a fair allocation of resources and where people are satisfied with the outcome of resource distribution particularly, because this relates to the overall development of people.[30] This is supported in the United Nations 1958 Resolution 1161, stating that where there is "a balance and integrated economic and social development …" it "would contribute towards the promotion and maintenance of peace and security, social progress and better standings of living, and the observance of and respect for human rights and fundamental freedoms".[31] Bearing this in mind, Botswana is the second most peaceful country in Africa according to the 2024 Global Peace Index,[32] the least corrupt country and 70% of its land is tribal with 25% owned by the state and 5% privately owned.[33]

In outlining the notion of distributive justice, Nameda et al lay out two types of resource distribution: reward distribution, which has to do with allocating resources for work done; and responsibility distribution, which describes the sharing of burdens and responsibilities.[34] For some, distribution of resources cannot be isolated from economics as the latter often determines the share of production through market exchange processes, which often, is utilised in giving little attention to redistribution and its impact on social justice and equity.[35] The reality is that wealth and income are concerned with numerous economic, political and social activities classified as market or non-market activities.[36] Simply put, individuals with access to and control of market opportunities are

29 Cook and Hegtvedt, supra note 24, 221.

30 Nameda et al, supra note 26, 435.

31 Balanced and Integrated Economic and Social progress, Resolution 1161(XII), adopted by the United Nations General Assembly 158.

32 Vision of Humanity (2024) Global Peace Index. Available at: https://www.visionofhumanity.org/maps/#/ (consulted 24 October 2024).

33 Krassov, Oleg Igorevich (2022) *Land Law in African Countries*. Moscow: Norma, 318.

34 Nameda et al, supra note 26, 435.

35 Iqbal, Ali and Muljawan, supra note 1, 44.

36 Ibid.

likely to accumulate wealth consequently, reflecting a capitalist system. For scholars such as Iqbal et al, a capitalist system is characterised by free market activities and distribution of income and wealth, which are considered just.[37] However, the socialist system considers market activities as being exploitative and that the distribution generated in the market system is unjust and hence, advocates for socialism in ensuring effective redistribution as a means to attain justice.[38] Greater clarity is provided on this in the discussion that follows.

3 An Overview of Redistributive Justice

As previously mentioned, redistributive justice may be understood as the (re)distribution of resources and opportunities, often, in instances where there was, or is a skewed distribution of resources. The initiative to redistribute often occurs through economic policies or social programmes aimed at promoting development and prohibiting inequality. According to Ennser-Jedenastik, different social programmes are often based on redistributive justice principles such as equity, equality or need.[39] The principle of equity provides that the benefits received should be proportional to one's contribution. In other words, those who contribute more, should be given more if they are unable to provide for themselves due to, for example, loss of unemployment or disability.[40] The principle of equality provides that each member of society or group should be treated equally, receiving the same support irrespective of social status, income, contribution or need. For Ennser-Jedenastik, "the equality principle is said to be dominant when the maintenance of social harmony and good social relations between individuals is the primary goal of a group".[41] The principle of need provides that those who are worst-off, should have help extended to them. In other words, those with the greatest need "should receive the largest amount of assistance" thus, prioritising individual development and welfare.[42] The need principle is independent of nativism in instances where the need is defined within economic terms as opposed to ethnic or racial terms.[43]

37 Ibid.

38 Ibid.

39 Ennser-Jedenastik, Laurenz (2018) Welfare Chauvinism in Populist Radical Right Platforms: The Role of Redistributive Justice Principles. *Social Policy Administration* 52(1): 294.

40 Ibid at 296.

41 Ibid.

42 Ibid.

43 Ibid at 298.

In politics, redistribution of resources is often associated with welfare chauvinism whereby, there is a need to prioritise native-born citizens. In this instance, welfare benefits are granted exclusively to certain persons based on the criteria of citizenship, race, ethnicity or religion. This position is classified as a leftist stance,[44] which is likely to support corruption and foster discriminatory, exclusionary or selective allocation of resources. Consequently, the implementation of such an approach fails to support social inclusion and affects redistributive justice by undermining equity, social reform and development for all members of society. Although most radical political parties take this stance, some appear to be premised on the underlying principles of social justice, which ought to anchor on fair distribution of social benefits and burdens.[45] This perspective provides that all benefits should be distributed equitably irrespective of ethnicity, race or citizenship.[46]

For Davidoff, any proposal that aims to further distribution standards is unacceptable and thus, he supports states working towards ensuring greater equity between citizen, and further argues that any proposal or action aimed at increasing "wealth, health, industrial growth, and so forth of a society while maintaining the status quo in regard to the distribution of those values have been judged improper or unjust".[47] In essence, this perspective suggests that public policy proposals should rather aim to bridge the gap between those who have much and those who have little. In other words, there should be consideration of equity with respect to the huge gap between the wealthy and the impoverished.[48] Accordingly, redistributive justice entails the fair (re)allocation or (re)distribution of wealth and resources within a society, involving policies on welfare programmes, affirmative action to address economic inequalities and providing support to marginalised groups.

4 Bearing of the Right to Development on Corruption, Social and Redistributive Justice

The draft Covenant on the Right to Development defines development as "[...] a comprehensive civil, cultural, economic, environmental, political and

44 Ibid at 294.
45 Ibid at 295.
46 Ibid at 297.
47 Davidoff, Paul (1975) Working Toward Redistributive Justice. *Journal of the American Institute of Planner* 41(5): 317.
48 Ibid at 317.

social process" aimed at improving or advancing the well-being of people.[49] This process should give people a feeling that something has changed, and convey optimism, progress and improvement of their conditions as human beings. Furthermore, it must convey emphasis of social change in ensuring the enjoyment of improved livelihood and better quality of life.[50] This process should leave people with a sense of empowerment collectively and individually by providing opportunities to equip themselves with the productive capabilities necessary for sustaining livelihood.[51] The process must indeed, be transformative. Despite the perception that it is a subjective concept, the process for development is one that entails change and within the context of social groups, development denotes an ongoing enhancement in the ability to adapt and coordinate both internal and external relationships.[52]

The RTD is defined in Article 1(1) of the Declaration on the Right to Development. The definition is mirrored in Article 4 of the draft Covenant.[53] It is anchored in Articles 1(3) and 55 of the Charter of the United Nations and in Articles 27(1), 28 and 29 of the Universal Declaration of Human Rights.[54] Its legal status can also be traced to the International Covenant on Civil and Political Rights and the International Covenant on Economic, Social and Cultural Rights.[55] In fact, the international bill of human rights broadly embodies elements of the RTD notably, through the incorporation of, for instance, economic, social and cultural rights among others.[56]

Article 22 of the African Charter on Human and Peoples Rights (African Charter) states that

---

49 Draft International Covenant on the Right to Development—Report by the Chair-Rapporteur of the Working Group on the Right to Development, Zamir Akram (Pakistan) Human Rights Council A/HRC/54/50 54th Session, 6 October 2023.

50 Muhammad, Ibrahim; Wasiu, Sanusi Abdul and Gado, Muddassir Ahmad (2023) Corruption and its Impact on Socio-Economic Development in Selected Countries of Africa. *African Journal of Politics and Administrative Studies* 16(2): 29.

51 Ngang, Carol Chi (2019) Systems Problem and a Pragmatic Insight on the Right to Development Governance for Africa. *African Human Rights Law Journal* 19(2): 390–393.

52 Muhammad, Wasiu and Gado, supra note 50, 2.

53 Draft Covenant on the Right to Development, supra note 49.

54 Kimber, Norman (2023) The Human Right to Development: Historical and Contemporary Linkage to Colonialism. Master of Studies in Law, University of Western Ontario, 2.

55 International Covenant on Economic, Social and Cultural Rights (ICESCR), Resolution 2200A(XXI), adopted by the UN General Assembly 1966; International Covenant on Civil and Political Rights (ICCPR), Resolution 2200A(XXI), adopted by the UN General Assembly 1966.

56 Aziz, Muhammad Rashid; Arif, Sardar and Bannian, Bushra (2023) Historical, Regional and International Law Perspectives on the Right to Development: An Overview. *Pakistan Social Sciences Review* 7(3): 626.

> All peoples shall have the right to their economic, social and cultural development with due regard to their freedom and identity and in the equal enjoyment of the common heritage of mankind. States shall have the duty, individually or collectively, to ensure the exercise of the right to development.[57]

The African Charter recognises the RTD as legally binding and enforceable.[58] Some of the state parties have gone further to incorporate the right in their respective national constitutions.[59] In the interpretation and application of Article 22, the Court in the *Ogoni* case held that the right of the Ogoni people where not protected by the state of Nigeria and that their RTD was consequently, violated.[60] In interpreting Article 22, the African Commission on Human and Peoples' Right in the *Endorois* case held that Kenya had the burden to provide favourable conditions for the development of the Endorois community; that the Endorois were entitled to an equitable distribution of the benefits that derived from the game reserve and that they suffered violations of Article 22.[61]

Development and human rights are interdependent and mutually supportive in that sustainable development for instance, cannot occur without full respect for human rights. Likewise, in the absence of development the full enjoyment of human rights cannot be realised. Realisation of the RTD thus, entails the enjoyment of civil and political as well as economic, social and cultural rights.[62] To achieve this, states have a duty to develop appropriate national policies aimed at improving the well-being of their populations and individually, promote participation in the development process and enjoyment of the benefits of development.[63]

---

57 African Union, African Charter on Human and Peoples' Rights, adopted in Nairobi, Kenya, on 27 June 1981. OAU Doc CAB/LEG/67/3 Rev. 5 (1981).

58 Aziz, Arif and Bannian, supra note 56, 628.

59 See for example, Sect 24(a)(iii) of the Constitution of the Republic of South African, Sect 30 of the Constitution of the Republic of Malawi of 1998, Art 58 of the Constitution of Democratic Republic of Congo of 2006 and Art 43 of the Constitution of Kenya of 2010. Aziz, Arif and Bannian, supra note 56, 628.

60 *Social and Economic Rights Action Centre* (SERAC) *and Another v Nigeria* (*Ogoni* case) Comm 155/96 (2001) AHRLR 60 (ACHPR 2001).

61 *Centre for Minority Rights Development (Kenya) and Minority Rights Group International on behalf of Endorois Welfare Council v Kenya* 276/2003.

62 Alasttal, Abdelrahman; Maskun, Abdul and Sakharina, Iin Karita (2023) The Role of the United Nations in Protecting the Right to Development in Occupied Palestine. *Legality: Jurnal Ilmiah Hulum* 3(1): 139.

63 Kimber, supra note 54, ii.

In 1998, the Intergovernmental Open-ended Working Group on the Right to Development was established with the mandate to oversee the process of drafting a binding treaty on the RTD.[64] In 2020, the Working Group released the draft Convention on the Right to Development,[65] subsequently, renamed the International Covenant on the Right to Development. On matters relating to social and redistribution justice, the Preamble to the draft Covenant buttresses the role of development in improving human wellbeing.[66] In seeking to realise development, it acknowledges obstacles, including poverty, inequality and corruption, which must be eliminated.[67] As discussed earlier, social justice aims to ensure equal social, economic and political rights and opportunities whereas, redistributive justice aims to redistribute resources, wealth and opportunities to everyone. Against this background, it is argued that the draft Covenant embodies social and redistributive justice. This is supported by sections of the Preamble, emphasising on:

- Equality of opportunity for development;
- Civil, cultural, economic, environmental, political and social processes fall within the scope of development aimed at advancing the well-being of everyone; and
- Active, free and meaningful participation of everyone in the development process and in the fair distribution of benefits.[68]

There are other provisions in the draft Covenant that mirror social and redistributive justice. These provisions include Article 4(2), Article 5(3) and Article 12(2).[69]

Corruption has a direct negative impact on development outcomes.[70] It hinders development efforts through theft, misappropriation, expropriation and mismanagement of state resources for private benefit. Consequently, for most countries in Africa, high rates of corruption are perpetuated through misappropriation of state resources, causing a direct negative impact on both development and governance.[71] It is generally accepted that developing countries that experience high poverty rates, low economic growth, political instability

64 Teshome, Roman Girma (2022) The Draft Convention on the Right to Development: A New Dawn to the Recognition of the Right to Development as a Human Right. *Human Rights Law Review* 22(2): 1.

65 Ibid.

66 Draft Covenant on the Right to Development, supra note 49.

67 Ibid.

68 Ibid.

69 Ibid.

70 Muhammad, Wasiu, and Gado, supra note 50, 29.

71 Kimenyi, Mwangi et al (2021) Foresight Africa: The Continent's Greatest Challenges and Opportunities for 2011. *Brookings*, 30–31.

and poor healthcare are most vulnerable to corruption.[72] Consequently, alongside affecting the well-being of people, the widespread perpetration of corruption in economically impoverished or developing countries could lead to low public sector salaries due to fiscal distortions and deprivation of state revenue; affects risk management efforts by undermining decision making processes and resource allocations for the identification, assessment and management of risk.[73]

Corruption indeed, aggravates pre-existing challenges faced by a state. For instance, considering how corruption does not promote development, the rate of poverty in a state are likely to increase when corruption increases. This is supported by the notion that corruption has greater devastating consequences in poor or developing countries than in developed or rich countries.[74] For example, the 2023 United Nations list of least developed countries includes the Democratic Republic of Congo.[75] The Democratic Republic of Congo is amongst the countries with the highest corruption rates globally as per Transparency International Corruption Perception Index (CPI),[76] and the second country to Nigeria with the highest number of people living in extreme poverty.[77] In light of this statistics, the link between corruption and development is supported by Desta who outlines the relationship between high corruption and developing countries, which has a negative impact on economic growth, social justice and contributes towards political instability.[78] Desta however, notes that corruption is not a conundrum of exclusively developing countries.[79] Statistics show that corruption does exist in developed countries as well.[80] Desta's emphasis is that in countries that are grappling with economic underdevelopment, political instability and social injustice are likely to be witnessed.[81]

72 Desta, Yemane (2019) Manifestation and Causes of Civil Service Corruption in Developing Countries. *Journal of Public Administration and Governance* 9(3): 23–24.

73 Ibid at 29.

74 Ibid at 23–24.

75 UN List of Least Developed Countries. *UN Conference on Trade and Development*. Available at: https://unctad.org/topic/least-developed-countries/list (consulted 28 July 2014).

76 Transparency International (2023) Corruption Perceptions Index: Democratic Republic of Congo. *Transparency International*. Available at: https://www.transparency.org/en/cpi/2023/index/cod (consulted 30 July 2024).

77 Galal, Saifaddin (2024) African Countries with the Highest Share of Global Population Living below the Extreme Poverty Line in 2024. *Statista*. Available at: https://www.statista.com/statistics/1228553/extreme-poverty-as-share-of-global-population-in-africa-by-country/ (consulted 28 July 2024).

78 Desta, supra note 72, 32.

79 Ibid at 32.

80 The Transparency International CPI reveals that Denmark, Sweden, Germany and Finland and United States also experience corruption.

81 Desta, supra note 72, 32.

Considering the above, it is indisputable that corruption can hinder developing and poor countries from the realisation of the RTD. The Preamble to the draft Covenant highlights the obstacles, to realising the RTD, including poverty, inequality and corruption.[82] As a remedy, Article 13 of the draft Covenant provides for state parties' duty to cooperate. Article 13(4) particularly, provides that state parties recognise the need—

> to create a social and international order conducive to the realization of the right to development by, inter alia:
> [...]
> j) Eliminating illicit financial flows by combating tax evasion and corruption, reducing opportunities for tax avoidance, enhancing disclosure and transparency in financial transactions in both source and destination countries and strengthening the recovery and return of stolen assets.[83]

Highlighting corruption as one of the hindrances to the realisation of the RTD, the draft Covenant enshrines in Article 18, a preventative measure against corruption, requiring states parties to individually and jointly;

a) promote and strengthen measures to prevent and combat corruption;
b) promote, facilitate and support international cooperation and technical assistance in the prevention of and fight against corruption [...];
c) promote integrity, accountability and proper management of public affairs and public property;
d) ensure financial integrity and transparency.[84]

As with any international treaty, there are limitations to the above cited provision. First, the provision does not compel states to any obligation in preventing or suppressing corruption. For a state that has high corruption rate, there is little likelihood to adhere to this provision. Second, there is no specific enforcement mechanism if states parties fail to adhere to the provisions of the draft Covenant. Despite this, one of the significant benefits pertaining to the prevention and suppression of corruption is that the draft Covenant promotes cooperation among states in combating corruption. This is particularly, evident in Article 13(j) on the recovery and return of assets. Although the draft Covenant is not final, some states have entered into agreements aimed at recovering and returning assets. For example, the Framework for the Return of Assets from

82 Ibid.
83 Ibid.
84 Ibid.

Corruption and Crime in Kenya (FRACCK) is a multilateral initiative between Kenya, the United Kingdom, Switzerland and Jersey.[85] Another multilateral agreement is that between Nigeria, Switzerland and the World Bank to repatriate the assets of the late Sani Abacha.[86] These agreements have successfully let to the return of assets. For example, at least USD 3.7 million located in an account in Jersey was returned to Kenya;[87] and at least USD 32 million returned to Nigeria.[88] Although multilateral agreements indicate effectiveness, African states must demonstrate political will towards these agreements given the prominence of illicit financial flows in offshore accounts.

Regarding the realisation of the RTD and the elimination of obstacles to development, states may co-operate by formulating development policies aimed at realising this right.[89] Specifically referencing developing countries, the draft Covenant recognises that international co-operation is important for the economic development of developing countries, and that cooperation among these countries must be based on the principles of equality, self-determination and economic development as a means to attain economic independence.[90] The emphasis on co-operation is to provide support to countries regardless of their size or wealth in an attempt to ensure that they participate and enjoy the benefits of international trade for their own economic development and social progress.[91] Importantly, and notwithstanding the need for co-operation, every state has the duty and the right in determining their social development or progress,[92] which however, is hindered by corruption as illustrate in the next section.

85 FRACCK Agreement with Kenya Illustrates that Partnership is Essential when the Disposal of Confiscated Assets should Benefit Development. *Basel Institute on Governance*. Available at: https://baselgovernance.org/news/fracck-agreement-kenya-illustrates-partnership-essential-when-disposal-confiscated-assets (consulted 30 July 2024).

86 Ajakaye, Rafiu (2017, 6 December) Nigeria Inks Deal to Repatriate $321M of "Stolen Funds". Available at: https://www.aa.com.tr/en/africa/nigeria-inks-deal-to-repatriate-321m-of-stolen-funds/989895 (consulted 30 July 2024).

87 Stolen Asset Recovery Initiative. Available at: https://star.worldbank.org/asset-recovery-watch-database/windward-trading-40220150350-case (consulted 23 October 2024).

88 Stolen Asset Recovery Initiative. Available at: https://star.worldbank.org/asset-recovery-watch-database/2010-halliburton-nigeria-bribery-settlement-agreement-us325-million#disclaimer (consulted 23 October 2024).

89 Kimber, supra note 54, ii.

90 Balanced and integrated economic and social progress. See also Article 13 of the Draft International Covenant on the Right to Development.

91 Aziz, Arif and Bannian, supra note 56, 630.

92 Ibid at 630.

5 Synopsis of Corruption and Its Impact on Development in Africa

Corruption is often described as the abuse of power for private or personal gain.[93] Though general, this description is limited as it unnecessarily narrows down corruption to the misuse of public power for private gains. Corruption is also understood in different ways and in different forms.[94] Conceived a bit more broadly, corruption can be understood as a behaviour or conduct that can be perpetrated by an individual or a consortium with devasting consequences on others, institutions and on a country.[95] For the most part, it can be described as a practice, perception and attitude.[96] Notwithstanding the varying understandings, corruption should by no means, be limited to public officials. In describing corruption, it is imperative for the concept to not be seen exclusively as a set of practices, but rather as a framework in interpreting what is considered ethical or harmful.

There are various contributing factors that influence corruption. For Jungo et al, one of the contributing factors towards the systematising of corruption in Africa is the low levels of education by the populations across the continent, militarisation of political systems and influence of the state in the economy, which according to scholars, contribute to the looting of public funds.[97] For them, corruption is even far higher in countries that are considered poor thus, making it difficult for those countries to progress economically.[98] This is made worse in instances where there is mismanagement of resources, and weak economic policies, which in turn leads to increased inequality and poverty rates on the continent.[99]

Irrespective of the different perceptions on or factors influencing corruption, the latter has a negative impact on growth and development in any country. From a socio-economic perspective, corruption does not benefit any society. It only enriches a few individuals and their allies, resulting in societal

93 Munyai, Anzanilufuno (2020) *Overcoming the Corruption Conundrum in Africa: A Socio-legal Perspective*. Newcastle upon Tyne: Cambridge Scholars Publishing, 3–4.

94 Graycar, Adam (2015) Corruption: Classification and Analysis. *Policy and Society* 34(2): 87–96.

95 Saputra, Farhan and Saputra, Ebit Bima (2021) Measures of Corruption: Needs, Opportunity and Rationalisation. *Journal of Law Politics and Humanities* 2(1): 42–43.

96 Aluko, Opeyemi Idowu (2020) Breaking the Cycle of Corruption in Nigeria: The Myth and Reality. *Journal of Co-operative and Business Studies* 5(1): 116.

97 Jungo, João; Madaleno, Mara and Botelho, Anabela (2023) Controlling Corruption in African Countries: Innovation, Financial Inclusion and Access to Education as Alternatives Measures. *International Journal of Social Economics* 50(6): 766–767.

98 Ibid.

99 Ibid.

discontent and loss of trust in the political system. This is premised on how corruption enables political elites in using their positions for personal gains.[100] Furthermore, from a socio-economic point of view, developing countries get affected by virtue of an increasing number of individuals living outside the financial system because of high corruption rates. This may be due to the consideration that money is the lubricant for corruption and illicit activities such as money laundering, bribery and tax evasion.

Considering the discussion on RTD above, it is worth noting that irrespective of a country's level of development, corruption hampers development processes and initiatives mostly through the diversion of public funds. Generally, the effects of corruption are most common in the public sector usually, through looting, stealing or misappropriating of funds for private use instead of for the public interest.[101] Considering the different forms it may take to understand its impact, one must recognise the political, social, and economic conceptual facets of corruption.[102] From a social perspective, corruption erodes the social fabric. It affects the underprivileged significantly by exacerbating their struggles and need for basic education, healthcare, water and sanitation amongst other things. The deprivation widens the inequality gap, making the rich richer and the poor poorer, resulting in the marginalised being excluded.[103] From an economic perspective, corruption has enormous consequences on developing countries thus, impedes economic growth, distorts markets, and deters foreign investment opportunities amongst other things.[104] From a political point of view, corruption weakens government structures, undermines the rule of law, and erodes public trust.[105]

For Gök, corruption in Africa was introduced during the colonial era considering how pre-colonial Africa was established on strong ethical values on social justice and compliance.[106] Whether or not accurate, the statistics demonstrate that following independence from colonial rule, corruption has been a massive

---

100 Mlambo, Daniel et al (2019) Corruption and its Implications for Development and Good Governance: A Perspective from Post-Colonial Africa. *Journal of Economic and Behavioural Studies* 11(1): 39.

101 Aluko, supra note 96, 115.

102 Ibid at 116.

103 Jayalakshmi, H. and Kachhi, Z. (2024) Strategies for Combating Corruption in Poverty Alleviation. In: Yakubu, I.N. (ed) *Examining Corruption and the Sustainable Development Goals*. Pennsylvania: IGI Global, 255.

104 Ibid.

105 Ibid.

106 Gök, Adem (2021) Determinants of Corruption: The Case of sub-Saharan Africa. *Ankara University Journal of Political Sciences* 76(2): 524.

hurdle to prospects for development[107] and prevented Africa from achieving continental economic growth.[108] Gök further notes that colonialism was a source of grand systematic corruption in sub-Saharan Africa in the sense that the process of subjugation contaminated existing ethnical values, checks and balances and indigenous standards that existed in various regions.[109]

Many years later in post-colonial Africa, corruption has resulted in numerous fragile and underdeveloped economies and the exploitation of public funds and institutions for private gains.[110] In other words, the prevalence of corruption in Africa undermines integrity, democratic principles, accountability, morality and fairness as well as weakens democratic governance, resulting in socio-economic underdevelopment across the continent.[111] When corruption undermines governance, it distorts public policy, the public and private sectors and also economic growth.[112]

The culture of corruption deprives states from exploring substantial political, economic and social development particularly, where corruption is systemic and entrenched in all levels of governance.[113] It is therefore, a misconception that it is only corruption perpetrated by public officials that is detrimental to society. Corruption in the private sector equally has the same detrimental effects.[114] For Africa, it is no surprise that the more prevalent corruption becomes, internal problems are followed by political instability.

It is generally accepted that bad governance in Africa is born from high levels of corruption due to its direct contribution to socio-economic underdevelopment. Countries with high levels of corruption are prone to experiencing high levels of poverty and unemployment, which is worsened when decision makers use their powers for personal gains.[115]

Notwithstanding various anti-corruption efforts, the prevalence of corruption has proven to abort such efforts and their effectiveness, particularly where it (corruption) is promoted by corrupt leaders who engage in theft,

---

107 Muhammad, Wasiu, and Gado, supra note 50, 33.

108 Mlambo et al 2019, supra note 100, 39.

109 Gök, supra note 106, 524.

110 Mlambo, Daniel; Mubecua, Mandla and Mlambo, Victor (2023) Post-Colonial Independence and Africa's Corruption Conundrum: A Succinct South African Critique Post-Democratisation. *Insights on Africa* 15(2): 186.

111 Muhammad, Wasiu, and Gado supra note 50, 25.

112 Gök, supra note 106, 524.

113 Mlambo, Mubecua, and Mlambo 2023, supra note 110, 185.

114 Duri, Jorum (2020) Overview of Corruption and Anti-Corruption in sub-Saharan Africa. *CHR Michelsen Institute*, 14.

115 Gök, supra note 106, 525.

misappropriation or embezzlement of public funds, nepotism and money laundering.[116] Corruption in Africa is unmistakeably plain, with the funds lost in the process, depriving the countries of needed essential services such as education, housing and healthcare among others.[117] As a consequence, states' failure to provide economic freedom and access to basic resources results in the erosion of public trust in the principles of equality, neutrality, accountability, representativeness, and the fair allocation of resources,[118] components or attributes that fundamentally ground the exercise of the RTD.

In extreme cases of corruption, owing to the fear of losing power or fear of prosecution and confiscation of their wealth, some African leaders resort to violence thus, disrupting democracy and adherence to the principle of accountability.[119] For example, in his thirty-seven year rule, the former President of Zimbabwe, Robert Mugabe had swirled allegations of corruption, which became one of the basis for his forced removal from power in 2017.[120] In other examples, Mobuto Sese Seko of Zaire (now DRC) is believed to have looted millions of US dollars during his tenure.[121] Frederick Chiluba of Zambia was implicated in the misappropriation of millions from taxpayers,[122] Teodoro Theodorin Nguema Obiang, Vice President of Equatorial New Guinea has been under investigation for corruption with an order issued in 2023 to seize his assets.[123]

Despite various anti-corruption instruments, one of the major challenges in Africa in the fight against corruption is either attributed to the lack of active political will or poor oversight mechanisms. The 2023 Transparency International CPI in the public sector revealed that corruption thrives due to weakened judicial systems and a decline in public officials being held accountable

116 Example Omar al-Bashir sentenced to two years of corruption and Ehud Omert convicted of bribery. See also Muhammad, Wasiu, and Gado, supra note 50, 33.

117 Mlambo, Mubecua, and Mlambo 2023, supra note 110, 185.

118 Ibid.

119 Ibid at 188.

120 BBC (2021) British American Tobacco Negotiated Bribe for Mugabe, New Evidence Suggests. *British Broadcasting Corporation*. Available at: https://www.bbc.com/news/world-58517339 (consulted 31 July 2024).

121 Newton, Michael (2010) *Crime and Criminals*. New York: Infobase Publishing, 78.

122 Shacinda, Shapi (2007) Zambia's Chiluba Hit with 23 Million Pounds for Graft. *Reuters*. Available at: https://reuters.com/article/world/zambia-s-chiluba-hit-with-23-million-pounds-for-graft-idUSL04300150/ (consulted 31 July 2024).

123 Skrdlik, Josef (2023) South Africa Seizes Teodoro Nguema Obiang Mangue's Superyacht. *Organized Crime and Corruption Reporting Project*. Available at: https://www.occrp.org/en/daily/17327-south-africa-seizes-teodoro-nguema-obiang-mangue-s-superyacht (consulted 29 July 2024).

for their actions thus, seemingly increasing impunity for corruption.[124] When this happens, the vulnerable and the marginalised are primarily affected in that their access to justice is restricted by dint of the rich and powerful haven captured the justice system.[125] This reality regrettably allows access to justice mostly to the rich who are capable of paying bribes. This restriction of justice for the impoverished and the marginalised sustains inequality and thus, hinders the realisation and enjoyment of the RTD.

The 2023, the Transparency International CPI data reveals that the least corrupt country in Africa is Seychelles with a score of 71, ranking 20 out of 180 countries while other least corrupt African countries include Cape Verde, Botswana and Rwanda, ranking 30, 39 and 49 respectively.[126] By a 2022 survey conducted by Afrobarometer, a greater number of Cape Verdeans hold the view that some public officials are involved in corruption including the police and judicial officers.[127] In terms of the enjoyment of freedoms, the 2023/2024 survey by Freedom House scored Cape Verde at 91 out of 100 thus, signalling being free (not necessarily completely free) in the Global Freedom Score calculated taking into account political rights, and civil liberties.[128] At the time of writing, there was no study on democracy score conducted. There was also no democracy score conducted in Botswana, however in terms of the Global Freedom Score, Botswana scored 72 out of 100 and thus, considered free.[129]

In contrast, the African countries rated as most corrupt according to Transparency International 2023 CPI are Somalia, South Sudan and Equatorial Guinea.[130] In terms of the 2023/2024 Global Freedom Score, Equatorial Guinea scored 5 out of 100 thus classified as not free, scored zero in political rights, and 5 out of 60 in civil liberties.[131] Similarly, Somalia was classified as not being free with a score of 8 out of 100, a score 2 out of 40 for political rights, and 6 out of 60 for civil liberties.[132] South Sudan had the worst score of the three

124 Transparency International (2023) Corruption Perceptions Index. *Transparency International*. Available at: https://www.transparency.org/en/cpi/2023 (consulted 29 July 2024).

125 Ibid.

126 Ibid.

127 Afrosondagem, Summary of Results: Afrobarometer Round Survey in Cabo Verde 2002.

128 Freedom in the World (2024) Carbo Verde. *Freedom House*. Available at: https://freedomhouse.org/country/cabo-verde/freedom-world/2024 (consulted 29 July 2024).

129 Freedom in the World (2024) Botswana. *Freedom House*. Available at: https://freedomhouse.org/country/botswana/freedom-world/2024 (consulted 29 July 2024).

130 Transparency International 2023, supra note 125.

131 Freedom in the World (2024) Equatorial Guinea. *Freedom House*. Available at: https://freedomhouse.org/country/equatorial-guinea/freedom-world/2024 (consulted 29 July 2024).

132 Freedom in the World (2024) Somalia. *Freedom House*. Available at: https://freedomhouse.org/country/somalia/freedom-world/2024 (consulted 29 July 2024).

countries with a score of 1 out of 100 thus considered not free, a score of -3 out of 40 for political rights and 4 out of 60 for civil liberties.[133] According to the Afrobarometer survey results released in 2024, a greater number of Sudanese revealed that some public officials are involved in corruption including civil servants, the police, judicial officers, traditional and religious leaders. The results revealed that majority of the Sudanese believe that corruption increased tremendously in the past year.[134] It is important to emphasise that as of 2024, there is ongoing conflicts in South Sudan and Somalia.[135]

The discussion on corruption illustrates that it is a complex phenomenon, involving complex contributing factors and an overall negative impact on social justice, redistributive justice and realisation of the RTD. Although corruption is rife and may remain on the rise for years to come, the efforts of African countries in eradicating the pandemic ought to be recognised. However, a concerning aspect indicative of the data highlighted above is that in some African countries like South Sudan and Somalia, corruption is not only rife, the countries' level of democracy are also considerably low, which affects the populations' freedom and the exercise of their civil and political rights. In such instances and conditions, realisation of the RTD will be a herculean task.

6 Specific Examples in Africa

The preceding discussions outlined the conceptual frameworks on corruption, social justice, redistributive justice and the RTD. The analysis on the selected countries that follows, is intended to demonstrate the extent of corruption, their commitment to the RTD, and efforts, if any, towards social and redistributive justice. According to the 2023 Transparency International CPI, South Africa ranked 83 out of 180 countries with a score of 41 out of 100.[136] South Africa's lowest CPI score was captured in 2016, ranking 64 out of 176 countries with a score of 45 out of 100.[137] Notwithstanding these results, Corruption Watch,

133 Freedom in the World 2024: South Sudan. *Freedom House.* Available at: https://freedomhouse.org/country/south-sudan/freedom-world/2024 accessed 29 July 2024 (consulted 29 July 2024).

134 Sudan Polling Statistics Centre (2024) Afrobarometer Round 9 Survey in Sudan 2022: Summary of Results. *Afrobarometer*, 45–47.

135 See World Report 2024.

136 Transparency International 2023, supra note 125.

137 Transparency International (2016) Corruption Perceptions Index. *Transparency International.* Available at: https://www.transparency.org/en/cpi/2016 (consulted 30 July 2024).

a non-profit organisation reporting corruption in South Africa, reported in 2024 that:

- 65% of South African participants indicated scepticism of law enforcement agencies in effectively combating corruption;[138]
- Participants concur that the demographics mostly affected by corruption include unemployed youth (75%), women and children (70%), those living in rural areas (69%) and people living with disabilities (68%);[139]
- Participants consider the areas mostly affected by corruption are housing and land (73%), protection of communities (69%) and quality education (68%).[140]

Considering the perception of corruption and the effect of apartheid, it is no surprise that South Africa is rated the most unequal country in the world in terms of income, wealth or standard of living.[141] In 2023, the World Bank Gini coefficient ranked South Africa as the country with the highest income inequality in the world.[142] With the available data on corruption and inequality, South Africa recognises the outcomes that the RTD can yield. In fact, South Africa is one of the 29 countries that voted in favour of the draft Covenant on 12 October 2023.[143]

South Africa has been engaged in numerous efforts focused on social and redistributive justice. This includes the constitutional provisions on progressive realisation of socio-economic rights enshrined in the Bill of Rights;[144] the Growth, Employment and Redistribution strategy adopted in post-apartheid South Africa and the Broad-Based Black Economic Empowerment (BBBEE) policy intended to address the economic inequalities created by the apartheid regime (effective to date).[145] The BBBEE policy aims to empower the majority of black South Africans who were oppressed by the apartheid regime. Shava explains that the BBBEE policy seeks to reallocate wealth by changing the functioning of different sectors with a primary focus to transform the economy

138 Corruption Watch (2024) The Impact of Corruption: Insights from a Perception and Experience Survey. *Corruption Watch.* Available at: https://www.corruptionwatch.org.za/wp-content/uploads/2024/05/Corruption-Watch-Report-Experiences-and-Perceptions_FINAL.pdf, 17 (consulted 30 July 2024).

139 Ibid at 23–24.

140 Ibid at 25–26.

141 McKeever, Matthew (2023) Social Stratification and Inequality in South Africa. *Sociology Compass* 18(2): 1.

142 Ibid.

143 United Nations Human Rights Council (2023) The Right to Development (A/HRC/54/L.27).

144 Sects 26 and 27 of the Constitution of the Republic of South Africa of 1996.

145 Shava, Elvin (2016) Black Empowerment in South Africa: Challenges and Prospects. *Journal of Economics and Behavioural Studies* 8(6): 161.

to enable black South Africans actively participate in economic activities and promote economic growth.[146]

In the 2023 Transparency International CPI, Rwanda ranked 49 out of 180 countries with a scope of 53 out of 100,[147] whereas in 2022 it ranked 54 with a score of 51.[148] In addition to Rwanda's ranking among Africa's top five least corrupt countries,[149] it also ranks as one of the countries with the lowest poverty rates in Africa. In terms of the 2024 extreme poverty line data on African countries, Rwanda scored the lowest with 0.8%.[150] In seeking to redress the effects of the 1994 genocide and its root causes, the impact of corruption and the need for social justice, Rwanda has undertaken several initiatives that reflect efforts towards social and retributive justice. For example, the *Ubudehe* programme was developed to "bolster the decentralization process in Rwanda while contributing to poverty reduction and promoting community cohesion and reconciliation".[151] This is critical, considering the heinous acts of genocide and its underlying root causes of wealth distribution and corruption associated with historical and socio-economic inequalities.[152] The programme is set to complement Rwanda's Social Protection programmes by addressing the socio-economic developmental challenges the country is confronted with.[153] The programme is unique in the sense that it is a home-grown model with a grassroots approach in addressing community socio-economic challenges through participatory mechanisms and the promotion of citizen ownership.[154]

Another initiative is the Land Tenure Regularisation introduced by the post-genocide Rwandan government to address historical inequalities in access to land and its ownership; and to promote economic development.[155] One

---

146 Ibid.

147 Transparency International 2023, supra note 125.

148 Transparency International (2022) Corruption Perceptions Index. *Transparency International*, 2022. Available at: https://www.transparency.org/en/cpi/2022 (consulted 30 July 2024).

149 According to the 2023 Transparency International reports, the least corrupt African countries in terms of rank are Seychelles (No 20), Cape Verde (No 30), Botswana (No 39), Rwanda (No 49), and Mauritius (No 55).

150 Galal, supra note 76.

151 Local Administrative Entities Development Agency (LODA) (2024) Obudehe. *LODA* Available at: https://www.loda.gov.rw/ubudehe (consulted 30 July 2024).

152 See Ngoga, Thierry Hoza (2009) A Quick, Cost-Effective Approach to Land Tenure Regularisation: The Case of Rwanda. *International Growth Centre*, 1–11.

153 LODA, supra note 152.

154 Ibid.

155 Ngoga, supra note 153, 3–4.

of the benefits of the programme is that it provides women the opportunity for land ownership. Other benefits include land tenure security, access to formal credit, improved land management and natural resource and agriculture management.[156] Another initiative is Vision 2050 with goals that envisage economic growth with a GDP per capita of over USD 12,476 and improved quality and standard of life.[157]

Other African countries have experienced challenges relating to efforts towards social and redistributive justice. One can assume that in instances where corruption is rife, such initiatives may result in the disproportionate distribution of socio-economic opportunities. Nevertheless, the one hindering factor that all countries in Africa experience is corruption. Over and above this, the outlined initiatives and many others[158] are in line with the aspirations set out in the Draft Covenant on the Right to Development. The initiatives demonstrate the need to equitably distribute wealth, promote social inclusion and reduce poverty.

7 Conclusion

According to Transparency International CPI reports, corruption remains rife in Africa.[159] Consequently, this compromises Africa's efforts towards development aspirations. The chapter made two primary finding: (1) that the persistence of corruption will negatively impact the binding obligations set out in the prospective Covenant on the Right to Development, a reality acknowledged in the Covenant; and (2) that the draft Covenant is grounded on social and redistributive justice. Adherence to the obligations set out in the draft Covenant entails the effective management of state resources, which unfortunately, is weakened by corruption and in turn, erodes the rule of law and good governance and hence also hampers realisation of the RTD.

It is important however, to acknowledge existing efforts by some African countries like South Africa and Rwanda in seeking to achieve social and redistributive justice and hence, guarantee that the obligations contained in the draft Covenant on the Right to Development will eventually be fulfilled. Having said that and based on the primary findings, the following recommendations

156 Ibid at 12–15.

157 Republic of Rwanda, Vision 2050 (2015) 1–11.

158 In South Africa, the National Development Plan and the Reconstruction and Development Program. In Rwanda, the National Strategy for Transformation.

159 Transparency International 2023, supra note 125.

may be considered: First, all African states must adopt comprehensive legislative framework and strengthen existing anti-corruption institutions. Second, African states must adopt and strengthen asset recovery multilateral agreements and systems in order to seize and return property siphoned to offshore locations. Third, in light of colonialism perpetuating unequal distribution of wealth and resources, efforts must be adopted towards social and redistributive justice mechanism with the view of implementing future obligations set out in the draft Covenant on the Right to Development.

References

African Union, African Charter on Human and Peoples' Rights, adopted in Nairobi, Kenya, on 27 June 1981. OAU Doc CAB/LEG/67/3 Rev. 5 (1981).

Afrosondagem, Summary of Results: Afrobarometer Round Survey in Cabo Verde 2002.

Ajakaye, Rafiu (2017, 6 December) Nigeria Inks Deal to Repatriate $321M of 'Stolen Funds". Available at: https://www.aa.com.tr/en/africa/nigeria-inks-deal-to-repatriate-321m-of-stolen-funds/989895 (consulted 30 July 2024).

Alasttal, Abdelrahman; Maskun, Abdul and Sakharina, Iin Karita (2023) The Role of the United Nations in Protecting the Right to Development in Occupied Palestine. *Legality: Jurnal Ilmiah Hulum* 3(1): 138–156.

Aluko, Opeyemi Idowu (2020) Breaking the Cycle of Corruption in Nigeria: The Myth and Reality. *Journal of Co-operative and Business Studies* 5(1): 115–125.

Aziz, Muhammad Rashid; Arif, Sardar and Bannian, Bushra (2023) Historical, Regional and International Law Perspectives on the Right to Development: An Overview. *Pakistan Social Sciences Review* 7(3): 624–634.

Balanced and Integrated Economic and Social progress, Resolution 1161(XII), adopted by the United Nations General Assembly.

Bhugra, Dinesh; Tribe, Rachel and Poulter, Daniel (2022) Social Justice, Health Equity, and Mental Health. *South African Journal of Psychology* 52(1): 3–10.

Braveman, P. (2016) Health Difference, Disparity, Inequality, or Inequity—What Difference Does It Make What We Call It: An Approach to Conceptualizing and Measuring Health Inequalities and Health Equity. In: Buchbinder, M.; Rivkin-Fish, M. and Walker, R.L. (eds) *Understanding Health Inequalities and Justice: New Conversations Across the Disciples*. Chapel Hill: University of North Carolina Press.

British American Tobacco Negotiated Bribe for Mugabe, New Evidence Suggests. *British Broadcasting Corporation*. Available at: https://www.bbc.com/news/world-58517339 (consulted 31 July 2024).

Centre for Minority Rights Development (Kenya) and Minority Rights Group International on behalf of Endorois Welfare Council v Kenya 276/2003.

Combley, Roz (2011) *Cambridge Business English Dictionary*. Cambridge: Cambridge University Press.

Constitution of the Republic of South Africa, 1996.

Cook, Karen and Hegtvedt, Karen (1983) Distributive Justice, Equity, and Equality. *Annual Review of Sociology*, 9: 217–241.

Corruption Perceptions Index (2022) *Transparency International*. Available at: https://www.transparency.org/en/cpi/2022 (consulted 30 July 2024).

Corruption Perceptions Index (2023) *Transparency International*. Available at: https://www.transparency.org/en/cpi/2023 (consulted 29 July 2024).

Corruption Perceptions Index (2016) *Transparency International*. Available at: https://www.transparency.org/en/cpi/2016 (consulted 30 July 2024).

Corruption Perceptions Index (2023) Democratic Republic of Congo. *Transparency International*. Available at: https://www.transparency.org/en/cpi/2023/index/cod (consulted 30 July 2024).

Corruption Perceptions Index (2023) Rwanda. *Transparency International*. Available at: https://www.transparency.org/en/cpi/2023/index/rwa (consulted 30 July 2024).

Corruption Watch (2024) The Impact of Corruption: Insights from a Perception and Experience Survey. *Corruption Watch*. Available at: https://www.corruptionwatch.org.za/wp-content/uploads/2024/05/Corruption-Watch-Report-Experiences-and-Perceptions_FINAL.pdf, 17 (consulted 30 July 2024).

Davidoff, Paul (1975) Working Toward Redistributive Justice. *Journal of the American Institute of Planner* 41(5): 317–318.

Desta, Yemane (2019) Manifestation and Causes of Civil Service Corruption in Developing Countries. *Journal of Public Administration and Governance* 9(3): 23–24.

Distributive Justice. *Cambridge Dictionary*. Available at: https://dictionary.cambridge.org/dictionary/english/distributive-justice#google_vignette (consulted 29 July 2024).

Draft International Covenant on the Right to Development—Report by the Chair-Rapporteur of the Working Group on the Right to Development, Zamir Akram (Pakistan) Human Rights Council A/HRC/54/50 54th Session, 6 October 2023.

Duri, Jorum (2020) Overview of Corruption and Anti-Corruption in sub-Saharan Africa. *CHR Michelsen Institute*.

Dutta, Subha Deep (2020) *Company Law: Based on Company Act 2013, Including Company Amendment Act* 2020. Uttar Pradesh: Shree Vinayak Publication.

Ennser-Jedenastik, Laurenz (2018) Welfare Chauvinism in Populist Radical Right Platforms: The Role of Redistributive Justice Principles. *Social Policy Administration* 52(1): 293–314.

FRACCK Agreement with Kenya Illustrates that Partnership is Essential when the Disposal of Confiscated Assets should Benefit Development. *Basel Institute on Governance*. Available at: https://baselgovernance.org/news/fracck-agreement

-kenya-illustrates-partnership-essential-when-disposal-confiscated-assets (consulted 30 July 2024).

Freedom in the World (2024) Botswana. *Freedom House.* Available at: https://freedomhouse.org/country/botswana/freedom-world/2024 (consulted 29 July 2024).

Freedom in the World (2024) Carbo Verde. *Freedom House.* Available at: https://freedomhouse.org/country/cabo-verde/freedom-world/2024 (consulted 29 July 2024).

Freedom in the World (2024) Equatorial Guinea. *Freedom House.* Available at: https://freedomhouse.org/country/equatorial-guinea/freedom-world/2024 (consulted 29 July 2024).

Freedom in the World (2024) Somalia. *Freedom House.* Available at: https://freedomhouse.org/country/somalia/freedom-world/2024 (consulted 29 July 2024).

Freedom in the World (2024) South Sudan. *Freedom House.* Available at: https://freedomhouse.org/country/south-sudan/freedom-world/2024 accessed 29 July 2024 (consulted 29 July 2024).

Galal, Saifaddin (2024) African Countries with the Highest Share of Global Population Living below the Extreme Poverty Line in 2024. *Statista.* Available at: https://www.statista.com/statistics/1228553/extreme-poverty-as-share-of-global-population-in-africa-by-country/ (consulted 28 July 2024).

Gök, Adem (2021) Determinants of Corruption: The Case of sub-Saharan Africa. *Ankara University Journal of Political Sciences* 76(2): 523–546.

Graycar, Adam (2015) Corruption: Classification and Analysis. *Policy and Society* 34(2): 87–96.

Hage, S.M.; Mason, M. and Kim, J. (2011) A Social Justice Approach to Group Counselling. In: Conye, R.K. (ed) *The Oxford Handbook of Group Counselling.* Oxford: Oxford University Press.

Hart, David (1974) Social Equity, Justice and the Equitable Administrator. *Public Administration Review* 34(1): 3–11.

Huang, Karen; Greene, Joshua and Bazerman, Max (2019) Veil-of-Ignorance Reasoning Favors the Greater Good. *PNAS—Psychological and Cognitive Sciences* 116(48): 23989–23995.

International Covenant on Civil and Political Rights, Resolution 2200A(XXI), adopted by the UN General Assembly 1966.

International Covenant on Economic, Social and Cultural Rights, Resolution 2200A(XXI), adopted by the UN General Assembly 1966.

Iqbal, Munawar; Ali, Salman Syed and Muljawan, Dadang (2007) Advances in Islamic Economics and Finance. *Proceedings of 6th International Conference on Islamic Economic and Finance.*

Jayalakshmi, H. and Kachhi, Z. (2024) Strategies for Combating Corruption in Poverty Alleviation. In: Yakubu, I.N. (ed) *Examining Corruption and the Sustainable Development Goals.* Pennsylvania: IGI Global.

Jungo, João; Madaleno, Mara and Botelho, Anabela (2023) Controlling Corruption in African Countries: Innovation, Financial Inclusion and Access to Education as Alternatives Measures. *International Journal of Social Economics* 50(6): 766–786.

Kimber, Norman (2023) The Human Right to Development: Historical and Contemporary Linkage to Colonialism. Master of Studies in Law, University of Western Ontario.

Kimenyi, Mwangi et al (2021) Foresight Africa: The Continent's Greatest Challenges and Opportunities for 2011. *Brookings*, 30–31.

Lissowski, Grzegorz; Tyszka, Tadeusz and Okrasa, Wlodzimierz (1991) Principles of Distributive Justice: Experiments in Poland and American. *The Journal of Conflict Resolution* 35(1): 98–119.

Local Administrative Entities Agency (LODA) (2024) Obudehe. *LODA*. Available at: https://www.loda.gov.rw/ubudehe (consulted 30 July 2024).

McKeever, Matthew (2023) Social Stratification and Inequality in South Africa. *Sociology Compass* 18(2): 1–14.

Mlambo, Daniel; Mubecua, Mandla and Mlambo, Victor (2023) Post-Colonial Independence and Africa's Corruption Conundrum: A Succinct South African Critique Post-Democratisation. *Insights on Africa* 15(2): 184–202.

Mlambo, Daniel et al (2019) Corruption and its Implications for Development and Good Governance: A Perspective from Post-Colonial Africa. *Journal of Economic and Behavioural Studies* 11(1): 39–47.

Muhammad, Ibrahim; Wasiu, Sanusi Abdul and Gado, Muddassir Ahmad (2023) Corruption and its Impact on Socio-Economic Development in Selected Countries of Africa. *African Journal of Politics and Administrative Studies* 16(2): 23–46.

Munyai, Anzanilufuno (2020) *Overcoming the Corruption Conundrum in Africa: A Socio-legal Perspective*. Newcastle upon Tyne: Cambridge Scholars Publishing.

Nameda, Akinobu et al (2023) Distributive Justice and Development: Toward an Integrative Understanding of Reward and Responsibility Distributions. *Journal of Moral Education* 52(4): 435–452.

Newton, Michael (2010) *Crime and Criminals*. New York: Infobase Publishing.

Ngang, Carol Chi (2019) Systems Problem and a Pragmatic Insight on the Right to Development Governance for Africa. *African Human Rights Law Journal* 19(2): 365–394.

Ngoga, Thierry Hoza (2009) A Quick, Cost-Effective Approach to Land Tenure Regularisation: The Case of Rwanda. *International Growth Centre*, 1–11.

Okello, Anne (2023) In Seychelles, Majority Support Gender Equality, Think Greater Efforts are Needed. *Afrobarometer: Dispatch No 703*.

Picard, Louis; Mogale, Thomas and Corrigan, Caitlin (2024) *The South Africa State transformed? Sanctions, negotiations, and elite pacts 1975–2018*. Cape Town: UCT Press.

Rawls, John (1971) *Theory of Justice*. Cambridge: Harvard University Press.

Rosen, Michael and Young, Annemarie (2018) *What is Right and Wrong? Who Decides? Where Do Values Come From? And Other Big Questions*. London: Hachette Children's Group.

Saban, Liza Ireni (2016) *International Disaster Management Ethics*. New York: State University of New York Press.

Saputra, Farhan and Saputra, Ebit Bima (2021) Measures of Corruption: Needs, Opportunity and Rationalisation. *Journal of Law Politics and Humanities* 2(1): 42–50.

Shacinda, Shapi (2007) Zambia's Chiluba Hit with 23 Million Pounds for Graft. *Reuters*. Available at: https://reuters.com/article/world/zambia-s-chiluba-hit-with-23-million-pounds-for-graft-idUSL04300150/ (consulted 31 July 2024).

Shava, Elvin (2016) Black Empowerment in South Africa: Challenges and Prospects. *Journal of Economics and Behavioural Studies* 8(6): 161–170.

Skrdlik, Josef (2023) South Africa Seizes Teodoro Nguema Obiang Mangue's Superyacht. *Organized Crime and Corruption Reporting Project*. Available at: https://www.occrp.org/en/daily/17327-south-africa-seizes-teodoro-nguema-obiang-mangue-s-superyacht (consulted 29 July 2024).

Social and Economic Rights Action Centre (SERAC) *and Another v Nigeria* (*Ogoni* case) Comm 155/96 (2001) AHRLR 60 (ACHPR 2001).

Stolen Asset Recovery Initiative. Available at https://star.worldbank.org/asset-recovery-watch-database/windward-trading-40220150350-case (consulted 23 October 2024).

Stolen Asset Recovery Initiative. Available at: https://star.worldbank.org/asset-recovery-watch-database/2010-halliburton-nigeria-bribery-settlement-agreement-us325-million#disclaimer (consulted 23 October 2024).

Sudan Polling Statistics Centre (2024) Afrobarometer Round 9 Survey in Sudan 2022: Summary of Results. *Afrobarometer*, 45–47.

Teshome, Roman Girma (2022) The Draft Convention on the Right to Development: A New Dawn to the Recognition of the Right to Development as a Human Right. *Human Rights Law Review* 22(2): 1–24.

The Constitution of Kenya, 2010.

UN List of Least Developed Countries. *UN Conference on Trade and Development*. Available at: https://unctad.org/topic/least-developed-countries/list (consulted 28 July 2014).

United Nations Human Rights Council (2023) The Right to Development (A/HRC/54/L.27).

Vision of Humanity (2024) *Global Peace Index*. Available at: https://www.visionofhumanity.org/maps/#/ (consulted 24 October 2024).

Yusuf, Hakeem and van der Merwe, Hugo (2021) (eds) *Transitional Justice: Theories, Mechanisms and Debates*. New York: Taylor and Francis.

CHAPTER 16

An Assessment of Armed Conflicts and Insurgencies as a Hindrance to the Right to Development in Africa

Linda Mushoriwa

1 Introduction

The right to development has been defined as

> the right to a process of development, consisting of a progressive and phased realization of all the recognized human rights, such as civil and political rights, and economic, social and cultural rights (other rights admitted international law) as well as the process of economic growth consistent with human rights standards.[1]

One of the problems that continues to hinder growth and development on the African continent is armed conflicts and insurgencies. The African Union (AU) acknowledges in its founding document, the Constitutive Act that "the scourge of conflicts in Africa constitutes a major impediment to the socio-economic development of the continent and of the need to promote peace, security and stability as a prerequisite for the implementation of our development and integration agenda […]".[2]

The AU "Agenda 2063: The Africa We Want" framework for development (Agenda 2063) was adopted by the AU Assembly in 2015 in commemoration of the 50th anniversary of the AU's predecessor, the Organisation of African Unity (OAU) and the strides made by the AU since its inception. Agenda 2063

1 Report of the Independent Expert on the Right to Development (Arjun Sengupta) (Report 2 of the Independent Expert), 17 August 2000, A/55/306, Para 16.

2 Constitutive Act of the African Union adopted in Lomé, Togo on 11 July 2000, Preamble.

 | DOI:10.1163/9789004734357_017

is the AU's 50 years development blueprint,[3] which reaffirms the right to development and equality.[4]

This chapter examines 3 of the 7 aspirations for the development of the African continent as expressed in Agenda 2063. These are "a prosperous Africa based on inclusive growth and sustainable development" (Aspiration 1), a "peaceful and secure Africa" (Aspiration 4) and "an Africa whose development is people driven, relying on the potential of African people, especially its women and youth, and caring for children" (Aspiration 6). It analyses the progress made by AU member states in implementing the selected aspirations and their related goals and attributes the slow pace of implementation to the persistent threats to security in Africa, which significantly hinder the continental agenda for development, as seen through the lens of the conflict in Mozambique which began in 2020. This is done within the context of the evolving dynamics of the conflict, including the internal displacement of people from the Cabo Delgado region, the use of child soldiers,[5] and the withdrawal of the Southern African Development Commission Mission in Mozambique (SAMIM) in July 2024. The chapter also analyses the draft International Covenant on the Right to Development that was submitted by the United Nations (UN) Human Rights Council to the UN General Assembly in October 2023 for negotiation and adoption.[6]

A number of scholars have commented on the resurgence of armed conflicts in Africa,[7] the AU and its regional economic communities' (RECS) role

---

3 African Union Commission (2015) Agenda 2063: The Africa we want. *African Union*. For a detailed overview of Agenda 2063; see Mushoriwa, L. and Njieassam, E. (2023) COVID-19 and the Implementation of Aspiration 1 of the African Union's Agenda 2063: The Case of South Africa, Zimbabwe and Eswatini. In: Onuora-Oguno, A. (ed) *Promoting Efficiency in Jurisprudence and Constitutional Development in Africa*. Cham: Springer Nature, 57–61.

4 AU Agenda 2063, supra note 3, 43.

5 Human Rights Watch (2024, 15 May) Mozambique: Child Soldiers Used in Raid on Northern Town. Available at: https://www.hrw.org/news/2024/05/15/mozambique-child-soldiers-used-raid-northern-town (consulted 6 December 2024).

6 United Nations (2023, 12 October) Morning—Human Rights Council Adopts Five Resolutions, Submits to General Assembly Draft International Covenant on the Right to Development for its Negotiation and Adoption, and Extends Mandate on Burundi. Available at: https://www.ungeneva.org/en/news-media/meeting-summary/2023/10/le-conseil-adopte-cinq-resolutions-dont-celle-transmettant (consulted 6 December 2024).

7 See for example, Davis, I. (2022) *Armed Conflict and Peace Processes in Sub-Saharan Africa*. Oxford University Press; Adelakun, O. (2023) Gender Mainstreaming in Post-Conflict Reconstruction in North-East Nigeria. In: Onuora-Oguno, A. (ed) *Promoting Efficiency in Jurisprudence and Constitutional Development in Africa*. Cham: Springer Nature, 95–118.

in resolving conflicts on the continent[8] as well as the Agenda 2063 framework and the right to development.[9] This chapter contributes to the available body of knowledge by providing an up to date analysis and insights into how conflicts hinder development in Africa through the negative impact it has on lives and livelihoods, including through displacements and how this ultimately affects the African peoples' right to development enshrined in the African Charter on Human and Peoples' Rights[10] and the draft Covenant on the Right to Development. Section 2 analyses the right to development within the context of Agenda 2063. Section 3 examines the draft Covenant on the Right to Development. Section 4 assesses how conflicts hinder the right to development, and section 5 makes some concluding remarks.

2 Agenda 2063: the Africa We Want and the Right to Development

2.1 *The Rio Declaration on Environment and Development*

The Agenda 2063 framework document reaffirms among others, the right to development and the commitment to ensure a conducive space for nationally tailored policies and programmes.[11] The Rio Declaration on Environment and Development adopted at the Earth summit in 1992 by 178 UN member states, encompasses 27 principles intended to guide country efforts in fostering sustainable development.[12] Of relevance to this chapter is Principle 3, which provides that "The right to development must be fulfilled so as to equitably

---

8 Institute for Security Studies (2021, 26 March) What can the AU do About the Conflict in Mozambique? *ISS PSC Report*. Available at: https://issafrica.org/pscreport/psc-insights/what-can-the-au-do-about-the-conflict-in-mozambique (consulted 7 December 2024); Birhan, Aemro Tenaw (2024) The African Union and Conflict Resolution: Challenges and Prospects. *Social Science and Humanities Journal* 8(3): 34576–34585; Aboumbeng, Asumbeng Sunday (2017) AU and SADC Involvement in Conflict Resolution in the Democratic Republic of Congo (DRC): Testing the AU's Principle of Non-Indifference. University of Johannesburg Master of Arts Thesis.

9 See for example, Stevens, Clydenia (2019) Reviving the Right to Development Within the Multilateral Trade Framework Affecting (African) Countries to Actualise Agenda 2063. *African Human Rights Law Journal* 19(2): 470–493; Mosala, Seshupo (2024) Pan-Africanism and the Right to Development in Africa: A Critical Analysis of Agenda 2063. *African Renaissance* 21(2).

10 African Charter on Human and Peoples' Rights adopted in Nairobi, Kenya on 27 June 1981 OAU Doc CAB/LEG/67/3 Rev.5 (1981), Art 22.

11 AU Agenda 2063, supra note 4, 43.

12 United Nations General Assembly, Report of the United Nations Conference on Environment and Development, Annex 1, Rio Declaration on Environment and Development. Available at: https://www.un.org/en/development/desa/population/migration/gene

meet developmental and environmental needs of present and future generations".[13] Reference to the Rio principles in Agenda 2063 is significant in that it highlights the fact that development is not just an aspiration, but a fundamental human right.

2.2 *Agenda 2063: the Africa We Want Framework for Development*

This section discusses the relevant Agenda 2063 aspirations and how their successful implementation is key to the realisation of the right to development for the peoples of Africa.

2.2.1 Aspiration 1: a Prosperous Africa Based on Inclusive Growth and Sustainable Development

The aspiration for a prosperous Africa has its basis in the AU Constitutive Act, which enshrines as one of the AU's objectives to "promote sustainable development at the economic, social and cultural levels as well as the integration of African economies".[14] Aspiration 1 of Agenda 2063 envisages an Africa that is prosperous, which prosperity has its basis on inclusive and sustainable growth and development. It embodies the aspiration for "A high standard of living, quality of life and well-being for all citizens", entailing that by 2063, at least half of AU member states are ranked within the high category on the human development index (HDI) and that all African countries should be providing basic income security for the elderly.[15] When the Agenda 2063 was adopted in 2015, 18 African countries ranked either in the high or medium category on the HDI. These included Botswana, Gabon, Ghana, Mauritius, Namibia, South Africa, and Zambia.[16] All 10 countries with the lowest HDI are in Africa, including Burkina Faso, Burundi, Chad, Mali, Mozambique and Niger.[17] In the 2023–2024 Human Development Report, 23 African countries were classified as having a very high, high and medium HDI, including; Angola, Botswana, Eswatini,

---

ralassembly/docs/globalcompact/A_CONF.151_26_Vol.I_Declaration.pdf (consulted 7 December 2024).

13 For a detailed overview on Principle 3 see Molinari, C. (2015) Principle 3: From a Right to Development to Intergenerational Equity. In: Vinuales, J. (ed) *The Rio Declaration on Environment and Development: A Commentary*. Oxford: Oxford University Press, 139–156.

14 Constitutive Act, Art 3(j).

15 AU Agenda 2063, supra note 4, 160.

16 United Nations Development Programme Human Development Report 2015 (2015, 1 January) Work for Human Development. Available at: https://hdr.undp.org/system/files/documents/hdr15standaloneoverviewen.pdf (consulted 7 December 2024), 28–30.

17 Ibid at 31.

Mauritius, Namibia, South Africa, Zambia, and Zimbabwe.[18] These latest figures show that the target goal to have at least half of African countries ranked in the high category is far from being met, as only Seychelles was categorised as having a very high HDI.[19] Only 6 countries namely; Algeria, Botswana, Egypt, Libya, Mauritius, South Africa and Tunisia ranked in the high HDI category.[20] 10 of the 11 lowest ranked countries are African countries, which include Chad, Central African Republic, Mali and Mozambique.[21]

The criteria used in measuring HDI are long and healthy life, knowledge and a decent standard of living. The indicators for these dimensions are life expectancy at birth, expected years of schooling for children of school entering age and average years of schooling for adults 25 years and older, and gross national income per capita.[22] Failure to reach the HDI targets as stipulated in Agenda 2063 can be attributed to the corresponding failure by AU member states in making significant strides in key areas of development, including education, health and work. In the second Continental Progress Report on Agenda 2063 Implementation, the overall performance in some priority areas like income, jobs, decent work, poverty, inequality and hunger was weak and failed to meet the 2021 targets in the Agenda 2063 framework.[23] The overall performance on Goal 1 was 31%, a significant decline from 56% recorded in 2019. There was a rise in unemployment from 11% in 2013 to 15% in 2021. This was attributed to a contraction in the expected growth of African economies. The prevalence of undernourishment was high at 24%, against a 2021 target value of 9%.[24] Other overarching drivers of the weak performance with respect to Goal 1 include the global macro-economic stress resulting from the COVID-19

18 United Nations Development Programme Human Development Report (2023–2024) Breaking the gridlock: Reimagining cooperation in a polarised world. Available at: https://hdr.undp.org/system/files/documents/global-report-document/hdr2023-24reporten.pdf (consulted 7 December 2024), 274–276.

19 Ibid at 274.

20 Ibid at 275.

21 Ibid at 276.

22 Herre, Bastian and Arriagada, Pablo (2023, 1 November) The Human Development Index and related Indices: What They Are and What We Can Learn from Them. *Our World in Data.* Available at: https://ourworldindata.org/human-development-index#article-citation (consulted 7 December 2024).

23 African Union Development Agency-NEPAD (2022, February) Second Continental Report on the Implementation of Agenda 2063. Available at: https://au.int/sites/default/files/documents/41480-doc-2nd_Continental_Progress_Report_on_Agenda_2063_English.pdf (consulted 7 December 2024), 16.

24 Ibid at 15.

pandemic; and economic hardships that necessitated a shift in investment priority from the Goal 1 priorities to other areas that needed attention.[25]

Economic growth does not necessarily translate into higher human development.[26] It is however, established that work enhances human development by providing incomes and livelihoods, reducing poverty and ensuring equitable growth.[27] It is therefore, understandable that one of the priority areas under Agenda 2063, Goal 1.1 is income, jobs and decent work.[28] This is commensurate with the notion that work is broader than jobs, hence it includes informal sector ventures. Although there was a rise in unemployment, it was reported that AU member states took some steps to alleviate the situation including Egypt, Madagascar and Togo.[29] It is pertinent to note that the countries that managed to implement programmes to foster economic growth and sustainable development are those that are not experiencing armed conflict. It reiterates the point highlighted in this chapter that there is a mutual link between economic development and peace and security. The effects of armed conflict including the displacement of people and destruction of infrastructure in turn stifles development.

2.2.2 Aspiration 4: a Peaceful and Secure Africa

The inclusion of Aspiration 4 in Agenda 2063 is plausible when one looks at the prevalence of armed conflicts on the continent. At the time of writing, Africa comes second to Asia in terms of the number of armed conflicts, with non-international armed conflicts currently taking place in Burkina Faso, Cameroon, the Central African Republic, the Democratic Republic of the Congo, Ethiopia, Mali, Mozambique, Nigeria, Senegal, Somalia, South Sudan and Sudan.[30] One of the goals under Aspiration 4 (Goal 13) is to ensure that "peace, security and stability is preserved". A target is to ensure that "Effective

25 Ibid at 16.

26 United Nations Development Programme (2015) Fact Sheet Human Development Index: Human Development Report Work for Human Development. Available at: https://www.undp.org/sites/g/files/zskgke326/files/migration/dk/UNDP_Denmark_HDR_2015_Fact_Sheet.pdf (consulted 7 December 2024).

27 Ibid at 3.

28 AU Agenda 2063, supra note 4, 160.

29 AU-NEPAD, supra note 24, 16.

30 Geneva Academy (2024) Today's Armed Conflicts. Available at: https://geneva-academy.ch/galleries/today-s-armed-conflicts#:~:text=Africa%20comes%20second%20in%20the,Somalia%2C%20South%20Sudan%20and%20Sudan (consulted 6 December 2024).

mechanisms to address the root/structural causes of violent conflict are in place by 2025".[31]

The AU has clearly failed to meet this target as there are currently, no effective mechanisms in place to address the root causes of the conflicts by 2025. Key drivers of violent conflicts in Africa have been identified to include "weak governance, historical animosities, exclusionary politics, contested legitimacy, resource competition, external factors, globalized conflicts and extremist ideologies".[32] In Mozambique for example, the conflict has been fuelled by the discovery of natural gas in the Cabo Delgado region which in turn, led to perceptions of worsening marginalisation and inequalities by the local communities who had to be relocated to pave way for the gas exploration project.[33] The three instruments the AU relies on in responding to the violent conflicts on the continents are diplomacy, mediation and peace support operations, which extend to its regional economic communities.[34] The AU's mandate on conflict resolution obtains from the Constitutive Act, which provides as one of its main objectives, to "promote peace, security, and stability on the continent".[35] In line with this objective, in 2002, the AU adopted the Protocol relating to the Establishment of the Peace and Security Council (PSC Protocol).[36] The PSC Protocol empowers the Peace and Security Council (PSC) to deploy a peacekeeping mission to a member state; recommend to the Assembly intervention in a member state pursuant to Article 4(h) of the Constitutive Act and approve modalities for such intervention.[37] It reiterates that in making decisions pertaining to responding to conflicts, the PSC shall be guided by the principle of

31 AU Agenda 2063, supra note 4, 153.

32 Gilpin, R. (2016) Understanding the Nature and Origins of Violent Conflict in Africa. In: Aall, P. and Crocker, C.A. (eds) *Minding the Gap: African Conflict Management in a Time of Change*. CIGI Publications, 21.

33 Matsinhe, Sozinho Francisco (2021, 29 April) An Overview of the Conflict in Cabo Delgado: Narratives, Causes and Strategies on the Way Forward. *ACCORD*. Available at: https://www.accord.org.za/analysis/an-overview-of-the-conflict-in-cabo-delgado-narratives-causes-and-strategies-on-the-way-forward/ (consulted 6 December 2024); Chingutoane, Énio Viegas et al (2021, October) Strategic Options for Managing Violent Extremism in Southern Africa: The Case of Mozambique—Situation Report. Maputo: Friedrich-Ebert-Stiftung, 8–10.

34 Suzuki, Sanae (2020) Exploring the Roles of the AU and ECOWAS in West African conflicts. *South African Journal of International Affairs* 27(2): 173.

35 Constitutive Act of the African Union, supra note 2, Art 3(f).

36 Protocol Relating to the Establishment of the Peace and Security Council of the African Union, adopted by the 1st Ordinary Session of the AU Assembly of Heads of State and Government in Durban, South Africa, 9 July 2002.

37 Ibid at Art 7(b–f).

"[…] respect for the sovereignty of Member States".[38] In terms of Article 4(j) of the PSC Protocol, the PSC is mandated to intervene in member states in accordance with Article 4(h) of the Constitutive Act.[39]

Since its inception in 2000, the AU has deployed a total of 22 peacekeeping missions including the AU Mission in Burundi (2003–2004), AU Mission in Somalia (2007–2022), AU Transition Mission in Somalia (since 2022), the African-led International Support Mission in the Central African Republic (2013–2014) and the AU-UN Hybrid Mission in Darfur (2008–2021).[40] The RECs also deploy peacekeeping missions, including the two missions by SADC, the SADC Prevention Mission to Lesotho (2018) and the SADC Mission in Mozambique (SAMIM 2021–2024).[41] Notwithstanding the involvement of the AU and its RECs in peacekeeping missions, what is lacking are effective mechanisms to address the root causes of conflicts and in turn curb the resurgence of armed conflicts on the continent. The ineffectiveness of the AU peace and security architecture stems mainly from the fact that the existing instruments on responding to conflicts are reactionary rather than preventive. In addition, AU member states have shown a tendency to resist intervention by the AU and RECs based on territorial integrity.[42] A prime example is how the Mozambican government initially resisted intervention from SADC when the Cabo Delgado conflict broke out.[43]

Goal 14 of Agenda 2063 envisages "a stable and peaceful Africa", including the target to "silence all guns by 2020". The pledge to silence the guns in Africa by the year 2020 was made by African leaders in 2013 in the OAU/AU 50th Anniversary Solemn Declaration.[44] The pledge was followed by two initiatives,

38 Ibid at Art 4(e).

39 Ibid at Art 4(j).

40 Allen, Nate (2023, 9 August) African-Led Peace Operations: A Crucial Tool for Peace and Security. *African Centre for Strategic Studies*. Available at: https://africacenter.org/wp-content/uploads/2024/05/African-Led-Peace-Operations.pdf, 1–12, 5 (consulted 6 December 2024).

41 Ibid at 5.

42 Djilo, Felicite and Handy, Paul-Simon (2022, 11 May) Africa's Solutions to Conflict are in Crisis. *Institute for Security Studies Today*. Available at: https://issafrica.org/iss-today/africas-solutions-to-conflict-are-in-crisis (consulted 6 December 2024).

43 International Crisis Group (2021, 11 June) Stemming the Insurrection in Mozambique's Cabo Delgado. Available at: https://www.crisisgroup.org/africa/southern-africa/mozambique/303-stemming-insurrection-mozambiques-cabo-delgado (consulted 6 December 2024).

44 African Union (2013) 50th Anniversary Solemn Declaration. Available at: https://au.int/sites/default/files/documents/36205-doc-50th_anniversary_solemn_declaration_en.pdf (consulted 6 December 2024).

a PSC open session under the theme, "On silencing the guns: Pre-requisites for realising a conflict-free Africa by the year 2020" held in April 2014;[45] and a retreat under the theme "Silencing the guns in Africa: Building a roadmap to a conflict-free continent", which took place in Durban in April 2014.[46] Participants at these two events acknowledged that identifying and addressing the key drivers of conflict was a prerequisite to silencing the guns in Africa and the successful implementation of the roadmap to silencing the guns. In 2020 the AU adopted "silencing the guns" as its theme for the year.

Unfortunately, the sound of guns has continued to reverberate across the African continent[47] with the conflict in Cabo Delgado erupting the same year in 2020,[48] the conflict in Sudan which started in 2023,[49] the ongoing conflicts in the Democratic Republic of Congo,[50] and the Central African Republic[51] among many others. By the end of 2020, it became clear that the target to silence the guns in Africa by 2020 could not be achieved and the AU extended this target to 2030.[52] The pledge to silence the guns highlights the AU's recognition of the fact that conflicts stifle development. Looking at the prevailing state of conflicts in Africa at the time of writing this chapter, it can be stated

45 African Union Concept Note (2014, 24 April) On Silencing the Guns: Pre-requisites for Realising a Conflict-Free Africa by the Year 2020 for the Open Session of the Peace and Security Council of the African Union, AU New Conference Centre, Addis Ababa. Available at: https://www.peaceau.org/en/article/open-session-on-silencing-guns-pre-requisites-for-achieving-a-conflict-free-africa-by-2020 (consulted 6 December 2024).

46 African Union Press Release (2024, 29 April) Silencing the Guns in Africa: Building a Roadmap to a Conflict Free Continent. Available at: https://au.int/sites/default/files/newsevents/pressreleases/25651-pr-com-durban-silencing-guns.pdf (consulted 6 December 2024).

47 Mushoriwa, Linda (2023) The African Union's Quest for a "Peaceful and Secure Africa": An Assessment of Aspiration 4 of Agenda 2063. *Law, Development and Democracy* 27(2003): 64.

48 Matsinhe, supra note 34.

49 Armed Conflict Location and Event Data (2024, 14 April) One Year of War in Sudan. Available at: https://acleddata.com/2024/04/14/sudan-situation-update-april-2024-one-year-of-war-in-sudan/ (consulted 6 December 2024).

50 UN News (2024, 27 June) UN Mission Boosts Presence in Central African Republic's Conflict-Stricken Southeast. Available at: https://news.un.org/en/story/2024/06/1151566 (consulted 6 December 2024).

51 UN News Strife in Central African Republic Could Turn into Religious War and Spill Over Borders, UN Warns. Available at: https://www.un.org/africarenewal/news/strife-central-african-republic-could-turn-religious-war-and-spill-over-borders-un-warns (consulted 6 December 2024).

52 Mushoriwa, supra note 48, 66–67; Louw-Vaudran, Liesl (2022, 28 June) Can Africa Stay on Target to Silence the Guns by 2030? *Institute for Security Studies Today*. Available at: https://issafrica.org/iss-today/can-africa-stay-on-target-to-silence-the-guns-by-2030 (consulted 6 December 2024).

with certainty that by 2030 the target to silence the guns in Africa would not have been achieved. Silencing the guns in totality is not realistic especially, taking into consideration the factors that act as key drivers of the conflicts as highlighted above. However, AU efforts thus far and the significant role by RECs in responding to the conflicts across the continent are noteworthy.

2.2.3 Aspiration 6: an Africa Whose Development is People-Driven

Aspiration 6 of Agenda 2063 envisages an Africa in which the people especially, women and the youth, play a pivotal role in driving development, and children are well catered for. This is in sync with the Constitutive Act, which enshrines the objective to "promote and protect human and peoples' rights in accordance with the African Charter on Human and Peoples' Rights and other relevant human rights instruments".[53] It embodies the right to development enshrined in the African Charter, which provides that:

1. All peoples shall have the right to their economic, social and cultural development with due regard to their freedom and identity and in the equal enjoyment of the common heritage of mankind.
2. States shall have the duty, individually or collectively, to ensure the exercise of the right to development.[54]

The right to development is implied in Article 22 of the Universal Declaration of Human Rights[55] and is also explicitly enshrined in African Youth Charter[56] and in the Protocol on the Rights of Women[57] in Africa among other instruments within the African human rights system. It is commendable that the AU recognises the importance of women, youth and children in shaping the developmental trajectory on the continent. This is the first time an AU framework or blueprint has expressly mentioned that development of the continent ought to include women and the youth, who have previously been marginalised.[58] In 2016, the AU adopted the theme "Year of human rights with particular focus

53 AU Constitutive Act, supra note 36, Art 3(h).

54 African Charter on Human and Peoples' Rights adopted in Nairobi, Kenya on 27 June 1981 OAU Doc CAB/LEG/67/3 Rev.5 (1981), Art 22 (1 and 2).

55 Universal Declaration of Human Rights, UN General Assembly Resolution A/RES/217(III), adopted in Paris, France on 10 December 1948, Art 22.

56 African Youth Charter adopted by the 7th Ordinary Session of the AU Assembly of Heads of State and Government in Banjul, the Gambia on 2 July 2006.

57 Protocol to the African Charter on Human and Peoples' Rights on the Rights of Women in Africa adopted by the AU Assembly of Heads of State and Government in Maputo, Mozambique on 11 July 2003, Art 19.

58 Hingston, Claudine Anita (2016) Towards Gender Equality in Africa *Journal of African Union Studies* 5(2): 39–49.

on the rights of women", which the then Commission Chairperson, Nkosazana Dlamini-Zuma affirmed was a reflection of the challenges and opportunities in advancing gender parity in Africa.[59] It is pertinent to note that Aspiration 6 is also in sync with the recognition by the AU that "no society can reach its full potential unless it empowers women and youth and removes all obstacles to women's full participation in all areas of human endeavors".[60]

Goal 17 of Agenda 2063 emphasises "Full gender equality in all spheres of life" with a priority focus on "women and girls empowerment" and a commitment to eliminate "violence and discrimination against women and girls".[61] The targets in this regard are gender parity in all AU institutions and RECs by 2030, a functional Annual High Level Panel on Women Empowerment by 2016, the establishment of a Fund for African Women by 2017 and the elimination of all forms of violence against women by the year 2030.[62] According to the second Progress Implementation Report, there was a moderate performance aggregate of 67% for the 2013 to 2021 period under review. Areas that registered significant achievement were the proportion of parliamentary seats held by women in African countries which recorded an increase from 21% in 2013 to 27.6% in 2021; proportion of women and girls subjected to sexual and physical violence dropped from 41.6% in 2013 to 21.2% in 2021 and the proportion of girls and women aged between 15 and 49 who undergo female genital mutilation witnessed a drop from 38% in 2013 to 27% in 2021.[63] The continent failed to reach the target of 39% women's ownership of secure title to agricultural land although there was an increase from 16% in 2013 to 23% in 2021.[64] With respect to individual member states, it is worth noting that countries that recorded significant achievements with respect to the Aspiration 6 goals, priority areas and targets are those countries that are not experiencing armed conflict.

The proportion of women representatives in parliament, regional and local bodies increased from 14.9% in 2014 to 27.41% in 2020 in Egypt; from 41.9% in 2013 to 47.4% in 2019 then to 47.75 % in 2021 in Rwanda; and from 10% in 2013 to 11 % in 2017 in Cote D'Ivoire.[65] In Mauritius, before 2010, 73% of leases were registered to men. In 2021, 34% of leases were registered to women, and

59 Ibid at 42.

60 Ndizera, Vedaste and Muzee, Hannah (2018) A Critical Review of Agenda 2063: Business as Usual? *African Journal of Political Science and International Relations* 12(8): 144.

61 AU Agenda 2063, supra note 4, 169.

62 Ibid at 169.

63 Ibid at 43.

64 Ibid at 43.

65 Ibid at 43–45.

35% joint registration.[66] In December 2012 the government of Cote D'Ivoire established the Support Fund for Women, with an initial amount of XAF 1 bn. By 2021 the fund had increased to XAF 25 bn and supported income-generating projects for 261 450 women.[67] In Chad, victims of sexual and other violence decreased from 15% in 2013 to 4.3% in 2021; and the proportion of women and girls who underwent genital mutilation decreased from 38.4% in 2013 to 34.2% in 2021.[68] In 2020, the government of Cote D'Ivoire facilitated psychosocial care for 5405 survivors of gender-based violence. In the same year, 391 survivors (70%) of gender-based violence received medical treatment within 72 hours.[69] The governments of Egypt, Chad, Lesotho, Mauritius, Cote D'Ivoire and Rwanda have all adopted legislation and policies to strengthen gender parity.[70]

It is agreed that the data used in compiling the implementation progress reports is not always reliable as not all member states provide the required information. In addition, some of the indicators for progress are contested.[71] Notwithstanding this, the available data is indicative of the link between peace and development. Countries in conflict like Mozambique, the DRC, Cameroon and Central African Republic do not feature on the list of countries that have made remarkable progress. Admittedly, other countries that are not affected by conflict like South Africa and Zambia also do not feature on the list of countries that have made outstanding progress with respect to Goal 13 of Aspiration 6. There are other factors that influence the rate of progress such as the deep-seated inequalities in South Africa, which are remnants of the apartheid-era legacy.[72] However, it is clear that there is a correlation between armed conflict and the lack of, or slow pace of development. This will be explained further when the Cabo Delgado conflict is discussed.

Goal 18 is focused on an "engaged and empowered youth and children" with the priority area being youth empowerment.[73] As Mpungose aptly observes, African youths have suffered for a long time from lack of inclusion in key issues with regards to their well-being, development and participation in

66 Ibid at 44.

67 Ibid at 43–45.

68 Ibid at 44.

69 Ibid.

70 Ibid at 43–45.

71 Mpungose, Luanda (2020, June) Africa's Diverging Approaches to Youth Inclusion and Participation. *South African Institute of International Affairs—Occasional Paper No 307* 18 and 24.

72 Francis, David and Webster, Edward (2019) Poverty and Inequality in South Africa: Critical Reflections. *Development Southern Africa* 36(6): 788–802.

73 AU Agenda 2063, supra note 4, 169.

important matters such as governance and democracy.[74] The inclusion of goal 18 in Aspiration 6 therefore, gives hope that Africa is moving towards ensuring full participation of the youth in key issues affecting their lives, communities, countries and the continent as a whole.

The second implementation progress report recorded a slight decrease in youth unemployment rate from 18.4% in 2013 to 17.6% in 2021. There was an increase in the proportion of children engaging in child labour from 15% in 2013 to 23% in 2021 While the percentage of children who fell victim to child marriage increased from 8% in 2013 to 18 % in 2021 and the percentage of children who fell victim to child trafficking also increased from 1.1% in 2013 to 3.3% in 2021.[75] Countries that recorded a significant decline in youth unemployment include Egypt, from 31.9% in 2013 to 16.4% in 2021. Mauritania recorded a significant decline in child labour for children aged between 10 and 17 years, from 7.8% in 2012 to 4.3% in 2017. The case of Mauritania, although commendable, highlights the problem of member states not regularly providing information used in compiling the implementation progress reports, as the latest data available was from 2017, 4 years before the last year under review which was 2021.

Although there was some progress with regards to Goal 18, the statistics highlighted above are a cause of concern as they show that the aspiration for an Africa whose development is driven by its youth is far from being realised. The youth in Africa are grappling with a myriad of problems including employment, which in turn is a key driver of poverty. This is despite a number of initiatives that have been implemented both at the national and continental levels to empower the youth, including through the African Youth Charter,[76] the Youth Decade Plan of Action,[77] the Roadmap for Harnessing the Demographic Dividend (2017),[78] the AU Year of Youth (2017)[79] and the African Plan of Action

74 Mpungose, supra note 71.

75 AU-NEPAD, supra note 24, 47.

76 African Youth Charter, supra note 56.

77 African Union (2024) Youth Development. Available at: https://au.int/en/youth-development (accessed 6 December 2024).

78 African Union Commission (2017) AU Roadmap on Harnessing the Demographic Dividend through Investments in the Youth. Available at: https://library.au.int/au-roadmap-harnessing-demographic-dividend-through-investments-youth (consulted 7 December 2024); African Union Declaration on the 2017 AU Theme Harnessing the Demographic Dividend through Investments in Youth Assembly/AU/Decl. 1(XXIX) July 2017; Mpungose, Luanda and Monyae, Lennon (2018) Carrying Forward the Momentum of the 2017 African Year of the Youth. *South African Institute of International Affairs—Policy Insights* 60. Available at: https://view.ckcest.cn/AllFiles/ZKBG/Pages/85/af4ed0259996fa2f91763e30ee8c30e04f878433.pdf (consulted 7 December 2024), 1–12.

79 Ibid.

for Youth Employment (2019 to 2023).[80] Due to space constraints, these initiatives will not be discussed in detail.

One of the factors that hinder youth empowerment is the lack of political will to implement the initiatives and policies adopted by the AU, its RECs and member states at the national level. In the second Implementation Progress Report, the level of implementation of the African Youth Charter for the continent was 74.4% in 2021. Although there was an increase from 66.5% in 2013, it fell short of the target of 100% by 2021.[81] This is partly attributable to the slow pace of ratification. With respect to the African Youth Charter for instance, at the time of writing this chapter, only 41 of the 55 AU member states have ratified the Charter.[82] Compared to the progress made with respect to empowering women and the youth respectively, it can be inferred that Africa's youths have indeed, been neglected. Mpungose observes that

> Africa's youth are a key yet neglected constituent in governance processes. Although there are sufficient frameworks guiding participation, policy remains focused on a rights-based approach without specifications regarding political and civic participation, levels of participation and capacity building. As a result, there is insufficient monitoring of and reporting on youth participation.[83]

It is a cause for concern that the implementation progress report does not consider the protection of children in line with the aspiration for an Africa that cares for its children. States have a duty to protect children from harm, including from the negative impacts of conflicts. States also have a duty of care, meaning that they are the upper guardians of children. The Convention on the Rights of the Child (CRC) defines a child as anyone who has not yet attained the age of 18 and provides that all children deserve special care and protection.[84] This includes protection from conscription into the military or armed groups as child soldiers. The CRC provides that "States Parties shall take all feasible measures to ensure that persons who have not attained the age of

80 African Union (2019–2023) African Plan of Action for Youth Employment Available at: https://au.int/sites/default/files/documents/38229-doc-apaye_final_eng_ok.pdf (consulted 7 December 2024).

81 AU-NEPAD, supra note 24, 47.

82 African Youth Charter Status List. Available at: https://au.int/sites/default/files/treaties/7789-sl-AFRICAN_YOUTH_CHARTER_0.pdf (consulted 7 December 2024).

83 Mpungose, supra note 71, 5.

84 Convention on the Rights of the Child, adopted by UN GA Resolution 44/25, on 20 November 1989, 44 UN GA Resolution Supp. No 49, UN Doc A/44/736, Art 1.

fifteen years do not take a direct part in hostilities".[85] The African Charter on the Rights and Welfare of the Child (African Children's Charter) further provides that no child may be recruited as a child soldier.[86]

Additional Protocol I and II to the 1949 Geneva Conventions adopted in 1977, prohibit the recruitment of children under the age of 15 into international and non-international armed conflicts.[87] Considering the prevalence of conflicts in Africa, and the incidents of children being recruited as child soldiers to engage in hostilities,[88] It would have been a step in the right direction for the implementation progress report to include progress achieved by AU member states in preventing and/or stopping the recruitment of child soldiers. This would align with the AU's aspiration that "The Africa of 2063 will be a continent where [...] children are nurtured and cherished".[89] The targets for 2063 with respect to goal 18 initially included ending all forms of violence against children by 2020, and ending the phenomena of recruitment of child soldiers by 2020.[90] With the commitment to silence the guns by 2020 having been missed, it follows that the targets to end all forms of violence against children and the recruitment of child soldiers, have also been missed. Children are the future of the continent. When their lives are affected by violence and recruitment of child soldiers amongst other violations; this has an adverse impact on the development of the continent. It is worth pointing out that the second implementation progress report does not include the recruitment of child soldiers as one of the indicators for Goal 18.[91]

85 Ibid at Art 38(2) and (4).

86 African Charter on the Rights and Welfare of the Child of 1990, OAU Doc CAB/LEG/24.9/49, Art 22(2).

87 Protocol Additional to the Geneva Conventions of 12 August 1949 and relating to the Protection of Victims of International Armed Conflicts (Protocol I) adopted 8 June 1977, Art 77(2); Protocol Additional to the Geneva Conventions of 12 August 1949, and relating to the Protection of Victims of Non-International Armed Conflicts (Protocol II) adopted 8 June 1977, Art 4(3)(c) and 4(3)(d).

88 Faulkner, Christopher (2024, 25 February) Why Child Soldiering Persists in Africa. *Georgetown Journal of International Affairs*. Available at: https://gjia.georgetown.edu/2024/02/25/why-child-soldiering-persists-in-africa/ (consulted 7 December 2024).

89 AU Agenda 2063, supra note 4, 40.

90 Ibid at 157.

91 AU-NEPAD, supra note 24, 139. The indicators used for Goal 18 are level of implementation of the African Charter on the Rights of the Youth by member states; rate of youth unemployment; percentage of children who are human trafficking victims, and percentage of children engaged in child marriage.

3 Draft International Covenant on the Right to Development

This section analyses the draft International Covenant on the Right to Development (draft Covenant) within the context of Aspirations 1, 4 and 6 and their stated goals and targets and highlights why despite Agenda 2063 and the UN Sustainable Development Goals (SDGs), it is still important for the International Covenant on the Right to Development to be adopted. In 2018, the UN Human Rights Council adopted Resolution 39/9, paving the way for "a draft legally binding instrument on the right to development".[92] The mandate to draft the Covenant was given to the Special Working Group on the Right to Development.[93] The draft Covenant draws from the UN Declaration on the Right to Development (the Declaration) adopted in 1986.[94] The Declaration conceived of development as an inalienable human right and accordingly, recognises that the human person should be at the centre of development initiatives. Article 1(1) of the Declaration provides that "The right to development is an inalienable human right by virtue of which every human person and all peoples are entitled to participate in, contribute to, and enjoy economic, social, cultural and political development, in which all human rights and fundamental freedoms can be fully realized".[95]

The draft Covenant also draws from other instruments including the Universal Declaration of Human Rights, the International Covenant on Economic, Social and Cultural Rights (ICESCR) and the International Covenant on Civil and Political Rights. The UN Working Group on the Right to Development published the first (zero) draft known then as the draft Convention on the Right to Development, in January 2020.[96] Although the draft does not create any new concepts, obligations or standards, it does indeed, create new international law obligations with respect to the formulation of rights and their

92 UN General Assembly, A/HRC/RES/39/9, on the Right to Development, adopted on 27 September 2018, Para 17(e).

93 Ibid at Para 17(e).

94 Declaration on the Right to Development Resolution A/RES/41/128 adopted by UN General Assembly on 4 December 1986.

95 Ibid at Art 1(1).

96 Draft Convention on the Right to Development (draft Convention) 17 January 2020, A/HRC/WG.2/21/2; Draft Convention on the Right to Development with Commentaries (the Commentary), 20 January 2020, A/HRC/WG.2/21/2/Add.1; see also Schrijver, Nicolaas (2020) A new Convention on the Human Right to Development: Putting the Cart Before the Horse? *Netherlands Quarterly of Human Rights* 38(2): 84–93; Teshome, Roma Girma (2022) The Draft Convention the Right to Development: A New Dawn to the Recognition of the Right to Development as a Human Right. *Human Rights Law Review* 22(2): 1–24.

associated obligations which have thus far been non-binding, into legally binding standards.[97]

The Preamble to the draft Covenant stipulates that state parties consider that "[…] peace and security at all levels is an essential element for the realization of the right to development and that such realization can, in turn, contribute to the establishment, maintenance and strengthening of peace and security at all levels".[98] This underscores the argument that conflict hinders development. The Working Group on the Right to Development released the revised draft in March 2022.[99] A notable change in the revised draft is the replacement of the words "human-rights based approach to development" with the words "human rights based development".[100] This was at the request of states from the Global South, which Nagakiri argues, was a regressive move.[101] This chapter disagrees with Nagakiri's view and asserts that human rights based development perceives development not as a charity enterprise but as part of efforts towards the realisation of human rights.

A human-rights based approach perceives development assistance given by donors as a means to facilitate the realisation of rights for the recipients of aid.[102] A human rights-based approach to development also presupposes that the need for capacity building and service delivery are not the prerequisites for development aid but that a state that needs the aid must meet conditions, including the upholding of minimum standards of human rights for its citizens.[103] Whilst it is not in dispute that states have a duty to uphold human rights, there is also general consensus that in recent years politically

97 Deutsches Institut fur Meunscheurechte (2020, October) First Draft of an International Covenant on the Right to Development. Position Paper. Available at: https://www.ohchr.org/sites/default/files/Documents/Issues/Development/Session21/Comments/3-3-gihr.pdf (consulted 6 December 2024), 2.

98 Draft Convention, supra note 66, Preamble.

99 UN General Assembly, Human Rights Council, Working Group on the Right to Development (2022, May) Revised Draft Convention on the Right to Development A/HRC/WG.2/23/2 (Revised Draft Convention); see also Nakagiri, Makoto (2022, 19 September) Struggles to Reconcile Theory and Politics: Comments on the Revised Draft Convention on the Right to Development. *EJIL Talk*. Available at: https://www.ejiltalk.org/struggles-to-reconcile-theory-and-politics-comments-on-the-revised-draft-convention-on-the-right-to-development/ (consulted 6 December 2024).

100 Revised Draft Convention on the Right to Development, supra note 96, Art 3(c).

101 Nakagiri, supra note 99.

102 Broberg, Marten and Otto-Sano, Hans (2018) Strengths and Weaknesses in a Human Rights-Based Approach to International Development: An Analysis of a Rights-Based Approach to Development Assistance Based on Practical Experiences. *International Journal of Human Rights* 22(5): 667.

103 Ibid at 668.

powerful states in the Global North have used aid as a tool to interfere in the internal affairs of states in the Global South.[104] The continued conditionalities attached to development aid arguably, constitute an extension of the legacy of colonialism during which countries from the Global South were subjugated on account of their being "uncivilised".[105]

Most countries in the Global South view the duty to cooperate internationally as one that prioritises the realisation of economic, social and cultural rights before civil and political rights in the sense that developed states should provide development aid, without conditionalities.[106] The wording "human-rights based development" as opposed to "human-rights based approach" is commensurate with the AU's goal for Africa, taking full responsibility to finance development on the continent (Goal 20) and the aspiration for "Africa as a strong influential global partner" as stipulated in Aspiration 7.

The revised draft also notably expanded on the international peace and security provision by adding a sub paragraph which stipulates that "States Parties undertake to promote peace and inclusive societies within their territories for the full realization of the right to development for all".[107] This is significant as it highlights the importance of states being proactive rather than reactionary in fostering peace, which in turn will reduce the incidents of conflict. The second revised text of the draft Convention on the Right to Development was released by the Working Group in January 2023.[108] Like the two previous drafts, the second revised draft draws on the Universal Declaration of Human Rights and the United Nations Declaration on the Right to Development as well as the nine core human rights treaties. The provision on international peace and development was retained as conceived in Article 22 of the second revised draft.[109] The Expert Drafting Group rejected a suggestion by the Holy See to

---

104 Apodaca, Clair (2017) Foreign Aid as Foreign Policy Tool. *Oxford Research Encyclopedia of Politics*, 1–19.

105 Anghie, Anthony (2007) *Imperialism, Sovereignty and the Making of International Law*. Cambridge University Press.

106 Whelan, Daniel (2022) The Right to Development. In: *The Oxford Research Encyclopedia of International Studies*. Oxford University Press.

107 Revised draft Convention on the Right to Development, supra note 99, Art 22(3).

108 United Nations General Assembly, Human Rights Council, Working Group on the Right to Development, Second Revised Text of the draft of the Convention on the Right to Development, With Commentaries A/HRC/WG. 2/24/2/Add.1.

109 Ibid at Article 22, Commentary A, Para 1.

delete the words “inclusive societies” on the basis that lack of inclusive societies is one of the key threats to peace and to the right to development.[110] The United Nations Office on Drugs and Crime suggested adding an undertaking in Paragraph 3 of the draft Article 22 to “significantly reduce illicit arms flows” before the words “promote peace”. The Expert Drafting Group however, did not accept this recommendation as it opined that it would be better to leave the provision broad rather than confining it to a specific mechanism for the promotion of peace.[111] The reference to human-rights based development rather than human rights-based approach to development was retained in draft Article 3(c). As in the previous drafts, some countries (Russia, Algeria, Iran, Egypt and China) were opposed to the words “human-rights based development” on the basis that the concept is controversial.[112] The Expert Drafting Group rejected the opposition expressed by these countries, noting as follows:

> the human rights-based approach practised by many donor countries, or their development agencies, requires recipients of development aid or assistance to ensure respect for human rights while implementing development projects, including through transparent and accountable institutions. While this is indispensable and intrinsic to the right to development, in such frameworks it is not generally considered the duty of donors to realize development and not impede it [...] Aid or assistance as loans designed to increase debt, with predatory conditionalities attached or requiring contracts for donor companies can violate the right to development of recipients.[113]

The Expert Drafting Group emphasised that “This lopsided deployment of human rights-based approach to development is contrary to the right to development that requires an equal focus on all three dimensions of obligations of States—internal, external, and collective”.[114] There is no consensus on the need for a covenant on the right to development between countries in the Global North and those in the Global South. Countries in theGglobal North like the United Kingdom and those under the auspices of the European Union, have consistently argued against the adoption of the Covenant on the Right to Development, advocating instead for countries to focus on achieving the

110 Ibid at Para 2.
111 Ibid at Para 3.
112 Ibid at Art 3, Commentary A, Para 1.
113 Ibid at Art 3, Commentary B, Para 2.
114 Ibid.

Sustainable Development Goals (SDGs).[115] This view is shared by Schrijver, who argues that the right to development already exists through Article 11 of the ICESCR and that state parties only need to take it seriously.[116] Nakagari argues with respect to the zero draft that it "attempts to change international law without consent of the international community, especially of Western donor States".[117] It is noted in this regard that development aid must not be confused with the right to development.[118] Teshome has aptly pointed out that the adoption of a universally binding treaty on the right to development would be significant, and that the merits of the draft Convention should be assessed based on not only its legal authority—whether or not a binding treaty is viable but also to what extent its normative content adds to the existing frameworks.[119] This chapter agrees with Teshome's view, and argues that the adoption of a legally binding treaty might result in AU member states taking their duty to implement Agenda 2063 more seriously. The jurisprudence of national courts,[120] the African Court on Human and Peoples' Rights,[121] and the African Commission on Human and Peoples' Rights[122] affirm that the right to development is justiciable.[123]

115 CETIM Press Release (2023, 31 May) The Convention on the Right to Development on the Right Track. Available at: https://www.cetim.ch/24th-session-of-the-wg-on-the-right-to-development/ (consulted 6 December 2024).

116 Schrijver, supra note 96, 93.

117 Nakagiri, Makoto (2021) The Zero Draft Convention on the Right to Development as a Non-consensual Lawmaking: International and Domestic Dimension. Master Thesis, Aix-Marseille University, 3.

118 CETIM Statement (2022, 29 June) Significant progress on the Draft Convention on the Right to Development. Available at: https://www.cetim.ch/significant-progress-on-the-draft-convention-on-the-right-to-development/ (consulted 6 December 2024).

119 Teshome, supra note 96; see also Feyter, Koen De (2013, April) Towards a Framework Convention on the Right to Development. *Global Policy Forum*. Available at: https://archive.globalpolicy.org/component/content/article/211-development/52393-towards-a-framework-convention-on-the-right-to-development.html (consulted 5 December 2024).

120 *Republic of South Africa v Grootboom*, Case No CCT 11/00 2000 (11) BCLR 1169; *Minister of Health v Treatment Action* Campaign Case No CCT 8/02 2002 (10) BCLR 1033; *Soobramoney v Minister of Health (KwaZulu-Natal)*, Case No CCT 32/97 1997 (12) BCLR 1696; Sentencia C-175/09, Colombia: Corte Constitucional, 18 March 2009.

121 *African Commission on Human and Peoples' Rights v Republic of Kenya*, Comm 006/2012, ACtHPR, 26 May 2017.

122 *Centre for Minority Rights Development (Kenya) and Minority Rights Group International on Behalf of Endorois Welfare Council v Kenya*, Comm 276/2003, 46th Ordinary Session of the ACHPR, 25 November 2009.

123 Teshome, supra note 96, 5.

4 "A Peaceful and Secure Africa?": the Cabo Delgado Conflict

The Cabo Delgado conflict began in October 2017 and escalated in August 2020 when insurgents took control of the town of Mocimboa da Praia.[124] Commentators have identified different factors as the drivers of the insurgency in Cabo Delgado. These include the radicalisation of young Muslims by preachers from Tanzania and Kenya,[125] marginalisation of the youth who are now demanding for their views to be considered seriously by the government,[126] unemployment, poverty and perceived neglect of the people of Cabo Delgado by the state[127] and external factors including Kenyan migrant militants to Mozambique.[128]

Although there are varied reasons for the conflict, it is not in dispute that the overarching driver of the conflict is the socio-economic problems that have resulted in poverty and human insecurity amongst the Mozambican population.[129] The discovery of natural gas in the Cabo Delgado area in 2010 brought hope to the local people who believed that this development would result in better employment opportunities and poverty eradication in the area.[130] Cabo Delgado is the poorest province in Mozambique, hence the discovery of natural gas in the region was perceived by the locals as a turning point.[131] Contrary to the people's expectations, the youth tried without success to secure employment in the gas companies which reportedly employed people from other provinces.[132] This led to disgruntlement amongst the local population especially, the youth who have been identified as the main instigators in the attacks.[133]

124 De Almeida, Tomas (2024, 10 October) 7 Years into the Conflict, Solutions to Displacement in Cabo Delgado Remain Elusive. *Internal Monitoring Displacement Centre*. Available at: https://www.internal-displacement.org/expert-analysis/7-years-into-the-conflict-solutions-to-displacement-in-cabo-delgado-remain-elusive/ (consulted 7 December 2024); see also Ntaka, Buyisile (2023) The Cabo Delgado Insurgency: A Symptom of Governance Failure in Mozambique. *African Journal of Governance and Development* 12(1): 28–29.

125 Ntaka, supra note 124, 31.

126 Hanlon, Joseph (2018, 19 June) Mozambique's Insurgency: A New Boko Haram or Youth Demanding an End to Marginalisation? *LSE Research Online*. Available at: https://eprints.lse.ac.uk/90103/ (consulted 7 December 2024).

127 Ntaka, supra note 125; Mutasa, Makaita Noel and Muchemwa, Cyprian Ansar Al-Sunna Mozambique: Is it the Boko Haram of Southern Africa? *Journal of Applied Security Research* 17(3): 332–351.

128 Ntaka, supra note 124; International Crisis Group, supra note 45.

129 Ntaka, supra note 124.

130 Matsinhe, supra note 34.

131 Ntaka, supra note 124, 31.

132 Hanlon, supra note 126; Ntaka, supra note 124, 30.

133 Hanlon, supra note 126.

The conflict has led to the displacement of approximately 1,3 million people in northern Mozambique.[134] There are approximately 9 000 internal displacements between 2017 and 2019; 592 000 in 2020 and 286 000 in 2022.[135] Due to relatively lower conflict levels owing to improvements in the security situation including the presence of SAMIM; there was a significant 86% decrease in internal displacement in 2023.[136] As at December 2023, there were 709 529 internally displaced persons (IDPs) across 264 locations in southern, central and northern Mozambique. About 76% of these IDPs were from Cabo Delgado alone.[137] According to more recent statistics, attacks in Mueda, Muidumbe, and Mocimboa da Praia have displaced 2,073 persons between 23 and 29 October 2024.[138] It has also been reported that the number of returnees is declining significantly due to a resurgence of violent attacks.[139]

The conflict in Cabo Delgado has resulted in a humanitarian crisis, with the affected people experiencing loss of livelihoods and increased vulnerabilities. The IDPs have faced a myriad of challenges including mental distress, separation of families and lack of civil documentation to enable them access essential services.[140] As at March 2024, 182 unaccompanied children and 154 missing children were registered.[141] Women without civil documentation are vulnerable to discrimination, harassment, sexual exploitation and abuse among other forms of gender-based violence. Men without civil documents are also vulnerable to arbitrary detention by armed forces, physical violence and harassment.[142] IDPs have many needs including access to education and health care, food and shelter.[143] Even those who have not been internally displaced

134 De Almeida, supra note 124.

135 Ibid.

136 Ibid.

137 International Organisation for Migration (2024, 26 September) Mozambique—National Displacement Profile (NDP) 2023. Available at: https://dtm.iom.int/reports/mozambique-national-displacement-profile-ndp-2023?close=true (consulted 7 December 2024).

138 International Organisation for Migration (2024, 4 November) Mozambique—Emergency Tracking Tool Report—Movement Alert #115. Available at: https://dtm.iom.int/reports/mozambique-emergency-tracking-tool-report-movement-alert-115-04-november-2024?close=true (consulted 7 December 2024).

139 Ibid.

140 United Nations Office for the Coordination of Humanitarian Affairs (OCHA) (2024) Mozambique: Displacement in Northern Cabo Delgado—Situation Report No 1 (as of 15 March 2024). Available at: https://www.unocha.org/publications/report/mozambique/mozambique-displacement-northern-cabo-delgado-situation-report-no-1-15-march-2024 (consulted 7 December 2024).

141 Ibid.

142 Ibid.

143 Reliefweb (2024, 5 September) Mozambique: 2024 Humanitarian Response Dashboard—Conflict (June 2024). Available at: https://reliefweb.int/report/mozambique/mozambi

bear the brunt of the conflict. Children have been exposed to violations including rape and other forms of sexual violence; attacks on schools and medical facilities; abduction and recruitment and use of children as child soldiers. According to UNICEF the conflict in Mozambique is considered to be one with critical child protection needs.[144] In May 2024, boys as young as 13 were used by the group locally known as Al-Shabaab to raid the town of Macomia.[145] In July 2024, Save the Children reported that the rising violence in Cabo Delgado was leading to an increase in the number of girls forced into early marriages through abduction by armed forces or given away by families in need of dowry.[146]

Armed conflicts not only threaten peace and security, but also foreign direct investment. The armed conflict in Cabo Delgado has led to disruptions in the natural gas projects in the region. On 26 April 2021, TotalEnergies declared *force majeure* on its LNG gas project. In addition, the company announced that it was withdrawing its entire staff from the site on the Afungi Peninsula following the attacks of 24 and 25 March 2021 on the town of Palma.[147] More than 3 years after the *force majeure* declaration, TotalEnergies has not yet resumed operations although it has indicated that work will resume, without giving a definitive date. In September 2024, the out-going Mozambican President Felipe Nyusi said, the company was waiting for the outcome of elections to resume operations so as to avoid uncertainties.[148] The presidential and parliamentary elections were held on 9 October 2024 and the ruling Frelimo

---

que-2024-humanitarian-response-dashboard-conflict-june-2024 (consulted 7 December 2024).

144 UNICEF (d.n.a.) UNICEF Response to Children Affected by Armed Conflict in Northern Mozambique. Available at: https://www.unicef.org/mozambique/media/4661/file/UNICEF%20response%20to%20children%20affected%20by%20armed%20conflict%20in%20northern%20Mozambique.pdf (consulted 7 December 2024).

145 Reliefweb (2024, 15 May) Mozambique: Child Soldiers Used in Raid on Northern Town. Available at: https://reliefweb.int/report/mozambique/mozambique-child-soldiers-used-raid-northern-town (consulted 7 December 2024).

146 Save the Children (2024, 3 July) Mozambique: Rising Violence Driving up Child Marriage in Cabo Delgado Province. Available at: https://www.savethechildren.net/news/mozambique-rising-violence-driving-child-marriage-cabo-delgado-province (consulted 7 December 2024).

147 TotalEnergies Press Release (2021, 26 April) Total Declares Force Majeure on Mozambique LNG Project. Available at: https://totalenergies.com/media/news/press-releases/total-declares-force-majeure-mozambique-lng-project (consulted 7 December 2024).

148 Club of Mozambique News (2024, 25 September) Mozambique: TotalEnergies is Waiting for Election Outcome to Resume LNG Project—Nyusi. Available at: https://clubofmozambique.com/news/mozambique-totalenergies-is-waiting-for-election-outcome-to-resume-lng-project-nyusi-267053/ (consulted 7 December 2024).

party's Daniel Chapo was declared the winner, to succeed Nyusi.[149] The opposition party led by Venancio Mondlane and civilians rejected the election outcome as fraudulent and this has led to widespread protests in the country.[150] Approximately 66 people had reportedly been killed during the protests as of 8 November 2024.[151] The post-election violence not only renders the anticipated resumption of operations in Cabo Delgado by TotalEnergies more uncertain, it also heightens the security threat of an already fragile Mozambique, which has to grapple with the armed conflict in the Cabo Delgado region.

4.1 *The Role of SADC in Stemming the Armed Conflict in Cabo Delgado*

SADC has been at the forefront of responding to the Cabo Delgado conflict. This is in line with the principle of subsidiarity, in terms of which the AU must defer to the RECs and only intervene when the RECs have failed or have requested the AU to intervene.[152] In June 2021, SADC approved the deployment of SAMIM and the peacekeeping mission was launched in August of the same year.[153] SADC approved the extension of SAMIM's mandate in October 2021 and in January 2022 and by April 2022, SAMIM was downscaled from an enforcement to a peacekeeping operation.[154] In August 2023, the AU Assembly extended SAMIM's mandate to July 2024.[155] The SAMIM's successes include

149 The Conversation (2024, 16 October) Mozambique's 2024 Elections: 9 Major Challenges that Will Face the New President. Available at: https://theconversation.com/mozambiques-2024-elections-9-major-challenges-that-will-face-the-new-president-240923 (consulted 7 December 2024).

150 AP News (2024, 2 November) Why Mozambique's Election Has Sparked Weeks of Protests and a Violent Crackdown by Police. Available at: https://apnews.com/article/mozambique-election-protests-violence-unrest-frelimo-e732c78af8f39f89862c85f408d40c75 (consulted 7 December 2024).

151 Reuters (2024, 8 November) Three Killed, 66 Injured in Mozambique Opposition Protest, Hospital Says. Available at: https://www.reuters.com/world/africa/three-killed-66-injured-mozambique-opposition-protest-hospital-says-2024-11-08/ (consulted 7 December 2024).

152 Djilo, Felicite and Handy, Paul-Simon (2021, 17 December) Unscrambling Subsidiarity in the African Union: From Competition to Collaboration. *Institute for Security Studies*. Available at: https://issafrica.org/research/africa-report/unscrambling-subsidiarity-in-the-african-union-from-competition-to-collaboration (consulted 7 December 2024).

153 SADC News (2021, 10 November) SADC Mission in Mozambique (SAMIM) in Brief. Available at: https://www.sadc.int/latest-news/sadc-mission-mozambique-samim-brief (consulted 7 December 2024).

154 Martin, Guy and Helfrich, Kim (2022, 4 April) SAMIM Deployment Extended and Mandate Altered. *Defence Web*. Available at: https://www.defenceweb.co.za/featured/samim-deployment-extended-and-mandate-altered/ (consulted 7 December 2024).

155 African Union (2024) Communiqué of the 1203rd Meeting of the Peace and Security Council held on 4 March 2024, on Updated Briefing on the Operations of the SADC

the confiscation of weapons, dislodging of insurgents from their bases and retaking control of captured villages.[156] This created an enabling environment for the flow of humanitarian aid, and the return of IDPs whose livelihoods were secured through the establishment of development projects.[157] Since the conflict began, more than 610 000 IDPs have returned to their homes.[158]

Despite these positive strides, there are other areas in which SAMIM did not achieve its objectives notably, in the fact that SAMIM did not train the Mozambican security forces, because the Mozambican government was not able to identify the training needs.[159] It has however, been explained that the Mozambican security forces received training from other stakeholders like the United States, a private security company (Benham) and the European Union.[160] The withdrawal of SAMIM has been described as premature. Following the May 2024 attacks in Macomia, Opperman and Pigou argued that SAMIM's withdrawal paved the way for the insurgents to regroup, which led to the resurgence of violence in the Cabo Delgado region.[161] For Opperman and Pigou, "SAMIM didn't achieve a battlefield victory. Instead, it stabilised vital parts of the province by displacing rather than neutralising insurgents. In the absence of a comprehensive counter-insurgency strategy and with time on their side, IS has manoeuvred to fight another day in Mozambique".[162]

Whilst acknowledging that SAMIM's withdrawal was premature, Sambo has argued that the withdrawal ought to be considered within the broader scope of the challenges in carrying out its mandate, including the lack of predictable, sustainable and sufficient financial resources.[163] Lack of funding is one

Mission in Mozambique (SAMIM). Available at: https://papsrepository.africa-union.org/handle/123456789/2048 (consulted 7 December 2024).

156 Chidzanjja, Chikondi (2023, 20 December) Situating the SAMIM Model Within the Pragmatic Peace Operations Approach. *ACCORD*. Available at: https://www.accord.org.za/analsis/situating-the-samim-model-within-the-pragmatic-peace-operations-approach/ (consulted 7 December 2024).

157 Mandrup, Thomas (2024, 24 April) Lessons from the SADC Mission in Mozambique (SAMIM). *ACCORD*. Available at: https://www.accord.org.za/analysis/lessons-from-the-sadc-mission-in-mozambique-samim/ (consulted 7 December 2024).

158 De Almeida, supra note 126.

159 Mandrup, supra note 157.

160 Ibid.

161 Opperman, Jasmine and Pigou, Piers (2024, 30 May) SAMIM Withdrawal from Cabo Delgado: Uncomfortable Truths. *Institute for Security Studies Today*. Available at: https://issafrica.org/iss-today/samim-withdrawal-from-cabo-delgado-uncomfortable-truths (consulted 7 December 2024).

162 Ibid.

163 Sambo, Manuel Francisco (2024, 15 May) Mozambique's "War on Terror": Why are Regional Troops Withdrawing? *Journal of Global Policy*. Available at: https://www.global

of the factors that hamper efforts by the AU and its RECs in responding to conflicts on the continent among other challenges. This has had a negative impact on socio-economic growth and development, hampered the successful implementation of Agenda 2063 and also compromised realisation of the right to development guaranteed to the peoples of Africa, including the people of Mozambique where prospects for realising the right are being eroded by the ongoing conflict.

The withdrawal of SAMIM has however, not created a complete security vacuum in Cabo Delgado. The Rwandan government entered into a bilateral agreement with the Mozambican government and deployed a joint peacekeeping force comprising of police and armed forces.[164] Rwanda is not a SADC member state but as an AU member state, its role in peacekeeping in Cabo Delgado is acknowledged and significant. The Cabo Delgado conflict as discussed above is a classic example of how conflict hinders development in Africa.

5 Conclusion

This chapter has highlighted the fact that the right to development is a universally recognised human right, and in this vein, it has examined the progress in implementation of the right through Aspirations 1, 4 and 6 of the AU developmental blueprint, Agenda 2063. The chapter has equally underscored the lack of, or slow pace of implementation of the Agenda 2063 aspirations and their related goals, which is partly attributed to the impact of the armed conflicts that are prevalent on the African continent. The analysis has sought to establish the fact that there is a link between peace and development by outlining the progress made by African countries in the implementation of Agenda 2063 between 2013 and 2022. The available data shows that those countries which managed to record significant progress with respect to the selected aspirations, are countries which are not experiencing conflict including Mauritius and Egypt. Using the conflict in Cabo Delgado as a case study, the chapter illustrates how armed conflicts and insurgencies not only threaten peace and

policyjournal.com/blog/15/05/2024/mozambiques-war-terror-why-are-regional-troops-withdrawing (consulted 7 December 2024).

164 Ministry of Defence, Government of Rwanda (2021, 10 July) Rwanda Deploys Joint Force to Mozambique. Available at: https://www.mod.gov.rw/news-detail/rwanda-deploys-joint-force-to-mozambique-1 (consulted 7 December 2024); Shield, Ralph (2024) Rwanda's War in Mozambique: Road-Testing a Kigali Principles approach to counterinsurgency? *Small Wars and Insurgencies* 35(1): 80–117.

security but also foreign direct investment and a hindrance to socio-economic development.

The UN has expressed pessimism at the possibility of the SDGs being met by the 2030 deadline. Like Agenda 2063, the SDGs are also anchored on development issues and the right to development. The Agenda 2063 aspirations and goals are directly aligned to the SDGs. For instance, Agenda 2063 Goal 17 aligns with SDG 5 which both envisage to "Achieve gender equality and empower all women and girls" while Aspirations 3 and 4 of Agenda 2063 align with SDG 16, which aims to "Promote peaceful and inclusive societies for sustainable development, provide access to justice for all and build effective, accountable and inclusive institutions at all levels." It is noted in conclusion that adoption of the Covenant on the Right to Development will be pivotal in reinforcing states' obligations on the right to development and in ensuring effective implementation of the development aspirations contained in Agenda 2063 and the SDG frameworks for development.

References

Aboumbeng, Asumbeng Sunday (2017) AU and SADC Involvement in Conflict Resolution in the Democratic Republic of Congo (DRC): Testing the AU's Principle of Non-Indifference. University of Johannesburg Master of Arts Thesis.

Adelakun, O. (2023) Gender Mainstreaming in Post-Conflict Reconstruction in North-East Nigeria. In: Onuora-Oguno, A. (ed) *Promoting Efficiency in Jurisprudence and Constitutional Development in Africa*. Cham: Springer Nature, 95–118.

African Charter on Human and Peoples' Rights adopted in Nairobi, Kenya on 27 June 1981 OAU Doc CAB/LEG/67/3 Rev.5 (1981).

African Charter on Human and Peoples' Rights adopted in Nairobi, Kenya on 27 June 1981 OAU Doc CAB/LEG/67/3 Rev.5 (1981).

African Charter on the Rights and Welfare of the Child of 1990, OAU Doc CAB/LEG/24.9/49.

African Commission on Human and Peoples' Rights v Republic of Kenya (Ogiek Case), Comm 006/2012, ACtHPR, 26 May 2017.

African Union (2013) 50th Anniversary Solemn Declaration. Available at: https://au.int/sites/default/files/documents/36205-doc-50th_anniversary_solemn_declaration_en.pdf (consulted 6 December 2024).

African Union (2019–2023) African Plan of Action for Youth Employment. Available at: https://au.int/sites/default/files/documents/38229-doc-apaye_final_eng_ok.pdf (consulted 7 December 2024).

African Union (2024) Communiqué of the 1203rd Meeting of the Peace and Security Council held on 4 March 2024, on Updated Briefing on the Operations of the SADC Mission in Mozambique (SAMIM). Available at: https://papsrepository.africa-union.org/handle/123456789/2048 (consulted 7 December 2024).

African Union (2024) Youth Development. Available at: https://au.int/en/youth-development (accessed 6 December 2024).

African Union Commission (2015) Agenda 2063: The Africa we want. *African Union.*

African Union Commission (2017) AU Roadmap on Harnessing the Demographic Dividend through Investments in the Youth. Available at: https://library.au.int/au-roadmap-harnessing-demographic-dividend-through-investments-youth (consulted 7 December 2024).

African Union Concept Note (2014, 24 April) On Silencing the Guns: Pre-requisites for Realising a Conflict-Free Africa by the Year 2020 for the Open Session of the Peace and Security Council of the African Union, AU New Conference Centre, Addis Ababa. Available at: https://www.peaceau.org/en/article/open-session-on-silencing-guns-pre-requisites-for-achieving-a-conflict-free-africa-by-2020 (consulted 6 December 2024).

African Union Declaration on the 2017 AU Theme Harnessing the Demographic Dividend through Investments in Youth Assembly/AU/Decl. 1(XXIX) July 2017.

African Union Development Agency-NEPAD (2022, February) Second Continental Report on the Implementation of Agenda 2063. Available at: https://au.int/sites/default/files/documents/41480-doc-2nd_Continental_Progress_Report_on_Agenda_2063_English.pdf (consulted 7 December 2024).

African Union Press Release (2024, 29 April) Silencing the Guns in Africa: Building a Roadmap to a Conflict Free Continent. Available at: https://au.int/sites/default/files/newsevents/pressreleases/25651-pr-com-durban-silencing-guns.pdf (consulted 6 December 2024).

African Youth Charter adopted by the 7th Ordinary Session of the AU Assembly of Heads of State and Government in Banjul, the Gambia on 2 July 2006.

African Youth Charter Status List. Available at: https://au.int/sites/default/files/treaties/7789-sl-AFRICAN_YOUTH_CHARTER_0.pdf (consulted 7 December 2024).

Allen, Nate (2023, 9 August) African-Led Peace Operations: A Crucial Tool for Peace and Security. *African Centre for Strategic Studies.* Available at: https://africacenter.org/wp-content/uploads/2024/05/African-Led-Peace-Operations.pdf (consulted 6 December 2024).

Anghie, Anthony (2007) *Imperialism, Sovereignty and the Making of International Law.* Cambridge University Press.

AP News (2024, 2 November) Why Mozambique's Election Has Sparked Weeks of Protests and a Violent Crackdown by Police. Available at: https://apnews.com/article

/mozambique-election-protests-violence-unrest-frelimo-e732c78af8f39f89862c85f408d40975 (consulted 7 December 2024).

Apodaca, Clair (2017) Foreign Aid as Foreign Policy Tool. *Oxford Research Encyclopedia of Politics*, 1–19.

Armed Conflict Location and Event Data (2024, 14 April) One Year of War in Sudan. Available at: https://acleddata.com/2024/04/14/sudan-situation-update-april-2024-one-year-of-war-in-sudan/ (consulted 6 December 2024).

Birhan, Aemro Tenaw (2024) The African Union and Conflict Resolution: Challenges and Prospects. *Social Science and Humanities Journal* 8(3): 34576–34585.

Broberg, Marten and Otto-Sano, Hans (2018) Strengths and Weaknesses in a Human Rights-Based Approach to International Development: An Analysis of a Rights-Based Approach to Development Assistance Based on Practical Experiences. *International Journal of Human Rights* 22(5): 664–680.

Centre for Minority Rights Development (Kenya) and Minority Rights Group International on Behalf of Endorois Welfare Council v Kenya, Comm 276/2003, 46th Ordinary Session of the ACHPR, 25 November 2009.

CETIM Press Release (2023, 31 May) The Convention on the Right to Development on the Right Track. Available at: https://www.cetim.ch/24th-session-of-the-wg-on-the-right-to-development/ (consulted 6 December 2024).

CETIM Statement (2022, 29 June) Significant Progress on the Draft Convention on the Right to Development. Available at: https://www.cetim.ch/significant-progress-on-the-draft-convention-on-the-right-to-development/ (consulted 6 December 2024).

Chidzanjja, Chikondi (2023, 20 December) Situating the SAMIM Model Within the Pragmatic Peace Operations Approach. *ACCORD*. Available at: https://www.accord.org.za/analysis/situating-the-samim-model-within-the-pragmatic-peace-operations-approach/ (consulted 7 December 2024).

Chingutoane, Énio Viegas et al (2021, October) Strategic Options for Managing Violent Extremism in Southern Africa: The Case of Mozambique—Situation Report. Maputo: Friedrich-Ebert-Stiftung.

Club of Mozambique News (2024, 25 September) Mozambique: TotalEnergies is Waiting for Election Outcome to Resume LNG project—Nyusi. Available at: https://clubofmozambique.com/news/mozambique-totalenergies-is-waiting-for-election-outcome-to-resume-lng-project-nyusi-267053/ (consulted 7 December 2024).

Constitutive Act of the African Union adopted in Lomé, Togo on 11 July 2000.

Convention on the Rights of the Child, adopted by UN GA Resolution 44/25, on 20 November 1989, 44 UN GA Resolution Supp No 49, UN Doc A/44/736.

Davis, I. (2022) *Armed Conflict and Peace Processes in Sub-Saharan Africa*. Oxford University Press.

De Almeida, Tomas (2024, 10 October) 7 Years into the Conflict, Solutions to Displacement in Cabo Delgado Remain Elusive. *Internal Monitoring Displacement Centre*. Available at: https://www.internal-displacement.org/expert-analysis/7-years-into

-the-conflict-solutions-to-displacement-in-cabo-delgado-remain-elusive/ (consulted 7 December 2024).

Declaration on the Right to Development Resolution A/RES/41/128 adopted by UN General Assembly on 4 December 1986.

Deutsches Institut fur Meunscheurechte (2020, October) First Draft of an International Covenant on the Right to Development. Position Paper. Available at: https://www.ohchr.org/sites/default/files/Documents/Issues/Development/Session21/Comments/3-3-gihr.pdf (consulted 6 December 2024).

Djilo, Felicite and Handy, Paul-Simon (2021, 17 December) Unscrambling Subsidiarity in the African Union: From Competition to Collaboration. *Institute for Security Studies*. Available at: https://issafrica.org/research/africa-report/unscrambling-subsidiarity-in-the-african-union-from-competition-to-collaboration (consulted 7 December 2024).

Djilo, Felicite and Handy, Paul-Simon (2022, 11 May) Africa's Solutions to Conflict are in Crisis. *Institute for Security Studies Today*. Available at: https://issafrica.org/iss-today/africas-solutions-to-conflict-are-in-crisis (consulted 6 December 2024).

Draft Convention on the Right to Development (draft Convention) 17 January 2020, A/HRC/WG.2/21/2; Draft Convention on the Right to Development with Commentaries (the Commentary), 20 January 2020, A/HRC/WG.2/21/2/Add.1.

Faulkner, Christopher (2024, 25 February) Why Child Soldiering Persists in Africa. *Georgetown Journal of International Affairs*. Available at: https://gjia.georgetown.edu/2024/02/25/why-child-soldiering-persists-in-africa/ (consulted 7 December 2024).

Feyter, Koen De (2013, April) Towards a Framework on the Right to Development. *Global Policy Forum*. Available at: https://archive.globalpolicy.org/component/content/article/211-development/52393-towards-a-framework-convention-on-the-right-to-development.html (consulted 5 December 2024).

Francis, David and Webster, Edward (2019) Poverty and Inequality in South Africa: Critical Reflections. *Development Southern Africa* 36(6): 788–802.

Geneva Academy (2024) Today's Armed Conflicts. Available at: https://geneva-academy.ch/galleries/today-s-armed-conflicts#:~:text=Africa%20comes%20second%20in%20the,Somalia%2C%20South%20Sudan%20and%20Sudan (consulted 6 December 2024).

Gilpin, R. (2016) Understanding the Nature and Origins of Violent Conflict in Africa. In: Aall, P. and Crocker, C.A. (eds) *Minding the Gap: African Conflict Management in a Time of Change*. CIGI Publications, 21–32.

Hanlon, Joseph (2018, 19 June) Mozambique's Insurgency: A New Boko Haram or Youth Demanding an End to Marginalisation? *London School of Economics Research Online*. Available at: https://eprints.lse.ac.uk/90103/ (consulted 7 December 2024).

Herre, Bastian and Arriagada, Pablo (2023, 1 November) The Human Development Index and related Indices: What They Are and What We Can Learn from Them.

Our World in Data. Available at: https://ourworldindata.org/human-development-index#article-citation (consulted 7 December 2024).

Hingston, Claudine Anita (2016) Towards Gender Equality in Africa *Journal of African Union Studies* 5(2): 39–49.

Human Rights Watch (2024, 15 May) Mozambique: Child Soldiers Used in Raid on Northern Town. Available at: https://www.hrw.org/news/2024/05/15/mozambique-child-soldiers-used-raid-northern-town (consulted 6 December 2024).

Institute for Security Studies (2021, 26 March) What can the AU do About the Conflict in Mozambique? *ISS PSC Report*. Available at: https://issafrica.org/pscreport/psc-insights/what-can-the-au-do-about-the-conflict-in-mozambique (consulted 7 December 2024).

International Crisis Group (2021, 11 June) Stemming the Insurrection in Mozambique's Cabo Delgado. Available at: https://www.crisisgroup.org/africa/southern-africa/mozambique/303-stemming-insurrection-mozambiques-cabo-delgado (consulted 6 December 2024).

International Organisation for Migration (2024, 26 September) Mozambique—National Displacement Profile (NDP) 2023. Available at: https://dtm.iom.int/reports/mozambique-national-displacement-profile-ndp-2023?close=true (consulted 7 December 2024).

International Organisation for Migration (2024, 4 November) Mozambique—Emergency Tracking Tool Report—Movement Alert #115. Available at: https://dtm.iom.int/reports/mozambique-emergency-tracking-tool-report-movement-alert-115-04-november-2024?close=true (consulted 7 December 2024).

Louw-Vaudran, Liesl (2022, 28 June) Can Africa Stay on Target to Silence the Guns by 2030? *Institute for Security Studies Today*. Available at: https://issafrica.org/iss-today/can-africa-stay-on-target-to-silence-the-guns-by-2030 (consulted 6 December 2024).

Mandrup, Thomas (2024, 24 April) Lessons from the SADC Mission in Mozambique (SAMIM). *ACCORD*. Available at: https://www.accord.org.za/analysis/lessons-from-the-sadc-mission-in-mozambique-samim/ (consulted 7 December 2024).

Martin, Guy and Helfrich, Kim (2022, 4 April) SAMIM Deployment Extended and Mandate Altered. *Defence Web*. Available at: https://www.defenceweb.co.za/featured/samim-deployment-extended-and-mandate-altered/ (consulted 7 December 2024).

Matsinhe, Sozinho Francisco (2021, 29 April) An Overview of the Conflict in Cabo Delgado: Narratives, Causes and Strategies on the Way Forward. *ACCORD*. Available at: https://www.accord.org.za/analysis/an-overview-of-the-conflict-in-cabo-delgado-narratives-causes-and-strategies-on-the-way-forward/ (consulted 6 December 2024).

Minister of Health v Treatment Action Campaign Case No CCT 8/02 2002 (10) BCLR 1033.

Ministry of Defence, Government of Rwanda (2021, 10 July) Rwanda Deploys Joint Force to Mozambique. Available at: https://www.mod.gov.rw/news-detail/rwanda-deploys-joint-force-to-mozambique-1 (consulted 7 December 2024).

Molinari, C. (2015) Principle 3: From a Right to Development to Intergenerational Equity. In: Vinuales, J. (ed) *The Rio Declaration on Environment and Development: A Commentary*. Oxford: Oxford University Press, 139–156.

Mosala, Seshupo (2024) Pan-Africanism and the Right to Development in Africa: A Critical Analysis of Agenda 2063. *African Renaissance* 21(2): 129–149.

Mpungose, Luanda (2020, June) Africa's Diverging Approaches to Youth Inclusion and Participation. *South African Institute of International Affairs—Occasional Paper No 307*, 1–28.

Mpungose, Luanda and Monyae, Lennon (2018) Carrying Forward the Momentum of the 2017 African Year of the Youth. *South African Institute of International Affairs—Policy Insights 60*. Available at: https://view.ckcest.cn/AllFiles/ZKBG/Pages/85/af4ed0259996fa2f91763e30ee8c30e04f878433.pdf (consulted 7 December 2024).

Mushoriwa, L. and Njieassam, E. (2023) COVID-19 and the Implementation of Aspiration 1 of the African Union's Agenda 2063: The Case of South Africa, Zimbabwe and Eswatini. In: Onuora-Oguno, A. (ed) *Promoting Efficiency in Jurisprudence and Constitutional Development in Africa*. Cham: Springer Nature, 53–75.

Mushoriwa, Linda (2023) The African Union's Quest for a "Peaceful and Secure Africa": An Assessment of Aspiration 4 of Agenda 2063. *Law, Development and Democracy* 27(2003): 55–92.

Mutasa, Makaita Noel and Muchemwa, Cyprian Ansar Al-Sunna Mozambique: Is it the Boko Haram of Southern Africa? *Journal of Applied Security Research* 17(3): 332–351.

Nakagiri, Makoto (2021) The Zero Draft Convention on the Right to Development as a Non-consensual Lawmaking: International and Domestic Dimension. Masters Thesis, Aix-Marseille University.

Nakagiri, Makoto (2022, 19 September) Struggles to Reconcile Theory and Politics: Comments on the Revised Draft Convention on the Right to Development. *EJIL Talk*. Available at https://www.ejiltalk.org/struggles-to-reconcile-theory-and-politics-comments-on-the-revised-draft-convention-on-the-right-to-development/ (consulted 6 December 2024).

Ndizera, Vedaste and Muzee, Hannah (2018) A Critical Review of Agenda 2063: Business as Usual? *African Journal of Political Science and International Relations* 12(8): 142–154.

Ntaka, Buyisile (2023) The Cabo Delgado Insurgency: A Symptom of Governance Failure in Mozambique. *African Journal of Governance and Development* 12(1): 21–42.

Opperman, Jasmine and Pigou, Piers (2024, 30 May) SAMIM Withdrawal from Cabo Delgado: Uncomfortable Truths. *Institute for Security Studies Today*. Available at:

https://issafrica.org/iss-today/samim-withdrawal-from-cabo-delgado-uncomfort able-truths (consulted 7 December 2024).

Protocol Additional to the Geneva Conventions of 12 August 1949 and relating to the Protection of Victims of International Armed Conflicts (Protocol I) adopted 8 June 1977.

Protocol Additional to the Geneva Conventions of 12 August 1949 and relating to the Protection of Victims of Non-International Armed Conflicts (Protocol II) adopted 8 June 1977.

Protocol Relating to the Establishment of the Peace and Security Council of the African Union, adopted by the 1st Ordinary Session of the AU Assembly of Heads of State and Government in Durban, South Africa, 9 July 2002.

Protocol to the African Charter on Human and Peoples' Rights on the Rights of Women in Africa adopted by the AU Assembly of Heads of State and Government in Maputo, Mozambique on 11 July 2003.

Reliefweb (2024, 15 May) Mozambique: Child Soldiers Used in Raid on Northern Town. Available at: https://reliefweb.int/report/mozambique/mozambique-child-soldiers -used-raid-northern-town (consulted 7 December 2024).

Reliefweb (2024, 5 September) Mozambique: 2024 Humanitarian Response Dashboard—Conflict (June 2024). Available at: https://reliefweb.int/report/mozam bique/mozambique-2024-humanitarian-response-dashboard-conflict-june-2024 (consulted 7 December 2024).

Report of the Independent Expert on the Right to Development (Arjun Sengupta) (Report 2 of the Independent Expert), 17 August 2000, A/55/306.

Republic of South Africa v Grootboom, Case No CCT 11/00 2000 (11) BCLR 1169.

Reuters (2024, 8 November) Three Killed, 66 Injured in Mozambique Opposition Protest, Hospital Says. Available at: https://www.reuters.com/world/africa/three-killed -66-injured-mozambique-opposition-protest-hospital-says-2024-11-08/ (consulted 7 December 2024).

SADC News (2021, 10 November) SADC Mission in Mozambique (SAMIM) in Brief. Available at: https://www.sadc.int/latest-news/sadc-mission-mozambique-samim-brief (consulted 7 December 2024).

Sambo, Manuel Francisco (2024, 15 May) Mozambique's "War on Terror": Why are Regional Troops Withdrawing? *Journal of Global Policy*. Available at: https://www .globalpolicyjournal.com/blog/15/05/2024/mozambiques-war-terror-why-are -regional-troops-withdrawing (consulted 7 December 2024).

Save the Children (2024, 3 July) Mozambique: Rising Violence Driving up Child Marriage in Cabo Delgado Province. Available at: https://www.savethechildren .net/news/mozambique-rising-violence-driving-child-marriage-cabo-delgado -province (consulted 7 December 2024).

Schrijver, Nicolaas (2020) A new Convention on the Human Right to Development: Putting the Cart Before the Horse? *Netherlands Quarterly of Human Rights* 38(2): 84–93.

Sentencia C-175/09, Colombia: Corte Constitucional, 18 March 2009.

Shield, Ralph (2024) Rwanda's War in Mozambique: Road-Testing a Kigali Principles approach to counterinsurgency? *Small Wars and Insurgencies* 35(1): 80–117.

Soobramoney v Minister of Health (KwaZulu-Natal), Case No CCT 32/97 1997 (12) BCLR 1696.

Stevens, Clydenia (2019) Reviving the Right to Development Within the Multilateral Trade Framework Affecting (African) Countries to Actualise Agenda 2063. *African Human Rights Law Journal* 19(2): 470–493.

Suzuki, Sanae (2020) Exploring the Roles of the AU and ECOWAS in West African conflicts. *South African Journal of International Affairs* 27(2): 173–191.

Teshome, Roma Girma (2022) The Draft Convention the Right to Development: A New Dawn to the Recognition of the Right to Development as a Human Right. *Human Rights Law Review* 22(2): 1–24.

The Conversation (2024, 16 October) Mozambique's 2024 Elections: 9 Major Challenges that Will Face the New President. Available at: https://theconversation.com/mozambiques-2024-elections-9-major-challenges-that-will-face-the-new-president-240923 (consulted 7 December 2024).

TotalEnergies Press Release (2021, 26 April) Total Declares Force Majeure on Mozambique LNG project. Available at: https://totalenergies.com/media/news/press-releases/total-declares-force-majeure-mozambique-lng-project (consulted 7 December 2024).

United Nations General Assembly Resolution A/HRC/RES/39/9, on the Right to Development, adopted on 27 September 2018.

United Nations General Assembly, Human Rights Council, Working Group on the Right to Development (2022, May) Revised Draft Convention on the Right to Development A/HRC/WG.2/23/2 (Revised Draft Convention).

United Nations News (2024, 27 June) UN Mission Boosts Presence in Central African Republic's Conflict-Stricken Southeast. Available at: https://news.un.org/en/story/2024/06/1151566 (consulted 6 December 2024).

United Nations News Strife in Central African Republic Could Turn into Religious War and Spill Over Borders, UN Warns. Available at: https://www.un.org/africarenewal/news/strife-central-african-republic-could-turn-religious-war-and-spill-over-borders-un-warns (consulted 6 December 2024).

UNICEF (d.n.a.) UNICEF Response to Children Affected by Armed Conflict in Northern Mozambique. Available at: https://www.unicef.org/mozambique/media/4661/file/UNICEF%20response%20to%20children%20affected%20by%20armed%20conflict%20in%20northern%20Mozambique.pdf (consulted 7 December 2024).

United Nations (2023, 12 October) Morning—Human Rights Council Adopts Five Resolutions, Submits to General Assembly Draft International Covenant on the Right to Development for its Negotiation and Adoption, and Extends Mandate on Burundi. Available at: https://www.ungeneva.org/en/news-media/meeting-summary/2023/10/le-conseil-adopte-cinq-resolutions-dont-celle-transmettant (consulted 6 December 2024).

United Nations Development Programme (2015) Fact Sheet Human Development Index: Human Development Report Work for Human Development. Available at: https://www.undp.org/sites/g/files/zskgke326/files/migration/dk/UNDP_Denmark_HDR_2015_Fact_Sheet.pdf (consulted 7 December 2024).

United Nations Development Programme Human Development Report (2023–2024) Breaking the Gridlock: Reimagining Cooperation in a Polarised World. Available at: https://hdr.undp.org/system/files/documents/global-report-document/hdr2023-24reporten.pdf (consulted 7 December 2024).

United Nations Development Programme Human Development Report 2015 (2015, 1 January) Work for Human Development. Available at: https://hdr.undp.org/system/files/documents/hdr15standaloneoverviewen.pdf (consulted 7 December 2024), 28–30.

United Nations General Assembly, Human Rights Council, Working Group on the Right to Development, Second Revised Text of the Draft of the Convention on the Right to Development, With Commentaries A/HRC/WG. 2/24/2/Add.1.

United Nations General Assembly, Report of the United Nations Conference on Environment and Development, Annex 1, Rio Declaration on Environment and Development. Available at: https://www.un.org/en/development/desa/population/migration/generalassembly/docs/globalcompact/A_CONF.151_26_Vol.I_Declaration.pdf (consulted 7 December 2024).

United Nations Office for the Coordination of Humanitarian Affairs (OCHA) (2024) Mozambique: Displacement in Northern Cabo Delgado—Situation Report No 1 (as of 15 March 2024). Available at: https://www.unocha.org/publications/report/mozambique/mozambique-displacement-northern-cabo-delgado-situation-report-no-1-15-march-2024 (consulted 7 December 2024).

Universal Declaration of Human Rights, UN General Assembly Resolution A/RES/217(III), adopted in Paris, France on 10 December 1948.

Whelan, D. (2022) The Right to Development. In: *The Oxford Research Encyclopedia of International Studies*. Oxford University Press.

CHAPTER 17

Conclusion: Envisaging Actualisation of the International Covenant on the Right to Development

Carol Chi Ngang

1 Some Concluding Reflexions

It is of essence, and indeed, worth drawing attention to the fact that where there is subject matter confusion and lack of clarity especially, regarding a discourse of immense contemporary relevance as the right to development that has been the target of gratuitous controversy, there is a rightist academic obligation to dispel those controversies and provide requisite clarity to enable robust and comprehensible engagements on the subject. The motivation to do so draws from the fact that, the right to development is envisaged to not only enable global balance, ensure equitable redistribution and hence, development justice but essentially also, guarantee a humanely satisfactory threshold of sustainable livelihood and better standards of living for the billions of peoples around the world who, in spite of their basic entitlement to the right to life with dignity, have over the centuries been left behind in impoverishment and vulnerability by political design.[1]

It is unthinkable that claims on the right to development will ever do the world any harm. In other words, it can never really go wrong asserting the right to development in a world that has through various global development agendas and initiatives, continually aspire to eradicate the obstacles and challenges that stand in the way to global sustainable development. Yet, despite universal recognition of the existence of that right, including in the African Charter on Human and Peoples' Rights adopted in 1981, the UN Declaration on the Right to Development adopted in 1986, and the Vienna Declaration and Programme

1 Mackloskey, Stephen (2020) Poverty is a Political Choice: A UN Rapporteur has delivered a Withering Critique of the International System. *Policy and Practice—A Development Education Review Issue 31*: 77–90; Hickey, Sam and Bracking, Sara (2005) Exploring the Politics of Chronic Poverty: From Representation to a Politics of Justice? *World Development* 33(6): 851–865.

 | DOI:10.1163/9789004734357_018

of Action adopted in 1993, the Arab Charter adopted in among other instruments under international law, the inalienable human right to development has suffered lack of implementation and enforcement. This has been exacerbated by the reticence among the majority of developed countries in endorsing the right to development in a legally binding instrument.[2]

The dynamics are however, shifting and interestingly, in the direction of a global rule of law framework following the drafting of the International Covenant on the Right to Development, which it must be emphasised, will become an integral constitutive instrument of the international bill of human rights alongside the Universal Declaration of Human Rights, the International Covenant on Civil and Political Rights and the International Covenant on Economic, Social and Cultural Rights. While adoption of the draft Covenant on the Right to Development by the UN General Assembly raises expectations that its coming into force will govern and regulate the global framework for development in terms of obligations that would have to be adhered to and complied with, implementation and enforcement thereof, is still not absolute. The apparent shades of grey that predominate and indeed, shape the global development landscape and the geopolitical interests that engineer the globalising world, necessitates an in-depth enquiry on how the International Covenant on the Right to Development will eventually be actualised when it becomes law.

The predominantly academic contributions in this book, responding to a broad range of interconnected issues, are intended to provide as much conceptual clarity as possible with respect to a proper understanding of the right to development and the extent to which implementation and enforcement are achievable. The discussions broadly focus on contributing factors to the effective realisation of the right to development. Where actualisation of the right to development has been confronted with challenges like in Africa, some of the impeding aspects have equally been explored with the hope that knowledge about them may become instrumental in shaping policy formulation and hence, appropriate legal frameworks for an enabling right to development dispensation both at the global, regional and domestic levels. The adoption and coming into force of the Covenant on the Right to Development will add to, and significantly enhance the international legal framework in harnessing the international dimension of the human right to development. The important question is how?

---

2 Kirchmeier, Felix (2006) The Right to Development—Where Do We Stand?: State of the Debate on the Right to Development. *Friedrich Ebert Stiftung—Dialogue on Globalisation Occasional Paper No 23*, 13–15.

2 Monitoring, Implementation and Enforcement

Every human rights treaty makes provision for or establishes a monitoring mechanism to ensure effective implementation and enforcement. For the Covenant on the Right to Development, a Conference of States Parties is established in accordance with Article 26, to monitor its implementation. The Conference of States Parties shall be composed of all states and international organisations that would have signed and ratified the Covenant and therefore, undertake and commit to its full realisation. The Covenant provides in concrete terms that:

> The Conference of States Parties shall keep under regular review the effective implementation of the Covenant and any related legal instruments that the Conference of States Parties may in the future adopt, and shall make, within its mandate, the decisions necessary to promote the effective implementation of the Covenant. To that end, the Conference of States Parties shall:
>
> a) Periodically examine voluntary reports by States Parties on the implementation of their obligations under the Covenant and the obstacles that they face in the realization of the right to development, in the light of the object and purpose of the Covenant. In this regard, the Conference of States Parties may refer such reports to the implementation mechanism contemplated under article 28 of the present Covenant;
>
> b) Promote and facilitate the open exchange of information on measures adopted by States Parties to address the realization of the right to development, taking into account the differing circumstances, responsibilities and capabilities of States Parties and their respective obligations under the Covenant;
>
> c) Promote, develop and periodically refine, in accordance with the provisions of the present Covenant, the methodologies and best practices for States Parties to assess the status of the realization of the right to development;
>
> d) Seek and utilize, where appropriate, the services and cooperation of, and information provided by, competent international organizations and governmental and non-governmental bodies;
>
> e) Consider and adopt regular reports on the status of implementation of the Covenant, and ensure their publication;
>
> f) Make recommendations on any matters relevant to the implementation of the Covenant, and ensure their publication;

g) Exercise such other functions within the scope of the Covenant as are required for the achievement of the object and purpose, as well as the aims, of the Covenant.[3]

It is envisaged that "At its first session, the Conference of States Parties shall establish an implementation mechanism to facilitate, coordinate and assist, in a non-adversarial and non-punitive manner, the implementation and promotion of compliance with the provisions of the present Covenant".[4] The implementation mechanism shall comprise of independent experts selected to serve in their personal capacity on the exclusive basis of moral standing and recognised subject matter competence and experience.[5] The actual nature of the implementation mechanisms in terms of composition and *modus operandi*, is still to be determined. However, even though the Covenant will become legally binding upon adoption and ratification, its tone is largely in favour of a soft law approach to implementation.

2.1 *Soft Law Approach to Implementation*

Treaty implementation is generally supposed to be achieved through political processes. Usually, and except otherwise stated, by acceding to or ratifying a treaty, states parties tacitly agree that they will be bound by the provisions thereof, and accordingly, undertake to adopt requisite domestic legislative and other measures and to take actionable steps to that effect. It necessitates states parties to integrate the provisions of the treaties they have committed to under international law into the domestic governance architecture and to roll out services, programmes and activities that will culminate in the full realisation of the treaty obligations. This is supposed to be achieved without much pressure. Like for all other treaties, the same is true for the Covenant on the Right to Development when it becomes legally binding on states parties.

Thus, with respect to the implementation mechanism's envisaged mandate in actualising the right to development, an important highlight regarding implementation is the Covenant's insistence on the pursuit of a "non-adversarial and non-punitive" approach. It implies that legal actions through court proceedings is not a desired option as far as the international dimension of the right to development is concerned. The soft law (non-adversarial) approach is

3 Draft International Covenant on the Right to Development—Report by the Chair-Rapporteur of the Working Group on the Right to Development, Zamir Akram (Pakistan) Human Rights Council A/HRC/54/50 54th Session, 6 October 2023, Art 26(1).

4 Ibid at Art 28(1).

5 Ibid at Art 28(3).

obviously strategic, intended on the one hand, to not dissuade ratification of the Covenant and on the other hand, because the right to development was originally not conceived to be confrontational and antagonistic especially, to the extent that every human person and all peoples' entitlement to development is genuinely respected. That is to say, if all relevant duty bearers refrain from actions and/or inactions that may impair enjoyment of the right to development, the context will not necessitate confrontational measures in asserting the right.

Mention must be made of the fact that it is the prerogative of every human person and all peoples as the subjects and beneficiaries of the right to development, to create development, which is conceived and understood in context as aspirations for improved well-being and the attainment of better standards of living in larger freedoms. The expectation in that regard, centres on setting development priorities appropriately, which entails eliminating obstacles to development, including by every conceivable measure, the often resource-intensive and time-consuming adversarial legal proceedings that may have the unintended consequence of derailing the development process. Under the reporting mechanism, states parties shall be enjoined to submit periodic country reports detailing out the measures they have taken as well as the obstacles they may be confronted with in the realisation of the right to development.

In a similar approach with the Declaration on the Right to Development, which has up till now, been the principal international instrument on the right to development, the draft Covenant on the Right to Development places emphasis on international cooperation as a mechanism for its actualisation. The Declaration on the Right to Development broadly articulates the need for international cooperation in realising the right to development, which must be sanctioned by full respect for the principles of international law in accordance with the UN Charter.[6] In addition to the commonplace triad duties to respect, protect and fulfil, the Covenant on the Right to Development enshrines the duty to corporate, including by non-state actors[7] in responding to the extensive listing of specific targets where separate and/or concerted actions are required in ensuring that the right to development is made a reality for everyone and for

6 Declaration on the Right to Development Resolution A/RES/41/128 adopted by UN General Assembly on 4 December 1986, Art 3.

7 A/HRC/54/84: Duty to cooperate and non-State actors—Thematic study by the Expert Mechanism on the Right to Development—Report of the Independent Expert on the Right to Development, Koen de Feyter, 5 July 2023.

all peoples.[8] The duty to cooperate entails in a nutshell, a genuine commitment to mobilise the requisite financial, material and human resources for development, the undertaking to eliminate obstacles that may impede the processes for development, and most importantly, the political will to formulate, adopt and implement the most appropriate people-centred and rights-based regulatory frameworks. It also necessitates mainstreaming human rights-based development into sane governance practices both at the national and international levels. These measures will create an enabling environment for the effective exercise and enjoyment of right to development.

Contemporary international law underscores the fact that international cooperation and hence, the duty to cooperate must adhere to the rules and principles that oblige respect for self-determination, permanent sovereignty over natural resources, sovereign equality of states and most crucially, the *erga omnes* obligation to respect human rights in their entirety. Under the international rule of law, the duty to cooperate needs diligent monitoring to ensure that it is not confused or misconstrued as entitling any peoples anywhere around the world to subjugate and patronise other peoples as has been the case over the centuries, resulting in legitimate claims on the right to development. The right to development should, in its international dimension, be understood also as a self-determination right of states to be left alone particularly, regarding making contextually relevant development choices that respond adequately to the realities on the ground and the livelihood circumstances and exigencies of their peoples.

In addition to prescribing the non-adversarial approach to actualising the right to development by the implementation mechanism that shall be set up, the Covenant also underscores the fact that the decisions of the Conference of States Parties shall be in the form of modest, non-binding recommendations. It means that states parties will have the discretion to comply or not to comply with the recommendations of the Conference of States Parties. It means also that implementation will hinge essentially on and be driven predominantly by the international law principle of *pacta sunt servanda*, necessitating agreements make in good faith to be kept. Applied to the Covenant on the Right to Development it principally, only entails a discretionary demonstration of good faith by states parties in advancing the right to development. While good faith is crucial to uphold as a principle of law in ensuring the protection of human rights, it is an aspiration that is often difficult to practicalize, necessitating in most instances, recourse to legal action as a matter of last resort in asserting

8 Draft Covenant on the Right to Development, supra note 3, Art 13.

universally recognised human rights, not excluding the right to development in the instance of a flagrant violation.

2.2 *Safeguard, Litigation and Remedial Measures*

Public international law, comprising of a broad and ever-increasing range of treaties generally aims to regulate relations between the states parties to those treaties. When the draft Covenant on the Right to Development is adopted and comes into force as a legally binding treaty, it will add to the extensive series of human rights treaty instruments and therefore, a recognised source of international law in accordance with Article 38 of the Statutes of the International Court of Justice (ICJ) and therefore, also subject to interpretation and enforcement by the Court.[9] Even though the Covenant on the Right to Development makes specific provisions for, and is largely in favour of a soft law approach to implementation as illustrated in the preceding section, there is no justification that recourse cannot be had to legal action in the event that a dispute arises relating either to non-compliance or contravention of the Covenant. In order that the rights enshrined therein are not gratuitously rendered susceptible to violation with impunity, the preference for a non-adversarial approach to implementation does not rule out the possibility of litigation. The Covenant explicitly states in this regard that

> Any dispute between two or more States Parties with respect to the interpretation or application of the present Covenant that has not been settled by negotiation may, upon agreement by the parties to the dispute, be referred to the International Court of Justice for a decision, unless another mode of dispute settlement is agreed upon by them.[10]

States parties to the Covenant on the Right to Development shall in accordance, have standing to bring their disputes before the ICJ on the basis that such states parties are also parties to the ICJ Statute in terms of Article 35(1) in addition to having made the declaration contemplated in terms of Article 36, acknowledging the competence of the Court. Thus, as a matter of last resort (where attempts at negotiated settlement have failed), the ICJ shall have both subject matter competence (protection of human rights, including the right to development founded in international law) and jurisdictional competence (envisaged in Article 36 of the Covenant) to entertain and adjudicate

9 Charter of the United Nations and Statute of the International Court of Justice, adopted in San Francisco, United States of America on 26 June 1945.

10 Draft Covenant on the Right to Development, supra note 3, Art 36.

on the matter relating to interpretation and enforcement of the Covenant on the Right to Development.[11] To this end, the mandate of the ICJ shall, besides interpreting the Covenant on the Right to Development and litigating on alleged violations of any of the provisions therein, include ordering for provisional measures where necessary[12] and giving advisory opinions on questions relating to conceptualisation of the right to development under international law.[13] The Court shall have the discretion regarding any dispute arising from the Covenant on the Right to Development, to make a determination on its jurisdiction as to whether or not, to litigate on the matter.[14]

It is a legitimate expectation that the judgments of the ICJ regarding disputes arising from the Covenant on the Right to Development and the remedies it would have to award, shall to the utmost extent conceivable, uphold and promote global development justice and advancement of the human right to development. The crafting of such remedies may include but not limited to reiterating the specific measures provided for in the Covenant on the Right to Development to the effect that effective realisation of the right to development obligates and mandates

1. States Parties [to] recognize that [...] Specific and remedial measures may include enabling the full, effective, appropriate and dignified participation of rights holders in decision-making processes, programmes and policymaking that affect their full and equal enjoyment of the right to development, without subjecting them to structural, environmental or institutional constraints or barriers.
2. States Parties [to] recognize that developing and least developed countries, owing to historical injustices, conflicts, environmental hazards, climate change or other disadvantages, including of an economic, technical or infrastructural nature, may require specific and remedial measures through mutually agreed international legal instruments, policies and practices for ensuring equal realization of the right to development by all individuals and peoples. Such measures may, as appropriate, include:
    a) Recognition of and respect for common but differentiated responsibilities and respective capabilities, in the light of different national circumstances;
    b) The provision of special and differential treatment;
    c) Preferential terms on trade, investment and finance;

11 Charter of the United Nations and Statute of the ICJ, supra note 8, Arts 35(6), 36 and 37.

12 Ibid at Art 41.

13 Ibid at Chapter IV et seq.

14 Charter of the United Nations and Statute of the ICJ, supra note 8, Art 35(6).

d) The creation of special funds or facilitation mechanisms;
e) The facilitation and mobilization of financial, technical, technological, infrastructural, capacity-building or other assistance;
f) Other mutually agreed measures consistent with the provisions of the present Covenant.[15]

3 Implications for the Global Balance of Power

With retrospection on the not-too-smooth path through which the concept of the human right to development has evolved from the initial reticence in recognising that such as right does exist, to presently been considered for legal protection in a binding treaty instrument under international law, a determining factor that ought to be considered is whether the legacy objective of seeking to create global balance,[16] would have been attained with the coming into force of the International Covenant on the Right to Development. Mihir Kanade affirms in the Foreword to this book that, "[…] the Covenant will have immense positive implications for the human rights project in general by establishing a normative framework that is built on the acknowledgement that development is not charity or a privilege but a human right of all individuals and peoples". He adds that "[…] the Covenant, once in force, will have great implications for how the international order is structured".

Over the past decades, several framework instruments have indeed, underscored and reiterated the need to prioritise the right to development and make it a reality for everyone and for all peoples.[17] Transition from the

15 Draft Covenant on the Right to Development, supra note 8, Art 15.

16 See for example Ngang, Carol Chi (2017) Differentiated Responsibilities Under International Law and the Right to Development Paradigm for Developing Countries. *Human Rights and International Legal Discourse* 11(2): 280–281; Šlaus, Ivo and Jacobs, Garry (2013) In Search of a New Paradigm for Global Development. *Cadmus Journal* 1(6): 1.

17 Transforming Our World: The 2030 Agenda for Sustainable Development Resolution A/RES/70/1 adopted by the United Nations General Assembly on 27 September 2015, Para 10; UN Declaration on the Rights of Indigenous Peoples Resolution 61/295 adopted by the General Assembly on 13 September 2007, Arts 21 and 23; Durban Declaration adopted at the World Conference against Racism, Racial Discrimination, Xenophobia and Related Intolerance held in Durban, South Africa on 31 August to 8 September 2001, Para 78; UN Millennium Declaration Resolution *A/55/L.2* adopted by the General Assembly on 8 September 2000, Preamble, Paras 11 and 24; Vienna Declaration and Programme of Action adopted by the UN World Conference on Human Rights UN Doc A/CONF.157/24 25 June 1993, Paras 1(10) and (11); Rio Declaration on Environment and Development adopted at the UN Conference on Environment and Development in Rio de Janeiro, Brazil

Millennium Development Goals framework to the Sustainable Development Goals dispensation does not fail to accentuate the fact that the global agenda cannot be achieved without recourse to the right to development. Central to the shared global commitment to realising the SDGs, the Transforming Our World framework document draws attention to the fact that conceptualisation of the goals contained therein was informed by the Declaration on the Right to Development.[18] While the Covenant on the Right to Development builds on, and strengthens the commitment to sustainable development, it notes in explicit terms that:

> States Parties, individually and jointly, undertake to ensure that:
> a) Laws, policies and practices relating to development at the national and international levels are aimed at and contribute to the realization of sustainable development, in a manner consistent with their obligations under international law;
> b) Their decisions and actions do not compromise the ability of present and future generations to realize their right to development;
> c) The formulation, adoption and implementation of all such laws, policies and practices aimed at realizing sustainable development are made fully consistent with the provisions of the present Covenant and other obligations under international law for realizing sustainable development.[19]

The discussion in chapter 4 provides more clarity on the right to development/sustainable development nexus. It can never be overemphasised that, human rights—the right to development inclusive—are moral entitlements that people claim for themselves by virtue of possessing those entitlements as birth-right endowments, which cannot be taken away or bargained for less than their inherent values. It is not incorrect as Sengupta notes that the right to development has often been perceived as a right for developing countries.[20] Looking at the right to development from this point of view does not imply

on 3 to 14 June 1992; Declaration on the Right to Development Resolution A/RES/41/128 adopted by the UN General Assembly on 4 December 1986; Principle 3; OHCHR (d.n.a) TST Issues Brief: Human Rights Including the Right to Development. *Joint Issue Brief.* Available at: https://sustainabledevelopment.un.org/content/documents/2391TST%20Human%20Rights%20Issues%20Brief_FINAL.pdf (consulted 18 December 2024).

18 Transforming Our World, supra note 17, Para 10.

19 Draft Covenant on the Right to Development, supra note 3, Art 24.

20 Sengupta, Arjun (2004) The Human Right to Development. *Oxford Development Studies* 32(2): 181.

that it pertains exclusively to developing countries but as the literature on the subject affirms, claims on the right to development have mostly emerged from and predominantly, advanced by developing countries on the basis of the historic disadvantage, exploitation and development injustices they have suffered.[21] Even as the Covenant on the Right to Development is envisaged to apply to everyone and to all peoples everywhere around the world, it cannot be denied that it will have more relevance to the peoples in the developing parts of the world who are systematically deprived of the right to development.

The adoption and coming into force of the International Covenant on the Right to Development therefore, creates expectation that it will no longer be business as usual as has been the case previously wherein, the right to development has been the object of contravention with impunity owing to the absence of a normative instrument guaranteeing its protection at the international level. As noted in the draft Covenant, the use of coercive measures like sanctions, economic sabotage, threats of war and military invasions which developed countries often resort to in constraining developing and least developed countries to submit to their values and perceptions of development shall subsequently, be read to constitute a violation of the right to development under international law.[22] It also means that a normative framework will henceforth, be established obliging commitment, responsiveness and accountability. It guarantees some measure of anticipation especially, for the teeming billions of impoverished, disadvantaged, marginalised and vulnerable persons and peoples around the world, including women and the youth as highlighted in chapters 9 and 12 respectively and well as indigenous peoples and children

21 Ngang, Carol Chi (2021) *The Right to Development in Africa* Leiden/Boston: Brill Publishers, 112; Whelan, Daniel; Kanade, Mihir and Puvimanasinghe, Shyami (2020) The Right to Development: Origins, History and Institutional Development. Available at: https://www.google.com/url?sa=t&source=web&rct=j&opi=89978449&url=https://www.ohchr.org/sites/default/files/Documents/Issues/Development/chapter-1-whelan-kanade-and-puvimanasinghe-history-and-evolution-of-the-rtd.docx&ved=2ahUKEwjosOXEtLGKAxVkSUEAHTYTIwwQFnoECBoQAQ&usg=AOvVaw3V9KoXP5zk6kww4JrgCqY (consulted 18 December 2024), 1–27; Adeola, Ramola (2018) The right to development under the African Charter: Is there an extraterritorial reach? In Ngang, C.C.; Kamga, S.D. and Gumede, V. (eds) *Perspectives on the Right to Development*. Pretoria: University of Pretoria Law Press, 34–36; Ouguergouz, Fatsah (2003) *The African Charter on Human and Peoples' Rights: A Comprehensive Agenda for Human Dignity and Sustainable Democracy in Africa*. Dordrecht: Martinus Nijhoff Publishers, 298; Dieng, A. (1987) Background to the Growth of the Right to Development: The Role of Law and Lawyers in Development. In: Nobel, P. (ed) *Refugees and Development in Africa*. Sweden: Scandinavian Institute of African Studies, 55.

22 Draft Covenant on the Right to Development, supra note 3, Art 14.

among other rights holders that when their right to development is violated, legal redress can be sought.

The anticipated adoption and coming into force of the Covenant on the Right to Development will however, not dramatically transform the global development landscape and make it more conducive and enabling. Like all legal instruments, the Covenant is not going to become self-actualising. It will not become a magic wand that will whisk away all the development challenges the world in confronted with. Its actualisation will require consistent concerted actions in creating the enabling people-centred environment and the rights-based conditions that allow for the constant improvement in living standards for everyone and for all peoples around the world.

4 Looking Forward to the Right to Development Dispensation

The International Covenant on the Right to Development does not only guarantee a full range of entitlements, it principally also imposes positive as well as negative obligations that must be adhered to in ensuring effective realisation thereof. While prohibiting actions and inactions that may impair realisation of the right to development, including the extraterritorial operations of third states as illustrated in chapter 6, states parties have the ultimate primary obligation to ensure that the guarantees on the right to development enshrined in the Covenant become reality for their peoples. It entails emphasising with vigour, the fair and equitable application of the rules of international law in regulating global development practices, including for example, in the areas of digital technological advancement as noted in chapter 10 and international trade where disadvantage for developing countries is largely perpetuated by developed countries as vividly explained in chapter 14. Actualising the right to development equally necessitates putting an end to conflicts. The analysis in chapter 16 sheds light on how conflicts impede development and consequently impair realisation of the right to development.

Envisaging an enabling dispensation governed by the Covenant on the Right to Development necessitates restating the nature of the right to development, which in essence is an embodiment of the interwoven and mutually reinforcing right to self-determination and the entitlement to permanent sovereignty over natural resources. The analysis in chapter 2 is instructive on this point. With the right guaranteed recognition and protection, state governments are equipped both with the sovereignty and the self-determination (without being coerced) in making appropriate policy choices that will guarantee effective exercise and enjoyment of the right to development. The

Covenant on the Right to Development accordingly, promises *Development as Freedom* as Amartya Sen[23] would put it, and that development justice is desirable and indeed, attainable.[24] Development justice enjoins state governments to adopt robust policy and regulatory measures at the national, regional and international levels in eradicating obstacles to development like the prevalence of illicit financial flows and corruption discussed in chapters 13 and 15 respectively.

The Covenant on the Right to Development is explicit in prohibiting constraining development practices, including those perpetrated by international organisations as illustrated in chapters 7 and 8. In a world that has historically and more so, is increasingly driven by the desire to exploit, development justice will certainly never be given on a platter of gold, it will only have to be exacted by those who lay claim to it. In other words, giving effect to the provisions of the International Covenant on the Right to Development is first and foremost, the primary duty of states, which must demonstrate the political resolve to guarantee enjoyment of the right to development to their peoples. Political resolve embodies on the one hand, genuine responsiveness in making the right to development a reality at the national level (chapter 11 illustrates how the right to development could be incorporated into domestic constitutionalism) and on the other hand, decisiveness in asserting the right to development at the international level.

While the international dimension on the right to development is envisaged to be achieved through cooperation and hence, the emphasis in the Covenant on the duty to cooperate, it is crucial to distinguish between mutually beneficial forms of cooperation and those that perpetuate dependency and are utterly lopsided and paternalistic in nature and therefore, diametrically opposed to the advancement of development justice. As clearly explained in chapter 5, caution is reiterated here against recourse to the skewed donor/recipient-oriented models to development cooperation, which evidently have no potential in leveraging realisation of the right to development.[25] Promoting the international dimension of the right to development is therefore, largely contingent on gainful development cooperation models based on mutually beneficial strategic partnerships that subscribe to the rules of international law and

23 Sen, Amartya (1999) *Development as Freedom*. Oxford: Oxford University Press.

24 Culp, Julian (2014) Global Justice and Development. Cham, Switzerland: Palgrave Macmillan; Asia Pacific Forum on Women, Law and Development (2019, July) We Need Development Justice. Available at: https://apwld.org/wp-content/uploads/2019/07/2019_Development_Justice_Brief_update.pdf (consulted 18 December 2024).

25 Ngang 2021, supra note 20, 83–152.

hence, equip cooperating states parties with the armoury of sovereignty and self-determination in making rational and sensible development choices. The Covenant on the Right to Development lists alternative models of development cooperation to choose from.[26]

References

Adeola, Ramola (2018) The right to development under the African Charter: Is there an extraterritorial reach? In Ngang, C.C.; Kamga, S.D. and Gumede, V. (eds) *Perspectives on the Right to Development*. Pretoria: University of Pretoria Law Press, 34–77.

Asia Pacific Forum on Women, Law and Development (2019, July) We Need Development Justice. Available at: https://apwld.org/wp-content/uploads/2019/07/2019_Development_Justice_Brief_update.pdf (consulted 18 December 2024).

Charter of the United Nations and Statute of the International Court of Justice, adopted in San Francisco, United States of America on 26 June 1945.

Culp, Julian (2014) Global Justice and Development. Cham, Switzerland: Palgrave Macmillan.

Declaration on the Right to Development Resolution A/RES/41/128 adopted by UN General Assembly on 4 December 1986.

Declaration on the Right to Development Resolution A/RES/41/128 adopted by the UN General Assembly on 4 December 1986.

Dieng, A. (1987) Background to the Growth of the Right to Development: The Role of Law and Lawyers in Development. In: Nobel, P. (ed) *Refugees and Development in Africa*. Sweden: Scandinavian Institute of African Studies.

Draft International Covenant on the Right to Development—Report by the Chair-Rapporteur of the Working Group on the Right to Development, Zamir Akram (Pakistan) Human Rights Council A/HRC/54/50 54th Session, 6 October 2023.

Durban Declaration adopted at the World Conference against Racism, Racial Discrimination, Xenophobia and Related Intolerance held in Durban, South Africa on 31 August to 8 September 2001.

Hickey, Sam and Bracking, Sara (2005) Exploring the Politics of Chronic Poverty: From Representation to a Politics of Justice? *World Development* 33(6): 851–865.

Kirchmeier, Felix (2006) The Right to Development—Where Do We Stand?: State of the Debate on the Right to Development. *Friedrich Ebert Stiftung—Dialogue on Globalisation Occasional Paper No 23*, 1–28.

26 Draft Covenant on the Right to Development, supra note 3, Art 13(4)(g).

Mackloskey, Stephen (2020) Poverty is a Political Choice: A UN Rapporteur has delivered a Withering Critique of the International System. *Policy and Practice—A Development Education Review Issue 31*: 77–90.

Ngang, Carol Chi (2017) Differentiated Responsibilities Under International Law and the Right to Development Paradigm for Developing Countries. *Human Rights and International Legal Discourse* 11(2): 265–288.

Ngang, Carol Chi (2021) *The Right to Development in Africa* Leiden/Boston: Brill Publishers.

Office of the High Commissioner for Human Rights (d.n.a) TST Issues Brief: Human Rights Including the Right to Development. *Joint Issue Brief.* Available at: https://sustainabledevelopment.un.org/content/documents/2391TST%20Human%20Rights%20Issues%20Brief_FINAL.pdf (consulted 18 December 2024).

Ouguergouz, Fatsah (2003) *The African Charter on Human and Peoples' Rights: A Comprehensive Agenda for Human Dignity and Sustainable Democracy in Africa.* Dordrecht: Martinus Nijhoff Publishers.

Rio Declaration on Environment and Development adopted at the UN Conference on Environment and Development in Rio de Janeiro, Brazil on 3 to 14 June 1992.

Sen, Amartya (1999) *Development as Freedom.* Oxford: Oxford University Press.

Sengupta, Arjun (2004) The Human Right to Development. *Oxford Development Studies* 32(2): 179–203.

Šlaus, Ivo and Jacobs, Garry (2013) In Search of a New Paradigm for Global Development. *Cadmus Journal* 1(6): 1–30.

Transforming Our World: The 2030 Agenda for Sustainable Development Resolution A/RES/70/1 adopted by the United Nations General Assembly on 27 September 2015.

UN Declaration on the Rights of Indigenous Peoples Resolution 61/295 adopted by the General Assembly on 13 September 2007.

UN Millennium Declaration Resolution *A/55/L.2* adopted by the General Assembly on 8 September 2000.

Vienna Declaration and Programme of Action adopted by the UN World Conference on Human Rights UN Doc A/CONF.157/24 25 June 1993.

Whelan, Daniel; Kanade, Mihir and Puvimanasinghe, Shyami (2020) The Right to Development: Origins, History and Institutional Development. Available at: https://www.google.com/url?sa=t&source=web&rct=j&opi=89978449&url=https://www.ohchr.org/sites/default/files/Documents/Issues/Development/chapter-1-whelan-kanade-and-puvimanasinghe-history-and-evolution-of-the-rtd.docx&ved=2ahUKEwjosOXEtLGKAxVkSUEAHTYTIwwQFnoECBoQAQ&usg=AOvVaw3V9KoXP5zk6kww4JrgCqY (consulted 18 December 2024).

Index

www.ingramcontent.com/pod-product-compliance
Lightning Source LLC
Chambersburg PA
CBHW070252260926
51849CB00001BA/279
9789004734340